W9-BQK-844

SEEDS OF FIRE:

CHINA AND THE STORY BEHIND THE ATTACK ON AMERICA

GORDON THOMAS

A Dandelion Books Publication
www.dandelionbooks.com
Tempe, Arizona

Copyright, 2001 by Gordon Thomas

All rights exclusively reserved. No part of this book may be reproduced or translated into any language or utilized in any form or by any means, electronic or mechanical, including photocopying, recording or by any information storage and retrieval system, without permission in writing from the publisher.

Published Worldwide
by Dandelion Books
with Anvil Studios
Tempe, Arizona

A Dandelion Books Publication
Dandelion Enterprises, Inc.
Tempe, Arizona

Library of Congress Cataloging-in-Publication Data
Thomas, Gordon
Seeds of Fire: China and the Story Behind the Attack on America
Library of Congress Catalog Card Number 2001088909

ISBN 1-893302-54-7

Dragon illustration by Terry Moody
Book design by Michele O'Hagan

Printed in the United States of America

Dandelion Books
www.dandelionbooks.com

ALSO BY GORDON THOMAS:

Non-Fiction:
DESCENT INTO DANGER
BED OF NAILS
PHYSICIAN EXTRAORDINARY
HEROES OF THE R.A.F.
THEY GOT BACK
MIRACLE OF SURGERY
THE NATIONAL HEALTH SERVICE AND YOU
THAMES NUMBER ONE
MIDNIGHT TRADERS
THE PARENT'S HOME DOCTOR (*with Ian D Hudson, Vincent Pippet*)
TURN BY THE WINDOW (*with Ronald Hutchinson*)
CANCER DOCTOR: THE BIOGRAPHY OF JOSEF ISSELS, M.D.
THE DAY THE WORLD ENDED (*with Max Morgan-Witts*)
EARTHQUAKE (*with Max Morgan-Witts*)
SHIPWRECK (*with Max Morgan-Witts*)
VOYAGE OF THE DAMNED (*with Max Morgan-Witts*)
THE DAY GUERNICA DIED (*with Max Morgan-Witts*)
ENOLA GAY/RUIN FROM THE AIR (*with Max Morgan-Witts*)
THE DAY THE BUBBLE BURST (*with Max Morgan-Witts*)
TRAUMA (*with Max Morgan-Witts*)
PONTIFF (*with Max Morgan-Witts*)
THE YEAR OF ARMAGEDDON (*with Max Morgan-Witts*)
THE OPERATION
DESIRE AND DENIAL
THE TRIAL: THE LIFE AND INEVITABLE CRUCIFIXION OF JESUS
JOURNEY INTO MADNESS
ENSLAVED
TRESPASS INTO TEMPTATION
GIDEON'S SPIES

Fiction:
THE THIRTEENTH DISCIPLE: THE LIFE OF MARY MAGDALENE
THE CAMP ON BLOOD ISLAND
TORPEDO RUN
DEADLY PERFUME
GODLESS ICON
VOICES IN THE SILENCE
ORGAN HUNTERS
POISONED SKY

Screenplays:
EMMETT (*with Gordon Parry*)
ENSLAVED (*with Kevan Barker*)
ORGAN HUNTERS
THE JESUS CONSPIRACY (*with Kevan Barker*)
CHAOS UNDER HEAVEN
ISSELS (*with Kevan Barker*)

For

Carol Adler

A publisher who understands writers

because first and foremost she is one.

Her enthusiasm and encouragement

have helped to make this book what it is.

In Buddhism there is an ancient adage:

ku-hai yu-sheng.

It means to survive in a world of suffering.

Carol has done so.

INTELLIGENCE SERVICES

ISRAEL

IDF .... Responsible for co-ordinating all intelligence for the General Staff of the Israeli Defense Forces. From time to time gives Mossad specific tasks.

AMAN .... Intelligence branch of the IDF with specific responsibility for gathering military, geographic and economic intelligence. Its prime focus remains the activities of Israel's Arab neighbors in the new millennium.

AFI .... Intelligence branch of Israel's Air Force. specializes in gathering signals, intelligence and aerial reconnaissance. By the year 2002, the latter will be largely replaced by satellite, leaving AFI's role to provide conventional air support intelligence.

BP .... Paramilitary-style border police in Israeli-occupied territories. Limited intelligence-gathering role.

NI .... Naval intelligence unit of all Israeli seaborne forces. Work includes monitoring Israel's coasts, updating foreign naval resources. Israel's Navy was equipped in 2000 with three Dolphin-class nuclear submarines.

GSS .... Also known as Shin Bet or SHABEK. Responsible for internal security and defense of Israeli installations abroad such as embassies, consulates and important Israeli organizations.

RPPC .... Research and Political Planning Center advises Prime Minister of the day and his policy makers on long-term strategy.

MOSSAD .... Premier service. Works world-wide, 1,500 full-time staff (2001). Has estimated back-up of 1 million in Jewish Diaspora.

UNITED STATES OF AMERICA

CIA .... Conducts covert operations, provides intelligence analysis for the incumbent President. Forbidden by Executive Order from conducting assassinations.

DIA .... Coordinates all military intelligence for the Joint Chiefs of Staff.

INR.................State Department's small intelligence and research department (1999 staff of approximately 500). Reports only to incumbent Secretary of State.

NIO.................Based in Pentagon. The National Imagery Office controls all U.S. satellite intelligence gathering. Constantly "tasked" by the CIA and DIA.

NRO.................Again Pentagon-based. Works closely with NIO and has specific responsibility for all satellite hardware and deployment.

NSA ....Operates from Fort George G. Meade, Maryland. Over the years its "spy in sky" image has given the National Security Agency a glamour once only the prerogative of the CIA. Specializes in signals intelligence, cryptography. Works closely with NIO on satellite intelligence gathering.

UNITED KINGDOM

GCHQ...........Its 7,000 (approx. 2001) staff acts as Britain's "invisible eye in outer space." Formally known as Government Communications Headquarters, it monitors and decodes radio, telex, fax and e-mail traffic in and out of United Kingdom. Regularly "tasked" by Britain's two main intelligence services.

MI6.................Also known as the Secret Intelligence Service. Staff of under 2,000 (2001) plans, carries out and analyzes worldwide clandestine operations and intelligence gathering.

MI5.................2,000 staff (2001). Britain's prime internal counter-espionage service. Specializes in monitoring all designated subversives in the country and conducts surveillance on a large number of foreign diplomats and embassies, including those of Israel.

RUSSIA

GRU:...............Glavnoye Razvedyvatelnoye Upravlenie provides Kremlin with military intelligence. Staffed with the best of the former Soviet surveillance.

FCS.................Renamed the Federal Counterintelligence Service, it is really the old KGB updated. Staff of 142,000 (2001). Focuses on border movement control, internal counter-intelligence, surveillance of all foreign diplomats, many journalists and businessmen. Has a powerful secret police division with units in every major city in Russia.

SVR.................Sluzhba Vneshnie Razvedaki runs world-wide, multi-layered intelligence-gathering operation. Specialist units gather political, industrial and commercial intelligence. Conducts covert operations, including assassinations.

CHINA

ILD ....Harmless-sounding International Liaison Department, the organization engages in a wide range of covert activities. Prime target is the United States.

MID ....Military Intelligence Department reports to the General Staff of the People's Liberation Army. Brief includes: updating all foreign military capabilities (especially the United States) and conducting satellite reconnaissance. Staff is attached to every PRC embassy and consulate.

MSS...............Founded in 1983, the Ministry of State Security is responsible for all counter-espionage within China. Has a fearsome reputation.

STD...............Based in Ministry of Defense, the large Science and Technology Department has two prime functions: to collate all signals traffic from the Chinese Navy and overseas embassies; to target primarily U.S. firms working at the cutting edge of military and civilian technology.

NCNA...........Nominally a news agency reporting on Chinese affairs. Has long been a cover for all other Chinese intelligence agencies engaged in clandestine activities.

FRANCE

DAS ....Miniscule (staff of under 50 in 2001). Focuses on assessing long-term defense planning work by other nations.

DPSD..............Direction du Production et de la Securite de la Defense. Responsible for gathering military intelligence abroad.

DRM ....At the coal-face of French satellite intelligence program. Divided into five sub-directorates. Reports directly to Prime Minister of the day.

DST ....The Directorate for Surveillance of the Territory is the largest and most powerful of France's intelligence agencies. Has several thousand employees. Operates both internally and overseas. Wide-ranging responsibilities include surveillance of all foreign embassies in Paris and conducting a large number of clandestine operations. Reports directly to incumbent Minister of the Interior.

DGSE.............Direction Generale de la Securite Exterieure. Brief is to gather industrial and economic intelligence, penetrate terrorist organizations and conduct old-fashioned spying.

SGDN ....Reports to the incumbent prime minister, the Secretariat General de la Defense Nationale, provides an overview of military intelligence developments in countries of interest to France.

JAPAN

NAICHO.......Part of Cabinet Research Office. Has a large budget to analyze defense policies of all major nations of interest to Japan.

MITI................Responsible for gathering commercial and economic data worldwide.

PSIA ....The Public Security Investigation Agency concentrates on counter-terrorism and counter-espionage. Primarily operates internally but increasingly by 2001 had developed a global approach.

CONTENTS

AUTHOR'S NOTE

While this book is necessarily a compression of experiences, it is totally based upon the truth of honest recall. The identity of a number of people has been protected, usually by a change of name or the omission of a detailed biography. They are still living in China or have relatives there. With good reason they fear for their lives.

Most of the interviews were with eyewitnesses never before questioned. As well as personal testimony, they provided a wealth of official records, memoranda, and private material: diaries, letters, faxes, and telexes. In the end it resembled a small college library.

The ranks of all members of the Chinese government and its officials, as well as the People's Liberation Army, are those they held at the time of this story.

A NOTE ON PRONUNCIATION

The pinyin system has been used for transcribing Chinese names. Thus Peking becomes Beijing. Introduced by the Communist party in the 1950s, the system needs a few pronunciation reminders. *Zh* is pronounced like the *J* in John; *q* like the *ch* in child; *c* like the *ts* in pats; *x* is always delivered with the same emphasis as the *s* in she. However, for the sake of clarity, Hong Kong, Xiang Gang in pinyin, remains.

1

The Third Millennium

DECEMBER 2000
WASHINGTON D.C.

George John Tenet, the Director of the Central Intelligence Agency on that cold winter's morning in December 2000 had told friends that among the many things he would miss when he came to relinquish office was the privilege of being chauffeur-driven from his headquarters in Langley's 219 acres of pleasant and partially-wooded Virginian countryside, along the banks of the Potomac River.

For the past year and a half he had held the office of America's chief official spymaster. Tenet had enjoyed many other small privileges that went with the job: the elevator that only he could ride up to his private office; his private dining room; the right to choose the wall color which complemented the neutral carpet in his office suite. And, of course, the vast expanse of desk, behind which so many of his illustrious predecessors had once sat to secretly rule over their world: William Joseph Casey; Stansfield Turner; William Egan Colby; James Rodney Schlesinger; Richard Helms; all the way back to the legendary, and probably the greatest of them all, Allan Welsh Dulles.

In between had come George Herbert Walker Bush, for less than a year — 30 January 1976 to 20 January 1977. Now he held an even more important position, the father of the present President of the United States. Officially he had no part to play in the new Administration. But everyone tutored in the ways of Washington knew his son would not make a single important move without consulting his father. Most important of all, the former President would set the agenda for the Administration's foreign policy. The first evidence of what that would be could come with the younger Bush's attitude towards the People's Republic of China.

In his year at the CIA, his father was still remembered by the paucity of information about his tenure as Director. No one could recall any major intelligence successes or failures on his watch; there was an absence of colorful talk to mark his days on the seventh floor. He concentrated on improving staff morale, something badly needed, and making his staff happy and keeping both himself and the agency out of the news. Viewed as an ambitious politician when he was appointed, from the day he arrived at Langley he set out to show that partisan politics had no place on his agenda. Battered by successive investigations, his staff breathed a collective sigh of relief; they even came to admire the way George Herbert Bush reached outside the agency to pick defeated Republican candidates to fill key jobs; inside Langley he promoted men who had demonstrated their ability in the lower ranks. Overall he had shown shrewdness and skills that revitalized the CIA at a time when it badly needed it.

The Washington intelligence community was collectively shocked when President Jimmy Carter, despite all the evidence he had received of George Bush's competency, promptly fired him. It was seen by many as an act of peculiar viciousness, a reflection that Carter was lacking in structured intellect. During his election campaign Carter had run against the CIA; he saw it as part of the Washington sophistication he held in high suspicion. To him Bush had stood for secrecy and was a Washington insider.

Bush kept his own contempt for Carter under careful lock and key, like so much else he did. But Tenet knew things about Bush that few others did. There was, for instance, his view of China. Tenet had told colleagues he was reasonably certain his son shared his father's views.

During his time at the CIA, and later as President of the United States, George Herbert Bush had shown an admiration for China's then supreme leader, Deng Xiaoping, along with barely concealed detestation for the Chinese students who had dared to oppose Deng and the other Old Men of the Long March who had created China in their own image: a hard-line Communist state in which the very word "democracy" had no translation into Mandarin. It still did not.

Almost certainly then, the incoming President of the United States, George W. Bush, would take the same view as his father about China.

One reason was that the incoming Administration viewed China as a vitally important trading partner, and was determined to see that European nations — especially Germany, France and the United Kingdom — would not seriously challenge that position. The new Bush Administration would balance that against knowing American memories were long. Many people could not easily forget or forgive what had happened in China a mere nine years ago — the shocking massacre of the young students of Beijing's universities in Tiananmen Square.

But there was still another reason, one far more demanding of Tenet's attention than the machinations of American businessmen seeking to deepen their collective foothold in China or the protests of American liberals.

China, through its Secret Service, CSIS, had proven itself a ruthless and competent enemy of the United States. It had carried out one of the most successful intelligence operations against the very heart of America's nuclear research establishment, one at the cutting edge of the nation's defenses. The facility is Los Alamos, where the two bombs had been developed which had destroyed Hiroshima and Nagasaki and ended World War Two.

For almost three years the FBI, under the personal command of its director, Louis J. Freeh, had probed and combed through every inch of Los Alamos, driven on by Attorney-General Janet Reno whose manner would be more remembered for a rasping voice than inspired leadership. It was Reno who had led all the network news shows earlier in 1999 with her exultant claim that a Chinese lab scientist working at Los Alamos, Dr. Wen Ho Lee, had been arrested as China's spy. The Taiwanese-born Lee had been incarcerated in solitary confinement in a Federal prison awaiting trial on charges he had passed nuclear warhead designs to CSIS, along with a library of CD-ROM stored documents which revealed what Reno had termed *"pretty well all that any enemy would need to know about our defense secrets."*

Tenet had not believed Lee was guilty from the time his own team made their own separate enquiries to those of the FBI. He had been proven right. In the closing weeks of 1999, Reno had been forced to order Lee's release from incarceration on the simple grounds that the FBI had uncovered no evidence even remotely substantiating any charge of espionage.

The fifty-eight felony counts against Lee were dropped and U.S. District Court Judge James Parker took the highly unusual step of publicly apologizing to Lee for *"government misconduct which has embarrassed the entire nation."*

Tenet was not the only one who wondered how much of the apology was generated by the persistent rumors which had percolated through the Washington intelligence community: that Lee's work at Los Alamos was so futuristic that, if he revealed even a hint, it would have monumental repercussions. Lee, ran the whispers, worked on what was known as Project HP — Holographic Portal. This took Los Alamos scientists at the Lawrence Livermore and Sandia laboratories into what can be called *"ET technology."*

The portal *"is designed to allow time travel across space-time and possibly interdimensionally. In effect it would allow the cliché of Star Trek to come true — to go where no man has gone before."*

That claim was made by Dr. Richard Boylan. He is no wild card cruising the Internet with crackpot theories. Dr. Boylan is a respected behavioral scientist with proven contacts within the National Security Agency. NSA is responsible for any attempts to make contacts with extra-terrestrials. Dr. Boylan is also a renowned lecturer on the campus of California State University; his articles and papers are carefully studied within the Washington intelligence community.

Boylan is the first to have publicly raised the possibility that Lee was working towards making contact with life far beyond earth. For almost fifty years there have been repeated rumors that Los Alamos was engaged in such work but no one has been able to pinpoint it as the probability Dr. Boylan claims.

Boylan, who lives in Sacramento, California, has closely monitored what goes on at Los Alamos — in itself no easy task. Analyzing what his sources have told him, Boylan has concluded that the "nuclear secrets" which Lee was alleged to have misappropriated, were in reality *"a code phrase for all kinds of secret advanced technology such as antigravity propulsion and psychotronic-remote influencing devices."*

Long before Tenet had joined the CIA, the agency had been engaged in a search for such devices. The project was known as MK-ULTRA and it had been designed to find out if it were possible to brainwash people. It had been the first planned, sustained and systematic assault on the human psyche and, until then, certainly the most sinister activity ever engaged in by any agency of the United States government. The CIA in the 1960s had conducted a series of horrific secret programs to discover ways to manipulate human behavior.

Those who survived carry the scars to this day of what was done to them by the CIA as its agents obsessively pursued methods of controlling human behavior, and were fully supported by some of America's best known and most respected scientists and doctors. In return for huge sums of money, they agreed to disregard their sacred oath to harm no patient. Many of their victims died as a result of the experiments performed upon them. But there were also survivors.

One of them is Kathleen Ann Sullivan. Years ago she began to contact the author of this book providing, a little at a time, glimpses of the CIA's careful and systematic assault on her psyche. It became clear that not only was her story true, but that she had been the victim of perhaps the most sinister activity ever engaged in by an organ of the United States government. At the time, still filled with dread of what might next happen to her, Kathleen was not ready to go public. She broke off contact. Then, in late May 2001, she decided to reopen it. She did so by providing a sworn declaration about what she had suffered. There is no comfortingly simple explanation as to why she decided to speak out. Except one. Her need to tell the full truth about what happened to her. Checked against all the known facts, her story at the very least is a footnote to the lack of accountability in the democracy that the United States prides itself in upholding. No words can better her own description of what she endured:

"I am a 45-year old U.S. survivor of the CIA's MK-ULTRA Program and other sub-projects that dealt with breaking and controlling subjects' minds and wills. I was first exposed to the personnel working on these projects when I was three years old. I was not able to begin to break away from their and their associates' control until I received outside help beginning in the mid-1980s.

"I have been in active, therapeutic recovery for over twelve years. My diagnoses are Dissociative Identity Disorder (D.I.D., formerly M.P.D.) and Post-Traumatic Stress Disorder (P.T.S.D.), delayed. I suffer horribly from anxiety, for which I am on Social Security Disability. Since I began remembering and becoming co-conscious with my altered states of consciousness, I have been repeatedly, voluntarily hospitalized due to major depression and suicidal tendencies, for which I am now on medication.

"Just recently I have decided to come out of hiding and go public about what was done to and through me. I finally have realized that I can't keep hiding … that leaves me only a shell of a life to live. I'm tired of hiding and I'm tired of living in fear.

"The CIA sought to break the minds and wills of their subjects and create altered states of consciousness that they could then train and control. I was one of their subjects. The experiments were all too successful in my mind and life. Some of the things they did to me to break my will and control my mind and life were: forced druggings — including opium, Thorazine, hallucinogens and experimental drugs; electrical shock and torture — including bare live wires, stun guns, stun belts and several series of ECTs designed to shatter my personality and fragment my memories; forced harm to animals; light probes (done in darkened rooms, usually); occult ritualized torture and *horrification; sensory deprivation, sometimes combined with drugs — including in padded rooms, buried coffins, large black boxes, and saltwater tanks; drowning and resuscitation; hanging and resuscitation; threats made against myself, my pets and the lives of my loved ones; starvation; isolation; false imprisonment; hypnosis; being put in small crates or cages, some electrified.*

"Other forms of ritualistic, methodical, pre-planned torture included being forced to witness assaults on others, including children and babies; being forced, beginning at my age 4, to harm others in controlled alter-states; being forced to perform and assist in illegal pornography, to be sold on the black market; being forced to assist in breaking the minds of child victims (aka 'programming'); being forced to act as a prostitute, sometimes as a lead-in to assassinations; being forced to participate in "black-op" assassinations, many of them overseas; being placed in an adult-sized gyroscope and spun to split my personality further; being spun on a table-like device (aka 'spin-programming'); being covered with insects in enclosed containers.

"Most of the acts I was forced to perform that were filmed were later used to blackmail me into silence and further cooperation.

"Whenever I was caught remembering, either by my handler or by others assigned to keep an eye on me, I was then transported to a facility where I was forcibly given more drugs and ECT applications. These repeated regimens further shattered my memories and kept me controlled and amnesic. They continued until I finally remembered enough to make myself safer.

"Other acts were perpetrated against me, but this is all I can remember at this time. I attest that the above is completely true and correct."

Today Kathleen Sullivan lives in a retirement community near Chattanooga, Tennessee. Ironically her neighbors include two retired intelligence officers. They exchange polite greetings with Kathleen but little more. For her part she feels they have *"gradually become quite human towards me."* In going public, she hopes that other victims will emerge from *"the prisons of their minds and finally bring out all the truth. Not just some of it. All of it."*

Kathleen and untold others like her were part of a carefully coordinated CIA program that was involved in finding ways to control human behavior. The most telling evidence that the CIA failed is that Kathleen Sullivan has somehow survived to tell her story of that dark time in American history.

In mental institutions across the United States, in a psychiatric hospital attached to Canada's respected McGill University, and later at CIA safe houses in Germany, the mentally ill, suspected Soviet spies, double agents and even prostitutes, were subjected to a whole battery of gross experiments. Many never recovered from their maltreatment. The suspected Soviet spies and double agents were executed and buried in the forests of post-war Germany. American citizens who had been experimented upon in North America were either kept in asylums or cast aside; to this day some of them still live in the twilight zones of their minds, the result of what they suffered. MK-ULTRA was an extension of a program the Nazis had first instituted and the Soviets and Chinese had later refined. Some of the CIA work had been conducted at Los Alamos. When news finally surfaced in 1973 of what the CIA had been doing, there had been long nights of shredding behavior-modification techniques. The papers at Langley had then been incinerated in electric-powered furnaces in the basement.

The subsequent Congressional hearings had assured a stunned world that this could never happen again.

Whatever his feelings about what had been done by his predecessors — views that George Tenet kept to himself — he knew that while MK-ULTRA was officially dead, its legacy would not go away. It had surfaced again with the revelations about the break-in at Los Alamos.

But after Dr. Wen Ho Lee was arrested, the rumors surfaced. Was Los Alamos not only at the cutting edge of nuclear research — how to make smaller and even more lethal bombs than those that had destroyed Hiroshima and Nagasaki — but was it also once more the home for the successors of those who had been the most respected scientists in their day and who, in return for vast funding, had made a Faustian bargain with their ethics and personal morality to work in MK-ULTRA?

Were the holographic portal, anti-gravity propulsion and psychotronic remote influencing devices a logical extension for what MK-ULTRA had tried and failed to find? Was that why Lee had been so hurriedly released from nine months of incarceration, having been treated with the same isolation and severity as a prisoner on death row? Was it ultimately the fear that, if he was put on trial he would, in his own defense, become a whistle-blower unequalled?

Would Lee, for instance, have revealed all he knew about the ultra-secret laboratory — code-named S4 — carved into the base of the Papoose mountain? The mountain is deep inside the now infamous Area-51 on the Nellis Air Force Base in central Nevada. The area is known in scientific circles at Los Alamos as "Dreamland."

It has been whispered that what goes on there is the experimental groundwork for the mind control of the future — that, in the lab, experimental techniques far beyond anything publicly known today are being worked upon. These, so the rumors go, include brain implants and the creation of robots with electronic brains able to dominate man. Again, such rumors are not completely fanciful. Kevin Warwick, Professor of Cybernetics at the University of Reading, England, and a world authority on the subject is certain that *"machines will one day become the dominant life form on earth."* In other words, secret intelligence will be controlled by artificial intelligence. Is that the world "Dreamland" is trying to produce?

From time to time scientists from Los Alamos have been flown to the laboratory. Before doing so, each one was reminded again of the "total secrecy" clause in the contracts — and the severe penalties that would follow if they ever revealed what was inside the lab.

The installation is built into the Papoose mountain. It has nine entrances, each the size of an aircraft hangar door, positioned at an angle matching the configuration of the mountain. Each door is coated with a sand-textured paint to make it blend with the side of the mountain and desert floor. Not even the most powerful satellite surveillance camera would spot the doors.

Kathleen Ann Sullivan

To Whom It May Concern:

I am a 45 year old female, U.S. survivor of the CIA's MKULTRA and other subprojects that dealt with breaking and controlling subjects' minds and wills. I was first exposed to the personnel working on these projects when I was three years old. I was not able to begin to break away from their, and their associates', control until I received outside help beginning in the mid-1980's.

I have been in active, therapeutic recovery for over twelve years. My diagnoses are Dissociative Identity Disorder (D.I.D., formerly M.P.D.) and Post-Traumatic Stress Disorder (P.T.S.D.), delayed. I suffer horribly from anxiety, for which I am on Social Security Disability. Since I began remembering and becoming co-conscious with my altered states of consciousness, I have been repeatedly, voluntarily hospitalized due to major depression and suicidal tendencies, for which I am now on medication.

Just recently, I have decided to come out of hiding and go public about what was done to and through me. I was assaulted over three years ago for "talking" on a Canadian radio program (CKLN) about what was done to me, who did it, and how I was used as an adult by the CIA to do illegal activities for them and their associates. I finally have realized that I can't keep hiding . . . that leaves me only a shell of a life to live. I'm tired of hiding and I'm tired of living in fear.

My deceased father -- William Thomas Shirk Sr.; CIA grandfather -- James F. Cochran of Laureldale, Pennsylvania; and their associates, some of whom were Nazi war criminals brought to the US by the CIA; sought to break the minds and wills of their subjects, mostly children, and create altered states of consciousness that they could then train and control. I was one of their subjects. The experiments were all too successful in my mind and life.

Some of the things they did to me to break my will and control my mind and life were:

*Forced druggings – including opium, Thorazine, hallucinogens and experimental drugs
*Many sexual assaults over many years
*Electrical shock and torture – including bare live wires, stun guns, stun belts, and
  several series of ECT's designed to shatter my personality and fragment my memories
+Exposed to radiation
+Forced to harm animals
*Light probes (done in darkened rooms, usually)
*Occult ritualized torture and horrification
*Sensory deprivation, sometimes combined with drugs – including in padded rooms,
  buried coffins, large black boxes, and saltwater tanks
+Drowning and resuscitation
+Hanging and resuscitation
*Threats made against myself, my pets and the lives of my loved ones
+Starvation
*Isolation
+False imprisonment
*Hypnosis
+Being put in small crates or cages, some electrified

Affidavit from Kathleen Sullivan, an MK-Ultra survivor.

*Other forms of ritualistic, methodical, preplanned torture
*Being forced to witness assaults on others, including children and babies
*Being forced, beginning at my age 4, to harm others in controlled alter-states.
*Being forced to perform and assist in illegal pornography, to be sold on the black market
*Being forced to assist in breaking the minds of child victims (aka "programming")
+Being forced to perform in bestiality films, to be sold on the black market
*Being forced to act as a prostitute, sometimes as a lead-in to assassinations
- Being forced to participate in "black op" assassinations, many of them overseas
- Being placed in an adult-sized gyroscope and spun to split my personality further
+Being spun on a table-like device (aka "spin programming")
+Being covered with insects in enclosed containers
- Being forced to watch my beloved daughter be assaulted and tortured (she also
  developed M.P.D. and blessedly remembers little of her childhood)

Most of the acts I was forced to perform, that were filmed, were later used to blackmail
me into silence and further cooperation.

One of my children was forcibly taken away from me – I was made to believe that he
would not be harmed if I cooperated. My daughter, who probably is not physically
mine, was also used to blackmail me into cooperating and not trying to run away. (I
was told that if I tried to break control, my then-husband -- her father – would receive
custody and then they would be able to do anything they wanted to her, at any time.)
Because of these threats and concerns for my children, I did not try to break away when
I did remember and realize what was happening to me.

Whenever I was caught remembering, either by my then - handler husband (Alfred John
Dow of Lawrenceville, Georgia) or by others assigned to keep an eye on me, I was then
transported to a local facility where I was forcibly given more drugs and ECT
applications. These repeated regimens further shattered my memories and kept
me controlled and amnesic. They continued at least into the end of the 1980's and
may have continued into the early 1990's, before I finally remembered enough to
make myself safer.

Other acts were perpetrated against me, but this is all I can remember at this time. I
attest that the above is completely true and correct.

Sincerely,

Kathleen Ann Sullivan

Kathleen Ann Sullivan

- Done to me as an adult
+ Done to me as a child
* Done to me as a child and continued in my adult years

The Pentagon, or any other U.S. government intelligence agency, flatly refuses to discuss the work at the lab. All that is known of what is inside is that it is heavily guarded by marksmen on duty behind its portals with orders to shoot dead anyone who attempts to enter the hangar doors.

Whether Lee visited the lab and learned its secrets will never be known. In return for the dropping of those 59 charges against him, he guaranteed never again to speak about his work.

But could the work at the lab fit the analysis of Professor Warwick? *"The frontiers of space can be seen in a different way when the frailties and limitations of humans are removed. This will be achieved well before 2050. The human race will probably by then be surpassed by a network of intelligence machines that were created by humans. In doing so those creators will have orchestrated the destruction of the human race."*

Is that what the "Dreamworld" lab is doing? Was Lee one of those involved in "ET Technology"? The only certainty is that his silence shields the others.

No one knows if Tenet or any of his predecessors has ever visited the lab. All his colleagues will say — under an absolute guarantee of anonymity — is that whatever the CIA director saw and learned on his own visits to Los Alamos, he would share with no one. Boylan believes that Tenet may have had a *"glimpse into another world; that what he had learned had both frightened and intrigued him."*

George Tenet also knew that though Lee had not been a CSIS spy, China's Secret Intelligence Service had carried out its penetration of Los Alamos almost certainly with the help of another foreign intelligence service. On paper that service was deemed to be the closest of all friendly intelligence agencies to the American intelligence community. The service was Mossad, the external intelligence agency of Israel.

When Tenet had come into office, he had read two documents written by his predecessors. The first was penned by William Casey on March 21, 1984. *"A nation creates the intelligence community it needs. America relies on technical expertise because we are concerned to discover rather than secretly rule. The Israelis operate differently. Mossad, in particular, equates its actions with its nation's survival."*

The second document was written by Robert Michael Gates a mere week after he became Director of the CIA on December 15, 1986. *"Mossad's most celebrated director, Meir Amit, has said that Mossad should live by the credo 'Israel first, last and always. Always. We must never be caught going through the pockets of our friends. The key word is caught'."*

Commenting on that adage, Gates had detailed Mossad's increased penetration of the United States through economic, scientific and technological espionage. A special Israeli unit code-named "AL" — Hebrew for "above" — had been set up to prowl through California's Silicon Valley and Boston's Route 128 for high-tech secrets.

In his report to the Senate Intelligence Committee, another of Tenet's predecessors, Bobby Ray Inman, had identified Israel as one of six foreign nations with a "government-directed, orchestrated and clandestine effort to steal U.S. military and economic secrets."

Tenet had not forgotten that another on the list was China. Now, though he still could not prove it in a way that a court of law would demand proof, he was very certain that the Los Alamos operation had been a joint venture between Mossad and CSIS. For China the accruing benefits had been easy to understand: access to secrets that no other country possessed. For Israel those secrets were also beyond price. But to share them with China, Israel had demanded an extra price: access to other technology that China was developing which would give Israel a lead over its Arab neighbors in such vital areas as agriculture, water desalination and the other requirements that would ensure the country would continue to prosper and blossom in the arid landscape of their forefathers. Israel would also receive China's latest weapon technology, as advanced as that of the United States.

George Tenet, so his friends later said, had thought long and hard about how much of all this he should reveal to the Bush transition team. Those same friends had no doubt that, as his limousine eased its way through the traffic on its nine-mile journey into Washington, the question would still be uppermost in his mind.

Tenet knew this morning that he could have been driven on the first stage of his journey back into civilian life. When he had finished briefing the transition team on secrets some may have merely suspected and others would have no previous idea about, his work as Director of Central Intelligence could be all but over.

Soon a newcomer would enjoy his privileges. And, for George Tenet, the most satisfying had been the right to be driven anywhere he wanted to go in this state-of-the-art limousine which would pass on to his successor. The Lincoln Continental was the latest model; its CIA chauffeur had passed the most demanding driving course in the world. By his right knee, within instant reach, was a compartment containing a pump-action shot gun. The car's armor had added some 2000 pounds to the Lincoln's original weight. An armored rear partition and windshield had been integrated into the body shell. The doors were similarly protected, as was the roof.

The titanium-ceramic armor had been tested to withstand a 155 mm shell airbursting overhead, or a ten-pound mine detonating under the chassis. All the windows were proofed against 50-caliber armor piercing bullets.

Built into the passenger compartment was an oxygen mask and fire-suppression system, a global positioning indicator accurate to within one meter, and a jam-resistant satellite communications switchboard which could reach CIA headquarters, the Pentagon or the Oval Office in the White House. It could also contact Air Force One anywhere in the world at the press of a button.

In the event of the limousine's tires being shot out, the Lincoln would still be able to maintain a speed of 60 mph on the steel rims of its wheels.

The Lincoln had replaced the Oldsmobile that former directors had used. Inside the vehicle, George Tenet felt as invulnerable as it was possible to be.

Seated in the back seat heading towards the Beltway may well have been the moment when, as he had so often done before, he reached for his hand-tooled leather attaché case to study the briefing papers, the ones he would use this time to address the transition team. Each document was in its own coded file. Each briefing paper ran to no more than three pages, the maximum length Tenet liked briefs to be.

All bore the acronym: "Bigot List." This was a definition that the material was for a small select group of people entitled to see reports from a particularly sensitive agent or from an espionage operation. Apart from the President of the United States, the material was seen by the National Security Adviser, the White House Chief of Staff, the White House Chief Legal Counsel, the Attorney General and the Secretary of State.

Each document also carried the standard stamped classification: "Top Secret." This signified that it included material whose disclosure could be expected to cause either exceptionally serious national security damage or create international political damage.

That the transition team would now be privy to such data was a calculated risk Tenet had taken. Despite the picket line of restrictions surrounding each document (and he would preface his introduction by saying no document would be left behind), he knew there was always the possibility of a leak to either the *Post* or the *New York Times*. That had always been the nature of secrecy in Washington.

Two of the documents concerned the Russian Mafia.

The first dealt with the Mafia's relationship with the Mossad. It contained the revelation that the Israeli agency could soon be asked to move its European headquarters in Holland following highly embarrassing claims that Mossad had been secretly buying plutonium and other nuclear materials from the Russian Mafia. The allegation had come from a CIA agent in Amsterdam who had picked it up from Intel, the small but formidable division of Dutch intelligence.

Intel operated from a deep bunker near Amsterdam's Central Railway Station; the bunker had ironically been built to shelter the Dutch Royal Family in the event of a Soviet nuclear attack on the city at the height of the Cold War.

The CIA agent's report said that most of the nuclear material had been stolen by the Mafia from Russian weapons labs such as Chelyabinsky-70 in the Ural Mountains and Arsamas-16 in Nizhini Novorod, formerly Gorky.

Senior Mossad officers had insisted to Intel that precisely because the deadly materials were stolen, their agents had purchased them from the Russian Mafia. It was the only sure way to stop the material from being sold to Islamic and other terrorist groups.

While conceding that the Mossad claim was plausible, Intel investigators had become convinced the nuclear materials had been secretly shipped out of Amsterdam's Schipol Airport to boost Israel's own nuclear weapons manufacturing plant at Dimona in the Negev Desert. Already stockpiled there were an estimated 200 nuclear weapons.

For Tenet, knowing Mossad was trafficking with the Russian Mafia had rekindled a nuclear nightmare that has never quite gone away. While the Cold War doctrine of MAD — mutually assured destruction — was a thing of the past among the super powers, in its place was a more dangerous scenario where nuclear know-how and materials were on sale. It was capitalism, Wild East style, in which organized crime syndicates and corrupt government officials worked in league to create new markets for nuclear materials — a bazaar with some of the world's most dangerous weapons on offer.

Much of the work of tracing the stolen nuclear material was done at the European Trans-Uranium Institute (ETUI) in Karlsruhe, Germany. There, scientists used state-of-the-art equipment to track whether stolen materials had come from a military or civilian source. But the CIA agent in Amsterdam conceded *"it's like trying to catch a thief who has never been fingerprinted."*

To head off undoubtedly awkward questions should Mossad's own fingerprints be found, the Israeli service's director general, Efraim Halevy, had made a secret visit to Holland to explain Mossad's role to Intel. The Dutch service was still not convinced. The CIA report concluded that Intel had recommended to the Dutch government that Mossad should be asked to move its European headquarters in the El Al complex at Schipol Airport. Mossad had been based there for the past six years. From second floor offices in the complex — known at Schipol as "Little Israel" — eighteen Mossad officers run European operations.

The second part of the Russian Mafia report also dealt with its unusual relationship with Israel. The report detailed Israel's decision to allow a Russian Mafia boss, Seymon Yukovich Mogilevich, to travel on one of its passports. CIA's London Station had attached an MI5 report which described Mogilevich as *"one of the world's top criminals. Substantial sums of hard currency have been provided to Saddam Hussein by this man from the sale of Iraqi oil allowed to be sold under United Nations' sanctions. Mogilevich has laundered the money around the world for Saddam."*

The report detailed how one of America's largest and oldest banks, the Bank of New York, has been caught up in a maelstrom of money laundering orchestrated by Mogilevich. It was in the records of the conservative and, until now, well-regulated institution, that the first clues had emerged about the secret deal Saddam had struck with the Mafia baron.

The Bank of New York was the end of a "laundering" journey. Once "clean," the money was used by Mogilevich to provide Saddam Hussein with billions of U.S. dollars in hard currency.

The Saddam deal was only a small part of an unprecedented money-laundering operation. Banks as far apart as Germany and Australia had formed part of the money laundering chain Mogilevich had created. The CIA now believed Mogilevich had the financial resources available through his global criminal network to equal that of a medium-sized nation.

He had entered the Western financial world in 1988 when the Bank of New York began to aggressively seek business in Russia. Their contact man in the former Soviet Union was Bruce Rapport, a Swiss banker. Born in Haifa, Israel, the 50-year old Rapport ran an investment brokerage out of a modest office in Geneva. He operated in, among other places, Oman, Liberia and Haiti before setting up in New York.

Within five years he had established himself, through investments, as one of the Bank of New York's biggest individual stockholders. Using that position he offered to open doors for the bank in Russia. At some point Mogilevich saw his opportunity to use the Bank of New York for money laundering.

The CIA report revealed that investigators have now traced close to $5 billion that was laundered through one bank account in one month in 1999. All told, over $10 billion had passed through the account in the next six weeks.

Like a number of other Russian criminals, the CIA had taken steps to ensure that Mogilevich was barred from entering the United States or Britain.

Meantime, he continued to travel between Moscow and Budapest. No criminal activity was too small to catch his eye. As Jews prepared to leave the former Soviet Union for Israel, he told them they would need hard currency in the West. He took their art, jewelry and other valuables and sold them. They never saw him again.

While George Tenet remained uncertain what action if any the transition team would take on such matters once its members assumed power, he was certain they would be stunned by the documents he would present to them. Who could not be, he had told his aides before setting off to brief the team. Many of the documents dealt with the activities of Mossad. But that could not be helped. Long before Tenet had come to be Director of Central Intelligence, Mossad had been a problem for the United States. Equally, his own confidential briefings about the transition team members showed that a number had strong anti-Israeli leanings.

What would they say, for instance, to his detailed revelation that Israel had obtained three German-built submarines capable of launching nuclear warheads and hitting any target within a 900-mile range of its shores?

Each Dolphin-class submarine could carry 24 cruise missiles. Equipped with nuclear warheads, each missile would have a destructive power greater than the Hiroshima bomb. Displacing 1,720 tons and costing $350 million apiece, the combined destructive power of the three submarines gave Israel a total seaborne nuclear arsenal equal to its already powerful land and air capability.

Already successful missile test firings have been carried out by two of the submarines in the Indian Ocean.

The CIA report on the submarines revealed that the National Security Agency in Washington and U.S. Navy surveillance had placed two of the submarines patrolling some 500 miles off the Persian Gulf in early December 1999. The third submarine had been pinpointed at its dockyard in Haifa. It was expected to take up its station in the Mediterranean shortly.

All three submarines had begun their journey from the German dockyard at Kiel on April 21, 1999.

A few days before, over 100 Israeli sailors had arrived in the port city. They had been booked into small hotels near the Howaldstwerke Deutsche Werft shipyard. There, under tight security, the three submarines had been built. Shipyard workers believed the boats were for the German Navy. Only the yard's top management and the German Ministry of Defense knew the submarines were for Israel.

At dusk on April 21, the Israeli sailors arrived at the shipyard. They were members of an elite group known as "Force 700." Each man had been trained to crew the nuclear subs. Part of that training had been in the United States. The men of Force 700 divided up into 35 officers and ratings for each submarine. In addition, each boat carried five "specialists." They would be responsible for the cruise missiles that would be fitted to each vessel once it reached Israel.

Their journey to the Navy dockyard at Haifa would have been impossible without the covert support of the Madrid government after discreet pressure had been applied by President Clinton. The Spanish government's permission was required for the submarines to pass through its territorial waters on the journey to Israel.

Tenet planned to explain how both Washington and Madrid were assured that the submarines would not be equipped with cruise missiles with nuclear warheads. Then he would add that, not for the first time, Israel had duped both Spain and Washington.

Critical to masking its true intentions had been a number of secret visits Mossad Director Efraim Halevy made to both Madrid and Washington earlier in 1999. He had been chosen by Israeli Prime Minister Ehud Barak because Halevy is a former Israeli ambassador to Brussels and a seasoned diplomat.

He took charge of Mossad in 1995 — a time when Israel believed Iran would have the capability of launching a nuclear strike against Israel by 2002. Halevy had helped to convince the Israeli government it must develop a seaborne nuclear capability able to destroy military targets in Iran, Iraq or Libya.

In 1997, the order for the submarines was placed with the German shipyard. No one was told that the nuclear warheads for the cruise missiles would come from Israel's nuclear arsenal in the Negev desert.

Halevy's visit to Madrid was to obtain agreement for the three submarines to stay as close as possible to the Spanish coastline during their passage to Haifa. Spain, according to the CIA document Tenet would reveal to the transition committee, only agreed after President Clinton had reassured Madrid that the submarines would have no nuclear capability.

The three Dolphin-class subs, each 176-feet long, were allowed to negotiate Spanish waters. A few days later they reached their pens at Haifa. By then Halevy had persuaded Madrid and Washington to approve of the submarines carrying out sea trials in the Atlantic. The submarines once more passed through Spanish territorial waters. Out in the Atlantic the boats headed south. They passed around the Cape of Good Hope into the Indian Ocean. Off the coast of Sri Lanka the submarines conducted their program of test firings.

Using conventional warheads, the missiles hit Israeli targets moored some 900 miles away. The program of tests was completed while the Camp David negotiations were failing.

Unlike some of his predecessors, George Tenet knew the importance of holding his audience from the outset, preferably with a story that had a positive outcome. So he intended to re-create for them an intelligence operation which showed, despite the great technological advances of the past few years, that *humint*, intelligence gathered by spies on the ground, was still of critical importance. He would tell them the story of the Rockets of North Korea.

On July 15, 2000, a plump-cheeked Libyan in a silk suit and hand-tooled leather shoes sat down for lunch at the Hunbon Restaurant in central Pyongyang, the finest in North Korea. The man was Abu Bakr Jaber, and his host was Kim Sol, president of the state-owned Chongchengang Arms Corporation. The company built ballistic missiles, the Na-Dong weapons.

Abu Bakr Jaber was Libya's defense minister. He had traveled via Madrid and Basle in Switzerland to collect from banks where Libya held accounts with drafts to the value of $500 million. The money was to pay for thirty-six Na-Dong rockets and their launchers.

The deal had been completed earlier on that July morning when the bank for the arms corporation confirmed the drafts were in order.

Sol and Jaber had been driven across the city to the Hubon restaurant where only the elite of the Workers Party ate, paying with US dollars, the only currency the restaurant accepted.

Dining off thinly sliced beef, fatty duck, lobster and chicken, barbequed at their table on tiny gas cookers, and washed down with Japanese beer and sake, the two men had paid no attention to the young and smartly-dressed couple seated a few tables away. They were German BND intelligence agents who had tracked Jaber from the time he had flown from Tripoli on an Alitalia flight to Rome. From there they had tailed him to Madrid and Basle and finally to Pyongyang.

Flashing their wads of dollars, the couple gave the appearance of wealthy tourists to the guards at the restaurant door who made sure no North Korean could enter unless his name was on the restaurant table booking chart.

Twenty-four hours later, having made the obligatory visit to Pyongyang's Taeson department store, a run-down version of similar stores in the West, the couple had left North Korea having shown their German passports at the airport.

Within a few hours, Konrad Portner, head of the BND, had informed George Tenet and other NATO intelligence chiefs of the deal brokered in the Korean capital.

A month later the first consignment of missiles and their launchers arrived in the Libyan capital. From Tripoli they had been dispersed along the Mediterranean coast, targeted on NATO bases in Spain, Italy, Greece and Turkey. The rockets were also within range of Israel.

The weapons were similar to Scud missiles and could carry conventional, nuclear or chemical weapon warheads.

In his "red alert" message to Tenet and NATO chiefs, the BND chief stated that Libya had stockpiled both chemical and biological weapons. The arsenals were based in underground bunkers in the country's desert hinterland. Libya had obtained the North Korean missiles only months after the United Nations sanctions against the country were lifted. That had followed Colonel Gadaffi's decision to hand over two former Libyan intelligence officers suspected of involvement in the Lockerbie bombing.

The presence of the thirty-six weapons ensured Libya was now one of the most powerfully-armed nations in the Mediterranean.

The Na-Dong missiles had the sophisticated technology that was much sought after by rogue states denied access to Western arms. North Korea was known to have also supplied Iran with Na-Dong missiles.

In January 2000 Indian customs officials seized a North Korean freighter with a concealed cargo of missile guidance and navigation systems. Indian naval intelligence initially believed the systems were destined for Pakistan. But an investigation by the CIA revealed the cargo was destined for Libya. The failure of that attempt to import the North Korean missiles led to them being flown by air.

A German BND officer had flown to Tripoli and told Libya that NATO was aware of the missiles being in Libya and that unless they were immediately mothballed, Libya faced a pre-emptive strike. Libya had been left in little doubt it would come from Israel. Within a week the missiles were back in their packing cases.

Like most incoming Presidents and foreign heads of state he had met in his career, George Tenet suspected that President George W. Bush would relish nothing more than an insider's view of the one spymaster who had bedeviled the CIA and other Western intelligence agencies during the long years of the Cold War. His name was Markus Wolf and he had been head of the foreign intelligence service of the Ministry of State Security of the German Democratic Republic: the Stasi.

For most of his professional life Wolf had been known to other intelligence services as "the man without a face," a tribute to both his skills at disguise and his ability to stay in the shadows. Finally, Britain's MI6 had managed to snatch a photograph of him.

Wolf was now retired and living in Berlin where so many of his German agents had also found homes. But with the skills that continued to make him so formidable, Wolf had only recently let slip the full extent of how many old Stasi agents were still living undercover in a number of European countries including Britain and the United States and Canada. So far Wolf had refused to name them — despite the blandishments of the CIA to offer him a new identity and life in California. But Tenet still hoped that perhaps one day Wolf could be persuaded to finally come in from the cold.

A story like that, Tenet knew, would most certainly lighten the mood at the meeting he was being driven to. And he was certain no one present would fail to see the bittersweet irony in the attempt to bring Wolf to the United States, when set against the determination of previous Washington Administrations to keep another spy incarcerated until the end of his life in a Federal prison. The man was Jonathan Pollard.

Tenet had ordered a briefing paper prepared that dealt with demands Jonathan Pollard should be released. Pollard had been sentenced to life imprisonment after he had been found guilty of being the greatest traitor in the history of the United States. Compared to Pollard, the damage done by other U.S. spies during the Cold War, it was said at his trial, "pales into insignificance."

Pollard had been a civilian senior analyst in the most secret Navy Field Operational Intelligence Office in Suitland, Maryland. The post required top-security clearance because Pollard had access to the most highly classified files in the entire U.S. intelligence community. In the time he had spied for Israel, Pollard read and copied and transmitted every worthwhile secret the United States possessed.

Since his imprisonment, the all-powerful Jewish lobby in Washington had battled tirelessly to have Pollard released. The Conference of Presidents of Major Jewish Organizations, a consortium of fifty-five groups, had lobbied the White House. The consortium argued that whatever Pollard had done could not be called high treason *"because Israel was then and remains now a close ally."* They planned to use the same arguments once President Bush was in the Oval Office.

Further pressure would also come from many American leading Jewish religious organizations demanding freedom for Pollard. The most vociferous would undoubtedly be the powerful Reform Union of American Hebrew Congregations.

Harvard Law School Professor Alan M. Dershowitz, who had served as Pollard's lawyer, had already called for *"the need to correct this long-standing miscarriage of justice. There is nothing in Pollard's conviction to suggest he had compromised the nation's intelligence-gathering capabilities or betrayed world-wide intelligence data."*

George Tenet intended to tell the transition team how wrong Dershowitz had been.

Dershowitz, who had also worked for the defense of O. J. Simpson and knew the value of striking at the right time, had first made his appeal to have Pollard freed after a crucial moment in the Israeli-Palestinian Wye River Conference in Maryland in October 1998. Israel's then Prime Minister, Benyamin Netanyahu, said it would be difficult for him to *"convince my own people unless there is some give and take."*

Clinton had asked, *"What kind of give and take, Bibi?"*

Netanyahu replied: *"Well, there is Pollard for a start … you know he is a cause célèbre in my country."*

Clinton said: *"The best I can do is to order a review of the case."*

Tenet intended to reveal to the transition team that he would have resigned if Pollard were freed. Tenet knew he was not the only one who had joined in the battle over Pollard's future. Four retired U.S. admirals, one who had served as a director of U.S. Naval Intelligence, had circulated a paper within the Washington intelligence community that bluntly stated Pollard's release would not only be *"irresponsible to the highest degree, but also a victory for the clever public relations campaign waged for the worst traitor this country has had."*

Tenet would tell the transition team: *"Pollard stole every worthwhile intelligence secret we have. We are still trying to recover from what he did. We have had to withdraw dozens of agents in place in the former Soviet Union, in the Middle East, South Africa and friendly nations like Britain, France and Germany. The American public just doesn't know the full extent of what he did."*

Ironically, Pollard in his youth made no secret of his support for Israel. The youngest son of an award-winning microbiologist, his family and friends have described his near obsession with *"the power of Mossad."* At Stanford University he said he was *"waiting for the day when Israel will call upon me."* Nobody took him seriously; many thought he was a fantasist. For that reason the CIA rejected his job application, dismissing him as a *"blabbermouth."*

But the agency also saw that he had an extraordinary gift as an analyst. This talent allowed Naval Intelligence to overlook his other faults.

His former chief, David Muller, had publicly said *"Pollard was a genius when it came to breaking down complex data. He was a one-off in every sense of the word. With hindsight we all should have listened to the alarm bells ringing. Pollard had a drug habit. He had huge debts. He lived well above his salary. In every sense he was a prime target for a foreign intelligence service to recruit."*

No other U.S. spy in modern intelligence has generated such controversy as Jonathan Pollard. Now forty-six years of age and incarcerated in a maximum security jail for the rest of his life, no one publicly still knows the full extent of the damage he did after he was recruited in November 1984 for Israel.

Over eleven months Pollard had raped U.S. intelligence. His trial was told *"over 360 cubic feet of top secret paper was transmitted to Israel."* They gave Israel's government a unique overview of U.S. operations throughout the world.

Pollard was arrested on November 21, 1986, outside the Israeli embassy in Washington. He elected to plea-bargain rather than face a full trial. The U.S. government agreed with alacrity; no state secrets would have to be revealed, especially about the extent of Israeli espionage. After the plea bargain the Justice Department supplied the court with a sworn declaration signed by Casper W. Weinberger, then Secretary of Defense, which detailed by categories some of the intelligence systems that had been compromised.

Pollard was sentenced to life in prison. He divorced his wife, Anne (who had been sentenced to five years imprisonment for being his accomplice), and converted to Orthodox Judaism. In 1994 he married, in prison, a Toronto schoolteacher named Elaine Zeitz. Esther Pollard, as she was from then on known, became the spearhead of the campaign to have her husband freed. She planned now to lobby the Bush Administration.

Tenet intended to tell the transition team that: *"If it is the last thing I do, it is to convince you that Pollard must remain locked away. Much of what he knows is still in his head. Some of what he stole is still in use by the CIA. The reason the key to his cell was thrown away until he dies is that he would be useful to Israel. They would just have to show him something and Pollard would know how to extrapolate from it. A man like that does not lose his touch because he is locked away. To even think of seeing Pollard within the context of the 'big picture' in the Middle East would be unthinkable."*

The only remote possibility that he might go free or at least have his sentence shortened was if Mossad were to reveal in full, as part of an exchange deal, the role Israel played in what was undoubtedly the most stunning espionage operation with China's CSIS which had led to the penetration of Los Alamos.

Approaching the Washington suburbs, Tenet's mind may well have dwelled on the irony that only a few minutes from his route lived two of the people who had become the unwitting victims of that operation. On Sundays they would nod to each other as they took their places in the pews of the same church in which they worshipped. But, behind that polite greeting, George Tenet knew a great deal more about them than William and Nancy Burke Hamilton could ever have realized.

The Hamiltons had been born into an era, the Thirties, when Norman Thomas, the black liberal rights leader, was the nation's conscience — the voice of the mute, the advocate of the dispossessed, a prophet who spoke out against injustice while others fled into silence.

Bill had steadfastly refused to yield his own idealism to despair and integrity was in his blood, in the marrow of his bones. In Nancy he had found a soulmate ready to tackle grotesque inequalities, conspicuous waste, gross exploitation and poverty. Both subscribed to the belief that the secret to the good life was to have the right loyalties and to hold them in the correct scale of values.

The couple had grown up through many of the pivotal events which had made America what it was: the bus boycott at Montgomery, Alabama; Little Rock; Russia launching its first Sputnik; the founding of the John Birch Society; and freedom riders in Dixie. Later had come the Bay of Pigs; Kennedy confronting Khrushchev in Vienna; John Glenn orbiting the earth; and the Cuban missile crisis. Then: Apollo 11 landing on the moon; Chappaquidick; the Chicago Seven trial; and, of course, Watergate.

All these events helped to shape the Hamiltons' attitude to life; to test their faith and belief in the strength of justice.

It would be easy for those they did not admit into their close-knit working and private lives to dismiss them as dull, and perhaps even colorless. Those were the people who did not see the glint in Bill's eyes when he felt he was being railroaded, or the way Nancy pursed her lips when she felt that there was "*something not quite right here.*" It was easy to make wrong assumptions about them: the less-than-fashionable way they dressed, their taste for simple foods. If people felt there was an apple-pie mentality about them, that was fine by the Hamiltons. They were that increasing rarity in Washington and elsewhere in the United States: patriots. They were content to be no more, no less.

They may well have lived out their lives, Tenet had said to colleagues in the U.S. intelligence community, in comfortable anonymity if William Hamilton had not received a telephone call on a day as cold as this one in December 2000.

The call had come on February 10, 1983, to the offices of Inslaw, a small company Hamilton and his wife co-owned. The caller was Madison "Brick" Brewer, a senior official at the Justice Department. Inslaw developed software programs in its offices on Washington's 15th Street NW. Earnest Midwestern-ers, there was something endearingly old-fashioned about them in their soft drawls, courtesy and quiet determination to see if their latest invention would secure for them what Bill called *"at last our place in the world."*

Their expectation was based on how they had transformed a software pro-gram, Promis — Prosecutors Management Information Systems — into some-thing very different. It was now called Enhanced Promis and it had the poten-tial to turn the Hamiltons into multi-millionaires.

Their creation of Enhanced Promis also seemed to them the perfect way to repay their patriotism — and make a fair profit from their hard work. They wanted the United States government to be their first client. This decision exemplified their own unassailable belief in the Constitution and those it served. They spoke of their creation with an excitement usually seen in new parents for their child.

On that February day in 1983 the call to William Hamilton from Brewer thrilled the Hamiltons. As the Justice Department Project Manager, Brewer had considerable power over the future of Enhanced Promis. In one of the many twists the story was about to assume, Brewer had once worked for Inslaw. Bill Hamilton had fired him because of "good cause." A circumspect man of few words, Hamilton had never elaborated in public his feelings towards Brewer. For his part, Brewer had maintained a stoic silence. But on that February day all was cordial between both men.

During the call, Hamilton was to recall Brewer had said that the Justice Department would have no objection to Inslaw going into *"all necessary detail"* to how Enhanced Promis worked to the visitor that Brewer was going to send over by cab from the Justice Department. His name was Dr. Orr and he was from Tel Aviv.

To Bill Hamilton his forthcoming visitor was potentially further proof that *"Justice was going to go on playing it fair and square."*

Bill Hamilton had written a letter to the Department of Justice detailing the improvements made to the original, public-domain Promis, asking the Depart-ment to waive rights it *"might claim to the Enhanced version."*

On August 11, 1982, a Justice lawyer replied: *"To the extent that other enhance-ments (beyond the public domain Promis) were privately funded by Inslaw, and not specified to be delivered to the Department of Justice under any other contract or agree-ment, Inslaw may assert whatever proprietary rights it may have."*

The Hamiltons saw the letter as clear-cut: Enhanced Promis was their cre-ation to profit from. They would later be comforted by the clarification offered by the then deputy attorney-general Arnold Burns, that *"our lawyers (at DOJ) are satisfied that Inslaw's lawyers could sustain the claim in court that we had waived those proprietary rights."*

Completely reassured that profits that would accrue from the considerable sums they had invested in Enhanced Promis were theirs alone, Bill and Nancy Hamilton had constantly updated Enhanced Promis. In his submission to the Justice Department, Bill Hamilton had eloquently argued that the need for such software was all too evident:

"The United States government, the most powerful government in the world, has internal information systems which are mired in the archaic technology of the 1960s. There is a Department of Justice database, an Attorney General's database, and an IRS database. Every arm of government has its own database. But none of them can share information. That makes tracking offenders almost always difficult and building cases against them a long and bureaucratic task."

Hamilton acknowledged that in the past efforts had been made to deal with the problem when Inslaw had been a non-profit corporation funded entirely through government grants and contracts. Its prime client in those days had been the Law Enforcement and Assistance Administration, LEAA. Through public funding Inslaw had developed the original program, calling it Promis.

When President Carter closed down the LEAA, the Hamiltons bought and converted Inslaw to a for-profit corporation. They set to work using their own money to continue to upgrade the original Promis. So significant had been the many improvements made that the Hamiltons had renamed the software Enhanced Promis.

The technically-minded at the Department of Justice readily understood how significant the changes had been to create Enhanced Promis. Bill Hamilton explained that the public domain Promis had run on Burroughs, Wang and IBM machines, all of which used 16-bit architectures. But Enhanced Promis operated on a 32-bit architecture and ran on a DEC VAX microcomputer. To those baffled with technology, Bill Hamilton had said that *"the difference is like comparing a Ford Edsel to a Rolls Royce."*

But everyone at the Department of Justice grasped that Enhanced Promis had a staggering 570,000 lines of computer code, allowing it to integrate with innumerable databases without a need to reprogram. In essence, Enhanced Promis could convert data into priceless information on a scale never before imagined. Hamilton, long accustomed to the ways of the government, knew that *"anyone in Washington will tell you that information, when wielded with finesse, is power — and Enhanced Promis is the most powerful of computer tools."*

No one at the Justice Department disagreed with him.

Enhanced Promis went far beyond the original public domain version. It could not only handle the case management and tracking workloads of large urban jurisdictions, but enabled prosecutors to keep detailed track of cases and individuals entered into the labyrinth of the U.S. criminal justice system. Further, it would also keep an eye on all their known associates who had so far evaded prosecution: Mafia bosses, drug barons, arms dealers, money launderers, crooks of every kind. Enhanced Promis could keep an electronic check on them all. The Hamiltons knew in certain hands it also had the potential to be the most effective espionage tool modern intelligence had ever used.

It did not depend on some satellite in outer space to do so, or by obtaining court orders to implement wiretaps. The appeal of Enhanced Promis was its essential simplicity. It tracked data held confidentially in other databases. Once a target subject had been identified, the software would tap into the services he used: bank and telephone company records, the water department, credit card companies, travel itineraries and various utility services that are essential to make life go smoothly.

In his presentation to the Department of Justice, Hamilton had explained:

"If a target person suddenly started using more water and more electricity and making more phone calls than usual, it would be reasonable to assume he had guests staying with him. Enhanced Promis could then start searching for the records of his friends and associates. If any of those were found to have stopped using their own essential utilities, then it could be surmised that he or she might be staying with the original target. So the net would widen. Enhanced Promis has the capability to conduct simultaneous searches on 100,000 persons. If they are suspected of being linked to the original suspect, the software can search all the police and crime records in the country, for the original target and all his known or suspected associates. The software is also sophisticated enough to uncover details which would reveal the true identity of anyone using an alias. It could then discover all the contacts that alias has made. And so on. In theory, Enhanced Promis has the ability to track every citizen in the United States by accessing their personal data files. The barest details of their lives would be sufficient: a birth certificate, a marriage license, a driver's license, an employment record."

The Hamiltons had heard disquieting tales of how government officials would casually ruin a career over a late drink at an embassy or slyly tarnish a reputation over dinner. But none of this had touched them personally and therefore they never had to question their relationship with the Justice Department. Enhanced Promis would guarantee their own future; just as other discoverers of great inventions had been honored and remembered. It was a touching conceit for a couple who had none of the airs and graces of Washington.

On almost every occasion he telephoned, project manager "Brick" Brewer had some nugget to impart. Attorney General Edwin Meese III had praised Enhanced Promis. Deputy Attorney General Lowell Jensen had called it *"one of the great discoveries of this century."* Brewer himself had said that the Hamiltons should be proud of what they had achieved.

Now, on that bleak February morning in 1983, he had more good news. The Hamiltons would have a chance to show off Enhanced Promis. Would the Hamiltons give Dr. Orr a demonstration of how Enhanced Promis worked? Very likely, added Brewer, Dr. Orr would go back to Israel not only impressed with what he would have seen, but also ready to urge his own ministry to buy the software to keep track of Israeli criminals.

The Hamiltons were elated. Waiting for their visitor, Dr. Orr, they made sure that their modest offices and research and development area were ship-shape. Both lived by the credo that first impressions are the ones that matter. Nancy made sure there was fresh coffee in the pot and the china they used for visitors was laid out. There were cookies on a plate. The staff had been briefed on the importance of Dr. Orr's visit. After a final check that everything was in order, Bill and Nancy sat back to await his arrival. They had never met someone from

Israel before and certainly not someone as important as Dr. Orr. His prominence spoke for itself in the way Brewer had arranged matters so quickly.

The company's staff was all on hand to greet their visitor and, like Bill and Nancy Burke Hamilton, they could barely conceal their excitement. All those years of research and development, of following Bill's cheerful cry of *"back to the drawing board,"* and Nancy's ever-ready cups of coffee to sustain flagging energy: it all seemed to have been worthwhile.

Dr. Orr arrived by cab. Muffled in a top coat and wearing a cap with earmuffs, he was a striking figure. With the build of a wrestler and a bone-crunching handshake, he had a voice to match: guttural and heavily accented, his words broken by a smile that never seemed to go beyond his lips. But the most striking thing about Dr. Orr were his eyes. They reminded Bill of *"a computer — tracking everything. It was quite uncanny and intimidating. Impressive too."*

Flanked by Bill and Nancy, Dr. Orr was taken on a tour of the offices where Enhanced Promis had been patiently created — chip by chip, microcircuit by microcircuit. Bill Hamilton's office had been chosen for the formal presentation. He explained to his visitor how an Enhanced Promis disc could select from myriad alternatives the one that made most sense; how it eliminated deductive reasoning because, as Bill put it, *"there are too many correct but irrelevant matters to simultaneously take into account for human reasoning. Our software can be programmed to eliminate all superfluous lines of enquiry and collate data at a speed beyond human capability."*

It was virtually the same presentation that had hooked the senior staff of the Justice Department.

Dr. Orr's questions were few and the sort the Hamiltons expected to be asked. Could Enhanced Promis be adapted to different languages? It could. Had Inslaw patented it? Of course: it was the first thing its inventors had done. Was it expensive? Yes, relatively so. But it was worth the price.

Bill Hamilton remembered that Dr. Orr had given another of his quick smiles that never left his lips. Then, as swiftly as he appeared, the man from Tel Aviv had gone, driving away in a cab down 15th Street.

It was only then that Nancy Hamilton remembered they had not asked Dr. Orr how and where he could be contacted. Bill was reassuring. "Brick" Brewer, their contact at the Justice Department, would surely have Dr. Orr's address in Tel Aviv.

They both agreed that Dr. Orr's visit had been memorable. *"No small talk. He just asked the questions which mattered. He was a man you could do business with."*

Not for a moment did they suspect he was the world's leading spymaster. His real name was Rafi Eitan and, for a quarter of a century, he had been deputy director of operations for Mossad, Israel's legendary secret intelligence service.

Rafi Eitan's spying operations against the United States had reached a high point some five years before, far to the west of where the Hamiltons had awaited his arrival. As with several of his espionage missions against the United States, Eitan had been accompanied by a trusted subordinate, Yosef. He was an aeronautics engineer, more used to spending his working day standing over a drawing board and working on blueprints than being exposed to the rigors of the desert.

On that August morning the furnace heat of the Nevada desert reminded Yosef of his own desert village on the other side of the world, in Israel's Negev wilderness. Already with the sun barely above the horizon, his shirt and pants were soaked with dark patches of perspiration that also ran down his pinched cheeks and chin.

The area where they stood was part of the highly secure government base on the Nevada Test Site. It would become known as Area 51, and is located some 125 miles north of Las Vegas. Close to where Eitan and Yosef stood, years later would be constructed the underground lab, C-4, hidden under the Papoose mountain.

Yosef wondered how Rafi Eitan showed no signs the one hundred degree-plus temperature was affecting him. He still wore the serge two-piece he had purchased in Tel Aviv and had never changed out of since arriving in California two days before. Squat and barrel-chested and still in his early forties, Eitan was myopic and almost totally deaf in his right ear from fighting in Israel's War of Independence in 1948.

In his inside breast pocket was a letter of introduction signed by Israel's then prime minister, Menachem Begin, a one-time street fighter who had risen to become one of his nation's most astute politicians. The letter said that both Eitan and Yosef were attached to the University of Tel Aviv where they were carrying out studies on the effect of "climactic conditions on electromagnetics in relation to aerodynamics." Rafi Eitan was named as "*Professor Isaak Goldstein*"; Yosef was identified as "*Dr. Solomon Kublemann.*"

Their journey to California started when a Jewish scientist who had once worked at the Moscow Institute of Radio Engineering, had managed to leave Russia in 1973 at the height of the Yom Kippur War. Although Israel's pilots flew America's most advanced jet attack aircraft and were as skilled in aerial combat as their US counterparts, Israel had lost 109 aircraft in the first eighteen days of the conflict. Most were shot down by radar-guided ground-to-air missiles and anti-aircraft batteries. What made it more galling was that the Syrian and Egyptian ground gunners were all too clearly poorly trained.

Yet evasive maneuvers by Israel's pilots to avoid Arab missiles had proven to be disastrous; all the turning and twisting drilled into them at flying school to slow down an incoming missile actually made the aircraft more vulnerable to ground fire.

It was during the post-mortem into the war, held within the walled citadel of the *kirya*, the Israeli Defense Force headquarters in Tel Aviv, that Rafi Eitan heard about the Russian engineer and the papers he had stolen from the Moscow Institute. Eitan was no scientist. Even the title of the paper, to which his attention had been drawn, made his eyes glaze: "*Method of Edge Waves in the Physical Theory of Diffraction.*" After several readings, his own staff said the paper also made no sense to them.

Eitan discovered the engineer, Pyotr Ufimstev, had recently been set free from his CIA safe house in Washington and was working for the U.S. Department of Defense.

Yosef was given the task of "*coming alongside*" Ufimstev. Yosef had little difficulty in infiltrating the Russian groups Ufimstev frequented. In Yosef's later words Ufimstev's paper, even translated into English, was "*one that only a nerd's nerd could make sense of.*" Yosef was no nerd. After days of patient study and cross-checking the meaning of what Ufimstev was claiming, Yosef found what he had been looking for.

On pages 35–38 of what Ufimstev had written was an analysis of a century-old formula created by the Scottish physicist, James Clark Maxwell. This had later been expanded by the German electromagnetic expert, Arnold Johannes Sommerfeld.

Both Maxwell's and Sommerfeld's calculations were the reason Rafi Eitan and Yosef had come to the United States. Six years after the disastrous Yom Kippur War, the United States had come up with an aircraft capable of beating any Arab radar ground defenses. It had been developed by the Lockheed Aircraft Corporation.

It was the Stealth fighter-bomber.

It had taken Israel eighteen months of lobbying at the highest level in Washington to allow Eitan and Yosef to witness the first test flight, the only outsiders given such permission. It was tangible evidence of the close relationship that existed between Washington and Israel.

The combined skills of Abraham Feinberg, the most powerful Jewish fundraiser for the Democratic Party in the United States, along with the political skills of Robert McNamara, a former Secretary of State for President John F. Kennedy, had been required to ensure Eitan and Yosef would have ringside seats at this historic moment.

Even Rafi Eitan, who knew most things, later admitted he did not know the full details of how the lobbying had eventually led them, via the Department of Defense and the Pentagon, to be present at the test flight.

On arrival at Los Angeles airport, Eitan and Yosef had been driven across the city to downtown Burbank where the Lockheed Aircraft Corporation had the most secret of all its high-security research centers. Simply known as the "Skunk Works" — named after the Andy Capp character "skunk" — it was a windowless two-story building. Its walls were thick enough to resist the most powerful eavesdropping equipment on board Soviet spying trawlers in those days patrolling off the coast of California.

Formally known as the Lockheed Advanced Development Project Center, The Skunk Works was where the Stealth aircraft had gone through its many development stages.

Rafi Eitan had briefed himself fully on the Skunk Works role within the Lockheed aeronautical empire. Founded by Kelly Johnson, long one of the key aerodynamicists in American aviation, Johnson had designed the U-2 spy plane and a small air force of other secret airplanes earning Lockheed the nickname of being the CIA's "toy maker."

Johnson's close relationship with the CIA was in marked contrast with the one he had with what he called *"those goddamned Air Force blue suits."*

Rafi Eitan, ever ready to reveal a piece of information which appeared to be "insider" data, regaled Lockheed executives over dinner with accounts of some of Mossad's previous operations. Eitan was a gifted storyteller — anyone who had heard his version of how Mossad had captured Adolf Eichmann in Argentina would vouch for that.

Then, in a switch of mood, he described his visit to Auschwitz-Birkenhau; how a tangible sense of evil permeated the place. Other concentration camps he had visited seemed like survivals from the receding past, like something from blurred black-and-white newsreels. But Auschwitz was different. He had gone there on a winter's day and what had struck him was the sheer size of the place: It was a place for killing on an industrial scale, a place of factory murder, of mass production slaughter, of assembly lines that ended at the door to the ovens. What had made it so indelible in his mind was that Auschwitz came from the same world that had produced autobahns and Volkswagens, I.G. Farben and domestic gadgets from Krupps.

His audience had sat in silence — who could not? — as he explained that close to over a million-and-a-half people had been exterminated at Auschwitz, an average of eight hundred men, women and children each day for five years. Put another way, it meant that every twenty-four hours some thirty-two tons of flesh, bone and cartilage had been destroyed.

He did not tell them that was the prime reason that had shaped his thinking, making him Israel's master spy. If what he did helped to ensure Auschwitz would never again happen to his people, then it justified all the deceit, lying and double-dealing his work required.

In California he stuck rigidly to his *"cover of the academic who drank little and occasionally interspersed the conversation with a risqué story."* The Lockheed executives regarded him *"as a great guy."*

Next morning Rafi Eitan and Yosef were among the team of Lockheed engineers and scientists and senior officers from the CIA and the United States Air Force who found themselves out in the Nevada desert at the test site over which the Stealth prototype would perform.

A Lockheed executive had told Rafi Eitan that the site was half the size of Israel and, standing there in the scorching Nevada desert heat, Eitan found it easy to believe. The site stretched as far as his eye could see. Far beyond the horizon, soldiers patrolled the chain-link fence line, making sure no unauthorized person could tell what was going on inside the site.

Though it was still only 8:30 a.m., the temperature was well over the 100-degree mark. In an hour it would be too hot to stand close to the reflected heat from the trucks parked amidst the puff-balls bouncing across the scree as if they were being hit by invisible billiard cues.

The vans contained radar technicians and a small army of Lockheed executives and those from the Central Intelligence Agency and Pentagon officers. Rafi Eitan and Yosef were in a van where technicians were glued to their scopes ready for the signal the test was underway. Far out in the desert waited Marines equipped with ground-to-air Hawk missile launchers. Their tracking equipment was so powerful it could detect a buzzard riding on thermals thirty miles away. The Hawk missile crews were briefed to score a "kill" on the Stealth prototype: the aircraft was so secret it was still only known as Have Blue.

At the core of the plane's complex set of computers was a powerful anti-radar device. The brief for the Marine gunners was to locate the aircraft when it was still at least fifty miles away, then to push all the lock-on buttons on their missiles. In a combat situation, this would have almost certainly signaled the destruction of the aircraft.

Eitan had been both astonished and excited when he learned Lockheed engineers had provided the missile crews with precise details of the prototype's flight plan. Eitan would remember one engineer had said "to make it easier for them, we're giving them the exact flight plan. It's as if I had pointed a finger at a spot in the sky and said aim at that point and you'll score a hit. Except there won't be one."

The risk from such confidence failing was huge. If a Hawk's missile-homing system registered a "hit," it meant the entire Stealth program was back to the drawing board. Tens of millions of dollars had already been invested by Lockheed in the project. If the test failed, no one could be certain whether the company was ready to risk more. For Eitan and Yosef their hope of finding an aircraft that would give Israel its vital air superiority would be over. And, since the near disaster of the Yom Kippur War, Eitan was certain it was only a matter of time before the Arabs would attack again. And next time their ground defenses would be better trained and equipped, thanks to Russian help.

Both Israelis were only partially encouraged by the reactions of the observers. The Lockheed team exuded confidence. No tracking system in the world, they murmured to each other, would be able to locate the Stealth airplane. It had the capability to deflect radar beams like a bulletproof shield so that no missile or homing device would be able to "see" its approach. On the missile's tracking system, even one as sophisticated as the Hawk's, the radar profile of the aircraft would appear to be no bigger than that of a sparrow.

That was the theory, and half of the Pentagon radar experts went along with it. But the other half, and they included members of the CIA's Science and Technology Division, felt this was what one called "aerodynamic hogwash." The mood among the cynics around Eitan was that Lockheed was engaged in a slick piece of salesmanship designed to pour untold millions more dollars into a project that so far had only been demonstrated on a forty-foot wooden model. The model had been placed on top of a pole on a radar test range. The test had hardly been conclusive.

The two camps — what Eitan called "the for and againsters" — had come to Nevada with their views unchanged. The demonstration was to settle the matter.

But for Eitan there was another issue. He did not know much about the finer points of radar technology; in fact, in his own later words, "*most science left him cold.*" But, with the instinct that made him a great intelligence officer, he sensed — "*just sensed*" — that Lockheed "*could be on to something.*"

His role at the test site was not to take sides between the "*bad-mouthing and you-better-believe-it groups.*" His job was to pick up every item of hard information he could. Yosef, with the trained mind of an engineer who knew what was, and was not, important to note — was there to guide him.

Rafi Eitan was equipped with a minute buttonhole-sized camera Mossad's technicians had designed. It had twice the speed of a Minnox but was totally silent and could shoot hundreds of frames without re-loading. To work it, all Rafi Eitan had to do was to brush his jacket as if flicking away a speck of dust. Another flick and the mini-camera would stop filming.

In the run up to the test, he had visited several of the vans asking intelligent but non-threatening questions to the Lockheed and Pentagon officers. The camera had behaved perfectly.

They had told him all the Marines manning the Hawk missiles had been told their target had a "*black box in its nose which would emit powerful beams to deflect incoming radar signals.*" The gunners were confident it would still not deflect their tracking system. In the words of one, "*this Lockheed plane is a dead duck once it takes off.*"

To decide whether there had been a "kill" each missile crew would monitor its tracking system on radar scopes inside their windowless command vans. But a Pentagon officer and a Lockheed executive each would stand outside the command vans and confirm that the prototype aircraft had passed overhead.

At 9:05 a.m., a Pentagon officer peering through binoculars murmured into a lipmike: "*I have bogey at eight. Chaser estimated five behind.*" The Pentagon officer confirmed the sighting.

Translated, it meant the Lockheed spotter had located the Stealth prototype at 8,000 feet. Some five miles behind was a T-38 chase plane. It was there to ensure, in the event of the Stealth developing a problem such as an engine malfunction requiring it to be talked down to a safe landing, the T-38 would act as its shepherd.

Suddenly a blip appeared, flying along the same track which the prototype had flown a good two minutes earlier — and was now some fifty miles distant.

Years later Rafi Eitan would remember the exchanges that followed inside the command van.

A Pentagon officer turned to the Lockheed team and sighed. "*It's the T-38.*"

Big and unmistakable on the radar scopes the chase plane passed noisily overhead.

A CIA officer shrugged and added: "*Looks like your gizmo came down some place out there before it could be killed.*"

Then the Lockheed spotter who had run into the van spoke. "*Gentlemen, either all your radars are on the blink or I have just witnessed a piece of history. I saw with my own goddamned eyes Have Blue pass directly overhead. The dish on the van*" *did not move a fraction of an inch. Neither did the missiles."* The Pentagon observer confirmed this to be true.

Rafi Eitan almost smiled. His secret camera had recorded the strange diamond-shaped plane which had passed overhead; the radar dish that had not moved; the motionless missiles and the scanner screens still remaining blank until the chase plane had arrived on the scene.

His spying mission against the United States had proven to be as successful as the test flight of the Stealth prototype on that August morning in 1979.

But despite the invaluable data Eitan and Yosef returned with to Tel Aviv, Israel's aircraft manufacturers, who had been adept at turning other secrets Eitan had stolen into hardware for the defense of their country, were unable to duplicate the Stealth bomber. They were still trying to do so by the time Eitan would have long gone from Mossad leaving only the memory of his operational skills that had once more revealed themselves during his visit to Inslaw.

But as they waved goodbye to the bogus Dr. Orr on that February afternoon, Bill and Nancy Hamilton were only filled with a trusting belief that, through their visitor, their world was about to change.

The senior staff at the Justice Department had full knowledge of who Rafi Eitan really was when he visited Inslaw in 1983. That he had once more traveled under a false name on a fake passport is proof of what he would later admit: that he had developed a *"good understanding"* with those officials.

This was itself remarkable, given that the CIA had recently warned the U.S. intelligence community that Israel was beginning to target sensitive projects in the United States that were being developed for the country's military and intelligence agencies. But, Rafi Eitan had been received as a welcome visitor to the Justice Department, which was happy to make the arrangements for him to visit Inslaw.

By 1983, within the U.S. intelligence community, it was also common knowledge that Rafi Eitan was no longer master-minding operations for Mossad but was now in charge of an even more secret Israeli organization. It was called LAKAM and it operated out of Israel's Ministry of Defense in Tel Aviv. LAKAM was responsible for collecting scientific and technical intelligence from other countries, both friendly and hostile. It did so through every means Rafi Eitan could devise. A lifetime in espionage had made Eitan the most formidable stealer of secrets.

In Tel Aviv, LAKAM was formally known as the Bureau of Scientific Liaison, quickly shortened to its Hebrew acronym of LAKAM. Created in 1960, its role was to be the Israeli Defense Ministry's own spy unit. Mossad regarded LAKAM as the proverbial *"new kid on the block."* The senior agency had made strong attempts to have LAKAM closed down. But Rafi Eitan, relishing his new opportunity to run things *"just the way I wanted them run,"* resisted Mossad. He was helped by powerful friends in Israel's political and intelligence community. Among them was Shimon Peres, then Israel's deputy Defense Minister. Rafi Eitan had set up LAKAM offices in New York, Boston, Los Angeles and Washington. Every week LAKAM staff dutifully shipped boxes of technical journals back to Tel Aviv. As Eitan later said, "*a good read of a magazine tells you more what's going on than all the cocktail party circuit chatter.*"

His first success at LAKAM had been organizing the theft of nuclear materials from the Numec Reprocessing Plant at Apollo, Pennsylvania. Sufficient quantities of fissionable materials had been spirited out of the plant by LAKAM operatives to enable Israel to create its own nuclear arsenal at Dimona in the Negev Desert.

On his trip to Numec, Rafi Eitan had posed as an Israeli government "*inspector*" for the "*peaceful use*" of nuclear materials. "*His full-time job,*" he had told Numec employees, was as "*Director of the Department of Electronics, University of Tel Aviv, Israel.*" There was no such post — nor was there ever a "Dr. Cohen" at the University — the person Rafi Eitan had claimed to be in his Numec foray.

Rafi Eitan had taken pains to ensure that if a background check were made by the Hamiltons, they would be satisfied. There was indeed a real Dr. Orr who had been a prosecuting attorney with the Israeli Justice Department. But Dr. Orr had long since retired and was living in Jerusalem.

Rafi Eitan had simply borrowed his name and created a false identity for himself, including a passport with the help of Mossad's forgers.

With the thoroughness that typified all he did, Israel's super spy had briefed himself fully on Hamilton: how he had been sent to Vietnam to devise a network of electronic listening posts to monitor the Viet Cong as its forces moved through the jungle; how he had devised a computerized Vietnamese-English dictionary which had proven to be a powerful aid to translating Viet Cong messages and interrogating prisoners. In many ways, Hamilton was one of the founding fathers of modern day surveillance.

Bill Hamilton would later recall that period as "*the time when the revolution in electronic communications — satellite technology and microcircuitry — was changing things in a big way: faster and more secure encryption and better imagery were coming on line at increasing speed. Computers grew smaller and faster; more sensitive sensors were able to separate tens of thousands of conversations. Surveillance was coming into its own.*"

After Vietnam, Hamilton had joined the National Security Agency, NSA, itself at the coalface of surveillance. Driven by the exigencies of World War II, and then the Cold War, the National Security Agency was created in 1952. Hamilton found himself working in an organization with acres of computers, electronic listening posts located around the world, and a fleet of spy satellites circling overhead. NSA could eavesdrop on the communications of both friends and enemies, including American citizens.

At his introductory briefing to NSA, he was told that "*news of an invasion, an assassination or a coup overseas can be flashed from the point of interception to the President's desk in minutes. The latest performance data from Soviet missile tests can be recorded and analyzed. Even the radiophone conversations of top Soviet and Chinese officials can be snatched from the atmosphere.*"

With its current budget of $2 billion and more than 60,000 employees, the NSA easily eclipsed all other U.S. intelligence organizations. Yet it operated, and still does, in almost total secrecy.

George Tenet realized that Rafi Eitan's visit to Inslaw could only have been arranged by a senior official in the Justice Department. William Hamilton had no doubts. He told this author in a telephone interview in December 1999, that Brewer had made the arrangements.

Separate confirmation came from Meir Amit, a former director-general of Mossad. In an interview with the author in 1998, he said: *"when push came to shove, the CIA made sure we were kept in the picture; that anything new that came their way which they could share with us, share it they would. Often their political masters didn't know this. But why should they? They are often only temporary stewards of government. The intelligence community often remains in power for a decade, often longer. It was on that basis that we could work closely together. To understand that is to see the world in a new way. Not the world of elected government. But a far more powerful one, the one that lies beneath."*

Rafi Eitan's visit to Inslaw had been to confirm that Enhanced Promis possessed an extraordinary intelligence gathering capacity.

Dressed in his favorite chain-store suit and shoes, he had cultivated, during his visit, an unassuming air. Long ago he had learned that *"in my business you don't want to try and impress. My work calls for many things, but being high profile or boastful are not requirements."*

Certainly on that February afternoon in 1983, there was nothing about Rafi Eitan that suggested his legendary cold-blooded ruthlessness and cunning, his ability to improvise at ferocious speed or his inborn skill at outwitting even the best-laid plans. Instead he was polite, listening intently, his square block of a head tilted to one side.

Only later would Bill Hamilton realize that he and Nancy had been in the presence of a *"man who knew how to act the part perfectly. Not one of us who met him would ever have guessed who he was or what was going on in his mind: how to steal Enhanced Promis."*

The Justice Department had already secretly sent a copy of the software to the CIA for evaluation, a move that flagrantly broke the terms of the contract it had with Inslaw.

CIA programmers, in a secret report to the agency's then Director, William Casey, concluded Enhanced Promis *"can satisfy our requirements because of the versatility of the software, i.e., the ability to use Enhanced Promis' automated tailoring subsystem to adapt the software to track any kind of information in an extraordinarily fast way. It has the capability of being of high value to every agency in the U.S. intelligence community and can be installed on nuclear submarines of the United States and Great Britain. Further, a reduced-function version can be created for sale to suitable foreign governments."*

The closest ties the CIA had were, and are, those with the State of Israel.

Now, over sixteen years later, being chauffeur-driven into Washington, George Tenet had by all accounts run the CIA with credible distinction. He was as thoroughly briefed as any director could be on the software. Only weeks ago, at the

Clinton-Ehud Barak-Yasser Arafat summit in an Egyptian seaside resort, he had taken time out to carefully question the one man who could help fill in the gaps from the Israeli side about Enhanced Promis. He was Danny Yatom, the former director-general of Mossad and, in 2000, Prime Minister Barak's personal adviser on security.

Yatom, a bull-necked figure with an ability to conjure up the past had taken Tenet back to 1984, the year that Israel once more found itself in crisis. It was also the year that Rafi Eitan was at the height of his cunning.

A new Arab Intifada was about to begin at a time when Rafi Eitan's fortunes had become mixed.

On the plus side he had pulled off another major intelligence coup against the United States. In what can only be described as a mesmeric series of moves, Eitan had recruited the most important spy Israel had ever placed within the U.S. intelligence community, the American-born Zionist, Jonathan Pollard. Eitan's fertile mind had begun to focus on how he could obtain the Enhanced Promis software — and how it could then be used by Pollard to increase and further his treachery.

But while Eitan's superiors in Israeli intelligence admired his skill in running Pollard, there were those among his peers who thought the old spymaster was *"heading for the hill."* Never a political animal, Rafi Eitan did not fit into the way things were done by the new men at the top of Israeli intelligence. For his part, his service to his country had left him with little more than a pension to look forward to. More and more he began to ponder how he could ensure the financial future of his wife and himself. Their home on Shay Street in north Tel Aviv was comfortable but there was little money in the bank.

Then, just as the Justice Department and the CIA had seen the Enhanced Promis software as a powerful weapon, so did Eitan. With it Israel could keep track of its enemies. But he also saw another possibility. While the system would provide invaluable intelligence to Mossad and other Israeli intelligence services, it could also be marketed along the lines the CIA programmers had originally suggested: in a limited version to other countries. And that marketing would be a private venture that would, Eitan hoped, solve all his financial problems for the future.

Eitan told no one about his plans to get for himself a piece of the action, but he began to put together a scheme which he hoped would make him among the richest men in the world of secret surveillance.

Meantime, there was still a need to continue to keep Jonathan Pollard betraying his country as part of Eitan's fine-tuned plan to use Enhanced Promis for Israel and his own needs.

Within a month, Rafi Eitan's plan was in place. He had put together a small team of former LAKAM programmers. They deconstructed the Enhanced Promis disc that Eitan had obtained from a source he still, in 2000, refused to reveal. All he would say to this author in December 1999 was *"it is best to leave such matters unsaid until certain people are out of prison."* After Eitan's programmers had done their deconstruction work, there was no way for the Hamiltons to claim ownership of what Enhanced Promis had now become. Eitan decided to keep the original name *as it sounded like such a good marketing tool to explain what the system could do if you were in the surveillance industry.*

The programmers had added what Eitan called *"a final trick."* This was a "trapdoor" in the new system, a microchip which would allow Eitan to know what information was being tracked by any user of the system. He could sit in Tel Aviv and keep tabs on the world.

Eitan opened his *"little black book in which I keep all the most useful names."* Under "B-M" he found the man he wanted — Ari Ben-Menashe. An Iranian Jew by birth, Ben-Menashe had risen high in the Israeli intelligence community — ending up as adviser on counter-terrorism to the government of Yitzhak Shamir. Unfailingly polite, with a liking for First Class air travel and deluxe hotels, he fitted more the public's perception of a James Bond type of spy rather than the less colorful ones Mossad's upper echelon preferred. Ben-Menashe found himself out of work. The call from Rafi Eitan, he would recall to the author in May 2001, was *"very welcome. I went to his office."*

What followed has all the trappings of a Hollywood movie. But not only does Ben-Menashe insist that every word is true; so do Rafi Eitan and a number of well-placed members of the U.S. intelligence community the author spoke to about what happened after Ben-Menashe visited Rafi Eitan.

"Rafi said we can use this program to stamp out terrorism by keeping track of everyone. But not only that. We can find out what our enemies know, too."

I stared at him for a moment. Suddenly I realized what he was talking about. "Ben zona ata tso dek!" Son of a bitch, you're right, I exclaimed. All we had to do was 'bug' the program when it was sold to our enemies.

"It would work like this: A nation's spy organization would buy Promis and have it installed in its computers at headquarters. Using a modem, the spy network would then tap into the computers of such services as the telephone company, the water board, other utility commissions, credit card companies, etc. Promis would then search for specific information. For example, if a person suddenly started using more water and more electricity and making more phone calls than usual, it might be suspected he had guests staying with him. Promis would then start searching for the records of his friends and associates, and if it was found that one had stopped using electricity and water, it might be assumed, based on other records stored in Promis, that the missing person was staying with the subject of the investigation. This would be enough to have him watched if, for example, he had been involved in previous conspiracies. Promis would search through its records and produce details of those conspiracies, even though the person might have been operating under a different name in the past — the program was sophisticated enough to find a detail that would reveal his true identity.

"This information might also be of interest to Israel, which is where the trap door would come into play. By dialing into the central computer of any foreign intelligence agency using Promis, an Israeli agent with a modem need only type in certain secret code words to gain access. Then he could ask for information on the person and get it all on his computer screen.

"*Rafi Eitan did not want to risk having a trap door developed in Israel. Word might leak back that the Israelis had been bugging software and then handing it out to others. Eitan decided it would be best if a computer whiz could be found outside the country.*

"*I knew just the man for the job. Yehuda Ben-Hanan ran a small computer company of his own called Software and Engineering Consultants, based in Chatsworth, California. I had grown up with him but I didn't want him to know that I was scouting him for a possible job. I had to sound him out, to find out if he was a blabbermouth.*

"*When I called on him, I told him I was in California on holiday and had decided to look him up. We chatted about our days as kids, and he introduced me to his wife, a Brazilian Jew. I decided he was right for the job — he was not conspiracy-minded, and it was unlikely his suspicions would be aroused. Five days after I left, he was approached by an Israeli man who hired him to build an external access to a program. Yehuda wasn't told what the program was all about. He was simply given blueprints and set about his work for a $5,000 fee.*"

In May 2001, in a telephone conversation with the author, Yehuda Ben-Hanan initially said he "*did not know Ben-Menashe, have never met this man.*" Later he admitted he had been questioned about "*this matter some years ago, and I have nothing more to say.*"

Others would adopt the same closed-mouth position. One is the former United States Attorney General in the Reagan Administration, Edwin Meese III.

A rotund lawyer with strong conservative beliefs, he would rise and fall from power because of his political connections. As a young lawyer in the district attorney's office in northern California's Alameda County, he supervised the arrests of over 700 participants in U.C. Berkeley's Free Speech Movement and helped to put down anti-draft protests. While these publicized actions made him few friends among Sixties liberals, his reputation as a law and order man brought him to the attention of the most politically powerful man in California, Governor Ronald Reagan, who chose Meese as a member of his cabinet.

When Reagan became President, Meese followed him to The White House in 1982 as special counsel. Three years later, Meese became the top law enforcement official in the country when Reagan appointed him Attorney General. And yet, within the next three years, Meese would come under heated criticism and become a liability to the Republican Party for his questionable business dealings, including those with Earl Brian, a soon-to-be key character in the theft of Enhanced Promis. In 1988 Meese was finally hounded out of office in a wake of ethical violations and the results of an internal government investigation that found Meese demonstrated "*conduct which should not be tolerated of any government employee, especially not the Attorney General.*"

Central to the charge was Meese's entangled relationship with another old friend of Reagan, Earl W. Brian, who also became a friend of Rafi Eitan.

During Ronald Reagan's second term as Governor of California (1971–1974), Brian had served as Secretary of Health. One of his many skills was a fluency in Farsi, the language of Iran. After leaving the Reagan Administration, Brian began to explore business possibilities in Iran. He could see it would take time to find his way into the closed community that Khomeini and his ayatollahs were planning to establish as an anti-West regime. Sensing the moment was not right to pitch for business, Brian returned to California to seek the Republican nomination for the U.S. Senate. A year later, after losing the primary, he met with Ronald Reagan to discuss his new career as a businessman.

Reagan proposed that Brian should put together a Medicare plan for the Iranian government. It was one of those quixotic ideas the new President of the United States was prone to come up with. He told Brian that a version of Medicare would show Iran a *"positive side of America,"* and so improve the United States' image in the region. In a memorable phrase, Reagan told Brian *"if Medicare works in California, it can work anywhere."*

Brian agreed to *"give it a try"* and resolved to market the proposal through his holding company, the Biotech Capital Corporation. Through what was essentially a financial holding company, Brian also controlled a number of other companies. One was called Hadron which specialized in marketing computer systems. Ursula Meese, the wife of Edwin Meese, had raised the money to help launch Brian's business career. Privately wealthy, Ursula Meese had no doubt seen an opportunity to increase the value of her portfolio of stocks. She and her husband were especially interested in seeing how Hadron could find its place at the forefront of what Ursula had called *"the new technical frontier opening up in the development of packaging computers to retrain and retrieve information, particularly in the justice system."*

Over dinner, shortly after his appointment to the White House, Edwin Meese had told Ursula and Brian about Enhanced Promis. He had heard about the system during a visit to the Justice Department.

Edwin Meese and Brian had a long-standing working and social relationship from the time they had worked in the cabinet of Ronald Reagan when he was Governor of California. That relationship had continued when Reagan became President of the United States. It was Meese who had arranged for Earl Brian to have his own office in the White House while he launched himself on the business world. Brian took full advantage of being able to make his calls — anywhere in the world — via The White House switchboard.

Over that dinner, Meese had set in motion another sequence of events with a remark. *"Now, wouldn't it be great if Hadron could get hold of marketing Enhanced Promis outside of the Justice Department's requirements,"* Brian later recalled Meese saying.

The prospect stuck in Brian's mind. Whenever he met with prospective investors in Hadron, he hinted that the company was about to acquire a piece of software of *"great promise."*

By then the CIA had taken its first steps to use Enhanced Promis. They had secretly arranged to install the software in the Bank of International Settlements in Basle, Switzerland to keep track of electronic fund transfers to combat money-laundering and other criminal activities, including drug trafficking, securities and banking frauds and political pay offs. The CIA also began to furnish the software to its agents in the field to track data.

Inevitably, given his close connections to the U.S. intelligence community, Rafi Eitan had come to learn of these developments and Brian's hopes to become involved with Enhanced Promis.

The two men had met when Rafi Eitan was the Israeli helmsman steering what became known as Irangate, the arms-for-hostage deal, a debacle that had swept Jimmy Carter out of office and allowed Reagan into the White House.

Rafi Eitan decided to invite Brian to Israel. They struck up an immediate rapport. Eitan would remember *"Earl was hooked on stories like how I caught Eichmann and had one of my agents dress up as a woman to go into Beirut and kill the last of the murderers of the athletes at Munich. And for sure I liked to hear about Earl's life in the fast lane in Hollywood."*

Friends though they had become, Rafi Eitan still thought *"Earl's idea of Medicare for Iran was just about the craziest thing I had heard for a long time."*

Just as he had researched Bill Hamilton's background, Rafi Eitan had continued to update himself on Brian's career. With the help of Ursula Meese's money and her husband's Washington contacts, Brian had managed to establish Hadron as a computer systems contractor for the United States government. In all, the company had some thirty other contracts, many of them with U.S. intelligence agencies, including the CIA. Through his growing connections in the intelligence community, Brian had heard more about the Enhanced Promis system. Further details came from his visits to the White House to see his old friend, President Reagan. Insiders in the former Reagan Administration recalled how Brian and the President would have a cosy chat on just about everything going on.

Almost certainly that was how Brian first discovered that the President had tasked the NSA — which by now also had a copy of Enhanced Promis, supplied by the Justice Department — to use the program to penetrate the global banking industry.

A secret memo prepared by the then Special Assistant to the President for National Security Planning, ordered NSA *"to penetrate banks to combat money-laundering and other criminal activities including drug trafficking, illegal sales of high technology to the Soviet Union and gun running to terrorist and guerrilla groups."*

NSA was instructed to secretly install Enhanced Promis in all major wire transfer clearing houses in the United States and Europe, including the Clearing House Interbank Payment System in New York.

It was against this background that Rafi Eitan had planned his trip to Inslaw. Before visiting the Hamiltons he had again met Earl Brian, this time in Washington. At the end of their meeting, Eitan repeated his invitation for Brian to visit him in Tel Aviv. Brian accepted.

Rafi Eitan then went on to visit Inslaw posing as "Dr. Orr." Back in Israel he made plans to exploit the arrival of Brian.

Brian arrived as the Intifada raged on. But the street battles were some distance from Eitan's home on Shay Street.

At some stage in those relaxed hours in Rafi Eitan's living room, filled with artifacts and quality art, Brian had readily answered his host's carefully posed questions about Enhanced Promis and how it was being used by the United

States to fight crime and terrorism. He also revealed the steps he had taken to try and get *"a piece of the action"* (the words Rafi Eitan later recalled Brian using) for Hadron.

To do this Brian had moved Hadron's facilities to Newport, Rhode Island, so that he could be closer to the Navy's Undersea Systems Center. Brian hoped the proximity would enable him to one day get the contract to install Enhanced Promis on board Trident nuclear submarines. Rafi Eitan recalled his guest describing the software's use as being *"for the gathering and dissemination of intelligence information."*

Brian explained how the software could, for example, store the unique sonar signature of every Russian submarine. Artificial intelligence on board a Trident could perform the targeting calculations to destroy the enemy submarine.

Brian had hinted, Rafi Eitan later recalled, that Enhanced Promis could also be adapted for the firing of nuclear-armed missiles from a submerged Trident, a technique known as *"over the horizon"* at targets within the Soviet Union or China. The software was also programmed to include details of the defenses around a target, along with the advanced physics and mathematics needed to ensure a direct hit.

To Rafi Eitan it was *"all like playing a computer game."* He also assumed that Brian was being so free with details because: *"We both knew that Israel always received from the United States more information than Washington shared with other countries. In Washington we were top of the list for getting anything that would be helpful to us."*

Rafi Eitan did not know — neither, he said, would he have been troubled if he had known, that much of what he was learning was still on the highly classified list in Washington. But he said the value of Enhanced Promis for the small Israeli Navy and its powerful air force was all too obvious.

When it was time for Brian to return home, Rafi Eitan had arranged for him to keep track of what Inslaw was currently doing to improve the Enhanced Promis model he had been shown by Bill and Nancy Hamilton on that bleak February afternoon in Washington.

In his long life as an intelligence operative, Rafi Eitan had an unbreakable rule: *"Keep everyone you meet on tap. You never know when he or she can be useful."*

Back in Washington, Earl Brian continued to work himself deeper into the Reagan administration. Around the White House he was a commanding figure, always ready to tell a good yarn about his days as a combat physician in Vietnam. The President later said it was like having his own real-life M*A*S*H hero on the premises: Brian had a limitless fund of stories which would have made good plot lines for the television series. Certainly, Brian lost no opportunity to appear around the Oval Office with a chest full of ribbons.

Some cynics on the Reagan staff thought this was Brian's attempt to divert attention from his recent questionable dealings. Before moving into the White House, the Securities and Exchange Commission had cited him for issuing press releases designed to inflate stocks in his company.

Eventually this would lead to him being found guilty of fraud and sentenced to a 57-month term in a federal penitentiary. At the time this book was written — May 2001 — Brian was coming to the end of his sentence. He stead-fastly refused to discuss his time at the Reagan White House or his involvement with Enhanced Promis and the small but significant part one of his companies, Hadron, had played in showing the capability of the Israeli-doctored software once it had been fitted with its Trojan horse trap door.

With the trap door in place, there was still a need to test-market the new version of Enhanced Promis. Israel's neighbor, Jordan, was chosen as the place. A small U.S. sales company, Hadron, sold and installed the program in military headquarters in Amman. The Jordanians were delighted to see how easy it was to track Yasser Arafat and the PLO. In Tel Aviv, Rafi Eitan was able to see just who the Jordanians were tracking but also, through Enhanced Promis, he was able to learn many of Jordan's own defense secrets, sucked up through the ingenious trap door chip. These were passed on to Mossad.

Hadron's involvement with Rafi Eitan was short-lived. He needed a super salesman for his global market offensive. The only man with all the qualities Eitan wanted was the newspaper tycoon, Robert Maxwell.

Maxwell was no ordinary run-of-the-mill millionaire. Physically a Falstaffian figure, Maxwell had a gargantuan appetite for everything: food, wine and women. Unwilling to enter into any permanent affair, he chose to satisfy his sexual needs through high-priced prostitutes. In every city he visited, his aides had call girls on hand to satisfy his needs. Like many despots, he worked anti-social hours, waking exhausted aides in the small hours to execute some minor whim that had come into his head. His chauffeur once had to drive half-way across London to bring Maxwell a brand of ice cream that he fancied. On other occasions he would arrive in the newsroom of his flagship tabloid, the UK-based *Daily Mirror*, and terrorize the night staff by taking charge of production. He sacked people without warning, rewarded others with unexpected gifts. Unpredictable, volcanic in temper, he ruled by fear from which no one was safe. His own sons were publicly abused by him and his wife treated as a drudge.

But to the rich and powerful his lack of manners, his sexual peccadilloes, his unsavory eating habits, his often shambolic dress style: all these were of little consequence because of the power he wielded through his global publishing empire. Like William Randolph Hearst, he strode the newspaper world like an emperor; like Hearst, Maxwell had a xenophobia, in his case a dislike of the United States. Maxwell was a Zionist. He believed that the United States had not done enough to help the Jews flee from the Nazis in the run-up to World War II. He also resented what he saw as an attempt to Americanize post-war Europe. But, like so much else about him, Maxwell kept such views secret.

All his life, Maxwell had cultivated the rich and famous to help him promote his publishing interests and political aspirations. In Britain in 1964, his contacts with its government had seen him return as a Labor Member of Parliament. His election had opened doors for him in Washington. He became a frequent visitor to the White House. Among those he came to know was Senator

John Tower. Tower had regaled Maxwell with stories of how he had helped to get George Herbert Bush into Congress.

On a visit to Israel, it was to Eitan that Maxwell revealed his own dislike of America. Eitan, who had no such antipathy, noted the tycoon's feelings and decided that *"one day that could be useful to know."*

Maxwell was heavily committed to Israel. He owned its daily tabloid, *Maariv*, and had set up a number of manufacturing companies in the coastal strip between Tel Aviv and Haifa. One was called Degem Computers. It primarily served as a useful cover for Mossad operatives in Central and South America.

In the United States, Maxwell had also set up a raft of small companies that were a spin-off of his own gigantic Pergamon Press in Britain. A number of those companies were based in Virginia and Arkansas. Among board members were several former members of intelligence agencies.

Eitan had no problem in convincing Maxwell that he should take his place on the Enhanced Promis gravy train.

By then Robert Maxwell had already become the most powerful informer Mossad had ever recruited. Maxwell had volunteered his services at the end of a meeting in Jerusalem with Shimon Peres shortly after Peres had formed a coalition government. One of Peres' aides would recall the encounter as *"the ego meets the megalomaniac. Peres was haughty and autocratic. But Maxwell just drove on saying things like 'I will pour millions into Israel'; 'I will revitalize the economy.' He was like a man running for office. He was bombastic, interrupted, went off on tangents and told dirty jokes. Peres sat there smiling his Eskimo smile."*

Recognizing that Maxwell over the years had developed powerful contacts in Eastern Europe, Peres arranged for Maxwell to see Nahum Admoni, Mossad's then Director General. The meeting took place in the Presidential Suite of the King David Hotel in Jerusalem, where Maxwell was staying. Maxwell and Admoni found common ground in their Central European backgrounds; Maxwell had been born in Czechoslovakia (which had led Peres to utter one of his few remembered jokes: *"He's the only bouncing Czech I know with money."*). Both men shared a burning commitment to Zionism and a belief Israel had a God-given right to survive. They also enjoyed a passion for food and good wine.

Admoni was keenly interested in Maxwell's view that both the United States and the Soviet Union had a similar desire to achieve global domination, but through significantly different approaches. Russia included international anarchy as part of its strategy, while Washington saw the world in terms of "friends" and "enemies" rather than nations with conflicting ideological interests. Maxwell had offered other insights:

The tycoon had painted portraits of two men of particular interest to Admoni. Maxwell said that after meeting Ronald Reagan, he came away with the feeling that the President was an eternal optimist who used his charm to conceal a tough politician. Reagan's most dangerous failing was that he was a simplifier and never more so than on the Middle East where his second or third thought was no better than his original shoot-from-the-hip judgment. Maxwell had been among the first Europeans to meet Reagan, doing so within three months of the new president taking office.

In his travels, Maxwell had also met William Casey and judged the CIA director as a man of narrow opinions and no friend of Israel. Casey was running a "can-do" agency with outmoded ideas about the role of intelligence in the current political global arenas. Nowhere, in Maxwell's view, was this more evident than in the way Casey had misread Arab intentions in the Middle East.

These views coincided exactly with those of Nahum Admoni. After the meeting, they drove in Admoni's unmarked car to Mossad headquarters where the tycoon was given a personally conducted tour of some of the facilities by the director general.

Maxwell had soon shown his worth. His power and position allowed him to go anywhere. He was welcomed in the offices of the most powerful presidents, dictators and heads of state. All he learned, he passed on to Mossad. He also kept his promise to energize the Israeli economy. He set up publishing and printing works and opened computer companies.

On visits to Israel, Maxwell was feted like a head of state; he was a regular guest of honor at government banquets and was given the finest accommodations. But Mossad had taken the precaution of being prepared, should the proverbial "hand that fed it" suddenly withdraw its largesse.

Discovering Maxwell had a strong sexual appetite and, because of his massive size, favored oral sex, Mossad arranged that during the tycoon's visits to Israel he was serviced from one of the stable of prostitutes the service maintained for blackmail purposes. Soon Mossad had acquired a small library of video footage of Maxwell in sexually compromising positions. The bedroom suite of the hotel where he stayed had been rigged with a concealed camera.

In late 1984 Rafi Eitan flew to Paris to meet Maxwell. The tycoon was at his most expansive, ordering champagne and oysters to his suite in the Ritz Hotel. After dinner the talk had turned to the business at hand. Maxwell said he would use Degem Computers to launch Israel's stolen and doctored version of Enhanced Promis.

There was no doubting Maxwell was a brilliant marketer of Enhanced Promis or, as far as Mossad was concerned, of the effectiveness of the system. The service had been the first to obtain the program and it had been a valuable tool in its campaign against the Intifada. Many of its leaders had left Jordan for safer hideouts in Europe after several had been assassinated in Jordan.

A spectacular success came when an Intifada commander who had moved to Rome called a Beirut number that Mossad's computers already had listed as the home of a known bomb-maker. The Rome caller wanted to meet the bomb-maker in Athens. Mossad used Enhanced Promis to check all the travel offices in Rome and Beirut for the travel arrangements of both men. In Beirut further checks revealed the bomber had ordered the local utility companies to cut off service to his home. A further search by Enhanced Promis of the local PLO computers also showed the bomber had switched flights at the last moment.

It did not save him. He was killed by a car bomb on the way to Beirut airport. Shortly afterwards, in Rome, the Intifada commander was killed in a hit-and-run accident.

Soon other examples would create complete satisfaction of the efficiency of Enhanced Promis as a powerful weapon with which Mossad could fight terrorism.

In the months which followed, Maxwell continued to sell the version that Rafi Eitan's programmers had reconstructed around the world. Using the same pitch — *"what I have is better and cheaper than anything else on the market"* — Maxwell persuaded the South African regime to purchase the software to track black revolutionary groups. A planned strike by black miners protesting apartheid was stopped when the software was used to track down the strike leaders through their required identity passes. All were incarcerated without trial.

In Guatemala the system was sold after Maxwell had personally demonstrated how it could track all opponents of the regime. Using the software, some 20,000 government opponents were rounded up. They were either killed or joined the ranks of "the disappeared."

Maxwell rampaged through South America hawking Enhanced Promis. The security forces of Brazil, Columbia and Nicaragua all bought the system. In Tel Aviv, Rafi Eitan's technicians knew who had been arrested even before the families of a regime's opponents were picked up.

Maxwell launched his sales offensive into the very bastion of security — the Swiss banking world. He persuaded Credit Suisse Bank to install the Israeli version. Through the trap door installed in the system, Rafi Eitan could learn many of the secrets of sensitive bank accounts. The data was passed on to Mossad. Often the depositors were Israeli millionaires who had opened overseas accounts, illegal under the country's strict financial controls. *"After finding out who had lodged overseas deposits, they were approached to make a donation to help Israel. If they refused they were exposed — and faced heavy fines and imprisonment."*

Maxwell's greatest coup was to persuade the Soviet Union to accept the system. Through the secret trap door microchip, Enhanced Promis was able to access Soviet military intelligence. The information passed to Mossad made it probably the best-briefed service on Russian intentions.

Next, South Korea, Australia and Canada were persuaded by the tireless Robert Maxwell to buy the software.

He might have gone on forever but for the fact that, massive though the sales were, Maxwell's cut did not give him enough to save his publishing empire. Even worse, he started to throw his weight around Tel Aviv. He behaved like a modern day pharaoh. But his boasting and bluffing had finally become too much. "Time was running out for Maxwell," Rafi Eitan was to recall.

More dangerous for Maxwell, Mossad decided his instability could become a threat to their operations. A senior *katsa,* a field agent, code-named Shimon Goldstein was assigned to track the tycoon's trips.

Early in 1985, Maxwell made another, his third, visit to Beijing. Once more he stayed in one of the guest houses the regime reserved for its most important visitors.

According to Goldstein's report, Maxwell met over several days with leaders of China's computer industry, which was beginning to expand. According to Goldstein, present at some of those meetings were senior members of CSIS, China's secret service. As usual Maxwell was expansive as he described the undoubted qualities of Enhanced Promis. But while the Chinese were undoubtedly impressed, they wanted to know more. Goldstein would recall in his subsequent report that one of the Chinese computer experts mused if the software was powerful enough to penetrate the vaunted security that the United States had long placed around its most sensitive establishments. Maxwell had no doubt: there was no place on earth that could defend itself against the trap door in the version of Enhanced Promis he was selling. What about Los Alamos, one of his hosts was later reported by Goldstein to have mused; was even Los Alamos no longer impenetrable? Maxwell had laughed and said that even Los Alamos' defenses, like the walls of Jericho, would tumble under the electronic power of Enhanced Promis.

In revealing details about the trap door, Maxwell had broken a strict order never to reveal its existence. The most likely explanation is that he now betrayed its existence because he was so desperate to make a sale from which he would obtain more money to try and save his newspaper empire. If there was one final turning point in the self-destruction of Robert Maxwell, it was that moment in Beijing.

The Chinese government placed an order for six sets of software — a sale worth $9 million. The key to the secrets of Los Alamos was cheap at that price.

Returning to Israel, Maxwell had begun to display even more disturbing traits. Maxwell told Mossad Chief Admoni he should start employing psychics to read the minds of Mossad's enemies. He began to suggest targets for elimination. All these requests were firmly but politely parried by Admoni. But within Mossad questions began to be asked about Maxwell. Was his behavior only that of a megalomaniac throwing about his weight? Or was it a precursor of something else? Could the time soon come when, despite all he had done for Israel, Robert Maxwell had become sufficiently mentally unstable and unpredictable to create a serious problem?

In Tel Aviv, Robert Maxwell was full of his usual bombast over his success in Beijing. And Rafi Eitan, as always, wanted to know what he liked to call "*chapter and verse*" about the trip. He listened without comment as Maxwell had described his host's interest in Los Alamos and how he had convinced them that with Enhanced Promis they could learn its inner secrets. But now, back in Israel, Maxwell was not so sure. More than once he asked Rafi Eitan if it was really possible for the software to do that. Goldstein would recall that Rafi Eitan smiled and shrugged. Who could tell?

But already an idea had begun to take root in the fertile mind of the spymaster.

Rafi Eitan was about to begin on what he hoped would be his greatest triumph yet. He planned to penetrate deep into the very heart of America's nuclear arsenal using his doctored version of Enhanced Promis to do so. He devised a plan for Robert Maxwell to sell the software to Los Alamos. The device would contain the trap door which was so brilliantly designed it could not be detected; if deconstructed, the trap door would simply disappear.

It was Maxwell's close connection to the late Senator John Tower — who would eventually be rewarded with a seat on Maxwell's Macmillan publishing company in New York — which opened the door to Los Alamos. During his sales patter in Los Alamos, Maxwell let drop that Enhanced Promis was already being used by MI5 in Northern Ireland to track the IRA and the movements of political activists like Gerry Adams. His listeners were suitably impressed at being given a privileged peek into a secret world — and at the same time reinforced the almost magical power of Enhanced Promis. This time Maxwell did not tell them about the secret trap door microchip.

After his first visit to Los Alamos, Maxwell flew to Israel to report to Eitan that the Sandia National Laboratories would be the most likely to buy Enhanced Promis. Sandia was primarily responsible for arming U.S. nuclear submarines.

Only a very few knew that, in another part of the sprawling Sandia laboratory complex, in an area Maxwell would never be allowed to enter, the first halting steps had been taken into studying the feasibility of what Dr. Richard Boylan would later call "time travel and teletransportation." The work was under the supervision of a senior Los Alamos physicist, Dr. Robert Lazar, and had been given the code name of Project Galileo. Part of Lazar's work had also been conducted out at the ultra-secret S-4 lab close to where, all those years before, Rafi Eitan had witnessed the first flight of the Stealth aircraft. None of this Maxwell had an inkling of. The tycoon was, according to Rafi Eitan, "a very focused man. He never took his eye off the ball he was after."

Already the system that Eitan's programmers had adapted from the one Inslaw had originally developed, had proven to be a winner. Maxwell had sold it to a number of countries around the world. He had contracts pending that would eventually raise $500 million in Britain, Australia, South Korea, Canada, Russia, Poland and China. Eitan's dream of becoming the hard-currency millionaire of the computer surveillance world was coming true.

Maxwell, as usual in Israel, was received like a potentate, excused of all airport formalities and welcomed by an official greeter from the Foreign Office on what would turn out to be his last visit. Maxwell treated the man the way he did all his staff, ordering the official to carry his bags and to sit beside the driver. Maxwell also demanded to know where his motorcycle escort was and when told it was not available, he threatened to call the prime minister's office to have the greeter fired. At every traffic stop, Maxwell harangued the hapless official and continued to do so all the way to his hotel suite. Waiting was Maxwell's favorite prostitute. He sent her running; there were far more pressing matters than satisfying his sexual needs.

In London Robert Maxwell's newspaper empire was in even more serious financial trouble. Soon, without a substantial injection of capital, it would have to cease operations. But in the City of London where he had previously always found funding, there was a resistance to go on providing it. Hard-nosed financiers who had met Maxwell, sensed that behind his bluster and bully-boy tactics was a man who was losing the financial acumen that in the past had allowed them to forgive so much. In those days he had raged and threatened at the slightest challenge. Bankers had curbed their anger and caved in to his demands. But they would no longer do so. In the Bank of England and other financial institutions in the City, the word was that Maxwell was no longer a safe bet.

Their information was partially based on confidential reports from Israel that Maxwell was being pressed by his original Israeli investors to repay them the money that had helped him to acquire the Mirror Group of newspapers. The time limit on repayments had long gone and the demands from the Israelis had become more insistent. Trying to fend them off, Maxwell had promised them a higher return on their money if they waited. The Israelis were not satisfied; they wanted their money back now. This was why Maxwell had come to Tel Aviv: he hoped to cajole them into granting him another extension. The signs were not good. During the flight, he had received several angry phone calls from the investors threatening to place the matter before the City of London regulatory body.

There was a further matter for Maxwell to be concerned over. He had stolen some of the very substantial profits from the sale of Enhanced Promis that he had been entrusted to hide in Soviet bloc banks. He had used the money to try and save the Mirror Group. Maxwell had also already stolen all he could from the newspaper's staff pension fund.

Once his thefts of profits from the software program were uncovered, he would find himself confronting some very hard men, among them Rafi Eitan. Maxwell knew that would not be a pleasant experience.

From his hotel suite, Maxwell began to strategize. His share of the profits from Degem's marketing of Enhanced Promis would not be able to stem the crisis. Neither would profits from *Maariv*, the Israeli tabloid modeled on his flagship *Daily Mirror*. But there was one possibility, the Tel Aviv-based Cytex Corporation he owned, which manufactured high-tech equipment. If Cytex could be sold quickly, the money could go some way to solving matters.

Maxwell ordered Cytex's senior executive, the son of Prime Minister Yitzhak Shamir, to his suite. The executive had bad news: a quick sale was unlikely. Cytex, while holding its own, faced increasing competition. This was not the time to take it to the market. To sell would also throw skilled people out of work at a time when employment was a serious problem in Israel.

The reaction provoked a furious outburst from Maxwell as his last hope of rescue faded. Tactically he made an error in lambasting the prime minister's son, who now told his father that Maxwell was in serious financial trouble. The prime minister, aware of the tycoon's links to Mossad, informed Nahum Admoni. He called a meeting of senior staff to see how to deal with what had become a problem.

Later it emerged that several options were discussed.

Mossad could ask the prime minister to use his own considerable influence to mobilize his own resources and contacts to find money to bail out Maxwell. This was rejected. Shamir had a strong sense of self-preservation and now wished to distance himself from Maxwell.

Another option was for Mossad to approach its highly-placed contacts in the City of London and urge them to support a rescue package for Maxwell. At the same time, Maxwell-friendly journalists in Britain could be encouraged to write supportive stories about the financially troubled tycoon.

Again those suggestions were discounted. Reports Admoni had received from London suggested that the City would welcome the end of Maxwell and that few journalists outside Mirror newspapers would dream of writing favorable stories about a tycoon who had spent years threatening the media.

The final option for Mossad was to break off all contact with Maxwell. There was a risk there: Maxwell, on the evidence of his present unpredictable state of mind, could well use his newspapers to actually attack Mossad. With the access he had been given, that could have the most serious consequences.

On that somber note, the meeting concluded that Admoni would see Maxwell and remind him of his responsibility to both Mossad and Israel. That night the two men met over dinner in Maxwell's hotel suite. What transpired between them would remain unknown. But hours later Robert Maxwell left Tel Aviv in his private plane.

On a blistering hot day in January 1985, Robert Maxwell lumbered down the steps of his private Lear jet at Albuquerque airport. Behind him an aide carried the magnate's bulky briefcase, emblazoned with Maxwell's initials in gold leaf. This was the tycoon's second trip to Albuquerque in the past four months.

The first trip had been an exploratory one, made at Eitan's suggestion, to see if there was a potential market for the Enhanced Promis software to be sold to one of the many laboratories and research centers operating within the Los Alamos complex.

Maxwell had discovered on his first visit there that there was a long-standing requirement at Los Alamos for the latest compatible database software.

On his initial visit, Maxwell had presented himself as President of "Information on Demand," a company incorporated in Virginia. However, the nature of the man had not stopped him from boasting that he was the single most powerful newspaper magnate in the world and that, through his parent holding company, he controlled an interlocking web of companies that were there to exploit what he called *"the cutting edge of technology that our company in Israel has developed."*

What followed has so far remained under strict secrecy in FBI files.

But eighteen heavily redacted FBI documents in the possession of the author and obtained under the Freedom of Information Act, provide sufficient clues to piece together a startling new slant to the botched investigation by the FBI into the later thefts from Los Alamos of its most sensitive nuclear secrets in a joint operation by Mossad and CSIS – using Israel's doctored Enhanced Promis software Robert Maxwell had sold Beijing.

Even today, in 2001, seventeen years later, those FBI documents make fascinating reading into the mindset of the FBI. One marked "Secret: From SAC Albuquerque 105c-3262," like all the others still so sensitive that parts of it are blacked out, contains this paragraph:

"On 8/13/84 (blacked out) Sandia National 67C Laboratories, Albuquerque, NM one of the individuals who originally brought this information to the attention of the FBI, and the fact that NSA (National Security Agency) might wish to establish liaison with the Bureau."

Another document marked "This entire communication is classified SECRET: Subject: Robert Maxwell Dba," refers to an interview with Information On Demand's Chief Executive, Sue Rugge. The date is deleted.

A key paragraph reads: "According to RUGGE, the (deleted) has been a client of IOD for at least ten years and it would be impossible to recall all the information requested by them, except for the last year. RUGGE advised she does not know if any of the requests of the (two lines redacted)."

The first deletion, according to the author's FBI sources, referred to the Central Intelligence Agency. The second two-line redaction the sources say refers to Mossad and Maxwell's association with it.

Other documents refer to the FBI attempts to track Maxwell's various corporations in the United States. What was discovered is again heavily censored.

The sensitivity of those investigations can be discovered from a telex to the "Director, FBI, Washington D.C." It is from the FBI Albuquerque field office. It states: "The matter redacted was placed in a closed status."

On 8/9/84, the New York FBI office sent a "SECRET" memo to "Director FBI: subject: ROBERT MAXWELL (OO:AQ) *was now being placed in an RUC status."*

Like all the other documents, portions of this are heavily redacted.

A document dated 6/29/84, addressed as "SECRET" to "Director FBI, Washington, D.C.," from "SAC, San Francisco," is deemed so sensitive that, when it was requested by the author under the Freedom of Information Act in 1999 all four pages were redacted, apart from the concluding line: "*San Francisco taking no further action."*

FBI sources who worked on the Maxwell investigation at the time and cannot be named on the author's guarantee they would remain anonymous in return for information, confirmed Maxwell was being investigated because of his Mossad connections. One said their investigations were cut off at the highest possible level — President Reagan.

Reagan is today in an advanced state of senile dementia. The secrets in those FBI documents remain safe — until somebody finds a way to have them made public.

In April 2001, the author was provided by Inslaw with a document that goes a long way to confirm the extent of Maxwell's role. The document was prepared by the company's attorneys and submitted to the U.S. Senate Committee on the Judiciary. Headed: "*Role of the late Robert Maxwell in the dissemination of Promis on behalf of Israeli Intelligence*," the document stated:

"*Maxwell had been a long-time intelligence operative for Israel. According to Ari Ben-Menashe, a former Israeli intelligence officer, Maxwell also assisted Israeli intelli-*

gence and Rafi Eitan in the dissemination of the proprietary Promis software to the intelligence and law enforcement agencies of other governments, particularly in Eastern Europe, the former Soviet Union, the United Kingdom and certain countries in Latin America, and to international commercial banks.

"In August 1985, Maxwell incorporated in the Commonwealth of Virginia a tiny national defense publishing house, Pergamon-Brassey's International Defense Publishers of McLean, Virginia. In 1987, Pergamon-Brassey's hired two senior computer systems executives who resigned at the same time from the Meese Justice Department's Justice Data Center. The proprietary IBM mainframe version of Promis had been operating at the Justice Data Center since the early 1980s. Maxwell's six-employee Pergamon-Brassey's was chaired by former U.S. Senator John Tower and included on its board of directors a recently retired four-star U.S. Army General who had headed the Southern Command in Panama during the Reagan Presidency, and a retired British Major General. Its president was a recently retired U.S. Air Force Colonel.

"When George Vaveris resigned his estimated $90,000 a year Senior Executive Service position as Director of the Justice Data Center to become Vice-President for Technical Services at the tiny Pergamon-Brassey's, he reportedly confided to a colleague at the Justice Department that his compensation at Pergamon-Brassey's would be in excess of $200,000 a year.

"In December 1981 Hadron, Inc. acquired Telcom International as a wholly-owned subsidiary. Billy R. Morris, the President of Telcom International, had been employed at the CIA until 1977. According to a former Hadron executive, Telcom International was staffed entirely or almost entirely by former CIA employees. Billy R. Morris was a close friend of King Hussein of Jordan, and Hadron did not buy Telcom International for its telecommunications expertise, according to this former Hadron executive.

"At the time of its acquisition by Hadron, Telcom International had an office in Amman, Jordan, according to Hadron's annual reports.

"The fact that a Hadron subsidiary had an office in Amman, Jordan, in the early 1980s and the alleged closeness of the subsidiary's President to the King of Jordan added to the plausibility of the claim by Ari Ben-Menashe that shortly after Rafi Eitan acquired the version of Promis, he arranged to sell a copy of it to the military intelligence agency of Jordan, in secret support of an Israeli communications intelligence initiative. The Israeli objective was allegedly to gain secret electronic access to Jordanian military intelligence dossiers on Palestinians."

Back in London from the U.S. in the spring of 1991, Maxwell, against all the odds, seemed to be succeeding in holding on to his newspaper group. He was likened to an African whirling dervish as he went from one meeting to another seeking financial support. From time to time he called Mossad to speak to Admoni, always informing the director general's secretary that the "big Czech" was on the line. The sobriquet had been bestowed by Mossad on Maxwell after he had been recruited. What was said in those calls would remain unknown.

On September 30, 1991, further evidence of Maxwell's bizarre behavior came when he telephoned Admoni. This time there was no disguising the threat in Maxwell's words. His financial affairs had once more taken a turn for the worse and he was being investigated in Parliament and the British media, so long held at bay by his posse of high-priced lawyers and their quiver of writs. Maxwell then said that unless Mossad arranged to bail him out, he could not be sure if he would be able to keep secret all he knew. The threat was crude and clear.

On October 29, 1991, Maxwell received a call from the Israeli embassy in Madrid. Maxwell was asked to come to Spain the next day and, according to former Mossad agent, Victor Ostrovsky, "*his caller promised that things would be worked out and there was no need to panic.*" Maxwell was told to fly to Gibraltar and board his yacht, *The Lady Ghislaine*, and order the crew to set sail for the Canary Islands "*and wait there for a message.*"

Robert Maxwell agreed to do as instructed.

On October 30, 1991, four Israelis arrived in the Moroccan port of Rabat. They said they were tourists on a deep-sea fishing vacation and hired an ocean-going motor yacht.

On October 31, after Maxwell reached the port of Santa Cruz on the island of Tenerife, he dined alone in the Hotel Mency. Shortly afterwards Maxwell returned to his yacht and ordered it back to sea. For the next thirty-six hours *The Lady Ghislaine* kept clear of land, cruising at various speeds. Maxwell had told the captain he was deciding where to go next. The crew could not recall Maxwell ever showing such indecision.

On his third cold night at sea, newspaper tycoon Robert Maxwell called upon God to save him as he prowled his state cabin aboard *The Lady Ghislaine*. The luxury yacht was named after his daughter, the one person in the world to whom he had ever shown a semblance of affection. She was asleep in her Manhattan apartment, 3,000 miles away, unaware her father's tyrannical rule was in deadly peril.

On every front he faced financial disaster. His European newspaper, recently launched in the United States, was losing $1,400,000 a month. Wage checks for staff were about to be dis-honored by one of his London bankers, the Midland Bank. Another bank, Goldman Sachs, were demanding a bank draft for $50 million to cover loans made to Maxwell's company. NatWest, another British bank, were threatening foreclosure unless they received a substantial payment on the $400 million debt Maxwell had accrued. Swiss bank, Credit Lyonnais, and the Irish merchant bank, Guinness Mahon, were all demanding repayments totaling close to half a billion dollars.

To try and meet these demands Maxwell had stolen another $70 million from the Mirror Group pension fund before flying to the Canary Islands. The fund, his only source of immediate cash, was now almost empty. It had originally contained over $1.3 billion dollars to ensure the retirement security of his 23,400 employees. The fund had been their employer's first act of plunder. Stealing their future had not for a moment troubled him. What had driven him on to steal was what he had once called "the sheer excitement of the deal"; accompanying it had been the publicity from which he fed, and was never quite satiated.

On this night out in the Atlantic he owned interests in newspapers, publishing, television, printing and electronic data-bases around the world that had a paper value of $5 billion. But, set against that, he had debts of over $3 billion that needed to be serviced if he were to remain solvent. But like the pension fund, the financial pyramid he had created of interlinked companies, of bank accounts that were kept in perpetual orbiting — one supporting the other — all were beginning to fall to earth with the same relentless succession as the dark cold waves lapping against the hull of his yacht.

In those first two days at sea, every phone call he received on his satellite phone brought bad news. Bankers Trust and Chase Manhattan Bank were pressing for repayment. Citibank had joined in with their demand for $45 million to be paid back within seven days.

On the newspaper front, the *New York Daily News* was losing circulation by the day; advertisers were failing to continue to buy space and those who had, were demanding refunds because the newspaper had failed to meet its guaranteed circulation targets.

In his three days at sea, he had learned of further steps to plunge his empire into bankruptcy. Lehman's Bank had sensed that Maxwell's empire was in serious trouble. Mark Haas, the Lehman's banker who had advanced close to $200 million to Maxwell, had now demanded *"repayment within 24 hours."* The demand had been attached to an International Recall Note, a document that is guaranteed to send a red alert to any bank.

Maxwell's response offers a clue to his departure from reality. He ordered one of the yacht's stewardesses to come to his suite to spread L'Oreal No. 7 over his hair and color his eyebrows with a black eye pencil — just as his valet had unfailingly done back in London before Maxwell had left his penthouse in the Mirror Group headquarters and set forth to spend another day cajoling, manipulating and threatening the bankers of the world.

But they were no longer ready to be compliant or threatened.

Moments after the stewardess had completed her ministrations, Maxwell received another call — the one he had banked so much upon. It was from his son, Kevin, in London. He simply said: *"Rothschilds say they can't help."* One of the most powerful banking dynasties in the financial world had, after days of consideration, turned its back on Maxwell's request for a rescue package.

Kevin Maxwell had more bad news. "Dad, I am sure a lot of them are going to follow Lehmans and pull the plug on us. They're talking of selling our collateral."

Those were stocks and shares in Maxwell's companies which had been pledged and re-pledged, as well as Mirror Group Pension Fund certificates that in reality now had no trade-in value.

Usually, given such news, Maxwell would fly into a rage, cursing whoever had told him. But this time Kevin was to recall, his father said, *"Don't worry, I'm working on it."*

By satellite phone he ordered borrowings from one bank to be once more switched to another. Smaller debtors like Barclays Bank, who had just refused to honor a check for $1.5 million, were brushed aside. In London, Citibank had sent a senior banker to squat outside the office of Maxwell's financial controller until he received a bank draft for $40 million. It never materialized.

On his third night at sea came another mortal blow. Goldman Sachs had fulfilled their threat and sold 2.2 million shares Maxwell had lodged with them as collateral to recover some of their outstanding loans. Worse yet, Goldman Sachs were threatening to sell the remaining 24.2 million shares of Maxwell holdings they held for what they could get.

"*Everyone wanted their pint of blood,*" Kevin Maxwell would later say. "*Everyone wanted to speak to Dad.*"

But, in those closing hours of his third night at sea, the phone connections to *The Lady Ghislaine* was no longer working.

"*It was as if Maxwell had suddenly disappeared from the face of the earth,*" was how his then London secretary, Charlotte Thornton, was to remember. "*In the mounting chaos, a number of us still clung to the wild hope that Robert Maxwell would pull something out of the bag.*"

Unknown to anyone on board, Maxwell clung to the promise he had received from Shabtai Shavit, the current director general of Mossad. He had been told that at sea *The Lady Ghislaine* would rendezvous off the coast of West Africa with another boat. He would be handed by its captain a sealed envelope. Inside would be a banker's draft to the value of one billion U.S. dollars drawn on an account in Credit Suisse in Geneva, Switzerland.

From his own financial dealings, Maxwell would have known that the Swiss bank was one that Mossad used to transfer secret funds.

But was Shavit's promise, given to Maxwell before he had left Israel, no more than a ploy to try and placate Maxwell? Unusual though the exchange at sea would be for any normal business transaction, it would appeal to Maxwell's own sense of adventure. This was how he would expect Mossad to behave!

Victor Ostrovsky, a former Mossad agent, would later indicate that the promise of financial salvation for Maxwell, was part of a carefully conceived plan. In his book, *The Other Side of Deception*, Ostrovsky has documented how Maxwell had over the years provided finance for many of Mossad's operations in Europe. The money came from his newspaper pension fund.

"*They got their hands on the pension funds almost as soon as he obtained the* Daily Mirror *and its associate newspapers,*" claimed Ostrovsky.

The former spy later claimed that Maxwell had reached his "*sell-by date in terms of balancing his usefulness against his shameless bully-boy tactics in Israel. Mossad could not go on allowing that. Nobody kicks around the head of Mossad.*"

When Ostrovsky's allegations had surfaced, he found himself the victim of a grubby smear campaign in which Maxwell had played an important role. Part of the reason was that the former agent had publicly hinted at Maxwell's connection to Mossad. In doing so, he had also described some of its operational methods and also named a number of serving officers.

Israel's Prime Minister Yitzhak Shamir asked Maxwell to mobilize his powerful media resources to destroy Ostrovsky's credibility. Ostrovsky became the object of a smear campaign in the Maxwell media, including the Tel Aviv tabloid *Maariv,* which Maxwell had bought.

But, though the first person to publicly identify Robert Maxwell's links to Mossad, Ostrovsky had by no means revealed the full story.

Ostrovsky believes the fate of Maxwell was decided when he had continued to threaten and browbeat Mossad, ordering the agency to *"arrange for him to have all the funds he needed to cover what he had stolen."* Ostrovsky claims that implicit in that demand was Maxwell's threat to publish in his newspapers hitherto secret details of Mossad operations.

Victor Ostrovsky would later state *"a small meeting of right wingers at Mossad headquarters resulted in a consensus to terminate Maxwell."*

If Ostrovsky's claim is true — and it has never been formally denied by Israel — then it was unthinkable that the group was acting without the highest sanction and perhaps even with the tacit knowledge of Yitzhak Shamir, the man who had once had his own share of killing Mossad's enemies.

Now, in October 1991, the matter could only have become more urgent for Mossad with the publication of a book by the veteran American investigative reporter Seymour M. Hersh, *The Samson Option: Israel, America and the Bomb,* which dealt with Israel's emergence as a nuclear power. News of the book had caught Mossad totally by surprise and copies were rushed to Tel Aviv. Well researched, it could nevertheless still have been effectively dealt with by saying nothing; the painful lesson of the mistake of confronting Ostrovsky's publisher should have been absorbed. But there was one problem: Hersh had also identified Maxwell's links to Mossad. Predictably, Maxwell had taken refuge behind a battery of lawyers, issuing writs against Hersh and his London publishers. But for the first time he met his match. Hersh, a Pulitzer Prize winner, refused to be cowed. In Britain's Parliament, more pointed questions were being asked about Maxwell's links to Mossad. Old suspicions surfaced. MPs demanded to know, under parliamentary privilege, how much Maxwell knew about Mossad's operations in Britain. For Victor Ostrovsky, *"the ground was starting to burn under Maxwell's feet."*

Sometime on the night of November 4, 1991, Robert Maxwell left his cabin and went up on deck. A swell was running. He wore only a night-shirt. He made his way to the stern of the yacht. He may have stood there for a few moments. What was going through his mind no one will ever know. The deck area where he stood was not covered by the security cameras dotted around the rest of the yacht — and which were monitored from the bridge.

Near where Maxwell stood was a telephone fixed to the rail. In recent days it had rung several times for Maxwell when he had stood there, staring out to sea as he dictated his increasingly desperate orders to his son Kevin in London, trying to save the Maxwell empire from sinking into the financial morass which engulfed it.

But on that cold, blowy November night with no stars visible to lighten the seascape, if not Maxwell's mood, the phone did not ring.

How long he stood there, a massive three-hundred pound figure, the wind tugging at his night-shirt and his hair, no one will know.

Did he suddenly cry out? Did he struggle to keep his balance? Did he grab at the hand rail? No one on board will ever know. The wind was up. Those on duty on the bridge were staring ahead.

Then suddenly Robert Maxwell, a man who had survived through greed and corruption, who had spied for Mossad, who had then threatened the one agency he must have known could not be threatened, was no longer a problem for the spy masters who had controlled him.

He had vanished beneath the cold Atlantic swell.

When Maxwell's body was eventually recovered and brought ashore in Tenerife, three Spanish pathologists were assigned to perform an autopsy. They knew the importance of Maxwell; he was their first true world celebrity to be opened up and have his organs examined.

A high-ranking member of the Israeli Cabinet called the Israeli ambassador in Madrid. He was told *"a distinguished Israeli citizen — Robert Maxwell — has been lost at sea in a tragic accident."*

In the meantime the Maxwell family, his widow and two sons — his daughter would only learn later of their father's death — were informed of Maxwell's fate.

While Maxwell lay naked *"like a beached whale"* on an autopsy table surrounded by the three pathologists poised to open up his bloated body, matters moved swiftly. From Madrid came urgent orders from both the Minister of Health and the Foreign Minister to the Governor of the Canary Islands.

The body was to be *"suitably embalmed"* and prepared to be flown in its coffin to Tel Aviv within hours.

Embalming is a complicated process and requires the draining of all blood from the body and the removal of all vital organs. This was done. The organs were only briefly forensically examined by the pathologists. They filled the cadaver with embalming fluid. Maxwell's organs, including his brain, were shoved back into his stomach. The corpse was sewn up. Maxwell was then placed in a coffin. The casket was sealed, as per international requirements, and taken to the airport for the five-hour flight to Tel Aviv.

On November 10, 1991, Maxwell's funeral took place on the Mount of Olives in Jerusalem, the resting place for the nation's most revered heroes. It had all the trappings of a state occasion, attended by the country's government and opposition leaders. No fewer than six serving and former heads of the Israeli intelligence community listened as Prime Minister Shamir eulogized: *"He has done more for Israel than can today be said."*

A year later, in October 1992, in what it claimed was a *"world exclusive,"* headlined *"How and Why Robert Maxwell was Murdered,"* Britain's Business Age magazine claimed that a two-man hit team crossed in a dinghy during the night from a motor yacht which had shadowed *The Lady Ghislaine*. Boarding the yacht, they found Maxwell on the afterdeck. The men overpowered him before

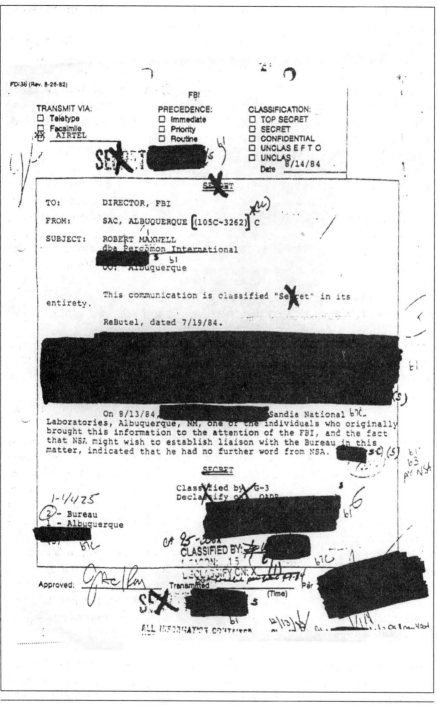

FBI documents on Robert Maxwell
To this day, many remain redacted as part of the ongoing cover-up this book reveals.

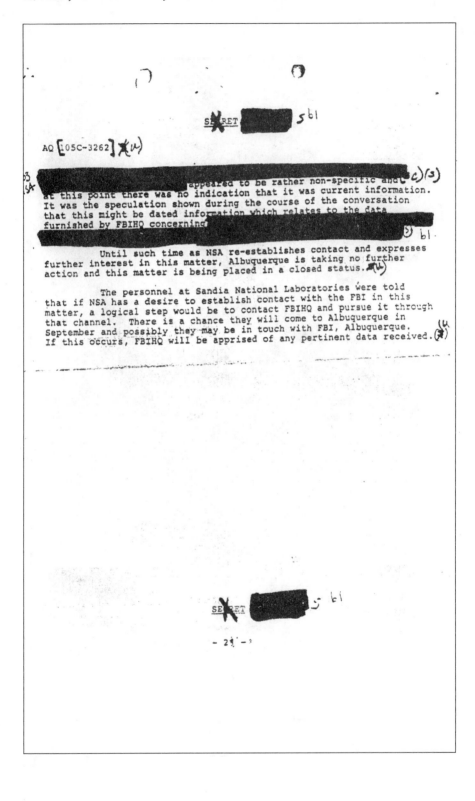

SECRET

AQ [105C-3262]

appeared to be rather non-specific and at this point there was no indication that it was current information. It was the speculation shown during the course of the conversation that this might be dated information which relates to the data furnished by FBIHQ concerning

Until such time as NSA re-establishes contact and expresses further interest in this matter, Albuquerque is taking no further action and this matter is being placed in a closed status.

The personnel at Sandia National Laboratories were told that if NSA has a desire to establish contact with the FBI in this matter, a logical step would be to contact FBIHQ and pursue it through that channel. There is a chance they will come to Albuquerque in September and possibly they may be in touch with FBI, Albuquerque. If this occurs, FBIHQ will be apprised of any pertinent data received.

SECRET

- 2 -

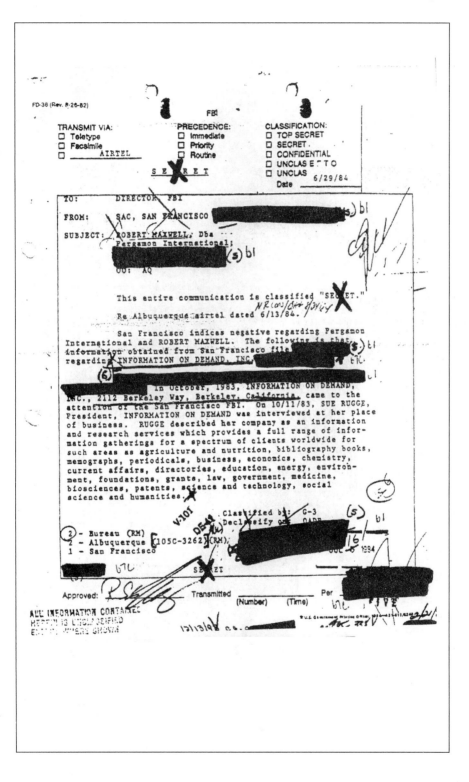

FD-36 (Rev. 8-26-82)

FBI

TRANSMIT VIA:
☐ Teletype
☐ Facsimile
☐ _____ AIRTEL

PRECEDENCE:
☐ Immediate
☐ Priority
☐ Routine

CLASSIFICATION:
☐ TOP SECRET
☐ SECRET
☐ CONFIDENTIAL
☐ UNCLAS E F T O
☐ UNCLAS

S E X R E T

Date 6/29/84

TO: DIRECTOR, FBI

FROM: SAC, SAN FRANCISCO

SUBJECT: ROBERT MAXWELL, Dba
         Pergamon International;

         OO: AQ

This entire communication is classified "SECRET."

Re Albuquerque airtel dated 6/13/84.

San Francisco indices negative regarding Pergamon International and ROBERT MAXWELL. The following is that information obtained from San Francisco file regarding INFORMATION ON DEMAND, INC.

In October, 1983, INFORMATION ON DEMAND, INC., 2112 Berkeley Way, Berkeley, California, came to the attention of the San Francisco FBI. On 10/11/83, SUE RUGGE, President, INFORMATION ON DEMAND was interviewed at her place of business. RUGGE described her company as an information and research services which provides a full range of information gatherings for a spectrum of clients worldwide for such areas as agriculture and nutrition, bibliography books, memographs, periodicals, business, economics, chemistry, current affairs, directories, education, energy, environment, foundations, grants, law, government, medicine, biosciences, patents, science and technology, social science and humanities.

Classified by: G-3
Declassify on: OADR

2 - Bureau (RM)
2 - Albuquerque (105C-3262)(RM)
1 - San Francisco

Approved: _____   Transmitted _____ (Number) (Time)   Per _____

ALL INFORMATION CONTAINED
HEREIN IS UNCLASSIFIED
EXCEPT WHERE SHOWN

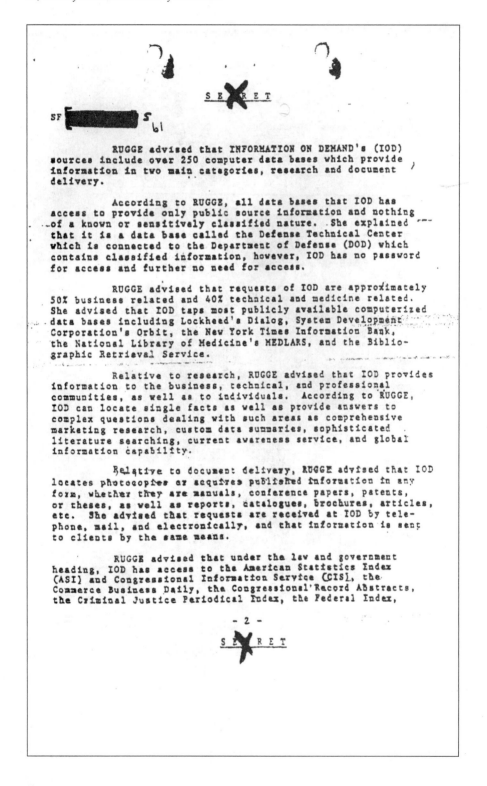

S E C R E T

SF ▮▮▮▮▮▮ s_{61}

RUGGE advised that INFORMATION ON DEMAND's (IOD) sources include over 250 computer data bases which provide information in two main categories, research and document delivery.

According to RUGGE, all data bases that IOD has access to provide only public source information and nothing of a known or sensitively classified nature. She explained that it is a data base called the Defense Technical Center which is connected to the Department of Defense (DOD) which contains classified information, however, IOD has no password for access and further no need for access.

RUGGE advised that requests of IOD are approximately 50% business related and 40% technical and medicine related. She advised that IOD taps most publicly available computerized data bases including Lockheed's Dialog, System Development Corporation's Orbit, the New York Times Information Bank, the National Library of Medicine's MEDLARS, and the Bibliographic Retrieval Service.

Relative to research, RUGGE advised that IOD provides information to the business, technical, and professional communities, as well as to individuals. According to RUGGE, IOD can locate single facts as well as provide answers to complex questions dealing with such areas as comprehensive marketing research, custom data summaries, sophisticated literature searching, current awareness service, and global information capability.

Relative to document delivery, RUGGE advised that IOD locates photocopies or acquires published information in any form, whether they are manuals, conference papers, patents, or theses, as well as reports, catalogues, brochures, articles, etc. She advised that requests are received at IOD by telephone, mail, and electronically, and that information is sent to clients by the same means.

RUGGE advised that under the law and government heading, IOD has access to the American Statistics Index (ASI) and Congressional Information Service (CIS), the Commerce Business Daily, the Congressional Record Abstracts, the Criminal Justice Periodical Index, the Federal Index,

- 2 -

S E C R E T

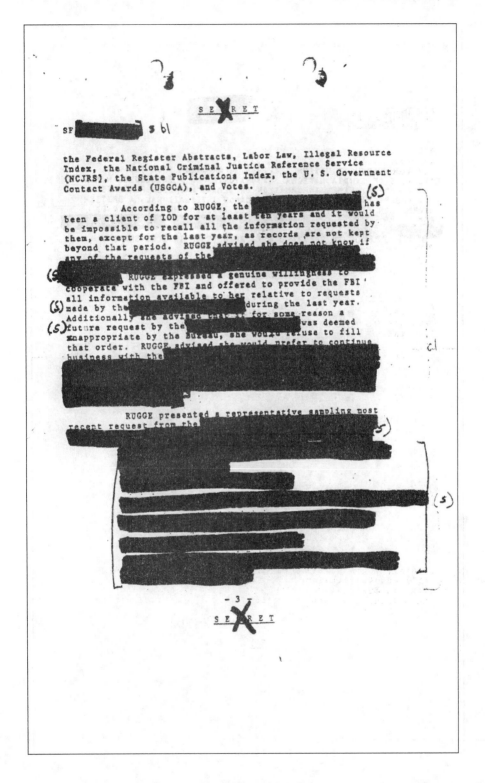

SE⊗RET

SF ▮▮▮▮▮ 8 b1

the Federal Register Abstracts, Labor Law, Illegal Resource
Index, the National Criminal Justice Reference Service
(NCJRS), the State Publications Index, the U. S. Government
Contact Awards (USGCA), and Votes.

According to RUGGE, the ▮▮▮▮▮▮▮▮▮▮ has
been a client of IOD for at least ten years and it would
be impossible to recall all the information requested by
them, except for the last year, as records are not kept
beyond that period. RUGGE advised she does not know if
any of the requests of the ▮▮▮▮▮▮▮▮▮▮▮▮▮ (S)

▮▮▮▮▮▮ RUGGE expressed a genuine willingness to
cooperate with the FBI and offered to provide the FBI
all information available to her relative to requests
made by the ▮▮▮▮▮▮▮▮ during the last year.
Additionally she advised ▮▮▮▮▮ for some reason a
future request by the ▮▮▮▮▮ was deemed
inappropriate by the Bureau, she would refuse to fill
that order. RUGGE advised she would prefer to continue
business with the ▮▮▮▮▮▮▮▮▮▮▮▮▮▮▮▮▮▮▮▮

RUGGE presented a representative sampling most
recent request from the ▮▮▮▮▮▮▮▮▮▮▮ (S)

- 3 -

SE⊗RET

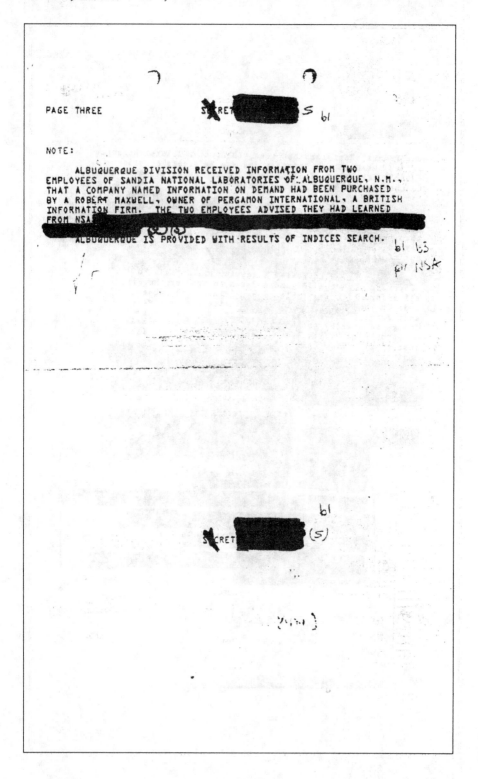

PAGE THREE   S⬛CRET ⬛⬛⬛⬛ S ʙₗ

NOTE:

     ALBUQUERQUE DIVISION RECEIVED INFORMATION FROM TWO
EMPLOYEES OF SANDIA NATIONAL LABORATORIES OF ALBUQUERQUE, N.M.,
THAT A COMPANY NAMED INFORMATION ON DEMAND HAD BEEN PURCHASED
BY A ROBERT MAXWELL, OWNER OF PERGAMON INTERNATIONAL, A BRITISH
INFORMATION FIRM. THE TWO EMPLOYEES ADVISED THEY HAD LEARNED
FROM NSA⬛⬛⬛⬛⬛⬛⬛⬛⬛⬛⬛⬛⬛⬛⬛⬛⬛⬛⬛⬛⬛⬛⬛⬛⬛⬛⬛⬛⬛⬛⬛⬛
ALBUQUERQUE IS PROVIDED WITH RESULTS OF INDICES SEARCH.   ʙₗ ₆₃

         for NSA

S⬛CRET ⬛⬛⬛⬛ (S)   ʙₗ

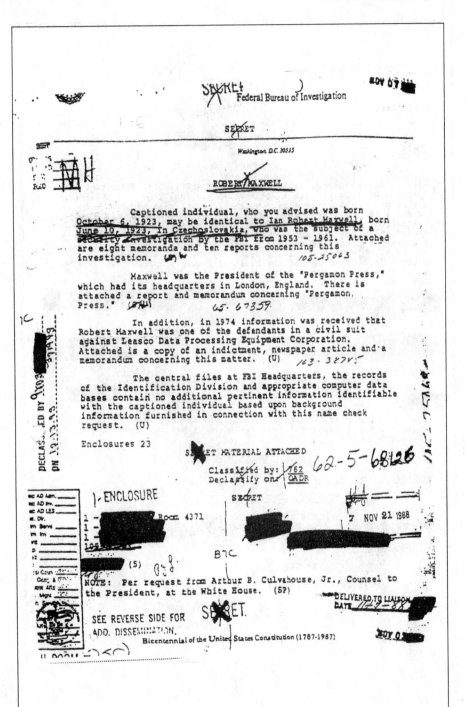

SECRET
Federal Bureau of Investigation

SECRET

Washington D.C. 20535

ROBERT MAXWELL

Captioned individual, who you advised was born October 6, 1923, may be identical to Ian Robert Maxwell, born June 10, 1923, in Czechoslovakia, who was the subject of a security investigation by the FBI from 1953 - 1961. Attached are eight memoranda and ten reports concerning this investigation. 105-25063

Maxwell was the President of the "Pergamon Press," which had its headquarters in London, England. There is attached a report and memorandum concerning "Pergamon, Press." 65-67359

In addition, in 1974 information was received that Robert Maxwell was one of the defendants in a civil suit against Leasco Data Processing Equipment Corporation. Attached is a copy of an indictment, newspaper article and a memorandum concerning this matter. (U) 163-3877

The central files at FBI Headquarters, the records of the Identification Division and appropriate computer data bases contain no additional pertinent information identifiable with the captioned individual based upon background information furnished in connection with this name check request. (U)

Enclosures 23

SECRET MATERIAL ATTACHED   62-5-68126

Classified by: 162
Declassify on: OADR

1- ENCLOSURE   SECRET

1   Room 4371   7 NOV 21 1988
1
1
100

(5)

B7C

NOTE: Per request from Arthur B. Culvahouse, Jr., Counsel to the President, at the White House. (SP)

DELIVERED TO LIAISON
DATE 11-9-88

SEE REVERSE SIDE FOR   SECRET.
ADD. DISSEMINATION.
Bicentennial of the United States Constitution (1787-1987)

SECRET ███████ -S b1

AQ [105C-3262] (↓↓)

54704, with Telephones (415) 644-4500 and (800) 227-0750. The president of this firm is a woman known as SUE RUGGE. The nature of this firm is that it is a firm which has compiled data base information and for a fee will provide them to customers. The data base information relates to a wide variety and to the best of their knowledge is not classified in any manner. However, it includes information concerning government and various available means of tapping government information data bases. The information provided by the Sandia employees was received from employees of the National Security Agency (NSA) and has to do with the purchase of Information On Demand, Inc., by one ROBERT MAXWELL, the owner of Pergamon International, a British information firm. According to NSA, ███

███████████████████████████████ (S)(S) b1 b3 p₁ NSA

The information received from these Sandia employees is ██

computerized data bases on behalf of the Soviets.

b₁ b3 p₁ NS

Albuquerque indices are negative regarding Pergamon International, ROBERT MAXWELL, Information On Demand, Inc.████

███████   b7C

According to the Sandia employees, there is a New Jersey Pergamon International Office; however, they did not know where it was located. (S)(S)

LEADS

NEW YORK CITY DIVISION

    AT NEW YORK CITY, NEW YORK

    Search indices regarding Pergamon International, ROBERT MAXWELL, Information On Demand, Inc.████████████ b7C

NEWARK DIVISION

    AT NEWARK, NEW JERSEY

    Will check indices as set forth for New York Office.

SECRET ██████████ (S) b1

- 2 -

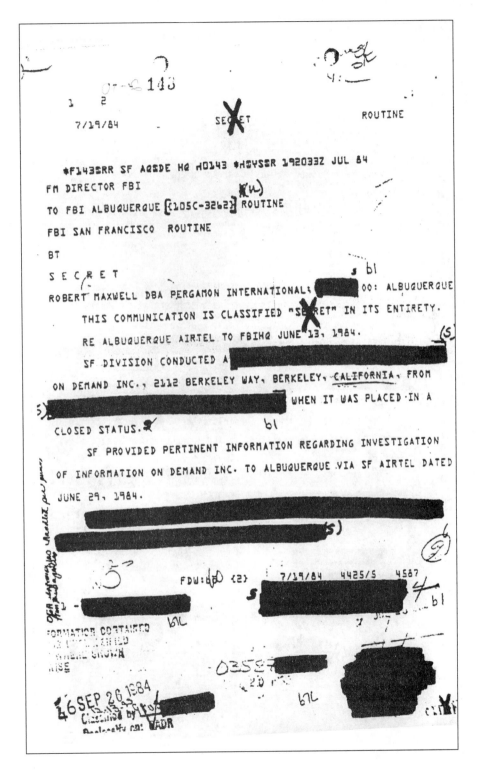

0--Q 143

1   2

7/19/84   SE~~ET   ROUTINE

#F143SRR SF AQSDE HQ H0143 #HSYSSR 192033Z JUL 84

FM DIRECTOR FBI

TO FBI ALBUQUERQUE (105C-3262) ROUTINE

FBI SAN FRANCISCO ROUTINE

BT

S E C R E T

ROBERT MAXWELL DBA PERGAMON INTERNATIONAL;   00: ALBUQUERQUE

THIS COMMUNICATION IS CLASSIFIED "SECRET" IN ITS ENTIRETY.

RE ALBUQUERQUE AIRTEL TO FBIHQ JUNE 13, 1984.

SF DIVISION CONDUCTED A

ON DEMAND INC., 2112 BERKELEY WAY, BERKELEY, CALIFORNIA, FROM

WHEN IT WAS PLACED IN A

CLOSED STATUS.

SF PROVIDED PERTINENT INFORMATION REGARDING INVESTIGATION

OF INFORMATION ON DEMAND INC. TO ALBUQUERQUE VIA SF AIRTEL DATED

JUNE 29, 1984.

FDW: (2)   7/19/84   4425/S   4587

FORMATION CONTAINED

SEP 26 1984

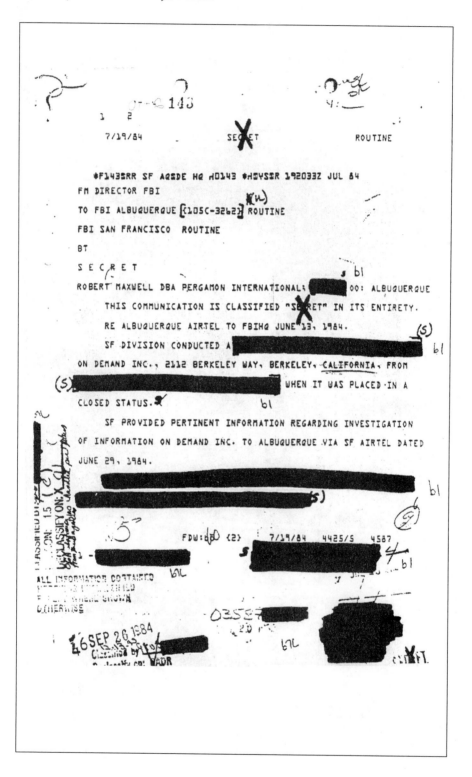

7/19/84   SECRET   ROUTINE

#F143#RR SF AQ#DE HQ HO143 #H#YS#R 192033Z JUL 84

FM DIRECTOR FBI

TO FBI ALBUQUERQUE (105C-3262) ROUTINE

FBI SAN FRANCISCO ROUTINE

BT

S E C R E T

ROBERT MAXWELL DBA PERGAMON INTERNATIONAL; ███████ 00: ALBUQUERQUE

    THIS COMMUNICATION IS CLASSIFIED "SECRET" IN ITS ENTIRETY.

    RE ALBUQUERQUE AIRTEL TO FBIHQ JUNE 13, 1984.

    SF DIVISION CONDUCTED A ████████████████████████

ON DEMAND INC., 2112 BERKELEY WAY, BERKELEY, CALIFORNIA, FROM

████████████████████████ WHEN IT WAS PLACED IN A

CLOSED STATUS.

    SF PROVIDED PERTINENT INFORMATION REGARDING INVESTIGATION

OF INFORMATION ON DEMAND INC. TO ALBUQUERQUE VIA SF AIRTEL DATED

JUNE 29, 1984.

FDW: ██ (2)   7/19/84   4425/S   4587

ALL INFORMATION CONTAINED
HEREIN IS UNCLASSIFIED
EXCEPT WHERE SHOWN
OTHERWISE

SEP 26 1984

SECRET

PAGE TWO DE HQ 0143 SECRET

(S) b1

C BY: 5806: DECL:OADR

BT

i

SECRET

THE WHITE HOUSE
WASHINGTON

October 7, 1988
(Date)

TO: FBI, LIAISON

FROM: ARTHUR B. CULVAHOUSE, JR.

SUBJECT: FBI Investigations

Subject's Name: MAXWELL, ROBERT

Date of Birth: 10/6/23   Place of Birth: _____

Present Address: _____

We request: _____   Copy of Previous Report

            X   Name Check   _____   Expanded Name Check

            _____   Full Field Investigation   TO IRS TO FBI

            _____   Limited Update

This person named above is being considered for:

            _____   White House Staff Position

            _____   Presidential Appointment

            X   ACCESS

Attachments:

            _____   SF 85 1   2

            _____   SF 87, Fingerprint Card

            _____   SF 85, Supplement

Remarks/Special Instructions: BUSINESS ADDRESS
                                Publisher
                                Mirror Group Newspaper Ltd.
                                Holburn Circus
                                London ECIP1DQ
                                United Kingdom
                                PPT#: B 252462

ALL INFORMATION CONTAINED
HEREIN IS ██████████
DATE 12-13-93 ██████

62-5-68126

PLEASE EXPEDITE

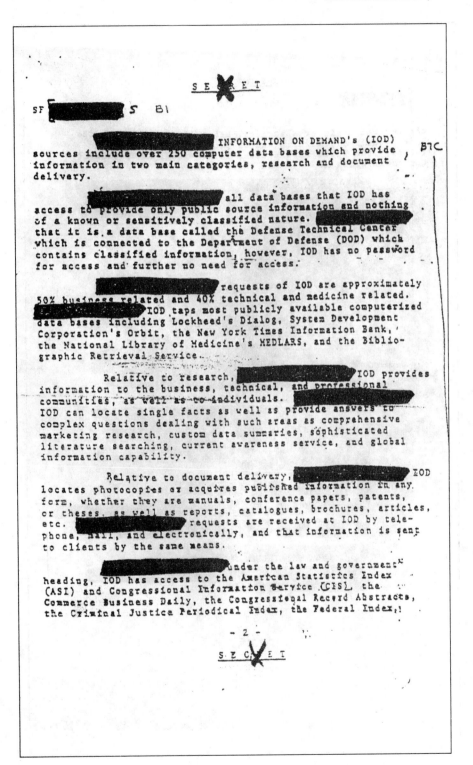

S E C R E T

SF [redacted] S B1

[redacted] INFORMATION ON DEMAND's (IOD) B7C
sources include over 250 computer data bases which provide
information in two main categories, research and document
delivery.

[redacted] all data bases that IOD has
access to provide only public source information and nothing
of a known or sensitively classified nature. [redacted]
that it is a data base called the Defense Technical Center
which is connected to the Department of Defense (DOD) which
contains classified information, however, IOD has no password
for access and further no need for access.

[redacted] requests of IOD are approximately
50% business related and 40% technical and medicine related.
[redacted] IOD taps most publicly available computerized
data bases including Lockheed's Dialog, System Development
Corporation's Orbit, the New York Times Information Bank,
the National Library of Medicine's MEDLARS, and the Bibliographic Retrieval Service.

Relative to research, [redacted] IOD provides
information to the business, technical, and professional
communities, as well as to individuals.
IOD can locate single facts as well as provide answers to
complex questions dealing with such areas as comprehensive
marketing research, custom data summaries, sophisticated
literature searching, current awareness service, and global
information capability.

Relative to document delivery, [redacted] IOD
locates photocopies or acquires published information in any
form, whether they are manuals, conference papers, patents,
or theses, as well as reports, catalogues, brochures, articles,
etc. [redacted] requests are received at IOD by telephone, mail, and electronically, and that information is sent
to clients by the same means.

[redacted] under the law and government
heading, IOD has access to the American Statistics Index
(ASI) and Congressional Information Service (CIS), the
Commerce Business Daily, the Congressional Record Abstracts,
the Criminal Justice Periodical Index, the Federal Index,

- 2 -

S E C R E T

S E C R E T

SF ████████ 5 81

the Federal Register Abstracts, Labor Law, Illegal Resource
Index, the National Criminal Justice Reference Service
(NCJRS), the State Publications Index, the U. S. Government
Contact Awards (USGCA), and Votes.

- 3 -

S E C R E T

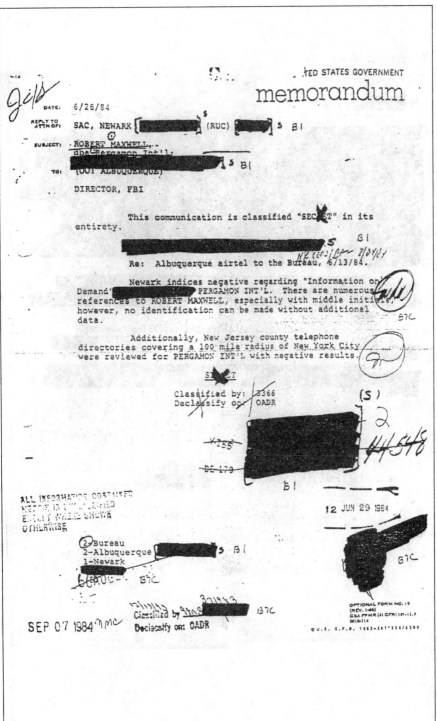

UNITED STATES GOVERNMENT

memorandum

DATE: 6/26/84

REPLY TO ATTN OF: SAC, NEWARK ▮▮▮▮ (RUC) ▮▮▮ S B1

SUBJECT: ROBERT MAXWELL, dba Pergamon Int'l; ▮▮▮▮ S B1

TO: (OO: ALBUQUERQUE)

DIRECTOR, FBI

This communication is classified "SECRET" in its entirety.

▮▮▮▮▮▮▮▮▮▮ S B1

Re: Albuquerque airtel to the Bureau, 6/13/84.

Newark indices negative regarding "Information on Demand" ▮▮▮▮ PERGAMON INT'L. There are numerous references to ROBERT MAXWELL, especially with middle initials, however, no identification can be made without additional data.

B7C

Additionally, New Jersey county telephone directories covering a 100 mile radius of New York City were reviewed for PERGAMON INT'L with negative results.

SECRET

Classified by: /3366
Declassify on: OADR

(S)

B1

ALL INFORMATION CONTAINED
HEREIN IS UNCLASSIFIED
EXCEPT WHERE SHOWN
OTHERWISE

12 JUN 29 1984

②-Bureau
2-Albuquerque ▮▮▮▮ S B1
1-Newark
B7C

B7C

Classified by ▮▮▮▮
Declassify on: OADR B7C

SEP 07 1984

OPTIONAL FORM NO. 10
(REV. 1-80)
GSA FPMR (41 CFR) 101-11.6
M10-114
☆U.S. G.P.O. 1983-381-514/6301

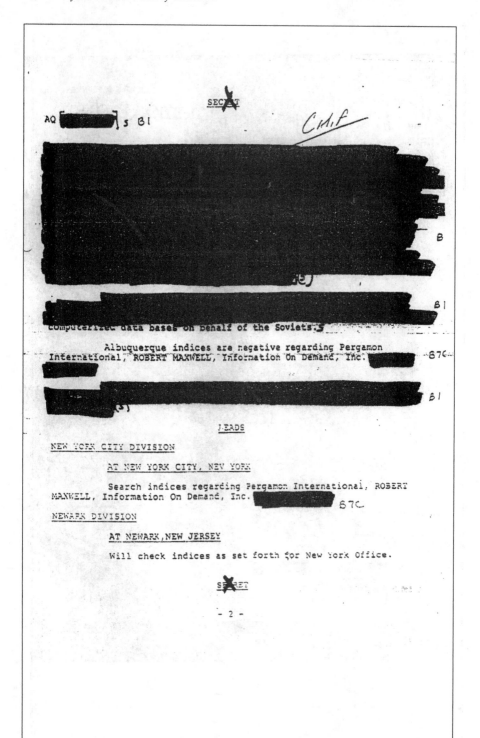

SECRET

AQ [   ] s B1

Chief

B

B1

computerized data bases on behalf of the Soviets.

Albuquerque indices are negative regarding Pergamon International, ROBERT MAXWELL, Information On Demand, Inc.   B7C

B1

LEADS

NEW YORK CITY DIVISION

AT NEW YORK CITY, NEW YORK

Search indices regarding Pergamon International, ROBERT MAXWELL, Information On Demand, Inc.   B7C

NEWARK DIVISION

AT NEWARK, NEW JERSEY

Will check indices as set forth for New York Office.

SECRET

- 2 -

FEDERAL BUREAU OF INVESTIGATION
COMMUNICATION MESSAGE FORM

143

PAGE 1 OF 2

DATE	CLASSIFICATION	PRECEDENCE
7/19/84	SECRET	ROUTINE

SF149IRR SF AQIDE HQ H0143 #45H5ER 1920337 JUL 84

FM DIRECTOR FBI

TO FBI ALBUQUERQUE ▓▓▓▓ ROUTINE B1

FBI SAN FRANCISCO ROUTINE

BT

S E C R E T

ROBERT MAXWELL DBA PERGAMON INTERNATIONAL; ▓▓▓ OO: ALBUQUERQUE

THIS COMMUNICATION IS CLASSIFIED "SECRET" IN ITS ENTIRETY.

RE ALBUQUERQUE AIRTEL TO FBIHQ JUNE 13, 1984.

▓▓▓▓▓▓▓▓▓▓▓▓▓▓▓▓▓▓▓▓▓▓▓▓▓▓▓▓▓▓▓▓▓▓▓▓▓▓

▓▓▓▓▓▓▓▓▓▓▓▓▓▓▓▓▓▓▓▓▓▓▓▓▓▓▓▓▓▓▓▓▓▓▓▓▓▓

▓▓▓▓▓▓▓▓ S   B1

SF PROVIDED PERTINENT INFORMATION REGARDING INVESTIGATION

OF INFORMATION ON DEMAND INC. TO ALBUQUERQUE VIA SF AIRTEL DATED

JUNE 29, 1984.

▓▓▓▓▓▓▓▓▓▓▓▓▓▓▓▓▓▓▓▓▓▓▓▓▓▓▓▓▓▓▓▓▓ (S)

▓▓▓▓▓▓▓▓▓▓▓▓▓▓▓▓▓▓▓   B1

DO NOT TYPE MESSAGE BELOW THIS LINE

DRAFTED BY	DATE	ROOM	TELE EXT
FDV:▓▓ (2)	7/19/84	4425/5	4587

1 - ▓▓▓▓▓▓▓▓▓▓▓▓▓▓▓▓▓▓▓▓▓▓▓▓▓▓▓▓▓▓▓▓ B1

B7C   JUL 26 1984

ALL INFORMATION CONTAINED
HEREIN IS UNCLASSIFIED
EXCEPT WHERE SHOWN
OTHERWISE

SEP 26 1984
Classified by ▓▓▓
Declassify on: OADR

DO NOT FILE WITHOUT COMMUNICATIONS STAMP

JUL 8 1983
B7C

SECRET

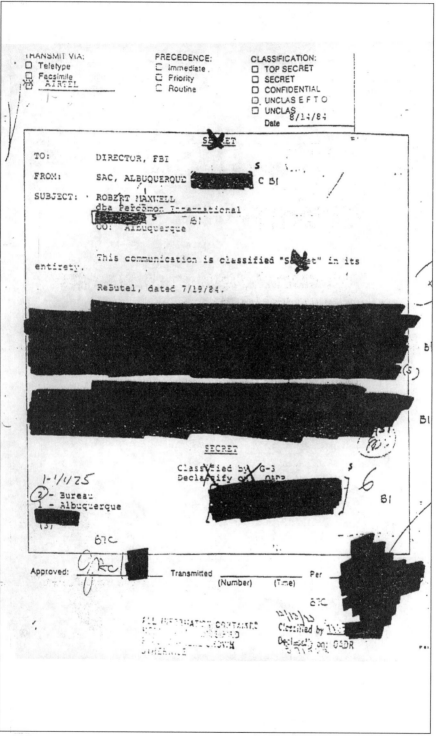

SECRET

TO: DIRECTOR, FBI

FROM: SAC, ALBUQUERQUE

SUBJECT: ROBERT MAXWELL
           dba Pergamon International
           OO: Albuquerque

This communication is classified "Secret" in its
entirety.

ReButel, dated 7/19/84.

SECRET

Classified by G-3
Declassify on OADR

2 - Bureau
1 - Albuquerque

Approved: _____   Transmitted _____   Per _____
                                      (Number) (Time)

ALL INFORMATION CONTAINED
HEREIN IS UNCLASSIFIED
EXCEPT WHERE SHOWN
OTHERWISE

Classified by
Declassify on: OADR

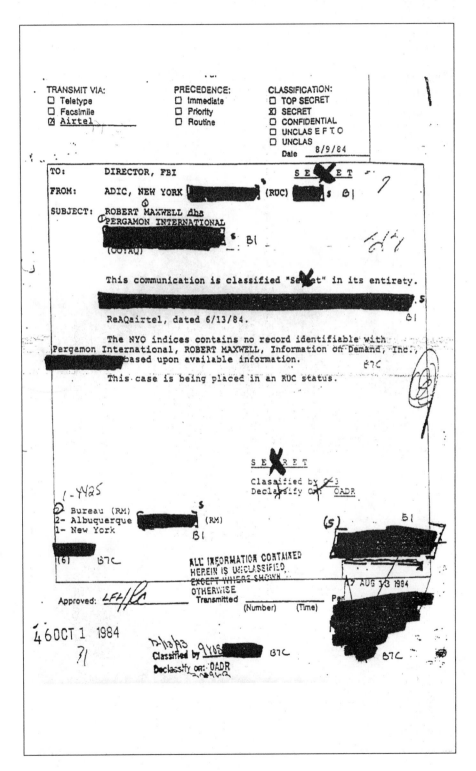

TRANSMIT VIA: PRECEDENCE: CLASSIFICATION:
☐ Teletype   ☐ Immediate   ☐ TOP SECRET
☐ Facsimile   ☐ Priority   ☒ SECRET
☒ Airtel   ☐ Routine   ☐ CONFIDENTIAL
                                           ☐ UNCLAS E F T O
                                           ☐ UNCLAS
                                           Date 8/9/84

TO: DIRECTOR, FBI   S E ✗ E T

FROM: ADIC, NEW YORK [   ]   (RUC) [   ] S B|

SUBJECT: ROBERT MAXWELL aka
           PERGAMON INTERNATIONAL
           [   ] S B|
           (OO:AQ)

           This communication is classified "Secret" in its entirety.

           [   ] S
                                                           B|
           ReAQairtel, dated 6/13/84.

           The NYO indices contains no record identifiable with
Pergamon International, ROBERT MAXWELL, Information on Demand, Inc.,
based upon available information.   B7C

           This case is being placed in an RUC status.

                              S E ✗ E T
                              Classified by O-3
                              Declassify On OADR

1-4425
② Bureau (RM)   B|
2- Albuquerque [   ] S (RM)   (S)
1- New York   B|
(6)   B7C   ALL INFORMATION CONTAINED
                   HEREIN IS UNCLASSIFIED
                   EXCEPT WHERE SHOWN
                   OTHERWISE   AUG 13 1984
Approved: LFL/RC   Transmitted _____ Per
                              (Number) (Time)
460CT 1 1984
   71   Classified by 9Y68   B7C   B7C
               Declassify on: OADR

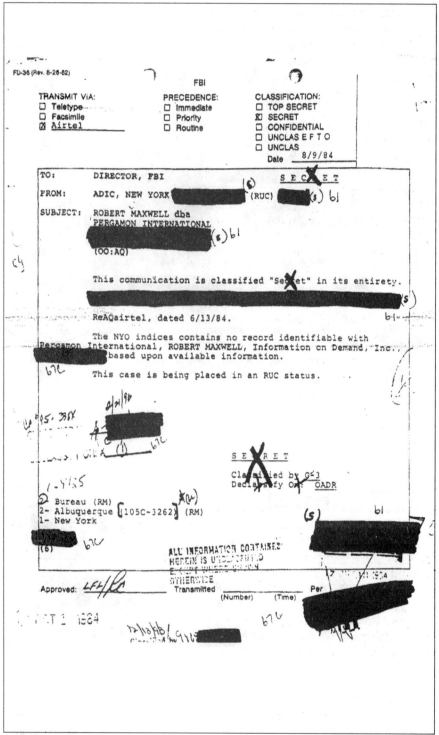

FD-36 (Rev. 8-26-82)

FBI

TRANSMIT ViA:
☐ Teletype
☐ Facsimile
☒ Airtel

PRECEDENCE:
☐ Immediate
☐ Priority
☐ Routine

CLASSIFICATION:
☐ TOP SECRET
☒ SECRET
☐ CONFIDENTIAL
☐ UNCLAS E F T O
☐ UNCLAS

Date 8/9/84

TO: DIRECTOR, FBI   S E C R E T

FROM: ADIC, NEW YORK   (RUC)

SUBJECT: ROBERT MAXWELL dba
         PERGAMON INTERNATIONAL

         (OO:AQ)

This communication is classified "Secret" in its entirety.

ReAQairtel, dated 6/13/84.

The NYO indices contains no record identifiable with Pergamon International, ROBERT MAXWELL, Information on Demand, Inc., based upon available information.

This case is being placed in an RUC status.

S E C R E T

Classified by G-3
Declassify On: OADR

2- Bureau (RM)
2- Albuquerque (105C-3262) (RM)
1- New York

(6)

ALL INFORMATION CONTAINED
HEREIN IS UNCLASSIFIED
EXCEPT WHERE SHOWN
OTHERWISE

Approved: _____ Transmitted _____ Per _____
                   (Number)   (Time)

he could call for help. Then, *"one assassin injected a bubble of air into Maxwell's neck via his jugular vein. It took just a few moments for Maxwell to die."*

The magazine concluded the body was dropped overboard and the assassins returned to their yacht. It would be twelve hours before Maxwell was recovered — enough time for a needle prick to recede beyond detection as a result of water immersion and the skin being nibbled by fish.

In his powerful book, *"Maxwell: The Final Verdict,"* Tom Bower, an English investigative journalist, makes the valid point that discovering the cause of Maxwell's death depended on meticulous police investigation.

Key questions have still to be answered: Why was the door to Maxwell's cabin locked from the outside? Had he done so himself before going up on deck? Had somebody locked it after he had gone? What had happened to the key? It was never found on Maxwell's body, or on deck.

Why had Maxwell gone up on deck? Had he just gone for a breather? Or had he been lured up there? Why had it taken so long to raise the alarm? Twelve hours would elapse before his body was recovered. Yet the senior Spanish pathologist who conducted the post mortem was to record in his findings: *"The evidence points to the body having been dead longer than it was in the water."*

Bower accuses the Spanish police of being *"negligently unsuspicious. Tests were not conducted on the yacht's rails, decks or walls. The seals (to Maxwell's cabin) were removed and the stewardesses allowed to clean up the mess. If any clues to his disappearance were to be found on the cabin's carpets or furniture, they were swept aside as the two girls cleaned the room."*

The only certainty is that, as Bower says, Maxwell's death spawned *"tales of intrigue, unidentified frogmen, a mystery ship, radio intercepts, intelligence-service rivalries, unauthorized weapons deals, stolen gold, secret bank accounts, money laundering...and ultimately murder."*

Given the identity of the corpse, nothing should have been discounted.

Now, nine years later, driving into Washington, Tenet knew those FBI documents about Robert Maxwell could go some way to providing the Bush transition team with highly persuasive evidence that it was not the hapless Dr. Lee who had been the Chinese Secret Service spy inside Los Alamos — but the Israeli version of the Enhanced Promis software that Robert Maxwell, with the full approval of Rafi Eitan and undoubtedly Israel's political masters, had sold to China.

Tenet could not know if the transition team, once in office, would demand that the previous FBI enquiry, so badly bungled, together with the posturing of Clinton's Attorney General, Janet Reno, would now be reopened and the truth finally made public. There could be no doubt that the truth had been discreetly buried because of the need to build a new relationship with China following the massacre of those students on Tiananmen Square.

Tenet knew that how much would ever emerge depended in part on two Canadian Mounties. For months now they had doggedly been probing what exactly lay behind that funeral eulogy of Israel's prime minister that Maxwell had done more for that country than anyone knew, as his massive corpse was lowered into the stony ground of Mount Olives in Jerusalem.

Room 713 is a cheerless one in the Royal Canadian Mounted Police Security Investigations Unit, headquartered in the Ottawa suburb of Vanier, Ontario. For sixteen months it had been the office of two senior investigators, Sean McDade and Randy Buffam. Both highly experienced detectives, they had been given the assignment of discovering how the Israeli-doctored Enhanced Promis had come to be sold some eight years before by Robert Maxwell to the Canadian Secret Intelligence Service, CSIS.

By October 2000, their search had taken them thousands of miles, traveling often in the utmost secrecy. It had brought them into close contact with the CIA and agents of Britain's MI5 and MI6 and the dark and dangerous world of the Russian Mafia and its money-laundering activities. But they had also come to realize their trail had been discreetly blocked at every turn whenever they came close to the truth.

All their efforts, for instance, to bring Rafi Eitan to Ottawa from his home on Shay Street in the northern Tel Aviv suburb had been politely declined by the Israeli government. They said Eitan was now a private citizen who had been previously interviewed years ago by the Israelis who now saw no need for the old spymaster to be brought to Canada to answer the many new questions McDade and Buffam wished to put to him — and which Eitan only could answer. For his part, the two investigators knew Eitan, who was now an advisor to the Castro regime, had taken considerable precautions to avoid flying anywhere near Canadian air space on his regular trips to Havana.

On their visits to Washington, the two Mounties had spoken with Bill Hamilton no fewer than thirty-two times. Everything he had told them had checked out. But that had not helped them either.

On one of their trips they had met with the former lead investigator of the House Judiciary Committee, John Cohen. He had not minced his words: *"There is a putrid stench that reaches across party lines in Washington and involves cover-ups by various administrations and foreign governments, specifically Israel's. Though tens of millions of dollars have been spent investigating the 'Inslaw affair,' they have all failed for one reason only. Very powerful people do not wish the truth to get out."*

On that October morning, back from yet another trip to the United States, the two investigators believed they now knew the truth — but could never prove it in terms of providing the kind of evidence a court of law would demand. They knew that a Trojan horse, or back door, had been fitted into the Israeli-doctored software sold to CSIS and many other intelligence services. They knew with bitter hindsight that, from the beginning, they had been sent on a Mission Impossible that had taken them deep into the world of covert and undetectable surveillance in which Enhanced Promis played a key part in the new age of communications warfare.

For those past sixteen months they had immersed themselves in the story of how Enhanced Promis had been stolen and wound up in the hands of the spy agencies of the world where it had become, and remained a powerful tool.

In Holland Intel used it to track the activities of the Russian Mafia as it shipped arms and drugs through Schipol Airport. In Germany the BND, the nation's equivalent to the CIA, used the software to follow the trail of nuclear materials out of the former Soviet Union into the Middle East. In France the security services used Enhanced Promis to track terrorists in and out of Africa and elsewhere. In Spain, the software was used to keep tabs on the Basque terrorist movement. In Britain, MI5 used it to watch the movements of the scores of Middle East groups who had set up base in the suburbs of London. In Northern Ireland it became a weapon for the security services tracking the IRA as its members came and went across the border with the Irish Republic. In Scotland it formed a database for what became the long-running investigation into the terrorist destruction of Pan Am 103. In Hong Kong, Britain's MI6 used the program to track the Triads and agents from the People's Republic. In Japan, Enhanced Promis was used to interdict the links between the Japanese underworld and its counterparts in North Korea and Mainland China. In South Africa, where Israel had already sold the system, Enhanced Promis was used to track white extremists. The same software served a different purpose in Sweden: there it was used to maintain a watch over foreign diplomats in the country, especially those from Eastern Europe who might be using their political immunity to set up arms traffic networks through Sweden. And, of course, Mossad used Enhanced Promis to maintain its intelligence stranglehold over its neighbors. Using the system, Mossad was able to track all the communications the Jordanians had with all its Arab neighbors.

To this day, Enhanced Promis remained in place around the world as an unseen agent of the secret services.

McDade and Buffam had studied every previous investigation by U.S. law enforcement agencies, private detectives, congressional investigators and U.S. customs. They had read every affidavit and judgment handed down by some of the most powerful courts in the United States. Typical had been the verdict by the United States Congress Judiciary Committee. *"The theft of Enhanced Promis is surrounded by conspiracy, fraud, witness tampering, retaliation against witnesses, interference with commerce by threats of violence. Violations of the Racketeer and Corrupt Organizations Act. Transportation of stolen goods, securities, monies. Receiving stolen goods."*

But most serious of all had been the accusation that *"a foreign power — the state of Israel — had been engaged in active espionage against the United States by the illegal use of the Enhanced Promis software."*

Following up on that accusation which both Mounties now knew to *"be utterly true"* had taken them deep into the shadowy world of international espionage.

On that October morning in 2000, they had no doubt what they had discovered. It was in McDade's written memo to his superiors: *"If made public, it conceivably will cause a major scandal in both Canada and the United States. More than one U.S. Presidential Administration will be exposed because of their knowledge and complicity in what did happen. There is no doubt that high-ranking Canadian govern-*

ment officials were also involved. These persons had used the Enhanced Promis software to launder the money they received from helping to arrange the sale of Enhanced Promis to CSIS. The Israeli Mossad may have modified the original stolen software by Rafi Eitan ('Dr. Orr') which was the 'first back door.' Later it became a 'two-way back door,' allowing the Israelis access to top U.S. weapons secrets at Los Alamos and other classified installations in the United States. The Israelis now possess all the nuclear secrets of the United States. Compared to this espionage coup, it can be categorically stated that the Jonathan Pollard case is insignificant."

While he typed his memo on a secure PC, McDade suspected that across the world, in Tel Aviv, the gist of his words would soon be on the desk of the latest in a long line of Israeli spymasters who had been keeping a close eye on the events which had followed Rafi Eitan's visit to Inslaw on that cold day in February 1983.

The Israeli's name was Danny Yatom. Once the head of Mossad, he was now the personal security adviser to Israel's prime minister, Ehud Barak. Both Mounties knew that Yatom had the skills needed to keep the lid on what Israel had done.

Among the many remarkable things about Danny Yatom was that only two years ago in March 1998, when he had been head of Mossad, he had been sacked by the then prime minister, Benyamin Netanyahu, for running two operations which had left Mossad's reputation in tatters and the service's morale at its lowest-ever ebb.

At the age of fifty-one, Yatom's career seemed over. The spy chief with the ruthlessness of a street fighter found the only decision he had to make was when to lop off the heads of flowers in his garden close to the electrified fence marking the border between Israel and Jordan.

His white-walled home, standing on the very ground where the spies of Gideon, the Old Testament warrior, had prepared their missions, was no longer a place from where Yatom organized the operations which finally led to his downfall. Then Netanyahu had been ousted. Ehud Barak, an old friend of Yatom's, had taken his place. Within weeks Yatom was back in high office.

He was again one of the most powerful figures in the Israeli intelligence community. His office was close to that of the prime minister and his swipe card gave him access to the other most important offices in Israel. He was privy to more secrets than almost any other person in Israel.

Since his appointment he had read all the Israeli intelligence files on Enhanced Promis and compared them with what he had learned the two Mounties were uncovering. His information on their progress came from his own well-placed contacts in Washington. On the organization charts newspapers try to piece together and publish those sources that have remained among the empty spaces.

Like Yatom they took their anonymity seriously. Their reasons for helping Yatom can best be said as a real and genuine desire to protect Israel.

They had provided Yatom with the latest intercepts of the emails that McDade had been sending to his contacts in the United States. Yatom sensed a desperation in McDade's lack of progress; it was there in the copies of his messages. They were sent from a return address marked "*Simorp*," which was Promis spelled backwards. McDade invariably signed himself "*Hunter*."

Yatom, a man steeped in tradecraft, found the Mounties' methods amateurish.

One of the emails had been to a woman who lived in Southern California. Her name was Cheri Seymour and she doubled as a private investigator and freelance journalist.

Yatom already knew a great deal about Seymour. A petite, attractive and unassuming middle-aged woman, she had been tracking the story of Enhanced Promis for several years. There was nothing remarkable in that. The Hamiltons had tried to mobilize any media interest they could. But most reporters had given up, driven to do so by the sheer complexity of the story — and often the outlandish claims by some of those attached to it.

But Seymour had stuck with her enquiries and had reached the point where she felt able to send her findings to John Cohen, the former lead investigator to the House Judiciary Committee. But by then the Committee had closed down its investigation, delivering their harsh judgment against the Department of Justice.

Weeks later, unknown to Cohen or Seymour, her findings had been slipped to a Mossad *katsa*, field agent, in Washington. He had forwarded it to Tel Aviv in an Israeli embassy diplomatic bag. From there it had come onto Yatom's desk.

One name had caught his eye: Michael Riconoscuito. Rafi Eitan had mentioned he had met him in Beirut while Eitan was on a Mossad mission. Riconoscuito had claimed he was working for the U.S. Drug Enforcement Agency in Lebanon. Eitan had reported that Riconoscuito had "*rambled on*" about working from a safe house in Cyprus for the DEA. On this November morning in 2000, Riconoscuito was still in a U.S. Federal prison on what he had claimed, according to one of McDade's emails "*as trumped-up charges to keep him silent about Enhanced Promis and his related activities to it.*"

It appeared from the "*Simorp*" intercepts which had come to McDade that Riconoscuito was again hinting he knew a great deal more than had emerged so far about how the software had been used to rob Los Alamos of its most sensitive secrets. If that were true, then it would make sense of other reports from Yatom's contacts inside British intelligence.

Seated in his tan leather armchair in his office, Yatom knew there were many in the Israeli intelligence community who marveled at the way he had come back as a more powerful figure than before. Once more his lifestyle was what he had been used to as head of Mossad: handling a number of problems that every day called for fine judgment.

There was, for instance, the business of how Hezbollah had kidnapped Hanan Tannenbaum in Switzerland. He was a former Mossad officer. Yatom had sent him to Zurich with the prime minister's approval to discover links between Hezbollah and Iranian arms dealers and financiers who were believed to be the godfathers behind the second Intifada in the West Bank and Gaza.

Tannenbaum — who in the past had used a number of aliases and passports on other missions to Switzerland — operated out of Mossad's station at Schipol Airport, Amsterdam.

When he had been head of Mossad, Yatom had used Tannenbaum on the operation that had finally led to his own downfall. Tannenbaum had been one of the team who, in 1998, planned to bug the apartment of Abdullah Zein, the man Mossad believed was Hezbollah's fund-raiser in Europe. At the time Zein was living in Liebefeld near Berne, Switzerland.

When the mission failed, Tannenbaum managed to escape to Israel. But in September 2000, Yatom had sent Tannenbaum back to Switzerland to uncover those links between Iranian arms dealers.

Yatom was now certain that a "mole" inside a Swiss police agency had tipped off a Hezbollah team that had snatched Tannenbaum and spirited him out of Switzerland. While Barak had publicly called the kidnapping a "Mafia act," Hezbollah's leader, Sheykh Nassan Nasrallah, had taunted the prime minister: "*If you want to know how we did it, go and search.*"

What troubled Yatom was how quickly Tannenbaum's cover had been blown. With his background as an artillery colonel in the IDF and his fluency in German and French, his cover had been well nigh foolproof. Officially he was a consultant to one of Israel's leading arms manufacturers, The Rafael Corporation. Ten days before he had been snatched, he had reported to his Mossad controller that he had developed important contacts. That was the last anybody in Israel heard of him. The other question that troubled Yatom was just how Hezbollah had managed to smuggle Tannenbaum out and back to southern Lebanon. The latest intelligence placed him in Lebanon's Beka'a Valley. If that were true, Yatom would ruefully admit, then Hezbollah had carried out a kidnapping that Mossad itself would find hard to equal in its ruthless audacity.

Yatom might well doubt that Mossad would find someone with the capability of carrying out such an operation from the proof copy of the advertisement on his desk. Its heading came to the point:

"*The Mossad has openings. Only you in your heart of hearts know you are capable of thinking differently, in doing more than you thought you could.*"

Applicants were invited to contact a box number. The advertisements would appear in Hebrew-language newspapers across the world. While preference would be given to Jews, Mossad was ready to consider anyone. Candidates were required to have proven computer skills, superb physical fitness and a proven ability to analyze. Women recruits would have to face another test: a readiness to use sexual entrapment.

The rules for that had been laid down many years ago by a former Mossad chief, Meir Amit. He had stated that "*a woman agent should be ready to sleep with the enemy. Use sex for the good of her country. What she will be asked to do takes special courage. If she is married, she must betray her marriage vow. But she is not a prostitute. She is living up to the ideal of her profession — intelligence work.*"

Danny Yatom suspected that the advertisement would attract people for all kinds of reasons. There would be the misplaced glamour of working for a secret intelligence. Some would be attracted by the sense of adventure. Some would hope that being in Mossad would enhance their status. Undoubtedly a few would want what they believed to be the secret power Mossad would give them.

None of these were acceptable reasons for even being accepted for a preliminary interview. Those who passed that test would have shown they had a calm and clear, far-sighted judgment and a balanced outlook.

His fears that the advertisement would produce many who did not possess those qualities were to be proven right. Out of the thousands who applied, only a handful were sent on to the Mossad training school at Herzilia, a seaside resort south of Tel Aviv, to begin their three-year course.

But all this was only a digression. Yatom's main concern on that November morning was how far could the two Mounties, Sean McDade and Randy Buffam, get with their investigation into Enhanced Promis? How would they react to the information they had received months before from London?

On March 3, 2000, two Scotland Yard officers, Sergeant Adnan Quershi and Detective Constable Sean Reardon had flown Business Class on the British Airways flight from London's Heathrow Airport to Toronto. Each carried a bulky leather briefcase which they had stowed in the overhead rack. Seasoned travelers, they had eaten little and had drunk copious amounts of water. They knew that once they reached Toronto they would be expected to begin work at once.

Waiting to escort them through Immigration and Customs formalities were McDade and Buffam. The two Yard men were greeted with warm handshakes and a marked deference.

They had come to Canada to brief McDade and Buffam on the wider implications of the Mounties' investigation into the Promis affair. The Canadians had been in telephone contact with the officers for some weeks; the introduction had been brokered by the MI6 "resident" in Canada.

Once clear of the airport, their baggage stowed in the trunk of McDade's car but clutching their briefcases, the two men had been driven to the RCMP building in McArthur Avenue in Vanier.

There, in Room 713, for the next two days, apart from short breaks for sleep at a local hotel, Quershi and Reardon briefed McDade on all that British intelligence knew had happened since Rafi Eitan had visited Inslaw, posing as "Dr. Orr."

Those bulging briefcases they had guarded so carefully on the long flight to Canada contained a treasure trove of files all marked "Most Secret." One buff-colored file dealt with Robert Maxwell's role as Israel's super salesman of Enhanced Promis. It contained hard evidence of how the tycoon had managed to sell it to China.

The Mounties' worst fears were all in the files. The documents filled in the gaps in the winding trail they had followed across America that had included a visit to the Cabazon Indian Reservation in California. In that unlikely setting, a joint venture had been set up between the small group of Mission Indians who occupied the reservation and the Wackenhut Corporation whose long-time connections with the CIA were well documented in the MI5 file. Some of

Wackenhut's staff were former CIA or FBI agents, or had worked for other agencies within the U.S. intelligence community.

McDade and Buffam had readily seen why the reservation had been chosen. For a start it was remote. Then, under California and Federal exemption laws, all Indian reservations enjoy a special status that makes them all but sovereign nations and, in the words of one document, "*are free to govern within the confines of the reservation without outside intervention.*" For Wackenhut, who had created yet another version of Enhanced Promis, the Cabazon Reservation was the perfect place to complete the work.

But by then Maxwell had his eyes on China. While Wackenhut would sell its version of Enhanced Promis to other RCMP departments, China had ended up purchasing the Israeli-doctored version from Maxwell.

Their visitors from London were to reveal more. They produced British Intelligence's file on Michael Riconoscuito. These detailed his visits in Lebanon, including his involvement with drug runners. There were also details of the Eurama Trading Company working out of Nicosia, Cyprus. The company was a joint front for both MI6 and the CEA/CIA operations against Middle East drug traffickers into Europe and North America.

Everything the RCMP investigators had learned from their own interviews with Riconoscuito in a Florida Federal prison was restated in the British intelligence file on him.

For long hours, McDade and Buffam could only have listened agog as their visitors from London confirmed so much of what they had themselves picked up in all those weary months of trudging across the United States, seemingly receiving support for their investigation from U.S. agencies, but in reality finding themselves being side-tracked.

The more they listened, the more they realized that Cohen, the former congressional committee investigator had been right: there was indeed a "*putrid stench*" emanating from the greatest cover-up that involved not only the governments of the United States and Canada but others around the world.

Having laid out all they knew, the two officers from London turned their attention to the matter that primarily concerned them: the damage done to joint U.S./U.K./Canadian intelligence operations, not only as a result of China acquiring the Israeli-doctored Enhanced Promis software, but how it had been used to remove the secrets from the very heart of the West's defense against its new potential threat — China. That had been done with the complicity of Israel.

Already as the millennium opened, there was disturbing evidence that any serious attempt to disinter the truth of how Enhanced Promis had been stolen from the United States had been effectively blocked.

Would the new Bush Administration have the courage to demand that the investigation be reopened? Or would the new President continue to allow China and Israel to get away with the greatest scam in the history of secret intelligence? Will what has become known as the Tiananmen Trump continue to be played by the new men in power in Washington and Beijing?

See page 7 - 10

Computer Law Association
30th Anniversary Program
May 3-4, 2001
Monarch Hotel, Washington, D.C.

World Computer and Internet Law Congress
Presentation

"Managing the Global Digital Information Technology
Explosion"

INSLAW, Inc.

Luncheon Address by William A. Hamilton
May 3, 2001

"The Largest Global Software Theft In History"

Documents that confirm how the greatest computer theft
in the history of the world was perpetrated — and by whom.

1

Thank you for inviting me to speak at this 30th Anniversary program of the Computer Law Association.

Nancy Burke Hamilton, my wife and the mother of our six children, and I are the principal owners and officers of INSLAW, Inc. Both Nancy and I will be pleased to answer any questions you may have.

The topic of my talk is "The Largest Global Software Theft In History." It is a story of copyright infringement by the U.S. Department of Justice, the entity responsible for enforcing the criminal prohibitions against copyright infringement. Nancy measures the duration of INSLAW's problem by the age of the youngest of our six children, who was born when the infringing began. Brendan is about to leave home for college.

INSLAW began as a vendor of legal case management software in January 1973, over 28 years ago. During the 1970's, INSLAW developed several successive generations of the PROMIS case management software product for public prosecution agencies, principally under contracts and grants from the U.S. Justice Department's now-defunct Law Enforcement Assistance Administration (LEAA). LEAA's mission was to help state and local governments do a better job in combating crime, particularly street crime. PROMIS helped prosecutors identify and give priority to the small proportion of offenders who account for a disproportionate volume of the workload of the court system, and to quantify the reasons for case attrition.

Under amendments to the U.S. Copyright Law that took effect in January 1978, the author of software, no matter what the source of the funds, is automatically vested with five exclusive rights from the moment the software is created and fixed in tangible media so long as the computer program is original and meets the low threshold of creativity necessary for copyright protection.

One of the five copyright rights vested exclusively in INSLAW as the author of PROMIS is the right "to reproduce the copyrighted work in copies." Another of the five copyright rights vested exclusively in INSLAW is the right "to prepare derivative software based on the copyrighted work." Still another of the five copyright rights vested exclusively in INSLAW is the right "to distribute copies of the copyrighted work."

Under the U.S. Copyright Law, none of the five rights can be deemed to have been waived unless the author of the software makes an explicit, written waiver of the particular right in question.

The mechanism used by the U.S. Government to obtain the so-called "data rights" it wishes to obtain under federal contracts for software development is to incorporate into its software development contracts selected clauses from the Federal Acquisition Regulations that convey certain license rights to the government from the software vendor.

In PROMIS software development contracts with INSLAW, the LEAA and the Justice Department incorporated a standard data rights clause under which INSLAW granted the Federal Government a license to make an unlimited number of copies for the government's internal use of the particular version of PROMIS developed under the contract in question. Neither LEAA nor the Justice

2

Department, however, ever obtained a license from INSLAW to prepare derivative works based on the copyrighted work, or to distribute copies of the software outside the U.S. Government itself.

In 1980, Congress decided to abolish LEAA and the Justice Department, accordingly, notified INSLAW that its contract with LEAA for the upkeep and upgrade of PROMIS would end as of May 1981.

There were by then dozens of large urban local district attorneys' offices using PROMIS. Unless INSLAW found a way to continue PROMIS upkeep and upgrade services after the LEAA funding of those services ended in May 1981, these prosecution offices could eventually encounter software "bugs" without having any way of obtaining corrections for such latent defects. Moreover, the software would gradually become obsolete because there would be no vendor to add essential new functions and features, to make PROMIS easier to use, or to upgrade PROMIS to take advantage of the new computing platforms of the 1980's such as the very powerful 32-bit architecture computers.

To resolve this problem, INSLAW decided to invest private, non-government funds in continuing the upkeep and upgrade of PROMIS as of May 1981, and to recover its investment both by charging annual fees to existing PROMIS users for software support, and by selling licenses to the privately-enhanced version of PROMIS to new customers.

I was concerned, however, that district attorneys who had not obtained PROMIS free in earlier years when LEAA was subsidizing the effort might not understand why INSLAW was suddenly charging PROMIS license fees. I was concerned that some of these local prosecutors might in fact complain to their congressmen or senators about having to pay INSLAW when their colleagues in other cities and counties had obtained PROMIS in earlier years at no charge.

I thought one way to minimize this potential problem would be to make sure that the Justice Department understood what INSLAW was about to do and why. Therefore, in the fall of 1980, INSLAW's counsel and I briefed the Chief Operating Officer in the Carter Administration's Justice Department, Deputy Attorney General Charles B. Renfrew. That Deputy Attorney General stated that he had no problem with INSLAW's plans.

In addition to local District Attorneys Offices, INSLAW had also by then licensed PROMIS to one of the legal divisions at the Headquarters of the Justice Department, the Land and Natural Resources Division; and had licensed a 16-bit architecture version of PROMIS to two large U.S. Attorneys Offices. Beginning in May 1981, many of the local District Attorneys Offices, as well as the Land and Natural Resources Division at the Justice Department, bought annual subscriptions to INSLAW's PROMIS software support services. These subscriptions recognized INSLAW's ownership of all enhancements created under the subscription program.

INSLAW used private non-government funds during the second half of 1981 to create the 32-bit architecture VAX version of PROMIS. At the time INSLAW created the VAX version of PROMIS, INSLAW had no federal contract requiring its delivery.

3

In March 1982, INSLAW won a competitive contract to install the 16-bit architecture version of PROMIS in 20 of the largest U.S. Attorneys Offices on government furnished computers and to provide a temporary PROMIS computer timesharing service to the 10 largest U.S. Attorneys Offices using a computer of INSLAW's choice located at INSLAW. INSLAW chose to use one of its VAX computers to provide the temporary PROMIS timesharing service via leased telephone lines to each of the 10 largest U.S. Attorneys Offices.

In April 1982, INSLAW's counsel and I briefed the Reagan Administration's first Deputy Attorney General, Edmund Schmultz, on the fact that INSLAW had invested over one million dollars in private non-government funds during the previous 12 months in PROMIS upkeep and upgrade services and intended to offer licenses to a new version of PROMIS, called PROMIS 82, to any local, state, federal or foreign prosecution office that was interested. We asked this Deputy Attorney General for a letter stating that the Justice Department understood what INSLAW was doing and did not object. After a number of meetings between Justice Department officials and INSLAW's counsel, INSLAW obtained such a letter in August 1982, signed by an Associate Deputy Attorney General.

The General Services Administration, at the time, had authority over the Federal Government's acquisition of computer software. By the fall of 1982, GSA evidently understood at a very high level the potential for using PROMIS to prepare derivative software applications for the U.S. Government. In a letter dated October 14, 1982 to the Comptroller General of the United States, the Deputy Administrator of the GSA, Ray Kline, made the following comments about PROMIS:

> Although this system was designed for state and local government legal case tracking, it has been modified to track inmates in jail, parcels of land, tort cases in New York State, and is in use in all 94 U.S. Attorneys Offices and several other federal agencies. This system could be further modified to track welfare recipients or any function requiring tracking.

One important error in the GSA letter, however, was the erroneous description of PROMIS as "a federally-owned case tracking system." This mistake by the number two official in the agency responsible for the U.S. Government's procurement of software may help explain the government's infringement of INSLAW's PROMIS copyright rights, but it would not diminish the government's liability because copyright infringement is a strict liability tort and intentions do not matter.

Beginning in late 1982, the Justice Department attempted to force INSLAW to deliver the 32-bit VAX version of PROMIS that INSLAW had been operating on one of its own computers to support the 10 largest U.S. Attorneys Offices through leased telephone lines.

There was, however, no requirement under the May 1982 contract with the U.S. Attorneys Offices for INSLAW to deliver to the Justice Department the version of PROMIS that INSLAW had been using for the temporary computer timesharing services.

Therefore, I declined to deliver the VAX version of PROMIS unless the Justice Department first modified INSLAW's contract to recognize that the Justice Department had no right to use this version of PROMIS unless it paid license fees to INSLAW. I cited the "sign off" letter from the

4

Deputy Attorney General's Office in August 1982 as evidence that the Justice Department had already recognized INSLAW's rights in this regard.

The Justice Department officials responded that the sign off letter had no relevance. They continued to insist that INSLAW deliver the VAX version of PROMIS.

In February 1983, while this controversy was still ongoing, the U.S. Attorneys' Project Manager telephoned me and asked if I would be willing to demonstrate the VAX version of PROMIS to someone he described as a public prosecutor from the Ministry of Justice in Tel Aviv, Israel by the name of Dr. Ben Or. The Justice Department project manager told me that Dr. Ben Or was heading a project to computerize the Israeli public prosecution offices and might be interested in buying the VAX version of PROMIS from INSLAW. INSLAW provided a several hour demonstration and briefing for the Israeli visitor in February 1983. The Israeli visitor was enthusiastic about the VAX version of PROMIS but the visit never led to a sale of PROMIS to Israel - - at least it did not lead to a sale by INSLAW or any agent authorized by INSLAW.

The Justice Department eventually modified INSLAW's PROMIS contract in April 1983 in order to obtain delivery of the VAX version of PROMIS, promising to negotiate the payment of license fees, once INSLAW provided evidence of the privately-financed enhancements contained in the VAX version, and assuming, of course, that the Justice Department decided in the meantime to substitute the 32-bit VAX version of PROMIS for the 16-bit version of PROMIS that INSLAW had been contracted to install in the 20 largest U.S. Attorneys Offices.

Also in April 1983, the Chairman of Hadron, Inc., a computer systems vendor to U.S. intelligence and military agencies, telephoned me seeking to buy INSLAW. He told me that Hadron had been promised the U.S. Government's case management software business as a result of its contacts at the highest levels of the Reagan White House but needed title to PROMIS in order to exploit the opportunity. When I declined to discuss the sale of INSLAW, the Hadron Chairman told me: "We have ways of making you sell." Hadron was then controlled by a holding company headed by Earl W. Brian. Brian had served in the California cabinet of Governor Ronald Reagan. At the start of the Reagan Presidency, Brian also served on a cabinet-level committee known as "Pro-Comp" for pro-competition.

In May, June and July 1983, the Justice Department rejected every approach suggested by INSLAW for substantiating INSLAW's claim about privately-financed enhancements in the VAX version of PROMIS, while refusing to tell INSLAW why it was rejecting INSLAW's proposed methodologies. At the same time, the Department directed INSLAW to substitute the 32-bit VAX version of PROMIS for the 16-bit version of PROMIS in the then impending installations in the 20 largest U.S.

6

INSLAW's counsel and I met with Deputy Attorney General Jensen in December 1985 in an effort to determine whether the Justice Department intended to stand behind Sposato's letter. Jensen declined to intervene. Jensen also volunteered at our meeting that he had never been impressed with any generation of INSLAW's PROMIS software, beginning with his days as the District Attorney in Alameda County, California. Jensen told me that the FBI had the only advanced technology for case management at the Department of Justice, a claim to keep in mind in light of information summarized later in this presentation.

5

negotiated prior to the contract for use in accumulating INSLAW's charges for its PROMIS computer timesharing service. This Justice Department Contracting Officer unilaterally decided in the spring of 1983 to pay a much smaller monthly fee to INSLAW for the PROMIS timesharing services than the amount INSLAW had been billing under the negotiated formula.

Using the timesharing billing algorithm and two other sham contract disputes concocted at the same time in mid-1983, the Justice Department eventually withheld almost $1.8 million in payments for services rendered by INSLAW, forcing INSLAW to file for bankruptcy protection in February 1985.

In a meeting with the Reagan Administration's new Deputy Attorney General, D. Lowell Jensen, shortly after INSLAW filed for bankruptcy protection, INSLAW counsel sought and obtained Jensen's commitment to have a disinterested Justice Department lawyer attempt to unravel the contract problems that had propelled INSLAW into bankruptcy. The Department's internal procurement counsel, Janis Sposato, thereafter conducted the negotiations on behalf of the Justice Department. The negotiations took place during 1985, the first year of INSLAW's bankruptcy.

At the first negotiation session, I asked that the PROMIS license fee issue associated with the April 1983 contract modification be added to the agenda. Sposato reluctantly agreed, but insisted on first addressing the computer timesharing billing algorithm problem and resolving that problem before proceeding to any other issues. Sposato also insisted on placing the PROMIS license fee issue at the bottom of the list of the items for negotiation.

INSLAW had programmed its timesharing computer to accumulate PROMIS usage data in accordance with the negotiated algorithm. After the Justice Department repudiated the negotiated algorithm, INSLAW had to improvise "rules of thumb" to substantiate the fairness of the timesharing charges. After lengthy meetings over a period of months, INSLAW successfully accomplished this objective but Sposato refused to accept the result on the grounds that her "client" or "people" would be unhappy. Most of the negotiation sessions in 1985 addressed this single issue.

INSLAW discovered later that its peak charges for the PROMIS timesharing service were actually less than the amount the Justice Department had estimated the timesharing service should cost, based on an internal written estimate made by the Department before awarding the contract to INSLAW in March 1982.

The negotiations were clearly going nowhere. In November 1985, Sposato sent INSLAW a letter demanding that the bankrupt company repay the government almost $700,000 in what Sposato claimed had been overpayments to INSLAW under the contract. Sposato also included an intriguingly worded additional demand in her letter, a demand that I did not understand at the time but believe that I may now understand and that may have a lot to do with the government's misappropriation of PROMIS:

> INSLAW will recognize that the United States has the right to unrestricted use of the software obtained or delivered under this contract for any federal project, including projects that may be financed or conducted by instrumentalities or agents of the Federal Government such as its independent contractors. [Emphasis added]

6

INSLAW's counsel and I met with Deputy Attorney General Jensen in December 1985 in an effort to determine whether the Justice Department intended to stand behind Sposato's letter. Jensen declined to intervene. Jensen also volunteered at our meeting that he had never been impressed with any generation of INSLAW's PROMIS software, beginning with his days as the District Attorney in Alameda County, California. Jensen told me that the FBI had the only advanced technology for case management at the Department of Justice, a claim to keep in mind in light of information summarized later in this presentation.

Rebuffed by Deputy Attorney General Jensen in December 1985, INSLAW hired litigation counsel and brought suit against the Justice Department in the U.S. Bankruptcy Court in June 1986.

When a company files for Chapter 11 protection, there is an automatic stay which enjoins creditors from taking any action against the assets of the estate. The government forfeits its sovereign immunity if it is a creditor and if it violates the automatic stay. During the first year of Chapter 11, the Justice Department repeatedly described itself as INSLAW's largest creditor. INSLAW alleged that the government forfeited its sovereign immunity and that the Justice Department violated the automatic stay by continuing to exercise dominion and control over the 32-bit VAX version of PROMIS, without paying license fees to INSLAW as required under the April 1983 contract modification.

In early 1988, following several weeks of trial the previous year, the U.S. Bankruptcy Court ruled that the Department of Justice "took, converted, stole" the VAX version of PROMIS "through trickery, fraud and deceit" and then attempted "unlawfully and without justification" to force INSLAW into liquidation in order to prevent INSLAW from litigating the government's theft of PROMIS. The court also found that the government had expanded the number of U.S. Attorneys Offices using PROMIS from 20 to the 40-plus largest. The court ordered the government to pay INSLAW approximately $8 million in PROMIS license fees and legal fees and expenses.

The Justice Department accused the bankruptcy judge of bias and appealed his ruling to the U.S. District Court. In November 1989, the U.S. District Court issued its own 44-page opinion affirming the findings of the Bankruptcy Court, stating that even the evidence that is not in dispute between the Justice Department and INSLAW virtually compels the findings of the bankruptcy court.

The Justice Department next appealed the INSLAW case to the U.S. Court of Appeals for the District of Columbia. In May 1991, the U.S. Court of Appeals overturned the decisions of the bankruptcy and the district court, largely on a technical jurisdictional basis without addressing the merits of the dispute.

In September 1992, the House Judiciary Committee published an investigative report entitled *The INSLAW Affair*, which was endorsed by all of the Democrats and opposed by all of the Republicans. The Committee stated that it had independently confirmed the earlier judicial finding that the Justice Department stole PROMIS, and had supplemented the earlier judicial finding with investigative leads suggesting that private sector friends of the Reagan Administration, including Earl W. Brian, may have sold and distributed stolen copies of PROMIS "domestically and overseas" "for their personal financial gain and in support of the intelligence and foreign policy objectives of the United States." The Committee's number one recommendation was for Attorney General Barr immediately to compensate INSLAW.

Attorney General Barr declined to take action on any of the Committee's recommendations pending the outcome of an investigation that he had earlier commissioned a retired federal judge to conduct. However, following the November 1992 election of President-elect Clinton, Attorney General Barr recused himself in the INSLAW case on the grounds that he was returning to a law firm which had, in the meantime, been representing Earl Brian in the retired judge's investigation.

Attorney General Reno eventually released a heavily redacted version of the retired judge's report, redacted to remove information relating to national security. The report exonerated the Justice Department of any wrongdoing. Several months later, in September 1994, Reno issued her own report declaring that the Justice Department was not only blameless but also did not owe INSLAW any compensation.

In May 1995, the U.S. Senate, under the leadership of Senator Orrin Hatch, passed a Congressional Reference resolution ordering the U.S. Court of Federal Claims to conduct a hearing on whether the United States owes INSLAW compensation arising from the government's use of PROMIS, either as a matter of law or of equity. The measure automatically waived technical defenses available to the government such as sovereign immunity and statutes of limitation.

In August 1998, the Chief Judge of the U.S. Court of Federal Claims, the court which coincidentally has exclusive jurisdiction over copyright infringement claims against the United States, sent an Advisory Report to the Senate stating, in part, that INSLAW owns the copyright rights to PROMIS, that INSLAW never granted a license to the government to produce derivative software products, and that the United States would have infringed INSLAW's copyright rights if the government had in fact prepared any PROMIS-derivative software. The Advisory Report noted, however, that there was no "indication" in the hearing record that the government had prepared any derivative software.

By way of explaining the lack of any such indication in the hearing record, the court's Hearing Officer had erroneously ruled, at the urging of the Justice Department and prior to the conduct of much discovery, that PROMIS is in the public domain and that the government had therefore been free to do whatever it wished with PROMIS. INSLAW obtained a reversal of this ruling on appeal but failed to obtain an opportunity to conduct discovery under the correct legal standard.

Approximately six months after the Chief Judge issued his Advisory Report to the Senate, Gordon Thomas, a British author and journalist, published an authorized history of Israel's Mossad intelligence service entitled *Gideon's Spies: the Secret History of the Mossad*. The Israeli government granted Thomas access to living former top officials of the Mossad, including Rafi Eitan, who had been Deputy Director of the Mossad for almost a quarter of a century. *Gideon's Spies* reports startling admissions by Rafi Eitan regarding INSLAW's PROMIS software, including the following:

8

- Eitan had become acquainted with Earl Brian during Brian's business trips to Iran in the 1970's. Brian was, even at that early point in time, telling this high ranking Israeli intelligence official about his ideas for making money from INSLAW's PROMIS software.

- Eitan invited Earl Brian to visit him in Israel -- presumably following the election of Ronald Reagan as President of the United States. As noted earlier, Brian had served in Governor Reagan's California Cabinet.

- When Brian visited Eitan in Israel, Brian was "white face angry" because he had recently discovered that the U.S. Justice Department had already misappropriated PROMIS for an intelligence application, that of tracking money laundering, without Brian's knowledge and without Brian's participation in the profits.

- Exploiting Brian's closeness to the Reagan White House and Brian's determination to find a way to make money from INSLAW's PROMIS, Eitan told Gordon Thomas that he arranged for the Reagan Administration to provide PROMIS to Israeli intelligence. Israel then prepared the second unauthorized derivative software product for use in intelligence.

- Israeli intelligence modified PROMIS to keep track of intelligence information about terrorists, integrated this PROMIS-derivative software with artificial intelligence software designed to support automated correlations of intelligence data, and installed the PROMIS-derivative system on computers that contained a "trap door", i.e., an extra microchip designed to enable signal intelligence penetration of the databases created from the use of the software.

- Israeli intelligence had Earl Brian make the first sale of this PROMIS-derivative software, through Hadron, Inc., which Brian then controlled, to military intelligence in Jordan. Israeli intelligence then used the trap door to copy and download Jordan's intelligence information on Palestinian terrorists.

- Rafi Eitan then turned to the British publisher Robert Maxwell to sell this PROMIS-derivative software to intelligence agencies throughout the world, as part of U.S. and Israeli espionage against these foreign governments. Maxwell sold over $500 million worth of PROMIS-derivative software to intelligence agencies of such U.S. allies as Canada, Great Britain, Australia, and South Korea, as well as to the Soviet KGB and a Polish intelligence agency.

- U.S. Government agencies also used PROMIS-derivative software to track intelligence information. Included among those agencies were the FBI, the DEA and the CIA.

- Israeli intelligence, operating out of the Israeli embassy in Washington, D.C., successfully penetrated PROMIS databases in U.S. Government agencies as part of Israeli espionage against the United States.

In January 2000, nine months after the March 1999 publication of *Gideon's Spies*, an investigator in the foreign counterintelligence section of the Royal Canadian Mounted Police telephoned me to tell me that the RCMP's National Security Investigation Section was conducting an investigation into whether the RCMP had acquired a stolen copy of INSLAW's PROMIS and, if it had, whether the copy contained a trap door through which Canada's national security may have been compromised. Nine years earlier, in January 1991, Canada's Federal Department of Communications had written to INSLAW to inquire whether INSLAW had a French-language version of PROMIS because various federal agencies in Canada were using INSLAW's PROMIS but only had the English-language version, while Canada has two official languages. In response to questions from INSLAW, the Department of Communications stated that the RCMP was using INSLAW's PROMIS to support 900 different locations and that another agency was using PROMIS to support five locations. Soon thereafter, the Department of Communications apologized for having written to INSLAW, claiming that Canada had never acquired INSLAW's PROMIS and denying that it had told INSLAW that the RCMP was using any software called PROMIS.

For its part, the RCMP insisted that the new investigative case management software that it began deploying in 1983 had been developed internally by RCMP staff.

During the January 2000 telephone call, the RCMP investigator told me that the Canadian Government had made certain "untruthful" statements in 1991 when it insisted that the RCMP's own employees had internally developed the new case management software and when the Canadian Government insisted that it had thoroughly investigated the matter. This investigator told me that the RCMP's new case management software had materialized "out of nowhere one day," rather than having been developed internally, and that this January 2000 investigation was the first investigation ever conducted by the Canadian Government.

Later during 2000, the same RCMP investigator told me that the RCMP's case management software is based on INSLAW's PROMIS software and that INSLAW's PROMIS was shipped to Canada by Strategic Software Planning Corporation in Cambridge, Massachusetts.

Under prodding from the House Judiciary Committee, the CIA had years earlier admitted to the Committee having software called PROMIS but insisted that it was not INSLAW's PROMIS but instead software by the same name that the CIA had purchased from Strategic Software Planning Corporation in Cambridge, Massachusetts.

If Robert Maxwell made the sale of INSLAW's PROMIS to Canada on behalf of Rafi Eitan but a CIA software supplier shipped the goods to Canada's RCMP, Maxwell may have been one of the "instrumentalities or agents of the Federal Government" who "financed or conducted" projects involving INSLAW's PROMIS, as referenced in Janis Sposato's November 1985 letter to INSLAW.

In January 2001, *Insight Magazine*, a conservative weekly news magazine affiliated with the *Washington Times Newspaper*, published a four-part series on an eight-month long investigation conducted by RCMP foreign counterintelligence officers in the United States during 2000 relating to the PROMIS software. The series, which is available on the world wide web at http://www.insightmag.com/, reported on admissions made by RCMP investigators to American

10

citizens they interviewed while in the United States. These admissions include the fact that the RCMP is using the PROMIS software; that U.S. nuclear secrets were stolen from the Los Alamos National Laboratory through a foreign government's exploitation of a PROMIS-derivative database at Los Alamos; and that the directors of four allied intelligence agencies (the CIA, the British MI6, Canada's CSIS, and Israel's Mossad) met at Los Alamos in December 1999 under the codename "unique elements" because these four agencies use the same software and one of the four agencies had discovered a technical problem with the software. *Insight Magazine* reported that it had independently confirmed the meeting in Los Alamos with sources in the U.S. Government.

In a letter to me on March 26, 2001, the Officer in Charge of the RCMP's National Security Investigation Section confirmed that the RCMP's national security investigation of INSLAW's PROMIS software is still underway.

Shortly after Robert Maxwell died in 1991, an anonymous source at the Justice Department sent word to me that the Justice Department has documentation on two PROMIS sales by Robert Maxwell totaling $30 million, that INSLAW should be able to obtain this documentation under the Freedom of Information Act because Maxwell's death would prevent the government from interposing the privacy act as justification for withholding the documents, and that INSLAW's acquisition of the documents would end the ability of the Justice Department to continue the coverup.

Eventually, INSLAW obtained from the FBI under the Freedom of Information Act a heavily redacted copy of a foreign counterintelligence investigative report by the FBI field office in Albuquerque, New Mexico in 1984 on Robert Maxwell's sale of PROMIS in New Mexico. The investigation was triggered by a complaint to the FBI by employees at the Sandia National Laboratory, who voiced concern that while Maxwell was selling PROMIS in New Mexico through Pergamon International, another Maxwell-controlled company was selling unclassified U.S. Government information to the Soviet Union. There are two U.S. intelligence agencies located in New Mexico - - the nuclear intelligence units of the Sandia and the Los Alamos National Laboratories.

In 1984 and 1985, Rafi Eitan was concurrently serving as the Israeli spymaster for Jonathan Pollard, a U.S. Navy intelligence analyst who used a computer terminal in his office in Suitland, Maryland to access databases in U.S. intelligence agencies in order to steal secrets for Israel. Pollard's main espionage assignment from Rafi Eitan was reportedly to steal U.S. nuclear secrets. As noted earlier, Rafi Eitan boasted that Israeli intelligence had penetrated PROMIS databases in U.S. Government agencies as part of Israeli espionage against the United States.

Rafi Eitan also claims that the FBI implemented PROMIS-derivative software. During the first seven months of 1983, INSLAW marketed PROMIS to the FBI. INSLAW and the FBI officials responsible for the development of the first Bureau-wide investigative case management system had a number of technical meetings at the FBI and at INSLAW during the first half of 1983. One of the meetings was with the foreign counterintelligence arm of the FBI, which the FBI told INSLAW was slated to be the first recipient of the new software. In early July 1983, the FBI telephoned me to tell me that its computer system staff had recommended a contract with INSLAW to use PROMIS as the

11

basis for the FBI's first enterprise-wide case management system. Immediately after giving me this information in early July 1983, the FBI broke off communications with INSLAW for four or five months, without offering any explanation. When INSLAW and the FBI finally met again in November 1983, the FBI told INSLAW that it had decided to use its own staff to develop the new software internally and that it had almost completed the development during the four or five month interval since the last previous communication with INSLAW. This is presumably the system that Deputy Attorney General Jensen described in his December 1985 meeting with me as the only advanced technology for case management in the Department of Justice.

When the U.S. Court of Federal Claims authorized a panel of outside software experts to compare FOIMS to PROMIS in 1996, the FBI claimed that it had not retained the first 10 years of the FOIMS source code, making any such comparison of dubious value.

The new FBI case management system, called FOIMS (Field Office Information Management System) apparently began operation in 1985. In October 1985, FBI agent Robert Hanssen, a computer savvy FBI agent who was reportedly instrumental in the introduction of the new system into his foreign counterintelligence division, allegedly began spying for the Soviet Union. According to the FBI complaint, Hanssen made extensive use of the FBI's computerized case management system in his alleged espionage for the Soviet Union. The FBI also alleges in the complaint that Hanssen gave the Soviet Union a technical manual in 1987 on the U.S. intelligence community's secure network for on-line access to intelligence databases.

According to several INSLAW sources in the U.S. Government, the CIA deployed a derivative of PROMIS, beginning in 1983 or 1984, as the standard on-line database software for the gathering and dissemination of intelligence information by U.S. intelligence agencies, the intelligence components of the U.S. Armed Forces, and U.S. law enforcement agencies. The technical manual that the FBI alleges that Hanssen gave to the Soviet Union may, therefore, have been related to the use of PROMIS as the standard software of the U.S. intelligence community.

In early 1993, with assistance from an investigator on the House Judiciary Committee staff, INSLAW identified its February 1983 Israeli government visitor from a photographic lineup. It was Rafi Eitan. Shortly before the March 1999 publication of *Gideon's Spies*, Rafi Eitan confirmed to Gordon Thomas that he had taken a taxi from the U.S. Justice Department to INSLAW in February 1983 for a demonstration of the VAX version of PROMIS that the Justice Department was about to steal.

Irrespective of how or why the Justice Department misappropriated PROMIS, there is a solution available that would not require the government to admit any wrongdoing or to reveal intelligence sources and methods: the Justice Department, on behalf of the U.S. Government, can purchase a retroactive global license to PROMIS, including the right to prepare derivative software and to distribute PROMIS and PROMIS-derivative software.

IN THE UNITED STATES COURT OF FEDERAL CLAIMS

INSLAW, INC., A Delaware Corporation,)
WILLIAM A. HAMILTON, and NANCY BURKE)
HAMILTON,)
)
            Plaintiffs,)
      v.   )
)
THE UNITED STATES,)
)
            Defendants.)
_____)
	Congressional
	Reference
	No. 95-338X
	(Judge Miller)

RECEIVED

JUN 19 1996

P.M.K. & M.

DECLARATION OF RICHARD D. DAVIDSON

I, Richard D. Davidson, declare as follows:

(1) I am a Supervisory Special Agent in the Federal Bureau of Investigation (FBI), assigned to the Freedom of Information-Privacy Acts Section, Document Classification Unit at FBI Headquarters, in Washington, D.C. Among my responsibilities are the review of FBI information for classification purposes as mandated by Executive Order (EO) 12958,[1] and the preparation of affidavits and/or declarations in support of exemption claims asserted by the FBI under (b)(1) of the Freedom of Information Act, 5 U.S.C. § 552 (FOIA). I have been designated by the Attorney General of the United States as an original Top Secret classification authority and declassification authority pursuant to EO 12958, sections 1.4 and 3.2.

---

[1] 60 Fed. Reg. 19825 (1995).

(2)   It is the responsibility of the Document
Classification Unit to which I am assigned to review documents
responsive to FOIA requests to insure that classified national
security information is redacted prior to release of the
documents.   I understand that in the above-captioned case, the
plaintiffs, through the civil discovery process, are seeking an
unredacted copy of the document attached hereto as Exhibit A
which was provided to plaintiffs Inslaw, Inc. and William
Hamilton in January 1994 in response to a FOIA request made by
those plaintiffs.

(3)   In connection with this lawsuit, the Document
Classification Unit was requested to re-review Exhibit A to
determine whether any of the withheld classified information
could be released in accordance with the new Executive Order
12958 regarding classified national security information.[2]   I
have personal knowledge of the re-review and, based on the new
Executive Order and information received from the National
Security Administration, certain additional information may be
released to the plaintiffs.   Attached hereto as Exhibit B is a
copy of the re-reviewed document in question.

(4)   The redacted information contained in Exhibit B
that is marked in the margin as "b1" is being withheld from
plaintiffs on the basis of 5 U.S.C. § 552(b)(1) because such
information (a) is specifically authorized under criteria

---

[2]   Exhibit A originally was reviewed and redacted in
accordance with Executive Order 12356 which was in effect at the
time of the review.

established by Executive Order 12958 to be kept secret in the interest of national defense or foreign policy and (b) is in fact properly classified pursuant to such Executive Order.

Under penalty of perjury, I declare the foregoing to be true and correct.

Executed this _13_ day of June, 1996.

Richard D. Davidson
Supervisory Special Agent
Document Classification Unit
FBI Headquarters
Washington, D. C.

3

INSLAW, Inc.

1125 15th Street, N.W., Washington, DC 20005-2707
(202) 828-8600 FAX (202) 659-0755

William A. Hamilton, President

MEMORANDUM

To: Gordon Thomas

From: Bill Hamilton

Date: September 23, 1999

Subject: Chinese Acquisition of Nuclear Intelligence Information From the Los Alamos National Laboratory on the W-88 Warhead

---

1.   Enclosed is a self-explanatory article from the front page of today's *New York Times*. Please note the following statement: "That convinced investigators that the espionage had occurred between 1984, when the final design for the W-88 was approved, and 1988, when the Chinese document was dated."

2.   In the *Samson Option*, Seymour Hersh refers to the fact that the Los Alamos National Laboratory and the Sandia National Laboratory have each had nuclear intelligence units since the 1960's when the CIA delegated some of its representatives in this area to the two labs.

3.   The FBI office in New Mexico conducted a foreign counterintelligence investigation during the first half of 1984 of Robert Maxwell for the sale of computer software in New Mexico. The 18-page document that INSLAW obtained from the FBI is heavily redacted for national security reasons but includes a reference to an FBI interview of someone employed at the Sandia National Laboratory. My FOIA requests had asked the FBI for any documents relating to Robert Maxwell's sale and/or distribution of computer software products, including PROMIS.

4.   Jonathan Pollard, whom Seymour Hersh describes as Israel's first nuclear spy, was arrested by the U.S. Navy in approximately November 1985 and charged with espionage for Israel and Rafi Eitan. Edwin Meese was Attorney General at the time and he sent a team of Justice Department lawyers to Israel in 1986 to meet with the Government. The delegation from the Meese Justice Department included Joseph DiGenova, the U.S. Attorney for the District of Columbia and several senior prosecutors from the Criminal Division at Justice Department Headquarters.

5.   In approximately March 1987, Defense Secretary Caspar Weinberger sent a highly classified letter to Chief Judge Aubrey Robinson of the U.S. District Court in Washington, D.C. informing the Chief Judge, who was personally handling the plea bargaining and sentencing case of Pollard, of the immense damage that Pollard did to the United States through the intelligence information he stole

Memorandum to Gordon Thomas
September 23, 1999
Page 2

from the Government and gave to Rafi Eitan and Israel. Acting on the classified Weinberger memorandum, Robinson sentenced Pollard to life imprisonment, notwithstanding Pollard's guilty plea and cooperation with prosecutors.

6.　　In January 1988, U.S. Bankruptcy Judge George F. Bason, Jr., published his findings of fact and conclusions of law from INSLAW's litigation against the Justice Department in 1987, finding that the Justice Department "took, converted, stole" millions of dollars worth of PROMIS "through trickery, fraud and deceit."

7.　　In February 1988, the U.S. Court of Appeals for the District of Columbia, which is the appointing authority for the fixed-duration terms of federal bankruptcy judges, denied Judge Bason's application for reappointment even though statistics of the Administrative Office of the U.S. Courts reveal that virtually every bankruptcy judge who seeks reappointment is granted reappointment.

8.　　In the spring of 1988, Ronald LeGrand, then Chief Investigator for the U.S. Senate's Committee on the Judiciary, visited Nancy Hamilton, my wife, and me at INSLAW and passed on information about our case from someone whom he described as a trusted friend for 15 years. LeGrand told us that the INSLAW case is a lot dirtier for the Justice Department than Watergate was and that it had compromised the Justice Department at every level. He said that D. Lowell Jensen, the California native who began Reagan's first term as the Presidential appointee in charge of the Criminal Division, had engineered INSLAW's problems with the Justice Department from within the Criminal Division in order to "get INSLAW out of the way and gave the business to friends." LeGrand gave us the names of several very senior Criminal Division Officials whom his source claimed knew the whole sordid story. LeGrand urged INSLAW to use the subpoena power of its case against the Justice Department to take the depositions of these three people. One was the ranking career prosecutor responsible for terrorism, espionage and extradition; one was the career prosecutor in charge of extraditions, who reported to the aforementioned prosecutor; and one was the highest ranking career prosecutor in the Criminal Division.

9.　　Chief Judge Aubrey Robinson assumed control of INSLAW's litigation against the Justice Department after Judge Bason's term ended in February 1988.

10.　　Soon after INSLAW issued subpoenas for the three senior Criminal Division officials, in the spring of 1988, Chief Judge Robinson, acting *sua sponte*, quashed the subpoenas pending the outcome of the Justice Department's appeals of Judge Bason's January 1988 rulings. One of the three Criminal Division officials, the career Deputy Assistant Attorney General in the Criminal Division with responsibility over criminal cases involving espionage, terrorism and so forth, headed the delegation to Israel in 1986 on the Pollard Case.

Memorandum to Gordon Thomas
September 23, 1999
Page 3

11.   Elliot Richardson filed a Petition for a Writ of Mandamus lawsuit against Attorney General Dick Thornburgh for ducking his responsibilities to enforce the federal criminal law in the INSLAW case, and focused in the lawsuit on the Justice Department's failure to investigate the information supplied by LeGrand.

12.   The *New Republic Magazine* did an article on the INSLAW case, focusing heavily on the information that the Hamiltons obtained from LeGrand and the failure of the Justice Department and/or Congress to investigate. *The New Republic* later published a letter to the editor from Senator Sam Nunn, Chairman of the Senate Permanent Subcommittee on Investigations, confirming that LeGrand had made essentially the same claims to his investigators but that LeGrand had refused to identify the Justice Department trusted source for his information.

13.   INSLAW filed its initial lawsuit against the Justice Department in U.S. Bankruptcy Court in June 1986. INSLAW's litigation counsel was Leigh Ratiner, a partner in the law firm of Dickstein, Shapiro & Morin.

14.   In October 1986, the Senior Management Committee of Dickstein, Shapiro and Morin met and decided to fire Leigh Ratiner, a partner for 10 years, and two months later, Dickstein, Shapiro & Morin told INSLAW it had reassessed the evidence and concluded that INSLAW could not sustain its claim of government misappropriation of INSLAW's software.

15.   In October 1986, Attorney General Meese and Deputy Attorney General Arnold Burns each spoke with Leonard Garment, a senior partner and member of the Senior Management Committee at Dickstein, Shapiro and Morin, about the INSLAW case, according to a sworn Justice Department answer to an INSLAW interrogatory. In 1989, *Barron's* quoted Garment as saying that he had actually spoken to Meese that month about Israel, not INSLAW. Garment also told another self-professed journalist, who repeated the information to INSLAW, that his October 1986 communication with Meese regarded a back channel communication with Israel on a national security issue of concern to both Israel and the U.S. Department of Justice, *i.e.*, Pollard.

FOR BACKGROUND
PURPOSES ONLY

December 22, 1999

The Honorable Orrin G. Hatch
Chairman
U.S. Senate Committee on the Judiciary
Room SD-224, Dirksen Senate Office Building
Washington, D.C. 20510-6275

The Honorable Patrick J. Leahy
Ranking Minority Member
U.S. Senate Committee on the Judiciary
Room SD-224, Dirksen Senate Office Building
Washington, D.C. 20510-6275

Dear Chairman Hatch and Senator Leahy:

When the Senate passed a Congressional Reference resolution and bill by unanimous consent in May 1995 for INSLAW, Inc. and the two undersigned principal owners and officers of INSLAW, Inc., it ordered the U.S. Court of Federal Claims to conduct a hearing on INSLAW's claims for compensation arising from the government's use of INSLAW's PROMIS prosecutive case management software product, and to send an Advisory Report to the Senate on whether the United States owes INSLAW any further compensation either as a matter of law or of equity and, if so, in what amount.

The U.S. Court of Federal Claims not only has exclusive jurisdiction over Congressional Reference claims against the United States but, as you probably are aware, it also has exclusive jurisdiction over copyright infringement claims against the United States. In May 1998, a three judge Review Panel of the U.S. Court of Federal Claims, the entity that constitutes the appellate authority in a Congressional Reference case, ruled that the Court's Hearing Officer had erred when she made a determination that the PROMIS software is in the public domain and that the government was free therefore to do whatever it wished with PROMIS. The Review Panel ruled that INSLAW owns the copyright to PROMIS, that the government never obtained a license from INSLAW to make modifications to PROMIS, including modifications for the purpose of creating derivative software products, and that the government would have infringed one of INSLAW's exclusive rights under federal copyright law if it modified PROMIS in order to create derivative software products. Noting in its ruling that INSLAW had failed to prove that the government had produced PROMIS-derivative software products, the Review Panel characterized the Hearing Officer's mistake as an error of no consequence and therefore refused INSLAW's request for a new hearing.

FOR BACKGROUND
PURPOSES ONLY

Memorandum to the Record
December 22, 1999
Page 3

1.   **Earl Brian, during visits to Iran in the 1970's as a private businessman, first disclosed to Rafi Eitan his interest in the money-making potential of INSLAW's PROMIS computer software.**

During Ronald Reagan's second term as Governor of California, 1971-1974, Earl W. Brian served as Secretary of Health and Secretary of Health and Welfare, successively.

After leaving the California Administration of Governor Reagan, Brian began to seek business in Iran. In 1974, Reagan's final year as Governor, Brian resigned to seek the Republican nomination for the U.S. Senate. In early 1975, after losing the Republican primary, Brian began working on a proposal to Iran for a new health care system, according to an article in the *Sacramento Bee* on January 12, 1975.

Brian's interest in PROMIS as early as the 1970's was matched by an interest in PROMIS during the late 1970's on the part of Edwin Meese, another official from the California Administration of Governor Reagan who exhibited a strong interest in the PROMIS software during the interval between the end of Reagan's second term as Governor of California and the start of Reagan's first term as President of the United States. Edwin Meese, who was Governor Reagan's Chief of Staff when Brian was Secretary of Health and Welfare, closely followed INSLAW's work with PROMIS during the late 1970's while serving as Director of the Center for Criminal Justice Research at the University of San Diego, and Meese viewed INSLAW's work with PROMIS as one of the most important developments in the administration of justice nationally, according to the transcript of Meese's luncheon speech on April 22, 1981 to a national meeting in Washington, D.C. of INSLAW's PROMIS Users Group.

In January 1981, the month of Reagan's first inauguration as President, Edwin Meese's family established certain business and financial ties with Earl Brian. That month, Brian had the initial public offering of Biotech Capital Corporation, the financial holding company through which Brian controlled a number of companies including Hadron, Inc., a government contracting company that specialized in computer systems work. Ursula Meese, Edwin's wife, borrowed money from Edwin Thomas, a close friend of Earl Brian and a White House subordinate of Edwin Meese, and used the proceeds of the loan to buy shares in the initial public offering of Brian's holding company. Meese was then working in the White House as Counselor to President Reagan.

At a dinner meeting in Montreal on February 23, 1981, Earl Brian told a prospective Canadian investor in Hadron that Hadron's future growth would come from a "new technical frontier" in "packaging computers to retain and retrieve information" about the "justice system," that Hadron intended to carry out these plans through its acquisition of a prepackaged software products company in the administration of justice field, and Brian described the company that Hadron intended to acquire as having "great promise [PROMIS?]," according to the contemporaneous

Memorandum to the Record
December 22, 1999
Page 4

handwritten notes of John Belton, a Canadian stock broker and investor who participated in the dinner meeting with Brian.

2.   **During Earl Brian's first visit to Rafi Eitan in Israel, Brian revealed his anger at his recent discovery that the U.S. intelligence community had misappropriated INSLAW's PROMIS software, without Brian's knowledge and apparently without Brian's ability to share in the profits, and had successfully modified PROMIS to track money laundering in the banking system instead of law cases in the court system.**

Brian evidently expected to profit from every use of PROMIS by the federal government during the Reagan Administration, as implied by Rafi Eitan's admissions to Thomas. Brian's complaint about the U.S. intelligence community's use of PROMIS in the banking system, therefore, has two possible implications: first, that Brian did not, at least initially, share in the profits from the U.S. intelligence community's sale of PROMIS to banks and, secondly, that the use of PROMIS for intelligence collection in the banking system began before the Reagan Administration. Rafi Eitan described this U.S. Government use of PROMIS as tracking "money laundering and other criminal activities," according to Thomas' affidavit. As explained in the next several paragraphs, that PROMIS intelligence application apparently refers to a highly classified U.S. intelligence project to track electronic funds transfers in the banking systems, a project that evidently began as a CIA HUMINT (Human Intelligence) collection project and became an NSA SIGINT (Signal Intelligence) collection project early during the first term of President Reagan.

In 1981, the first year of the Reagan Administration, the CIA arranged for the installation of software called PROMIS in the Bank of International Settlements in Basel, Switzerland, according to an article in the *Economist* magazine of the Japanese-language newspaper *Mainichi Shimbun* on January 30, 1996. This PROMIS application involved keeping track of electronic funds transfers in order to combat money laundering and other criminal activities, including drug trafficking, securities and banking frauds, and political payoffs, according to the article. Any CIA project that used the PROMIS software to collect intelligence information would have been a HUMINT collection project whereby someone employed in the targeted institution, such as a CIA asset, would periodically copy data from the computer system and give the copied data to the CIA.

Former insiders in the Reagan Administration have occasionally referred publicly to a major new Reagan Administration intelligence initiative in the banking system, officially dubbed "Follow the Money," but have described the Follow the Money initiative as an NSA SIGINT collection project, rather than as a CIA HUMINT project, and have described the Reagan Administration's SIGINT penetration of the banking system as having begun in 1982 rather than in 1981.

In 1982, President Reagan tasked NSA with the on-line, real time SIGINT penetration of the banking industry, according to the testimony of Dr. Norman A. Bailey before the Senate Judiciary

Memorandum to the Record
December 22, 1999
Page 5

Committee on August 17, 1989. Bailey, who was Special Assistant to President Reagan for National Security Planning, testified that NSA's SIGINT penetration of banks enabled the U.S. Government to combat money laundering and other criminal activities, including drug trafficking, illegal sales of high technology to the Soviet Union, and gun running to terrorist and guerilla groups. In a PBS-TV documentary entitled *Follow the Money*, which aired on July 12, 1989, Bailey said that NSA's Follow the Money SIGINT penetration of the banking industry resulted, very early in Reagan's first term, in the installation of computer tracking software in major wire transfer clearinghouses in the United States and Europe, including CHIPS (Clearing House Interbank Payment System) in New York City. Bailey referred to the computer software as "powerful computing mechanisms."

By 1986, three key members of Reagan's cabinet were pressing to expand NSA's SIGINT penetration of the banking system to include the approximately 400 major commercial banks that comprise the interbank payment system, according to a White House e-mail message to Colonel Oliver North of the National Security Council staff on June 5, 1986 from one of his colleagues, David Wigg. The e-mail message identified the three Reagan cabinet members as CIA Director Casey, Attorney General Meese, and Defense Secretary Weinberger. Portions of the e-mail message were declassified and made public during the investigation of the Iran/Contra scandal. According to the aforementioned testimony by Bailey before the Senate Judiciary Committee, by the late 1980's, the U.S. intelligence community had successfully penetrated a number of major commercial banks including "the Bank of Credit and Commerce International, Banco de Occidente of Colombia, Uruguayan banks and such American banks as Chase, Citibank, Continental Illinois and others..."

When the NSA, in 1982, took over the task of tracking electronic funds transfers in the banking system, it, like the CIA before it, evidently used the PROMIS software. The World Bank, for example, began to use the VAX version of PROMIS to track electronic funds transfers during the second half of 1983, according to a sworn statement to INSLAW on November 15, 1995 by Steven R. McCallum, who had worked in the World Bank's computer center in 1983. Toward the end of President Clinton's first year in office, Dr. Bailey, who is often referred to as the author of the Reagan Administration's NSA penetration of the banking industry, reportedly contacted a novelist for advice on how to create a fictionalized account of two real life projects involving NSA's use of the PROMIS software in the banking system. Bailey told the novelist that the two NSA PROMIS projects were known as SPRINT and SWIFT. Bailey contacted Jack Cummings, who became a successful novelist while pursuing a business career in real estate in Florida. Cummings then shared the information with a lawyer friend in Los Angeles with whom he had frequently spoken about the PROMIS software and INSLAW. The Los Angeles lawyer is a long time associate of the principal owners of INSLAW.

When the Reagan Administration assigned to NSA the U.S. intelligence community's responsibility for the use of PROMIS in the banking system, Brian may have acquired an opportunity to influence the Reagan Administration's selection of the banking industry software contractor for

*FOR BACKGROUND
PURPOSES ONLY*

Memorandum to the Record
December 22, 1999
Page 7

in Cambridge, Massachusetts, the same vendor whose name appears in connection with the CIA's alleged use of INSLAW's PROMIS, as explained later in this memorandum. The RCMP eventually claimed that its own employees internally developed its new PIRS case management software.

4.   The U.S. intelligence community modified misappropriated copies of PROMIS for its own internal use, including specifically within the FBI and the DEA, and the CIA directly distributed copies of the U.S. intelligence community's version of PROMIS to other governments in support of a U.S. espionage program.

A third channel for the distribution of intelligence versions of PROMIS, ~~with server accounts of D. G. Elliott and two others~~, was a channel controlled directly by the CIA. In its September 1992 Investigative Report entitled *The INSLAW Affair*, the House Judiciary Committee reported that the CIA admitted that it had purchased for its own internal use copies of a PC-based project management software product called PROMIS from Strategic Software Planning Corporation in Cambridge, Massachusetts. That is the same vendor from which the Canadian government eventually claimed to have bought software called PROMIS, after initially notifying INSLAW that the Royal Canadian Mounted Police and other agencies were using INSLAW's PROMIS.

In September 1993, however, CIA Director James Woolsey told INSLAW Counsel Elliot Richardson that the CIA uses software called PROMIS to keep track of the intelligence information that it produces and that the CIA's PROMIS is identical to the PROMIS software that NSA uses to keep track of the intelligence information produced by NSA. Richardson memorialized Woolsey's admissions in a follow up letter to the CIA Director dated October 1, 1993.

NSA's PROMIS software, like INSLAW's PROMIS software, operates on IBM mainframe computers rather than on IBM PC's, the computing platform for the project management software called PROMIS marketed by Strategic Software Planning Corporation. Although CIA Director Woolsey said that the CIA and the NSA use the identical PROMIS software to keep track of their intelligence information, NSA insists that its own employees internally developed its PROMIS software and that NSA never distributed its PROMIS software outside of NSA.

INSLAW obtained additional information about the CIA's role in the distribution of PROMIS from an INSLAW customer. In the early 1990's, Norma DiGiacinto was the office manager for the Washington, D.C. area litigation office for one of the largest property and casualty insurance companies in the United States. That company then operated INSLAW's case management software in all of its litigation offices nationwide. DiGiacinto explained to INSLAW that a member of her family had ties to the CIA and that she would, as a favor to INSLAW, attempt to find out about the U.S. intelligence community's alleged use of PROMIS. When the Justice Department took her deposition in 1996, DiGiacinto admitted having provided most of the following information to INSLAW, admitted that she took the information very seriously, and volunteered that she had

FOR BACKGROUND
PURPOSES ONLY

Memorandum to the Record
December 22, 1999
Page 8

become fearful for her safety because of her role as a conduit of the information. DiGiacinto denied, however, knowing anyone at the CIA or even knowing the identity of the person who repeatedly gave her information to provide to INSLAW. The essence of what DiGiacinto provided to INSLAW concerned the PROMIS distribution channel directly controlled by the CIA. The following italicized paragraphs provide the highlights of the information that DiGiacinto provided to INSLAW:

> *There was a long-standing requirement in the U.S. intelligence community for compatible data base software. The CIA obtained a copy of PROMIS from the Justice Department in order to evaluate it against this requirement. The CIA concluded that PROMIS could satisfy the requirement because of the versatility of the software, i.e., the ability to use PROMIS' automated tailoring subsystem to adapt the software to track any kinds of information in conjunction with any kinds of work flow processes, and because of the extraordinarily fast way that the PROMIS software could search for and retrieve relationships between one matter and all the other business of the organization.* [This latter feature refers to PROMIS' on-line cross references which each customer specifies and INSLAW then automatically implements at the time of implementation and which rely on an INSLAW trade secret to perform searches of massive databases with extraordinary speed.]

> *The CIA integrated PROMIS with another piece of software and then deployed the extended version of PROMIS to virtually every agency of the U.S. intelligence community, even using PROMIS to track nuclear materials and long-range missiles in the United States and abroad.*

> *The first deployment of the U.S. intelligence community's version of PROMIS was on board the nuclear submarines of the United States and Great Britain.*

> *The CIA also appointed someone named Lindsey, at a facility in Herndon, Virginia, to produce a reduced-functionality version of the U.S. intelligence community's PROMIS for sale to foreign governments. Earn Brian sold this extended version of PROMIS under the name PROMIS Plus to Egyptian Military Intelligence, which paid for it with U.S. Foreign Military Assistance funds. Brian made the sale through a company that appears to be a CIA holding company*

> *There is another intelligence community application of PROMIS that is much more sensitive than the applications already described. The only persons authorized to disclose this particular application are the four statutory members of the National Security Council - - the President, the Vice President, and the Secretaries of State and Defense.*

Memorandum to the Record
December 22, 1999
Page 9

According to DiGiacinto, the first deployment of the version of PROMIS that the CIA misappropriated for internal use within the U.S. intelligence community was to U.S. and British nuclear submarines for an intelligence application. The following paragraphs provide corroboration from government documents and from an on-the-record admission from an official Naval Sea Systems Command spokesperson for a PROMIS intelligence application on board the nuclear submarines of the United States. As explained in the following paragraphs, this initial internal use of PROMIS within the U.S. intelligence community evidently began in 1984, at least a year after Robert Maxwell evidently began selling the terrorist-tracking version of PROMIS to foreign governments, including Canada.

Hadron, Inc. was a computer systems contractor for the U.S. government. Earl Brian controlled Hadron through his holding company, Biotech Capital. Hadron had 30-40 contracts with U.S. intelligence agencies, according to Brian's deposition testimony to the House Judiciary Committee on September 20, 1990. Hadron also had contracts in the early 1980's for computer systems work on the Trident nuclear submarines, according to Hadron's annual reports. The fact that Hadron had field offices in Newport, Rhode Island, where the Navy's Undersea Systems Center is headquartered, and in Groton, Connecticut, a major port for U.S. nuclear submarines, suggests that Hadron's work on the computer systems of U.S. nuclear submarines was an important focus of Hadron's business in the early 1980's.

Robert A. Duffy, the executive responsible for much of Hadron's submarine contract work in the early 1980's, told INSLAW that the Navy was about to deploy the first commercial-off-the-shelf computers to U.S. nuclear submarines when he resigned from Hadron in late 1983, and that he believed that the Navy intended to select VAX 11/780 computers for the deployment to the nuclear submarines.

The Navy did in fact deploy VAX 11/780 computers to all of its nuclear submarines, installed software called PROMIS on them, and used the VAX 11/780 version of PROMIS for an intelligence application. In response to questions from a reporter for *Navy Times* in 1993, an official spokesperson for the Naval Sea Systems Command stated that the Navy had installed software called PROMIS on VAX 11/780 computers on board both its attack submarines (the SSN's or Sub-Surface Nuclear submarines) and its ballistic missile submarines (the SSBN's or Sub-Surface Ballistic Nuclear submarines), that the Navy used this PROMIS software "for the gathering and dissemination of intelligence information," and that the Navy deployed PROMIS to the submarines "in the early 1980's." The reporter memorialized these statements in his contemporaneous 1993 notes and in a sworn statement to INSLAW in 1995.

If the deployment of the VAX 11/780 version of PROMIS to the nuclear submarines could not have occurred prior to 1984, as indicated by the former executive responsible for Hadron's computer systems work on the U.S. nuclear submarines, but took place in "the early 1980's," as

FOR BACKGROUND
PURPOSES ONLY

Memorandum to the Record
December 22, 1999
Page 10

disclosed by the Naval Sea Systems Command spokesperson, then the deployment of the VAX 11/780 version of PROMIS to the U.S. nuclear submarines had to have occurred in 1984.

The Navy's Undersea Systems Center in Newport, Rhode Island advertised in the *Commerce Business Daily* in 1987, three years after the Navy evidently began the deployment of PROMIS to U.S. nuclear submarines, and again in 1990 for an engineering vendor to support the use of its PROMIS software in conjunction with the "combat system" on board both the Navy's attack submarines and the Navy's ballistic missile submarines. The advertisements refer to the use of PROMIS in "over the horizon computer delivery," presumably of nuclear submarine-launched ballistic missiles fired from the U.S. SSBN ballistic missile submarines "over the horizon" to targets in the former Soviet Union, and in the computer-delivery of "fire control," presumably of missiles fired from U.S. SSN "attack" submarines against Soviet ballistic missile submarines.

The firing of nuclear-armed missiles from a submerged submarine "over the horizon" against targets in the former Soviet Union would presumably require the on-line retrieval from the PROMIS intelligence database of detailed information about the Soviet target and the defenses around the Soviet target; the calculation of the exact location of the U.S. SSBN submarine from which the submarine-launched missile is to be fired, including the submarine's depth, longitude and latitude; and the application of rules from advanced physics and mathematics to determine how to fire the missiles in order accurately to hit the target. Artificial intelligence software could presumably automate such calculations, and could constitute the second piece of software that DiGiacinto said was integrated with PROMIS before the deployment to the nuclear submarines.

Computer delivery of fire control may refer to the use of computer software and databases in underwater attacks against soviet ballistic missile submarines in time of war. The PROMIS database could, for example, store the unique sonar signatures of every submarine of the former Soviet Union. Once a targeted Soviet submarine was positively identified, through a search of the PROMIS intelligence database using the submarine's unique sonar signature, artificial intelligence software could perform the firing calculations in order to enable the submarine to destroy the Soviet ballistic missile submarine with missiles fired from a submerged U.S. SSN submarine. William Casey, who was President Reagan's CIA Director at the time of the deployment of PROMIS to U.S. nuclear submarines in 1984, boasted that during his tenure as Director, the CIA had produced "better techniques for monitoring Soviet ballistic missile submarines," according to Bob Woodward's book *Veil: The Secret Wars of the CIA 1981-1987*. The CIA's National Underwater Reconnaissance Office provided the CIA with a direct way to influence intelligence programs on board U.S. nuclear submarines, according to *Blind Man's Bluff: the Untold Story of American Submarine Espionage* by Sherry Sontag and Christopher Drew.

FOR BACKGROUND
PURPOSES ONLY

Memorandum to the Record
December 22, 1999
Page 11

The Navy's Undersea Systems Center claims that its own employees developed its PROMIS software, that its PROMIS is used for inventory tracking of equipment, and that its PROMIS has never been distributed to any U.S. nuclear submarine.

The integration of an on-line intelligence database system into the command and control system of a combat unit such as a nuclear submarine is referred to within the U.S. military as C3I, *i.e.*, the integration of Command, Control, Communications and Intelligence. Improvements in C3I systems were among the highest priorities of the five-point strategic defense buildup announced by President Reagan and Defense Secretary Weinberger during the first year of the Reagan Administration. As noted earlier, Weinberger was also one of the three Reagan Administration cabinet officers actively supporting the expansion of NSA's Follow the Money initiative in June 1986 to include approximately 400 major commercial banks.

Another example of the use of on-line intelligence database software and artificial intelligence software as integrated components of military command, control and communications systems relates to a system that Lockheed Aircraft deployed in the cockpit of the F-117 Stealth Fighter beginning in November 1984, the same year when the Navy deployed a comparable version of PROMIS to the nuclear submarines. This intelligence database application in the cockpit of the F-117 Stealth Fighter appears to be based on INSLAW's PROMIS, as explained in the following paragraphs.

Lockheed developed the F-117 at its Burbank, California Skunk Works for the U.S. Air Force and the CIA. Ben Rich, the Lockheed Vice President in charge of the Skunk Works at the time of the development of the F-117, described in a book entitled *Skunk Works* how Lockheed engineers developed a sophisticated on-line intelligence database system in the cockpit of the F-117. The intelligence database would be updated en route with the latest satellite-acquired intelligence about enemy missile and radar systems, according to *Skunk Works*. Rich described how the intelligence database software would automatically route the aircraft around the most dangerous enemy radar and missile threats, automatically turn the F-117 at certain angles to maximize its stealthiness at dangerous moments during a mission, and even automatically drop the aircraft's two bombs on the mission's targets.

Artificial intelligence software in the cockpit would presumably be used to direct such maneuvers based on information produced by the aircraft about its longitude, latitude and altitude, and on information from the cockpit's intelligence database about the mission's threats and targets, including the locations and ranges of enemy radar and missile sites. According to Rich's book, the Air Force was so impressed with the on-line intelligence database software in the cockpit of the F-117 Stealth Fighter that it later ordered the deployment of the software to all U.S. attack aircraft.

Memorandum to the Record
December 22, 1999
Page 12

Rich also claims in *Skunk Works* that Lockheed's engineers in Burbank developed this on-line intelligence database system in only 120 days time, a feat that implies the use of a highly versatile prepackaged application software product such as PROMIS.

In the Fall of 1996, on the eve of the 50th Anniversary of the U.S. Air Force, the publisher of the then-planned U.S. Air Force's official commemorative book telephoned and wrote to INSLAW to invite INSLAW to join other enumerated major U.S. Air Force software vendors, including Microsoft, Oracle and Sybase, in placing advertisements in the 50th Anniversary publication. INSLAW had, however, never sold software to the U.S. Air Force.

A high school classmate of INSLAW's founder and chief executive officer, who is a retired U.S. Air Force Colonel and test pilot with a doctorate in aeronautical engineering, happened to see a volume of documentation on software called PROMIS in an F-117 Stealth Fighter project office at McClelland Air Force Base in California in September 1994 while consulting on the F-117's fiber optic network.

One former U.S. intelligence official, who is not willing to provide sworn testimony, told INSLAW that the Air Force Systems Command at Wright Patterson Air Force Base in Ohio employs more PROMIS computer programmers than INSLAW, and that Lockheed Aircraft has been a major consumer of INSLAW's PROMIS software.

According to several other sources currently or formerly associated with U.S. intelligence agencies, INSLAW's PROMIS was literally the missing piece of software for the U.S. military's SMART (Special Management Automated Reasoning Tool) Program, and SMART is the sum of the PROMIS tracking software and artificial intelligence software. The first installation of the SMART version of PROMIS was on board U.S. nuclear submarines, and the SMART version of PROMIS has been installed in the cockpits of U.S. aircraft, according to these same sources.

5.   While serving as a business partner of Earl Brian and the Reagan Administration in worldwide sales of the PROMIS software to foreign governments, Israeli intelligence also penetrated PROMIS databases in U.S. Government agencies as part of Israeli espionage against the United States.

While Rafi Eitan, presumably in his capacity as Anti-Terrorism Advisor to the Israeli Prime Minister, was serving as a business partner for Earl Brian and the Reagan Administration in the sale of over half a billion dollars worth of PROMIS licenses to governments throughout the world, Rafi Eitan, in his capacity as Director of Israel's LAKAM intelligence agency, was simultaneously serving as the Israeli spymaster for Jonathan Pollard.

*FOR BACKGROUND
PURPOSES ONLY*

Memorandum to the Record
December 22, 1999
Page 13

Until his arrest by the U.S. Navy in November 1985 for espionage for Israel, Pollard was a civilian intelligence analyst at the Navy's Anti-Terrorism Alert Center in Suitland, Maryland. According to press accounts of the Pollard case, Pollard was using a computer terminal on his desk at this U.S. Navy intelligence facility to search computerized databases of U.S. intelligence agencies for information that he had been directed by Rafi Eitan to steal for Israel.

Eitan used Israeli intelligence officials stationed in the Israeli embassy in Washington, D.C. to liaise directly with Pollard on espionage assignments to Pollard, a circumstance that matches Eitan's description of the way in which Israeli intelligence exploited PROMIS databases in U.S. Government agencies.

When Eitan made his admissions about governments to which Maxwell had sold PROMIS, Eitan neglected to admit sales of PROMIS that Robert Maxwell made to U.S. Government agencies, as reflected in the following paragraphs.

The FBI conducted a foreign counterintelligence investigation of Robert Maxwell, doing business as Pergamon International in New Mexico in 1984, for the sale of computer software products "including but not limited to the PROMIS computer software product." The words in quotation marks were the words that INSLAW used in its Freedom of Information Act (FOIA) request that prompted the FBI to produce a copy of the above-mentioned foreign counterintelligence investigative report. The FBI redacted most of the text in the copy of the report it sent to INSLAW, citing the need to protect U.S. national security secrets.

The portions of the investigative report that the FBI did not delete for national security reasons reveal, however, that the FBI office in Albuquerque, New Mexico was the office of origin for the investigation, that FBI sources for the investigation included two employees at the Sandia National Laboratory in New Mexico, and that these two FBI sources had expressed concern about Maxwell's sale of PROMIS because another company owned by Maxwell was simultaneously selling unclassified U.S. Government data to the Soviet Union.

According to several apparently unrelated sources in the U.S. intelligence community, each of whom has provided information to INSLAW that has proved to be consistently reliable, Maxwell's sales of PROMIS in New Mexico in 1984 were to the Los Alamos National Laboratory and the Sandia National Laboratory, and the aggregate dollar value for the sales to the two U.S. national nuclear weapons laboratories in 1984 exceeded $30 million. In the normal commercial world, such a large software license dollar amount would indicate a large number of copies of PROMIS and/or a large number of staff who would have access to the PROMIS software.

Beginning in the late 1960's, "much of the United States' primary analysis of nuclear intelligence had been shifted from the CIA to the design and engineering laboratories for nuclear

FOR BACKGROUND
PURPOSES ONLY

Memorandum to the Record
December 22, 1999
Page 14

weapons at Los Alamos and Sandia" in New Mexico, according to Seymour Hersh's expose on Israel's nuclear arsenal, which is entitled *The Samson Option*. Moreover, the Los Alamos National Laboratory reportedly designs nuclear warheads for missiles on board U.S. nuclear submarines, and the Sandia National Laboratory does the engineering work to "weaponize" those designs by implementing them into the delivery systems of the nuclear submarines. Finally, the Los Alamos National Laboratory also develops artificial intelligence software for the automated analyses of intelligence information, according to the testimony of Brian Bruh, then Director of a U.S. Treasury Department intelligence agency known as FinCEN, before the House Appropriations Subcommittee on Treasury, Postal Service, and General Government of March 9, 1993.

The following circumstances suggest that Robert Maxwell's sale of PROMIS to the U.S. Government in New Mexico in 1984 included the first PROMIS licenses for internal use within the U.S. intelligence community, *i.e.*, the sale of the VAX 11/780 version of PROMIS for operation on board U.S. nuclear submarines:

- The year when Maxwell made his sale to the U.S. Government in New Mexico, *i.e.*, 1984, coincides with the year of the first internal deployment of PROMIS within the U.S. intelligence community;

- The CIA engineered the decision to use PROMIS as the standard database software within the U.S. intelligence community, used the submarine version of PROMIS as the first deployment of the U.S. intelligence community's new standard version of PROMIS, and had long ago begun to rely on the Los Alamos National Laboratory and the Sandia National Laboratory for much of the United States' nuclear intelligence work;

- As explained more fully later in this memorandum, Brian probably initially planned to have Hadron make the sales of PROMIS to the U.S. intelligence community but Brian probably could not use Hadron to make the initial sales in 1984 for the following reason: Independent Counsel Jacob Stein was that year investigating Attorney General-Designate Edwin Meese's failure to disclose certain business ties with Earl Brian and searching for evidence of whether Meese had influenced the U.S. Government to award any contracts to companies controlled by Brian;

- Eitan admitted that Israeli intelligence had successfully penetrated PROMIS databases in unidentified U.S. Government agencies as part of its espionage against the United States, a feat that would be more feasible if Eitan and Maxwell were directly involved in PROMIS sales to U.S. Government agencies;

FOR BACKGROUND
PURPOSES ONLY

Memorandum to the Record
December 22, 1999
Page 15

- Eitan directed Maxwell's sales of PROMIS while serving simultaneously as Israel's spymaster for Jonathan Pollard, and Pollard carried out his espionage assignments for Eitan, in part, by accessing computerized databases in the U.S. intelligence community;

- The submarine version of PROMIS supported nuclear targeting, and Eitan used as Pollard's controller, Israeli Air Force Colonel Aviem Sella, who was reportedly one of Israel's top nuclear targeting experts; and

- The inclusion of licenses for copies of PROMIS for every U.S. nuclear submarine could help explain why Maxwell allegedly obtained such a large aggregate amount of PROMIS license fees, *i.e.*, over $30 million, for the sales in New Mexico in 1984.

The reason that Rafi Eitan used Colonel Aviem Sella, "perhaps Israel's top air force expert in nuclear targeting and the delivery of nuclear weapons," as Pollard's controller was that "new missile targets inside the Soviet Union," "for Israel's own "advanced Jericho missile system," "required increased intelligence" "and Sella's mission was to help Pollard gather the essential information and then evaluate it," according to Seymour Hersh's book in Israel's nuclear arsenal entitled *The Samson Option*. According to Hersh, "Israel would need the most advanced American intelligence on weather patterns and communications protocols, as well as data on emergency and alert procedures."

The U.S. Department of Justice "took, converted, stole" the VAX 11/780 version of PROMIS from INSLAW through a campaign of "trickery, fraud and deceit" during the winter and spring of 1983, according to the fully litigated findings of fact of two federal courts, the U.S. Bankruptcy Court for the District of Columbia in January 1988 and the U.S. District Court for the District of Columbia in November 1989. The House Judiciary Committee, in its September 1992 Investigative Report, *The INSLAW Affair*, independently confirmed the government's theft of PROMIS, almost 18 months after the U.S. Court of Appeals for the District of Columbia had overturned the decisions of the two lower federal courts on a jurisdictional technicality, without addressing the merits of the dispute.

In February 1983, early in the Justice Department's campaign of "trickery, fraud and deceit," the Justice Department sent Rafi Eitan to INSLAW for a demonstration of the VAX 11/780 version of PROMIS, although the U.S. Justice Department falsely introduced him to INSLAW as Dr. Ben Or of the Israeli Ministry of Justice in Tel Aviv. INSLAW did not discover the real identify of its Israeli visitor until the House Judiciary Committee revealed in its Investigative Report, *The INSLAW Affair*, almost 10 years later, that the Justice Department had documented the transfer of some version of PROMIS to a Dr. Ben Or of Israel in May 1983. That was only a few weeks after the Justice Department had taken delivery from INSLAW of the VAX 11/780 version of PROMIS.

Memorandum to the Record
December 22, 1999
Page 17

Independent Counsel explained that his decision resulted from his inability to find any evidence that Meese had influenced the award of federal contracts to Brian.

Allowing Robert Maxwell, an Israeli intelligence contractor, to make the first sales of PROMIS in 1984 for internal use within the U.S. intelligence community may have allowed Brian to circumvent the problem caused by the Independent Counsel's 1984 investigation of Meese's relationship to Brian, while satisfying Brian's determination to profit from sales of PROMIS, but it could also have jeopardized vital U.S. national security interests. One illustration of the risk to U.S. national security interests relates to the W-88 nuclear warhead, the most advanced nuclear warhead in the U.S. arsenal. The Los Alamos National Laboratory completed the design of the W-88 in 1984 for future deployment on Trident II nuclear submarines. No later than 1988, the People's Republic of China had acquired the specifications to the W-88 from an unknown source. If Los Alamos included in a PROMIS database specifications for the W-88 nuclear warhead, Rafi Eitan may have been able to use Pollard to steal such specifications. The Government of Israel has been an important source of the People's Republic of China's acquisition of advanced military technology, according to a recent Congressional Investigative Report on Chinese espionage entitled *The United States House of Representatives Select Committee on U.S. National Security and Military/Commercial Concerns with the People's Republic of China* dated January 3, 1999.

The prosecution of Jonathan Pollard in 1986 and 1987 for espionage for Rafi Eitan and Israel would, under the circumstances, have presented both political and institutional conflicts of interest to the Meese Justice Department. Such conflicts of interest may explain the facts summarized in the remaining paragraphs of this memorandum.

In October 1986, both Meese and his Deputy Attorney General, Arnold Burns, discussed the INSLAW case with Leonard Garment, then a Senior Partner at Dickstein, Shapiro and Morin, the law firm that had filed INSLAW's lawsuit against the U.S. Department of Justice for the theft of the VAX 11/780 version of PROMIS several months earlier. The Justice Department disclosed these communications in sworn answers to INSLAW's interrogatories in 1987. Garment, however, never disclosed the communications to INSLAW.

Earlier that same year, the Government of Israel had hired Garment to represent Israeli Air Force Colonel Aviem Sella, the nuclear targeting expert whom Rafi Eitan used as Pollard's controller.

Garment had a luncheon meeting with Deputy Attorney General Arnold Burns on October 6, 1986 during which Burns complained of INSLAW's strategy in the litigation against the Justice Department, and implied that a settlement might be forthcoming if INSLAW's litigation strategy were to change, according to the September 1989 Investigative Report of the Senate Permanent Investigations Subcommittee. One week after the luncheon meeting, Dickstein, Shapiro and Morin

FOR BACKGROUND
PURPOSES ONLY

Memorandum to the Record
December 22, 1999
Page 18

fired the partner in charge of the INSLAW case, according to the same Senate report. About two months after that, the law firm sent a letter to INSLAW giving INSLAW the choice of abandoning its claims for PROMIS license fees or finding new litigation counsel.

Garment initially maintained to the press that his October 1986 discussions with Meese were about a foreign policy issue involving Israel rather than about INSLAW, according to an April 4, 1988 interview of Garment published in *Barron's Financial Weekly*, entitled "Rogue Justice -- What Really Sparked the Vendetta Against INSLAW."

LINK7500 675331

FROM:

TO:

ADVISORY

Michael Riconosciuto is one of the original architects of the PROMIS backdoor. PROMIS was a people-tracking software system sold to intelligence organizations and government drug agencies worldwide. The global dispersion of PROMIS was part of a U.S. plot
to spy on other spy agencies.
Riconosciuto, who was Director of Research for a Wackenhut-Cabazon Indian joint venture, oversaw a group of several dozen people who worked out of business offices in nearby Indio, California. According to the testimony of Robert Booth Nichols, a CIA age
nt associated with Meridian International Logistics and connected to Music Corporation of America (MCA), Riconosciuto was in frequent contact with Bobby Inman, Director of the National Security Agency (NSA) and then Deputy Director of the Central Intelli
gence Agency (CIA), during this time.
Since intelligence computers are, for security reasons, usually not connected to external networks, the original backdoor was a broadcast signal. The PROMIS software was often sold in connection with computer hardware (such as a Prime computer) using a s
pecialized chip. The chip would broadcast the contents of the existing database to monitoring vans or collection satellites using digital spread spectrum techniques whenever the software was run.
Spread spectrum techniques offer a way to mask, or disguise, a signal by making it appear as "noise" with respect to another signal. For example, one may communicate covertly on the same spectrum as a local TV broadcast signal. From the point of view of
a TV receiver, the covert communication appears as noise, and is filtered out. From the point of view of the covert channel, the TV signal appears as noise. In the case of the PROMIS broadcast channel, the signal was disguised as ordinary computer noise-
-the type of stuff that must be reduced for TEMPEST certification in the U.S. In spread spectrum frequency communication, the transmitted spectrum is much wider than what is really necessary. In digital communication, the transmission widths of digital signals are expanded so that many "bit periods" are needed to represent one bit
at baseband. This results in an improvement in the signal-to-noise ratio. Spread spectrum techniques are used extensively in covert military communications and secure satellite systems.
The covert communication channel operates off a pseudo-random binary sequence, such as a stream cipher. Stream ciphers differ from block ciphers such as DES (the Data Encryption Standard) widely used in banking.
A block cipher applies a static transformation to a fixed block of data. The DES algorithm, for example, encrypts a 64-bit block of data using 64-bit keys. (The

Message Ref: █████████ 1 (continued)

effective key si.... actually 56 bits, since every eighth bit is considered a
parity bit and
is discarded.) In DES electronic code book (ECB) mode, each 64-bit block of
data is encrypted separately from every other block. In cipher block chaining
(CBC) and cipher feedback (CFB) mode, the encryption of the current data block
is dependent on prev
ious data blocks. But under any one of these three DES modes, the transformation
of a given data sequence with a given DES key will nevertheless result in the
same ciphertext, regardless of the time the encryption takes place.
A stream cipher, by contrast, applies a time- varying transformation to
individual digits or bits of data. "Time-varying" means the same sequence of
plaintext data bits seen at two different points in time will be encrypted to a
different sequence of cip
hertext data bits.
To illustrate this for a simple case, suppose we are doing encryption using
simple XOR rules of addition, adding keybits k to plaintext bits x on a bit by
bit basis to obtain cipher bits y: $y = x + k$. XOR addition follows the rules
0+0 = 0
0+1 = 1
1+0 = 1
1+1 = 0.
Suppose the plaintext data is "1011". The current key might be "1010". Then the
ciphertext data is
1011+1010 = 0001.
The ciphertext "0001" gives no information about the original plaintext. The
plaintext could have been any one of $2^4 = 16$ possible sequences of 0s and 1s.
To restore the original plaintext, we XOR the ciphertext "0001" again with the
key "1010" to obtai
n
0001+1010 = 1011.
In a stream cipher, the keystream will typically be different at different
points of time. This the encryption of a repeated plaintext "1011" might take
the form

time 1: 1011 + 1010 = 0001
time 2: 1011 + 1111 = 0100
time 3: 1011 + 0011 = 1000
and so on for other times. In this example, the "time- varying transformation"
takes the simple form of a time- varying keybit stream.
The most famous stream cipher is the Verdam cipher, or "one-time pad", which
follows the encryption scheme just described. If the current time is i, the
current plaintext bit is x(i), and the current key bit is k(i), then the
ciphertext bit is $y(i) = x(i$
$) + k(i)$. The number of key bits, N, must exceed the number of plaintext bits M:
N>M. The bits in the keystream sequence k(1), k(2), . . . , k(N) must be
independently and uniformly distributed, and are used only once and then
disgarded (hence "one- time
pad"). Of course, this scheme--while not breakable by cryptanalysis--has other
security problems. It requires both parties to have a copy of the current key,
and the key to be kept secret from all hostile parties. This in turn requires
that the keys be
generated, stored, and communicated in a totally secure manner--a massive
problem in itself. So one-time pads are typically only used in "hot lines", such
as the old Red Telephone between Moscow and Washington, D.C. that was installed
with the hope that
a little jawboning could help avert nuclear war. ("Can we talk?")
Practical cryptography for digital and analog communication thus uses "keystream
generators" which typically determine the keystream as some function f of an
underlying key K, and the current state of the system s(i):
$k(i) = f(K, s(i))$.

Message Ref: 6▇▇▇▇▇ Page 2 (continued)

This key stream k(i) can be added to the original bit stream to produce a new (encrypted) stream (as is done in "direct sequence" spread spectrum systems). Or the key stream can be used to make the carrier frequency hop around within the spread sprectrum

bandwidth (as is done in "frequency hopping" systems). Many variations and combinations are possible.

Like many people associated with PROMIS (including Earl Brian, the man who sold it around the world), Michael Riconosciuto is in jail. Riconosciuto was convicted on charges relating to the construction of a methamphetamine lab. Michael Riconosciuto appears in a recent manuscript The Last Circle by "Carol Marshall" (whose real name is Seymour). Much of the book is based on interviews with, and files purloined from, Riconosciuto. Part of the subject matter of The Last Circle invo

lves the West Coast activities of "The Company", a paramilitary drug dealing operation using ex-law enforcement and ex-intelligence personel that was based in Lexington, KY, in the late 78s and early 80s. However, because The Last Circle makes extensive

use of Riconosciuto's files, it is also concerned with many other activities, including in particular a biowarfare project undertaken by the Wackenhut-Cabazon Indian joint venture. ("The Company" itself is the subject of another book entitled The Bluegra

ss Conspiracy by Sally Denton.)

Riconosciuto wrote me in regard to a speech I gave to the Libertarian Party of Colorado on digital cash on April 28, 1997. I have added some comments with respect to the issues mentioned.

May 8, 1997

M. Riconosciuto

21389-086 Med. A-1

Box 819

Coleman, FL 33521

"Orlin,

▆▆▆▆▆▆▆▆ has been sending me some of your published material for some time. I have some questions concerning your talk on digital cash.

"First a little of my background. I started with computers when a "laptop" was an IBM porta-punch. My first serious computing experience was on an IBM system 1620. I went from there to the IBM 7090/7094 systems and from there to the then "new" IBM 360 fa

mily. I missed the 370 generations, because during that time my responsibilities had me in a position where comp center staff handled all my data processing. I have been on the DEC/PDP systems since they first came out (PDP 8, PDP 10, PDP 11) and stayed

with them as they matured into the VAX system. My programming experience runs the gamut from absolute coding sheets in unit record type systems, to top down/structured programming. I have been at this for awhile. I am not impressed by the Intel/MS standa

rd that has taken over the computing world. Although I might note that Windows NT has suspicious similarity to the VAX/VMS operating system.

"Up until six months ago I had access to a computer and the latest literature because of my inmate job assignments in facilities management and prison industries. We had a high end Pentium CAD set up in facilities and a network connection on a Data Gener

al Avion system in Unicor prison industries. I also had the responsibility of maintenance on a Honeywell building automation control DDC-HVAC system.

"As a direct result of the TV interview with the Germans I was pulled off my premium inmate job and re- assigned to the duty of picking up cigarette butts in the recreation yard for $5 per month. This was inspite of exemplary job assignment reports and n

o disruptive behavior incidents."

Message Ref: ▆▆▆▆▆▆▆▆Page 3 (continued)

[paragraph omitted]

"The point of all this is to make it clear that I am not that far out of touch with the current state of the art.

"This brings me to the first question that I want to ask about your digital cash speech.

"1) In your reference to the "discrete logarithm problem" are you taking into consideration the Donald Coppersmith work? Coppersmith developed a computationally feasible way to take discrete logarithms back in the 80s. Needless to say, this work has been

played down, but it has been in the open literature."

[Comment: The discrete log problem is the problem of finding x such that $g^x = y$ mod n, for a given y, g, and n. Here x is the discrete logarithm of y to the base g. Since this is hard to do, one can form a public/private key system with x as the private

(secret) key and $y = g^x$ mod n as the public key.

[Of course, the hard-to-do job of taking discrete logarithms may not be the only way to approach a given problem. The security of Diffie-Hellman, to which I referred in my speech, is apparently based on discrete logarithms, but is susceptible to a simple

attack by a person in the middle of the communication process. In Diffie-Hellman, Alice generates x and send Bob g^x mod n. Bob generates y and sends Alice g^y mod n. They both then calculate $g^{(xy)}$ mod n as the session key. (The best an observer can d

o is calculate $g^{(x+y)}$, without taking discrete logarithms.) However, if Eve controls all communication between the two, she can substitute her own parameters, and decrypt both sides of the conversation before forwarding the messages. Be this as it may,

Diffie introduced a simple variant of this process—called Station to Station (STS) protocol—which completely eliminates the man-in-the-middle attack.

[Riconosciuto refers to the work of Coppersmith [1], [2] in finding discrete logarithms. Coppersmith greatly increased the efficiency of finding discrete logs in fields of characteristic 2 (which use digits 0 and 1, and thus are efficient in programming)

, so that the modulus has to be of the order of $n = 2^{1000}$ to be secure.]

"2) You of course are aware that RSA type algorithms are no more secure that the modulus is difficult to factor. Are you aware of the latest advances in . . . differential cryptanalysis and meet in the middle techniques? Are you aware of the work by Lens

tra . . . et al with their methods of quadratic sieves etc?"

[Comment: Riconosciuto is refering here to several types of cryptanalytic attacks. Differential cryptanalysis and meet-in-the- middle generally refer to attacks on DES, while the work of Lenstra is directly relevant to RSA.

[The methods of Lenstra [3], Cohen and Lenstra [4], and Pomerance, Rumely, and Adleman [5], use Fermat's Little Theorem (or its analog in extension fields of rational numbers) and Gauss and Jacobi sums to test for primality.

[The quadratic sieve for factoring n has running time of the order of $\exp((\ln n \ln \ln n)^{.5})$. A slightly faster method is [6] the number field sieve, which has running time of the order of $\exp((\ln n)^{(1/3)} (\ln \ln n)^{(2/3)})$.]

"3) Have you ever heard of the Hilbert spectral processing technique and its application to high speed factoring systems?

[Comment: I'm not sure exactly what Riconosciuto has in mind here. But communication signals can be decomposed into addable parts using systems of orthogonal functions such as Fourier series or Walsh functions.

[Riconosciuto may be referring to the results of Xiao and Massey [9], who characterize correlation-immune functions in terms of their Walsh transforms.]

"4) Are you familiar with fast elliptical encryption methods?"

[Comment: I did not refer to these in my speech as they are fairly complex. Elliptic curve cryptosystems stem from the work of Neal Koblitz [7] and others.

[The analog of taking a power in modular arithmetic is multiplication on elliptic curves. So the analog of the Diffie- Hellman problem in the elliptic

curve world is to find the integer n such that nB = P, where B and P are points
on an elliptic curve. H
ere n can be thought of as the "discrete logarithm" of P to the base B. Elliptic
curve cryptosystems are believed to offer equal security at shorter key
lengths.]
"5) Do you remember the hard knapsack problems of Merkle and Hellman and how
they fell?"
[Comment: Knapsack problems were so- named because they resemble the problem of
fitting a number of items k into a total volume V—like packing a knapsack..
They have the characteristic that they are NP- complete, so that theoretically
an encryption sche
me could be constructed from them that is not solvable in polynomial time (with
respect to k). However, the original Merkle-Hellman knapsack was broken by
Shamir. So Riconosciuto is suggesting that implemented discrete log systems may
have hidden weaknes
ses much like the original knapsack encryption systems. There is a knapsack
system due to Chor and Rivest that hasn't been broken yet, to my knowledge.]
"This should be a good place to start. Let me know if you receive my letter.

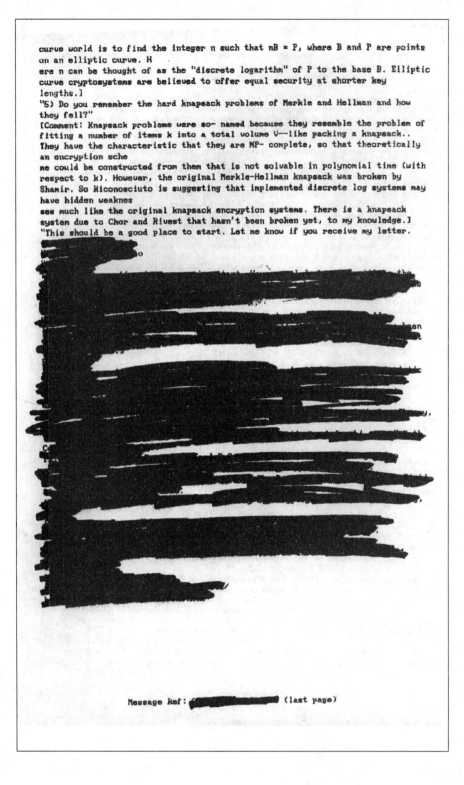

Message Ref: ▇▇▇▇▇▇▇▇▇ (last page)

REPORT OF SPECIAL COUNSEL

NICHOLAS J. BUA

TO

THE ATTORNEY GENERAL

OF THE UNITED STATES

REGARDING THE ALLEGATIONS OF INSLAW, INC.

NICHOLAS J. BUA

HELENE B. GREENWALD
JOSEPH H. HARTZLER
CHARLES D. KNIGHT
DEAN J. POLALES
DAVID S. ROSENBLOOM

March 1993

THIS DOCUMENT HAS BEEN REVISED
IN ORDER TO DELETE MATERIAL
THE DISCLOSURE OF WHICH IS
PROHIBITED PURSUANT TO
RULE 6(e) OF THE FEDERAL
RULES OF CRIMINAL PROCEDURE

U.S. Department of Justice

Federal Bureau of Investigation

In Reply, Please Refer to
File No. 190-NY-244726

26 Federal Plaza
New York, New York 10278
December 20, 1994

William A. Hamilton
Inslaw, Inc
1125 15th street NW
Washington, D. C., 20005

RE: Information on Demand, Inc.
FOIA REQUEST

Dear Mr. Hamilton:

Reference is made to my letter dated May 23, 1994, in which you were advised that cross-references responsive to your Freedom of Information Act (FOIA) request on the above-captioned subject had been referred to the Federal Bureau of Investigation's Security Classifying Officer (FBI's SCO) for classification.

The classification review of the cross-references has been completed and the review pursuant to the FOIA has also been completed.

Enclosed are copies of two (2) pages. Excisions have been made on these pages and the remaining fifty-eight (58) are being withheld in their entirety in order to protect information which is exempt from disclosure pursuant to the following subsection of Title 5, United States Code, section 552:

(b) (1) (A) specifically authorized under criteria established by an Executive order to be kept secret in the interest of national defense or foreign policy

(B) are in fact properly classified pursuant to such Executive order.

(b) (7) records or information compiled for law enforcement purposes, but only to the extent that the production os such law enforcement records or information

190-NY-244726

(C) could reasonably be expected to constitute an unwarranted invasion of personal privacy

(D) could reasonably be expected to disclose the identity of a confidential source, including a State, local, or foreign agency or authority or any private institution which furnished information on a confidential basis, and, in the case of a record or information compiled by a criminal law enforcement authority in the course of a criminal investigation or by an agency conducting a lawful national security intelligence investigation, information furnished by a confidential source

(b)(2) related solely to the internal personnel rules and practices of an agency;

You may appeal this denial by writing to the CO-DIRECTOR, Office of Information and Privacy, Room 7238,MAIN, United States Department of Justice, Washington, D. C., 20530, within thirty (30) days from receipt of this letter. The letter and the envelope should be clearly marked "Freedom of Information Appeal" or "Information Appeal". Please cite the name of the office to which your original request was directed.

Sincerely yours,

William A. Gavin
Deputy Assistant Director
in Charge

By: *James J. Roth*
James J. Roth
Principal Legal Advisor

2

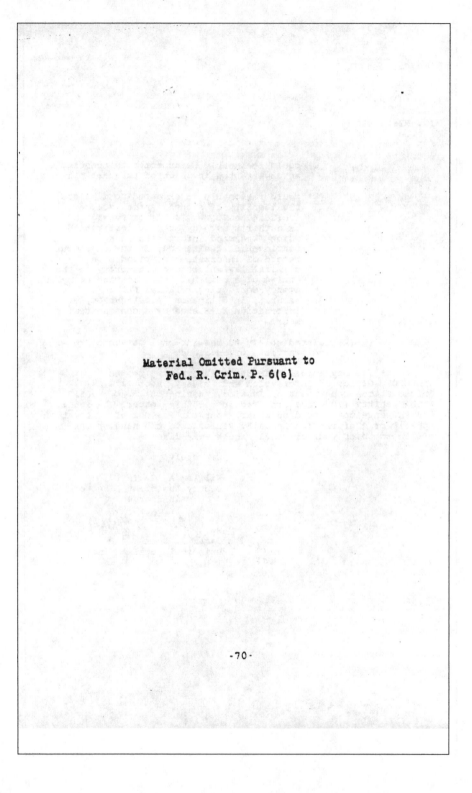

Material Omitted Pursuant to
Fed. R. Crim. P. 6(e)

reported directly to Ed Meese. He also arranged White House tours to woo investors in his government contracting company, Hadron Inc., according to a Canadian investment banker who took a tour.

But these seemingly random historical connections between Inslaw, Hadron, the Reagan White House and Earl Brian take on a new meaning when considered in light of the "October Surprise," the persistent allegation that the Reagan campaign negotiated with Iranian officials to guarantee that US hostages would not be released before Reagan won election in 1980.

The October Surprise theory hinges in part on alleged negotiations between the Reagan campaign and the Iranians on the weekend of Oct. 17P 21, 1980, in Paris, among other places.

The deal, according to former Iranian President Abol Hassan Bani-Sadr, ex-Israeli spy Ari Ben Menashe, and a former CIA contract agent ▮▮▮▮▮▮▮▮▮▮▮▮, included the payment of $40 million to the Iranians.

According to several sources, Earl Brian, one of Reagan's close advisors, made it quite clear that he was planning to be in Paris that very weekend. Ben Menashe, who says he was one of six Israelis, 12 Americans and 16 Iranians present at the Paris talks, said, "I saw Brian in Paris."

Brian was interviewed by Senate investigators on July 28, 1992, and denied under oath any connection with the alleged negotiations.

He told the investigators he did not have a valid passport during the October 1980 dates.

But according to court documents and interviews, Brian told Canadian investors in his newly acquired Clinical Sciences, Inc., that he would be in Paris that weekend. Brian acquired controlling interest in Clinical Sciences in the summer of 1980. Clinical Sciences was then trading at around $2 a share. Brian worked with Janos P. Pasztor, a vice president and special situations analyst with the Canadian investment bank of Nesbitt, Thomson, Bongard Inc., to create a market of Canadian investors for the stock.

Pasztor later testified in court documents that Brian said he would be in Paris the weekend of October 17 to do a deal with the Pasteur Institute (a medical research firm).

Two other brokers, Harry Scully, a broker based in Halifax, Nova Scotia, and John Belton, a senior account executive with Nesbitt-Thomson from 1968 to 1982 who is suing Nesbitt-Thomson and Pasztor for securities fraud, also claim that they were told that Brian was in Paris that weekend.

But if Brian went to Paris to see the Pasteur Institute, he seems to have missed his appointment. An investigation by the Royal Canadian Mounted Police into Clinical Sci-ences stock transactions revealed that the Pasteur Institute had never conducted business with, or even heard of Brian.

▮▮▮▮▮▮▮▮▮▮▮▮▮▮▮▮▮▮▮▮▮▮ Pasztor said, "These are political questions and I don't want to become involved." He refused further comment. Brian contends that the dates of his trip were in error and that he went to Paris in April 1981, not October 1980. But the passport he turned over to Senate investigators did not contain a French entry or exit stamp for April 1981.

Through his lawyers, Brian refused ▮▮▮▮▮▮▮▮▮▮▮▮

processing procurement or that would be likely users of PROMIS, and we have been unable to find any indication that the Agency ever obtained PROMIS software."

But a retired CIA ███████████████████████████████ that the DOJ gave PROMIS to the CIA. ███████████████████████████████ ████████████████████████████ █████████

How was the CIA involved? According to ████████████████████ ity, the agency accepted stolen goods, not aware that a major scandal was brewing. ████████████ ████████████████

But the CIA was not the only place where illegal versions of PROMIS cropped up. Canadian documents (held by the House Judiciary Committee ████████████████ place PROMIS in the hands of various Canadian government agencies. These documents include ████████ ██

And, of course, the software was transferred to Rafael Etian's anti- terrorism unit in Israel. The DOJ claims it was the LEAA version, but former Israeli spy Ben Menashe and others claim it was the 32-bit version. According to Ben Menashe, other government departments within Israel also saw PROMIS, ██████████████████ Dr. Earl Brian. In a 1991 affidavit related to the bankruptcy proceedings, Ben Menashe claimed: "I attended a meeting at my Department's headquarters in Tel Aviv in 1987 during which Dr. Earl W. Brian of the United States made a presentation intended to facilitate the use of the PROMIS computer software."

"Dr. Brian stated during his presentation that all U.S. Intelligence Agencies, including the Defense Intelligence Agency, the Central Intelligence Agency, and the National Security Agency and the U.S. Department of Justice were then using the PROMIS computer software," Ben Menashe continued. ██████████████████████████████████ the Israeli government has admitted that Ben Menashe had access to extremely sensitive information during his tenure at the Mossad.

Asked why Israeli intelligence would have been so interested in Inslaw and PROMIS, Ben Menashe said, "PROMIS was a very big thing for us guys, a very, very big thing ... it was probably the most important issue of the '80s because it just changed the whole intelligence outlook. The whole form of intelligence collection changed. This whole thing changed it." PROMIS, Ben Menashe said, was perfect for tracking Palestinians and other political dissidents.

(Ben Menashe's superior during this period was Rafael Etian, or Dr. Ben Orr, as he was known during his 1983 visit to Inslaw.)

Apparently, Israel was not the only country interested in using PROMIS for internal security purposes. Lt. Col. Oliver North also may have been using the program. According to several intelligence community sources, PROMIS was in use at a 6,100-square-foot command center built on the sixth floor of the Justice Department. According to both a contractor who helped design the center and information disclosed during the Iran- Contra hearings, Oliver North had a similar, but smaller, White House operations room that was connected by computer link to the DOJ's command center.

TO

the World Bank's Headquarters in Washington, DC. One of the two still had his notebook containing handwritten diary entries from his years at the World Bank's computer center. According to these individuals, the World Bank acquired the VAX version of PROMIS in approximately June 1983 for use in tracking international message flows between the World Bank and its member governments, on the one hand, and between the International Monetary Fund and the international banks, on the other hand. Neither of these two former World Bank computer specialists knew how or from whom the two international financial institutions had acquired the VAX version of PROMIS. INSLAW initially disregarded this lead because the tracking of international message flows was outside the traditional law department application domain for PROMIS. INSLAW reevaluated the lead, however, when a current U.S. Government employee, who knew nothing about the information INSLAW had earlier received from the two former World Bank employees, told INSLAW years later that the Justice Department had disseminated the proprietary VAX version of PROMIS to the World Bank in June 1983 as part of a U.S. intelligence initiative. According to this source, D. Lowell Jensen, then Assistant Attorney General for the Criminal Division, was personally involved in the dissemination to the World Bank, as were various officials of the Justice Department's Office of Security and the CIA. In the June 1993 rebuttal to the report by Justice Department Special Counsel Nicholas J. Bua, INSLAW summarized the backgrounds and claims of three of INSLAW's confidential witnesses about the spring 1983 dissemination to the two international financial institutions.

▓▓▓▓▓▓▓▓▓▓▓▓▓▓▓▓▓▓ informants are fearful of reprisals f▓▓▓▓▓▓▓▓▓▓
▓▓▓▓▓▓▓ and are, therefore, unwilling to submit to interviews ▓▓▓▓▓▓▓▓▓▓▓ officials.
▓▓. For example, the
▓▓
▓▓▓▓▓▓▓▓▓▓▓▓▓▓▓▓▓▓▓▓▓▓▓▓▓▓▓▓▓▓▓▓▓▓▓▓▓

In light of the fact that the World Bank and the International Monetary Fund present more accessible targets for obtaining such proof than U.S. and foreign intelligence agencies, ▓▓▓▓▓ recently contacted ▓▓▓▓▓▓▓▓▓▓▓▓▓▓ has investigated the U.S. intelligence community's penetrations of other financial institutions. Within two days of the initial meeting, ▓▓▓▓▓▓ that he had been able to confirm from his own sources at the World Bank and the International Monetary Fund that the Justice Department had disseminated the VAX version of PROMIS to these two international financial institutions as part of a U.S. intelligence community initiative and that this PROMIS Trojan horse initiative was spearheaded by the National Security Agency. Because of the NSA's alleged involvement, any contemporaneous Justice Department record of the dissemination, such as that which is alluded to in the narrative about witness #2 in Exhibit B ▓▓▓▓▓▓▓▓▓▓▓▓▓▓▓▓▓▓▓▓▓▓▓▓▓▓ to be highly classified and, consequently, stored in one of the Office of Security's Sensitive Compartmented Information Facilities (SCIF's). ▓▓▓▓▓▓▓▓▓▓▓▓▓▓▓▓▓▓▓▓▓▓▓▓▓▓▓▓▓▓▓▓▓ an ▓▓▓▓▓▓▓▓▓▓▓▓▓▓▓▓▓▓▓▓▓▓▓▓▓▓▓▓ation. Copies of two ▓▓▓▓▓▓▓▓▓▓▓▓▓▓▓▓▓▓▓▓▓▓.

FROM

prosecution to Rafi Eitan in exchange for his purported cooperation in the U.S. Justice Department's criminal investigation of the Pollard espionage case. ████████ went to Israel in 1986 as part of the U.S. Government delegation to interview Rafi Eitan and other Israeli Government officials involved with ████████ espionage against the United States.⁴

████████████████ seeking the appointment of an Independent Counsel to investigate Meese, Jensen, Brian, and Garment. ████████████████████████ n. The Public Integrity Section declined to ████████████████████████████████ , according ██ of ██ r. The Public ████████████████████████████),████████████████████

██ in ██ the ████████████████████████████████ c. ████████ , however, denies that he ever made such statements to the Bua investigators and ██ ██ ██ to. The Justice Department deleted all reference to this actual sworn testimony from the Bua Report, ascribing the deletions to the requirements of grand jury secrecy laws.

During the December 16, 1993 meeting with Assistant Associate Attorney General Dwyer, ████████ disclosed the existence of two additional extremely sensitive sources, whose existence ████████ had not previously disclosed to the Justice Department. ████████████ e. Each has independently corroborated key elements of ████ ████ detailed claims about the role of Israeli intelligence ████████████████. ████████ o presented a document to Mr. Dwyer, authored by a self-evidently credible source, outlining how the Justice Department can proceed to obtain sworn testimony from one of these two additional sensitive sources.

3. The Alleged Distribution of the VAX Version of PROMIS to the World Bank and the International Monetary Fund

Immediately after acquiring the VAX version of PROMIS from INSLAW in April 1983, the Justice Department apparently secretly and illegally disseminated a copy of the VAX version to the World Bank and the International Monetary Fund. In February 1991, Danny Casolaro, an investigative journalist, introduced INSLAW to two former computer systems specialists from

▬▬▬▬ Ari Ben-Menashe claims that Robert Maxwell --whose handling agent he was-- sold Promis to the Soviets.

[Answer] ▬▬▬▬▬▬▬▬▬▬▬ the booby-trapped software was sold to the GRU, the Soviet military intelligence service. Meanwhile, the Israelis discovered that the Americans were selling arms to Saddam Husayn. Speaking through Ben-Menashe, Shamir warned the CIA: Either you stop, or we will denounce you to the Russians. The sales continued. And as if by chance, the GRU's computers were mysteriously out of order for a week. It is likely that the Soviets dismantled and dissected their machines.

▬▬▬▬ Did the sales continue?

[Answer] Under the name of Promis or some other name, it was sold to Egypt and Cyprus and throughout the Middle East. In Australia. In Southeast Asia. To the World Bank. To two French banks: the Credit Lyonnais and the BNP. To the Swiss banks, including the UBS. Why spy on the banking system? Two reasons. First, to protect the dollar and keep an eye on competing currencies. The second reason dates back to 1981 and the fight against the laundering of drug money. That was the "Follow the Money" operation launched by Reagan. ▬▬▬▬▬▬▬▬▬ the DGSE (the intelligence service) had acquired Promis. Whatever the case, the DST (the counterespionage agency) got its hands ▬▬▬ microchip that downloads data from computers. In addition, obviously, the software found room for all its applications within the U.S. institutions themselves: from the CIA to the FBI and from the Air Force to the Navy--the nuclear-powered submarines and stealth bombers are equipped with them. Not to mention the laboratories where nuclear tests are simulated.

▬▬▬▬ To everyone's surprise, the Clintons are part of the story!

[Answer] Jackson Stevens--Arkansas billionaire, financial backer of the Democratic Party, and a friend and partner of the Clintons in the Whitewater real estate scandal--sells (surprise) Promis software! In short, he took up the torch from Californian Earl Brian. Vince Foster, the White House attorney who was linked with Stevens and even more so with the Clintons, committed suicide on 20 July 1993. A few days earlier, he had requested two files: one on the NSA and the other on Promis. His secretary confirms this--it was she who opened them and put them in the safe. They were never seen again. The safe had been cleaned out.

2

The Tiananmen Trump

JANUARY 1991
WASHINGTON, D.C.

In those first two weeks of 1991, despite the frenetic pace of events, time itself appeared to pass in slow motion as the entire world waited to see if there would be war with Iraq. In Washington hopes rose and fell as predictably as the flags on government buildings.

In one building, the State Department, the last acts of diplomacy were being played out. Secretary of State James Baker and his staff detailed for those diplomats still able to reach Saddam Hussein — Arabs mostly, with a sprinkling of Europeans — the horrors awaiting Iraq if hopes died. It was a portrait of high-tech warfare the likes of which had never been seen: "smart bombs" with their own video cameras to show the very moment prior to impact, and guided missiles that could cruise down the streets of Baghdad looking for a particular building to destroy. It was the world of Buck Rogers finally come true. Nothing, and no one, those diplomats were told, could resist such a show of force.

But Saddam remained unimpressed. He saw himself as the avenger of the Arab people, chosen by Allah to redress the slights visited on Arabs for generations.

As the hours ticked by to the deadline for war set by the United Nations for Tuesday, January 15 — and interpreted by Washington as expiring at noon Eastern Standard Time on that day — it became increasingly clear that Washington was conducting a dialogue with the deaf. Yet, anxious to show it was doing everything to avert what Saddam was predicting would be *"the mother of all wars,"* the Bush administration was, for the most part, conducting its efforts as publicly as possible.

The exception was its dealings with the hard-line Communist regime in Beijing. There, extraordinary secrecy prevailed. Only a handful in the administration outside President George Bush and Secretary Baker were aware of the precise ebb and flow of the discussions. These were first intended to persuade China to refrain from vetoing the United Nations resolution to use sanctions against Iraq shortly after it had invaded Kuwait and then, when the trade embargo failed, to persuade China to support a second resolution authorizing force to be used to expel Iraq from Kuwait.

The reasons for the secret dealings with China were rooted in the administration's embarrassment at having to depend on Beijing for support, coupled with a sense of pragmatism, which had come to permeate the Bush presidency more than any of its recent predecessors. To grasp that reality it is important to understand that both U.N. resolutions had been proposed in the high-minded guise of "restoring" Kuwait's democratic right to exist as a sovereign nation. Those Americans who squinted into the desert sun and spoke of being ready to fight "a just war" — one that would be swift and decisive, short and sweet, a Panama perhaps, but never another Vietnam — rarely paused to consider that democracy, as they understood it, had never existed in Kuwait. At best the Gulf Kingdom was a family-run dictatorship that employed foreign labor under often harsh conditions: workers' passports were confiscated to stop them leaving until their contracts expired; abuses of basic human rights were commonplace. In some ways Kuwait was as repressive as the People's Republic of China.

Yet China, as a permanent member of the U.N. Security Council, had the power to effectively wreck Bush's determination to go to war unless Iraq obeyed the January 15 deadline.

For the President, Saddam had become a personal nemesis and a *casus belli*. At times the rhetoric from the White House was as fierce as that coming from Baghdad.

Bush had also learned much from his most recent experience of war. On December 20, 1989, he had ordered U.S. forces into Panama to arrest its de facto head of state, General Manuel Noriega. The U.N. General Assembly had denounced the invasion as a *"flagrant violation of international law."* But for the administration, and indeed many Americans, the lofty ends justified the means: The invasion of Panama would stop the drug traffic into the United States; it would restore "stability" in the region. And, of course, it would "restore democracy" to Panama.

By the time the Persian Gulf crisis was engaging President Bush, the reality of his intervention in Panama was all too plain. Federal agencies were reporting that the drug traffic there was running at pre-invasion levels. Stability was as far away as ever in the region, and the prospect of a truly democratic Panama even further. And America itself continued to be branded as a bully and aggressor because of the invasion.

Bush knew he could not once more risk being accused of dangerous arrogance in assuming the role of the world's policeman by confronting Saddam. Consequently, since the very beginning of the Gulf crisis, he had worked hard to put together a coalition of Arab and non-Arab states to deal with Iraq. While he had made it clear that America would provide the bulk of the firepower, and in military terms would call the shots, it would do so with the blessing of the world. To that end it became critically important for Bush to be able to count on China.

The irony of the situation was most certainly not lost on the President.

Bush knew from the very beginning that the sheer speed and success of the Iraqi war machine depended, in significant measure, on China. In the past five years, the People's Republic had equipped it with 1,500 T-65 tanks, 9,000 Red

Army antitank weapons, 150 F-7 jet aircraft, 12 million artillery shells and mines, and over 4 billion rounds of small-arms ammunition.

More sinister, China had sold to Iraq large quantities of lithium 6 hydride, a key component in the manufacture of a hydrogen bomb. Throughout 1990, the China National Non-Ferrous Metals Import-Export Corporation had shipped several dozen sealed plastic bottles of the grayish-white granular substance to Baghdad. Each bottle held 250 grams of lithium 6 hydride. The bottles were packed in lead and encased in metal barrels, each weighing 200 pounds. Each barrel had a label stating the substance was for use in the Iraqi medical industry.

On arrival in Baghdad, the barrels were distributed to Iraq's three nuclear facilities.

By the time Saddam invaded Kuwait, China had provided him with the means to produce a dozen hydrogen bombs. Each had an estimated destructive capacity of approximately fifty times that of the device released over Hiroshima.

With the lithium 6 hydride, several score Chinese scientists and technicians had traveled to Iraq. A number had helped China successfully build its own hydrogen bomb in 1967. Their presence, like the export of the lithium 6 hydride, was a breach of the U.N. Nuclear Non-Proliferation Treaty. But China had never signed that agreement.

Despite knowing all this, the President was still determined to parley with China. With Saddam firmly in his gunsight, Bush was ready, according to his aides, to *"deal with just about anyone if it meant putting an end to the Baghdad bully."*

The President, long castigated as a wimp, was preparing himself for a massive act of expediency, one that would reveal the kind of ruthlessness most doubted he possessed. Only those who had served under the President when he was director of the Central Intelligence Agency (CIA) knew that Bush had the steel to balance the fate of a few against what he saw as the greater good for America.

In this case the few were students: young Chinese who had tried in their homeland less than two years before to stage a revolution Bush had been reluctant to support, despite the fact that its genesis was the one word now being increasingly used in Washington to justify intervention in the Persian Gulf — democracy.

In those first weeks following Saddam's occupation of Kuwait the unmistakable whiff of a nation preparing for war was added to the atmospheric pollution of Washington. It was part gung-ho, part fear, and part resignation and even resentment that it should have come at such a time.

The Persian Gulf crisis came in the wake of the collapse of Communism in Eastern Europe, and while the bone-picking continued over America's intervention in Panama. Yet the Iraqi action that burst upon the capital, catching unawares the powerful and the pretenders alike, had the potential to be more widespread than the quicksand of Vietnam.

The consensus in Washington was that deep in his fortified command bunker in Baghdad, Saddam had put into operation the first stage of a plan to reshape the Middle East in his image and create mayhem for the world's economic and political processes. Immediately at stake were Western oil supplies and the survival of Israel. Over both loomed the prospect of an even deeper worldwide recession, accompanied by the prospect of *jihad*, holy war, with Saddam leading hordes of fanatical fundamentalists in a struggle to the death against all Arab moderates and infidels in the region.

Saddam was no mere desert tribesman with grandiose dreams. He commanded the fourth most powerful military force on earth: a million men under arms, six thousand battle tanks in addition to those the Chinese had provided. With it came not only a potential nuclear capacity but also one of the world's largest stockpiles of chemical and biological weapons. There, too, China had played a key role, providing some of the ingredients and expertise.

In intelligence-gathering terms there was no great secret about any of this information. But the French and British security services, like the CIA, saw no real threat. Most agreed Saddam was *"protecting himself"* — the words are from a leaked report of the Service of External Documentation and Counterespionage [SEDCE], the French security service, in July 1990 — against Iran. Only Israel continued to warn about Saddam's probable intentions. But, not for the first time, Tel Aviv was out of favor in Western capitals. Its warnings were seen as self-serving.

The very day before Saddam invaded Kuwait, the CIA sent Bush a briefing paper on the region. It categorically stated that Iraq posed *"no immediate military threat."* Barely able to control his anger at such a grave intelligence miscalculation, the President had ordered, days after the invasion, a line drawn in the sands of Arabia across which Saddam would move at his peril.

The drift to war accelerated as through Washington's prism Saddam increasingly became the unacceptable face of Arab nationalism. For Bush it was soon all too clear that Iraq's leader was imbued with the Nietzschean principle that power is a good in itself. But the President determined America would disabuse Saddam of that idea, with the support of the rest of the world.

To maintain the moral high ground, Bush and Baker and their aides worked the phones out of Washington to cajole, remind, and reason or plead with nations to support the United States in a tough stand against Iraq.

Australia was quickly followed by Holland, Pakistan by Japan, Morocco by Egypt. The nations of NATO joined what remained of the Warsaw Pact. Mother Russia herself said she would support U.N.-approved action to drive Saddam out of Kuwait.

Finally only China still vacillated over the use of force in the two weeks before the U.N. deadline expired. While expressing its concern over Saddam's action against Kuwait, the Beijing regime continued to combine such talk with veiled criticism of an American-driven military action to remove Iraqi forces.

The longer China hesitated, the stronger grew the article of faith in Washington that the success of what was being planned — all-out war — depended on persuading the aged leadership in Beijing to support such action. No one in the administration undervalued the necessity of achieving this.

For a decade China had depended on arms sales to the Middle East and loaning out its technical expertise as yet another way to try and balance its embattled economy. In 1990, it had sold over $300 million worth of military hardware to Iraq, Iran, and Syria. That had also strengthened its political position as to what Premier Li Peng had called *"the new true friend of the Arabs."*

With the collapse of Marxism-Leninism in half a dozen countries in Eastern Europe, the People's Republic saw itself as the one surviving bastion against democracy. By definition, it had long held true in Beijing that anything bad for the United States was good for China.

Yet in its very role as Communism's great survivor, China had given the United States a hold over it. Within the upper echelons of the Bush administration this advantage had come to be known as the Tiananmen Trump. The card had been slipped into the State Department's diplomatic deck following the massacre of students in Beijing's historic Tiananmen Square on June 3, 1989.

For the preceding fifty-five days those students, encouraged by a million, and more, of their fellow citizens, had called for basic human rights in a unique and most dramatic way. They had peacefully called for democracy in the face of one of the world's currently most intransigent regimes. Young men and women with names often difficult to pronounce and, at best, an imperfect grasp of English had held the entire world in thrall.

There was Wuerkaixi, then a twenty-one-year-old bantam cock, whose dark good looks and all-knowing smile went with the California-style denims he wore. The anchor men of the network evening news shows — Rather, Jennings, and Brokaw — hung on his every word. He did not disappoint them. His swashbuckling manner and confrontational style epitomized what was happening on Tiananmen Square. Within a week of first appearing there, Wuerkaixi received the ultimate accolade: His face appeared on T-shirts around the world.

Wang Dan achieved similar instant fame. At the time barely twenty years old, his wan face and physical frailty fitted the popular image of the fearless intellectual. His sweatshirts, baggy pants, and hand-me-down black cotton shoes became a style imitated on campuses around the world. His words were endlessly quoted. He had become the latest folk hero for a voracious media.

So had Chai Ling, an elfin-faced twenty-three-year-old. Her matchstick figure strode across the television screens of mesmerized nations. It somehow did not matter that what she said had to be translated. In any language it was a recognizable clarion cry, one that reflected her boundless energy and good humor. She was the revolution's La Pasionaria — and hauntingly pretty, too.

There was Liu Gang, tall, slim, and almost handsome, with a liking for Western-style casual clothes that could have come off the rack at Sears. He was the pensive-faced twenty-eight-year-old in the TV group shots of the student leaders — the brilliant, if at times quixotic, thinker, who knew which emotional button to push.

In those same group shots there sometimes appeared a young couple: Yang Li and his girlfriend, who like many of the student activists preferred to be known by one name, in her case her forename, Meili. Yang Li had the unfathomable face of a thousand generations of peasants, a physical reminder he was, indeed, the first of his farming family to have reached higher education. Meili had the pale skin of a city girl and the manner and mores of the middle class. They made a striking couple.

There was Yan Daobao. His tall and languid appearance masked a sharp political mind. To revolution he brought the broadening experience of a spell in California. With it came a preference for being known by his forename, Daobao.

Among them they had dominated the world's airwaves, showing themselves the natural masters of the news bite, the telling quote, and the dramatic decision timed to gain their cause the widest possible exposure. They had seemed unstoppable. The seeds of fire burning in their souls had appeared strong enough to sweep away their aged rulers and the deeply repressive system they had created fifty years before to control the world's most populous nation.

For those fifty-five days in Beijing, and elsewhere in China, it had appeared the students were going to succeed in overthrowing their recent past in the full glare of the media army drawn to witness what was happening.

No one — not the reporters on the spot, their editors at their desks — stopped to ask if this could really be allowed to happen, not just by China's rulers, but by all the other Western leaders, who each had a vested interest in ensuring that the status quo remained.

There was Britain with its vast trading ties to China. Her Majesty's then-prime minister, Margaret Thatcher, had made it plain that she wanted nothing — and no one — to threaten those trade links. Her attitude found its echo in Paris, Bonn, and all those European capitals where governments approved massive business deals with China, on any given day worth billions of dollars.

This attitude found its ready supporters in Washington, in all the corridors and offices where profit ruled supreme, where the view of China was primarily that of a vast untapped market. Its people — already more numerous than the combined populations of the United States, the Soviet Union, and all of Europe — represented a nation ready for Western investment and know-how. Every year twelve million more Chinese were born, each one adding to the attraction of the marketplace.

The students had threatened all this by using a word they insisted would shake off that cruel jibe of Karl Marx: that their country was *"a carefully preserved mummy in a hermetically sealed coffin."*

The word was democracy.

To emphasize the importance of their demand, the students had chosen as their rallying point the ninety-eight acres of Tiananmen Square. Larger than St. Peter's Square in Rome or Red Square in Moscow, larger than any square on earth, Tiananmen is still widely held among the superstitious people of China to be the very core of their world; they believe those who hold this *"square of heavenly peace"* will also control China's destiny.

For those fifty-five days, the square became the setting for unprecedented confrontation. On the one side were the students, who drew their strength from the truism that history for the Chinese is not an objective account of the past, but an endless morality tale, in which the characters must be explicit heroes and villains. Opposing them were those who believed it was their historical duty to ensure that China remained a world unto itself.

Among much else, at stake was China's place in tomorrow's world — whether it would become the next Pacific superpower in the twenty-first century, and what role the United States would have in guiding it there.

Weeks before the first student marched, in the small colony of embassies in China's capital, expectations had reached fever pitch. The diplomats knew from what people were saying, and sensed from the attitude of Chinese officials, that momentous events were taking place, that the founding fathers of the communist regime were increasingly locked in a deadly power struggle. Yet China, as they also knew, remained what it was at the time of the emperors: a country where mystery is a cult, secrecy a religion.

Ambassadors asked each other how they could penetrate the bamboo walls when their embassies were like so many fortresses permanently under siege by the agents of Public Security. The *Gonganbu,* who followed their every move, listened shamelessly to their telephone conversations, vetted their telexes, opened their mail, and interrogated their domestic staff daily.

American diplomats worked, albeit often uneasily, alongside their Soviet counterparts. The envoys of Britain and France found themselves in the same *hutongs,* the alleys of Beijing, as their colleagues from Poland and Romania. Australia's diplomats dogged the paths of the Japanese. The envoys of Iran and Iraq hurried after each other. It was, remembers one European diplomat, *"rather like something out of Alice in Wonderland."*

Yet at first it often seemed to the diplomats that their governments were not heeding what was being reported. In London, Washington, and elsewhere, China watchers in foreign ministries disagreed about what the portents meant; politicians tried to fit the pieces into their constantly changing global jigsaws.

But many weeks before the first public call for democracy rose over Tiananmen Square, a number of governments knew what was about to happen and, like the United States, had decided their responses would be dictated by wider considerations. For America, among much else, there was the need to maintain its CIA listening posts on the Sino-Soviet border and build upon its ever-expanding trading links with China. For the Soviet Union, there was the question of what effect the students would have on Mikhail Gorbachev's historic state visit to China. For Australia and other countries around the Pacific Rim, there were equally pressing economic and political questions to be considered.

In every capital city with ties to China, preparations on how to react gathered momentum with what was happening on the university campuses in Beijing. There, student factions were increasingly penetrated by the intelligence services of the superpowers, and their every change of plan became quickly known in Washington and Moscow. It was, said one intelligence officer there, the most penetrated student movement since the sixties. Those reports all helped leaders such as George Bush come to a decision.

While the world watched the unfolding drama in Tiananmen Square, President Bush was secretly balancing pressures from the CIA and his military and economic advisers on the one hand to do nothing to endanger the administration's links to the Beijing regime, and from the American people on the other to support the students.

In the end, political pragmatism prevailed. In Washington, London, and other capitals, decisions were taken that however harshly the Chinese leadership chose to deal with the students, those leaders would not be ostracized for long. There would be official condemnation, of course, if only to defuse public anger over their actions. But it must not go beyond that: Political, military, and economic relationships with China were too important to be seriously disrupted.

In all the places where they could reasonably have expected a firm commitment of support — Bush's Oval Office, Thatcher's Downing Street, and the offices of other leaders who fell into line — the students had become for all practical purposes expendable by those fateful days in June 1989.

They were crushed with a savagery that, for sheer ferocity equaled that displayed by Genghis Khan when he brought China into the Mogul Empire in 1263. Some seven hundred years later the descendants of Khan's warriors, serving in the People's Liberation Army, mangled the living beneath their tank treads and machine-gunned civilians in numerous cities and towns far from Beijing. People were burned alive or drowned. Afterward, the dead were cremated in great pyres whose stench lasted for weeks.

After watching them die on prime time television, President Bush issued carefully worded protests. He sounded genuinely anguished. But the economic sanctions he finally imposed on China were even more ineffective than those in force against Iraq in those opening weeks of 1991.

In 1989, China's leaders, weaned on a lifetime of violent retribution, were no doubt surprised and relieved at how light their punishment proved to be for crushing the principle over which now, eighteen months later, the United States was pledged to wage war against Iraq.

In January 1991 the Beijing leadership knew that the last vestiges of China's ostracism after the Tiananmen Square massacre were effectively at an end. Already, China was trading vigorously not only with the Middle East, but also with many other countries that had condemned its murderous actions in June 1989. Only the United States had continued to show a certain reluctance to forgive, if not quite forget. But the old men in Beijing could afford to wait.

Experience told them their moment was surely coming. China's humiliations by Western imperialism during the nineteenth century, its subjection to invasion and pillage by a succession of foreign warlords, and, more recently, attempts to remove the rigid Communism they had imposed on the Middle Kingdom — all this was about to be avenged. America, the old men told each other, needed China more than China needed the United States. But Bush would have to pay a price, because China, too, had a Tiananmen Trump in its deck.

In those crucial two weeks before the U.N. deadline for war with Iraq arrived, both sides began to play their trumps for all they were worth.

The Chinese understood Bush. He had lived among them. His mind-set was closer to theirs than most other Western leaders'. He would understand their complexity, what they would want in return for their support. Besides, their demand would be no great surprise to the President, just as he could not have been astonished at how they had finally dealt with the students in June 1989. The Chinese leaders knew at that time that the President had a very clear understanding of what they would do. The CIA and other intelligence agencies had warned him. That he had chosen to act as he had, issuing little more than the mandatory protest, was an encouragement to play their Tiananmen Trump as calculatingly as any riverboat gambler.

In Washington the anonymous men of the State Department China Desk met their counterparts from the People's Republic's embassy a few blocks from the White House.

They made their separate ways along one-way Jackson Place to climb the six steps that lead up to the door of number 716, a government-owned brick townhouse with a long history of hosting clandestine meetings. The 113-year-old building, whose four stories seem out of proportion to its narrow frontage, had been the base for Vice-President Nelson A. Rockefeller's investigation into the CIA's notorious domestic activities in the Sixties. It had been here, too, that a former CIA director, Admiral Stansfield Turner, had briefed Bush's predecessor, Ronald Reagan, about the close intelligence links between China and the United States when it came to spying on Russia in the days when Moscow was still the perceived enemy.

The precise cut and thrust of the negotiations — who first said what, who first went back for fresh instructions, who first bluffed and counterbluffed — is a matter of conjecture. One China Desk hand who was privy to some of the discussions likened it to *"playing poker blindfolded."*

Yet it was no winner-take-all game. Both sides knew they could walk away as victors.

On the conference table was a very simple premise. In return for Beijing's support at the United Nations, the United States would make no public objection to China's "final solution" for all their student leaders who had been imprisoned without trial after the Tiananmen Square massacre. Beijing had now decided they were to stand trial the day after the deadline against Iraq expired. If the cynicism of the move stuck in American throats around the table, none showed it. This, after all, was what real politics was all about.

Besides, those matchstick-like figures on Tiananmen Square who had less than two years before dominated the news were, perhaps thankfully, largely forgotten. Almost certainly there would be no public clamor over their fate. A fearful world had something bigger now to occupy its attention: the ever-advancing countdown to conflict in the Persian Gulf, the imminent possibility of the first full-scale war since Vietnam — so Secretary Baker's men and the diplomats of China told each other as they examined the advantages of cooperation.

Finally it was done. The Chinese could have their show trials without protest from Washington. Bush would have Beijing's support for a war like no other.

When it emerged that the President, in return for China's support, intended to say or do nothing to condemn such a flagrant mockery of what he held dear — democracy — one of China's foremost dissidents, Liu Binyan, scholar-in-residence at the Woodrow Wilson International Center for Scholars in Washington, wrote an impassioned plea. He asked Bush to remember there was no real difference *"between the butchers of Beijing and the bully of Baghdad."*

Liu documented in the *New York Times* how, since the onset of the Persian Gulf crisis, China had skillfully manipulated the event to its advantage *"and rescued itself from being the pariah of the world. The U.S., Japan and the European (business) community, as well as the World Bank and the Asia Development Bank, are lifting sanctions and restrictions on access to China without any substantial improvement in human rights."*

He listed a number of leaders in China's pro-democracy movement who had disappeared into the country's pernicious prison system. Liu pleaded with Bush to remember *"these men are pleading for freedom for all of us. Please don't forget them so easily."*

There was no response from the White House or from anyone else in the administration.

A decision had been taken. The Tiananmen Trump had been played by both sides.

This is the untold story of how the trump card was created from that noblest of motives, a desire for democracy, and the basest of motives, its suppression.

3

Seeds of Fire

The six-story structure on the corner of M and First streets in the southeast quadrant of the city is known as Federal Building 213. It resembles a warehouse and appears no different from all the others around the old Washington Navy Yard on the bank of the Anacostia River. It is, however, enclosed by a fence strengthened to resist a Beirut-style car bomber, and its gates are guarded by armed men.

There are further indications that this nondescript building houses some of the most important elements in America's strategic defense network. The first is the blue-and-white sign above the main entrance: NATIONAL PHOTOGRAPHIC INTERPRETATION CENTER. The second is the massive air-conditioning plant bolted to one side of 213. Seventy-five feet long and rising through floor after floor of bricked-in windows, the system cools the computers inside the building. Some are the size of a room, others of a house. The real monsters run the length of an entire floor. Day and night they sift and scan millions of pieces of information, slotting them into place among billions of items already stored in the database.

The computers are sophisticated enough to correct distortion coming from the imaging sensors aboard the satellites the United States has positioned in space, eliminate atmospheric effects, sharpen out-of-focus images, turn them into three-dimensional objects, enhance the contrast between objects and their backgrounds, and, if need be, remove them totally from their surroundings for closer inspection. The computers also eliminate sun glare, take away shadows, and image objects totally obscured by cloud by using infrared radar. They can even use their radar "lenses" to penetrate the earth and locate a thermonuclear rocket secure in its silo, or missiles hidden in a tunnel.

The processors and photo interpreters make sense of what the computers uncover. They draw facts out of darkness by applying the art of informed conjecture. Among them on an average day the technicians study a million prints. In this building the truth was first established about the Chernobyl meltdown, Libya's poison gas factory, Iraq's use of chemical weapons in its war with Iran, and Pakistan's nuclear weapons. Those who work here kid each other they will be the first to see Doomsday.

On the third floor are the China watchers. As well as monitoring its military installations — missile silos, air bases, weapons factories, nuclear reprocessing plants — they keep track of China's agricultural and industrial development, its oil and gas production. They look for anything that can provide further insights into the country's present situation.

They study images varying from landscapes of twisted pines and misty waterfalls — the Shangri-la of ancient scrolls — to the arid steppes of the Gobi. The majestic topography does not interest them. They are looking for such clues as a new railroad spur, unfamiliar vehicle tracks around a factory, freshly dug earth near an air base. From past experience the technicians know such signs can speak volumes.

Now, eighteen months before the events in Tiananmen Square would become ingrained in the memory of untold millions of people, one of the photo interpreters assigned to keep watch over Beijing processed a sequence of satellite photographs taken from high over the city. They showed an area several miles to the west of the great square, which was as usual filled with milling crowds of sightseers.

The balding American with a degree in computer sciences knew that to those Chinese visible on his photographs, the square was the core of their world. At its very center, a little blob on the sat-photo, was the gate called Tiananmen. From it, a mere pinhead, was suspended the photo of Mao Zedong. It was a reminder that after nineteen centuries of European rule, fifty years of Communism continued to exercise its iron control over the people.

Today, what was happening on Tiananmen did not concern the technician. His interest lay in what was occurring in the city's western district. First he used an infrared scanner, rather like a microscope, to search every microdot of each print for details. He constantly checked against previous photos of the vicinity and he observed a change since he had last "tasked," or searched, the area.

On the keyboard of his video display unit, he tapped in instructions that gave him access to the computer in which all of China is reduced to digital imagery.

Moments later, on the screen appeared a high-definition three-dimensional image of a military barracks in a corner of the district. Its parade square was filled with hundreds of soldiers. The technician pressed a tab to produce a hard copy from the laser printer beside the screen. A 24" x 24" photo appeared in seconds. He keyed the next image onto the screen. In all he made fifteen prints. He arranged them on a viewing frame on the wall and peered intently at them, rather like a surgeon studying X-rays.

Next he fed further instructions to the computer. Onto the screen came a succession of close-up images of some of the soldiers. Their heavy winter clothing was clearly visible. Again he made hard copies, and then clipped them beneath the others on the viewing screen. He typed in a further command. Onto the screen came a star bedded in cloth. It was an enlargement of a shoulder-tab of an officer's uniform.

The technician took a print and compared it against a number of others, trying to match the blow-up with epaulets on the photos. He began to select photographs, laying them out on a long table beside the printer. After a while he started to make notations on the prints, using a marker pen to draw circles, arrows, and boxes around various objects. Finally he assembled the prints into a set. Then he began to type on the keyboard.

"Nineteen photographs processed. They cover various resolutions. No cloud cover or atmospheric distortion. Photo sequence (1–8) shows the People's Liberation Army Barracks Number Four in Wangshow District, West Beijing. Photo sequence (9–13) shows it is currently HQ of the 27th Army. Photo sequence (14–19) indicates elements of the Army are leaving. They are probably being sent to Tibet...."

His report completed, the technician electronically transmitted it. Simultaneously it would appear in the Central Intelligence Agency's Office of Imagery Analysis at Langley and in the Analysis Center at Bolling Air Force Base operated by the Defense Intelligence Agency.

From there it would make its way up through the intelligence community — the generic term for all U.S. intelligence agencies and departments of which the director of Central Intelligence is the most senior officer — until finally, if deemed important enough, it would form part of the President's Daily Brief, a summary of the most sensitive and exclusive of gleaned intelligence.

The last time the technician's work had appeared on the brief had been when he had processed details about the previous year's student unrest in Beijing. Then, the satellite cameras had clearly caught the reaction of the Beijing authorities, a massive crackdown with widespread street arrests. Since then there had been no noticeable sign of student activity.

The technician began to study the latest images from the Zhongnanhai compound in Beijing.

The satellite cameras had again photographed a group of old men shuffling along the towpath beside their private lake. The interpreter's task was to identify who was present and who was missing from the Chinese leadership. The intelligence analysts at Langley, the State Department, and other federal agencies had learned to tell a great deal from a man's presence or absence on the towpath, from whom he walked beside or avoided. When a man was not there, was he sick? Or out of favor? Or even dead?

The technician knew this report would have an eager reader in Vice-President George Bush, soon, barring an unforeseen disaster, to become the forty-first President of the United States. When he was director of Central Intelligence, Bush had insisted he be shown every intelligence item about China, however inconsequential. The old men of Zhongnanhai had long been a Bush fixation. He had been known to call at the oddest hours for more details about their latest sightings. He was like a birdwatcher. No matter how many times he saw them shuffling along, George Bush wanted to know more.

MONDAY, NOVEMBER 7, 1988
ZHONGNANHAI COMPOUND
BEIJING

Some of those old men walked with the help of tubular steel frames. Others used sticks fashioned from the hardwoods of the rain forests bordering Burma and Vietnam. Their movements were measured, like those of automatons, as metal and wood supports clunked over the ground. Several needed the assistance of a nurse; each woman was young and physically strong. Following at a distance, male attendants propelled electrically driven wheelchairs equipped with oxygen cylinders should any of the aged leaders require resuscitation. Behind came the ambulances. Over fifty people were required as backup for this evening stroll by men who looked like ghosts in faded photographs.

They were the survivors of that most epic of feats, one almost unequaled in the annals of war: the Long March of 1934. They had made an unforgettable two-year journey of six thousand miles — across mountain ranges and provinces larger than most European states. Theirs was at once a strategic military retreat, an escape from the terrible reality of brother killing brother, and a major and significant Communist migration, leading to eventual nationhood. When it began on October 16, 1934, 86,829 soldiers, each one solemnly counted and promised a special role in his country's future, headed out across China. Few, even their leaders, knew their destination. Many would die before it could be reached.

One of the first decisions of the surviving cadres after Mao Zedong proclaimed a new China on October 1, 1949, was to create their compound in the lee of the Forbidden City, from which the Emperors had ruled for seven hundred years.

The 250 acres of Zhongnanhai had been turned into one of the most fortified enclaves on earth.

Today there are guard posts in the most unexpected of places: cut into the trunks of trees, each niche just large enough for a man to wedge himself in position; in the wooden pavilions dotting the parkland; concealed in shrubbery. There are sensors, tripwires, and remote cameras. No aircraft is permitted to overfly. Only helicopters ferrying the old men to and from their summer palaces in the hills to the west of the city disturb their peace in the middle of one of the world's most congested cities.

Their homes are scattered along the eastern shore of the lake. Many are the size of palaces, with often thirty and more bedrooms, swimming pools, and Jacuzzis. They are furnished with artifacts removed from the Forbidden City. Each mansion has its retinue of servants and guards, who live on the northern side of the lake in several barracks-like buildings screened by trees.

There are over a hundred varieties of trees and shrubs planted in the grounds, each a reminder of the vegetation the old men saw on the Long March.

The leaders' workplaces overlook the western lakeshore. Mao had ordered the lake stocked with carp. Initially, a hundred thousand were dumped there; over the years the number of protected fish increased to several million. The water is dark with their feces, and on a summer's day an unpleasant smell rises from the lake.

The few foreigners admitted to this sanctum: diplomats, visiting dignitaries, are generally brought to the prime minister's compound.

The uniform style of its buildings and the careful alignment of the shrouding roofs create a feeling of unassailable authority.

The architecture, say his enemies, and they are many, had been carefully ordered by the country's first minister, Li Peng. At sixty-one years of age, the dominant parts of his character had intensified, creating in him a near megalomania, a preoccupation with his astrological calendar, and a fascination with fungi — the most potent mushrooms prepared in a broth, which he drank slowly to regenerate his essential *Qi*, which all Chinese believe to be the driving force of life.

He also had two obsessions. One was flying his kite. He had the most elaborate silk kite in all Zhongnanhai. In the summer months, when the air was thick and moist and warm, he would spend hours sending it spinning, the tails flowing in perfect concentrics, creating the swirling circles of the master calligrapher he was.

The other obsession, one guaranteed to darken his face, was the students of China. In his mind their education, instead of inspiring gratitude, had made them question the authority he represented. He had crushed them before; he would do so again. Yet he also secretly feared them, and he had prepared accordingly.

Beneath the compound's rolling lawns and paved walkways, one finds a place still more secret and inaccessible. It can be reached only from inside the homes and offices of the old men. Should the day come and the high walls of Zhongnanhai be breached, this would be their escape route, through steel doors in the basement of each building to elevators descending to a railway platform. The old men, their families, and others chosen to go with them would board a train that would haul them fifteen miles underground to an airfield in the Western Hills. From there they would be flown to one of several other protected enclaves to continue to rule China.

The train is permanently manned and ready to move at short notice.

Until recently, the old men had every reason to believe they would never have to use it. They had created a dictatorship like no other. It was the most perfect of all control systems: the people watching the people. Those who reported any deviation from the Party line — and the Party had one for everything, from sex to marriage, from birth to the actual form of approved funeral — were given extra food and privileges. Generations of children had been encouraged to inform on their parents and teachers, on anyone who stepped outside the defined limits of what is permissible. The system had always been at the core of what is still the world's most profound revolution.

It had begun with Mao's promise of *"socialistic transformation"* of the economy. His stated goal was to equal, and then surpass, the industrial capacity of Great Britain, the country that had been China's only peer in industrial production at the turn of the century and had inflicted some of the worst humiliations on China.

Initially Mao's vision had enjoyed widespread popular support. China was ready to make a dramatic leap into the modern age.

Then came the plan to merge the country's agricultural cooperatives into the so-called People's Communes. The new system led to massive population dislocation, violence, and famine. Economic blight swept the land. Some twenty-seven million people died.

Mao, his paranoia more acute than ever, launched the Cultural Revolution. He mobilized the youth of China to do his bidding. Millions of teenagers wielded power far beyond their understanding. Deng Xiaoping and other leaders were exiled.

The lesson of how to use the nation's young was not lost on Deng when he regained power in the wake of Mao's death. Deng too wanted to see China a world economic power. To achieve this goal, he courted China's much-maligned intellectuals. He also set about winning over the country's younger generation, that half of the nation's population born after the founding of the People's Republic. They now numbered some 650 million articulate and ambitious men and women under thirty. Encouraged by Deng, they increasingly gave voice to demands for higher education, good jobs, decent housing, and protection against arbitrary exercises of authority. Above all they demanded the right to at least a modicum of expression. They asked for some form of democracy.

For a while it seemed as if Communism and the right of choice would coexist. Foreign investment flowed into the country. Private enterprise thrived, especially in the consumer sector. China's brightest and best were encouraged to study abroad. Harvard University reported Beijing University was among the top ten feeder schools in the world for America's graduate programs. But the sheer pace of the changes and the problem of a state and private sector operating in tandem created tensions.

Nowhere were these tensions more keenly felt than among the old men in Zhongnanhai. Some said the freedoms created a loss of ideological control; that the very authority of the Party was in danger of being swept away. Others argued the loosening of restrictions was the unavoidable consequence of reform. The debate became fiercer, the battle lines more clearly drawn.

Once more the students became a focal point for the divided leadership. They were increasingly at the forefront in challenging the monopoly of the Party to make policy. The students wanted greater economic reforms, faster. They demanded political pluralism, now. They insisted on full human rights, not merely a relaxing of restrictions, and at once. They wanted democracy, immediately.

Some of the old men cautiously supported them. Others, like Li Peng, ferociously argued that even a tinge of democracy would eventually destroy the China they had created. They pointed to what was happening in Russia. The first sign of democracy was threatening to topple the Kremlin itself.

These evening walks along the lakeside, once a chance to relax at the end of a day, had become often tense occasions.

Among those leaning on the arm of a nurse was Yao Yilin, seventy-two years old. His clothes hung on him. With his head of gray cobwebs and crumpled cheeks, he looked like a scarecrow. Only his eyes remained sharp; they watched from their corners, giving his face a shifty look. When he was happy, he whistled through his teeth, though no one had ever seen him laugh. When he was angry, his skin, already taut, drew tighter around his eyes and mouth.

Yao was a hardliner, who said the greatest danger China faced would be for its people to forget their recent past. For Yao, there could be no compromise with the uncompromising discipline that had made China the great alternative to Soviet Marxism. His voice was even more querulous on those occasions when Hu Yaobang joined the group on the towpath.

In 1982, Deng had confirmed Hu as his successor, appointing him Party Secretary. Hu stunned everyone, inside and beyond Zhongnanhai, by placing himself at the forefront of not only economic reforms but also political changes. He began to attack official ideology, the hitherto sacred totem. He defined Marxism without the usual Leninist imperatives. He set about shaking the Party to its core.

Within four years he had swept the country toward a new society that few could have dreamed possible. The students hung on his every word. Young voices gave throat to one demand: democracy. There were near riots as hundreds of thousands challenged the Party's authority. Deng was forced to send in battalions of police. The leading demonstrators were either shot or sent to labor camps. Many were children of senior cadres. The elders of Zhongnanhai personally petitioned Deng to sack Hu. Reluctantly he did. But he insisted there would be no further punishment.

Hu had continued to promote Western ideas, encouraging China's youth to imitate the lifestyle of America's and Europe's young. Hu himself had visited Western fashion shows and gone to premieres of foreign films.

As usual the former Party Secretary general walked unaided. Hu's Western-style clothes somehow increased his resemblance to an ornamental garden gnome. He had a pointy chin and solemn dark eyes that darted everywhere, from the carp in the lake to the guards trailing behind the old men. Hu had once joked to President Carter's foreign affairs adviser, Zbigniew Brzezinski, who was now a member of President Bush's Foreign Intelligence Advisory Board, that inside Zhongnanhai some people didn't feel safe.

As the daylight began to fade, one man continued to move briskly among the others. The gossip, hearsay, speculation, and complaints flowed around him like water around a rock. No one asked what he thought. People had learned not to do that.

Qiao Shi was unusually tall for a Chinese, almost six feet. But he stooped, rumor had it, as a result of too many hours as a child spent studying the written Chinese language. Through native intelligence and sheer will, he had found his key to the world of radicals, strokes, phonetics, and recensions. The discipline of learning and remembering was a good training for his present position. As director of the Chinese Secret Intelligence Service, CSIS, he had been China's spymaster for the past fourteen years. He was on this day close to his sixty-fifth birthday, still with a taste for French cognac and Cuban cigars. But his laughter never quite reached his eyes. He had a way of making people's heads turn. It was more than a curious magnetism. It was an ability to suggest he could see what they were thinking.

He ran intelligence networks that extended across the Pacific into the United States and Europe and back again through the Middle East into China. He was a chief with hundreds of spies in place and a budget for bribery and blackmail rivaled only by those of the CIA and KGB. He answered only to Deng Xiaoping. The labor camps of central China were filled with those who had dared to challenge Qiao.

Because of who he was, even the most senior of the cadres treated him with respect. No one would have dared to point out that for a man in his position, he was a poor dresser; often his chain-store socks did not match. He usually looked as if he had gone to a shop in one of the city's alleys and reached for the first garments at hand. People assumed there was a purpose to this style, other than eccentricity.

They reminded themselves Qiao had always been a sly one. His entire career consisted of adroit, low-key moves; he had moved from one ministry to another with the minimum of notice. One day he had been a diplomat, the next entrenched as head of state security.

The essential certainty concerning Qiao was that he knew all the secrets, the peccadilloes and personal shortcomings within the leadership. He knew who was already corrupted, who could be corrupted. He knew the exact state of Deng Xiaoping's health and how long he was likely to remain in office. Qiao had his spies everywhere.

Now his agents were reporting that the students once more showed signs of unrest. Qiao had urged that their leaders should be arrested. Deng Xiaoping had refused. He had made it clear he would do nothing until the outcome of the struggle between two of the other old men.

One was Li Peng.

The other was Zhao Ziyang, the new Party Secretary. Recently Zhao had taken to wearing tinted glasses in his thick frame spectacles. His enemies — like the prime minister's, they too were many and multiplying — said this was a further sign of his affection for Western standards. Tinted glasses went with Zhao's wardrobe of silk suits, his fondness for Kentucky bourbon and reading Bismarck. At seventy, Zhao remained perfectly cast in the traditional role of the wise adviser who did not flinch from telling Deng hard truths. For years he and Li Peng appeared politically twinned. They sat side by side in the Politburo and on the review stand for the great parades on Tiananmen Square; they shared the toasts at important state banquets. Li Peng's remoteness seemed the ideal foil for Zhao's ebullience.

Their friendship was now dead. Some said it was over on that summer's day in 1987 when Deng decided Zhao would have Hu Yaobang's post. Like everyone else, the prime minister recognized it was Deng's way of anointing Zhao as his new successor.

Zhao had surrounded himself with some of the ablest of China's young scholars and technocrats. Many had studied abroad. Others came straight from China's universities into the think tanks he established around Beijing. They had produced a raft of proposals for further economic and political changes. These included freeing prices and disposing of state-owned companies into private ownership.

Zhao skillfully removed from office many conservatives who protested these ideas were as reformist as Hu's. He did so at the time Deng announced he was retiring from the day-to-day political scene to concentrate on managing the affairs of the Central Military Commission. No one doubted the commission's importance in the country's affairs, but everyone also knew the commission could run perfectly well without Deng constantly at the helm.

Deng Xiaoping, the great architect of change, had cleared the stage for an epic struggle, one as titanic as any Mao had engineered. Recognizing that the Marxist-Leninist praxis, the unity of theory and action, no longer commanded universal respect as the only way to social reconstruction, the country's supreme leader had deliberately decided on a monumental gamble: to risk China returning to political instability while a murderous struggle continued around him as to whose policies would lead the nation into the next century, Zhao's or Li Peng's.

In appointing Zhao as Party chief, Deng plainly indicated his own preference. Yet in allowing Li Peng to apply the brake, Deng was also showing he was not prepared to allow unrestricted political dissent to outpace economic reform.

The grain deficit, the pork shortage, and every kind of bureaucratic malfeasance had become an issue. So had the rising expectations of the people. Li Peng argued these were far beyond the state's capacity. He had recently said *"ideological flexibility"* had reached *"maximum tolerance"*; China was already in an inflationary spiral that was in danger of going out of control.

Zhao had continued to urge that China should allow free enterprise to flourish. He called for more foreign investment and for China to *"embrace the world."* That was, he said, the only way to curb inflation and unleash economic dynamism, create a true market economy, ensure growth, and satisfy the ever-louder demand for democracy.

For the young intellectuals, especially the country's students, his had been a vision for China's Camelot. At first it seemed that Zhao would sweep all before him. But a year after he had proclaimed his ideals, inflation and corruption continued to increase. Finally the students had started to criticize Zhao for not doing more to curb both.

Li Peng had increasingly attacked what he branded *"revisionist innovations"* and condemned Zhao for leading the nation's youth dangerously astray.

Zhao needed the students' support to convince his opponents in Zhongnanhai that the monolithic world they had all created was doomed and that social rebirth was only possible by recognizing *"we are not in the situation envisaged by the founders of Marxism."* The Party Secretary had begun a recent speech to the Politburo by saying:

"We cannot blindly follow what the books say. China's only way forward is for a prolonged period of non-socialist economic growth."

Li Peng condemned such ideas as *"an ideological formula largely devoid of ideological content"* and Zhao's approach as *"an open threat to the Party."*

Deng had listened impassively.

Clearly, all three saw that the country's students were both pawns and trumps in the developing crisis.

4

Illusions

THURSDAY, NOVEMBER 10, 1988
BEIJING

Some of those students pedaled down the avenue toward the massive gateway of Beijing University. It was late afternoon, the light already fading. With them was Cassy Jones, an American. She was a contract teacher, one of a number from overseas on campus who taught mostly languages. They were known as foreign experts.

Cassy was a couple of inches taller than most of the other cyclists and, at thirty, almost a generation older. Yet her freckles and lithe figure made her look like a student, even if no one on campus had her flaming red hair. As usual, it was braided into a ponytail. It gave her face a leaner and more determined look.

For as long as she could remember, China had held a fascination for Cassy. As a teenager she had been drawn to its exotic etiquette. At the end of high school she went on to study its language at college, majoring in Cantonese. Postgraduate studies improved her Mandarin. Several universities offered her positions. In the next six years she taught at several.

Cassy had voted Democrat until George Bush. She had supported his bid to be President because she knew he had spent time in China. She had cheerfully told some of the students she would have voted for any American politician who wanted to know more about their country.

Her attitude made Cassy one of the most popular foreigners on campus among the students. As usual, several vied to cycle close to her, to practice their English by asking more questions about life in America.

Among them was Li Yang, the first member of his peasant family to have made it to university. The twenty-year-old cycled effortlessly, his calf muscles hardened from a childhood spent toiling in his parents' rice field on the banks of the Yangzte River. Li had a brother, Bing, who was a soldier in the People's Liberation Army.

Next to Li rode his girlfriend, Meili, a petite twenty-year-old who liked wearing colorful scarves. Cassy was struck by how well the girl fitted the old Imperial image of beauty, the perfect oval face inset with almond-shaped eyes and rosebud lips. Meili's skin was pale. Cassy supposed her indoor pallor was a further attraction for the son of laborers.

Beside them the slight figure of Wang Dan pedaled steadily. In his padded jacket, baggy pants, and black cotton shoes, he looked the archetypical student. As usual the twenty-year-old was engaged in serious debate with those around him, his eyes glinting with passion behind the heavy frames of his glasses.

Yan Daobao rode alongside Cassy. His tall, muscular appearance contrasted with his soft way of speaking. But Cassy now knew that Daobao's languid ways masked a sharp political mind and determination. Like the others around her, he passionately believed China must embrace democracy if it were to take its rightful place in the world. As usual he cycled with one hand resting lightly on her shoulders, despite the rule that forbade any physical contact between foreigners and students.

There was so much Cassy was still coming to terms with about Daobao. The intensity of his feelings. The way he spoke to her, looked at her, touched her. She remembered only too vividly how they had met the day after she had arrived on campus and gone to the English Department.

The department appeared deserted, its bare corridors and stairs echoing like those of some abandoned monastery. The library was well stocked, with books in a dozen languages rising from floor to ceiling.

Cassy became aware a young Chinese had entered the library. He stood inside the door, watching her, arms folded. She smiled quickly and turned back to the shelves.

He told her where she could find Shakespeare and Dickens.

He had a gentle voice for someone so big and strong. She was also surprised by the American accent. Cassy asked if he was another foreign expert.

He shook his head and introduced himself, family name first, Chinese-style: Yan Daobao. He had spent the summer visiting a cousin at "Thomas Wolfe." He smiled his shy smile. *"They never let us read about our own decadence."*

Cassy let it pass, not wanting to be drawn into criticizing her host country. She asked if the library stocked Norman Mailer. He nodded. After a pause he asked her name and why she was there. In fluent Mandarin she told him.

His smile broadened. *"A foreign expert who speaks our language. Very good."*

As simply as that, their friendship had begun.

For the next hour Daobao led Cassy from one section to another, pulling out volumes, commenting and smiling. She was happy to let him.

At the poetry section she selected Schopenhauer's *World as Will and Idea* and said the book should be filed under philosophy.

Daobao took it from her and began to riffle through the pages.

Cassy looked into his face and said Schopenhauer argued that chance meetings often produced the most powerful sexual impulses.

Daobao said that was a very important observation.

The library door flew open. A short man in Mao jacket and baggy trousers stood on the threshold, his glasses glinting in the hard neon lighting. He rushed toward them, speaking Mandarin with such speed she barely understood him.

All she clearly caught was his name and position: Pang Yi, political officer.

Daobao calmly stepped between her and Pang Yi, who continued to scold. They had no right to be here! The library was closed until term opened! Why were they here? A foreign woman and a student? That was not permitted!

Daobao abruptly thrust the book into Pang's hands, nodded to Cassy, and walked out of the library. She followed, leaving Pang speechless.

At the end of her first day of teaching, Daobao waited in the corridor outside the classroom. He asked if she would like to come to an art exhibition. He was frank.

"It will be very boring. Party-approved art. I have to go. It is Comrade Pang's little punishment. He knows I hate art. Especially state-approved art. But if you come, it will be more bearable."

Laughing, she accepted.

At the entrance to the exhibition they found a scroll containing another of Mao's edicts. *"Art, for art's sake, art which transcends class or Party, art which stands as a bystander to, or independent of, politics, does not in actual fact exist."* The paintings reflected this sterile canon: portraits of healthy, smiling, pink-faced workers; landscapes filled with tractors; and the centerpiece, a huge oil painting of a hydroelectric plant with high-tension power lines draped across the countryside. There was not an abstract or nude to be seen.

As they left Cassy said, *"Schopenhauer would have hated the paintings."*

Daobao admitted he had returned to the library and borrowed the book. He had sat up most of the night reading it. He had wanted to know more about sexual impulses.

His directness continued to captivate her. Two nights later he took her to dinner in a restaurant behind the Friendship Hotel. They stayed until closing time. He cycled back with her to the hotel. After they dismounted, without a smile, with no word, but with great seriousness, he took her hands and gently removed them from her bicycle handlebars. She gave him no encouragement. He looked steadily at her. She thought he was like someone about to leap from a precipice, hoping she would catch him, not knowing if she would. He leaned down and gently kissed her on the mouth.

It seemed the most natural thing when she kissed him back.

In the evenings and on weekends they went for walks in the city's parks. They took the cable lift up Fragrant Hills, hoisted through the air in twin chairs to the summit, serenaded by loudspeakers playing "The Blue Danube" and other Strauss waltzes, and they strolled through the parkland at the peak. There were never any awkward silences between them.

She only fell silent when he expounded his views on China. Daobao said it was a country never designed for the social engineering of Communism. The promises to end poverty and backwardness had led to a system in which corruption was endemic. Fraud and open profiteering were an increasing problem. Only the other day a senior official in the oil distributing ministry was discovered receiving kickbacks of $1 million to divert fuel to the black market. How many more like him were hiding in the bureaucratic woodwork? Only full democracy, Daobao said, could flush out those profiteers.

Cassy thought Daobao could be very naive at times.

Beyond the Beijing University campus gate more cyclists merged with the group. Cassy thought again how in his California-style denims Wuerkaixi looked like another foreign expert. She still found it hard to believe he was a leading activist. The son of an important party official in remote Turkestan, Wuerkaixi had been raised and protected in the shadow of the Party. Yet when he entered Beijing Normal University the year before, he had quickly established himself as a radical.

He had spoken about the *"intellectual failure"* of Communism. How it had underestimated the importance of ethnicity and nationalism. How its policies were derived from a fatal misunderstanding of human nature. How it had failed to understand the basic craving for the right to self-expression and, above all, to enjoy political choice. How the Party failed to understand the connection between mass economic prosperity and the individual desire for personal freedom. How Communism had turned out to be a tragedy. Born out of impatient idealism, it promised a better and more caring society. Instead it had created oppression.

An hour after leaving the university, the cyclists reached Changan Avenue, the city's main thoroughfare. They slowly passed a long strip of billboards advertising sewing machines, vacuum cleaners, refrigerators, ovens, washing powders, and, always, family planning.

Daobao explained the signs concealed the site of Democracy Wall.

In 1978 a worker had displayed a handwritten poster offering the first public criticism of Mao. Others followed. Soon every city had its Democracy Wall. One of the most popular posters was a translation of the American Declaration of Independence: *"We hold these Truths to be self-evident, that all Men are created equal, that they are endowed by their Creator with certain unalienable rights, that among these are Life, Liberty, and the Pursuit of Happiness."* Democracy Wall had become the focus of a spontaneous, grass-roots movement for human rights in China.

Daobao continued speaking, his voice low and somber. He described how after four months the army had been sent to tear down the posters. The tension deepened his voice, driving him on. The past, she sensed, had left a deep scar on his psyche.

His parents, he explained, never understood about democracy. The family had a roof over their heads and sufficient food. They had not expected any more. His uncle, his mother's youngest brother, a teacher and a bachelor, seemed different. Every day after class he went to Democracy Wall to join in the protests. His school *danwei* or unit, expelled him. Short of imprisonment, there could be no greater punishment.

Cassy knew everyone in China must belong to a *danwei,* the place where they study or work. Even the youngest child in nursery school had to belong. Without a *danwei* affiliation a person was not allowed the basics of life. Instead, he or she literally became a non-person with no entitlements and no future within the state's all-embracing, all-constricting frame.

His uncle would have starved had Daobao's mother not taken a portion from her own family's bowls to feed him. An informer reported this kindness to the street *danwei* committee, who warned Daobao's mother that her family's food allowance would be reduced unless she stopped. His mother had hidden his uncle's bowl, feeding him secretly late at night. But the *danwei* was still after revenge. His uncle was a scholar, while its members were mostly uneducated. They deepened his public humiliation by making him stand before them to confess his crimes.

After six months, his uncle's school *danwei* said he could have a job at the school — cleaning toilets. Children he had taught were encouraged to spit on him. They were still doing so when he committed suicide. No one was allowed to go to the cremation except the family, because the *danwei* decided anyone who had advocated democracy should receive the minimum of mourning.

Daobao looked at Cassy and said all that must be very hard to understand. She nodded. It was.

They reached the staff entrance of one of the city's hospitals. A porter led them to a door at the end of a short corridor and pressed a bell-push. There was a faint hum, and the door slid open. Cold air rose from the darkness. Cassy found herself in a concrete chamber. In the far wall was a steel door, opened by pressing another button. Beyond was a tunnel.

Daobao explained they were in the city's nuclear defense system. Mao had ordered it built in 1969 when he thought the Russians were going to attack. Every major city in China had its network of shelters.

The group moved through one tunnel after another, each isolated by its steel doors, each section lit by the same low-wattage lights. At regular intervals were intersections with cross tunnels disappearing into the darkness. There was a distant humming sound. Daobao said it was the air conditioning.

They finally reached a large chamber with rows of benches, sufficient seating for hundreds. In one corner stood a podium. Daobao explained the place was originally intended for cadres to lecture the people on the virtues of Communism while they sheltered from a Soviet atomic holocaust.

Cassy shook her head, bewildered. The others settled themselves on the hard seats. She joined them.

Daobao walked to the podium, his head almost touching the curved roof. He stood for a moment, running a finger around the collar of his shirt, as if he wanted to free something inside. When he spoke, it was with a sudden certainty.

He reminded them they wanted so very little, and not for themselves, but for all those they spoke for. Applause swept the chamber. He silenced it with a wave of a hand. He said the time was fast approaching when they would again take to the streets. They must be ready to lay down their lives. That was a small price to pay for democracy.

For the first time Cassy felt uneasy.

His voice filling with passion, Daobao added they could be sure that the Western democracies would support them, and none more so than the next incumbent of the White House, George Bush. Daobao said he was certain the future President would understand how important it was to support the students in their aspiration to see China shake off the shackles of fifty years of stultifying Communism.

Once more Cassy thought how naïve Daobao could be.

SAME DAY, SAME TIME
HOSPITAL OF TRADITIONAL MEDICINE
BEIJING

Five floors above the chamber, in a small and hopelessly cluttered office, worked Professor Jia Guangzu, sixty-three, director of the hospital's "traditional medicine" department for the past nine years. He and his staff dispensed treatment that was far removed from modern Western concepts. A short man with a high domed forehead, the professor appeared a powerful advertisement for the figurine of the Longevity Goddess on the desk. Her ageless marble face rose above the mound of paperwork and medical products.

Jars were filled with slivers of deer antler for treating flatulence and scales of lizard skins for curing apoplexy. Vials contained the powder of pearls he prescribed as a tranquilizer. Tiny containers of snake oil for blood pressure, and bottles of anti-asthma pills made from the intestines of water rats, stood alongside sachets of crushed caterpillar, given for night sweats. There were pretty little boxes of powdered tiger bone for hypertension, tubes of ginseng jelly for baldness, extract of oxen penis to improve bone marrow, and frog essence to treat constipation.

Tongue diagnosis was Professor Guangzu's specialty. He could tell at a glance whether a stomach was not behaving properly, whether the fissure in a tongue indicated cancer or chronic hepatitis. Nowadays, people didn't always show proper respect for this ancient and, to Professor Guangzu, totally reliable method. If they did they wouldn't write the kind of curt and time-wasting letters he had to answer.

The State Insurance Office was challenging the cost of procedures. Could he explain an increase of a *yuan*, less than a dime, for burning the powdered root of the artemisia plant on the skin of a psoriasis sufferer? Or an extra *yuan* for every anesthetic performed by acupuncture?

The penny-pinching of the bureaucrats at times made Professor Guangzu wish he had taken up the offer to train the "barefoot doctors," the physicians who tramped the countryside, going from one commune to another, treating villagers. He envied them and their freedom.

Jenny, his daughter, had written that whenever she mentioned the scheme, her American colleagues were genuinely amazed to hear that young doctors were prepared to dedicate their lives to working in primitive conditions and living among illiterate peasants.

Sometimes he thought Jenny had become too Americanized. She had been in Los Angeles for over two years and was halfway through her postgraduate surgical studies. Her letters were increasingly filled with descriptions of what she called *"the good life"* in California: its supermarkets with their abundance of cheap food; low-cost fuel and cars. Their apartment was four times the size of what she and Zhong, her husband, could hope to rent in Beijing. It even had two separate bathrooms and a gas-fired barbecue on which she grilled steaks, each larger than a month's meat allowance for either of them in China.

Too much protein, he had gently reminded her, was bad for the blood. Zhong would confirm that. His son-in-law was a researcher, working on a cure for cancer.

The professor was glad they had gone to study abroad; he would be pleased when they returned. Jenny and Zhong had important roles to play in using what they had learned to benefit China. He also wanted his grandson, Peter, born in America, to grow up Chinese, not someone exposed to the lifestyle of southern California.

And, though he would never admit it to them, he would be glad to have them home because he was lonely. Since his wife had died ten years ago and Jenny, his only child, had gone to the States, there had been no one person he could really talk to except Hu Yaobang. But his evenings with his old friend were infrequent. Despite his loss of office, Hu was still involved in Politburo affairs.

Professor Guangzu would have liked to discuss with Hu the newspaper clippings Jenny had enclosed with her last letter. There was a story about how an immigration judge in San Francisco had granted political asylum to a Chinese couple who asserted they had fled Beijing after the man's wife had been forced to have an abortion under the Chinese government's policy that each family should have no more than one child. The issue had triggered a fierce debate in the United States. The professor suspected Hu would growl and ask what all the fuss was about — and how resisting Chinese family policies could amount to "political dissent."

Professor Guangzu felt that of more interest to the former Party chief would be the newspaper report that to supply the vast Chinese appetite for new airplanes, the Boeing Company and the McDonnell Douglas Corporation had launched a campaign to sell China four hundred planes in the next decade. Hu had always said China was one of the last great frontiers of air travel as a people used to crowding on trains discovered the convenience of planes.

Professor Guangzu had no doubt that the next President of the United States would want to do nothing to rock such a massive deal. Jenny had kept him informed on Bush's campaign for the White House. What had struck the professor was the way Bush wasted no opportunity to say how *"fundamentally important"* China was to the United States. Time and again the words appeared in the pile of news clips from Jenny on his desk. On some she had scribbled next to Bush's references to China: *"Can we really believe him?"*

Jenny, her father thought, had become for him that most baffling creature, a *radicalized* American, ready to tilt at all kinds of authority. She was like those students who met in the nuclear bunkers: Full of heady talk and dreams of changing their world. He was not altogether against that. But a country like China could not be changed overnight.

Professor Guangzu began to deal with his correspondence. It included a large envelope that bore the seal of the Office of the Party Secretary for Beijing. Professor Guangzu had met him once, at a reception for a visiting delegation of

Soviet doctors. The secretary had struck him as short on grace, humor, and temper. Hu had growled that the secretary was Deng's lapdog.

Professor Guangzu had wondered if such outspokenness had contributed to Hu's downfall. Nor had Hu learned to control his outbursts of volcanic temper. In a man of his years that was medically dangerous. It could precipitate a stroke or heart attack. But Hu refused to take the extract of pig's liver the professor had prescribed.

Professor Guangzu opened the envelope. It contained a revised disaster plan for Beijing, a blueprint for coping with any foreseeable calamity. His hospital had been designated to deal with victims from Tiananmen Square.

5

Secrets

At this hour, 6:30 A.M., only the tip of the Washington Monument is touched by the morning sun. Across the river the headstones remain in shadowy rows on Arlington's cemetery hill. The three men in the black government car each knew someone laid to rest beneath the stone markers.

The Oldsmobile had bulletproof windows, an armor-plated body, and anti-mine flooring. Only the official car of the President of the United States has similar protection. The Oldsmobile came with the job of Director of Central Intelligence (DCI).

William Hedgecock Webster had held the post since March 3, 1987. Occupying a corner of the back seat, reading in repose he remained genuinely intimidating. Perhaps it was because of his aura of total formality: his formal blue suit, his formal way of initialing each page before he read.

Under Webster, the CIA remained the nation's leading intelligence analyst, the unseen arm of U.S. foreign policy, frequently dealing with people the State Department found it diplomatically inappropriate to converse with.

But the presidency of Ronald Reagan was about to end, and after twenty months in office Webster had certainly read the newspaper speculation as to whether he would remain as the nation's chief intelligence officer in the forthcoming administration of President George Bush.

The best the press and media had ever said about Webster was that he was "safe"; under him there would be no more of the madcap missions that had enlivened and clouded the tenure of his predecessor, William Casey. Reporters described Webster as having *"brought to the CIA an abiding concern for efficient administration,"* turning the agency from *"being democracy's not very secret policemen into an annex of the Library of Congress."*

Bush had once run the CIA. Would he want to have the agency continue to operate on Webster's guidelines, or would he want to rekindle old fires and once more make the CIA more aggressive? The director knew that the answer, and his future, would become clearer after his first meeting of the day. It was another briefing to the transition team that was looking at the CIA for the new administration. This morning the subject was China.

Before the car entered the George Washington Parkway, Webster had read the NID, the National Intelligence Daily, an agency-produced summary of the main overnight intelligence developments, and the PDB, the President's Daily Brief, which contained the most sensitive and exclusive items from all U.S. intelligence agencies.

Among them was a report on the Chinese government's deal with Britain's Cable and Wireless Company to purchase fiberoptic communication equipment, sophisticated enough to ensure it was virtually secure against electronic bugging. The system was to be used to completely rewire the Zhongnanhai compound.

When China first tried to buy the equipment three years earlier, President Reagan personally convinced Prime Minister Margaret Thatcher that the sale would seriously hamper the CIA's intelligence gathering. The agency often shared with Britain information it obtained in the People's Republic. Mrs. Thatcher canceled the contract.

In a DCI EYES ONLY memo Webster had inherited from a predecessor, Admiral Stansfield Turner, the agency's policy of spying on its allies was clearly encouraged. Turner wrote that *"no one could surprise like a friend."* Mrs. Thatcher's approval of the deal once more showed that.

Webster had learned that Mrs. Thatcher had recently reminded her cabinet of China's continued readiness to allow two U.S. monitor stations to operate on Chinese territory a mere three-hundred miles southeast of Semipalatinsk, long the main test center for Russia's nuclear weapons. The facilities gave technical intelligence gatherers in Washington an invaluable "window" on the Soviet Union. Mrs. Thatcher also noted the overall increase in America's trade with the People's Republic. The message was clear: She was not going to allow Britain to miss an opportunity like the Cable and Wireless deal.

The CIA had long ensured Zhongnanhai was liberally sprinkled with electronic bugs. Lives had been risked to plant the listening devices in the compound's buildings and trees and along the paths surrounding its lake. CIA officers regularly left the U.S. embassy in the city's legation quarter to drive past Zhongnanhai. Their cars carried diplomatic number plates and were fitted with gadgetry to "vacuum" conversations gathered by the bugs. Though the Chinese Secret Intelligence Service electronically swept Zhongnanhai with regularity, Webster took pride in knowing that for every device located, another soon took its place.

Bush had laid great store on information obtained from bugging the Chinese leadership compound when he was head of the U.S. Liaison Office in Beijing in 1975 and, a year later, director of the CIA. He had spent many hours of his twelve-month stint in his suite on the seventh floor at Langley reading the intercepts of the old men who run China.

Webster was determined to convince Bush the Cable and Wireless deal was not a mortal blow, like those that had decimated U.S. intelligence gathering in Iran and Lebanon. As well as Zhongnanhai's ground bugs, ultra sophisticated hardware in space made him privy to military and political secrets being discussed by China's leaders.

Their words were sometimes snatched out of the air by aircraft hurtling through the earth's outer atmosphere at twice the speed of sound. What they missed, other equipment silently garnered.

A hundred miles out in space, satellites routinely observed the tidal wave of China's two hundred million city dwellers surging to work. The satellite sensors were so sensitive they could distinguish between the beeping and honking of the three-wheelers and the jingle of bicycle bells or separate the everyday sounds of China's villages, home for two-thirds of all the world's farmers. Their cameras were so powerful they could, if required, have identified the type of fur on Li Peng's hat or the tint in Zhao Ziyang's glasses.

Between 1,000 and 10,000 miles further out in space were more satellites, endlessly monitoring China's radar, measuring its ranges, frequencies, and power levels. At 23,300 miles — the geosynchronous orbit, where objects in space remain stationary in relation to the ground — were yet more continually listening to, among much else, the microwave-link telephone conversations between members of China's widely scattered People's Liberation Army. At 60,000 miles, a quarter of the way to the moon, a solitary satellite waited, ready to capture the first double-flash of a thermonuclear device being activated in one of China's launch sites.

Webster had been told by the National Security Agency, like every DCI at his first briefing: If a farmer slaughtered a pig in China's remotest province, within minutes NSA could provide a playback of the animal's screams.

Primarily, though, the system was to support politics at its highest level. The result of its eavesdropping helped to create U.S. foreign policy, shape a suitable diplomatic response, and exploit differences.

For some months now Webster had been using it to help him decide how to take advantage of the increasing dissension within Zhongnanhai. A key question was whether Deng Xiaoping was still sufficiently skilled to play off the warring factions and ensure that the political structure of China did not crumble.

Webster had asked the agency's China analysts to predict how far Deng would allow matters to go. The great upheavals of the past had led to huge loss of life; there had been at least a million executions in the campaigns of the early 1950s, an estimated 28 million deaths in the Great Leap Forward, 100 million uprooted or killed in the Cultural Revolution. Would Deng allow Zhao Ziyang's policy conflict with Li Peng to provoke another slaughter?

Most crucial of all, what would be the role of the People's Liberation Army in dealing with such a conflict? Would the PLA side with Zhao or Li Peng? Or would the army remain aloof until the power plays within Zhongnanhai were clearly resolved? So far, despite overtures from both Zhao and Li Peng, the commanders of the seven military regions had given no indication what they would do.

However, General Yang, commander of the 27th Army, the largest of the PLA's forces, had now spoken out about the need to control the students should they take to the streets. The electronic net cast over China had enabled

Webster to learn that the general had begun to canvas for support among his fellow commanders. He had told them that if there were trouble, the 27th was ready to deal with the situation *"by whatever force is necessary."*

The CIA's analysts saw the students as responsible for much of the erosion of Party authority. Licensed and encouraged by Mao, at first they were the vigorous voice of proletarian power. Then they began to act autonomously, and eventually mindlessly. Finally, on April 5, 1976, they had rampaged through Tiananmen Square, with Mao himself the target of their fury. Deng Xiaoping became a hero, calling their action *"a popular uprising."* He had stamped his imprimatur on the legitimacy of mass protest in the heart of the capital. He had done so again when the Democracy Wall movement briefly flowered. It had helped consolidate his political position.

Agency analysts still disagreed whether Deng had cynically exploited the students or had been forced to suppress them by the conservatives of Zhongnanhai as the price for their support.

Now, a decade later, a new generation of students had emerged determined to transform their motherland.

CIA files contained details about their leaders. Wuerkaixi was described as *"a super activist. Image conscious and prepared to lead from the front. Not all students like his confrontational style."* Wang Dan was *"working to create an independent student union movement."* Yang Li was *"one of the leading student strategists."* Yan Daobao was *"a militant."* Liu Gang, a twenty-eight-year-old physics major at Beijing University, was characterized as *"brilliant, if at times a quixotic thinker."* Chai Ling, a twenty-three-year-old graduate student at Beijing Teacher's University seemed *"a born revolutionary — more committed than most of her male compatriots."*

The student leaders were credited with being *"well spoken"* and *"choosing their targets shrewdly. They draw moral strength from nationalism, the hard facts to support their arguments from the* Wall Street Journal. *They cite the Pope on the strategic struggle against social evil and know how to exploit Gorbachev's perestroika for their own ends."*

The files repeatedly stated that the student leaders knew how to take an issue, human rights, and show that the basic denial of choice was what ultimately separated Communism from Democracy and would, in the end, doom it.

An analyst had noted that in China *"the State monopoly on mass communications, the lack of a multiparty system, and the absence of a genuine market economy, allowed student leaders to constantly reiterate that a nation which shaped so many of the laws of civilization should now be allowed to live within their framework."*

It was a heady philosophy. But was it strong enough to change the course of China's political life? And, most crucial for Webster, should he recommend to the new administration that the United States begin to support the students in their aims? Should Bush encourage them to push for greater reform, freedom of speech, assembly, and association? Or should the incoming President be told to curb his support for their democratic aims so as not to weaken the growing commercial and other ties linking the two countries?

The United States had played an important part over the past decade in helping China to become the fastest growing economy in the world. American corporations had made huge profits from doubling or even quadrupling the incomes of millions of Chinese and giving them a better standard of life. Yet with the GNP of the People's Republic still only averaging $350 a year per capita, more huge profits were to be made from business joint ventures. Americans were digging mines and operating luxury hotels in China. The lure of the market was often its sheer size: A manufacturer had only to sell one can of cola in a year to each of those billion Chinese to become very rich. In addition there was the bonus of paying low wages; the average Chinese industrial wage was about $60 a month, less than a day's salary in the United States. There was also the attraction for U.S. investors of training cheap labor with American technology, making China still more dependent on the United States.

All these were important considerations in Webster's mind as he tried to decide what advice to give the President's team.

Shortly after 7:00 A.M. the Oldsmobile passed beneath a bold green-and-white overhead sign on the freeway:

Central Intelligence Agency
Intelligence Community Staff
Next Right

The CIA was the most conspicuous of the world's secret intelligence services, spreading itself over 219 acres of pleasant and partially wooded countryside along the banks of the Potomac. Its location, nine miles to the northwest of the White House, made it a landmark for pilots landing at Washington's National Airport.

Webster placed his files in a leather briefcase before the Oldsmobile passed the guard post at the entrance to Langley. Beyond, the headquarters building showed its age. The complex had been built in the late fifties, an era when concrete, not glass, was in architectural favour. Landscaping only emphasized the building's squared, bunker-like appearance. The $46 million extension added in 1982 appeared to be tacked on.

The agency itself had become a vast bureaucracy, with its own fiefdoms, each engaged in a constant struggle for office space and additional money. Webster regularly spent time trying to settle internal rivalry that mocked the verse from the Gospel of St. John inscribed on a marble wall in the lobby: AND YE SHALL KNOW THE TRUTH, AND THE TRUTH SHALL MAKE YOU FREE.

Beyond the plaque are five color-coded elevators, each programmed to stop only at certain floors. On the first six floors the corridor walls are white and bare. On the seventh floor the walls are paneled to match the light oak doors, and paintings hang the length of the corridor leading to the director's suite. No one can reach it without a computer-checked pass allowing use of the blue elevator.

Shortly before 7:30 A.M., Webster entered the conference room beside his office. Waiting there was his deputy, Robert Gates, a cautious professional who had risen through the ranks. Standing beside Gates was a gaunt, monk-like man, Brent Scowcroft. He was going to be Bush's national security adviser. With him were four other members of the transition team.

When they were seated, each with a copy of his position paper before him on the table, Webster told them: *"I am going to switch things around a bit. I want to start with the student situation. I want to show you why they are probably going to be the key to what we can expect."*

From this moment onward George Bush would be fully apprised of exactly what the students of China were planning. At each step they took he would be given a choice of options, which ultimately came down to two: to support or not support them. That was the bottom line, an updated version of President Truman's famous saying that the buck stops here.

It was an awesome responsibility, and as he began his briefing, Webster had no real idea how the next President would shoulder it. For his part the CIA director would be evenhanded, merely presenting the facts and being careful not to shade them with opinion. That could come later, if he were confirmed in his post.

WEDNESDAY, NOVEMBER 16, 1988
EMBASSY OF THE UNITED STATES OF AMERICA
BEIJING

The American Embassy compound is the largest in the legation quarter. It occupies most of one side of Xiu Bei Jie, a tree-lined avenue. Tall iron railings separate the ill-kept roadway, which is China's responsibility, from the pathways and lawns that are America's and as carefully tended as those outside any federal building in Washington.

During the hours of daylight, Chinese stop and peer through the railings. Perhaps they are envious so much ground should be landscaped when they could put it to good use rearing ducks or raising crops; perhaps they dream of going to a country that can afford to squander so much land.

The onlookers are quickly told to move on by the militia who patrol the avenue. The rifle-toting young men in olive uniforms and forage caps wear rubber-soled boots that enable them to move quietly. They are most numerous around the compound's entrance; there are always half a dozen watching everyone who comes or goes.

The real surveillance takes place in the car parked opposite. The vehicle contains Chinese intelligence service agents. Day and night they keep watch and are in radio contact with other CSIS cars positioned around the foreign legation quarter.

The CIA agents who make their sweeps around Zhongnanhai have long learned to accept being followed.

They work from a building in the compound known as Spook City, which has the appearance of a mansion in upstate New York. It has white walls and a solid-looking front door. Its windows have antibugging alarms, primed to go off if any listening device is trained on the glass. Hidden detectors warn of parabolic microphones directed against the building. The roof has a number of aerials.

The chancery is the most imposing building in the compound. Its exterior would grace an affluent American suburb. The ground-floor reception rooms are imposing. But behind the fire doors in the hall lies a warren of offices. Here, many of the embassy's 110 diplomats work in often crowded conditions. For them China is another hardship posting in the service of their country.

One of them, James Laracco, the counselor for economic affairs, saw the usual huddle of young Chinese standing outside the main gate of the compound. Since early morning they had been waiting to be interviewed by one of the consular officers, who would decide who should be given visas to travel to the United States. Muffled in scarves and padded overcoats and jiggling on their heels against the cold of a bright winter's day, they practiced their English on the bored marine in the guard house.

Laracco was a neat and meticulous man who brought to his work a formidable intellect, able to reduce the most complex issues to concise sentences. For most of this day he had been working on a report explaining some of the problems China would have to address during the first term of the Bush administration. The report was part of a briefing package for the President-elect.

Laracco wished Bush could be standing here with him, watching the young Chinese around the guard post. He would tell the next President they were part of the problem confronting China. There were millions more like them, educated and disenchanted. And out there in the vast hinterland were a far greater number, uneducated but equally disenchanted. They presented China's leaders with a growing threat.

The problem facing Laracco was how to convey that opinion without sounding alarmist.

His legal pad was already covered with his analysis of why ten years of economic reforms had failed. As usual, he had jotted down headings, the framework in which he would fashion and contain his arguments.

"Population: no motivation to work harder. Inflation: remains on the increase. Government has failed to curb corruption," Laracco had written. He began to expand his argument. *"The result is that the rising standard of living, and expectations, parallel the rising complaints. Past legacies continue to burden the country."*

He penned a judgment. *"The economy remains trapped in a no-man's land. On the one hand the reformers, led by Zhao Ziyang, are unable to move closer to a genuine market-oriented economy, while the conservatives under Li Peng are trying to return to total centralized control. It is a recipe for disaster."*

He believed the disaster could be triggered by China's greatest and most pressing problem: how to cope with its population growth.

It had needed almost 4,000 years for China to produce a population of five-hundred million. Yet in three decades, the 1950s to the 1980s, the figure had doubled. Mao had encouraged the soaring birth rate, arguing that the larger the population, the greater would be China's work force. It was a piece of Marxist dogma that did not take into account the basic problem of too many mouths and not enough food.

Mao had also introduced a public health program that had pushed the average life expectancy from thirty-two years in 1948 to sixty-four in 1988.

To counter the problem of longevity coupled with a population explosion, Deng Xiaoping had introduced the most stringent family planning in history.

Each city and province received quotas for the number of babies allowed to be born each year, and local committees decided which families should bear children. Every woman had to formally report her menstrual cycle; anyone who missed her period and was not on the approved list for having a baby was automatically sent to an abortion clinic.

These measures were intended to reduce China's rate of population increase to zero by the year 2000. But it continued to increase by twelve million a year, requiring a further seven million tons of rice to feed the extra mouths.

Laracco knew that a large number of Chinese now lived in semi-starvation with a daily calorie intake almost half that of the United States. The average Chinese male adult ate only fourteen pounds of meat a year, thirteen of fruit, twelve of fish. Women averaged half that quantity. The authorities insisted that was sufficient for them to live on.

Increasingly, the birth-control policy had run into opposition from the peasants, who made up 80 percent of the country. They claimed they had always been able to feed the large families they needed to work the land.

Once there had been sufficient work for unskilled hands. Now, slowly but surely, mechanization was making inroads. A tractor could do the work of fifty men; only one drove it, the others went on the employment scrap heap. But they still had to be fed. The economists feared the disaster could be triggered in rural China.

There, the number of adults unemployed now totaled nearly two-hundred million. By the end of the century it would be over three-hundred million, based on the present birth rate. Yet the government options were limited. To introduce unskilled labor into the economy would slow down expansion and create greater inflation. To do nothing for a growing untrained labor force would create further unrest. Yet China could not afford the costs of an ever-expanding welfare state. To feed and house so many unemployed would prove a tremendous challenge for any government. For China's it would be insuperable.

Laracco began to formulate his next point. He too saw the students as having a key role in China's future. They had learned from the mistakes of the past. He had little doubt that in any new protest movement they would be better organized and more persuasive and appealing. The inarticulate unemployed could well be swept along by the students' passionate entreaties. A brute force of such magnitude would be almost impossible to subdue. Then China itself would be engulfed by ferment. Foreign investment in the country would be destroyed.

Over the past decade $11.5 billion had been invested by the United States, Japan, and Europe in China.

Currently Portman Cos, the Atlanta-based developer, was engaged on a $175 million building project in Shanghai. The Dow Chemical Company had a $56 million contract to erect a processing plant near the seaport. The Texas-based Helen of Troy Corporation had contracts worth $68 million for hairdryers produced in China. The American Telephone and Telegraph Company was engaged in a multimillion-dollar joint venture with the Chinese to manufacture joint transmission systems in Shanghai. The General Foods Corporation had a similar deal to produce tapioca and instant coffee and other beverage mixes. American toy makers, garment makers, and distributors of cheap telephones, calculators, and radios from China had all helped to swell an investment program that was part of China's sensational ten-year romance with the West in general, and the United States in particular, that had begun when President Jimmy Carter normalized relations with China in 1979.

Despite his pessimism over what had happened in the past decade, Laracco still believed that the only way forward for China was for the United States to continue to draw the country into *a web of economic, technological and military ties which would prevent the Middle Kingdom from plunging back into internal struggle.*

He would recommend that the new administration should do nothing to encourage the students.

6

The Watch Keepers

THURSDAY, NOVEMBER 17, 1988
TIANANMEN SQUARE
BEIJING

Yang Bing found the cold most penetrating while standing guard on the roof of the Great Hall of the People in the center of Beijing. Bing was the twenty-four-year-old elder brother of one of Cassy Jones's students, the muscular Li. Bing shared the pride of their peasant parents that Li had been the first in the family to enter the portals of Beijing University. But nowadays Bing had little else in common with Li. Bing suspected part of the reason was because he was a member of the People's Liberation Army. Li could not understand the pride Bing felt being in its ranks.

Of the 3 million Chinese who were annually eligible for call-up, only 750,000 were accepted. Each conscript served three years. Those with an aptitude for soldiering were invited to stay and maintain the army's strength of 3.5 million. The remainder were discharged to the reserve. This force currently numbered 18 million highly trained men and women who could be swiftly mobilized to defend the motherland.

In a year Bing had moved from conscript to fighter. The promotion carried an increase of three *yuan*, making his pay the equivalent of $8.50 a month. He hoped to transfer to the officer corps; that would double his income.

Physically Bing was like his brother: short and stocky with powerful shoulders and legs and dark skin. Nevertheless, Bing found it painful to realize how different they had become. Li quoted what the Party called Bad Elements, banned writers and poets, and read copies of proscribed books. He attacked the government and even berated Deng Xiaoping. Bing had told Li such heresy would surely bring tears to their parents' eyes.

Bing knew Li's new friends were responsible. From the outset, he had felt uncomfortable with them. Wuerkaixi, in his American clothes and that all-knowing smile on his lips. Liu Gang, who also dressed like an American and drank out of a can. Chai Ling, who had looked disdainfully at his soldier's uniform. Yan Daobao, with his superior ways, and the American woman, Cassy, who asked her careful questions. The more she tried to make him talk, the more uneasy he had become. His political officer said foreigners were at their most dangerous when they are pleasant and smiling. Wang Dan didn't even smile. He just sat there, staring, only once in a while stirring himself to challenge some statement. And Meili, Li's girlfriend. Bing had never seen a Chinese girl so forward. She smoked and drank alcohol and wore makeup. Thankfully, in a few hours' time they would all be gone from his life.

This evening he would board the military train for the long journey across China to Tibet, to meet up with the rest of the 27th Army. Matters there were serious, his platoon leader had said.

Now, as dawn lit the curved roofs of the Forbidden City, Bing knew four more hours of duty remained. The rest of his platoon kept the same silent watch from the roof of one of the most massive buildings in the world. Bing had learned a million volunteers had needed only ten months to erect the Great Hall. The political officer had allowed a momentary smile to cross his face as he described this achievement as *"the power of the collective family to achieve anything the State wants."*

Li had called the Great Hall an architectural monstrosity, outdated and numbed in its own enormousness. That was a week ago, when his brother once more challenged what they had both been taught to believe. They had met in one of the cafés near the Beijing University campus, and Li had asked Bing if he knew that only 4 percent of the population were Party members.

In between mouthfuls of food Li had continued. *"We have sixteen million unemployed in our cities. Mostly young people with no faith in the Party. No faith in the leadership. No faith in anything. You know why? They are being robbed. There is one law for those in the Party, another for the rest. That's why the Party likes to keep its numbers so small. So that its members have more to share among themselves from their robbing."*

Bing had looked at Li, wondering what was happening to his brother. He asked Li what he was trying to do. Ruin his future? Betray their parents? Bing's sudden anger surprised himself.

Bing continued to scan the expanse of Tiananmen Square's ninety-eight acres of paving stones, each painted with a numeral for easy regimentation during official demonstrations. The square could hold over a million people. His political officer said there was no other like it on earth.

Li had seen it as the place where the Red Guards first pledged themselves to Mao in a delirium of flags. His brother had assumed the role of teacher. No one, he explained, had been spared from their violence. Scientists, lawyers, doctors, teachers, and, of course, intellectuals, all became victims. Reputations were ruined, lives laid waste. All that was good and innocent was destroyed. Ornamental trees and flowerbeds were dug up. Household pets were destroyed; there had been mounds of rotting cats and dogs in the streets of Beijing and other cities. Whatever Mao ordered had been carried out blindly, without a moment's thought. One day he decreed keeping goldfish was criminal, and the Guards had gone on the rampage, smashing fishbowls across the country. On another, Mao pronounced playing chess to be immoral. Millions of boards and pieces were burned. When Mao outlawed stamp collecting, many of the country's priceless collections had been destroyed.

How, Bing had asked, did Li know all this?

His brother gripped him by the shoulders. *"One of my teachers. He was there. He saw it all. He told us."*

He asked Li why he believed his teacher.

No one could lie about such things, Li said. Not about half a million people casually murdered and tens of millions starved to death. No one could lie about that.

In the strengthening light, Bing could make out the red banners and yellow stars draped across the pediments of the Museum of Chinese History and Revolution. He scanned the Forbidden City, studying its bridges, walkways, and gateways. Nothing disturbed its peace.

Soon the light was sufficiently bright for him to pick out individual faces in the first shoal of cyclists emerging from the *hutongs,* the lanes which lead into Changan Avenue, Beijing's version of Fifth Avenue. They kept a steady and near-uniform pace, ignoring the traffic policemen endlessly gesticulating from their little islands in the middle of the boulevard that ran for ten miles through the center of the city.

Bing focused on an area northeast of the Forbidden City. As usual, a pair of sentries stood at either end of a bridge over a lake, ready to repel anyone foolish enough to approach Zhongnanhai. On the near side of the bridge, a line of stakes rose like dragon's teeth from the water, encased in barbed wire, their points sharpened as a further determent. Having carefully scanned the water and the surrounding banks, Bing peered into the leadership compound.

A figure stood on the towpath. Bing made out the sharp and foxy face of Yang Shangkun, the country's president. For a man in his eighty-first year he still performed his *taijiquan,* the traditional morning martial arts exercise, with grace.

He was joined by another warmly clad figure. Bing did not need his binoculars to recognize Wu Yi, the vice-mayor of Beijing and Yang's mistress. She wore the bright blue tracksuit the president was rumored to have specially ordered for her from America.

Unaware they were being observed, the couple began to move around one another in graceful shadow play. Several hundred miles in space a satellite camera captured the moment and transmitted it, as part of the early morning sweep of the city, to the National Photographic Interpretation Center in Washington. The technicians responsible for monitoring China now had fresh orders.

They were to keep track of any signs of *"untoward student activity."* The order had come from CIA Director Webster and formed part of a general brief to the agency's operatives in China itself. President-elect Bush had specifically asked Webster to keep him personally updated on events in China with, according to one operative, *"particular emphasis on what those students might be thinking of doing."*

In ordering that, the incoming President was signaling that China's students were very much a matter of concern for him, though Webster still had no clear idea exactly how Bush intended to reflect that interest. The CIA knew that to second-guess the President-elect on the matter was as tricky as predicting events in China. The country's aged leadership had an uncanny knack of confounding outsiders. At the moment, Webster had been told, *"they are bumping over only small potholes on the road to reform."*

But those students could change everything.

SAME DAY, LATER
FOREIGN LEGATION QUARTER
BEIJING

The first meetings of the day, some over breakfast, were being held in various embassies as diplomats and professional intelligence officers resumed the endless task of trying to discover what the Chinese leadership was planning.

In the Canadian chancery on San Li Tun Lu, Ambassador Earl S. Drake was closeted with senior staff. The Secret Intelligence Service officer assigned to the embassy began by briefing them on the latest visit to Beijing by a Canadian-born rocket scientist, Dr. Gerald Bull.

Brilliant but with a fatally flawed personality, Bull, a sixty-year-old rocket weapons specialist, had fallen out with his own government, and subsequently his CIA paymasters. Bitter and angry, Bull had hired himself out to first the South Africans and then Iraq. He had promised Saddam Hussein to build a series of superguns, each with the capacity to fire a shell several hundred miles. Months ago Bull had come to China to discuss with the state armaments corporation, Norinco, how it could be part of that deal.

The intelligence officer reported on the outcome of the latest meeting between Bull and Norinco executives at the Beijing Hotel. In return for unlimited funding, Bull would design a gun capable of shooting small satellites into space for about 5 percent of the cost of a conventional rocket launch. The Chinese thought the gun had a huge military potential for themselves, and one they could profitably market to clients in the Middle East, apart from Iraq.

China's arms sales were a substantial part of its annual $80 billion exports. These were made possible by massive loan packages from the World Bank and the Manila-based Asian Development Bank. German banks had advanced $2.1 billion of export credits, and Japanese finance houses had loaned Chinese industrial directors almost $6 billion to keep exports flowing.

Not only could China be plunged into recession if the students created serious unrest, but foreign confidence in China's ability to honor its commitments would fade.

The Canadian intelligence officer suggested that if the students once more took to the streets, there could be a significant difference in their tactics this time. They might appeal to the West to openly support their demands. Canada could well find itself in the forefront of such an appeal. In the officer's view, *"that could rock more boats than a stiff breeze does on the St. Lawrence Seaway."*

It was agreed that monitoring the student activity should become an important part of Canada's intelligence presence in Beijing.

A similar decision had already been taken at the French embassy a few compounds further along the street. There Ambassador Charles Malo and his minister-counselor, Gerard Chesnees, had sat over breakfast with Nicholas

Chapuis, the cultural counselor. With them was the embassy's senior intelligence officer, who operated under the cover of being one of the French attachés.

Chapuis, a likable, glad-handing diplomat, had spent the previous day talking to students and their foreign expert teachers at one of the university campuses. He had learned of the meeting held in the nuclear shelter. In Chapuis's view, the students were *"muscle flexing."*

Ambassador Malo warned that nothing must be done *"in the name of France"* to encourage them. To do so would place at risk the thousands of contracts between French and Chinese companies amounting to $4 billion, much of it in low-wage light industry.

Similar sentiments were being expressed in missions as far apart on the political spectrum as the Soviet Union's and Australia's. In a score of embassies throughout the legation quarter, diplomats were beginning to focus their attention on the country's student population. In the words of Lindsay J. Watt, New Zealand's ambassador, *"these young folk had the potential to raise a whole storm — and when the dust settled there'd be no telling what had been blown away."*

SAME DAY, STILL LATER
ZHONGNANHAI

Next to the prime minister's compound stands a smaller one, dominated by a squarely-built building, surrounded by a paved area containing a helicopter landing pad and parking space for fifty cars. The building's roof is festooned with aerials similar to those visible on the American embassy's Spook City. It also has an inner courtyard with an ornamental pond and a landscaped miniature garden.

Qiao Shi ran China's Secret Intelligence Service from the only office with direct access to the courtyard.

Several other CSIS buildings are scattered throughout the city. Counterintelligence is on West Qiananmen Street. Foreign intelligence operates from a modern building near the city's main railway station. But the spying activities of several thousand men and women are coordinated from the office with its pleasing views of shrubs and bushes in the secluded courtyard.

Adjoining Qiao Shi's office is the computer room. Its many millions of details stored on tape include information about every Chinese student studying abroad and the country's 14,489 accredited diplomats posted around the world, along with the names of all foreign contacts they had in their communities.

Also on tape were the identities of all Chinese convicted of, or suspected of being involved with, drug trafficking, and records of the CSIS role in their discovery, especially in the United States. There CSIS had worked closely with the Drug Enforcement Agency and the Federal Bureau of Investigation.

It was a striking example of the hidden links and interdependencies between intelligence services. All were sworn to deny these bonds existed.

Cooperation with the United States resulted from a meeting between William Casey, then director of the Central Intelligence Agency, and Qiao Shi in December 1984. Casey was the first American intelligence chief to recognize the mistake of looking at China as merely a massive regional threat. With its nuclear weapons, long-range submarines, orbiting satellites, and intercontinental ballistic missiles, China had become a world power.

Casey had flown secretly to Beijing to meet Qiao. Among much else discussed had been how the power of China's drug dealers now matched that of the Mafia in the United States and the drug barons in Colombia. Chinese cartels controlled over 60 percent of New York's heroin market. Every major North American city had its Chinese godfather, Mandarins infinitely richer and more powerful than any dynasty emperor. An increasing amount of the cocaine from Colombia and the Golden Triangle in Southeast Asia was actually marketed by men whose lineage went back to the big-city opium dens in the 1800s.

None of this could have surprised Qiao Shi. Under his direction the CSIS had manipulated the drug traffickers of Asia to hook U.S. servicemen in Vietnam. But inevitably, with drug-taking respecting no barriers, China had found itself with a growing addiction problem, especially among its students. According to Casey, Qiao had proposed *"a joint intelligence venture"* to combat the traffickers.

A top-secret meeting was held at the Mandarin Hotel in Hong Kong between senior CSIS officers and a team from the CIA, FBI, and DEA in January 1985. As a result the U.S. agencies had continued to receive information from the CSIS about any drug-running operations targeted against the United States; in return the CSIS were provided with the names of all known Chinese traffickers.

CSIS help had produced some spectacular results, including the now celebrated Goldfish Aquarium case in San Francisco. A million pounds of heroin had been discovered wrapped in cellophane and condoms inside fish imported from Asia. American federal agents had taken the credit for the bust. Privately they admitted they could not have succeeded without the CSIS team that had trailed the consignment across the Pacific.

Qiao Shi had approved handing over valuable information CSIS possessed about the Triads. With an estimated million members scattered worldwide, the ancient Chinese secret societies were the largest drug traffickers on earth.

Nothing seemed too small or too much on the periphery of mainstream intelligence to escape Qiao Shi's notice.

Five years before, when unrest had first surfaced in Poland and Hungary, the intelligence chief had persuaded Deng Xiaoping to create a 400,000-man armed police force that would be directly under CSIS control.

Qiao Shi recognized that to operate effectively, the force must be trained and equipped like Western riot-control teams, with rubber bullets, tear gas, and water cannon. To defend themselves, his men must be dressed in the same kind of protective clothes used by specialist teams in America and Britain. He had spent hours studying videos of the British Army in Northern Ireland.

But Western firms continued to be discouraged by their governments from selling China the lightweight body armor, weapons, and training techniques needed to subdue rioting crowds. With the Cable and Wireless deal in place, China's diplomats in Washington had begun to suggest that the United States should be careful of losing more business to Britain.

The diplomats had been helped by an old and still powerful friend, former Secretary of State Henry Kissinger. More than any other American, he had been responsible for promoting U.S. investment in China, creating a specialist consultancy to do so. In the past five years billions of dollars had been channeled into the Chinese economy through Kissinger Associates.

To further encourage trade, Kissinger had created the prestigious American-China Society, with himself and former Secretary of State Cyrus Vance as co-chairmen. Board members included ex-Presidents Gerald Ford, Jimmy Carter, and Richard Nixon, former National Security Advisers McGeorge Bundy, Robert McFarlane, and Zbigniew Brzezinski, and former Secretaries of State Dean Rusk, Edward Muskie, Alexander Haig, and William D. Rogers.

Kissinger Associates had persuaded clients to invest heavily in China. Chase Manhattan Bank had recently invested $270 million in the Daya Bay Nuclear Power Plant, which had an integral role in producing China's nuclear weapons. Another of the bank's multi-million-dollar investments underwrote leases for the purchase of aircraft by the Civil Aviation Administration of China.

Kissinger had arranged for American Express, a company of which he was a board member, to invest $138 million in a thirteen-year loan to build an office complex in Beijing. At the same time he had arranged for another company of which he was a board member, the American International Group, to establish a joint venture with the People's Insurance Company of China to handle insurance and reinsurance on Mainland China. The business was currently worth $25 million annually. Atlantic Richfield, another client of Kissinger Associates, had invested $170 million to develop the South China Sea natural gas field.

On the military front, Kissinger had continued to play what was called by Qiao Shi his "China card," allowing the United States to help China to upgrade its satellites and purchase advanced missile guidance systems. One of these systems had been sold to the People's Liberation Army by the Israelis in 1987, with full U.S. approval. Currently Grumman Aviation had a contract to provide advanced avionics for the Chinese Air Force's entire fleet of F8-2 interception jets, while Garret Aerospace was providing the engines for the C-8 fighters, the air force's short-range interceptors.

Against these genuinely massive investments, Qiao Shi knew that the question of his riot-control gear was a trifling matter. But Henry Kissinger was not a man to miss a deal. He had told China's spymaster not only that he would receive the gear, but that U.S. investment would increase even further once George Bush was in the Oval Office.

Qiao Shi believed the ability of Kissinger Associates to lobby even more effectively within the Bush administration would be enhanced by the presence of two top officials who had been members of the multimillion-dollar consulting company that bore Kissinger's name.

They were Lawrence Eagleburger, who would take over the number two slot at the State Department and become one of President Bush's most trusted troubleshooters, and Brent Scowcroft, who had been director of the Washington office of Kissinger Associates. He would be Bush's national security adviser.

Together with James Baker, the two former employees of Kissinger Associates would form the policy-shaping "troika" around Bush.

Qiao Shi could reasonably have expected such close friends of China to allow nothing to upset the cordial business relationships between the two countries. Most certainly they would not permit a group of almost penniless students with radical views to disturb America's huge financial investment in China.

7
States of Mind

THURSDAY, NOVEMBER 24, 1988
WASHINGTON, D.C.

Outside the unprepossessing brick townhouse at 716 Jackson Place across from the White House, government cars came and went, depositing members of the Bush transition team. The dozen men strode briskly up the six steps into the building, glad to be out of the raw early morning air. After coffee, the men who would set the course for the next presidency settled themselves around the dining room table to listen to another briefing from Webster.

They had greeted the CIA director warmly, taking their cue from the President-elect. A few days ago Bush had asked Webster to stay on. There was now a new zest about the director. He no longer looked like a man who had been given bad news by his doctor, but someone with a new sense of life.

Webster extended a personal welcome to each team member. To John Tower, the designate secretary of defense, the director seemed like a host greeting a bunch of cronies, rather than the country's intelligence chief about to "*spill some more of other people's secrets.*"

The presence of John Sununu, the former governor of New Hampshire, showed the President-elect could continue to surprise; Bush had just appointed him to be his White House chief of staff. Webster knew that Sununu was strong-willed, often tactless, and inclined to charge full tilt. The director was ready to fend off any ideas Sununu might have of using the CIA on some Mission Impossible. There were problems enough as it was. The intelligence summary he had prepared contained an update on every major global sphere of trouble. It provided an overview of what was likely to happen between now and when Bush formally entered office in late January next year.

Next to the former governor sat James Baker. Bush had already made it clear that as well as being secretary of state, Baker would be his de facto deputy. Though Baker had little foreign policy experience, he was on a fast learning curve. Webster had told senior aides that Baker had "*a real grasp of the realities.*" The director planned to use the secretary as a sounding board for proposals he wanted Bush to endorse when he was in office.

The director had also made his own careful assessment of each member of the team, their strengths and weaknesses, who was a team player, who an out-and-out loner. It would help him decide who should be on the list for BIGOT, the slim buff folder with a double blue stripe on the cover that was hand-carried by a CIA officer to a small group of people in the highest echelons of government. The folder contained either reports from a key field agent or details about some forthcoming ultrasensitive intelligence operation.

So far only Baker had been approved for access to the list. Almost certainly Bush would want Brent Scowcroft, the man seated opposite Baker, to have access, too.

Scowcroft was the transition team's hardliner, with a penny-pinching manner that went all the way back to his days as a child in Ogden, Utah. Now, half a century later, his Mormon faith continued to sustain him in a lifetime spent behind Washington's closed doors. He liked to say he knew where all the bodies were buried. Since 1987 he had run the Washington office of Kissinger Associates. It had given him an insight into the financial interplay between the United States and China better than any other man's in the room.

Next to Scowcroft sat John Tower. Webster doubted if he would ever make it to office. The FBI checks the President-elect had insisted on for all his nominees had revealed Tower to be a womanizer with a drinking problem. Defense was no place for a man who could be blackmailed. But for the moment Tower was privy to what Webster was unfolding.

He took them on a world tour, moving from Latin and Central America to Asia and South Africa. The next stop was Russia.

Webster said the country was in trouble. He added emphatically: *big trouble*. As well as having many economic problems, Moscow was finding it increasingly difficult to maintain homogeneity; there were too many ethnic groups and autonomous republics seeking independence. Webster added, Gorbachev could be presiding over the collapse of Soviet Communism.

Tower shifted in his chair. *"He'd never allow that,"* Tower said. *"He'd have to go back to the old ways. Terror and mass deportation. Break the people before they get a chance to break the system."*

Webster hesitated. How far should he go? Should he tell them that only a week ago he had once more flown to London to interview a top-ranking KGB defector who had been brought out of Russia into Finland by M16? That for the past two years the man had been providing invaluable insights into Gorbachev's thinking? That the defector had told him that not only Russia, but the whole of Communist Europe, was on the brink? One wrong move and it could go either way: collapse, or end in bloody civil war.

This kind of intelligence, Webster decided, he didn't want to share with the transition team. This was still BIGOT-list, or President-elect's ears only information.

Webster turned his attention to China. Despite its huge army, nuclear weapons, and intercontinental ballistic missiles, it still had little ability to influence international events.

For the next half hour he gave them an incisive picture of China's attempts to improve its nuclear arsenal. Its most advanced missile, the CSS-4, now had a range of 10,000 miles and carried a 5-megaton warhead. By the early 1990s it would be able to carry multiple warheads. China's two other "showcase weapons," the CSS-3 and CSS-2, had, respectively, a 5,000-mile range and a 3-megaton warhead, and a 2,000-mile range and 2-megaton warhead.

"Any of these weapons on offer to their clients in the Middle East?" asked Tower.

Webster shook his head. Representatives of Israel, the only country with a worthwhile intelligence service still operating in Iraq and Iran, had assured him of that.

The director focused their attention on China's internal situation.

Ideological disagreement was deepening within the leadership. The outcome depended on whether the economy could remain on its ambitious course without inflation getting totally out of control. Yet if the economy remained on track, it would only increase the pressure for fuller democracy. That pressure was now beginning to come from outside the country.

Many of the forty million Chinese living overseas had been both wealthy and had kept their emotional links with their motherland. They had welcomed its reconstruction by pouring in money. In the past year alone $15 billion had been invested by Taiwan. In all, Chinese overseas investment totaled $70 billion. With it had come a call for greater democracy and the often thinly disguised threat to withdraw funding unless the demand was met.

The country's students were mobilizing. As usual, they were being led by those on Beijing's campuses, where a total of 180,000 students were in residence. There was still no clear indication of what they would do to push for democracy.

Webster said there was one question that would have to be faced and answered. Should the United States support the demands for democratization and encourage its allies to do so, or should it sit back and watch how political dissent would develop?

There was silence in the room. Then Baker said there was no need for him to remind everyone that as little as possible must be done to disturb America's economic, political, and intelligence links with China. The secretary of state-designate then demonstrated how well he had absorbed the briefing paper Webster had circulated.

"China faces two clear problems. One: Who will take over from Deng? None of the Politburo members has the power to prevail over others in a factionalized environment. Two: The Chinese government is not strong enough to regulate the economy even if it can be tough with political unrest. That unrest could increase as the benefits from reform reach their peak and the sources of economic growth become harder to predict."

Baker then summarized the report prepared by James Laracco, the counselor for economic affairs at the United States embassy in Beijing. Baker painted a portrait of a China in the grip of low efficiency and growing inflation, currently at 30 percent, with some food items at over 100 percent. Corruption was endemic, the credibility of the Party slipping, and the threat from student-led demonstrations growing more serious.

Bush turned to Baker. *"As soon as an opening arises, I want to go to Beijing."* He made a chopping hand motion. *"I want to sit down with Deng Xiaoping. I want to see where he's going."* Another chop. *"I want to see how far we can go with him."*

Webster nodded. He told the room that the aged Emperor Hirohito of Japan was finally at death's door; he could only survive, at most, a few more weeks.

Bush was smiling. *"Perfect. I go to the funeral, and on the way home I call in to see Deng."*

He once more chopped air.

WEDNESDAY, DECEMBER 7, 1988
BEIJING

In a tiny apartment in the north of the city, the morning routine of Kao Jyan and his mother absorbed them both. While he shaved, she pressed his olive-green uniform and burnished the stars on the collar and shoulder tabs until they gleamed as brightly as the jacket buttons. As he dressed, she prepared breakfast. While they ate, she reminded him again that no one else in the apartment block had a son in the People's Liberation Army.

Though a year had passed since it had happened, she still enjoyed telling people that he had been promoted to captain instructor at the National Defense University, and that General Zhang Zhen, its president, had personally chosen him to be one of the academy's tutors. One day, she would add, her son would be a general, as famous as old General Zhang. He was a survivor of the Long March, like her husband.

Jyan hated when people said he looked like his father, the same bony frame, eyes set deep in a long face. He preferred to think he had acquired his mother's gentle voice and caring ways. When he thought of his father nowadays, Jyan could only clearly remember his hands: calloused, broad-fingered, and practical. They had been able to mend anything. But they had been violent hands, suddenly lashing out, sending his mother and himself reeling. His father's rages had been swift and terrible right up to the day he had been killed in a road accident.

His mother recounted the respect a new neighbor had shown when she had told her about Jyan. He smiled, indulging his mother, knowing his position gave her an extra cachet on the local Street committee. As long as she seemed happy, so was he. Theirs was the close relationship that often develops between a widowed mother and an only son with no girlfriend.

At twenty-seven, Jyan had become the youngest instructor at the military academy Deng Xiaoping had opened in 1986. Deng had promised the campus would turn out a new kind of military professional. Its graduates would still have to understand the subtleties of Marxist-Leninist doctrine, but they must also be versed in computer sciences and information technology. Jyan lectured on military tactics in urban situations.

To celebrate his appointment, he had given his mother a Japanese radio. This morning, as usual, her twiddling with the knobs had awakened him. He had also bought the refrigerator in the corner of the living room, purchasing it from Number One Department Store in Wangfujing Street, where PLA officers receive a special discount. Another perk was his secondhand Nissan. The right to a car came with his post. The car could only be used for official business, and every week Jyan was allowed enough gasoline for the fifty-minute drive to and from the campus in the Western Hills.

Despite these signs of affluence and position, the lifestyle of Jyan and his mother had altered following his father's death. They had been moved to this high-rise near Coal Hill, a two-hundred-foot high man-made mound that is the highest point in Beijing. Their neighbors were factory workers, often crude and noisy, not at all like the office staff they had lived among when his father was chief assistant to Undersecretary Wang at the ministry.

The Wangs had lived a few doors from them, and in the year Shao-Yen's father arranged for her to go to film school, he had signed the papers for Jyan to enter the army. His mother had said this was the undersecretary's first move to groom him to be a husband for Shao-Yen. Until the day she left for America, his mother had hoped they would marry.

His mother was full of such romantic notions, which he found strange, because she could be so tough when sitting as a member of the Street committee. She would not hesitate to order a pregnant wife to an abortion clinic or forbid a worker to transfer from one shop floor to another. But when it came to his marrying she could be quite blind, not stopping to think that the Party would never allow him to wed someone like Shao-Yen. The social gap between the families was now too wide. Her father was firmly entrenched in the upper echelons; he and his mother had slipped to within a few rungs from the bottom. Perhaps that was why Shao-Yen had not written from America. She too was now in a very different world. He accepted that. But he hoped they would always be friends. He'd wondered if his mother really understood when he said he'd be quite happy with that.

She still regarded Shao-Yen's decision to leave China as beyond her understanding. How could anyone want to give up a secure and comfortable life to live among foreigners on the other side of the world? In many ways, he knew, she found Shao-Yen as bewildering as his cousin, Sue Tung. She had also gone to California, giving up a teaching career while leaving her husband behind.

He had always found Sue a pleasant and lively woman, and he had been surprised at the man she had married, who was cold and domineering. Jyan had assumed Sue's decision to go to America was her way of ending the relationship. Usually, though, it was a husband who left his wife at home.

Sue had written regularly. Her campus life seemed as pleasant as his. He'd read her letters to his mother. Recently Sue had mentioned an American, a man she called "my Rod."

His mother said she had no business getting involved with a foreign man. The Party strongly discouraged such relationships, even for Chinese abroad, she reminded him.

Now, as she cleared the breakfast table, she announced Sue was going to get divorced. His mother often kept important news until just before he left the apartment. Satisfied she once more had surprised him, she explained her sister had telephoned with the news.

Jyan sighed. As an officer he was allowed a telephone. But it, like the car, was only to be used on official business.

His mother looked around the room, her face still unlined in a body thickened by age.

"Young people think marrying is a game. They marry carelessly and divorce lightly. Your cousin should think of what's good for the country. A strong family is a strong country."

She looked at the mantel clock by which his father had regulated his life. The morning homily was over.

Sharply at seven, Jyan left the apartment and made his way to the forecourt. Early though it was, the first of the bamboo-framed strollers, each holding a swaddled baby, was already out, parked among the pedicabs and bicycles. His was the only car.

He drove west through the morning rush hour. In another thirty minutes it would almost be impossible to move any faster than the continuous flow of massed cyclists. Passing the heavily guarded gates of Zhongnanhai, he turned onto Changan Avenue. On his left was the Great Hall of the People.

This morning Jyan would lecture junior officers on how to clear Tiananmen Square in an emergency: an earthquake, a plane crash, or a major fire in the Great Hall or one of the other buildings in the area.

Jyan had helped devise a plan for troops to be quickly moved into the square by helicopter or through the network of tunnels that led to the nuclear shelters.

He would use time flowcharts to show how an efficient military operation must be able to clear the vast square in a matter of minutes, even in rush hour. Soldiers would block off all side streets, stopping all traffic except emergency vehicles. Other troops would divide the civilians in the square into manageable groups and shepherd them to safety. It would call for close coordination and good communications. Orders would have to be obeyed without fail. Given the panic that any disaster brings, many decisions would have to be made on the spot.

Jyan had tried to think of everything, including what should happen if Tiananmen Square once more became the focus for civil unrest. He would repeat to the class the standing instruction. The army would remain uninvolved unless the disturbance became sufficiently serious to threaten the safety of the nation. Then the army would move as it would against any enemy.

SUNDAY, DECEMBER 18, 1988
BEIJING

Cassy reminded Daobao that in a week's time it would be Christmas. As they walked among the stalls in the web of streets behind the windswept expanse of Jianquomen Avenue, he towered over her, his strong, hard-muscled body she had come to love wrapped in a topcoat he had bought in America. In his best student's voice, he recited that the 1978 constitution guaranteed people the freedom to believe or not believe in religion, but only atheism could be propagated.

She laughed, her hand brushing quickly against his, the only intimacy they dared risk in such a crowded place in broad daylight. The Street committees were always active in this district; its members had the authority to arrest them for any infringement of the Party's moral code. Public affection was regarded as bourgeois even for a married couple. Between a Chinese and a foreigner such open intimacy was a sign of decadence.

The law made relationships like theirs even more difficult. No foreigner could marry a Chinese who served in the army or the political departments of the Party or who worked *"with State secrets."* Diplomats, interpreters, and even tourist guides were also forbidden to marry non-Chinese. All others had to get permission from their local political officer.

Daobao pointed to one of the stalls. Plastic Father Christmases could be found among the bric-a-brac imported from Hong Kong.

She said she was surprised there was a market for such trinkets. He reminded her how fervently the United States had tried to convert China to Christianity in the last century. A few million "rice-bowl Christians," people who converted for a guaranteed bowl of church food, were still scattered around China. As long as they did not proselytize, they were left alone.

They turned into a side street selling aromatic spices and roots. The air was pungent and heavy.

Daobao pointed to a sack of bark, explaining it was officially sold to strengthen vitality. But men used it to improve their sex drive, even though to do so had been forbidden since Mao had said *"too much physical sex saps the revolutionary will."*

They came to the butchers. There were scores of stalls, each displaying its specialty. One was festooned with necklaces of frogs, pierced through still pulsating gullets and suspended by fore and rear legs. Another displayed trays of dessicated snakes and dried seahorses. Daobao said that when they were ground together, the powder was supposed to prevent women from giving birth to baby girls.

Cassy knew that for the Chinese birth is not the beginning of life, nor death its conclusion. Every new child formed another link in the endless chain of human perpetuity that stretches back further than anyone can recall and, it is fervently accepted, will continue until the end of time itself. To ensure the human chain's preservation, it was important to show respect for the dead. Traditionally, a son had always been thought better able to do so as well as ensuring the continuity of the family line.

As they walked away from the stall, Daobao said that no matter how hard the Party tried, it was impossible to shake off the prejudice against girl babies, especially in rural China. When Cassy asked what happened to them, Daobao looked uncomfortable. Finally he said many were killed at birth; those allowed to live were sold by their parents, usually when they reached puberty. The money was used for another pig or a piece of farm equipment, anything to make life easier.

She asked what happened to a girl when she was sold. Daobao breathed out slowly and said what had always happened: The child became a wife for an old man or ended up in a brothel. Cassy asked why the Party allowed this to happen. He pursed his lips and said many of the traffickers were cadres. Cassy asked how extensive the traffic was. Daobao gave another slow expulsion of breath; she had come to recognize this as a sign of his anger. The numbers ran into thousands, he said. *"Thousands in a year?"* she asked. *"In a month, perhaps even in a week,"* he replied.

"My God," she murmured, not knowing what else to say.

They walked past turtles and tortoises being carefully selected from boxes, quickly weighed, and casually dismembered. There was a stall with cages crammed with cats and kittens, mewing and scratching at the wire. Customers used sticks to poke them, trying to estimate how much meat lay beneath the fur. The stallholder expertly fished out the doomed animals and wrung their necks.

She reminded herself that what went on in the slaughterhouses of Chicago was really no different, and she tried to believe that the dogs on an adjoining stall, skinned from the neck down, their entrails in bags hanging from their necks, were no less off-putting than the sheep or pigs she had seen displayed by European butchers.

Several stalls were devoted to thrushes. Thirty or more were crammed in a cage. Further along ducks formed the display. There were hundreds of them, squashed head to tail in their cages, totally unable to move.

Beyond was a trader who had over fifty monkeys of all sizes. Despite herself, she stopped. The stallholder looked at her curiously. Daobao told her the creatures were killed for their brains. She turned away. *"There are times when I wonder if I'll ever understand your people."*

Daobao smiled. *"There are times when I wonder if we'll ever understand ourselves."*

Beyond, at the mouth of the street, a large group had gathered around a man selling footwear. Among them were Wuerkaixi and several other students.

Despite the cold, Wuerkaixi was wearing his California-style denims. He gave an all-knowing smile that at times seemed almost supercilious to Cassy. The cold had caused Wang Dan's spectacles to mist over and made him wrap his hands inside the sleeves of his padded jacket. As usual he was in debate with, among others, Liu Gang, who wore a scarf with his Western-style jacket and cords and sipped a soft drink as he listened. They all greeted Cassy politely.

She knew that all over the city little groups were meeting like this every day, and she had detected a growing confidence among them. Daobao had said the students were now too important, too well organized, for the Party to crush.

She wished she had his confidence.

MONDAY, DECEMBER 19, 1988
CENTRAL INTELLIGENCE AGENCY

Late in the afternoon, half a dozen men were in the conference room adjoining Webster's office. Each was an agency specialist on China who had come to the seventh floor to present his view on how Bush should respond when he went to Beijing.

The trip was at the top of his foreign travel agenda when he became President. From Zhongnanhai had come an indication Bush would be welcomed as an old friend. The visit would depend on the timing of the state funeral of Japan's Emperor Hirohito. Against all expectations, he was clinging to life.

A technician from the Political and Psychological Division had brought psycho profiles of China's leaders. It had been President Reagan's idea to have such evaluations videotaped, because he found film *"easier to digest than the written word."*

The tape of Hu Yaobang described his *"emotional disappointment and sense of isolation"* now that he was out of office.

Li Peng's video identified his supporters. Skilled editing had isolated one old face from another.

"Chen Yun. Aged eighty-four, so frail he has not appeared in public for ten months. He is moved everywhere by wheelchair," intoned the narrator as a series of computer-enhanced photographs showed a figure being wheeled beside the lake in Zhongnanhai.

Another ancient face filled the frame. *"Wang Zhen. Eighty-one years old and the former deputy chief of staff of the People's Liberation Army. Today he still exercises great influence on the PLA."*

The screen was filled with the face of an old woman. *"Deng Yingchao, widow of Chou En-Lai, who had been Mao's prime minister. She is the adoptive mother of Li Peng."*

The narration began to explore Prime Minister Li Peng's personality: *"For him power and the past are synonymous. The protégé of the old, they look to him to protect all they hold to be true."*

Zhao Ziyang's video began with pictures of him at a podium, addressing a large audience. The narration explained, *"He argues that change will be painful in the short term, but less painful than the agony China will face if there is no change."*

A montage followed of crowded street scenes, window shoppers, empty factory floors, and banks with closed doors. It ended with peasants walking wearily from fields. The commentary gave meaning to the images.

"There is panic buying. Inferior goods are being bought simply as a hedge against rising prices. There have been runs on the banks in Beijing, Shanghai, and elsewhere. Factory workers have downed tools. Peasants are being paid for their crops with promissory notes that do not fall due for a year or longer."

Finally a succession of photographs showed Deng Xiaoping over the years. The commentary acknowledged him as one of the most adroit politicians on the world stage. *"A manipulator, perhaps his greatest skill is being able to have others carry out his wishes. He has always been able to distance himself from the unpleasant."*

Deng was shown entering the Great Hall of the People, addressing the Politburo, waving to the crowds at a rally in Tiananmen Square, saluting at a military parade, clapping at massed ranks of children passing in review. Deng always appeared pensive. The commentary suggested a reason: *"He is haunted by the past. That one day, some one will try and destroy all he holds to be sacred — the Party he has fashioned in his image, the State he has created after his fashion, the China that reflects his image."*

The screen went to black.

Webster immediately took up where the narration ended. He said that barely a year ago Deng had announced China could not survive without dictatorship, that it was essential to the country's future. Yet the freedoms Deng had allowed were now encouraging writers, artists, academics, and, above all, the country's students, to increasingly and openly debate China's future. But where did that leave Deng's commitment to dictatorship? And, if he were to exercise it, what should be Bush's response as President?

MONDAY, DECEMBER 26, 1988
UNITED STATES EMBASSY
BEIJING

In Spook City it was business as usual for the handful of CIA officers who comprised the agency's Beijing station. Most of them had spent their Christmas Day making the rounds of other missions, listening and picking up the latest information. Their travels had yielded very little, except a few hangovers.

The exception was the man the others called Tom. He had spent his Christmas on a train returning from Nanjing. Ostensibly he had gone there to address the local business community in his guise as a member of the embassy's economic staff. In reality he had visited an asset, or informer, a student at Nanjing University.

Tom deemed what he had learned sufficiently important to encrypt and transmit to Langley: The students' union at Nanjing University, until recently moribund, was once again highly active. At a recent meeting attended by several hundred students, their leaders had said the economic situation was in a mess because of mismanagement by the central government.

"In our discussions, a [Tom's asset] said that the overwhelming reaction of the meeting was there must be change and that the students must lead the way," Tom reported to Langley.

8

The Roof of the World

FRIDAY, DECEMBER 30, 1988
LHASA, TIBET

High in the mountains Bing Yang flattened himself against the frozen scree, the fur lappets on his cap secure over his ears. The cap somehow gave his peasant's face a still more determined look, making him appear rather like his brother, Li, one of the student activists at Beijing University. And, just as much as Li was a radical, so Bing had become still more of a Party idealist. The short time he had spent in Tibet had convinced him of the danger China faced from political activism of any kind.

An automatic rifle was cradled in Bing's arms. The rest of the platoon was spread across either side of the track rising from the Kyi Chu River, which marks the southern boundary of Lhasa, Tibet's capital.

At this hour, seven in the morning, the sun was still a diffuse pink behind the brooding Tangla hills. Daylight comes to Lhasa two hours later than in Beijing, four thousand miles to the east. But in Tibet, as all over China, Beijing time prevails, a reminder that the meridians, and even the sun itself, remain obedient to the dictates of the rulers in Zhongnanhai.

Far down in the valley the bells on the yak herds tinkled. In the rarefied, crystal-clear air, sound, vision, and smell are all enhanced. With daybreak the moaning wind increased, sending spumes of snow swirling. Bing had never known such cold.

It had taken some of the soldiers days to become acclimatized. A few with persistent altitude sickness had been sent back to lower levels. But apart from a blistering headache on the first day, Bing had suffered nothing. He credited his good health to sipping green tea and breathing slowly.

They had all been told not to wash: water at this altitude irritates the skin and removes its natural oils, an essential protection against the ultraviolet rays.

The sky was so blue it appeared almost black. Across the valley the unwalled city seemed like a village, so overpowering was the massive structure towering over it. Whatever the time of day — pick dawn, blinding noon, or amethyst evening — it remained awesome and forbidding, a castle set upon a fortress set upon a mountain. Six hundred feet of sheer white walls ended in the glittering golden roofs of the Potala, once the home of the pontiff-ruler of Tibet, the Dalai Lama.

Wherever he turned, Bing's eyes were drawn back to its monstrous beauty, its thousand windows like air vents keeping it afloat. It was the most intimidating building Bing had ever seen.

He focused for the moment upon one of the mounds of enormous cabbages on the opposite riverbank. On previous mornings Tibetan women, wrapped in dark gowns, had come to take some of the vegetables, and the sound of their voices had carried clearly. Now there was only silence.

Trucks approaching the city had been halted at roadblocks in the next valley. Those attempting to leave Lhasa would be stopped by more checkpoints within the city. Lhasa was as isolated as Tibet itself, a secret, hermetic land, and had been for centuries.

Everyone knew why. Everyone was waiting for the sound to return.

It came again with a suddenness that brought low "aahs" from Bing and the men around him. The roar rushed across the windswept mountains, over forested slopes, and into the deepest of the gorges. It passed over the buildings China had erected as evidence of its determination to stay: a sports stadium, a revolutionary museum, a hospital, ugly apartment blocks. The sound surged over the old city, the Parkor, where many of the buildings were fifteen hundred years old, their exterior walls and windows protected from the sun by great drapes of black yak wool. The noise seemed to fill every corner of the sky. It was the sound of jet engines at full pitch.

A mile away, over the city, the three J-5s made another sortie. Swooping in over the Pala marshes to the east, they passed just above the tops of the temples before banking and climbing over the gilded roofs of the Potala. Even at this distance the sound of the turbojets was shattering.

Bing could well imagine the panic the MIGs were causing in the narrow streets. The shock waves from their engines would be powerful enough to shake the flowerpots and set ritual bells tingling in all those deep-set window frames, each lacquered the same shiny black. He had been told the black was to ward off evil spirits. It was beyond him how people could possibly be re-educated when they believed such nonsense.

The aerial maneuvers were timed to coincide with the end of morning prayers, when thousands of red-robed monks would be emerging. The intention was to panic counterrevolutionaries into fleeing before the 27th's main sweep.

The bulk of the army was deployed along Tibet's frontier with India. From its bases there, it was conducting operations against Tibetan guerrillas. As part of this drive, units of the 27th had been sent to Lhasa, which had long been the main center of resistance.

At a signal, tanks and troops would simultaneously move from the West Gate below the Potala, down the road from the Sera monastery in the north, and out through the network of canals in the east. Street by street they would drive forward, the soldiers checking every building.

Bing and the other soldiers spread-eagled on the mountainside were positioned to block any escape to the mountains by this one route deliberately left open. Any person fleeing would be a counterrevolutionary. Anyone who resisted was to be shot. But prisoners were needed as examples to the population that resistance was futile.

The planes re-formed for another run. They swooped below the jagged white mountain peaks, the rising sun behind them, so that in the town no one could see the fighters coming. They once more burst over Lhasa. In a tight roll over the river, the MIGs banked and hurtled toward the Potala. The planes' afterburners seemed to blend with the sun's rays, sending golden-red shards bouncing off the gleaming roofs.

Bing watched them vanish behind the mountains. The wind carried the sounds of panic from the town. People were running, men, women, and children, in their thick, dirty *chubas*, gownlike garments fastened at the waist with thick woolen belts. A few of the men wore Western-style jackets, the women invariably plaid head scarves. Faces were begrimed with years of smoke from the yak-chip fires that swirled from thousands of chimneys. They were running back into the squat, white-walled buildings where they lived or worked, running just as the briefing officer had said they would. Bing continued to watch, the cold now forgotten with the prospect of action finally here.

On the train journey from Beijing, the political commissar had lectured them over the loudspeaker in every carriage about what was happening in Tibet.

He said that ever since the People's Liberation Army *"liberated"* Tibet in 1950, to make it *"free from imperialist oppression and to consolidate the defenses of China's western borders,"* reactionaries had tried *"to arouse the people."* Many were students, who resisted all attempts to pacify them. They refused to speak Chinese and insisted upon worshiping at their shrines and temples, prostrating themselves before gods officially discredited since the country's liberation.

The center of all this religious madness was their obsessive desire to see the return of their living god, the *Kundum,* the Dalai Lama. He had fled when China occupied the country.

His supporters were well armed and dangerous. Their weapons had been discovered under *cairns,* only allowed to be erected in honor of local deities, and in *chortens,* burial mounds, supposed only to contain holy relics. Explosives had been found in prayer wheels and even concealed inside the felicity scarves Tibetans were still allowed to carry and exchange as symbols of reverence and respect. They were killing those Tibetans who wanted to attend the self-criticism public meetings the Party had introduced. They were murdering members of the PLA. In the past month fifty officers and men had been killed in separate incidents.

The commissar read out each name and described the manner of each death: a catalogue of shootings in the back, garrotings, knives slipped under rib cages, and bombs exploding under vehicles. The counterrevolutionaries had even entered a barracks and slit the throats of sleeping soldiers. Bing was properly horrified.

An hour after they had crossed the Yangtze into Tibet, he saw his first Tibetans. The train stopped to refuel at the foot of a valley. Halfway up its side a monastery clung to the cliffs, its white walls framed with conifers. Vultures were perched in the trees. The commissar described how Tibet's dead are left out in the open to be consumed by the huge predators.

The Tibetans struck Bing as undernourished and servile, shuffling out of his path as they murmured incantations and continuously turned the little prayer wheels in their hands. Curious, he stopped a man and asked to inspect one. The Tibetan silently handed it over. Bing saw it was a slim metal cylinder on an upright axle; a weight attached to the cylinder by a thin chain created a flywheel and made it easy to keep the wheel in motion with a movement of the hand. Inside the cylinder was a tiny scroll covered with characters. Bing handed back the wheel; the man bowed his head and walked away, rubbing the wheel to remove any trace of Bing's fingerprints.

At the monastery Bing watched pilgrims placing coins on stones and among the wool tufts on the pine trees. He felt uneasy at such piety and was nauseated by the sour smell of coagulated yak butter, used to form thousands of lamp wicks. There were statues sculpted from yet more yak butter, saints set in nests of gilded wood, and everywhere myriad-headed figures of carved godlings. Over them all rose the endless repetition of mantras and the twirling of prayer wheels.

Stuffed apes, bisons, and bears were propped against the monastery's colonnades. How, Bing asked himself, could people accept that these mangy figures had divine power? Or the living creatures many Tibetans carried, the puppies, kittens, and chattering monkeys? Animals should be eaten, not worshiped. How was it possible that the warm, brown Yangtze he had grown up alongside had its source in this strange and forbidding land?

All night the train climbed and climbed. In the darkness he stood in the corridor with Lee Gang, the brother of Liu Yang, the student at Beijing University. Lee Gang's tank was on one of the flatcars behind the carriages. It was strange, Bing mused, how siblings could be so different. Yang, with his penchant for Western-style clothes and drinking out of a can, was as unlike Lee as Bing now was from his own brother.

In the shared companionship of traveling, Bing told Lee Gang about the letter he had written to his brother before leaving Beijing, expressing concern over his growing radicalism. The young tank commander admitted he too was concerned over how university life had affected his own brother. He added that all the Party could do was try and make students see their errors. But if all else failed, they must be taught the hard lesson the 27th was being sent to administer to the reactionaries of Tibet.

Bing stared out at the icy void beyond the window. After a while he said it would be one thing to kill traitors, quite another their own flesh and blood.

Lee Gang considered. When he spoke his voice was certain. Revolutionaries could not be regarded as flesh and blood.

Bing felt an admiration for him, for his honesty, for his courage in being ready to choose between personal ties and the greater need of the national family.

They stood in silence listening to the bleating of the engine whistles, one up front, one at the rear, pulling and pushing them through the mountains, through the night, Bing hoping he would never have to discover if he had Lee Gang's, certainty.

Late the next day, the train stopped once more. Bing and several hundred other soldiers disembarked. Their role in the operation was explained to them by their company commander, Tan Yaobang. He had stood before them, his lean, strong face weatherbeaten, his close-cropped gray hair hidden by his fur hat. He had to shout to make himself heard above the wind. In the minutes before Tan led them into the mountains, Bing sought out Lee Gang and asked him to mail the letter to Li, counting out the money for the postage. He was increasingly anxious for Li to change his ways as soon as possible. He hoped the letter, with its reminder of all the "good things" the state provided, would convince Li to give up his radical ways and those dangerous student friends.

Tan set a brisk pace, making it hard to believe he was a man in his mid-fifties. They marched through the bitter night; at dawn they found what shelter they could. When they reached their destination Tan showed them how to burrow into the ground and make sure their equipment did not catch the sun as it rose and set. He permitted no fires, and they ate only cold rations. At night Tan had moved among them quietly retelling his own experience in Korea, when he had survived for days on a bowl of rice eaten each morning in similar sub-zero temperatures.

Now, huddling against the scree, watching the jet fighters disappear, Bing envied Liu Lee in the warmth of his T-69. Its commander had said the tank was not only equipped with the latest armaments, including a laser range-finder, but also possessed a heating system to keep out even Tibet's harsh winter.

As the MIGs returned to make a further pass, Bing focused on the opposite river bank. Several men had appeared. Some headed along a path downriver, others in the opposite direction toward the ferry crossing. There would be no escape either way. Tan had placed soldiers to intercept both tracks.

The remaining pair carried an oblong-shaped boat made of yak hide. They shoved it into the water and clambered on board. They began to row furiously, heading for directly below where Bing waited.

He released the safety catch on his gun, settling himself into a firing position. The wind sent flurries of snow whistling over the slope, momentarily obscuring his view of the river. On either side he heard the clicks of weapons being primed. From behind a rocky spur Tan called out they should not fire unless absolutely forced to do so. They must take prisoners.

The swirling snow eased, and Bing could once more see the boat battling against the current. Over his shoulder he glimpsed Tan crawling over the ground to the next group.

From the roof of the PLA headquarters compound in the center of the city, a signal rocket soared into the sky. It burst close to the vapor trail of the jets disappearing to the north.

Bing quickly focused on the West Gate. Lee Gang's T-69 rumbled into sight. More tanks were coming from the north. Platoons of soldiers were beginning their house searches. He swung back to look at the river.

The oarsmen were halfway across, rowing steadily, expertly picking their way through the eddies and swirls. The wind clearly carried their shouts of encouragement to each other.

Downriver, an armored personnel carrier appeared. Its machine gun started to fire at the Tibetans on the path. They fell in strange, lifeless heaps. From somewhere behind, Bing heard Tan's short, furious curse. The machine gun fell silent, its traversing barrel looking for new targets.

Bing could see the oarsmen plainly now, no longer shouting, saving their energy, concentrating on rowing.

The boat was lost to view as it came beneath an overhang. The wind momentarily eased as the sun rose above the mountains.

Vultures appeared above the dead Tibetans. They wheeled in a tight circle, their cries clear above the rush of water and the sound of vehicles moving deeper into the city. The machine gun fired another short burst, and several birds plummeted into the river. The others rose ponderously into the sky, flapping back across the water to settle in the rocks around Bing. Though the nearest vulture was some distance away, its fetid smell made his nose wrinkle.

Below him was the sound of sure feet hurrying over the treacherous ground. A little distance apart, the two oarsmen were moving crabwise across the scree, expertly going from one piece of cover to another.

One of the platoon rose, pointing his rifle, shouting for the men to stop. Without breaking his stride, the first Tibetan lunged forward, the impetus of his movement driving home his dagger.

Bing saw the look of surprise on the soldier's face. Then the rifle fell from his nerveless hands, sliding down the icy slope. Even as the soldier began to buckle, the Tibetan reached to free his knife. As he did so, half a dozen guns cut him down. He dropped where he stood, his face, an arm, and a leg shattered.

Soldiers rushed to tend their wounded comrade. Bing stumbled down the scree to take the second man prisoner. He was surprised to see how young he was; he could have been no more than sixteen. His chuba was torn and his hide boots split at the seams. Bing searched him, removing a crude dagger.

Tan came sliding down the scree in a torrent of furious words. He had wanted prisoners, not corpses, he roared. A dead Tibetan was worth nothing. He hurled the corpse down the scree, where it lodged in a gnarled tree a little way above the river.

There was a sudden rush of wings as the vultures swooped on to the tree. They fought with each other over the pickings, using their wings to keep their balance. Beaks and claws dug deep into the flesh, and the constantly flapping feathers sent sprays of blood into the air.

Tan ordered Bing and two other soldiers to take the prisoner to headquarters in the town. He detailed more men to form a stretcher party. The wounded man was no longer conscious. Blood seeped through the field dressing.

The prisoner began to sob, covering his face with his hands as the birds rose into the air, carrying away their spoil.

One of the soldiers prodded the youth with his gun, motioning him to walk in front. Behind Bing came the stretcher-bearers.

Tan used his field radio to summon a jeep to meet the ferry that would take them across the river.

By the time they reached the boat the soldier was coughing gobs of blood. The bearers laid him on the open deck and packed another dressing into his wound. It did not stop the blood running out of his mouth. When the blood began to freeze on his lips, giving them a grotesque, clown-like appearance, Bing realized the man was dead.

One of the escorts turned to the prisoner and punched him on the temple so violently that the youth collapsed against Bing. Bing hauled the Tibetan to his feet, carefully positioning himself between the youth and the others. He warned them not to touch his prisoner again. To reinforce the point, he placed a finger on the safety catch of his rifle.

The rest of the journey passed in uncomfortable silence, the others staring down at the dead man, Bing watching them.

On shore, the corpse was laid on the floor of the jeep. Bing motioned the youth to get in. The others followed, squashing into the back. Horn blowing, the jeep roared through the streets. Through the windshield and the yellow celluloid windows of the canvas sides, Bing could see the mounting panic. Soldiers were everywhere, driving the population before them.

The jeep roared across a bridge, past the guards at the entrance of the 27th Army headquarters, and onto the parade square.

Hours later, Bing continued to watch the square, known as the People's Ground, as it steadily filled with Tibetans. They had been assembling all morning under the watchful eyes of the soldiers. By noon, he calculated, there must have been over a thousand present.

Bing's prisoner stood on a loading platform in front of a large building with a beam and pulley used to haul grain and other supplies.

Bing stood with two other soldiers to one side of the platform. Pinned to its front was a bright red banner bearing the words JUSTICE IS THE PEOPLE'S RIGHT.

At a table on the platform sat PLA officers. Two Bing only knew by sight. The third was Lee Gang. Near him was the political commissar who had addressed the troops on the train journey. He continued to harangue the crowd as he pointed to the prisoner. This reactionary had tried to kill those who were there to protect them. He had betrayed the ideals in which they all believed.

The commissar walked over to stand beside the youth. With one hand he reached forward and twisted the boy's face toward the crowd. This was their enemy, he screamed. Bing saw the soldier operating the loudspeaker system frantically adjusting the amplifier as the commissar's voice rose. This was the enemy of the people! The commissar was drowned out by a howl from the speakers.

He thrust the microphone toward the youth's face and demanded a confession. The boy kept his head bowed. No sound came from the crowd. Liu Lee leaned forward and, in a sharp and peremptory voice, ordered the prisoner to confess.

The youth admitted he was a counterrevolutionary who had obtained arms from the imperialists and was the enemy of the Tibetan and Chinese peoples. When he had delivered his admission he stood with head lowered.

The commissar turned back to the crowd. They had heard him. What did they have to say?

Bing saw the Tibetans looking uneasily at each other, bowing their heads, murmuring softly. The commissar pointed to a woman near the front. What did she have to say? he demanded. Bing had seen the commissar speaking to the woman earlier. In a trembling voice she said the youth had committed crimes against Tibet.

The commissar scanned the crowd, alighting on a man; Bing had seen the commissar address him earlier too. The man gave the same answer as the woman. Twice more the commissar picked out people in the crowd who responded similarly. The woman was speaking again. The youth must die for betraying Tibet.

The cry was taken up by others.

Bing watched the commissar marching back and forth across the platform, extending his microphone toward the crowd so that it could pick up the shouts.

Suddenly, like the water gushing through a dam Bing had seen burst on the Yangtze, everyone was shouting in a sudden and unstoppable rush. The prisoner must die for betraying Tibet! The commissar raised his hand. The crowd fell obediently silent. He turned and faced the trio at the table. One by one the judges gave their verdict.

The commissar signaled for Bing and the other soldiers to climb onto the platform. When they had done so, he went to the rear of the platform and fetched a coiled rope with a noose already fashioned at one end. He gave his instructions quickly.

One soldier balanced on the shoulders of another to secure the rope to the beam. The noose dangled several feet above the youth's head. With Bing supporting the youth's feet, the other soldier forced his head into the noose. Until this moment he had not struggled. Now he began to thrash, fighting to break free of the hands that were preventing him from dying.

The silent crowd watched the contortions. Then, as the exhausted youth grew still, the commissar stepped forward and tapped the soldiers with his microphone. One by one they stepped back. The body started to turn slowly in the wind.

SATURDAY, DECEMBER 31, 1988
BEIDAIHE, CHINA

Shortly after dawn the helicopters lifted out of Zhongnanhai and into a sky the color of sturgeon. Each was filled with members of the Politburo. In loose formation the armada headed east into a sky made even grayer by the smoke from kilns and factories.

Soon the helicopters passed near the industrial coal-mining city of Tangshan. Thirteen years ago many of the leaders had flown there to inspect the damage after one of the worst earthquakes to strike China. Over two hundred thousand had been left dead, a million injured, and four million homeless. Now a new industrial colossus once more stood on the uncertain earth, the pollution from its thousand factories and coal-processing plants blotting out the horizon.

This morning the old men had other thoughts to preoccupy them. They had been summoned at short notice by Deng Xiaoping. For the past week China's supreme ruler had been resting at Beidaihe after another course of chemotherapy, an attempt to halt his slowly progressing cancer. Over the past year, Deng had recuperated between treatments at the coastal resort used only by the Party elite.

An hour after leaving Beijing, the helicopters descended over Beidaihe, passing over the imposing villas and wide streets lined with hibiscus and oleanders.

The resort had been built by the British for their diplomats at the turn of the century as an escape from the stifling heat of Beijing in July and August. Forty years of Communist occupation had not removed an atmosphere of empire. The landscape was dotted with mock Tudor residences and bungalows that looked as if they had been transported from the south coast of England. Beyond their guarded perimeters surged a sea as leaden as the English Channel in winter.

Deng's mansion stood on a headland to the north of the resort. The helicopters settled close to waiting limousines, and the Politburo members were driven to a conference hall.

When they were seated in heavy red-covered armchairs, replicas of those used for Politburo meetings in Zhongnanhai, Deng explained he had summoned them to hear the arguments for and against keeping China on its present economic course.

For the rest of the day, the room echoed to increasingly angry and divisive debate. Familiar positions were restated. Prime Minister Li Peng and his supporters insisted that "bourgeois liberalism" was undermining the very patriotism and socialist values on which the country depended for its future. Party Secretary Zhao Ziyang reiterated that with economic reforms must come new freedoms.

The arguments raged to and fro. Li Peng argued that the ability of the state to regulate the economy had been fundamentally weakened as a result of the decentralization of the *"economic decision-making power."* Zhao countered that the real problem was the failure to curb the corruption that continued to erode Party authority, something he too did not wish to happen.

Figures were bandied around the room. The population was increasing at an average of twelve million a year. Every twelve months the number of people China had to feed increased by more than the population of New York, Los Angeles, or London. Yet now there was already an *"excess of unemployed,"* 180 million manual laborers alone. Li Peng conceded they represented an *"explosive problem"* to the central government that was getting worse as the number of unemployed in urban areas grew.

Zhao insisted the only way to solve the problem was to create a virtually new political-economic system, one that would open its doors to Western ideas.

"Do that," rasped Li Peng, and China's *"ideological purity will be contaminated."* The time had come to curb the *"liberal economic reform policy"* and be ready to face the consequences. If that meant dealing firmly with unrest, so be it.

Late in the afternoon, Deng addressed the factions. In a long and rambling speech, he reviewed what had been said. He seemed to veer toward one point of view, then another. Finally he announced he wanted Zhao Ziyang to modify his policies; perhaps, after all, they had been too liberal, too early.

Li Peng had won a crucial victory.

9

Persuasion

Cassy wore a thickly padded jacket against the biting cold. Similarly clad, Daobao and Yang Li cycled on either side, leading her unerringly through the alleys as they headed diagonally across the city on this New Year's Day morning.

The two students from time to time smiled reassuringly at her. Daobao said again in his soft voice that there was nothing for her to worry about. She was just another foreign expert being shown around the back streets of Beijing by her students. Li nodded.

They emerged from a *hutong,* an alley, crossed an avenue broad enough to accommodate a passenger plane, and entered another lane of gray brick walls and doors made of tin or wood. Every *hutong* seemed to lead a self-contained existence; each had its small factories, shops, and restaurants. They maneuvered past handcarts stacked with produce. The already narrow and crowded alley was further constricted by tiny stalls set up in doorways. In the courtyards beyond, Cassy glimpsed pots and trays and window boxes: Anywhere seeds could be germinated, they were. Daobao explained that several families used one yard to grow produce or raise ducks. They shared a stall to sell their products and divided the profits.

Li had not spoken since breakfast, when he read them Bing's letter reciting the benefits the state provided and attacking student radicalism. When he finished, he folded the letter carefully and put it back in its envelope. Then he took a match and set fire to the paper, shielding the flames with his hands so the fire did not spread.

Cassy wanted to say that burning the letter would change nothing, that his pain would only go away when he could sit down with Bing and talk about their differences. But in the past weeks Li's whole attitude had changed. Even toward his girlfriend, Meili, he appeared distant, as if he wanted no one to get really close to him, nobody to know what he was really thinking.

Daobao said it was because Li was now one of the student movement's strategists. He had sounded so serious; Cassy had managed not to smile. True, the students were meeting in increasing numbers to air their grievances, but she still found little to suggest they were a cohesive movement. They seemed to be separate groups, most with no designated leader, although Wuerkaixi and Wang Dan often articulated the views of one group to another.

In these past weeks Cassy had walked with them through the streets and alleys, listening as they discussed the need for free speech and increased funding for education and teachers' salaries. None of these demands had struck her as representing a properly developed political theory, let alone a detailed blueprint for change. She had thought again they sounded so very young, so very trusting.

No one seemed to be thinking where all this was leading. Yet whenever she expressed a doubt, Daobao brushed aside her fears with the same certainty she had seen him show when boosting the confidence of others. At times it struck her that Daobao really believed he could shift the bureaucratic balance simply by repeating that one word often enough, *democracy*. It was as if the word had assumed magical proportions for Daobao, and he wanted everyone else to share that magic. He had told her he wanted to use democracy to *"only destroy the bad and make even better all that is good in our society."*

In pursuit of this vision, Daobao and Li had suggested she should make this long bicycle ride with them. Daobao said the diplomatic corps was bound to turn out in force to attend the New Year's Day concert in the Jianguo Hotel, and no one would be surprised at her presence, or when she introduced her companions. Foreign experts were always showing off their favorite students to other foreigners. Li had given her his half-smile. Sometimes it could be quite intimidating, she decided.

They pedaled through the street markets, tiny islands of capitalism, the air filled with the shrill of barter and the warble of birds carried in cages. She still had not grown used to the way an old man would hold a cage close to his face and trill to an imprisoned lark or finch. Girls with too much lipstick, and old women walking arm in arm, stared at her, not quite believing a foreigner was among them.

Cassy thought about the careful way Li watched the sudden moments of tension between Wuerkaixi and Wang Dan. Wuerkaixi was increasingly the swashbuckling go-getter, Dan the same reserved student she saw in class. He would not be rushed into anything. Li, she suspected, was trying to decide who would eventually win this battle of wills.

He maintained the same careful approach to Liu Gang. The physics student had thinning hair and rounded shoulders, giving him a scholarly appearance. She wondered if Gang's choice of Western-style sports clothes and drinking from a can was a conscious attempt to balance his seriousness.

Entering another *hutong*, Daobao said this was where the Cultural Revolution had actually started. The Red Guards had come straight from Tiananmen Square to destroy the eleven silk-weaving factories that had been in the alley for centuries.

She asked why they had done that.

He looked pained. Because they had been told to. Didn't she think that was the great national failing of the Chinese, that they always did what they were told?

She glanced at Li. He was staring resolutely ahead. There was no way of knowing what he was thinking.

Daobao pointed out men lounging outside the Exhibition Center. They were *Gonganbu*, the foot soldiers of the Ministry of Public Security, on the lookout for any suspicious contact between foreigners and Chinese inside the cavernous hall. It was one of the places, he said, where homosexuals risked breaking the law to meet. The *Gonganbu* received a special commendation for every one they caught.

She said she found the idea of rewards for arrests genuinely shocking.

Daobao shook his head. Homosexuality was still a serious crime. Last year Pang Yi, suspecting one of the teachers was homosexual, had arranged for the *Gonganbu* to send two men to pose as students. They came to class and slept in a dormitory for almost a whole semester, until they caught the teacher. He had been giving good grades to certain students in return for sex. Daobao said the man had been *"put up on the board."*

She had seen the public notice boards with photographs of offenders standing handcuffed between policemen. She asked what happened to the teacher.

Daobao took his time to answer. He said the man had been executed.

Cassy was too stunned to speak. Finally she asked what had happened to the students.

Daobao sighed and explained they were sent to a labor camp.

They pedaled in silence the length of a *hutong* before he returned to the subject, saying the Chinese were a very traditional people, especially about sex.

They entered another warren of alleys. Daobao pointed to a large, concrete-walled building ahead. The blinds on its ground-floor windows were drawn. A ramp sloped from the closed front door. Two cars were parked illegally on the sidewalk. Their blue-suited chauffeurs stood smoking and talking, ignoring passers-by. Daobao dismounted; the others followed.

Cassy asked what was in the building. Daobao told her to be patient. He and Li continued to watch the door.

It swung open. A man in a shapeless gray uniform emerged and called to the chauffeurs. Stamping out their cigarettes, they hurried into the building. They emerged with two trolleys stacked with chickens, sides of meat, boxes of fish, and crates of fresh vegetables and fruits. With them was a middle-aged woman, dressed incongruously in a bright blue tracksuit and fur jacket. Her feet were encased in expensive calf-length boots.

When the man in the gray suit reached the cars, he darted forward and opened the rear door of one. Without a glance or a word to anyone, the woman slid in. The flunky closed the door and rushed to help the chauffeurs load the second car. They drove off, and the man quickly wheeled the trolleys back into the building. The door closed behind him.

Daobao turned to Cassy. *"You have just seen privilege at work. Politburo members come here and take away stuff by the carload. It's all subsidized. A whole pig costs about the same as a few ounces of pork in the shops. A crate of whiskey less than a bottle."*

The familiar tension was back in his voice. He nodded toward the building.

"*This place is filled with the very best from all over the world. You can even get prawns here every day.*"

The tension made Daobao's face stiffen. Cassy knew prawns were a luxury available to ordinary Chinese only on New Year. Li mounted and pedaled away. They followed him.

There were several similar stores, Daobao explained. One stocked the latest foreign videos, another current bestsellers from New York and London. Each book was marked *Nei-bu*, restricted, meaning it could only be read by the purchaser or his or her immediate family. Some shops sold only the newest fashions from Paris, others, *objets d'art* from around the Pacific. One store stocked furniture from as far afield as Canada and Bavaria. Another offered the most up-to-date sports equipment.

It was privileges like these the students wished to change, Daobao said. Trotsky had been right when he said all revolutions started for the same reason: because some people had an unfair advantage.

Cassy reminded him Trotsky had also said those who started revolutions often had no clear aims or leadership. Daobao replied Trotsky had also written it was enough to have a common hostility against the existing regime. She saw the half-smile was back on Li's lips.

They crossed the broad expanse of Dongdan Street. Daobao pointed to an open doorway with strips of silver tinsel pinned to its lintel. Men and women were walking under the decoration into the building. "*They've decided they want to get married. So they come to a place like this. The Party operates hundreds of marriage bureaus around the country,*" Daobao said.

Li broke his long silence. "*The Party encourages marriages between people who have the correct political outlook and are prepared to work together for society.*" He gave *correct* and *together* a mocking obeisance.

"*Until quite recently the Party had the total right to decide if a couple were suitable for each other. Now it just 'advises.' You'd be surprised how many take that advice because they don't want to make what the Party calls a 'mistake.'*"

Passing the bureau's door, Cassy glimpsed a room filled with men and women sitting on hard-back chairs. A couple of middle-aged women emerged, giggling softly to each other, clutching forms in their hands.

Daobao called out to ask if they had found husbands. They looked at him, startled. Then they hurried away, their confusion plain. He grinned at Cassy.

"*My cousin met her husband at one of these places. She was fat and fifty and no man in her village would look at her. She had teeth like this.*" Daobao bared his gums in imitation of a rabbit chewing. "*The bureau matched her with somebody twenty years older. All they had in common was that he had the same kind of teeth!*"

They separated outside the Friendship Store on the corner of Ritan Road. Li had insisted it was a risk for them to go together to the hotel; the *Gonganbu* were bound to be out in force there, looking for foreigners. They would meet her in the lobby. Cassy thought again that China hadn't changed since the time of the emperors: It remained a country where mystery is a cult and suspicion a religion.

As she parked her bicycle in the hotel forecourt, two agents gave her a quick look before turning back to note the numbers of cars with diplomatic plates.

They did so openly. She wondered if this was another of those petty exercises of authority for its own sake.

After checking her coat, she went to the lobby. Its carpets were Indian, the furniture from half a dozen countries, and the staff recruited from the *hutongs* and sent through a hotel school. The Jianguo was intended to give its guests a feeling of familiarity, that this could be any hotel anywhere.

The lobby was set up for the regular Sunday morning concert. Tables were crowded together; those near the door were mostly occupied by Chinese managers and foreign technicians.

The managers sat primly straight, blinking about them, smiling politely at some booming remark delivered in the thick accent of central Europe. The technicians were dressed as if they had come straight from the factory floor, wearing tieless shirts and heavy jackets and trousers. Slavic-faced women were smothered in makeup and laughed a lot among themselves, matching their men beer for beer. The Chinese invariably sipped soft drinks.

The tables in the center were occupied by Western and Hong Kong businessmen dressed in sober suits like their Chinese guests. Their women were smartly dressed and coiffeured and smiled at one another a great deal while the men sat with heads close together, concentrating on completing a deal or settling a contract. For them the lobby was another office.

Between potted palms at one end of the room, the orchestra tuned up. The half dozen rows of molded plastic chairs facing them were already full.

Cassy recognized familiar faces. The Greek ambassador was deep in conversation with the Italian ambassador. She had met them at a social evening at the French embassy. A few seats away, the Hungarian first secretary sat beside his counterpart from Sweden. The two diplomats had arrived in Beijing at the same time as she had. Cassy had told Daobao she knew probably a dozen envoys. That had given Li the idea to come here with her.

He and Daobao were standing near the bar. She waved at them and began to edge past the tables, heading into the room. They moved across the lobby toward her.

She recognized Raymond Burghardt, the counselor for political affairs, and his wife, Susan, the First Secretary Billy Huff and his wife, Lorraine, at the American embassy table. Burghardt was talking to a florid-faced man with heavy jowls at an adjoining table. The others seated there were listening respectfully to the conversation. The man nodded in an oddly pedantic way.

"That's Troyanovsky, the Soviet ambassador. Last year he gave us a talk on diplomacy," Daobao murmured behind her.

Cassy was close enough now to hear Burghardt asking about the prospects for a Sino-Soviet summit. Troyanovsky was saying it was too early to know, but he'd heard that Bush was planning to visit Beijing soon after he was inaugurated. Burghardt smiled and said advance men from Washington had flown in a few days earlier to conduct a preliminary reconnaissance.

This time Li spoke. *"The one with jug ears next to the ambassador. That's Boris Kovik. Don't be fooled by his smile. He's KGB. Always hanging around the campus."*

Nearby a group with distinctly English accents were ordering more drinks.

Among them was Brian Davidson. The tall, fair-haired young diplomat was the press attaché at the British embassy.

Burghardt was saying he'd heard that Deng Xiaoping's doctors were starting a new course of chemotherapy. Troyanovsky said the drug was Russian.

Cassy realized the lobby was a familiar place for them all, one for exchanging information, for checking, verifying, or discounting rumors.

Li looked at Cassy and then toward a table that still had several vacant places. A couple of men sat toying with beers. One was strongly built with a clear complexion and an honestly happy smile. The other was solemn-faced with thick spectacles.

Cassy smiled at him, pointing at the vacant chairs and raising three fingers. The man nodded.

Cassy walked over to the table with Li and Daobao. She introduced herself and then the students.

The bespectacled man said he was Brendan Ward, second secretary at the Irish embassy, and his companion was Ian McGuinness, a plant manager with Siemens.

Ward ordered a waiter to bring drinks. Li sat next to the diplomat. As if it were the most natural thing in the world to say, he told Ward how very fortuitous it was he had met him, as he was planning a term paper on Ulster. One of the many issues he wanted to deal with was the Irish Republican Army's use of hunger strikers to make a political point. How, asked Li, did the strikers prepare themselves for fasting to death?

Ward looked at him quizzically. But before he could reply, the orchestra began its opening number.

As they settled to listen Cassy saw Li's half-smile again. She suspected it was there because she had maneuvered the introduction he had wanted.

MONDAY, JANUARY 2, 1989
CENTRAL INTELLIGENCE AGENCY

At the first 9:00 A.M. staff meeting of the New Year, Webster and his senior aides considered the Politburo meeting at Beidaihe. The National Security Agency had put together a full account. NSA staff supplement the work of CIA officers operating undercover from U.S. embassies and carry out the majority of eavesdropping operations abroad, regularly providing verbatim transcripts from high-level foreign government meetings.

Part of the report had come from satellite surveillance and the agency's own ultra secret and state-of-the-art collection technology. Some of the details had been confirmed by the National Reconnaissance Office, the low-profile agency with special responsibility for what its brief only called *"other overhead intelligence gathering."* This included the use of not only satellites but also spy planes. The NRO reported primarily to the Secretary of Defense. In practice, Webster controlled their activities. A portion of the report had been marked SCI, for Sensitive Compartmented Information, indicating that its content was especially sensitive and would only be seen by those on the BIGOT list, still only a handful in the incoming Bush administration.

Many questions were being discussed at the staff meeting: Would Party Secretary Zhao Ziyang become increasingly isolated? Or would he try even harder to push through his reforms? And if he did, would he appeal for public support? Would he continue, for instance, to use newspapers such as the *World Economic Herald* to promote his ideas? Published in Shanghai, the paper now had an influence far beyond the city. It was read in all the capitals of the world and recognized as an advocate for reform.

Would Prime Minister Li Peng, secure in his new power, simply ignore Zhao? Or would he take the first real opportunity to attack him publicly at the next meeting of the National People's Congress, China's parliament? It would be dangerous for the prime minister to do this and then discover that an insufficient number of delegates supported him. That would seriously damage Li Peng's credibility. It could even make Deng think again about supporting his prime minister in a power play against Zhao.

Fang Lizhi, the most astute of China's intellectuals and a physicist hailed as the country's Sakharov, had once more put his huge authority behind the call for human rights. Fang's strategies had underpinned the 1986–87 student political protests. As a result he had been dismissed as vice-president of the University of Science and Technology at Hefei. But because of his worldwide reputation, no other action had been taken. Fang had continued to run a highly vocal campaign for change from his Beijing apartment. An old friend of Zhao's, he demanded much that echoed the Party Secretary's beliefs. The day of the Beidaihe meeting Fang had written to Deng asking that he release all political prisoners.

"*Without the right to express democracy, there can be no development,*" he had concluded.

If Fang had made the appeal with Zhao's full approval, that undoubtedly placed the Party Secretary openly in sympathy with student demands and must surely further encourage their militancy. With Fang behind them, and Zhao behind him, would the students want to translate their demands into action?

Webster's analysts said that if they did, the most likely day they would choose was the coming May 4, the seventieth anniversary of an important date in China's recent history.

On May 4, 1919, four thousand students had marched into Tiananmen Square, protesting China's humiliation at the peace conference in Versailles. The victors of the First World War had decided that Japan, not China, should receive Germany's former territories on the Chinese coast. The students had chanted that China's humiliation was the result of a corrupt political system.

The May the Fourth Movement, the first recorded organized student protest in China, had swiftly grown to challenge the country's entire educational and social system. That summer too, Beijing had echoed with the call for unprecedented political change, an end to China's feudal rule and the introduction of rule by law. The chant for "democratic reform" had been heard in Tiananmen Square for weeks.

The protest had eventually led to the birth of the Communist Party, and May 4 had remained a highly emotive celebration in the Party calendar. But recently Deng had tried to play down its importance. His focus was on the coming October, the fortieth anniversary of the founding of the Chinese state.

Yet Webster and his staff knew that May 4 would prove critical, given the current mood of China's students.

It fell on the eve of the forthcoming Sino-Soviet summit; Gorbachev could find himself in Beijing in the middle of student upheavals. Would he want to postpone his historic meeting with Deng until Beijing's house was in order? Or would he use the student protests for his own purposes, to push the idea that even in China, Communism must change?

It would be unthinkable for Deng to cancel the May 4 celebration. But could he control it? And would Zhao use the occasion to invite further reforms? Would the students echo his demands? Would the Party Secretary be ready to set the youth on a path that could plunge China into chaos? Would Hu Yaobang emerge to support them? And how would the protest be stopped? What would the Army do? The commander of the 27th Army was still canvassing support from Tibet for his fellow commanders in China to take a strong line with any future unrest. Would he succeed?

Webster wanted as many answers as possible before Bush went calling on Deng.

He told his staff the key to China's future could once more be in the hands of young people who almost certainly did not understand the responsibilities they had. In every contact the agency had with them, the director stressed, absolutely nothing must be done to encourage them to believe the United States would do anything to support their aims.

10

Camelot, Almost

FRIDAY, JANUARY 6, 1989
BEIJING

Professor Guangzu waited outside the main hospital entrance for the car to collect him for dinner with Hu Yaobang. He wore a dark Mao jacket and a tieless white shirt closed to the top button. In an inside coat pocket was a slim case holding a set of acupuncture needles. He never went anywhere without them.

At the end of his last lecture of the day he had reminded his students to do the same. Several had smiled indulgently. Attitudes had changed since he was a student.

Over Tiananmen Square the fog was suspended like a false ceiling into which the colonnades of the Great Hall of the People, the Monument of the People's Heroes, and Mao's mausoleum abruptly disappeared. On the other side of Changan Avenue, he could just make out the huge portrait suspended from Tiananmen Gate, Mao's coal-black eyes staring with an intensity that seemed to send the mist swirling uneasily.

For centuries the gate had been the epicenter of authority. Beyond lay the old Imperial palaces, the Forbidden City, from which the emperors had ruled, convinced their moated domain was the very center of the universe and themselves divinely blessed to govern. They had rarely gone beyond the high palace walls, content to have their proclamations read from the balcony of the Gate of Heavenly Peace.

Almost forty years before, Professor Guangzu had stood with over a million other people before this imperial relic and listened to Mao promise a new China. Instead there had been brutality, waste, and terrible personal suffering.

Deng Xiaoping had finally said he would end all that. He had tried; no one would deny that. But he had failed; how could he not? The factional battles; the *"struggle between two lines,"* as the battle between the hardliners and moderates had once been called; the arrest of Mao's widow, Jiang Qing and her three leftist comrades, forever to be vilified as the Gang of Four; the endless turmoil within the Party and government; the removal of Hu from office: All this had created apathy, cynicism, and fear.

Hu's firing as Party Secretary had been a particular blow to liberal political reforms. Despite his puny size and a penchant for coloring his hair black and sometimes wearing outmoded "Kipper-style" neckties, Hu had been respected by both the students and the uneducated masses. They saw him as a politician with only China's best interests at heart. Yet he had been sacrificed by Deng in a carefully calculated move for Deng to remain in office. Not for the first time had the ultimate ruler of China shown he could be both highly manipulative and malevolent. In removing Hu, Deng had added to his own reputation as the Great Survivor, the man who had himself survived three political purges and lived virtually on a diet of dog meat and sixty extra-strong Panda cigarettes a day, and to hell with what his doctors said about exacerbating his cancer.

Yet despite Deng's promise to modernize, the idealism, the energy, and the almost messianic fervor that had imbued the early years of Communism were no longer there. No matter how hard Deng tried to rekindle the enthusiasm of the people for a political system, it continued to lose what remained of its original appeal.

Professor Guangzu knew that part of the reason was the country's plodding bureaucracy, the system that allowed petty officials to demand full explanations for every *yuan* that was spent. That attitude stifled even the most energetic of the young and spread resentment.

Some of his own students were now politically active. He had heard them talking of the need to clear their minds of *"outdated"* Marxist dogma and saying that *"complete Westernization"* was the only way to modernize. They attacked the absence of human rights. Many spoke with a passion that surprised him; medical students had never been at the forefront of protest. It had made him wonder what the student engineers and economists, the traditional activists, must be saying.

At the heavily guarded western gate to Zhongnanhai one of the sentries checked Professor Guangzu's name against a master list. Then the barrier was raised and the car drove slowly into a broad driveway close to the lake.

Hu's home was at the southern end, its roof low and sloped and finished with traditional tiles. Lanterns were suspended from the carport. A security man rose from his chair in a corner and came forward, nodding deferentially as Professor Guangzu alighted.

Hu opened the richly lacquered front door. He was dressed in a dark Western-style suit that hung on him incongruously, his wrists sticking several inches below the cuffs. His hair gleamed unnaturally black from a recent dyeing. Behind stood his wife, Li Zhao, a small trim woman with her long hair, still naturally black, coiled in a bun. She wore a full-length dress with a high Mandarin collar. To Professor Guangzu, she always looked like a dowager empress.

They greeted him warmly and led him in to dinner, not to the large dining room on the left of the hallway reserved for more formal entertaining, but to a small room opposite where the family ate. Its walls were hung with photographs of Hu as Party Secretary, with foreign leaders such as President Nixon and Prime Minister Thatcher. There was also a framed piece of Mao's calligraphy. Written on the Long March, it had been a wedding gift to Madame Hu.

The table was set with Chinese red-and-white porcelain. The family cook had prepared the food and stood ready to serve it.

Professor Guangzu was the only guest; the Hus rarely entertained nowadays.

The meal was simple but delicious: hot-sour soup followed by roast duck, grilled fish, and a dessert made from almond paste. Tea was served with each course.

While they ate, Hu delivered a discourse on various newspaper articles that had appeared in that day's *People's Daily*. He said it was not enough for Zhao Ziyang to predict that soon two-thirds of the country's economy would be outside state control. That still meant almost a third was in the hands of no fewer than 107 separate government departments. These were overstaffed and inept, Hu continued. What was needed, he added, was the *"kind of housecleaning that regularly occurs in the West."* There senior managers were fired when they failed; in China they were given more staff to create further chaos.

The more he spoke, the more excitable he became, half-rising from his chair, waving his hands to emphasize a point, his face purple, a vein throbbing in his temple. The sight alarmed Professor Guangzu.

Pausing only to drink tea, Hu switched direction.

That afternoon, he explained, he had attended a Politburo meeting where Qiao Shi, the country's intelligence chief, had again warned that the students were beginning to *"mobilize seriously."* Hu described how Qiao Shi had identified the student ringleaders including Wuerkaixi, Wang Dan, and Chai Ling.

Hu deftly sketched portraits of the leaders. Wuerkaixi, born in remote Turkestan, the son of a local Party official. The former Party Secretary growled, Wuerkaixi had all the fervor of one of those born-again Christians Hu had seen on TV. And he didn't like the way Wuerkaixi aped American dress! The professor smiled. Tonight, Hu was dressed like a Wall Street broker.

Wang Dan was the steadying hand among the students, Hu went on. And he put up with no nonsense from the flamboyant Wuerkaixi. Chai Ling's elfin face masked a true revolutionary's mind; if she had been on the Long March, she would have commanded a woman's battalion. Hu remembered Liu Gang from the last student protests in 1986–87, which had finally led to Deng dismissing Hu for speaking up for the students.

Among them, the dozen or so key student leaders had the intellect and determination to effectively mobilize the campuses.

Professor Guangzu sensed Hu's enthusiasm for what the students were doing — creating an atmosphere of growing confrontation with the authorities.

Among the latest demands the student leaders were circulating around the campuses was that the incomes and assets of every member of the Politburo and their relatives be made public. Hu said he had not been surprised this demand had brought angry protests from many of his fellow Politburo members: A number of them had substantial deposits in Swiss bank accounts and, through their families, considerable investments in stock markets around the world.

Qiao Shi had told the Politburo that the students wanted the ban on street marches lifted and the right to have their demands fully reported in the press.

This had produced even angrier murmurs, which had further increased when Hu had intervened.

Professor Guangzu asked what his host had said.

Hu smiled his impish, garden-gnome smile: He had told the Politburo that the student demands were reasonable. There had been an uproar. Cadres had shouted at him from all sides.

And Deng, asked Professor Guangzu, how had Deng responded?

Hu shook his head. Deng had just sat there following the debate, saying not a word.

And Zhao Ziyang?

Hu sounded almost resentful. Zhao had also sat there and said nothing, not even when Qiao Shi had stood up and insisted he should now be allowed to arrest the student leaders. The intelligence chief had remained on his feet staring fixedly at Deng.

Professor Guangzu asked about Deng's reaction.

Hu looked around the table, drawing on an imaginary cigarette in a passable imitation of Deng. After a while Deng had motioned Qiao to be seated and then said that the students should be allowed to go on making their plans, Hu reported. That had produced further murmurs. Deng had waved for silence. Then he had said, *"When we know who they all are and what they all want, we can deal with them."*

Hu slumped further in his seat, once more imitating Deng smoking.

Professor Guangzu asked what Zhao had said to that.

Hu raised a finger to his lips: nothing. When it came to the students, he continued, there was something about Zhao he no longer trusted. If it suited him, his successor as Party Secretary would sacrifice them just as ruthlessly as Deng had done for his own survival.

"Survival," Hu said in his high-pitched voice. *"That is all they are concerned with."*

Hu began to speak with passion. The students could continue to count on his total support; through him they could reach the very core of government, even Deng himself. Once more half out of his chair, his excitement plain, Hu said that despite Deng's decision to ease up on reforms, matters had progressed too far; expectations had been raised that could not be lowered.

Madame Hu rose to her feet and gently but firmly pushed her husband back into his seat, the way a mother might deal with an overexcitable child. Hu smiled sheepishly at her. Waiting until she had resumed her place, he continued more calmly. Deng had created a trap for himself: In ordering limited economic freedoms he had misjudged the mood of the people, who wanted full political freedom.

Hu once again began to rise from his chair. His wife turned toward him, shaking her head.

This time he ignored her. He said that if the people didn't get what they wanted, they would fight for it. Not just the students but all the people.

Hu sank back in his chair, staring in turn at each of them. His voice solemn, he promised he would lead the fight from within the Politburo.

SATURDAY, JANUARY 14, 1989
BEIJING UNIVERSITY CAMPUS

Late in the afternoon, from a window in Daobao's dormitory block, Cassy watched the students converging on the barracks-like building. Behind her, close to a hundred already sat on beds and on the floor and leaned against the walls. The air was foggy from cigarette smoke.

Daobao, Cassy was glad to see, had managed to kick the smoking habit. She could observe him at the far end of the room, standing tall and still, only his eyes taking in the steady stream of newcomers.

The dark-skinned Yang Li and his pale girlfriend, Meili, were among the other student leaders. Standing with Daobao, Li had confided to Cassy a few days ago that when *"this is all over"* he hoped to marry Meili and take her back to his home on the banks of the Yangzte River. Cassy had privately wondered how the daughter of a middle-class family would blend into the hard village life.

Li's words, *"when this is all over,"* reminded Cassy how far the students seemed determined to push for reform. This meeting was the latest in a number of gatherings in which the student leaders had promoted their demands.

Daobao had constructed a makeshift platform by resting planks on lockers laid on their sides. Wang Dan was gingerly testing his weight on the boards. He wore another of his seemingly unlimited supply of sweatshirts.

Outside the building, Cassy could see the students Wuerkaixi had ordered be posted to signal a warning in case Pang Yi or any other of the political officers should show up. In that event the student leaders would switch back to discussing the ostensible purpose of the meeting, science and art within the framework of the state.

When the dormitory was completely filled, students sat on each other's laps. Some of the girls perched on top of bedside lockers or curled up on window ledges.

Daobao had reserved a place for Cassy to one side of the platform. Satisfied it would hold his weight, Wang Dan raised his hand for silence.

He immediately launched a withering attack on the economic policies of the central government. He called it *"an economy where everyone sells and buys but no one creates anything."*

Other speakers followed, decrying *"the dead hands"* controlling policies that were designed *"to improve only their own fortunes."*

Finally, Wuerkaixi rose.

He flashed the all-knowing smile that had become as much his trademark as the California-made denims he wore like a uniform.

Cassy had to admit, when Wuerkaixi had the floor he was electrifying. Every gesture seemed perfectly timed; every flick of the eyes, pause, and inflection proclaimed him either a carefully rehearsed, or a born, orator.

He spoke fiercely about the leadership's luxurious life-style. His voice trembling with anger, Wuerkaixi began to describe how the leaders, *"not satisfied with their own embezzlement, encourage their children to pillage our nation."*

Wuerkaixi then cited how the Kang Hua Company, the largest in China, was *"deeply engaged in officially approved speculation"* under the stewardship of

Deng Xiaoping's son, Deng Difang. All the sons of the top leaders were engaged *"in one kind of racketeering or another,"* including the four sons of Party Secretary Zhao Ziyang.

"We are told to work hard and practice frugality while our leaders cheat us and future generations!" Wuerkaixi cried. *"That is why we have inflation! That is why our consumer goods are often of poor quality! That is why all of us here have a duty, to China itself, to go out and change the situation!"*

He stepped off the platform to thunderous applause.

Watching Wuerkaixi make his way out of the dormitory followed by Daobao and the others, Cassy thought again how this country was awash with resentment and anger, coupled to an awareness of who was responsible. The combination was a potent mixture that, if ignited, could spread with the speed of a brush fire.

11
Presidential Pragmatism

MONDAY, FEBRUARY 6, 1989
BEIJING

Cycling to work, Cassy sensed that throughout the city on this chilly winter's morning, millions of Chinese continued to repeat one word, *Bush*.

In a few days the newly elected President of the United States would come to Beijing, giving China the honor of being the second nation he would visit after his inauguration. The President and the First Lady would arrive from Tokyo after attending the funeral of Emperor Hirohito later in the month, but that would be largely a matter of protocol, not politics. Having the new leader of the Western world come for a state visit was being seen as a major political coup for China's leadership.

No one doubted that as well as the glittering pomp and ceremony, there would be some very tough bargaining that would have far-reaching implications for China's future. One of Cassy's friends, an American diplomat in Beijing, had reduced the Bush visit to two questions: "*Can the President and his hosts ensure that China continues its economic openness while not losing its ideological purity? Can China's leaders ensure that domestic factors be made to interact with external factors?*"

Other diplomats with whom Cassy was friendly, especially those from Europe, had predicted that Bush would go out of his way to convince his hosts that the last thing America wanted was to push Beijing backward, either to isolationism or into the arms of Moscow.

When she had told Daobao, he had been genuinely shocked. He said all the student leaders had hoped President Bush would deliver a clear statement asking for an acceleration in human rights in return for continued U.S. economic support.

Once more she had thought how naive the students were. She was certain their aspirations were low in the calculations of America's foreign-policy makers. Her U.S. diplomat friend had told her there was simply too much at stake to risk upsetting Deng Xiaoping and the other old men of Zhongnanhai.

A number of her Chinese friends said that the Bush visit was further proof of China's standing in the world. This feeling had been reinforced by the news of the Sino-Soviet summit scheduled for May, which would officially mark the end of the long freeze in relations between the Communist superpowers.

Cycling through the campus Cassy once more experienced a warm glow of pride in simply being an American. Students called out to her asking what Bush was like.

Her attempts to get her students to follow the prescribed curriculum were good-naturedly brushed aside in a bombardment of similar questions. Had Bush kept up with the Chinese language, which he had shown signs of mastering when he had been posted here as the American ambassador? Would he be able to force the pace of democracy? Would he speak out on human rights? Would he use what the Chinese press was now constantly referring to as his "old friendship" with Deng Xiaoping not only to promote trade, but to develop the idea that China must become a more open society?

Cassy repeatedly said the President was sure to be sympathetic on all such matters. Privately she was less certain. She had attended another meeting of the student leaders. Wuerkaixi had said it would be *"foolish and dangerous"* to expect anything from Bush because U.S. trade with China was now running at $14 billion a year. The President would say or do nothing to disturb that situation, Wuerkaixi predicted.

Now Yang Li had returned to the subject in his usual oblique way.

"Cassy," he began, *"I would like to ask a question."*

She had told everyone to call her Cassy. Li was one of the few students who did.

"Shoot," she said.

Several of the other students had turned to look at Li. Even before he spoke she realized that what he was going to say would be addressed to them. He had often done this before, using her as a conduit to make a point to the others. There were sides to Li she did not always like.

Li folded his arms before he spoke. *"Do you think President Bush understands that China is to Gorbachev what Europe was to Peter the Great, a stage for him to try out his new political thinking?"*

Cassy shook her head. *"I've no idea what the President thinks."* There was a deliberate sharpness in her voice. The idea that she was infallible on American foreign policy had begun to wear thin.

But Li continued to press. *"Many Chinese feel the visit of the Soviet leader is not only a rapprochement with our people, but represents the first real challenge to the new administration in Washington. If that is so, then Bush will most certainly do nothing to upset our leaders. Therefore all our expectations will be based on a false premise. So should we not try and make our views known to the President?"*

There were murmurs of agreement throughout the room. Conversations sprang up among several students as they debated what Li had said. From his desk in the back of the class Li gave her his half smile.

SAME DAY, LATER
THE GREAT HALL OF THE PEOPLE

In a salon in the Great Hall of the People, the full Politburo had assembled at midmorning on this Monday to discuss the Bush visit. As usual Deng sat to one side wreathed in cigarette smoke, taking little direct part in the discussion but not missing a nuance.

Foreign Minister Qian Qichen began by saying that the United States could no longer regard its relationship with China as being based upon a common opposition to Soviet expansion in the region. Americans now realized that China was at *"the takeoff stage."* Every U.S. company doing business in the People's Republic was anxious to develop those links, especially at the expense of the Japanese.

Murmurs of satisfaction came from those seated around the foreign minister. Many of the old men still bore the scars, and memories, of the war they had fought against the Japanese fifty years before.

As usual the Politburo were seated in a semicircle of armchairs, each with its stand ashtray on one side and spittoon on the other. Behind each chair sat key advisers, taking notes. In addition, behind Hu Yaobang's chair stood an official informally known as "The Coat Tail Puller." His sole function was to restrain Hu when the passion of his argument forced him to his feet. Deng had ordered the official to be present after Hu had stood up and addressed the Politburo, his face so suffused that he had alarmed his colleagues.

Now, however, Hu sat slumped in his armchair, listening as Qian Qichen continued to argue that Bush would be anxious to present the United States *"as an Asian power."* Sensing the bafflement of some of his listeners, the foreign minister explained the phrase: America wished to be a major partner in China's plans to replace Japan as the next superpower to emerge from the Pacific. Bush had indicated this desire by nominating James Lilley as his next ambassador to China. The diplomat had served in the region before and was known to be *"a friend of China's."* Henry Kissinger had spoken for Lilley. In the foreign minister's view, there could be no higher recommendation.

Kissinger Associates had been helpful over the Bush visit, as always, providing supplementary briefing papers on U.S. expectations and what the new administration was prepared to offer in return. The United States wanted to increase its economic ties with China. In return it would view with understanding how China resolved its internal problems. Stripped of all the verbosity that characterizes so many Kissinger Associates documents, it came down to that simple tradeoff.

Hu Yaobang bestirred himself to ask a question: *"What would Bush say about the East Wind deal?"*

A few months ago China had sold Saudi Arabia a supply of East Wind missiles, each with a range of two thousand miles. The deal had stunned the Reagan administration, which had until then clung to the belief that neither Beijing nor Riyadh would alter the balance of power in the Middle East without at least checking with the United States. Reagan had dispatched his Secretary of Defense, Frank Carlucci, to seek assurances that such missiles would not be sold to what Reagan had defined as *"the terrorist club"*: Libya, Iraq, Iran, and Syria.

In Beijing Carlucci found himself in a not unfamiliar position for a Western emissary: a victim of Chinese subtlety. The Chinese said, of course, they wished to do nothing to encourage the dangerous spread of missiles, overlooking the fact they had supplied Iraq and Iran with a vast quantity of Silkworm missiles capable of delivering poison gas warheads. But, Carlucci had been reminded, the Chinese take pride in being one of the world's masters of rocketry. And naturally they had a living to make, and such arrangements included selling their weaponry to North Korea, their friendly neighbor. What happened to such weaponry after that was really no concern of China's.

Every member of the Politburo knew what really happened. From the North Korean port of Nampo, the missiles and their support electronics were exported to the Middle East through CITIC, the Chinese trading-banking-industrial development corporation, many of whose key posts were filled by the sons of the old men in the salon.

Behind Hu's question was another: *"Would President Bush put aside his personal determination to say or do nothing to offend his hosts and ask about those arms transactions?"*

Deng's answer was brief. If his *"old friend"* so far forgot himself as a *"polite guest"* to pose an embarrassing question, he would be firmly reminded how it could harm friendly relations between the two countries.

Deng paused and looked around the semicircle of attentive faces. He settled on Zhao Ziyang.

"I will leave it to you to convey to the President our thoughts on the matter," Deng said.

The Party chief nodded.

Prime Minister Li Peng then raised the question of possible student protests during the President's visit.

Deng's voice was harsh. *"That must not happen."*

SATURDAY, FEBRUARY 26, 1989
BEIJING

Flanked by their advisers and aides, Deng Xiaoping and President Bush sat in the splendor of the Great Hall of the People. Around them hundreds of reporters and photographers waited to record the first exchange between the two leaders.

Deng began by expressing *"a very hearty welcome."* Then, as if he needed to remind himself, he added, *"Furthermore, we have been good friends for a long time."*

Bush then made one of his peculiar hand-chopping motions, as if he were practicing *taijiquan*, the martial arts exercise.

The small talk between the two leaders developed a surrealistic tone, with Deng saying Bush was *"quite an athlete"* and the President mumbling, *"I keep tryin', keep ridin' my bicycle."* Deng then said they had one thing in common, playing bridge, drawing from Bush the comment, *"You're too good for me."* That prompted Deng to remind the President they had never played together. Bush chopped more air: *"I gave up bridge a long time ago. Too complicated. Too difficult. You're the expert."*

Deng beamed his panda-smile. *"No, it is even more difficult for you to find time to play bridge. It's a tough job being President of the United States. You could be the champion of the world in terms of the business of state."*

Bush's hand movements went into overdrive. *"There is much change in the world, so many big things are happening. I've come here at an interesting time, both an opportunity and a challenge. I'm delighted that Mr. Gorbachev will come to China. It's a good thing."*

Both men then turned to the press corps and shook hands several times. After a few minutes White House minders and officials from the Chinese Information Ministry ushered out the media.

The leaders were left alone with their aides. Bush's included Secretary of State Baker and National Security Adviser Brent Scowcroft; Deng was flanked by Prime Minister Li Peng and Party Secretary Zhao Ziyang. There was a lengthening silence.

It was broken by Zhao saying how much they were all looking forward to the Texas-style barbecue Bush had invited them to attend as a climax to his visit. To give the occasion an authentic atmosphere, a large supply of Lone Star beer had been flown in, along with prime U.S. steaks and Idaho potatoes.

Deng apologized for not being able to attend, blaming his doctors, who insisted he must go to bed early. It was the only clue he gave that he was not in good health. Deng added that the Chinese Party would be led by Li Peng and State President Yang Shangkun.

Once more there was silence. Bush and his entourage knew why. China's most celebrated dissident, astrophysicist Fang Lizhi, had been included on the guest list in a belated move by Bush to appease what the President had called *"the liberal element"* in the United States.

Before leaving Washington, Bush had studied the CIA'S profile of Fang, described in the document as *"China's Andrei Sakharov."* It was a typical piece of work from the CIA's Political/Psychological Division, as heavy on the small details as it was on more important issues. Fang's *"good cheer and guilelessness"* were noted. So was his whinny of a laugh. His penchant for permanent-press slacks was recorded, together with the tortoise-shell glasses that gave him a slightly owlish appearance. Fang's *"political formlessness seems rooted in his personality."* He had become *"an icon"* to China's students. The document ended with extracts from Fang's more celebrated speeches calling for reform in China.

Fang was to be the token dissident at the banquet. He would be there to dispel a growing impression that the new administration had established what Fang himself had recently called *"a double standard on human rights,"* tough on the Soviet Union and soft on China.

Already Bush's spokesmen, confirming that Fang had been invited, had made it clear that Bush had no intention of actually meeting the dissident, any more than the President intended to raise the subject of human rights in his discussion with China's leadership.

It was Zhao Ziyang who raised the subject. He launched into what some

State Department officials came to call *"a tongue-lashing"* on the danger for anyone who meddled in the internal affairs of China.

While Bush sat somber-faced, hands clasped in his lap, Zhao delivered Deng's message that those Chinese dissidents who advocated Western-style democracy could cause the nation's economic reforms to fail.

"That will neither contribute to the stability of China's political situation, nor will it be conducive to the friendship between our two countries," Zhao concluded.

The warning shot drew no response from Bush. During the rest of the meeting the discussion concentrated on how America could improve its trade links with China. Li Peng predicted that by the time China absorbed Hong Kong in 1997, U.S. trade with the People's Republic could be around $20 billion a year, not only securing America's position as China's main business partner, but giving the United States an even greater power base in the Pacific.

Hours later when Fang and his wife set out by car to attend the barbecue at the Great Wall Sheraton, they were stopped by police and told their invitation had been canceled, almost certainly on the orders of Deng Xiaoping. Next day, as he left China, Bush expressed his "regret" that Fang had not appeared at the festivities. *"It has been quite a party, just like back home,"* he told his hosts before boarding Air Force One.

Even before the plane left Chinese air space, the first posters were being put up by the students around Beijing University. They demanded the right of *"full intellectual and political freedom"* and *"the right to meet whom we wish in the name of democracy."*

The students had finally delivered their first public proclamation.

Cycling to class, Cassy saw that Pang Yi and Beijing University's other political officers were already busy tearing down the posters. But no sooner had they removed one than another took its place.

MONDAY, MARCH 7, 1989
THE PRIME MINISTER'S RESIDENCE
ZHONGNANHAI

Prime Minister Li Peng faced an unpalatable truth on this windswept morning. In the past week posters calling for democracy had appeared on campuses throughout the capital and in other university cities. Many of the posters called for support for the May Fourth Movement and its demand for *"a new China."*

Students and intellectuals were being asked to give voice to the demands at a rally in Tiananmen Square in two months' time, May 4. The rally would commemorate the seventieth anniversary of that celebrated occasion in 1919 when a ragtag procession of students had made their way to the square to protest a corrupt political system.

Security Chief Qiao Shi had once more suggested a roundup of the student leaders. But this time Li Peng had ordered nothing must be done. Coincidentally with the rash of posters, those who championed reform, led by Party Secretary Zhao, had suffered further setbacks in the Politburo. Their rallying cry, *"a Free economy Frees everything,"* was no longer heard. And Zhao himself had become an object of suspicion in student and intellectual circles after Li Peng had arranged for his aides to leak to the Chinese and foreign media an account of the Party chief's "tongue-lashing" of Bush. Not only had the revelation rocked Zhao's credibility, but it had also, more importantly, restored the power of those Party elders, hardliners to the core, who until then had found themselves shunted aside as policy-makers. Back with a vengeance, wheezing and spluttering, they issued a common cry about the dangers that came from granting "too many freedoms, too fast."

Rather than have the student leaders arrested and risk public demonstrations, Li Peng intended to weaken them by destroying their one champion, Zhao Ziyang.

The previous day the prime minister had begun to do so from the podium of the National People's Congress, China's parliament. Then he had delivered a cleverly couched attack on "the shortcomings and mistakes in our guidance." It had sounded like classic Chinese self-criticism. But everyone present knew that the words were aimed at Zhao.

Now, as the prime minister pressed for a further attack on his rival, events in Tibet were coming to his aid. That country was gripped by the most serious violence since the Chinese occupation. Li Peng had sent orders to the 27th Army that the "correct solution" was "a full show of force."

MONDAY, MARCH 13, 1989
LHASA, TIBET

Yang Bing felt broken glass and slivers beneath his boots as he prodded open another dark, polished door with his rifle. The young soldier was deep inside the Jokka Kang, the most holy of all the temples in the Pankor, the old city. All around him was the sound of gunfire, sporadic now after twenty-four hours of street fighting with the thousands of Tibetan monks who had launched themselves, often with no more than primitive weapons, against well-equipped soldiers. The result had been a slaughter. Hundreds of monks had been shot down, thousands more wounded.

Bing's platoon was among those ordered to seek them out and kill them on the spot.

Many had sought sanctuary in the Jokka Kang, over thirteen hundred years old and housing the most famous of all the country's sacred statues.

The platoon had advanced through the rubble of the streets to reach the older walls of the temple. Its massive carmine-colored gate, covered with gold inscriptions in Tibetan, hung off its hinges; it had been struck by a round fired from one of the Chinese tanks that had swept through the city.

Beyond the gate a group of monks had pelted the arriving soldiers with stones from one of the brightly painted galleries. They had been quickly dispatched with machine gun fire.

The platoon had then sprinted into the building, their boots slipping on the stone-flagged floor, slick with the body oil of pilgrims who had prostrated themselves on the holy ground down the centuries.

Inside the temple the soldiers had split up to search the red-pillared galleries and the rooms leading from them.

Bing found himself advancing past butter lamps in every niche and chapels dank with yak-dung smoke. Everywhere there were paintings and carved statues of animals, birds, and flowers. Heavy steel curtains secured with large padlocks had blocked the way to the main chambers. The locks had been shot off and the curtains ripped aside. Beyond were many bodies.

An hour after entering the Jokka Kang, Bing had reached its upper gallery. Entering the room he saw that its windows had been blasted out, probably from aerial strafing. The bullets had dislodged replicas of dragon heads and bells made of copper-covered gold from their wall mountings.

The room itself appeared to be some kind of storeroom; it was filled with lacquered gold and vermilion furniture and the low square stools covered in satin that Tibetans like to sit on while drinking rancid-tasting buttered tea.

A monk was cowering in a corner of the room beside a broken dragon's head. He was young, probably no more than fifteen, and wore the robe of a novice Lama. Blood had congealed on his sleeve. The boy rose to his feet, his mouth working but no words coming.

Bing shook his head and motioned for the monk to sit down. Then Bing turned and left the room, closing the door behind him and marking it with a penciled red star to indicate it had been checked.

From another part of the temple came more bursts of gunfire.

SAME DAY
BEIJING

Two thousand miles away in Beijing, Jeanne Moore, an American-born editorial assistant on the English language *China Daily*, proofread the next day's editorial on events in Tibet. It began uncompromisingly:

"The Lhasa riots show how we must value a stable environment. Haste and impatience for progress on the question of democracy will only increase the sources of instability."

A tall, intense idealist, Jeanne was married to a Chinese academic, Jiang. She worked on the paper to maintain a standard of life that was close to her own upbringing. Her position often gave her *"a glimpse behind the scenes."*

After reading the editorial she telephoned her husband and read it out to him. Jiang gave no immediate reply. But when he spoke his voice was somber.

"We are entering a new and dangerous phase. The Party is determined that no one, inside or out, will succeed in challenging those who now control our destiny."

12

Death in the Politburo

FRIDAY, MARCH 8, 1989
THE GREAT HALL OF THE PEOPLE

Shortly after 9:00 A.M. a cavalcade of Red flags swept out of Zhongnanhai, crossed Changan Avenue, and entered the inner courtyard of the Great Hall of the People. Each limousine contained a member of the Politburo. The more decrepit were accompanied by a doctor and a nurse carrying an emergency medical kit. In the courtyard itself were parked ambulances from several of the hospitals in the immediate area, including the one where Professor Guangzu worked. More doctors and nurses accompanied the ambulances.

This was the first full meeting of the Politburo since Prime Minister Li Peng had attacked Zhao Ziyang before the country's parliament. The one person who could have intervened, Deng Xiaoping, had chosen not to be there to witness the ferocious verbal assault on the Party Secretary. Deng had later told the previous holder of that office, Hu Yaobang, that he stayed away because he *"wanted to live longer."*

Now China's supreme ruler and Hu walked unaided from their limousines into the Great Hall. Deng wore a custom-made charcoal-gray Mao suit. Hu had chosen to wear another of the Western-style suits he had made in Hong Kong. As usual, the trousers were pulled too high, revealing Hu's passion for bright red socks.

Although they chatted amicably, the atmosphere around them was tense. The aftereffects of the violence in Tibet continued to reverberate through the leadership. Hardliners such as Vice-Premier Yao Yilin and Li Xiaming, Party Secretary of Beijing and political commissar of the city garrison, a key post should anything like the Lhasa uprising occur here, saw events in Tibet as impinging directly on what was happening in China, part of a deep-seated conspiracy against the Party.

Despite his uncompromising warning to President Bush, which he had been ordered to deliver by Deng, Zhao Ziyang still believed the students were no more than idealists, intending no harm to the country, and no real threat to the leadership. In this view he was supported by, among others, Yan MingFu and Hu Yaobang.

Apart from his close friends Zhao and Hu, Mingfu was the only real moderate present. Like all converts, he was fervent in his belief, which he called *"the advocacy of government by conciliation."* A keep-fit enthusiast, the abstemious fifty-eight-year-old Mingfu shared with Zhao and Hu an interest in history and music, as well as in the need to propel China toward economic reforms. As usual, they ignored Vice-Premier Yao Yilin, an ultraconservative steeped in a lifetime of socialist central planning. He sat slumped in his chair, breathing noisily.

Beside the rough-tongued Yao sat another formidable figure, Li Xiaming. The squat, muscular sixty-three-year-old moved like the schoolboy boxer he had once been. His opponents called him *"Deng's lapdog."* In reality he was a powerful figure in his own right.

Prime Minister Li Peng, as usual, sat cold and aloof. But behind the deadpan gaze he had an eye for a pretty girl; legend had it that he personally chose all his female staff. Two of them stood close by, ready to bring any papers he might require.

Beside him sat Qiao Shi. The old spymaster once more looked as if he had slept in his clothes. Before coming into the room he had lit another of his eight-inch-long Cuban cigars.

Close to Deng sat Yang Shangkun, the state president, eighty-two. His trim figure was the envy of many of the others. They put it down to his long-running affair with Wu Yi, the vice-mayor of Beijing, who had a reputation for sexual athleticism.

As usual, the "Coat Tail Puller" was positioned behind Hu's chair. Seated along one wall of the salon were aides ready to take notes or produce documents for their masters.

The meeting began pleasantly enough. There were expressions of relief that the worst of the trouble in Tibet appeared to be at an end. State President Yang Shangkun was instructed to send congratulations for a job well done to his nephew, commander of the 27th Army.

Li Peng then addressed the Politburo. Reading from notes, usually extemporized on such occasions, the prime minister began to review what was happening on the campuses of Beijing and elsewhere. He painted a picture of students *"corrupted"* by *"overexposure to westernization"* who were becoming *"class enemies"* of the people. Once more they were threatening to destroy the very fabric of their society and were being encouraged to do so by intellectuals such as Fang Lizhi.

Li Peng then mounted an increasingly angry attack on China's most renowned astrophysicist, calling him *"arrogant,"* *"destructive,"* and *"a friend of bourgeois Western thinking."* He reminded his audience that Fang had written to Deng Xiaoping in February demanding the release of *"so-called political prisoners,"* and that finally the National People's Congress had decided *"after the most careful study"* there was *"no need now"* to free any prisoners.

The attack had gone on for some ten minutes, punctuated by murmurs of agreement from the hardliners, when Hu Yaobang first intervened.

He said it was wrong to lay the burden of blame on one man. China's problems were the result of the inability of some of those around him to recognize that with education had come an awakening that could not be stifled and must not be.

Half-rising from his seat, only to be gently but firmly tugged back down again by the watchful official, Hu asked rhetorically: Who would want to see a return to the time Mao had condemned all China's intellectuals as a *"stinking category"*?

Murmurs of support mixed with those of protest.

Li Peng continued criticizing Fang for his latest statement to an American newspaper, that the students *"are counting the days to May 4."* The prime minister said this comment was tantamount to *"encitement"* for the students to take over a celebration that belonged to the Party. The May 4 celebration was *"a patriotic event,"* which had paved the way for Communism. Any attempt to use it to promote *"this nonsense"* about democracy and other political ideas would be completely unacceptable.

There were cries of support from the hardliners.

Vice-Premier Yao Yilin's rasping voice said that *"the problem went all the way back to the schools. Teachers have forgotten the reason why they teach, to instill proper patriotism and true socialist values."*

Beijing Party Secretary Li Xiaming led the cries of support with a strong attack on those *"who want to pamper our youth with foolish ideas instead of pressuring them to be our next line of defense against the spread of bourgeois liberalism."*

To make absolutely clear who he meant, Li Xiaming turned and faced Hu.

Li Tieying, the Politburo member responsible for school education, had started to speak when again Hu intervened.

What Hu, the former Party Secretary, had listened to was a recipe for *"social disaster."* This was the way back *"to our dark ages of anti-intellectualism,"* when education had been run on the proverbial shoestring. Students had lived in abject squalor, and teachers had earned less than a road sweeper.

Suddenly Hu was on his feet, brushing aside the official tugging at his jacket. He had started to say something about *"the only hope for China"* when he stopped. For a moment longer he stood slack-mouthed. Then he collapsed halfway back into his chair before sliding onto the floor.

There was stunned silence, then near pandemonium. Some of the old men backed away as if they could not bear to be in the presence of mortal illness. Zhao Ziyang knelt beside Hu, helping Yan Mingfu to loosen Hu's collar.

Then the first doctors and nurses arrived. Hu was pronounced alive despite his major heart attack. He was placed on a stretcher and rushed from the salon to a waiting ambulance.

The Politburo meeting was abandoned. By then Deng Xiaoping had already left the salon. He had made no attempt to come near the stricken Hu.

SAME DAY, LATER
CENTRAL INTELLIGENCE AGENCY

On Webster's desk was a report marked CONFIDENTIAL, the lowest form of classification within the agency. It signified the material could *"reasonably be expected to cause some form of damage to the national security."*

The document was the combined efforts of the half-dozen Chinese-speaking agents who had accompanied Bush on his visit to China. On returning to Washington they had assembled in a fourth-floor conference room at CIA headquarters.

One of the agents was a veteran of the days when the CIA had shipped arms to the Afghan rebels via China. Another had in 1979 helped create the first intelligence ties with China. The high point had been China's agreement to the construction by the CIA Directorate of Science and Technology of two signal stations in western China, near the border with the Soviet Union. The stations were still keeping tabs on Russia's arms control agreements.

The report the agents had compiled was less dramatic than that. In their days in Beijing, in the guise of visiting newsmen, the CIA operatives had spoken to a number of students and their supporters.

Gullible and unsuspecting about who they were confiding in, several student leaders, including the voluble Wuerkaixi and the studious Wang Dan, had revealed enough to show that the students were only waiting for an excuse to demonstrate.

The report concluded that the students believed that by calling for democracy, they would automatically receive the endorsement of the Bush administration despite the President having gone out of his way in China to give them no such encouragement.

Having initialed the report and sent it on its way through the labyrinth of the Washington intelligence community, Webster ordered one of his assistants to draft in his name an encoded instruction to Beijing Station — housed in that splendid colonial-style mansion known as Spook City — in the embassy compound, to intensify its surveillance and penetration of all student activities.

The CIA had invested more, and had more to lose, in China than any other foreign intelligence agency. What Webster had once called *"a bunch of kids politically wet behind the ears"* were most certainly not going to be allowed to threaten that investment or the billions of dollars American businesses had placed in China.

SAME DAY LATER
HOSPITAL OF TRADITIONAL MEDICINE

Professor Guangzu continued to watch Hu Yaobang from the doorway of the intensive care room. Heartbeats moved across the monitor positioned near the bed. Hu's eyes, pupils slightly dilated from the drugs he had been given, watched the monitor, as if he realized his grasp on life had been reduced to the silent trace endlessly crossing the screen.

Hu had been brought to the hospital from the Great Hall of the People. Since his arrival, there had been the usual complete news blackout about his condition. Long ago Deng Xiaoping had ordered no bulletins would be issued if any of the leadership fell ill. If they died, he would decide when the announcement would be made.

Public Security agents had arrived soon after Hu, sealing off the second floor cardiac unit where he had been brought. Other patients had been moved out, and only essential medical staff were permitted on the floor.

Gathered round Hu's bed were the hospital's cardiac specialist and his team. Western-style medical equipment surrounded the bed. The continuous clicking and pinging of screen and control panels reassured the medical team that all was not lost. The specialist had recently spent a year in the United States and had outfitted his department with the latest monitoring equipment. However, other departments in the hospital offered a mixture of Western and traditional treatments.

Professor Guangzu suspected that in this starkly lit sterile room there was no room for *Qi, Yin and Yang,* the ancient beliefs he swore by, or for his understanding that successful treatment depended on accepting that humanity did not exist in a vacuum, but that life or death was only a minute part of the universe and could he influenced by everything else in the cosmos. Here, only state-of-the-art Western medicine prevailed.

Professor Guangzu saw that Hu had sensed his presence. But he waited while the team around the bed finished their business of checking instrument readings, drips, and the leads that ran to sensors attached to Hu's chest. Satisfied, the team withdrew, each in baggy white top and trousers, their plastic sandals flapping on the bare floor as they left the room. At the door the specialist spoke to Professor Guangzu.

"Please stay only a little time with him. He is very tired, and there is every chance of another heart attack. But we have done everything possible."

Professor Guangzu nodded. He well understood that behind the polite words was the unspoken order not to interfere in Hu's treatment. A request to have Hu transferred to his own department had been refused by the hospital administrator. The order from Zhongnanhai was that Hu must remain in the cardiology unit. The administrator had added, not bothering to hide the malice in his voice, that it was *"fitting"* that Hu, *"such an admirer of the West,"* should be treated only by its methods.

Stepping over the cables on the floor, Professor Guangzu reached the bed. For a moment he looked down at Hu. Like so many others he had seen who had come close to death, the professor saw in Hu's face a determination not to be torn from life.

"Well, my friend, how are you?" asked Professor Guangzu.

"The better for seeing you," Hu whispered.

"You must be careful. The heart is the center of all emotional activity and thought processes," Professor Guangzu reminded Hu. *"Tell me what happened before you collapsed."*

Hu described the scene in the Politburo. Professor Guangzu nodded. It was an all too familiar clinical story. Every practitioner of traditional medicine knew that a person was made up of the five basic elements: earth, fire, metal, water, and wood. And each element had its corresponding sound, color, and weather conditions. Within that framework diagnosis was made easier by remembering that wood always destroyed earth, earth destroyed water, water destroyed fire, fire destroyed metal, and metal destroyed wood.

None of the machines around the bed could hope to understand that lifestyle and emotions are all too often the underlying causes of ill health. Yet it was obvious to any exponent of traditional medicine.

In his anxiety to win over his fellow Politburo members, Hu had obviously generated so much inner anger that it had brought on a heart attack. The result had been a loss of positive vitality, *Qi*. The energy force had ceased to flow through the meridian that stimulated the heart. In turn, the deficiency had increased five of the Seven Moods — anger, anxiety, sorrow, fear, and horror — at the expense of the job that normally kept them in proper balance. The result had been the heart attack. Every textbook in traditional medicine would have confirmed these steps to diagnosis.

Professor Guangzu spoke to Hu. *"This is a cold day. So wood was needed to produce fire. And fire corresponds to the heart in the body. Some fire is good. Too much is dangerous. This time the fire created an imbalance in your body. Here, show me your tongue."*

Hu put out his tongue as far as he could. Professor Guangzu gave it a long, silent scrutiny. He placed three of his fingers on Hu's right wrist and touched Hu's left wrist with his forefinger to test the pulse there, then reversed the process. As he did so he closed his eyes, feeling, timing, and sensing, in all, twelve pulses in Hu's wrists.

"You certainly have an imbalance of Qi," said Professor Guangzu.

"Can you treat it?"

"Yes, of course. But you are not my patient."

Hu shook his head. *"This is my body. I will decide who will treat it."*

Professor Guangzu nodded. *"Very well. I will see what can be done."*

From his pocket he produced the case with his set of acupuncture needles. He quickly inserted them along the twelve body meridians that stimulate the heart. When the needles were in place, the professor twisted them in turn, setting them gently vibrating. After each movement he asked whether Hu had *"felt the presence of Qi."*

After a while Hu began to nod and say, *"I feel Qi."*

SAME DAY, SAME TIME
FOREIGN LEGATION QUARTER

Despite the security procedures news of Hu's heart attack quickly reached the foreign embassy quarter.

Soviet Ambassador Troyanovsky was in the middle of a planning meeting for the forthcoming Gorbachev state visit when the news came. He immediately thought, *"This is not going to create a potential problem for the visit. Hu had no real authority."* Nevertheless, Russian attachés were instructed to probe their Chinese contacts to discover how ill Hu was and what had been under discussion in the Politburo when he had collapsed.

First Secretary Kauokin, a KGB official at the embassy, began his own inquiries by calling Qiao Shi's office. An aide said the security chief was not available.

The American embassy learned of Hu's illness through its press and cultural attaché, McKinney Russell. He had heard it from Jeanne Moore. The *China Daily* editorial assistant had picked up the news from a contact in the hospital.

U.S. diplomats at once began working the phones, calling other friendly missions and sources in government. In a surprisingly short time they had pieced together an accurate account of what had happened. A report was faxed to the State Department.

By then most embassies also had an idea of what had occurred in the Politburo. It was left to French Ambassador Charles Malo to articulate the view of many foreign diplomats. He felt that *"Hu's illness was only significant in how the students would react."*

SAME DAY, EVENING
BEIJING UNIVERSITY

In the campus coffeehouse there was not a seat to be had. Students lined the walls, listening to Li Yang describing what had happened to Hu.

Cassy saw that the student leader's deep-felt emotions were clear. As he had stood up to speak Meili squeezed his arm, her face whiter than usual at hearing the news.

Until then Cassy had not realized what a powerful public speaker Li was; he had a vibrant voice and a way of repeating key phrases. He constantly reminded his listeners that Hu had been struck down supporting them; therefore they had a duty to support him. The best way to do this was to ensure that the May 4 gathering in Tiananmen Square would be a resounding success.

Somebody pointed out that the occasion fell only two weeks before the Gorbachev visit and that the leadership would be particularly anxious to ensure there would be no embarrassing demonstrations before such a historic occasion.

Li Yang gave another of his half-smiles.

THURSDAY, APRIL 13, 1989
WASHINGTON, D.C.

DCI Webster's reading on the way to work this morning included a report prepared by the FBI on Chinese intelligence activities in the United States. The FBI believed that *"countering spies from the PRC is a growing problem, one nearly as large as that posed by the Soviet Union and its allies."* The report claimed that the Chinese could be about to intensify their spying activities through the nearly nineteen hundred diplomats accredited to its Washington embassy and various consulates throughout the country, especially the one in San Francisco. The consulate there was *"ideally placed,"* the FBI report said, *"for Chinese agents to steal or illegally purchase data on weapons and systems technology"* from northern California's vast defense industry.

A number of the Chinese spies could be among the more than twenty thousand Chinese students at American universities, possibly coerced into spying for their country by threats against their families back home. Webster fully approved of the FBI recommendation that surveillance be increased on all Chinese students.

The FBI report also warned that some students might try to organize protests in the United States in support of the growing calls for democracy emanating from Chinese campuses. That would cause considerable embarrassment to Washington and the U.S. business community.

Webster knew that the FBI was not alone in expressing concern about China's students. The CIA's Moscow station had reported the Kremlin viewed with *"real concern"* the prospect of the students trying to embarrass Gorbachev during his state visit. From London had come evidence of *"anxiety"* within the Foreign Office that the students would interfere with Britain's delicate negotiations over the future of Hong Kong, due to be returned to China in 1997.

CIA officers in Paris and Bonn reported that the French and German governments were under increasing pressure from their business communities to do nothing to encourage China's students in their search for democracy.

One report, which had intrigued Webster, had come from the U.S. embassy in Dublin. It revealed that student leaders had visited the Irish embassy in Beijing and spoken to a diplomat there about the precise techniques needed to run a successful hunger strike. The diplomat, after stressing that the Irish government did not support such methods of protest, had given the students details of how the IRA manipulated public sympathy by such methods.

Webster doubted if the Beijing authorities would allow matters to go that far.

SATURDAY, APRIL 15, 1989
HOSPITAL OF TRADITIONAL MEDICINE

Late in the morning Professor Guangzu made another visit to the former Party Secretary, Hu Yaobang. He had come twice a day. They had been left alone by the medical team to talk. During each visit the professor had inserted his acupuncture needles. He was convinced his intervention was responsible for Hu's remarkable improvement.

Apart from the heartbeat monitor, all the other equipment had been removed from the bed. All that remained was the emergency bell-push.

Hu sat propped up by pillows, wearing an old-fashioned nightshirt, listening intently as Professor Guangzu explained how the day before Li Peng had been forced to break Deng Xiaoping's standing order about not discussing any illness of a Politburo member. The prime minister, cornered by the foreign press as he left Beijing for a visit to Japan, had admitted Hu was in the hospital but recovering.

Then, Professor Guangzu said, had come a most extraordinary disclaimer. From his coat pocket he produced a clipping from the *People's Daily* and read aloud to Hu.

"Li Peng said he wished to emphasize that the illness of Comrade Hu had nothing directly to do with the Politburo meeting he had been attending when he was taken ill."

The professor handed the item to Hu. *"You see, my friend, how worried your opponents are. They are frightened people will think they tried to kill you!"*

"When I get out of here, they will have more cause to fear me!" Hu replied.

They spoke for a little while longer, mostly about the need to spread reform; then the professor left, saying he would return in mid-afternoon for a further chat.

At noon Hu had his usual lunch of soup, noodles, and tea. Afterwards he slept for a while. At 1:00 P.M. a nurse made another check on Hu. These examinations occurred every fifteen minutes now that he was no longer on the danger list.

Hu awoke at some point after she had recorded her visit on his chart hanging at the foot of the bed. The demand of nature upon a full stomach was probably the reason. Hu should have used the bell-push and asked for a bedpan. Instead, he decided to make his own way to the bathroom adjoining his room. He was halfway across the floor when he collapsed.

The nurse found him when she made her quarter-past-the-hour visit. By then Hu was already dead from a second massive heart attack.

SAME DAY, MIDAFTERNOON
BEIJING UNIVERSITY

Cassy was describing the intricacies of English grammar when the classroom door burst open. Daobao stood there, a portable radio in his hand.

"Have you heard?" he burst out. *"Hu Yaobang is dead! The radio has just said so!"*

There was a scramble as students rushed to surround Daobao. Moments later Radio Beijing repeated the announcement it had first broadcast at 3:02 that afternoon. *"The death is announced of Hu Yaobang, the true Communist fighter and great proletarian revolutionary, a great Marxist whose life is forever to be glorious for his contribution to economic structural reform...."*

The announcement concluded with the assurance Hu *"was given all possible medical attention but to no avail. To our great sorrow he died at 0753 today."*

One small unresolved mystery concerned the reason why the authorities had altered the actual time of Hu's death. A possible explanation suggested that they moved back his passing by several hours so as not to give the impression of unseemly haste in announcing his death.

In a rush the students left the classroom, followed by Cassy. She saw that on the campus the first hastily scrawled messages of condolence were being stuck up, along with white flowers fashioned from tissue paper and bits of wire. The flowers were the first symbols of mourning for Hu.

As she followed Daobao across the campus, Cassy saw that hundreds of students were converging on the coffeehouse.

"What's going to happen?" Cassy asked as they reached the building.

"The time has come for action," Daobao replied.

She saw that the door of the coffeehouse was already smothered with messages.

"We have lost a true man," a student had scrawled in black ink on an old newspaper. *"Our champion has gone,"* read another. *"We have lost our great hope,"* said a third.

But even as she watched, the tone of the tributes was changing. Li Yang stuck up a message that read *"False men are still living. The wrong man has died."*

Meili affixed a scroll: *"Xiaoping is still alive at the age of 84. Hu Yaobang, only 73, has died first. Those who should die still live. Those who should live have died."*

Murmurs of agreement greeted this blunt statement.

Another student stuck a poster with an even simpler message beside the scroll: *"Hu's death shows Deng Xiaoping no longer has a mandate to rule."*

Cheers rose from the large crowd gathered before the door.

Suddenly there was a commotion at the back of the crowd as Pang Yi appeared with several political officers. They began to thrust their way toward the door, on which someone was pinning a paper banner bearing the words OUR DEMOCRACY DOOR.

"Take those down!" shouted Pang Yi.

"No!" Daobao said. *"They stay!"*

He forced his way to stand before Pang Yi. Behind Daobao the students formed a solid mass to protect the door.

For long tense moments Pang Yi and the other political officers stood their ground. Then, abruptly, they turned and walked away. There were muted cheers from the students, which Li Yang and Daobao quickly silenced.

By now Cassy estimated there were close to a thousand students milling outside the coffeehouse. Many were sticking more white paper flowers on tree trunks or weaving wreaths. Those closest to Democracy Door were asking each other what they should do next. Cassy sensed a feeling of uncertainty.

Suddenly Daobao's voice rose above the conversations.

"We march! Let us go to Tiananmen Square! There we can express our feelings to those who are responsible for Hu's death!"

SAME DAY, SAME TIME
THE GREAT HALL OF THE PEOPLE

News of Hu's death had been telephoned to the Politburo, which had resumed the session interrupted by Hu's collapse. This time Deng Xiaoping was not present. Li Peng was still in Japan. The discussion on education under the chairmanship of Zhao Ziyang was once more abandoned to discuss Hu's death.

Everyone present knew that the death of a leader provided the opportunity for public protest in the guise of mourning. It had not needed Vice-Premier Yao Yilin to remind those present in the salon of what had happened when Chou En-Lai, China's prime minister for a record twenty-seven years, had died of cancer in 1976. His death had come when Mao himself was on his deathbed. Radicals in the Party had tried to suppress any public mourning for Chou En-Lai on the grounds it was *"untimely."* Chou En-Lai had died in January. But by April, when the Chinese traditionally honored their dead during the Qing Ming Festival, there was no holding back the crowds. They had poured into Tiananmen Square in the tens of thousands, carrying wreaths and reciting poems of mourning for a popular and respected leader. At the same time they had expressed their opposition to Mao's hated wife, Jiang Qing, and the other radicals. What had begun as mourning swiftly gave way to angry political protest. Finally Qiao Shi had sent in his public security forces and armed police to clear the square. There had been considerable bloodshed and hundreds of arrests.

Now, anxious to avert mourning for Hu being used as an excuse to voice protest, the Politburo acted swiftly.

Li Xiaming and Yang Shangkun began to draft the official obituary to be broadcast by Radio Beijing. Qiao Shi's mastery of the language was called upon to convey the all-important right tone. Fulsome praise was the order of the day. Hu's *"loyalty"* to the Party was repeatedly praised. He was *"a great statesman"* who had *"conferred lasting benefits on the Party and the people."* He was a *"true revolutionary"*; not only China, but the world, would mourn.

Care was taken to make no mention that he had been ejected from office as Party Secretary two years before for supporting previous student demands. He was simply described as having *"continued to serve the Politburo to the very end of his noble life."*

The state president read the final draft to the Politburo. There was general agreement that it affirmed that Hu had remained true to Party ideology and in no way implied he had supported those who were *"liberal"* in the Western sense of the word. The eulogy was sent off to the studio of Radio Beijing.

The Politburo had been about to return to the education issue when the sound of chanting could be heard in Tiananmen Square.

Zhao Ziyang was among the first to reach one of the huge windows in the Great Hall.

Moving across the vast expanse of the all but deserted square were columns of students. Many were dressed completely in white, the symbol of deep mourning. Others wore white headbands. All carried white flowers or wreaths. The column leaders held aloft banners and huge photographs of Hu.

From the window the stunned Politburo could read the words on the banners.

"Hu Must be Rehabilitated," read one. *"There Must be an End to Spiritual Pollution,"* urged another. But the most common one repeated time and again the same demand: *"China is Entitled to democracy."*

Qiao Shi reportedly was the first to react. He went to a telephone to call the public security forces. Before he could do so, Zhao Ziyang intervened. The Party chief reminded everyone what Deng Xiaoping had said. There must be no rush to action.

"Let us see what they will do," concluded Zhao. *"Then we can decide what action to take."*

Like the others he turned back to the window to watch the students draping a twenty-foot-long white banner around the Monument to the People's Heroes. It was emblazoned with the words *"Soul of China."*

It was the first formal tribute to Hu. For a moment the banner fluttered alone on the pediment. Then Daobao and Li Yang hung their banner on the monument, proclaiming China was entitled to democracy.

In that gesture Hu's death became irrevocably linked to the students' demands.

SAME DAY, SAME TIME
TIANANMEN SQUARE

As dusk settled over Tiananmen Square, Daobao climbed on to the pediment of the Monument to the People's Heroes. Despite the chill of the evening, he wore only white cotton trousers, a white shirt, and a matching bandanna.

Cassy saw his face was flushed, a sign of the anger he felt.

On the Square, the students found ways to mock their Chinese guards. One way was to display fake Chinese slogans like this one. The words made no sense to the soldiers. Only when the page is turned sideways does this meaning become clear. This caused huge merriment among the students — and bafflement by the guards.

This is a copy of the song the students sang: "We Are Democratic Chinese."

Below, Daobao could see several hundred students looking up at him, with Cassy in their midst. The last of the visitors to the Mao Mausoleum paused to watch, then hurried on. Beyond, Daobao caught a glimpse of the brightly lit windows of the Great Hall and the tiny figures in them. Army sentries were standing around the square, uncertain what to do.

For a moment longer he surveyed the scene. He felt this was *"a supreme moment, when anything was possible."*

When he spoke his voice was calm and certain.

"Long live Hu Yaobang! Long live democracy! Long live freedom! Down with corruption! Down with bureaucracy!"

The first slogans had been articulated for the greatest challenge China's Communist rulers had ever faced. Behind the words were a decade of tension between economic reform and political stagnation.

They expressed a powerful idealism and a yearning for that most basic of freedoms, the right to live outside the limits set by Mao Zedong. Forty years before, he had defined democracy as no more than the right of *"anyone to speak out, as long as he is not a hostile element."*

Now, his voice growing in power, Daobao signaled the need to break free from that constricting bond. He continued to repeat the slogans. Those grouped around the great obelisk began to echo them, their voices blending in unison, giving the words a deeply moving and haunting effect.

Cassy felt at that moment she was *"part of history and privileged to be the only foreigner to be here to witness it."*

She was wrong. Watching discreetly nearby was the CIA officer, Tom. From now on either he or one of his colleagues would maintain a permanent watch on the activities in the square. Other intelligence operatives would closely monitor developments on the city's campuses. Their reports would enable the analysts, linguists, psychologists, and behaviorists at Langley to piece together what was happening. To help them to anticipate new events, still more agents would continue to "vacuum" up the mumbled words of China's leaders in their compound in Zhongnanhai, capturing their fears and growing fury over what had begun to unfold beyond the high walls of their compound. The technology of the most sophisticated intelligence-gathering agency in the world was being brought fully to bear on the last great secret society on earth.

13

Overtures

MONDAY, APRIL 17, 1989
BEIJING

Daobao called the brief appearance in Tiananmen Square by the students *"a testing. We wanted to see how the authorities would respond to a deliberate illegal action."*

The Chinese constitution recognized the right to demonstrate. But after the massive student protests of 1986–87, Li Xiaming, Party Secretary of the city, had introduced a by-law forbidding all public demonstrations that did not have the written consent of the Public Security Office. In practice it only issued permits for state-approved demonstrations.

On the seven-mile journey back to the campus on Saturday evening the students had been ebullient: There had been no move by the authorities to intervene.

Later Daobao promised a packed meeting in the coffeehouse, *"They will do nothing because we will insist we are only showing respect for Hu."*

Throughout Sunday the Beijing University campus students had divided their time between turning the campus into a sea of white paper flowers and wreaths while the best calligraphers prepared banners, and consulting student leaders on other campuses in Beijing.

Late on Sunday evening the student leaders came together in a lecture hall at the University of Politics and Law in the city's western suburbs.

Eyes blinking owlishly behind thick-framed glasses, Wang Dan read out a message from Fang Lizhi, who was an authentic hero to the students. *"The death of Hu is an opportunity for you to show the government you are unhappy with the present situation."* Hours before, Fang had issued a similar statement to foreign journalists who knocked on his door seeking comment on Hu's death. Fang's support was greeted with jubilation by the student leaders; they had long seen him as someone who could look beyond the immediacy of the situation and judge its long-term effects.

As if in anticipation of victory, Wuerkaixi wore a new denim jacket, a gift from one of the foreign expert teachers on campus. His smile was even more all knowing. In contrast, Yang Li had become still more withdrawn, as if the demands of being one of the movement's planners weighed heavily. Daobao remained his calm, gentle self, though admitting to withdrawal symptoms from having given up smoking.

Another student had given Wang Dan a stronger pair of shoes, but the near-sighted student leader steadfastly refused to abandon his sweatshirt and black baggy pants. He said proudly that his clothes were as distinctive a uniform as Wuerkaixi's. Chai Ling, as usual, had no time for such nonsense. Her slim legs were encased in a pair of old jeans, her face devoid of makeup.

At meetings, the student leaders also revealed the first hint of discord among them. Wuerkaixi, Daobao, and Yang Li were among those who called for all-out militancy: abandoning the classroom to demonstrate throughout the city's campuses, and then marching in force on Tiananmen Square. But even they had no clear idea what they would do there or how long they should stay.

At this Sunday night gathering Wang Dan and Liu Gang continued to lead the call for caution. Nothing must be done that would allow the authorities to say theirs was not an act of genuine mourning but only of protest. Dan urged they must move slowly and carefully, all the time trying to anticipate responses from the public and the leadership; they must constantly keep the memory of Hu to the forefront. Posters must call for Hu's remains to be placed in a coffin alongside Mao's in the mausoleum on Tiananmen Square. Other posters should tell Deng Xiaoping to admit he had made a mistake in dismissing Hu. But the content of the calligraphy *"must be dignified and appear non-threatening to the leadership. This will then place us in a position where the leadership will still feel unhappy with us, but will have to accept our motives for demonstrating."*

There would be time enough, Wang Dan added, to decide what to do after this opening maneuver. The important thing was to make *"a dignified statement"* to the memory of Hu Yaobang.

But now, on this Monday morning, a plethora of new slogans and posters had sprouted on campuses not only throughout the city, but across the country. While some paid respect to Hu, many strongly condemned the Party and its leaders. There were blunt attacks on the crisis in education and in the economy, the rampant corruption and the lack of morality among Party officials, the resistance of the leaders to genuine political reform, and the suppression of freedom in the media. Most startling of all, thousands of posters launched a personal attack on Deng Xiaoping.

Daobao and another student had been jointly responsible for organizing what they called *"our poster war."*

The militant students continued to plan. Wang Dan and the others who had urged caution were swept along by the determination and enthusiasm of Wuerkaixi.

The death of Hu Yaobang and the student protest in Tiananmen Square had produced a flurry of activity among foreign diplomats. Throughout Sunday they had composed appraisals and sent them to their foreign ministers.

Some of the judgments were based on reports from intelligence operatives. Agents from the CIA, the KGB, and European intelligence services had tapped their contacts on campuses — students and tutors, some of them "foreign experts" — to try and assess how the student leadership would respond to the former Party Secretary's death. Dogging their footsteps were Qiao Shi's agents on a similar mission. One European intelligence officer would recall that *"not since the good old days of Berlin at the height of the Cold War could I remember so many of us out on the hoof."*

Britain's ambassador, Sir Alan Donald, had dispatched to London a lengthy telegram clearly warning that Hu's death would be apotheosized by the students into a symbol for democratic reforms but was *"unlikely to change the balance of power among the leadership."*

Donald, a tough pragmatist behind his easygoing smile, had been in Beijing for less than a year. But his reputation as one of Britain's most astute diplomats in the Far East had been established from his time as political adviser in Hong Kong. The Chinese regarded the fifty-five-year-old Donald, who was fluent in Mandarin, as someone with whom they could do business. He had shown that by boosting Britain's bilateral trade to a new record £1.5 billion a year. With it had come an increase in joint ventures, especially in technology and manufacturing. Donald had also played a key role in encouraging the Chinese to believe Britain would do nothing to jeopardize the handing over of Hong Kong. Underscoring his telegram was a reassurance that Hu's death would not change Britain's deepening relationships with the Middle Kingdom.

The same sanguine view was being expressed to their government by other senior diplomats in Beijing. The student march on Saturday night was seen by Raymond Burghardt, the counselor for political affairs at the American embassy, as no more than *"letting off a little steam."*

However, by this Monday morning a rather different view was beginning to prevail in the embassy.

CIA officers had gotten wind of the meeting at the University of Politics and Law and learned of the rash of posters that had appeared overnight attacking Deng Xiaoping and the leadership. The intelligence officer known as Tom had returned to the embassy with photographic evidence showing the extent of the protest posters. He told colleagues that Beijing University campus *"is awash with banners calling for just about anything."*

Diplomats and intelligence officers making the rounds of the city's other campuses found the mood tense and expectant.

This feeling was confirmed by Jeanne Moore, the young American journalist employed on the staff of the Party's English language newspaper, *China Daily*. When Jeanne had come to work on Sunday, she had been given a copy of the Politburo eulogy for Hu Yaobang to translate into English. It had struck her *"as a fairly typical piece of leadership-speak."*

The mood in the newspaper's offices on Jintai Xilu was as tense as on the campuses.

Jeanne was sure that *"the editors knew, from their own conversations with Zhongnanhai, that Hu's death had caused great public speculation. In any other country this would be the major political story of the day, but this was China. Nothing could appear, would appear, without official sanction. And no one was going to give us that. The tension we all felt was caused by frustration at being forced to accept the situation.*

But we also sensed that the students could be up to something serious. It was the same feeling just before the 1986–87 uprising, the same edginess and expectancy."

She had called the paper's bureaus in Shanghai, Guangzhou, and Hang Zhou. They reported that Hu's death had led to posters critical of the Party and leadership appearing at local college and university campuses.

Leaving the office on Sunday night, Jeanne saw the staff bulletin board contained several expressions of sympathy over Hu's death. Impulsively, she had organized a collection among the staff to buy a wreath for Hu.

This Monday morning she had gone to a florist near the *China Daily* compound and purchased one fashioned from spring flowers. Walking from the shop, holding the large wreath in both hands, she had felt slightly foolish. She had no idea where she should place the tribute.

When she returned home her husband, Jiang, a distinguished academic, told her what the students next planned to do. Jeanne realized she had found the solution to what to do with the wreath. She told Jiang she had also decided to keep a diary *"to record all those things that were beginning to happen but would never find their way into print."*

Barr Seitz, a tall, ruggedly handsome Yale graduate and another of the foreign experts teaching English at Beijing University, knew on this Monday morning *"that the action was just around the corner, and I sure wanted to be part of it."* He confided that to the diary he had started since arriving in China.

Seitz, whose father, Raymond, was a senior State Department official in Washington, had come to Beijing the previous September after majoring in Chinese political science. Like most other foreign experts he received a monthly salary of $120 for teaching one class a week. He used his ample spare time to improve his written Chinese.

The first months of his diary mostly contained the standard impressions of any visitor to China: its living customs and cultural roots; how its astronomy and irrigation techniques are the envy of the world.

But gradually Barr's observations sharpened. He had brought something of his father's eye to the paradoxes of China. His diary was filled with questions about them: How can China answer to no one in agriculture, yet has to import grain? Why do its musicians, who have one of the best of all musical traditions, create some of the worst modern music?

Setting out to answer his own questions, Barr had developed a keen and sensitive ear for what was happening around him. What he had heard and seen in those weeks past convinced him the students *"are ready to blow."*

During the weekend a student had brought Barr home to meet his family. The youth and his parents had spent all their waking time talking about the portents of Hu's death.

Barr had once been struck by how *"desperately the Chinese asked for change. My hosts were simple people with no great aspirations, except to have more of what any American would regard as the basics of life: a TV, fridge, maybe even a car. They tried to fit Hu's death into that framework. Would his departure be used by the hardliners to cut back on such things or would it be used as a chance to push forward? I couldn't imagine that kind of debate taking place anywhere else. It was a forcible reminder just how different were the value systems here from back home."*

On the way back to the campus, the student had told Barr: *"You know those movies where the cavalry ride in and drive out the bad guys? Well, we are the cavalry. You want to ride with us?"*

Barr had smiled and said he would think about it.

By this Monday morning he had decided what he would do. He would try to get a part-time job with one of the U.S. TV network bureaus, which would be reinforcing their local staff to prepare news stories for the forthcoming Gorbachev visit. With his knowledge of the language *"and how this town works,"* the twenty-two-year-old figured he could hold his own *"with any of those media stars when it came to getting things done, Chinese-style."* Working with a network would also give him a chance to get an overview of where the *"student cavalry"* were heading.

Cassy Jones had spent most of Sunday walking around the campus, *"just sensing the mood."*

After Daobao had addressed the coffeehouse meeting, he had taken her aside.

"Cassy," he had said, his voice strangely formal, *"we must put on ice our feelings. There will be no time for personal relations for a little while. All my energy will be needed for what is to come."*

He had shaken her hand quickly and left. She realized then that she still *"had a lot to learn about Daobao's priorities."* Cassy did not yet know if she felt *"sad or a little angry at the way he had decided things."*

By Sunday afternoon the criticisms on the posters were more pointed, she noticed. Returning to the coffee shop, she listened while Meili had read aloud a lengthy poem listing Hu's accomplishments and criticizing the attitude of many of her fellow students. The poem reminded Meili's listeners that Hu had been removed from office because he had defended the students against the leadership. And yet, Meili intoned, why hadn't all the students supported him at the time? Now he was dead. And now was the time to honor all Hu had stood for.

Meili received sustained applause for her reading. Cassy was puzzled. In class Meili had not shown any great literary aspirations. Yet the poem had considerable artistic merit. When Cassy questioned her, Meili laughed.

"The poem was written by the best poet in Nanjing," she explained.

"But how did you get hold of it so quickly?" Cassy asked.

Meili laughed again. *"Easy. We have fax machines. Also computers and telephones. Wuerkaixi arranged it all."*

She looked fiercely at Cassy. *"You know what Mao said about war being the highest form of struggle for resolving contradictions? Well, we are getting ready for war."*

Now, on this Monday morning, Cassy could *"smell the whiff of action in the air."*

She had arrived to find her classroom empty. Daobao soon appeared and told her there would be no lessons for the foreseeable future. He too chose the metaphor of war to explain to her what the students were going to do.

"This is our first full day of action to bring about what we most want, your kind of democracy. You have fought many wars to obtain it. We are willing to do the same, but

not with weapons, only words. We think they are more powerful than any gun. People will listen to our words, and make this a peaceful war."

Once more he was gone before she could respond. For a while Cassy remained in the classroom alone. Then she walked out into the campus, where thousands of students were assembling with their banners and posters and photographs of Hu.

SAME DAY, SAME TIME
THE FOREIGN OFFICE
LONDON

Susan Morton, a coltish twenty-eight-year-old with chestnut hair that framed and softened her jaw and cheekbones, was a research analyst at the Foreign Office. China was her brief. She spent her day often reading secret messages about developments there and writing reports that helped influence how Britain should respond.

On her desk were copies of the latest newspapers from China and Hong Kong. Nothing caught her eye. There was also a small pile of diplomatic telegrams.

Ambassador Donald's was on top. Like all those reports the office receives from its 350 outposts, the one from Beijing was addressed to *"Prodrome."* The classical Greek for *"forerunner"* had been the office's telegraphic address for over a hundred years.

The telegram had been typed by Communications on a machine devoid of lowercase letters. Susan could have read the opening words from several feet away. *"THERE IS AN ECHO OF THE RECENT PAST BEGINNING TO REVERBERATE IN THE UNIVERSITIES...."*

Susan riffled through the other telegrams. There was nothing that could not wait. She turned back to Donald's message, reading it slowly with total concentration. It described the beginnings of a new student movement. The highly experienced diplomat believed that it could grow sufficiently powerful to confront the leadership in a way no previous movement had.

The students were calling for the separation of Party and state, the decentralization of power, the streamlining of bureaucracy, and the introduction of *"full legal standards."* They wanted *"a channel for their demands and the voice of the masses to constantly reach the higher levels."* They wanted *"social consultation and conversation"* with the leadership. If their demands were not met, they would take to the streets in increasing numbers. The death of Hu Yaobang had provided them with the perfect excuse.

In her analysis, Susan developed Ambassador Donald's prediction that Hu's death would be apotheosized into a symbol of democratic reforms. In her judgment, any protest would most probably be rooted in previous unsuccessful demands: the call in 1983 for an end to *"spiritual pollution"*; the demand in 1986–87 for an end to *"bourgeois liberalization."* Likely to be added to these would be demands for the rehabilitation of the victims of those previous campaigns, including Fang Lizhi's January request for the freeing of all political prisoners; demands for the disclosure of the private bank accounts of the top leaders and their families; demands for full freedom of speech and freedom of the press; and, of course, Hu's last demand for increased expenditure on education and better treatment of intellectuals.

Susan neatly encapsulated the probable effect of Hu's death on the leadership. In many ways he had never been a strong Party leader; he had only had a limited role in the actual shaping of the reform policies that had so dramatically altered the face of post-Mao China. Much of the credit for reform must go to Zhao Ziyang.

Susan reread her submission. Then she began to add to, rewrite, excise, and shape it, so that it fitted the office style, which has hardly changed over a century.

SAME DAY, LATER
THE GREAT HALL OF THE PEOPLE

Once more the Politburo had assembled to try and agree upon a policy document on education. Party Secretary Zhao Ziyang had summoned the leaders of China's eight supposedly democratic parties to join in the discussion. The parties were no more than symbols of the political system that had existed in China before Mao had taken over. Their leaders remained at the edge of the absolute power of the Party. But Zhao needed them there, to rubber-stamp his own liberal plan for the future education of China's youth.

Zhao had been speaking for some time in his reedy, somewhat high-pitched voice, when once more there was an intervention from Tiananmen Square. The first of thousands of students were approaching the square. They began to sit in an ever-expanding circle around the Monument to the People's Heroes as, one by one, their leaders draped banners and photographs of Hu over the pediment. The first of hundreds of wreaths were propped around the obelisk.

In the salon the Politburo watched what was happening with mounting anger. State President Yang Shangkun spoke for many when he said in his distinctive bullfrog voice that this must stop, *now*.

Once more Zhao used his authority. He pointed out the TV crews and photographers who were accompanying the marchers.

"*The world is watching,*" Zhao was later quoted as saying. "*Let us do nothing that will allow them to criticize us.*" Then faintly but with mounting fervor came the sound of thousands of voices singing the first verse of China's national anthem, followed by the first two verses of the "*Internationale.*"

SAME DAY, LATER
TIANANMEN SQUARE

Jeanne Moore had quickly persuaded her editors of the need to have a first-hand account of what was happening, even if they could not publish it. Several hours before, she had learned that students all over the city were planning to march to Tiananmen Square. Her editors had agreed, with the proviso she must do nothing to embarrass *China Daily*. They approved of her laying a wreath.

She went to her apartment in building 23 of the newspaper's compound, dressed in warm clothes against the subzero air, and took bus 9 to Tiananmen Square, arriving shortly after the first columns of marchers. She laid the newspaper's wreath at the foot of the obelisk, placing it among the other floral tributes.

Jeanne then began to write down her impressions. They would be among the first detailed accounts of the birth pangs of an extraordinary moment in China's history.

"A full moon is rising over the monument to revolutionary heroes. Tightly packed on the top platform, north side, students giving speeches, but very hard to hear, no loudspeaker. Students going hoarse trying to make themselves heard. The crowd, though incredibly pressed, was surprisingly civil and made an effort to be quiet to hear. The demands were for freedom of press and speech, for political pressure (to be free), for human rights, for multiparty system."

On the pediment of the monument, Yang Li continued to articulate these demands. Extending his hands dramatically toward the Great Hall of the People, he shouted:

"We demand you open the bank accounts of the leaders! Tell us how much you earn! Tell us how big are your bank accounts in Hong Kong, San Francisco, and Zurich!"

The first sustained burst of cheering came from the students.

"We demand you tell us about the bank accounts of your sons and daughters!" Li Yang continued to shout, his voice raw.

The cheering grew louder.

"And we demand you tell us about the bank accounts of your mistresses!"

A great wave of giggling and laughter rippled through the crowd.

To Jeanne the mood was *"part carnival, part political."*

Moving through the crowd, she noted that it was often impossible to hear what the students on the pediment were saying. *"On the grass at the edge of the square quite a few are playing cards. Some young women. But only three foreigners besides myself were in sight, three men, correspondents, who walked around together getting quotes. Every time they stopped to interview someone, a crowd formed. At one point they were joined by two policemen who pressed into the crowd and took notes. Over all this the full moon rose slowly against a slate blue sky."*

The foreign TV crews and photographers had by now departed. It didn't seem to be much of a story, largely because the authorities were doing nothing to stop the catalogue of criticism and demands coming from the pediment.

Reaching the east side of the square, Jeanne saw a score of buses and jeeps filled with armed police parked in front of the Museum of the Revolution. The police, like many of the students, were playing cards. The park benches were completely filled with lovers oblivious of their presence.

Jeanne wrote in her notebook: *"Young men lie with their heads in the laps of their girls, who often read them poetry. Just like any other night."*

It was not.

SAME DAY, LATER
ZHONGNANHAI

In the compound the lights burned late into the night. Prime Minister Li Peng had returned from Japan and had gone into a closed session with, among others, Beijing Party Secretary Li Xiaming, the rasp-voiced Vice-Premier Yao Yilin, and Qiao Shi, the country's intelligence chief.

Western intelligence sources, piecing together what was discussed, concurred that the meeting accepted Li Xiaming's urging to alert the commander of the 38th Army, currently responsible for the city's garrison duty, to place his troops at a state of readiness. At the same time the central military commissar should be asked to review troop displacements throughout the country. Particular attention should be paid to the possibility of withdrawing at least part of the 27th Army from Tibet should trouble develop in Beijing. The 27th had proven itself in urban warfare in Lhasa.

14

Surges

WEDNESDAY, APRIL 19, 1989
ZHONGNANHAI

Shortly after 4:00 A.M., alarm bells sounded throughout the compound. Moments later lights came on in the villas along the lake. The doors leading to the underground railway were opened in preparation for the evacuation of the country's octogenarian rulers. The train was made ready to take them under the earth to the airfield in the western suburbs. The unprecedented activity at this hour was recorded by a U.S. satellite and transmitted to Washington.

Four days had now passed since the first student demonstrations. In that time, as the electronic spying from outer space continued, U.S. intelligence operatives had worked their way in among the students. Often they posed as journalists, joining the genuine reporters who had begun to arrive in Beijing to write advance stories about the forthcoming Gorbachev state visit and were on hand at this early hour to witness events at Zhongnanhai.

Scores of Public Security agents took up positions inside the compound walls. They were equipped with the Western-style riot gear Qiao Shi had requested, which had just arrived, speeded on its way with the help of Henry Kissinger. Other guards began to assemble behind the lattice-work screen placed across the redlacquered entrance gateway to conform with the traditional belief it would ward off any evil spirits attempting to enter the compound under cover of darkness.

It was not spirits who were massing at the gateway, but over five thousand students. Their ranks stretched all the way back to Tiananmen Square, where another estimated fifty thousand had assembled throughout the night. They represented every university in the city. Until an hour ago they had been good-natured, singing songs and reciting poems to each other.

The previous day, Jeanne Moore had watched Yang Li walking around the pediment shouting into his megaphone. Like Cassy Jones, the American journalist was impressed by the student leader's skill at working an audience.

"Ask yourselves this! Why is it so hard to achieve democracy in China? Because the people in power have been nothing more than one form of dictatorship after another!"

A huge roar swept the square: *"Down with the Communist Party! Long live democracy!"*

Late in the evening, the mood had changed. As the chimes from the Telegraph Building on Changan Avenue began to ring the hour, with the opening bars of the Maoist anthem, *"The East Is Red,"* student leaders began to urge the crowd to sing the *"Internationale"* again.

All at once, Li, quickly followed by Daobao and Wang Dan, had left the pediment to move through the throng.

"Let's tell the leadership what we think! Let's tell them what we want!" they repeatedly cried out.

The chant was taken up around them. In a great surge the students had moved out on to Changan Avenue. Swept along, Jeanne continued to fill her notebook with impressions.

"Taxis and buses screeched to a halt. Cars began to pile up as the students blocked the entire width of the avenue. They were shouting all the time: 'Long live democracy!' 'Long live Hu Yaobang!' Bus passengers hung out of windows, bewildered and more than a little frightened by what was happening. A traffic policeman stranded on his platform appeared stunned. Then he reached for his two-way radio and began to speak."

The students surged past him, holding aloft red banners proclaiming DEMOCRACY.

As they surged along Changan Avenue, they started to sing patriotic songs. It was *"like something out of an epic movie"* to Cassy.

For the past two days she had hardly left Tiananmen Square. What little sleep she managed had been snatched on the steps of the monument. Students had shared their food with her. The previous day she had gone with their leaders across the square to present a formal petition of demands to the Politburo.

An officer emerged from the Great Hall of the People and told them they were breaking the law. She watched with pride as Daobao replied it was still permissible, as it had been under the emperors, to present a petition seeking redress for any legitimate case of discontent. The functionary had ordered them off the steps and stomped back into the building.

At that moment Wang Dan stepped forward. Raising a scrawny arm toward the building, the history student, now one of the mainsprings of the student movement, once more displayed a fine sense of occasion. He delivered a short, sharp warning to the back of the retreating flunky.

"Please tell your masters we can wait for days for an answer to our demands. After all, China has waited for centuries for democracy."

A great whoop greeted the words. Dan then organized the first sit-in of the demonstration. Hundreds of students had squatted on the steps, oblivious to orders from the PLA sentries to move on. The soldiers had finally given up.

To Cassy *"this was the first student victory. They had shown that a combination of determination, strict discipline, and sheer gutsiness could work."*

A second victory had swiftly followed. Late the previous evening three members of the National People's Congress had emerged from the Great Hall to reluctantly receive the petition. One of them promised to pass it to *"superior government departments."*

Watching a door of the Great Hall close behind them, Wang Dan reminded the students: *"The only way to achieve all we want is to stay here in the square. No matter what they threaten to do, we must not leave!"*

As word spread of the demonstration in Tiananmen Square, similar protests were under way in other cities. In Shanghai and all along the Yangtze Delta, students were on the march. From the port city of Tianjin, students had faxed support to their Beijing colleagues. From Nanjing had come another faxed message, calling for concerted action to remove *"the jackals and wolves who now hold sway. There is no time to wait! Now is the time to act!"*

As Jeanne Moore stood in the Wednesday morning darkness, the young reporter could see that among the students outside the gate of Zhongnanhai, the rallying call was being translated into action.

In the crowd she saw Wuerkaixi, Wang Dan, Daobao, and Yang Li leading the endlessly repeated chant.

"Li Peng! Come out! Li Peng! Come out!'

The last vestige of mourning for Hu Yaobang was lost in the deep, throaty cry of thousands of young voices demanding the appearance of the prime minister.

Through the lattice-work screen, Jeanne could see lights turning on all over the compound and shadowy figures running and shouting. Then scores of Public Security agents ran out of the gate and began to push the students back, advancing slowly shoulder to shoulder, forming a perimeter around the gateway.

For the moment there was silence. It was broken with Daobao's shout.

"Don't be frightened! Long live democracy!"

He turned and yelled at the police lines.

"Send for Li Peng! We have no quarrel with you! We only wish to speak to him personally!"

The police continued to move forward. But now the students were also on the move, their ranks shoving against the guards'. Locked together, the two masses surged back and forth.

Suddenly from the compound came the amplified voice of Security Chief Qiao Shi. *"Students! You have one minute to withdraw and return to your universities! If you do not, you will be arrested. The majority of you are the victims of a small number of people who are spreading rumors and poisoning your minds. Do not let them! Leave now! Go back to your campuses!"*

An uneasy silence once more fell over the students. Those around Cassy were murmuring to each other that they must not take protest too far. Many began to turn and walk away. She saw the defeated look on the faces of Daobao, Wang Dan, and the other leaders. Then, as they too turned and left, Cassy saw Wuerkaixi. He was moving quickly through the students, speaking quietly and urgently.

"Go back to the square. I shall address you there."

With those words the twenty-one-year-old education student had made his bid to establish his total authority over the students where the others had failed.

SAME DAY, LATER
NATIONAL PHOTOGRAPHIC INTERPRETATION CENTER

On the third floor of Federal Building 213, technicians continued to process the flow of information from satellites over Beijing and other sites in China. The images included not only the scenes in Tiananmen Square and in and around Zhongnanhai, but also what was happening in the various garrisons in the capital. Troops were being placed on standby, but so far none had been sent to the scenes of disturbance.

Elsewhere in Washington, the eavesdroppers of the National Security Agency were beginning to collate data coming from their sophisticated collection technology on the ground and in space over China. Among much else, they had picked radio traffic out of Zhongnanhai to Tibet ordering units of the 27th Army to be ready to return to Beijing at short notice.

The reports from the National Photographic Interpretation Center, together with those of the NSA, made their way upward through the multiple levels of the intelligence community, pausing to be read and initialed at places such as the National Reconnaissance Office — a highly secret, low-profile agency jointly managed by the Department of Defense and the CIA — the Bureau of Intelligence and Research, the State Department, the Defense Intelligence Agency, and the National Foreign Intelligence Board, on which all the heads of U.S. intelligence agencies sit. Finally the reports would make their way into the White House office in which the President's Daily Brief is composed.

The reports would give him a clear idea of what the students were doing and the options the Chinese leadership was beginning to formulate to deal with them. The President would be told that a military response was on the list of probable actions.

SAME DAY
TIANANMEN SQUARE

Daylight broke over Tiananmen Square to reveal an extraordinary sight. There were now close to a hundred thousand students spread over the slabbed ground. Some had set up tents to keep out the cold; others lay curled in sleeping bags or wrapped in blankets. Thousands of banners hung limp in the early morning mist.

Cassy thought the scene resembled *"a medieval pageant."* She had spent what remained of the night snuggling beside Daobao at the base of the Monument to the People's Heroes. He had hardly spoken to her; she had sensed his dejection over how quickly the students had turned and left Zhongnanhai. At dawn he had kissed her quickly on the cheek and gone off to join the other leaders at the pediment.

She could see them now, huddled around Wuerkaixi, nodding at what he was saying.

Wuerkaixi was telling them that *"our only hope is to use Article 35 to legitimize what we are doing."* This article of the Chinese constitution is a bill of rights giving every citizen the right to speak, publish, and, most important, organize *"a lawful assembly to demonstrate and to petition."*

Wuerkaixi then suggested a parameter for future demonstrations. *"We must remember to always acknowledge the right of the Party to lead and the impossibility of creating an American-style democracy in our society. What we want is change within the existing framework."*

While one of the students hurried away to get the exact wording of Article 35 and select key passages from it for more poster displays, Wuerkaixi addressed the gathering in the square for the first time.

It was a masterly performance. Wuerkaixi took control of the crowd at once by first addressing the hundreds of police and Public Security agents in their paramilitary uniforms who were lining the edges of the square.

"Do nothing, because we are doing no wrong! This is a lawful assembly under the constitution," Wuerkaixi shouted through one of the microphones that had begun to sprout all over the monument's pediment.

Several of the police smiled and waved good-naturedly.

Then he turned to the tens of thousands of students, many squatting on the ground eating breakfast. With the skill of a street-corner orator, Wuerkaixi seized upon something his audience could all readily see, the thousands of banners and posters.

Pointing to one cluster away to his left near the Mao Mausoleum, whose messages were an attack on the Four Basic Principles of the State, Wuerkaixi began a careful and measured attack.

First he ridiculed blind adherence to Mao's kind of Marxism. Mao had said that only one kind of political thinking was correct. Wuerkaixi insisted this was a *"direct violation of the freedom to think."* Next he challenged the *"blind adherence"* the leadership demanded to all it said or did. That was *"a dangerous autocracy."* Then Wuerkaixi delivered a rousing dismissal of the *"dictatorship of the proletariat,"* which gave the Party the right to suppress the people at any time with any kind of force it chose. Next he challenged the very concept of socialism as practiced in China. He described it as *"the greatest threat to reform, which is the only hope for the future of our country."*

The first sustained cheer of the day greeted this salvo.

Wuerkaixi then opened a freewheeling discussion, inviting his audience to step up to the pediment and address the crowd. Many did, speaking haltingly at first, then with increasing euphoria. Others, more cautious, wrote out their comments or criticism for Wuerkaixi to read aloud. He conducted the forum to which he brought a theatricality, strutting and flourishing his hands. Pausing briefly, he turned to Wang Dan and said: *"You see, all they needed is to be organized. Everything is going beautifully."*

So it seemed.

SAME DAY, SAME TIME
THE HOSPITAL OF TRADITIONAL MEDICINE

Professor Guangzu looked at the young doctors and students who stood respectfully silent in his office. They had approached him as he ended his early morning visits to patients, requesting they be allowed to send a delegation to Tiananmen Square with a wreath for Hu Yaobang.

"I have no objection to that," he told them. *"But I cannot allow you to stay there. Your place is here. If there is trouble and there are casualties, your work will be needed."*

One of the students, a thick-set man called Chen, had then made the suggestion that led to this lengthening silence. He proposed the hospital should set up and run a first-aid post in the square for any students who might need medical help.

Professor Guangzu knew this was easier to suggest than to do. It would need approval from the hospital administration, which would almost certainly refer the matter to higher authority, which most definitely would refuse to do anything to help the students. Yet the more he considered it, the suggestion seemed a sensible one, given the hospital's designated role in the latest disaster plan. To have a first-aid post would certainly help should there be the kind of trouble Madame Hu had predicted.

The professor had visited her late the previous evening, not in Zhongnanhai, but at 25 Kuaijisi Alley, a *hutong* behind the Forbidden City, where she and her husband had recently obtained a more modest dwelling for their retirement. The house had previously belonged to Madame Hu's family.

After her husband's death his widow had moved there, where it would be easier to receive the thousands of visitors who wished to express their condolences. Floral tributes had overflowed, filling houses along the length of the *hutong.*

During Professor Guangzu's time with her, Madame Hu had expressed her fears that the students would *"do something that will go beyond mourning."* She was anxious to avoid any demonstration that would diminish public respect for her husband.

Returning to the hospital late the previous night, the professor had walked through Tiananmen Square and felt that what was happening was summed up by a banner raised before Tiananmen Gate. It read: WE HAVE WOKEN UP.

Going about his morning ward rounds, he had seen through the windows that hundreds more students were walking or cycling toward the square. Mingling with them were older people, workers and the unemployed. They too carried banners proclaiming their status and demanding better conditions.

Professor Guangzu came to a decision. As part of their training under the city's disaster plan, the medical staff regularly took part in field exercises, going to Tiananmen Square or some other public place and setting up a field post. He had the authority to call a rehearsal any time.

Professor Guangzu ordered Chen and a number of other doctors and students to go to Tiananmen Square and prepare a medical facility post. They should remain there until he recalled them. If challenged, they should say they were on a training exercise.

SAME DAY, SAME TIME
THE NATIONAL DEFENSE UNIVERSITY
BEIJING

Driving past the checkpoint, Captain Instructor Kao Jyan entered the pleasant surroundings of the military campus, driving past well-tended lawns and a succession of white stone buildings. Waiting for him on the steps of the main building was an aide. He said Colonel Fan Zhichi, who was in charge of all instructors, had called an immediate meeting in the main lecture hall.

Jyan did not have to be told why. Passing Zhongnanhai, he had seen the street cleaners pulling down the last of the posters and banners the demonstrators had stuck to the walls of the compound. A patrolling policeman had told him what had happened. Turning on to Changan Avenue, Jyan heard the cheers coming from Tiananmen Square.

In the lecture hall Colonel Zhichi gave a full account of events overnight in Beijing and elsewhere.

"Lawless elements" were calling for the overthrow of the Party and had thrown bricks and bottles at the police. There had been disturbances in three military regions several hundred miles from Beijing. Army units there had gone to full readiness. The 38th Army was ready to move into Beijing. Units of the 27th Army would come from Tibet in a few days and would be based fifty miles from the capital.

But the order from Zhongnanhai made clear no military intervention would occur for the time being. When and if it came, the university's instructors would play their part in implementing the plan they had devised to bring in troops either by helicopter or through the network of tunnels beneath Beijing. Speed and determination would be the key to success.

SAME DAY, LATER
TIANANMEN SQUARE

Brian Davidson, the press attaché at the British embassy, and Brendan Ward, second secretary at the Irish embassy, disagreed over the size of the crowd in the square.

Ward, a solemn-faced twenty-seven-year-old blessed with an acerbic wit, estimated the number would comfortably fit into Lansdowne Road, the rugby stadium in his beloved Dublin. That made it around sixty-five thousand. Davidson, a tall, fair-haired twenty-five-year-old preppy, who had been born in Jamaica and raised in Northern Ireland, put the number *"as likely to overflow Wembley Stadium on Cup Final day,"* close to a hundred thousand.

The two diplomats had been firm friends from their first meeting, drawn to each other in part by a common understanding of the problems Britain faced in Ulster and an abhorrence of what the IRA represented.

Their embassies had sent them here, in Davidson's words, *"to do a little sussing,"* to find out what was happening. Behind his carefully nurtured mannerisms, snappy dress, and hard-won street savvy was a cool head. Fluent in Mandarin and with a good grasp of the nuances of Chinese politics, Davidson was a rising star in the British embassy compound. Ambassador Donald shared a view common among senior staff: Davidson could one day be British ambassador to China.

In Ireland's small and widely spread diplomatic service, Ward was also considered a comer. Unlike Davidson, he had *"no real love affair with China."* Lacking the language, he found the Chinese remained almost as great a mystery as they had been the day he arrived in Beijing.

But this morning one mystery had become a little clearer to the Irish diplomat, the purpose of the inquiries Daobao and Liu Yang had made about IRA hunger strike methods some weeks ago. Seeing the extent of the protest, for Ward *"the penny dropped. These people would go all the way, and that could include hunger strikes. There was a determination about them to succeed that was both inspiring and a little scary."*

He and Davidson continued to move slowly through the crowd, listening and noting down what was being said. Davidson reminded Ward that Mao had said violent protest was the logical continuation of politics.

Ward said the scene didn't look so much a potential battlefield, more like an outside version of a gathering of the gypsies in his own country. There was that same good-tempered watchfulness.

Other foreigners were also making judgments.

The Russian embassy had sent over a dozen diplomats, including Minister-Counselor Vladimir Kudinov and Counselor Anatoly Bykov. The Russians were moving determinedly across the square, pausing from time to time to compare notes. Kudinov found the situation *"a little hard to understand. For many it seemed to be an excuse for a day out."*

Boris Klimonko, the embassy's first secretary and a fluent Mandarin speaker, busily copied out the details of the floral tributes to Hu around the Monument of the People's Heroes. While the majority came from campuses, he found a surprising number from within the Party itself. Some of those had messages that could be construed as support for the students. The one from the *People's Daily*, the mass-circulation organ of the Party Central Committee, bore a thinly veiled reminder that Hu had said protest could be beneficial. A similar sentiment accompanied the massive wreath from the Communist Youth League, with which Hu had been so closely associated.

As Klimonko continued his basic intelligence gathering, students from the Central Institute of Fine Art arrived with a giant black-and-white framed photograph of Hu. They hoisted it on the monument's pediment, pointing it so that Hu's gnome-like face stared resolutely out over the heads of the crowd toward the portrait of Mao on Tiananmen Gate.

Raymond Burghardt, the U.S. embassy's counselor for political affairs, one of several American diplomats monitoring events, was suddenly struck by the *"vision that Beijing now had two very separate and rival sources of authority: Hu and his students, Mao and those in his mold."*

Others too were coming to the conclusion that two different versions of Communism were confronting each other. Among them were the growing number of foreign intelligence officers who had slipped out of the legation quarter to take stock for themselves.

Some, like the middle-aged and jovial Boris Kavik of the KGB, were easy to spot; moving through the throng, he shook hands and proffered cigarettes. Like the other Russians, Kavik was primarily concerned with discovering how long the students intended to stay in that square. Several told him they would remain until the planned May 4 rally. That would leave an eleven-day gap before Mikhail Gorbachev's state visit, due to begin on May 15.

Intelligence officers from the CIA and European intelligence agencies were trying to discover whether the Russians themselves were encouraging the demonstrations, either as part of the *"wind of change"* currently sweeping through the Soviet bloc and fanned by calls for democracy there, or to create what one intelligence officer called *"a little mischief, to wrong-foot the Chinese leadership before Gorbachev came."*

The CIA's Tom would report no evidence had so far emerged indicating either to be the case. The demonstrations appeared to be totally inspired and controlled by students.

Nevertheless, on this Wednesday in the vast, crowded expanse of Tiananmen Square, the local foreign intelligence community continued to watch the students and each other. Posing as newspeople or supportive onlookers, the agents continued to work their way into the trust of the students. They made no attempt to directly infiltrate its leadership on the monument's pediment, concentrating instead on those camped around it. No doubt flattered to be the object of such attention, the students spoke freely about their hopes and plans.

By midday the intelligence officers could confirm what diplomats such as Brian Davidson and Brendan Ward were reporting to their superiors: The demonstrations were going to continue and intensify.

SAME DAY, SAME TIME
SAN FRANCISCO

Shao-Yan Wang, the daughter of a high-ranking official in Beijing, watched the television pictures of the scenes in Tiananmen Square with mounting excitement. Time and again she thought she saw familiar faces as the camera panned over the crowd. The reporter kept saying this was a peaceful demonstration to mark the week of mourning for Hu Yaobang.

Shao-Yen realized the reporter clearly had little understanding of the Chinese language, or he would have understood the snatches of Mandarin she heard students shout at the camera.

"Hu Yaobang didn't have a foreign bank account!" cried one. Another said: *"Help us overthrow dictatorship."* A third, in a husky Beijing accent, appealed: *"People of the world, listen to us!"*

As the camera focused on the Mao obelisk, Shao-Yen saw a poster that would probably have meant nothing to foreigners but was full of portent for her. It read: TZU-HSI MUST NOW RETIRE. Empress Tzu-Hsi had continued to rule at the end of the nineteenth century long after she had promised to give up power. The poster was clearly a pointed reference to Deng Xiaoping's insistence on remaining in office.

All too soon the TV report was over. Shao-Yen telephoned her father in Beijing. She could hear the concern in his voice as he told her about the march on Zhongnanhai.

"That has never happened before," he said.

"What will happen now?" she asked.

"No one knows," he replied. *"But I fear there will be much more trouble. It is good you are not here."*

Something in his voice stopped Shao-Yen from telling him of her efforts so far to interest Americans in China's desire for democracy. One of Qiao Shi's agents could be listening. She had heard they monitored all calls to and from China.

After speaking to her father, Shao-Yen telephoned Chinese friends in the Bay Area to report what she had seen on TV and what her father had said, including his prediction of further trouble.

"We must all try and see what we can do to help," she concluded each time.

But no clear plan emerged. In many ways she and her friends seemed like all those students she had seen milling around Tiananmen Square, Shao-Yen thought.

SAME DAY, NIGHTFALL
TIANANMEN SQUARE

Professor Guangzu picked his way through the sprawling students. He could remember nothing quite like this. During the Cultural Revolution the square had been filled with the Red Guards, many of them as young as the students now occupying Tiananmen, and their violent slogans. More recently, in the 1986–87 demonstrations that had led to Hu's purging for supporting the students, the prevailing mood had also been of aggression.

But now *"a great peace"* hung over the square. To Professor Guangzu it seemed *"sufficient that the students were there. They kept on repeating the same chant, though none I spoke to could explain what the words actually represented. Beyond this call for democracy, there was no tangible thought-through political philosophy."*

Yet he recognized that the very vagueness of what the students were calling for was a strength. They could incorporate into their chants almost any demand that might help to bring about a change in the country's cultural system.

In the crowd of several hundred thousand, the professor noticed a considerable number of workers were also present. More were arriving. They repeatedly told the students that they had come to lend more support. Yet he could see little that would reinforce the concern Madame Hu had expressed, that the gathering would exploit her husband's death. The students' posters were no more than he had expected.

Reaching the first-aid tent, he learned his staff had not yet had to treat a single injury. He sat for a while and chatted with them. Shortly before 10:00 P.M. he left. There had still been no call for his staff to deal with any injuries. The crowd was one of the most well behaved he could recall.

Professor Guangzu had almost reached Changan Avenue when he saw thousands of students parading from the west side of the square, repeatedly chanting *"Bring us Li Peng!"* Recovering from the suddenness of what was happening, he joined the people running down Changan, the Avenue of Eternal Peace. Professor Guangzu sensed then that *"the time of tranquility was over."*

Among those leading the second charge to Zhongnanhai were Li and Daobao. The decision to carry the protest to the leadership compound again was spontaneous, they would insist. In Daobao's words, *"We had been sitting around all day waiting for a response to our demands. It made people excitable and frustrated."* Those emotions were joined by anger as the crowd ran along the street.

Once again the indefatigable Jeanne Moore was among them. As she was swept into the approach road to Zhongnanhai, she saw that at least a thousand police had formed lines further down the street. The crowd charged them at full tilt. The first line gave. Fifty feet further on, the second line held, then collapsed. Only one row of police stood between the mob and the gateway to Zhongnanhai.

Sensing victory was theirs, they paused. It was a mistake. Within moments the two broken police lines had reformed, cutting off the people still approaching from Changan Avenue. At the same time hundreds of police emerged from the compound, brandishing leather belts. Behind them were rows of armed militia.

Trapped between the two forces, the students lost their resolve. They turned and ran back through the re-formed police ranks. Reaching Changan Avenue, they squatted across the wide thoroughfare, completely disrupting traffic.

It struck Professor Guangzu as a pointless display.

SAME TIME, SAME DAY
LOS ANGELES

Professor Guangzu's daughter, Jenny, and her husband, Zhong, were engaged in another of their arguments.

Dr. Jenny Guangzu had the same nut-brown eyes as her father, but her hair was thick and black, like her mother's. People often found it hard to believe she was thirty and had been a qualified surgeon for the past four years. She looked like a pre-med student, and she was not bossy or arrogant as many expected a doctor to be.

Americans have such a funny way of speaking, she had told Zhong. Her husband said this was because they are often so badly educated; there was nothing worse than listening to adults talking like children, he had added.

Nowadays, Jenny realized, he complained about most things, especially on those days when the hospital where they both worked was half-shrouded in smog. No matter how often she told him the weather had been far worse in Beijing, he continued to find fault. When it wasn't the smog, it was the cholesterol in the food or the way the hospital was run and the profits it made.

Though her father had never said so, Jenny knew he was disappointed she had married Zhong. Her husband was too dogmatic for her father. Jenny had hoped America would liberate Zhong. Instead he had become increasingly more assertive that China offered a far more worthwhile lifestyle than America. Once more it had led to an argument.

This one had been triggered by one of the TV reports from Beijing. After watching it, Jenny had said that China could be on the verge of the great breakthrough to democracy. Significantly, the authorities appeared to be making no attempt to end the protest, which could indicate that the moderates within the leadership had managed to convince Deng Xiaoping to further extend reforms. They might return home to a country dramatically changed for the better.

"*For the worse!*" Zhong had stormed. If democracy meant the kind of capitalist world they lived in now, he wanted no part of it for China. Jenny looked around the living room of their apartment in West Hollywood. It contained a TV, stereo, a VCR, and good quality furniture. In the kitchen were a dishwasher, microwave, washing machine, and refrigerator. She didn't know one home in Beijing that was similarly equipped. Here there were no street committees snooping and prying. She could say and do what she liked.

The argument had followed a familiar path, with Jenny extolling the freedoms of America and Zhong becoming increasingly critical. They still had not resolved their differences when they fell asleep.

Author Gordon Thomas' special permit from the People's Liberation Party, allowing him to visit Tiananmen Square in the aftermath of the massacre. It enabled him to interview the commanders and troops who carried out the mass killings.

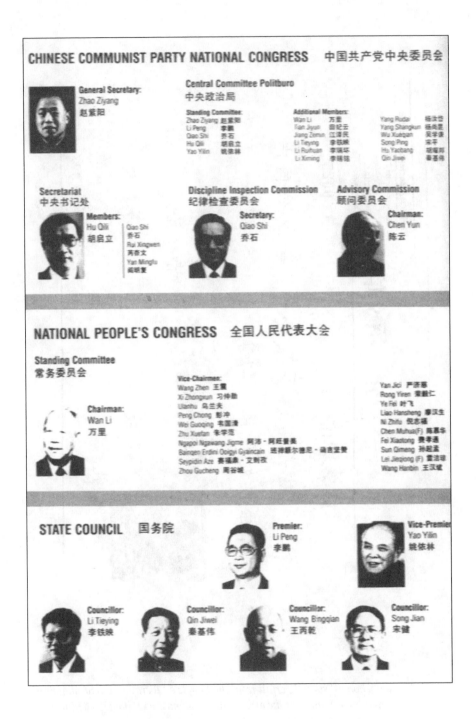

CHINESE COMMUNIST PARTY NATIONAL CONGRESS 中国共产党中央委员会

General Secretary:
Zhao Ziyang
赵紫阳

Central Committee Politburo
中央政治局

Standing Committee:
Zhao Ziyang 赵紫阳
Li Peng 李鹏
Qiao Shi 乔石
Hu Qili 胡启立
Yao Yilin 姚依林

Additional Members:
Wan Li 万里
Tian Jiyun 田纪云
Jiang Zemin 江泽民
Li Tieying 李铁映
Li Ruihuan 李瑞环
Li Ximing 李锡铭

Yang Rudai 杨汝岱
Yang Shangkun 杨尚昆
Wu Xueqian 吴学谦
Song Ping 宋平
Hu Yaobang 胡耀邦
Qin Jiwei 秦基伟

Secretariat
中央书记处

Members:
Hu Qili 胡启立
Qiao Shi 乔石
Rui Xingwen 芮杏文
Yan Mingfu 阎明复

Discipline Inspection Commission
纪律检查委员会

Secretary:
Qiao Shi
乔石

Advisory Commission
顾问委员会

Chairman:
Chen Yun
陈云

NATIONAL PEOPLE'S CONGRESS 全国人民代表大会

Standing Committee
常务委员会

Chairman:
Wan Li
万里

Vice-Chairmen:
Wang Zhen 王震
Xi Zhongxun 习仲勋
Ulanhu 乌兰夫
Peng Chong 彭冲
Wei Guoqing 韦国清
Zhu Xuefan 朱学范
Ngapoi Ngawang Jigme 阿沛·阿旺晋美
Bainqen Erdini Ooigyi Gyaincain 班禅额尔德尼·确吉坚赞
Seypidin Aze 赛福鼎·艾则孜
Zhou Gucheng 周谷城

Yan Jici 严济慈
Rong Yiren 荣毅仁
Ye Fei 叶飞
Liao Hansheng 廖汉生
Ni Zhifu 倪志福
Chen Muhua(F) 陈慕华
Fei Xiaotong 费孝通
Sun Qimeng 孙起孟
Lei Jieqiong (F) 雷洁琼
Wang Hanbin 王汉斌

STATE COUNCIL 国务院

Premier:
Li Peng
李鹏

Vice-Premier
Yao Yilin
姚依林

Councillor:
Li Tieying
李铁映

Councillor:
Qin Jiwei
秦基伟

Councillor:
Wang Bingqian
王丙乾

Councillor:
Song Jian
宋健

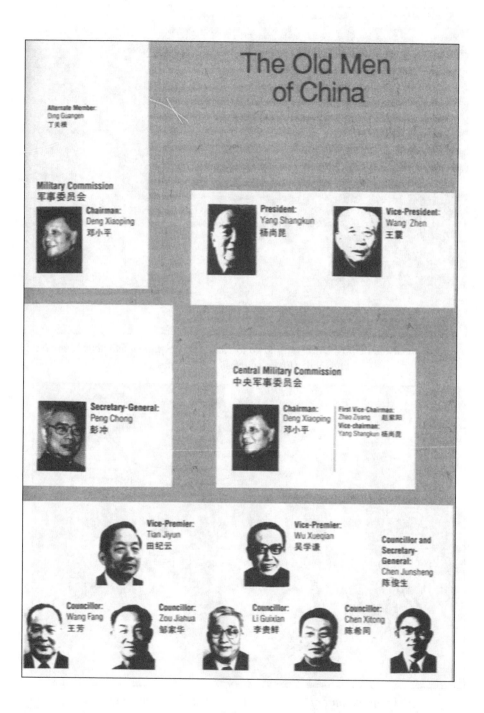

The Old Men
of China

Alternate Member:
Ding Guangen
丁关根

Military Commission
军事委员会
Chairman:
Deng Xiaoping
邓小平

President:
Yang Shangkun
杨尚昆

Vice-President:
Wang Zhen
王震

Secretary-General:
Peng Chong
彭冲

Central Military Commission
中央军事委员会
Chairman:
Deng Xiaoping
邓小平

First Vice-Chairman:
Zhao Ziyang 赵紫阳
Vice-chairman:
Yang Shangkun 杨尚昆

Vice-Premier:
Tian Jiyun
田纪云

Vice-Premier:
Wu Xueqian
吴学谦

Councillor and
Secretary-
General:
Chen Junsheng
陈俊生

Councillor:
Wang Fang
王芳

Councillor:
Zou Jiahua
邹家华

Councillor:
Li Guixian
李贵鲜

Councillor:
Chen Xitong
陈希同

Students leave Beijing University to go to Tiananmen Square a few days before the massacre. (Photo courtesy Cassy Jones).

In this dormitory building on the campus of Beijing University, student leaders met in secret from April, 1989 onward to plot their moves. Other students maintained guard by posing as soccer players.

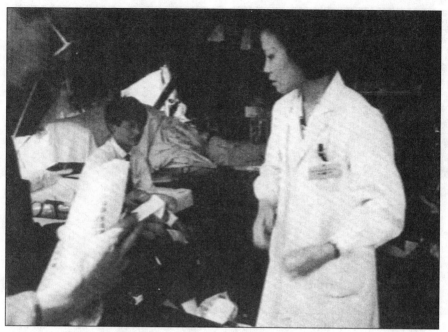

Dr. Jenny Guangzu in the field hospital she helped her father set up in Tiananmen Square. It was crushed by tanks in the massacre.

Another view of the field hospital set up by Professor Guangzu and his doctor daughter, Jenny, in Tiananmen Square.

PLA soldier Yang Bing (in second row, right) is photographed with his platoon in the suburbs of Beijing, two days before they went into action in Tiananmen Square. One of the soldiers is carrying a practice target.

The entrance to the Forbidden City.

*PLA junior officers at the National Defense University, near Beijing,
photographed in late May 1989, at target practice.
They would use their skills to deadly effect against the students.*

*Shao-Yen Wang, the actress daughter of a powerful member of the Chinese
hierarchy who had come to America to develop her career in Hollywood, found herself
caught up in a real-life drama. (Photo: Courtesy Shao-Yen Wang) At right: Shao-Yen
Wang today. She is a budding model in California. (Photo: Courtesy Hao Bing)*

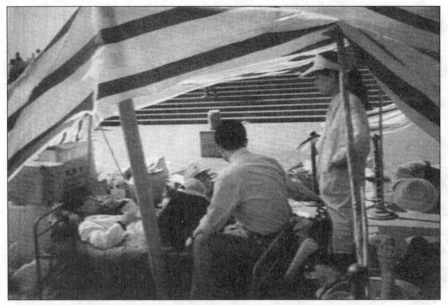

Dr. Jenny Guangzu and two student helpers are pictured on the morning of
Saturday, June 3, 1989, in their field hospital in Tiananmen Square.
The atmosphere is relaxed. No one suspected that 12 hours later they would be
engulfed with casualties before tanks crushed the hospital.

Another view of the square on the Saturday before the massacre.
There are no soldiers visible, but in the Great Hall of the People
thousands of troops were assembling.

Students camp out in Tiananmen Square. Many have with them their worldly belongings; many have also made wills bequeathing their possessions to relatives.

This was the students' Democracy Wall. The posters carried messages of support. But from where the students needed it most, world leaders, there was no encouragement. The West's rulers had other matters to consider, and the students were low down on the totem pole of pragmatic politics.

Newsmen wait. Many of the hundreds of reporters and TV crews in Tiananmen Square on Saturday, June 3, 1989, felt it was going to be a slow news day.

It is Saturday afternoon, June 3, 1989, and another student rally is in progress. It would be one of the last.

The cleared area is a place where student leaders could meet outside the crush in the square. In the background are the roofs of the Forbidden City.

The Goddess of Liberty — the very symbol of student aspirations — rises proud and defiant over Tiananmen Square on the night of Saturday, June 3, 1989.

In the "consult area" a group of student leaders including Li Yang (far right in spectacles) discuss their next move late on Saturday afternoon. But already the die had been cast by the aged rulers of China.

*The first confrontation. Troops arrive in a western suburb
late on Saturday afternoon, June 3, 1989, and form a line across the street.
Anyone attempting to cross will be shot.*

*Li Yang (foreground) leads a procession of students past the
Great Hall of the People on Saturday, June 3, 1989.*

Daobao and Li Yang's girlfriend, Meili, photographed in Tiananmen Square on the evening of June 3, 1989. Hours later they would be fleeing the might of the PLA soldiers — including Li's brother, Bing.

The Goddess of Liberty rises above the tens of thousands in the square on the Saturday afternoon of June 3, 1989.

Students assemble around the foot of the Mao monument in Tiananmen Square as they await the arrival of the army.

The Troops arrive in Tiananmen Square. There is a confrontation.

PLA tanks rumble into Tiananmen Square as the students try to stop them by sitting in their path. Later, many would be crushed for such bravery.

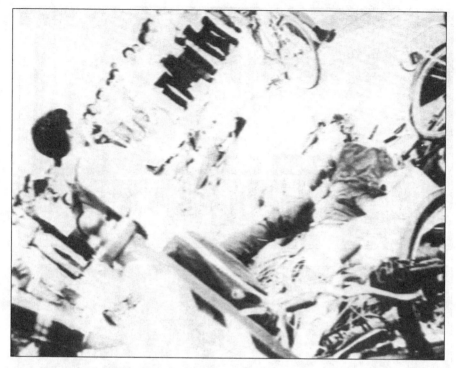

The bodies lie everywhere in and around Tiananmen Square.

The Beijing Government put up this poster to "commemorate" the "bravery" of the PLA in suppressing student "counterrevolutionaries."

Students at Beijing University read the official version of events.

*PLA Company Commander Tan Yaobang with author Gordon Thomas
in Tiananmen Square. In the background is the Great Hall of the People.
This, like other meetings with PLA officers, was arranged by the military commissar.*

Melinda Liu, a Newsweek
*correspondent whose reporting was one
of the highlights of media coverage.*

*Author Gordon Thomas talking to
one of the 100 eyewitnesses to China's
Night of Infamy that he interviewed.*

15

A Time of Decision

Standing below the pediment of the Monument to the People's Heroes late on Friday evening, Cassy felt that the entire city appeared on the move under cover of darkness. The demonstrations were in their sixth day.

Changan Avenue was lined with people, as it would be for any big parade. They were mourners for Hu Yaobang's funeral, which would take place late next morning in the Great Hall of the People. She estimated there could be over a million people waiting patiently to pay their respects. More were emerging from the alleys on either side of the broad avenue.

As midnight approached, a great stirring came from the crowd. In the distance Cassy and the others on the pediment heard the sound of singing growing louder.

Students from all the city's campuses had begun to march toward Tiananmen Square, chanting and singing, in columns of fifty to several hundred people each. Traffic police stood numb and helpless on their podiums at intersections. Public Security agents worked frantically to film and photograph faces in the advancing columns, then gave up, defeated by sheer numbers.

As they arrived on Changan Avenue, the student marshals with each column gave a brisk order. Picking up stride, the marchers burst into the Chinese national anthem: *"Rise up, you who refuse to be slaves."*

Her eyes brimming with tears of pride, Cassy turned to Daobao.

"You did it!" she said. *"You all really did it."*

"Everybody helped," Daobao grinned, watching the columns taking up their predetermined positions in the square. Nothing had been left to chance.

The planning had begun the night before, following the students' third failure to gain entry to Zhongnanhai. Over fifteen thousand students had tried to storm the compound. This time the police had sprung a well-prepared trap. They had emerged from the alleys around Zhongnanhai, waving the leather thongs they used for crowd control. At the same time, loudspeakers from inside the compound had unleashed a continuous denunciation, repeatedly calling the students *"reactionaries,"* a condemnation second in gravity only to *"counter-revolutionary"* in official-speak.

Half-deafened by the loudspeakers and stunned at the way the police suddenly attacked them, the students turned and fled. This time they were not allowed to go unmolested. They were chased and often severely beaten.

Professor Guangzu's first-aid post was soon filled with casualties. Several required hospitalization.

Hours later the rain had begun, washing away the blood on Changan Avenue. The downpour had also driven most of the students on Tiananmen Square back to their campus dormitories. They had left their posters and banners behind. Standing guard over the emblems was a token force of no more than five hundred students. Sodden and hungry, they had appeared to be no threat, and the police had ignored them.

"The protest movement had looked all but washed out," Jeanne Moore had recorded in her notebook. She had gone home to sleep. A few hours later, she received a telephone call from a contact at Beijing University. The rain had stopped, and fresh posters had gone up, demanding revenge and renewed action.

The messages on the posters had been composed by Meili, whose meticulous calligraphy had already become a hallmark of the demonstrations. Her latest messages were as uncompromising as always. *"The blood of our classmates must not have been given for nothing"*; *"Since the time of the First Emperor, we have lived under a dictatorship. This must end."*

By dawn on Friday the posters were being tacked up on every door, tree, and pole in the campus.

That morning Wang Dan and Wuerkaixi had addressed student leaders in the university's coffeehouse. Hundreds of students gathered outside to stop any attempt by the campus political officers to halt the meeting.

Wuerkaixi's denims looked as if he had slept in them. His voice was hoarse from hours of public speaking. Wang Dan's eyes were red-rimmed behind his spectacles. Though both of the student leaders looked exhausted, they had lost none of their verve.

Wuerkaixi reminded his listeners that the protest of 1986 had been led by provincial campuses such as Hefei and Changhai.

"That must not happen now," he insisted. *"It is our duty here in the capital to show leadership! We must control matters from here. In that way we will have a movement that will be coordinated and not diffuse as before."*

Wuerkaixi had then proposed they form a Beijing Students Solidarity Preparation Committee drawn from all the city's campuses.

Nine members were quickly elected: Wuerkaixi; Wang Dan; Chai Ling; her husband, Feng Conde; Liu Gang; Xiong Yan, a law student, whose job it would be to provide the legal arguments needed to justify protest; Yang Tao, a history student; Yan Daobao; and Yang Li. Among them they represented the entire spectrum of the students' points-of-view.

Wuerkaixi, Chai Ling, and her aggressive-voiced husband, Feng Conde, were the recognized militants. They could count on the support of Daobao, and

Li. Daobao found that giving up smoking had made him increasingly short-tempered, while Li now almost never showed that half-smile which had annoyed his brother Bing.

Wang Dan represented the articulate voice of moderation. While he was not against continued public demonstration, he wanted to operate strictly within legal constraints. To that end he was supported by Xiong Yan, who could recall the dry words of Chinese jurisprudence with no apparent effort. Yang Tao was another moderate, bringing a calming authority to discussions.

The first collective decision of the committee was to produce a manifesto. It bore all the *"marks of too many hands turning out too many characters,"* in the verdict of Barr Seitz, the young American foreign expert who taught English at Beijing University. For him the style of the manifesto *"was more like a Party document, but given the contents it was also a time bomb with the fuse lit."*

A big-character poster, called an *"Open Letter to Beijing College,"* listed the tactics. This Friday night every student in the city would march to Tiananmen Square. There they would remain until further notice. They would be fed and watered in rotation. There would be a call for volunteers to go on hunger strike.

After she read a copy of the poster, reporter Jeanne Moore sensed *"it was part of a new and very different game plan. The manifesto bore the signs of learning from past mistakes, of understanding the need to stiffen resolve now that the authorities had struck back. In many ways it was a declaration of war."*

Her judgment was affirmed by the intelligence operatives and foreign diplomats monitoring student activities. In the legation quarter three miles to the east of Tiananmen Square, reports were compiled and forwarded to Washington and elsewhere.

In the Beijing office of Kissinger Associates, staff sent an update on the demonstrations to the consultancy's office in Washington, with a copy to the American-China Society, housed in the same building in the capital. The report would be distributed by Henry Kissinger to his fellow board members, former Presidents Jimmy Carter, Richard Nixon, and Gerald Ford, as well as executive members Alexander Haig, Robert McFarlane, and Zbigniew Brzezinski. Some of the most powerful men in the United States had *"had their alarm bells rung,"* a Kissinger Associates employee would say.

President Bush's brother had also been alerted. Prescott Bush was a consultant to Asset Management, International Financing and Settlement Ltd. Its Chinese interests included financing the building of an $18 million country club in Shanghai, a wood-processing plant in rural China, and a satellite-linked computer database network based in Beijing. He was among the first of a growing number of U.S. businessmen who feared that the students' decision to take up permanent residence in Tiananmen Square until their demands for democracy were met could wreck all their carefully nurtured plans.

Throughout Friday, Daobao had played his part in ensuring that from now on, matters would go exactly as the committee ordained. While other members made telephone calls and sent faxes to provincial campuses asking them to send delegations to Tiananmen Square, Daobao and Yang Li had busied themselves with preparations for what was intended to be the largest demonstration since the Cultural Revolution.

An action committee had selected student marshals to supervise the marchers and songs for the columns to sing. As they passed close to the walls of Zhongnanhai, they would sing the *"Internationale,"* then, coming onto Changan Avenue, the opening verse of the national anthem with its call to rise and be free. Each student would bring sufficient food for several days and a bedroll.

Now, as Friday night passed into the first hour of Saturday morning, the totally disciplined columns continued to arrive in Tiananmen Square. The night was mild, the atmosphere tense. As the last of the columns arrived, the first of several thousand police were being bused onto Changan Avenue.

At 5:00 A.M., the voice of Chen Xitong, the mayor of Beijing, roared over the square's loudspeakers announcing that the area and the surrounding streets would be sealed in three hours for the funeral of Hu Yaobang.

From the pediment that had now become the source for all student pronouncements, Wuerkaixi calmly announced that the students were not going to leave but intended to hold their own funeral for Hu.

A great gasp swept the square and the crowd on Changan Avenue.

"All around me people are saying no one has ever dared upstage an official ceremony," Jeanne Moore scrawled in her notebook. *"Plans for the whole funeral have been carefully stage-managed to make it a Party-only occasion. No public viewing of the body to allow the focus to be Hu. No foreign delegations. Every one of the several thousand guests a Party member."*

With breathtaking bravado, Wuerkaixi had calmly announced the students intended to disrupt the single most important event in the Party calendar so far this year.

Minutes later Chen Xitong's voice once more spoke from the loudspeaker: The students must now leave.

At Wuerkaixi's order, everyone sat down in a concerted move. Around the monument, the student marshals locked arms. The student leaders waited on the pediment.

Police began to cordon off the square. Jeanne Moore, one of the few foreign reporters inside, continued to write furiously.

"The police are not armed, but some have removed their belts and are slapping them against their hands inches from the students' faces. In other places, the confrontations are more good-natured. When the police and students push against each other, the students embrace the police and chant 'People's cops should love the people! People's cops should join the people!' A group of spectators on a restaurant roof are urging the crowd to break through the police lines, singing for encouragement the Chinese national anthem. When they reach the words 'The Chinese people have reached a critical point, Let's march forward under the enemy bombardment,' the students and police, who have been on the point of violence, break out in laughter."

At 5:20 A.M., first light, Wang Dan and Wuerkaixi walked up the steps of the Great Hall of the People and knocked loudly on its center door. Three officers in dark Mao jackets appeared and said they were from the Funeral Organization Office. The senior officer started to express concern that all the Party's efforts to give Hu Yaobang a fitting funeral were now in jeopardy.

With one of his hand flourishes, Wuerkaixi said the students did not intend to disrupt the rites. But they had three demands. First, they wanted a firm guarantee there would be no police violence against anyone in the square. Second, they wanted a delegation to be admitted to view Hu's body to pay respects on behalf of all the students. Third, they wanted a complete explanation *"from the proper authorities"* for the police violence on Thursday night.

The official blinked furiously in the gathering light, then turned on his heels and walked back into the hall. He left the door ajar.

Wang Dan and Wuerkaixi sat on the stone steps, staring out at the endless rows of squatting students who had swung round to face the Great Hall.

Forty minutes later the senior official returned. The two students rose to their feet. In a strangled voice the functionary said the only demand that would be accepted was a guarantee for the students' safety.

"Then I must inform you," Wang Dan said in his most formal voice, *"that we will continue to stay here until further notice."*

Without waiting for a reply, he and Wuerkaixi walked back down the steps.

SATURDAY, APRIL 22, 1989
ZHONGNANHAI

At 9:00 A.M., Deng Xiaoping arrived from his compound half a mile to the north of Zhongnanhai. He made the journey underground, brought from beneath his mansion on board a red carriage.

At Zhongnanhai's underground station the carriage was coupled to others and pulled by a small but powerful electric engine the short distance to the cavernous bowels of the Great Hall. Elevators bore the supreme leader and his colleagues up to the salon where the funeral rites would be held.

Lesser guests had been escorted through a ten-deep cordon of police and soldiers outside in Tiananmen Square.

Realizing that Deng and Prime Minister Li Peng had, like the emperors of old, refused to show their faces to their subjects, the students were singing and chanting poems of praise for Hu mingled with cries of contempt for the Party leaders.

They had only broken off to fall into respectful silence when Madame Hu appeared with her family. With them walked Professor Guangzu. He felt the anger of the students *"was like a flame close to a box of dynamite. One mistake by the authorities and anything could have happened."*

Inside the Great Hall Madame Hu led the mourners in a slow file past her husband's coffin. Zhao Ziyang then delivered his eulogy, while Deng Xiaoping stood watching impassively. When the Party Secretary completed his carefully scripted remarks, Deng turned to Madame Hu, arms extended as if to offer condolence.

She waved him away. For a moment Deng stood, more ashen-faced than usual. Then he walked out of the salon, his face a mask. Li Peng and Zhao Ziyang quickly followed him.

As other mourners emerged into Tiananmen Square, many visibly flinched at the sea of flags and banners. The first thunderous chorus broke over them:

"We want dialogue! Down with dictatorship!"

The voices drowned out the funeral dirge coming through the loudspeakers. Then from the pediment Wuerkaixi called for silence. It came at once.

Cassy watched Wuerkaixi, Wang Dan, and Daobao walk slowly and purposefully across the square, the ranks of students parting before them. It reminded her of *"the showdown in High Noon."*

Wuerkaixi carried a rolled scroll in his hand. Reaching the steps of the Great Hall, they paused to turn and look at the silent crowd. Even the music had stopped.

Then they climbed the steps. Their slow, deliberate movements reminded Jeanne of *"Confucian officials of Imperial times submitting statements of moral criticism to the throne."*

The students knelt before the closed central door of the Great Hall. Slowly Wuerkaixi raised the scroll above his head. When he had done so, all three, in perfect harmony, chanted for Li Peng to enter into dialogue with the students. They continued to repeat this for half an hour. Then they turned and faced the still silent crowd.

"We have tried!" Wuerkaixi called out. *"We have really tried!"*

SAME DAY, LATER
SACRAMENTO, CALIFORNIA

Sue Tong was on her way to her postgraduate classes at Sacramento University when she heard the report on the all-news stations of how the students had disrupted the funeral.

The thirty-one-year-old cousin of the PLA Military Academy instructor Jyan had been in America for a year. In that time she had divorced her authoritarian Chinese husband and found new love with an American artist, Rod. They planned to marry this coming June.

She pulled her car into a gas station and phoned Rod. He had also heard the radio report.

"You think this will blow over?" Rod asked.

"No. This is only the beginning. There will be no stopping them after this," Sue predicted.

"You sound like you wish you were there."

"I do," she promptly said. *"I really do."*

There was a pause before Rod spoke. *"We've got a wedding date to keep."*

"I know," she replied. *"June fourth. I'll be there."*

"But you just can't drop everything and go to Beijing."

This time Sue was silent.

"What would you do if you went?" Rod gently pressed.

"I don't know right now, except just be there. Sometimes it's enough to show solidarity. That's very important to us Chinese, to support each other. You Americans are so independent. We draw strength from collective response."

"If you go, when will you go?"

"*I don't know. It's just I feel ... this tug to be there,*" Sue said.

"*If you go, you shouldn't go empty-handed. Those students are going to need help. Dollar help. Maybe you should start collecting from the Chinese community here.*"

Sue laughed. Rod's practicality was one of the things she loved about him.

"*I'll start today. If everyone only gives ten dollars, it could come to a lot!*"

"*You really think you can go and get back for the wedding?*" The date was now six weeks away.

"*Just let anyone try and stop me!*" Sue said.

Driving to the campus she began to plan her fund-raising strategy.

MONDAY, APRIL 24, 1989
FOREIGN LEGATION QUARTER

Judging by what was happening in the British embassy, Brian Davidson was certain the entire legation quarter was "*popping with a mixture of anticipation, excitement, and, no doubt, some apprehension that this business would really get out of hand.*" The demonstrations were now in their ninth day.

Throughout the weekend the press attaché had continued gathering information. After Hu's funeral, the students had paraded around Tiananmen Square. Late in the afternoon Wuerkaixi, in one of the changes of plan that would become a trademark of his leadership style and cause confusion and often resentment among other student leaders, ordered the majority of students to return to their campuses and rest. They would receive further orders by Monday morning.

Several students had been left to occupy the ground around the Monument to the People's Heroes.

On Sunday the litter-strewn square had been given over to the old men who normally flew their kites there. The graceful shapes had soared up to meet those high in the sky over Zhongnanhai. Among them was Premier Li Peng's.

Davidson had picked up hints of mounting tension inside the compound. He had reported to Ambassador Donald that his contacts were claiming the leadership was both "*divided and obsessed*" with how to handle the students.

Zhao Ziyang had ordered the police presence to withdraw immediately after the last official mourner had left the Great Hall on Saturday. The order had led to the students' peaceful departure.

"*Zhao was clearly promoting a hands-off approach,*" Davidson told Ambassador Donald. "*But the rumors were circulating that Zhao himself was behind the protest. The story wouldn't go away that he was using the students with an eye to actually seizing power.*"

"*There seemed no real basis for the story, but it was a dangerous one to have your name linked to,*" Ambassador Donald told the press attaché. "*What we are looking at here is perhaps the ultimate battle within the leadership, a power struggle between ambitious men and their competing visions of China.*"

The two hardliner vice-premiers, Qiao Shi and Yao Yilin, supported by Beijing Party Secretary Li Xiaming and Mayor Chen Xitong, had called an emergency meeting of the Politburo Standing Committee, a five-member "inner circle" who reported directly to Deng Xiaoping, for Monday evening. By then they wanted the police back in full strength around the square to keep the students out.

As reports came in of serious disturbances in the provincial cities of Xian and Changsha, the hardliners brought the meeting forward to Sunday morning, in Li Peng's office. Zhao was asked to attend. The hope, Davidson had learned, was to persuade the Party Secretary to *"see sense and support a tough line."* Instead Zhao had gone off to play a round of golf and then boarded the train taking him on an official visit to North Korea. The meeting had gone ahead without him.

Furious at Zhao's casual attitude, the hardliners were about to inform Deng when Li Peng suggested a different strategy. He would arrange for Deng to receive full reports on the near-riots in Xian and Changsha, so Deng could judge for himself the seriousness of the situation. Then he could be persuaded more easily to take action. In both cities *"student hooligans"* and *"unemployed hooligans"* had attacked government offices, overturned cars, and looted shops. Police had been stoned and fires started.

Davidson had learned many of the rioters had worn Mao buttons, an indication they had scant interest in the student demands for *"democracy."* The Maoists had gone on the rampage demanding a return to the policies of Mao, under which there had indeed been full employment and stable prices.

On Sunday evening Li Peng had gone to see Deng. As well as the riot reports, the prime minister brought a strongly worded letter from the Beijing Municipal Party Committee, demanding the *"strongest possible action to protect our city from reactionary elements."*

Davidson's contacts had given him an account of Deng's reaction. China's supreme leader had read the documents. For a while he had sat in silence, smoking. Then he had told Li Peng that the students must be stopped by whatever means necessary. If there had to be deaths, so be it, Deng was reported to have said.

SAME DAY, SAME TIME
CHINA DAILY COMPOUND
BEIJING

Jeanne Moore was transferring onto her computer, by far the most expensive item in her living room, the results of her Sunday spent on the Beijing University campus. It would form the basis for an article she planned to send to a Midwest newspaper. She was one of many foreign experts whose specialist knowledge had now been eagerly snapped up by the U.S. media, which sensed a major story developing. *China Daily*, however, had yet to publish anything about what was happening in Tiananmen Square or elsewhere in the country.

Jeanne had learned that the students had put up a poster listing by name and position officials who were relatives of senior Party and government personnel and demanding their removal. They had also hung posters outside the city's post offices claiming their telegrams to provincial universities seeking still more support were being intercepted.

A student in Baoding had telephoned Wang Dan to say a train had arrived from Tibet with units of the 27th Army. Baoding was fifty-four miles west of Beijing. Wang Dan had immediately sent students to spread the word around the factories and farming communes in the vicinity of Beijing. The workers were to be encouraged to support the students by allowing them to put up posters in work places and by sending delegations to Tiananmen Square.

Jeanne had completed typing her notes when an editor called from *China Daily*. The man's excitement and nervousness were all too plain. He told her that Deng Xiaoping had circulated instructions on how the Chinese media was to report the developing story.

"First, we must prepare our readers to accept Hu Yaobang made grave mistakes in the past few years," began the editor. *"We must be ready to report that Hu was not a true Marxist and criticize those who say he was."*

Jeanne remembered Zhao Ziyang had called Hu a true Marxist in his funeral eulogy. Now that the Party Secretary was in North Korea, the hardliners had clearly persuaded Deng to make his first serious criticism of his fellow official.

The editor continued. Deng had ordered the attack on Hu must emphasize he *"took a very weak stand during the campaign against spiritual pollution and wholesale Westernization."*

Hu's remains were still on their way to be cremated in his birthplace, but his reputation already *"was going up in smoke,"* Jeanne realized.

When the time came, her editor told her, China's media would blame Hu for everything that was happening. Future editorial policy had been clearly spelled out in one last chilling paragraph from Deng Xiaoping.

"We must mobilize the masses and use a mass campaign to stop the demonstration. Those people, plotters, behind the students must be reported and exposed."

To Jeanne it was obvious that Party Secretary Zhao was to be the ultimate target. It was the first clear evidence that Deng Xiaoping had finally decided who he wanted to be his successor. Premier Li Peng.

SAME DAY, LATER
WASHINGTON, D.C.

It was still Sunday in the capital when at noon the fax machine in CIA Director Webster's comfortably furnished home came to life with a message from his station chief in Beijing. The report was a detailed evaluation of the power struggle in Zhongnanhai. All the signs pointed to Deng preparing to use his prime minister as his instrument to crush the students on this, the ninth full day of demonstrations in China.

The unspoken question in the report was: *"What, if anything, should the United States do?"*

Webster knew what he must do. He called Secretary of State James Baker, who would tell the President. Only Bush could ultimately decide how, and at what level, the United States should respond to the decision of China's supreme leader to deal with the students.

WEDNESDAY, APRIL 26, 1989
DENG XIAOPING'S COMPOUND
BEIJING

At daybreak two Mercedes Benz limousines drove out of Zhongnanhai and headed north across the city, Prime Minister Li Peng in the lead car, closely followed by State President Yang Shangkun in the second. Both men preferred the custom-made German vehicles to the Red Flags used by other Politburo members.

Just south of Tiananmen Gate, the two cars pulled into a narrow alley, despite its signs warning not to enter. Fifty yards along the lane, a steel gate swung open and smartly dressed soldiers sprang to attention. The cars entered and drove down a tree-lined driveway before parking outside a dun-colored, unprepossessing building. This was Deng Xiaoping's home.

The two men were formally greeted by Deng's secretary and then escorted into the presence of the supreme ruler.

One account of what followed was subsequently pieced together by *New York Times* Beijing correspondent Nicholas D. Kristof. In this version Deng's early-morning visitors found their host in *"a grim mood, outraged by the ongoing protest and deeply alarmed at the prospect of further unrest."*

Deng's guests would do nothing to lighten his mood, nor, most certainly, did they wish to. Now that Deng had issued his guidelines to the media, they wanted him to go further, to put muscle into his order that the students were to be harshly treated, in print.

To encourage him, both men had brought evidence of how far matters had gone. On a tenth-century table, they unfurled posters Qiao Shi's agent had removed overnight from several of the city's campuses. Each carried a vitriolic personal attack on Deng. One poster described him as *"a little dwarf who has taken great power."* Another attacked him as *"the little bottle who approves big corruption."* (The bottle reference was a play on his given name, Xiaoping, which in spoken Chinese sounds like the words for "little bottle.") A third poster boldly stated: *"Under Deng, cadres are millionaires."*

Another account, from the files of a European intelligence service, portrayed Deng as sweeping the posters off the table and then walking around his office shouting that in socialist Europe, countries like Poland, whose rulers tolerated unrest, had paid a disastrous price in economic terms. Russia itself, Deng continued to fume, would go the same way unless the Kremlin showed something of the determination local commissars had in the Soviet Republic of Georgia, where thirty-one protesters had recently been summarily executed by troops.

Deng then railed against another student accusation, that he was the arch-practitioner of nepotism. One poster accused him of placing his wheelchair-bound son in charge of the China Welfare Fund for the Handicapped and then allowing him to use its charitable funds to finance a network of companies. Another poster proclaimed President Yang's cousin owed his job as chief of the army's General Political Department to family connections. Even Zhao had not escaped pillory. His son, Zhao Dajun, ran the Houhai Trading Company, which a poster claimed was *"recognized for its corruption."*

All this was a *"threat"* to China's future, Deng rasped through the smoke from his first cigarette of the day. *"This is not an ordinary student movement but turmoil. We must take a clear-cut stand and implement effective measures now to stop further unrest. We cannot let them have their way. This turmoil is a planned conspiracy to transform a China with a bright future into a China with no hope. What is at stake is the very future of the leadership and the socialist system."*

Deng's stenographer, the only other person present, continued to write down the diatribe as Deng's language grew more emotive. *"None of us wishes to see blood spilled, but it will be spilled if it is necessary. We must be ready to use a sharp knife to cut the tangled weeds."* The reference was a reminder of Deng's childhood work. Then he had cut weeds to allow rice to grow. Now he would order the students, dismissed in that phrase *"tangled weeds,"* to be cut down by one of the most powerful armies on earth.

Abruptly Deng led the others into the situation room adjoining his office. A flag-dotted wall map showed the current disposition of the PLA. No fewer than eleven armies stood guard on China's borders. The 2nd Army was on the border with Thailand; the 24th guarded against any threat from Pakistan; the 12th watched over China's flank with Burma. Nearer to hand were the 7th at Nanking and the 21st at Changshun. Even closer were the 28th and 38th armies and those first units of the 27th that had been brought back from Tibet and were now within fifty miles of Beijing.

Deng turned to his prime minister and the state president.

"We have several million loyal soldiers to do our weeding. We will allow them to start very soon."

He ordered the stenographer to transcribe his words. Like Richard Nixon, Deng liked to keep a record, but unlike the former president, China's leader did not make tapes. He feared any recording would be tampered with.

While they waited for the stenographer to return with transcripts, Li Peng and Yang Shangkun continued to play on Deng's paranoia by describing how the students had held a *"congress"* in the ruins of the Old Imperial Palace in the northeast corner of the city on the previous night. The outcome of the meeting was yet another student body, this one called the Provisional Beijing Students Union. Li Peng said it had only one aim: to force the government into a dialogue.

"Never!" Deng rasped. *"Never, never, never! To talk to these hooligans would be a sign of weakness."*

The note taker returned with the copies of the transcript, and the three leaders sat around the table in Deng's office.

While reading, according to a Western intelligence report, Deng began to fulminate once more over the allegations of nepotism. He reminded the others his son had been crippled when, as a student at Beijing University, he had been thrown out of a window by Red Guards.

"We must never see those days again," the supreme leader continued. *"That is why we must stop this now!"*

To do so, he proposed publishing *"a clear-cut"* editorial in the *People's Daily*, which would also be broadcast on state television and radio. Theoretically it should reach everyone in the land. Over a billion Chinese would know that the leadership would not tolerate any further threat to its invincibility.

While Li Peng and Yang Shangkun drafted thoughts for the editorial, Deng telephoned Xu Weichang, the most conservative of the ideologists on the Beijing Party Committee. Normally such an important policy document would have been written by Hu Qili, the Politburo member in charge of propaganda. But he was a known supporter of Zhao. Deng wanted no one to plead the Party Secretary's case.

Over breakfast, Xu Weichang drafted the core of a hard-hitting attack on the student movement, in Chinese, *xuechao.* Deng struck out the word and substituted *dongluan,* "turmoil," his favorite pejorative to describe the Cultural Revolution.

By midmorning the text had been completed and approved. It began by denouncing *"a planned conspiracy and turmoil"*; several thousand characters later, it appealed for *"all comrades of the Party and people throughout the whole nation to understand clearly that if we do not resolutely check this turmoil, our State will have no calm days."*

Xu Weichang left for the offices of the *People's Daily* while the others continued to plan.

Li Peng suggested that Deng should send a copy of the editorial to Zhao in North Korea and ask him to cable back his full endorsement of what was to be published. At the same time, the prime minister continued, copies of the text should be circulated to key Party and government officials.

"To wait until formal publication is too long," the prime minister insisted. *"We must show them we are now ready for full action."*

State President Yang gave his full support, and Deng quickly concurred.

All realized that by the time Party Secretary Zhao received his copy, the text would have been widely read, and therefore he would be in no position to argue for any changes. To ensure the *fait accompli,* Deng ordered that the editorial should lead the main national TV and radio news bulletins that evening. Immediately afterward it must be continuously broadcast for an hour over loudspeakers at all of the city's universities.

Throughout the morning the supreme leader continued to summon officials and plan an all-out counterattack against the students. Li Xiaming was ordered to arrange a rally the next day of the Party faithful in the Great Hall of the People to warn them of what Deng was repeatedly calling *"dongluan."* Qiao Shi was instructed to turn the full force of state security upon the students. They were to be infiltrated still further, and agent provocateurs were to be used to alienate public sympathy for the demonstrators. Yao Yilin was told to make sure that Zhao's supporters in Zhongnanhai knew that dissension would no longer be tolerated. Li Peng was given the task of briefing Foreign Ministry officials to convey to foreign diplomats that the crackdown was under way and that the world, in Deng's words, later reported by Nicholas Kristof in the *New York Times "should clearly understand we do not fear spilling blood, and we do not fear the international consequences."*

To prove the point Deng gave the order for twenty thousand soldiers of the 38th Army stationed in the suburbs to be prepared to move *"in minutes"* into the city. Over a thousand more policemen were sent to defend Zhongnanhai.

Like a Mafia godfather, the supreme leader was going to war by preparing for every possibility. He had orders sent to Jiang Zemin, Party Secretary of Shanghai, to stage a rally of support in that city and immediately close down the locally published *World Economic Herald,* which had become required reading in CIA Director Webster's suite and Bush's Oval Office, among other places. Other rallies were ordered to be held in cities throughout the country. Close to a billion Chinese were being once more ordered to show total obedience to the State.

Chain-smoking, Deng continued to pour out orders. Political officers at every university were to broadcast continued warnings throughout their campuses that further demonstrations would be met with *"the full force of the law."* Teachers were to be instructed to warn their pupils not to march; any teacher who refused was to be dismissed.

A poster campaign was to start at once attacking astrophysicist Fang Lizhi and his wife, Li Shuxian, both supporters of the students, as being two of the planners behind the unrest.

Finally, all posters, banners, and wreaths were to be removed from Tiananmen Square. At the same time there would be an official announcement that the period of mourning for Hu Yaobang was at an end.

"The students will have no further excuse to demonstrate," Deng said.

Shortly afterward Zhao called from the North Korean capital of Pyonayang to give his full approval of the editorial. The news was immediately circulated through Party and government channels. To all intents and purposes the leadership was united and the battle lines were drawn.

16

Power Plays

WEDNESDAY, APRIL 26, 1989
BEIJING UNIVERSITY

Despite the dormitory windows being closed, the relentless voice of Pang Yi continued to boom over the campus loudspeakers late in the evening. The political officer was using a tried and tested combination of threats and promises that had long been the backbone of all Party means of intimidation. The demonstrations were now in their eleventh day.

Pang Yi had said he understood the concern of the students for the country. But they should make their criticisms and suggestions to the Party through *"proper channels."* He could assure them everything would be most carefully listened to, and there would be no punishment for *"anyone voicing"* demands.

A hollow laugh had greeted the words.

"Demonstrations do not help. They only add to the chaos of society. You must not forget that the Party has always done its best for you," Pang Yi wheedled.

Then, abruptly changing mood, he had warned that any student who took part in any further marches would be expelled from the campus. It would effectively end his or her stay at the university. Jeers had greeted the threat.

Pang Yi's words had grown steadily more strident. Any further disobedience would lead to arrest and imprisonment. The political officer reminded them their support within the Party leadership had been seriously eroded by Zhao's decision to endorse the *People's Daily* editorial, which had been read out on TV and radio.

"You have no support. You have humiliated your families, your university, your country," Pang Yi continued. *"Your only hope of avoiding total disgrace and perhaps worse is to stop now. If you do so, the Party will be generous. It will forgive your transgressions. But if you continue, you will be destroyed. Because that is the will of the people. You cannot resist the people, or those who are there to defend them."*

Turning from the window, Yang Li addressed the students in the dormitory.

"The situation is serious," he said. *"Plainclothes police are everywhere. But I don't care if I am expelled or punished. I will fight on to the very end."*

A chorus of agreement came from the others.

"*What is happening shows the potential of our generation,*" Li continued. "*We are all trying to do something for our country. We must be prepared to sacrifice a great deal, knowing it is worthwhile.*"

Like all the other student leaders, Li showed signs of lack of sleep and irregular meals. He was hollow-eyed, and stubble gave his face an almost piratical look. But his determination to continue protesting came through in his voice. Despite its hoarseness, it sounded as confident as ever.

Outside the room was the sound of a door being slammed. Moments later Li saw another angry father storming out of the dormitory block, having failed to convince his son to agree not to demonstrate any more. All day the university administration had been busing in parents to try and persuade their sons and daughters to stop protesting. In almost all cases the parents had left defeated. It was the same story on other campuses.

The youth whose father had just left came into the room to say his parent had severed all ties with him and would send him no more money. Other students had been reporting a similar response. Li told the youth what he had said to the others: "*Don't worry about money. We will feed you for nothing. Once we have won our victory your parents will be proud of you.*"

Throughout the day students had been meeting in their dormitories to discuss tactics and give each other moral support. Many had been close to tears, partly from fear, partly from a sense of creating history. They had constantly reminded each other that Hu Yaobang had been removed from office in the first place because of his commitment to them.

Meanwhile, teachers had begged the students to give up. All the posters on the campus had been torn down by the political officers.

Students were summoned before the campus authorities and crudely threatened.

Then, just as some of the activists appeared on the point of giving up, fresh messages of support came from provincial campuses. These were swiftly circulated. Yang Li had told those in his dormitory that they had "*a solemn duty*" not to fail "*those who are looking to us for leadership.*"

"*Stay in the campus,*" roared Pang Yi over the loudspeakers. "*If you leave we cannot protect you against the reactionaries who are trying to ruin you. They are out there, plotting to use you to destroy all that is good in China. We only want to protect you.*"

The students greeted his words with a chorus of the national anthem.

Listening from his empty classroom, Barr Seitz, the American graduate teaching English, marveled at "*the courage of these students. They had nothing more than their voices, not a worthwhile weapon between them. They had simply convinced each other that if they were to succeed they must take risks.*"

Yet their leaders had not lost their coolness. After listening to the *People's Daily* editorial broadcast throughout the campus, Wang Dan had called a meeting of the Students Union Committee in the coffee shop. He had said that the editorial clearly indicated the pressures within the leadership but that it was important for the students to stay aloof from any power struggle going on in Zhongnanhai.

"Everything we do must be based on the constitution," he said.

Out of the meeting had come three new demands that would form the core of further confrontation with the authorities. There must be dialogue between the government and the Students Union Committee, and it must be on an equal footing. The government must apologize for all previous violence inflicted upon the students. From now on all the country's official media must give full and unbiased coverage to the students' activities.

In return, the students were prepared to fully support the Party in its *"correct"* way forward to promote socialism and reform.

The decision was a shrewd move to keep the protest within the framework of Article 35, the part of China's constitution that guaranteed free speech, yet still allowed the students to promote their aims.

Still more threats were being broadcast over the campus loudspeakers. Suddenly the functionary's voice was cut off. Over the loudspeakers came the voice of Wang Dan. Students at the engineering department had managed to bypass the secretary's microphone and allow Dan to broadcast from a makeshift studio. His message was defiant.

"Tomorrow we march! Tonight we prepare! Deng has said these are grave times. They are. So prepare yourselves. Write letters to your families. Prepare your wills. Prepare to support the correct path of leadership for the Party! Support security and reform. Long live democracy!"

A burst of cheers swept through the campus.

Standing at a classroom window of the all but deserted English Department, Cassy saw scores of Public Security agents led by Pang Yi running through the campus in search of the studio.

From dormitory windows students yelled abuse. Cassy thought *"it was like a World War II movie where the Allied prisoners taunted their German guards."*

Behind her she heard the door open. Daobao stood there. She was reminded of their first meeting in the building's library. Now, as then, she was surprised by his calm.

"Hi!" he said in his faintly American accent, walking into the room.

"Hi."

He came and stood beside her at the window and watched the security men rushing by.

"It won't matter if they find the studio," said Daobao. *"It was only meant to be another way to show them we will not be cowed. We have prepared everything as far as we can."*

She took his hand in hers as he continued to speak. *"The more they threaten us, the more we want to live freely."*

"But wanting and achieving are very different," Cassy said.

He took her by the shoulder, shaking her almost roughly.

"It will work this time. It has to."

He kissed her quickly on the mouth, and she felt his tears on her cheek. Then he turned and half ran from the classroom.

SAME DAY, LATER
THE WHITE HOUSE

The TV screens in the Oval Office were tuned to ABC, CBS, CNN, and NBC, which gave President Bush a chance to sample four presentations of the news. Only one channel had begun to carry live reports from China. Whenever the President paused in his punishing schedule to look, the CNN monitor seemed to be filled with young people on the other side of the world chanting slogans and waving banners. Bush understood enough Mandarin to grasp what they were demanding: democracy.

The President wondered how long it would be before the Beijing CNN team would be joined by the troika of U.S. network news: Dan Rather of CBS; Tom Brokaw of NBC; and Peter Jennings of ABC.

Among them the trio was watched by forty million Americans. Every night. If they went to Beijing and reported on what the students were trying to achieve, they could have a powerful effect on public opinion. The President knew it could force him to go public and offer some sort of support for the aspirations of the students. But until then he would say nothing.

It was no secret around the White House that National Security Adviser Brent Scowcroft, for one, wanted Bush to *"soft-pedal and weigh the long term"* — the words of one of Scowcroft's aides. No one had to be reminded that Scowcroft brought to his new post the same steely determination to have his way that he had displayed when running the Washington office of Kissinger Associates.

The consultancy could now count on another former employee, Lawrence Eagleburger, an Under-Secretary of State, to remind the White House of just what was at stake for the United States in China, those billions of dollars invested in scores of projects. Against them the idealism of those students on the CNN monitor seemed painfully inadequate.

SAME DAY, SAME TIME
CHINA DAILY COMPOUND

Jeanne Moore was typing a story for the Midwest newspaper. It was a reflective piece aimed at the op-ed page. Her words caught perfectly the mood of the city.

"Whatever happens next, politics in China will never be the same. The government has underestimated the silent majority," she typed on an elderly manual. *"The editorial has been dismissed with anger and contempt, not only by the students, but the public. In the meantime the students are now stockpiling food in their dormitories. They are going to war — and they are ready to die. A sense of crisis is everywhere. The city is as close to martial law as it could be without it actually being declared."*

Around her colleagues were collecting information they would not be allowed to publish in their own newspaper but were feeding to her.

There had been violence at a rally at the University of Politics and Law, where militiamen had attacked students. There had been running fights on the Normal University campus between students and campus security men. But there had also been clashes between students themselves over what the next move should be.

"Moderates at Qinghua University who have cautioned a wait-and-see approach have become the object of bitter anger among the more militant students," Jeanne typed. *"On other campuses professors and administrators have tearfully begged their students to return to class. But here in Beijing there's an overwhelming decision to march at dawn tomorrow."*

SAME DAY, SAME TIME
SACRAMENTO, CALIFORNIA

Sue, the Chinese postgraduate student, and Rod, her boyfriend, had abandoned any thought of sleep. Instead they sat in their pajamas on the couch before the TV set, switching channels in the hope of catching further news from China. On the coffee table before them were a radio tuned to an all-news channel and a jar almost filled with dollar bills, Sue's first efforts at fund-raising among her fellow Chinese. There was already over $1,000 in the jar. More was promised. Every donation had been entered in a notebook.

"There's a tremendous feeling of wanting to do something," Sue told Rod. *"It's like being back home."*

Sue wanted to collect $5,000 before she left for Beijing. But she had no idea how the money should be used.

There had been nothing on TV about China since the eleven o'clock news. But at midnight the radio commenced a live report from outside Beijing University, saying that several of the student leaders had fled their dormitory headquarters and gone into hiding, fearing they were about to be arrested. The radio reporter described how the campus gates were padlocked. On the railings someone had put up a poster: IN GOD WE TRUST.

Rod turned to Sue. *"It's going to be very dangerous, and it could be even more dangerous when you get there."*

"It's always been dangerous to protest in China," Sue replied. She tried to sound reassuring. *"But don't worry. Nothing they do can be as bad as the Cultural Revolution."*

Once more she took him back to that dark, turbulent time in her people's history. Then, the authorities had imposed a real reign of terror. What was happening now in China was *"probably no more than an intricate game of bluff and counterbluff,"* she said. *"Both sides will probably go on pushing hard. But if it comes to real violence, they'll also both pull back. No one in China today wants violence."*

Rod said he really hoped she was right.

SAME DAY, SAME TIME
THE MEDICAL CENTER, LOS ANGELES

In the anteroom of the operating theater suite Dr. Jenny Guangzu heard the anesthetist say, *"I'm going to tube him."* The daughter of one of China's foremost exponents of traditional medicine watched intently.

With surprising speed, the anesthetist pushed the tube in over the patient's tongue to provide a permanent airway into his lungs, then connected the visible end to the oxygen machine. The anesthetist squeezed the rubber breathing bag a few times as the patient breathed in. If he had been properly anesthetized, the action would halt voluntary breathing. She stopped squeezing for a moment. The man did not breathe. She resumed squeezing the bag.

From the OR came the sound of the same all-news station Sue and Rod were listening to. Some surgeons preferred to listen to music while operating; Jenny's boss liked to keep abreast of the stock market reports.

Scrubbed and gowned, Jenny followed him into the OR. The radio was on a trolley on the "non-clean" side of the room, isolated from the actual operating area by sterile curtains. The anesthetist and her trolley worked there because it was impossible to sterilize her cylinder and bottles.

The patient, a road accident victim with head injuries, was being positioned on the table. The two high instrument trays were wheeled into place and draped with sterile cloths. Other tables filled with sterilized equipment stood on the clean side of the OR.

Jenny checked that the endotracheal tube had not been disturbed. Beside her one of the nurses snipped away the man's hair, exposing the damaged skull.

"Guess your traditional doctors would do things differently," the surgeon said.

"Yes, they would," Jenny replied quickly. She suddenly felt protective of the kind of medicine her father practiced.

She had tried to call him several times in the past days. Each time the hospital switchboard in Beijing had said he was not available. When she had tried to ask the operator what was happening in the city, the woman had abruptly said a few troublemakers were giving the country a bad name.

Now, as the operation got under way, the radio carried a report from Beijing saying that night-shift workers in factories throughout the city had stopped work as a gesture of support for the students.

"This thing could rock the stock market," said the surgeon as he turned to the X-rays fixed to the viewing frame on one wall.

"It could also destroy a lot of lives," Jenny said grimly.

The surgeon squinted at her and said she should count herself lucky she was here.

That was the moment, Jenny later realized, when she decided she would return as soon as possible to China. She would leave Zhong and take Peter with her. They would move in with her father. The intuition she had inherited from her mother told her she was needed back home to play her part in China's destiny.

THURSDAY, APRIL 27, 1989
NATIONAL DEFENSE UNIVERSITY

At dawn Kao Jyan awoke and climbed out of the bedroll he had spread late the night before on the floor of his office. Like all the other instructors, Jyan had spent the night in the military academy, coordinating plans for the 38th Army to march into the city. This morning he would travel with a convoy of troops to the Great Hall of the People. Other troops would move into the network of tunnels beneath Beijing. The soldiers would be armed with assault rifles, though force was to be kept to a minimum. The intention was surprise.

Intelligence supplied by Public Security indicated the students did not plan to return to Tiananmen Square before midday. They would find the military waiting for them.

Over breakfast in the staff dining hall, Jyan reviewed the tactics with colleagues. *"These are kids,"* he said. *"They're not like the Tibetans, trained for this sort of thing. When we show up, they'll leave. They know they've had their fun and that now it's all over."*

Leaving the academy to rendezvous with the convoy, Jyan was still a little surprised by one decision. During the briefing for this operation it had emerged that units from a number of armies were placing a cordon around the city. To the perceptive captain instructor it indicated someone in Zhongnanhai *"was more nervous than necessary."*

Jyan thought again how foolish and ungrateful the students were. They represented only a minute part of society. Yet they had so much more than other people: education and an assured place in their society. He really could not understand their behavior. This democracy they wanted was something alien and dangerous and surely had no place in the China he knew.

SAME DAY, LATER
BEIJING UNIVERSITY

The sound of a bolt cutter snapping through the padlock broke the silence. Yan Daobao and Yang Li swung open the main gates of the campus. Behind them, stretching as far as they could see up the broad avenue, ranks of students gave a sustained cheer. The gates had been padlocked on Pang Yi's orders to keep them on campus. A similar measure had been taken at all other universities and colleges in the city.

Wang Dan stepped forward and read aloud, through a battery-operated bullhorn, Article 35 of the constitution. His amplified voice carried clearly in the still air.

When he finished, the accordionists from the music department struck up a brisk marching tune. Members of the various campus choral groups led the singing as the students marched out, once more on their way to Tiananmen Square.

At the same time students were emerging from the dormitories of the city's other forty-one universities and colleges in the same orderly manner. Fifty thousand in all were on the march. As they tramped through the streets, factory and office workers joined the columns, falling into step and lending their voices to the singing. Soon the number of demonstrators had doubled, then doubled again. Two hundred thousand and more were on the march, gathering still more people to them by the minute.

From her bedroom window in the Friendship Hotel, Cassy and several other foreign experts watched the scene. For most of the night they had debated what to do. The university administration had warned them to take no part in any demonstrations. Doing so would be a breach of contract and could lead to their arrest. But they had been told that they would also be breaking their contracts if they attempted to leave the country to go home. Some of the teachers had wondered whether they were being held hostage to deter their own countries from offering support for the students.

Barr Seitz found that suggestion fanciful. Better than most, he had an idea how the State Department would view the student protest: *"A real pain. What was happening was going to rock a lot of boats in Washington. The trade boat in particular. American businessmen would not like what they were seeing on their TV screens. Every step the students were taking was threatening to trample on a lot of deals. The last thing the State Department would be doing was to encourage what was happening. Indeed, Washington would be doing everything possible to keep a distance from the students."*

Barr, on the other hand, had every hope of getting into the thick of the action. The ABC-TV bureau in Beijing had promised him a job as a reporter, a runner for its correspondents, should the story *"really catch fire."*

Watching from the window of the hotel, he thought *"the flames were beginning to glow nicely."*

Despite the warning to stay away, Cassy knew nothing could stop her marching. She joined a group of hotel staff, which quickly became absorbed in one of the seemingly endless columns.

In one of them was Jeanne Moore. Despite the *"excitement, tension, and a feeling of not knowing what was going to happen,"* she maintained her reporter's cool eye for detail. She noted that none of the students carried identification, in case they were arrested. Their marshals used a prearranged set of hand signals and commands to direct and control the marchers. The music and singing were coordinated so that as the columns from various campuses began to merge with each other, they all played and sang the same patriotic songs.

Half an hour into the march, the students encountered their first opposition, a cordon of police stretched across an intersection. Wuerkaixi, at the head of the first column, turned and addressed the marchers.

"Do not be violent. But remember if blood is to be shed, we are all ready to do so."

The crowds lining the streets began to chant for the police to stand aside. The cordon broke, and the police, who a moment before had looked so threatening, were smiling and waving the students on their way.

Moving slowly through a hundred side streets, the columns flowed into the city's major avenue, completely stopping traffic. Workers poured from every alley, factory, and shop. From office blocks the length of Bingani, Diamen, and Dansishitiao avenues, clerks and typists ran to join the marchers or stood on the sidewalks flashing victory signs and cheering. Diplomats Brian Davidson and Brendan Ward this time agreed that close to a million were either on the march or cheering.

"This is serious," Davidson told his Irish colleague. *"The authorities have either got to do something to appease them or stop them right now."*

But from their vantage point on Changan Avenue, there was no sign of either happening.

It struck Brendan Ward that *"an official paralysis seemed to have set in. What police there were on duty just didn't know what to do. In the end they were simply brushed aside by this human juggernaut rolling through the city. Though they were completely unarmed there was something very intimidating about the way they marched, as if they knew they were unstoppable."*

By midmorning the entire area just north of Zhongnanhai across the width of the city was a seething mass moving inexorably south toward Tiananmen Square.

Time and again police lines broke, fell back, regrouped, and crumpled again. Many policemen simply faded into the *hutong,* cowed and defeated by the unstoppable formations.

As Jeanne's column skirted the northern wall of Zhongnanhai, passing along Jingshaw Road and then wheeling right on to Wangfujing Avenue, the entire staff of the China Art Gallery emerged to join the marchers. On Wangfujing a gang of steel erectors shinned down from the scaffolding to march. Moments later shop assistants streamed out of a department store to join them.

Scribbling as she walked, Jeanne noted: *"The slogans and songs were calculated to look and sound more Communist than the Party, more patriotic than the army, more law-abiding than the police. Nothing appeared planned: Clearly everything was. The banners down to the last characters stayed within the law. They all proclaimed support for true socialism. Every demand for democracy is buttressed with citations from the constitution. Most brilliant of all, they have taken Deng Xiaoping's own words and used them to telling effect. His own criticisms are now directed at corrupt Party officials."*

Swinging past the squad of police standing guard over the Beijing Hotel, the column burst into the theme from a popular Chinese television series, *"The Plainclothesmen."*

From a suite on the seventh floor, maverick rocket-gun scientist Dr. Gerald Bull was among the hotel guests watching. Most were businessmen whose thoughts were probably reflected in Bull's words to a colleague.

"The kids are a menace to their own country. Right now the last thing China wants is to get caught up in some fancy notions about democracy. That kind of talk will just get in the way of what China wants and is good at, making deals with the West."

Bull was back in Beijing to firm up his own deal with Norinco, the state-run arms conglomerate, to supply them with the technical know-how that would enable Norinco to secretly arm Saddam Hussein with long-range guns. Bull's only concern was that the demonstrations could escalate to the point where people like him would be told by their governments to stop trading with the Chinese *"until they sort out the students."* Bull had no doubt what should be done: *"Kick a few butts. Put their leaders in prison for a while."*

As if in answer to Bull's words, soldiers were jumping from trucks parked in front of the Great Hall of the People.

Stationed near the Great Hall, Captain Instructor Jyan knew the troops were too few and too late. There were fewer than a thousand lightly armed soldiers to stop the biggest demonstration he had ever witnessed.

There had been a clear failure of intelligence about the size of the crowd supporting the marchers. Thousands of people were scrambling out of every alley and side street to stand twenty deep along Changan Avenue. If they became violent, an entire army would be needed to hold them back. But by the time reinforcements could reach the area, it would be far too late. Jyan knew that the best thing to do would be to stage an orderly withdrawal.

Sensing the indecision of the soldiers, the crowd had occupied the stands in front of the Forbidden City and began to chant at the soldiers: *"Go home! Or join the march! Remember, the People's Army should love the people!"*

For a moment Jyan wondered whether the troop commander would order his soldiers to clear the area, if only to make a gesture that the army would not be so humiliated. But even as he turned to seek out his senior officer and caution him against such action, Jyan found himself swept aside by the first rank of marchers. In moments the soldiers were overwhelmed, escorted to their trucks, and ordered to climb back on board.

On a command from Wuerkaixi, the ranks then parted to form a corridor running east on Changan through which the troops could leave. As they ran the gauntlet, the visibly shaken troops were deafened by a continuous chant: *"Go home! Turn your guns into posters! This is the first nonviolent revolution in our history!"*

When the troops had gone and there was not a policeman in sight, Wuerkaixi led the student leaders to the pediment of the Monument to the People's Heroes. Dozens of foreign TV and radio crews and print-media reporters were using it as a vantage point to record what was happening. Through their microphones, Wuerkaixi deliberately addressed the world for the first time.

"This is China's history you are witnessing. We have come here to proclaim a simple truth. It is that we want change. We want democracy!"

He ordered the marchers to return to their campuses in the same orderly way they had come here.

To Brian Davidson it was "a masterly move." Wuerkaixi was showing leadership skills well beyond his years. He was saying, in effect, *"We have conquered Tiananmen, the very heart of the Party's power."* He wanted the old men in Zhongnanhai to know that from now on the students would come and go as they liked.

Watching the first ranks once more moving off, Wuerkaixi turned to Wang Dan and said: *"Hundreds of thousands of people have thrown cold water in the face of the leaders. Let us hope it has woken them up!"*

It had, but in a way even Wuerkaixi had not anticipated.

The brief exchange between the two leading student activists was carefully noted by a CIA operative, one of several foreign intelligence agents prowling the square. By this time, the thirteenth day of the demonstration, a cautious understanding appeared to have developed among the intelligence men. They took steps not to crowd each other, and made no attempt to blow each other's cover of either being bona-fide diplomats or news reporters. Several of the KGB men claimed they were from the Soviet news agency Tass, preparing reports for the Gorbachev visit, now less than two weeks away.

The students, their gullibility no doubt compounded by tiredness, answered questions freely, enabling the operatives to have a continuously updated picture of what was being planned.

The democracy movement had already become one of the most infiltrated and compromised protest movements in living memory.

The *"bunch of kids,"* as CIA Director Webster had once referred to them, were indeed no match for the experienced agents currently working the ninety-eight arid acres of Tiananmen Square.

17

Countermoves

Webster continued to brief the President in that soft, flat, emotionless voice some members of the cabinet found hard to follow. Bush clearly found it absorbing. The President sat listening intently to the CIA director. Those present included Secretary of State James Baker and some of his aides.

This May Day marked the seventeenth day of student protest in China. Over the past few days, events there had moved into the top spot in the intelligence summaries making up the President's Daily Brief.

Details had included the surprise announcement that had come hours after the students had marched back to their campuses. Radio Beijing had interrupted its programs to carry an announcement from the State Council, a body of ministers drawn from the upper echelons of government. The council pronounced it was *"ready to conduct dialogue with the students at any time."* In return the council asked that the students give up protesting.

Bush asked why the students kept marching in and out of Tiananmen Square, instead of just staying put and bringing matters to a head. One of Baker's aides suggested they *"were testing the temperature, seeing how far they could push before it came to a real shove back."*

Webster told the meeting that the latest intelligence gleaned from within Zhongnanhai indicated that disagreement among the leadership had reached a new intensity. The hardliners wanted a total crackdown now, with the student leaders arrested and sent to China's Gulag. One of the CIA's intercepts included China's spymaster, Qiao Shi, insisting his snatch squads could arrest all the leaders in a citywide swoop and so break the back of the movement. But once more Deng Xiaoping had hesitated.

Yet Deng's anger with the students had not diminished, cautioned Webster. Some reports reaching the CIA suggested it had increased. But Deng was a pragmatist, Webster reminded the others.

Mikhail Gorbachev would be arriving in Beijing for his four-day visit in two weeks. For Deng to behave harshly so close to such an historic event could create far more serious problems for him.

Bush suggested the turnout for the last student march must clearly have shown Deng the extent of public support for reform. China's leaders would want to do nothing that could turn that support to violence.

Webster concurred. The steady spate of EYES ONLY encoded faxes reaching him clearly revealed Deng's concern that if any of the student leaders were arrested, Beijing, and perhaps other cities, could rise in protest. That would totally destroy the careful mood of *"orderly calmness"* Deng wanted during the visit of the Soviet leader.

According to one aide present, Bush said Deng *"is in a real bind."* But the United States, insisted the President, would do nothing to make things more difficult. Any approach by the students to the U.S. embassy in Beijing for help was to be firmly refused.

That same source would later say, *"The President's view was that the reality was they [the students] were not going to achieve very much, and we don't want to be on the losing side. His view was that could set us back in all sorts of ways, politically and economically. The President saw our good relations with China as crucial to our influence in Asia and the Pacific Rim. That was the bottom line none of us was allowed to forget."*

On Friday, April 28, CIA agents in Beijing had slipped out of Spook City, their building in the embassy compound, to observe student leaders from every university, college, and institute in the city attending a meeting Wuerkaixi had called at Beijing Normal University.

The student leader had been as ebullient as always, flashing that all-knowing smile, slapping his fellow student leaders on the back. He had become the consummate leader.

Wang Dan, as always, was happy to take a secondary role. The intelligence operatives noted he looked paler than usual. So did Chai Ling. Like many of the student leaders, she was only able to snatch a few hours' sleep at a time, sleeping in a new place each night in case arrest orders were issued.

Wuerkaixi proposed the formation of yet another committee, the Autonomous Union of Students. It was a further shrewd move by the volatile yet hardheaded Wuerkaixi. By abolishing all previous committees, it allowed him to remove from the leadership those students he felt were moderates. In their place came young people ready to stage hunger strikes, to the death if necessary.

Webster's agents had reported that the meeting concentrated on how to exploit the forthcoming Gorbachev visit. Wuerkaixi said their most powerful weapon would be the ability to organize further demonstrations in the two weeks remaining before the arrival of the Soviet Leader.

"Rather than risk that, the leadership will want to talk to us," Wuerkaixi predicted. *"We must try and get as many concessions as possible now. After Gorbachev has left, it will be harder to deal with Zhongnanhai."*

Next day, Saturday, April 29, the President's Daily Brief had contained further evidence of how far the students were ready to challenge the leadership. Forty-five students had been invited to meet members of the State Council for a "dialogue." Almost all were members of official student unions subservient to the Party. Eager to make a point that it was willing to listen to demands, the leadership had invited Chinese TV to broadcast live what was being promoted as an *"important moment"* in the country's recent history.

Uninvited and unannounced, Wuerkaixi and Wang Dan arrived at the meeting in the Great Hall of the People, bounding up the steps and giving boxer salutes.

Stunned, yet unable to stop the moment's going out on national TV, the State Council had no alternative but to invite both students to join the discussions.

Wuerkaixi immediately began to repeat the now familiar demands for *"proper talks"* with Li Peng, a full public apology for all previous violence done to the students, and unbigoted reporting by the Chinese media.

The scandalized State Council members said all this was beyond their authority. Wuerkaixi stormed out of the meeting.

"The boy's a firebrand," Webster once more told Bush at the Monday morning briefing. The President made one of his hand-chopping movements and repeated the United States should do nothing to encourage Wuerkaixi.

After Webster completed his presentation, the President honed in on the issue that concerned him: the wider question of human rights that underscored the student demands and whether those demands were likely to interfere with the Gorbachev visit.

The issue of human rights had come into dramatic focus with the news the previous day, Sunday, April 30, that there had been demonstrations in the Chinese city of Changsha over the death sentences imposed on nine people involved in the disturbances there eight days before. Bush wanted to know whether the United States should protest about the sentences.

Baker advised against doing so, given that a few hours after the penalties were imposed, the U.S. embassy in Beijing had sent a telegram describing how the authorities were making *"every effort to defuse the student situation."*

Beijing Party Secretary Li Xiaming had publicly revealed his income and the jobs his children held. The city's Party Secretary earned $85 a month; his eldest daughter was an oculist, at $50 a month; her sister's paycheck as a medical technician was $35.

"By implication the Beijing Party Secretary was saying the students were way off base when it came to accusations that the Party's top officials were guilty of nepotism or lining their own pockets," Baker quoted from the telegram.

Bush made another hand-chopping motion and asked another question: Zhao Ziyang, the Chinese Party Secretary, was now back from North Korea, and was there any indication of how he might react, given the way he had been outmaneuvered over the now-notorious editorial in the *People's Daily?*

Webster said Zhao had summoned to his Zhongnanhai compound those in the leadership known to support him, including the key figure of Bao Tong, the secretary of the Politburo. The indications were that Zhao was planning to distance himself from the editorial and so gain favor among the students.

If the Party Secretary achieved that goal, Bush suggested, Zhao might be able to convince the students their *"kind of street protests"* would ultimately get them nowhere. They never had before, they never would, Bush added. He repeated again he was not against the students trying to get a better deal, but he also didn't want anything to wreck the Gorbachev visit.

Bush reminded the others Gorbachev had recognized that Communism was in a historical retreat, and that the only way for it to survive as a force was to allow more freedom in the lives of those it controlled. But unlike in central Europe, change could not be rushed in China.

Based upon his own firsthand experience, the President believed what was needed was a long-term process of increasing economic pluralism in which change would come slowly; otherwise China would continue to face strong confrontations within its borders. The United States was ready and eager to play its role in ensuring the economic success of China and take its own legitimate profit in the process.

Implicit in the President's words was that a bunch of students led by a hothead like Wuerkaixi must not he allowed to threaten that aim.

THURSDAY, MAY 4, 1989
BEIJING

Coming through Beijing airport, Melinda Liu, Asia editor of *Newsweek*, was already working, asking questions, absorbing the answers, forming her first judgments. She had followed the protest marches from reports coming into her bureau in Hong Kong, and at this stage she wanted to get a firsthand look at what was happening in Beijing. The demonstrations there were now in their twentieth day.

Liu was one of the best correspondents working the Asia beat. Shot up and shot at, she carried her physical scars like badges of honor; they were proof she was no barfly reporter but one who went out into the field to talk to guerrilla leaders, terrorists, and the warlords of the Golden Triangle. Quoted and admired by her peers, Melinda was the kind of reporter regimes feared.

Airport officials treated her with the respect due someone who had interviewed Deng and most of the Chinese leadership over the years. Her contacts in Beijing were the envy of most foreign intelligence operatives there.

By the time Melinda had arrived at her hotel, she knew she had once more timed her arrival perfectly. That very morning the students had actually delivered a formal ultimatum to Zhongnanhai. Either the Politburo Standing Committee met them, or there would be further demonstrations.

Her first call was to the government spokesman, Yuan Mu, a flunky she instinctively mistrusted. He stiffly said the government firmly rejected the ultimatum. He added that the students were being *"naive and impulsive."* He told her he was *"satisfied that there were people behind the scenes giving the students ideas in an attempt to create social upheaval."*

Yuan Mu would not be drawn further. But for Melinda *"it was the old bogeyman, Imperialist troublemakers being dusted down ready for another outing. Things must be getting out of hand when that bogeyman was being blamed."*

As she had been about to ring off, Mu added, *"We are not planning action against the students yet. If we take action now, it would be too soon."*

Melinda began to call her Chinese contacts in the state media to find out what Yuan Mu meant. She discovered the journalists were all taking part in yet another march to Tiananmen Square. Carrying banners calling for a free press, hundreds of reporters had joined more than forty thousand students. There had also been new demonstrations in a number of provincial cities.

A further hour of working the phones provided clear evidence Zhao Ziyang had made a daring and, for the Party Secretary, a potentially dangerous move. Appealing for calm and unity while addressing the governors of the Asian Development Bank that morning, Zhao had completely rejected the editorial in the *People's Daily* with its references to *"turmoil."*

He had told the bankers that *"student demonstrations are still under way in our cities. But I deeply believe the situation will become calm. There will be no great turmoil in China."*

The bankers she had reached to check the quote had been reassured by the words. But Melinda recognized they were not directed at Zhao's immediate audience in the Great Hall of the People. They were aimed directly at Deng Xiaoping and his claim that the student movement was *"turmoil."*

In the world of coded signals in which both Zhao and Deng lived, Melinda understood, this was *"tantamount to a declaration of war between the two men."* She could not remember anyone delivering such a public rebuke to the supreme leader.

SAME DAY, SAME TIME
NEW YORK

On the third floor of the ABC building at 47 West 66th Street in Manhattan, a sudden sense of urgency, unusual at this hour, 11:00 A.M., swept the newsroom that is the backdrop for *"World News Tonight,"* anchored by Peter Jennings. Every available reporter and producer was either working a phone or typing onto a computer screen.

What Bob Murphy, the Vice-President of TV news coverage, was repeatedly calling *"the China situation"* had finally burst upon the awareness of ABC. It had taken twenty days to do so.

Murphy had ordered a special *"World News This Morning Report,"* a bulletin that would cut into the network's morning output of game shows to give millions of Americans a picture of what was happening in Beijing.

Already Peter Jennings was at his massive desk, leafing through the news copy before him.

On the CNN monitor, one of twenty-eight in Jenning's vision, Chinese Premier Li Peng was telling the people of his country that the time had come to restore public order.

In the newsroom journalists were trying to decide what this meant. Martial law? A military crackdown? Or just more rhetoric?

Jennings shook his head. His caution is legendary. He would rather be second with the news than mislead his audience. Nothing he had read or heard had yet convinced him that China was about to crush the students with military force.

Moments later he delivered a crisp, no-nonsense update on what was happening in Beijing. He concluded by saying the city *"is rampant with rumors."*

By inference, Jennings not going to add to them.

SUNDAY, MAY 7, 1989
PEOPLE'S LIBERATION ARMY BARRACKS
WESTERN HILLS, NEAR BEIJING

Bing Yang struggled to follow what the political commissar was saying about the latest developments in Beijing. The more he listened, the greater was Bing's confusion. He suspected most of the other soldiers on the barracks square felt the same.

On the long train journey from Lhasa, the commissar had portrayed the students as little short of being counterrevolutionaries who would have to be dealt with by full military force. Now he was telling them that many students had given up protesting and were returning to their classrooms. Only at Beijing University and the Normal University had students continued to demonstrate.

Yet even those students were no longer considered now to be a serious threat, the commissar said.

Tan Yaobang, Bing's commander, demanded to know when they would be returning to Tibet. There was still real soldiering to do there. The commissar could not say. His orders were that the units were to remain at full readiness until further notice.

Throughout the hills to the west of Beijing other commissars were saying the same thing. Tens of thousands of troops were at full battle readiness to deal with a threat that seemed to have all but disappeared.

SAME DAY, SAME TIME
FOREIGN OFFICE
LONDON

Her desk covered with diplomatic cablegrams from the British embassy in Beijing, Chinese newspapers, and copies of the mimeographed leaflets the students had distributed, Susan Morton continued to look beyond the immediate events to forecast developments. Her carefully judged reports over the past few weeks had helped her Foreign Secretary keep abreast of events. She made a note that the demonstrations were now in their twenty-third day.

It was increasingly clear to Susan that this was shaping up to be a confrontation like no other in China's history. She interpreted the decision of most of the students to return to their campuses as only *"a chance to regroup"*; significantly, the protests continued at two key universities, Beijing and Normal. Even more important, the capital's citizens had continued to support the demonstrations. Many had even joined the fledgling Workers Federation, one of several new organizations born out of the protests, to challenge the position of the state-approved trade unions.

The latest diplomatic bag from the embassy in Beijing had brought to Susan's desk more samples of how radical the protest had become. A poster the Workers Federation was distributing simply asked a question: *"How much does*

Deng Pufang spend on gambling at the Hong Kong race course?" Deng Pufang was the son of China's supreme leader. Susan knew the answer, thanks to M16. Its officers in the colony had pieced together a detailed picture of Deng Pufang's wins and losses; right now he was on a losing streak.

Another poster proclaimed LONG LIVE THE PEOPLE! Susan knew that would be regarded by the leadership as *"highly subversive, tantamount to a call to insurrection."* Other leaflets sent to her for analysis called upon the Party to define its meaning of *revolution* and *reaction,* sacred words in the official lexicon. To even ask such questions was heresy. A cartoon now widely displayed around Beijing showed a Mandarin with an opium pipe; the caption read *"Democracy on high."*

But in judging the national mood and where it could be leading, Susan found most useful the poems that were being stuck up everywhere. They were a mixture of scorn, satire, and political argument. They helped bind together the strands of disparate dissent.

Yet in trying to cope with the pressure, the Party and its leaders were all too clearly seeing their options reduced. China under Communism, Susan wrote for her latest position paper, had *"always been a place that swings from thaw to freeze."* There had been a thaw, enough to allow the students to protest corruption and nepotism. Now the struggle had clearly reached a critical phase on both sides that could decide the next freeze.

Susan wrote: *"The leadership is clearly even more divided, while the students have continued to display a sharper political edge. In the division within Zhongnanhai, the role of Zhao has become crucial."*

The young analyst had spent hours studying the latest snippets of information about the Party Secretary. It had given her a clear picture of what Zhao had done since returning from North Korea.

Susan had underlined key phrases in the Party Secretary's pronouncements. *"The students have raised problems which must be resolved." "We must push forward with economic reform." "The way forward is by political restructuring." "Our students are by no means opposed to our fundamental system, rather they are asking us to correct mistakes in our work."*

For the past two days, Zhao had ordered such excerpts from his speeches to be featured on national TV and radio and the front page of the *People's Daily.* He had been careful to do it all, he kept insisting, in the *"name of harmony between us and the students."*

Susan had learned from information supplied by, among others, M16 and the CIA that Zhao's words had deeply angered Deng. One intelligence report described an angry confrontation in Zhongnanhai on May 6 between Li Peng and Zhao in which the prime minister accused the Party Secretary of *"portraying us as villains."* Zhao had calmly replied, *"If I made incorrect remarks I will bear the responsibility."*

Their row had carried on into a Politburo meeting the following day. The clashes there between hardliners and Zhao's moderates were the most bitter since the onset of the Cultural Revolution. In the end Zhao and his loosely knit group had refused to listen, driving Li Peng to brand them as betrayers of the Party.

Susan added to her position paper: The polarization has led to virtual paralysis in the leadership in dealing with the students. *"Deng is clearly fixated by the calendar. Mikhail Gorbachev will soon be in Beijing."*

Intelligence sources had told her that the students were planning a spectacular welcome for the Soviet leader, a massive hunger strike on Tiananmen Square.

MONDAY, MAY 8, 1989
CHINA DAILY COMPOUND

On this, the twenty-fourth day of the demonstrations, Jeanne Moore had concluded that *"we can't see any evidence that China has a formal government."*

Phone calls to ministries went unanswered. Requests for "guidance" on what could be published were ignored. *"No one seemed to know what to do or say,"* she had noted.

By late afternoon she had discovered, by calling her contacts at home, that the country was being effectively run by a small group, all survivors of the Long March. They had held their first meeting in Deng's compound that morning to decide what to do about the students. Each member of the group was a long-standing confidant of Deng's.

Once more Tiananmen Square had begun to fill. By noon the number was estimated at fifty thousand; hours later it had doubled, an influx of Beijing citizens joining the students. They told the police they had come to see the preparations for Gorbachev's visit. From all the buildings around Tiananmen Square hung Chinese and Soviet flags and emblems proclaiming mutual friendship. The police, *"having no clear orders, have done nothing. Most significantly, there are no soldiers to be seen,"* Jeanne had noted.

That seemed to confirm what she had gleaned from her sources in the U.S. embassy, that there was no agreement within Zhongnanhai to use military force. She had been told that Zhao was largely instrumental in stopping troops being sent. He had even managed to persuade some hitherto hardline members of the Politburo to support him, albeit reluctantly.

Earlier in the afternoon Jeanne had been assigned to translate an article by Zhao that would be published in the *People's Daily*. It promised human rights and argued for yet more reforms. Her own editor, a fervent Zhao supporter, and a man committed to liberalizing China, was ecstatic. He called Zhao's article *"a beacon that will light the way forward for the students and the Party."*

Now, Jeanne knew differently. She discovered by checking constantly updated obituaries in the newspaper's library that Deng's cabal were *"the hardest of the hardliners."* There was Deng Zhen, eighty-six, who walked with a frame; Chen Yun, eighty-four, who needed a wheelchair; Wang Zhen, eighty-one, who could not go anywhere without a doctor and nurse at his elbow. Yet despite their physical frailty, these men and the only woman Deng had allowed into the cabinet, Deng Yingchao, the widow of Chou En-Lai, were still extraordinarily powerful.

Jeanne had been told by her contacts in government that at the morning meeting Deng had demanded to know where he should draw a line. The cabal had all given the same response: There had been enough concessions. State President Yang Shangkun had added: *"We must not retreat from our duty, however harsh it must be."*

Jeanne's contacts had told her that afterward Deng had held lengthy telephone conversations with the commanders of the country's seven military regions. In her diary she had confided: *"Time is running out. But no one wants to believe it."*

SAME DAY
NEW YORK

In that other center of network news, the high-tech home of NBC in Manhattan, senior executives had passed on the China story. The visit of Mikhail Gorbachev to Beijing was, in their view, not a grabber for the evening news. And at ABC, executives reminded one another that Peter Jennings had been right to be cautious. Nothing was really happening in Beijing: When CNN showed another panning shot of the protesting crowds in Tiananmen Square, it was a big yawn. It certainly was not worth investing a million or more dollars in sending Jennings and his entourage just to cover that.

ABC's senior vice-president Rick Wald summed it up: *"The Chinese had already told us that the Gorbachev visit was entirely ceremonial. We sent reporters to cover that sort of thing, not a program."*

He could have been speaking also for NBC.

When the news reached the White House, there was a sense of relief around the Oval Office. The story really was not going to take off — no need for Bush to go public on what those students ten thousand miles away were doing.

Everyone assumed Dan Rather of CBS would also pass on the story.

SAME DAY, A LITTLE LATER
U.S. EMBASSY COMPOUND
BEIJING

Tom and the other CIA officers at the agency's Beijing station now knew that Deng Xiaoping had persuaded all his military commanders to mobilize their forces to deal with what the supreme leader was calling *"the greatest threat to the country I could remember."* One of the CIA operatives joked that Deng must be suffering from amnesia to have forgotten the Cultural Revolution.

On Tiananmen Square other intelligence operatives continued to infiltrate and probe, each with a clear agenda.

The Russians were primarily concerned with the effect the demonstrations could have on the Gorbachev visit, now only a week away. *"If this were happening in Moscow,"* one KGB man was overheard saying, *"The Red Army would have moved in and cleared everyone out."*

Intelligence operatives from other Soviet bloc countries — Romania, Bulgaria, Hungary, Czechoslovakia, and East Germany — were trying to establish if anyone was masterminding the demonstrations.

"They simply could not accept that this was planned and executed by the students," said Irish diplomat Brendan Ward. *"In their own countries, something so well*

organized and determined would have received some powerful driving force. What these people could not grasp was that the students were being motivated by that most powerful force of all, a need for democracy."

European intelligence agents, especially those of Britain, France, and West Germany, were concerned to discover what external support the students had, especially from Hong Kong and Taiwan. Three weeks into the demonstration these operatives had discovered not only that sizable sums of money were being smuggled in from Hong Kong and Taiwan to purchase food for the demonstrators, but that escape networks stretching for thousands of miles had been set up to smuggle students out of China before the authorities arrested them.

The intelligence officers realized that what had begun as a funeral rite for a beloved leader, Hu Yaobang, had assumed a far more significant meaning, one increasingly disturbing to foreign businesspeople. They had started to come to Tiananmen Square to see for themselves what was happening. Between them they had bankrolled China in the past decade with $37 billion. Twice that figure was scheduled to be placed in the country in the next five years. For men like George Kenneth Liu, chief executive in China of the giant General Foods Corporation, the situation was *"of deep concern."*

The view was being echoed by executives at the Chrysler Corporation's Beijing Jeep plant, the Philips Radio plant in the capital, and at C. M. Ericsson's telephone-equipment factory on the outskirts. In a score of foreign-managed corporations, there was growing unease over the possibility that the students could force the government into taking action that would lead to a global collapse of confidence in China's ability to manage its own affairs.

The reverberations from events in Tiananmen Square were not confined to Beijing's foreign business community. The unease had spread through the entire country. In Shanghai, the Volkswagen plant was producing at half capacity as workers there continued to march in support of the students. Along China's long southern coastal belt, foreign-financed clothing factories found their sewing machines increasingly idle for the same reason. It was the same in those plants producing electrical appliances, radios, and toys for the U.S. and European markets.

The situation was exacerbated, in the view of many businesspeople, by the increasing number of print and television reporters who had arrived to cover the Gorbachev visit and found themselves with a running story outside the hotel they had made their headquarters, the towering, monolithic Beijing, a few minutes' walk from Tiananmen Square.

Reporters from over 150 nations visiting the square all filed basically the same story. China was in the grip of something momentous. The outcome could either be another triumph for democracy, as in the Philippines, or a crushing failure, as in Burma. Was China on the verge of historic events like the Hungarian uprising of 1956 and the Prague Spring of 1968? Or was it about to plunge into some terrible abyss?

The correspondents and camera crews did not, could not, know. But there is nothing like a story that can go either way to dominate the media. Increasingly events in China did that around the world. Those reports led to deepening anxiety and concern among the global business communities, which began to exert still more pressure on their governments to either persuade the Chinese leadership to make some concessions, or make it absolutely clear to the students that they could expect no support.

"There was a lot of pressure from a number of sources," Britain's ambassador, Sir Alan Donald, acknowledged.

Tom, the CIA agent who had become almost a permanent presence in Tiananmen Square, put it more bluntly. *"If the Chinese were going to act, they should do so now. To the outside world it looked as if a bunch of kids were hijacking their government. No one could support that, even if it is done in the name of democracy."*

Those words reflected a policy decision taken in Washington by Webster. His agents would continue to probe the students but would provide them with no information in turn, such as that piece of news that Deng Xiaoping now had the full support of the army in crushing the demonstrations.

When measured against the wider interests of the United States and her European partners, the students were expendable. No one wanted them to die. But no one among those intelligence officers, businesspeople, and their governments would risk their own interests to ensure that the students succeeded.

SAME DAY, A LITTLE LATER
BEIJING AIRPORT

The long flight from California had been even more tiring than Jenny had expected. Thankfully, little Peter had slept for most of the journey. Even now she could not quite believe how swiftly events had happened.

Once Professor Guangzu's daughter had made the decision to go home, the Medical Center's administration in Los Angeles said she could have an extended leave of absence. Several colleagues had pressed sums of money on her. Zhong, her husband, had been coldly furious when she had told him she was leaving. He had refused to drive her to the airport. As she left the apartment, she had quickly shaken his hand. She knew then her marriage was effectively over.

During the flight she had wondered what she would tell her father. Now that she was there, she felt suddenly nervous. Should she phone him from the airport? Or just show up at the apartment?

Jenny turned to Sue Tung and sought her advice.

They had met on the flight, drawn to each other because they were the only two Chinese women among the passengers. In the long hours across the Pacific they had shared life stories. Sue had told her about the $10,000 she had collected and said she still had no clear idea of how it should be spent. Jenny had suggested Sue could ask her father what was needed.

"Don't just turn up. Call him," advised Sue as they lugged their cases through the customs hall. *"Parents hate surprises."*

Sue had decided to telephone Jyan as soon as she could. She was certain his position at the Military Academy would enable him to provide a clear report on the situation. She would also call Rod. Already she missed him. But she had promised to be back in Sacramento in time for their wedding.

Out in the airport arrivals hall, crowded as usual with hucksters trying to entice passengers to stay at certain hotels, the two women went in search of phones. Suddenly Jenny felt a tap on her shoulder. She turned to face her father.

"Papa," she gasped. "How did you know I was here?"

"Your husband called," Professor Guangzu said. He picked up Peter in his arms. "Hello, my little American," he smiled. "Do you speak any Chinese?"

The child shook his head. Professor Guangzu sighed and turned to his daughter. Jenny introduced Sue. The professor looked at both women.

"You come at a very interesting time," he finally said. "A very interesting and troubling time."

FRIDAY, MAY 12, 1989
BEIJING UNIVERSITY

One by one the chosen students made their way into the campus coffeehouse at midday, fifty volunteers who were prepared to starve themselves to death. Daobao and Yang Li had been among the first to step forward. But the other student leaders had insisted they were too important to be used for such a purpose.

Instead they had spent the morning of the twenty-eighth day of their protest helping to prepare a sumptuous farewell banquet for those who had promised to die. Cassy was among the other leaders who had prepared the food. Every table in the coffeehouse was filled with bowls of rice, meat, and fish. There were bottles of beer and the strong Maotai sorghum spirit. Everything had been donated by the people of Beijing.

Watching them eat, Cassy was close to tears, moved by the thought that in a country where widespread starvation was still common, these volunteers were going to use hunger as their final weapon to try and convince the regime to meet their demands for democracy.

The meal over, she joined other students escorting the volunteers to Tiananmen Square. As they cycled through the campus gates, Cassy wondered how many would ever return. Yet she could not believe the authorities would deliberately let them die in the full glare of the foreign media.

Watching them arrive on Tiananmen Square two hours later, Jeanne Moore recognized that publicity was the students' most powerful weapon. In all, she counted over four hundred volunteers drawn from campuses all over the city.

Once the reason for their presence became known there was sustained cheer from the tens of thousands who now permanently occupied the square.

Wuerkaixi ordered the volunteers to form ranks before the Monument to the People's Heroes. Then he administered a ceremonial oath, his voice close to breaking with emotion.

"You will all agree not to eat until we have obtained substantial, concrete, and real dialogue with the Party leadership, and until we receive official recognition that our cause is patriotic and democratic."

A chorus of agreement came from the volunteers. Wang Dan then addressed them, much to the visible irritation of Wuerkaixi. The relationship between the two leaders had become openly strained. Now Wang Dan brought a touch of farce to the proceedings. He said all the hunger strikers must also give up smoking. The news was greeted with a collective groan from the volunteers.

Wuerkaixi called the other leaders to meet with him in the roped-off space below the pediment that had become their "conference corner." He said Wang Dan was wrong to demand a smoking ban, that cigarettes would sustain the volunteers in the difficult times ahead. Daobao and Li then explained that they had learned that IRA hunger strikers such as Bobby Sands had survived so long by using nicotine to dampen down their hunger pains. Wang Dan relented and told the students they could smoke.

He then led them to the exact spot on the square where in two days' time State President Yang Shangkun was to formally welcome Mikhail Gorbachev. The volunteers sat down in ranks.

Once more Wuerkaixi addressed them.

"In this sunny, brilliant month of May you are going on a hunger strike. During this most beautiful moment of youth, you have chosen to put the beauty of life behind you…. You do not want to die. You would like to lead a good life because you are in the prime of your lives. None of us wants to die. Rather we would like to study hard. Our country is very poor. You will be leaving our country behind if you die."

Cassy saw that some of the onlookers were weeping openly as Wuerkaixi paused. She thought again how skilled he was at crowd manipulation.

Nearby Jeanne Moore and Melinda Liu were both writing down his words.

"Death is not our goal. But if the death of one person or a group of few would ameliorate lives of a larger group of people and succor the prosperity of our nation, we would not have the right to escape death."

Brendan Ward, one of the scores of foreign diplomats on the square, felt it was *"like being back in O'Connell Street, Dublin, listening to some of the great protest figures in my society."* Ward knew enough about what he called *"the politics of hunger"* to realize that the volunteers were deadly serious.

To Brian Davidson they had *"a touch of what the kamikaze pilots must have looked like."*

As Wuerkaixi spoke, the students put on white headbands bearing the words HUNGER STRIKE or DEMOCRACY WARRIOR. They stared fixedly at Wuerkaixi as he continued.

"Our country has already reached a stage where prices are soaring, official profiteering is rife, the mighty tower above, bureaucracies are corrupt, many of those with lofty ideals are lost, and social order grows worse by the day."

Raising his voice, Wuerkaixi declaimed: *"At this crucial point of life and death for our race and nation, compatriots, every compatriot with a conscience, please listen to our plea."*

When he stepped back there was total silence, the ultimate show of respect.

Then thousands of non-fasting students, still without speaking, formed a protective outer ring around those who were pledged to die to give meaning to what had been said. There was only the sound of weeping among the onlookers.

18

Turmoil on Tiananmen

SATURDAY, MAY 13, 1989
TIANANMEN SQUARE

Dressed in a beige safari jacket, chin thrust forward, Dan Rather once more set out to show why the CBS network thought he was worth almost $3 million a year as their anchorman for the evening news. It was the twenty-ninth day of the demonstrations.

Hours before, Rather had arrived from New York by what the airlines call *"the stagecoach route"* to the Orient, with stopovers in Paris and New Delhi. In Paris, Rather had heard the news that Panama was about to boil over — and here he was, on the far side of the world, with a major story, possibly *the* story, erupting in America's backyard. It had helped add to Rather's anxiety, so much so that having checked into Beijing's Shangri-La Hotel, where Chinese musicians in tuxedos played Brahms during the Happy Hour, Rather had gone at once to Tiananmen Square, accompanied by some of the seventy crew people needed to support him.

Flanked by his producer and director, Rather went directly to the Monument to the People's Heroes. For the next hour he explained to Wuerkaixi and Wang Dan why he was there and what he intended to do: *"make your cause fully known to the American people."*

The two student leaders listened politely. In the past few days other revered names of European broadcasting had beaten a path to them, seeking interviews, offering prime time exposure, shrewdly assuring Wuerkaixi that he was already a world-famous figure, so every word he said would be carefully listened to in the corridors of government. It was a heady prospect for a twenty-one-year-old who had counted his audience in hundreds until a few weeks ago.

The CBS team assured Wuerkaixi that the story would now be noted in the White House, and that Dan Rather was the very man to also get the American people all fired up. Wuerkaixi and Wang Dan promised the anchorman they would do everything possible to help him do that.

Shortly afterward Rather delivered in a dramatic, emotional voice, perfect for the occasion, his opening statement from the square.

"Gorbachev comes to China seeking to heal old wounds and neutralize America's strategic position in Asia. He is upstaged by striking students seeking to change the face of Communism. Getting to the center of the square means passing through an ocean of students, bicycles, loudspeakers, slogan-chanting, singing, and applause. Determination, not rage, is on the faces and in the voices. They defied a government order to be out of the square by the time Gorbachev arrives, and no one seems afraid. Police are around in force, but instead of breaking up the crowds, they broke into patriotic song, and the students sang back."

In those words Dan Rather had stamped his authority on the demonstrations. In New York, NBC and ABC news executives realized they had badly misjudged. While Panama, where Manuel Noriega had initiated a vicious physical assault on political opponents and thousands of U.S. troops were pouring into the Canal Zone, was indeed an important story, what was happening in China was not just news. It was history.

SUNDAY, MAY 14, 1989
TIANANMEN SQUARE

Late in the evening on the thirtieth day of the demonstrations for democracy, Professor Guangzu and his daughter, Jenny, walked among the hunger strikers, now two thousand strong. Themselves close to exhaustion after their long day in the square, they continued to check vital signs and then order medical students to carry away those strikers closest to collapse. Scores of other doctors were doing the same.

As soon as one stretcher was carried away to the hospital, another student lay down on the ground and prepared to die. Each time, Jenny felt fresh tears prick her eyes.

All around her, other doctors and nurses tried to control their emotions in the highly charged atmosphere. There were close to a million people in the square, listening to and commenting on the claims and counterclaims coming over the loudspeakers.

Daobao and Yang Li had set up the students' own relay system to broadcast speeches repudiating those put out by the Party from a studio in the Great Hall of the People.

Away from the hunger strikers, the atmosphere struck Cassy as *"part Coney Island, part state fair, part political convention."*

Vendors were selling food. The air was filled with competing rock music, and over everything blared the voices from the loudspeakers. They continued to give sharply differing accounts of the first real contacts between the student leaders and the authorities the previous evening.

For an hour they had met in a building opposite the gates of Zhongnanhai. Prime Minister Li Peng had sent Politburo member Yan Mingfu, the only real moderate in the government still openly supporting the students, to plead with Wuerkaixi and Wang Dan to order the students to leave the square. Unknown to those at the meeting, intelligence chief Qiao Shi had bugged the room. Throughout this Sunday the tape had been cleverly used to create the impression that the students were not really interested in reforms but simply wanted to shame China in the eyes of the world on the eve of Gorbachev's visit. The government broadcasts explained how Yan Mingfu had offered the students a place where they could continue their hunger strike in peace and had even offered an apology for *"past mistakes."*

Finally, the broadcast described how Yan Mingfu had made an almost tearful appeal. Through the loudspeaker had come his secretly recorded voice. *"If you insist on dividing the Party into factions, you should realize your action is going to seriously harm those of us who support reform. You will make it very difficult for Comrade Zhao Ziyang and all the other comrades working for what you all want."*

Qiao Shi had helped strengthen the suspicion that Party Secretary Zhao was using the situation in a bid for ultimate power.

Sensing this, Wuerkaixi had once more broadcast that the student leadership publicly distanced itself from everyone in the government.

In the past hours the young student leader had assumed almost a new personality. He no longer walked, but half ran everywhere, issuing orders, brooking no argument. The more the world's TV cameras were trained on him, the more theatrical Wuerkaixi became. To Cassy he *"was an actor who had found his stage."*

Other student leaders went about their business of running the protest with less show. Wang Dan huddled with others at the foot of the monument, his eyes blinking furiously behind his glasses as they reviewed strategy. Chai Ling was everywhere, urging students not to leave the square. Liu Gang, his Western-style sports clothes badly in need of cleaning, moved around the square, judging the mood. Yang Li's muscular frame seemed to be in perpetual motion as he prowled the square, quietly giving encouragement.

Daobao made regular forays from the monument to check on the supply of posters, food supplies, and the desperate need for more toilet facilities. Slit trenches had been dug on one side of the square and tents erected over them. But the trenches were filled to overflowing, and an overpowering stench drifted from the area. More trenches were now being dug. But with a million people now in the square it would not be long before they were also filled.

But to Jeanne Moore *"the situation had become a celebration of rejection and utter contempt for China's leaders, Zhao included. We are as close to revolution as we can be yet without a shot being fired."*

Now, this Sunday evening, she saw the government about to become further publicly humiliated. Through the crowd came Beijing's mayor, Chen Xitong and Li Xiaming, the city's Party Secretary. They were flanked by nervous aides and a phalanx of police. Reaching the Monument to the People's Heroes, and trying hard to ignore the scores of foreign TV cameras trained on them, both men appealed to the student leaders to withdraw from the square.

Wuerkaixi pointed dramatically to where the hunger strikers were.

"To leave will be for us to betray what they are doing!" he cried out. *"We will not leave until we have achieved our aims. Long live democracy!"*

The cry was taken up by the crowd. Visibly shaken, the delegation withdrew.

Shortly afterward the unmistakable voice of Qiao Shi came over the loudspeakers announcing the square was to be closed for the Gorbachev visit; all students must leave by three o'clock the following morning.

On the pediment, Wuerkaixi turned to Chai Ling. She grabbed one of the microphones and addressed the crowd.

"History demands we stay. And stay we will!"

She had spent hours writing and polishing what she would say. For ink she had used blood from a cut she had deliberately made in her arm, collecting the blood in a dish into which she dipped her calligraphy brush. The gesture was typical of the highly-strung young woman, whose strong sense of theater was only equaled by Wuerkaixi's.

Holding the parchment before her, Chai Ling's childlike voice carried to the furthest corners of the square. Under the impact of her words a stillness came over the crowd.

"People of China, we feel the purest patriotism! We offer the finest of our hearts and souls. Yet we have been described as 'rioting' and filled with 'ulterior motives' and being led by a 'small group of people.'"

Brian Davidson, the British press attaché, was among those who saw her pause and turn to face the portrait of Mao on Tiananmen Square.

"Honest citizens of China," she continued, *"each of you put your hand on your heart and ask the goodness that is in your heart, what are we guilty of? Are we rioting? No! We mean a peaceful demonstration! Yet our emotions have been manipulated time and again. We endure hunger to seek truth. But we are met with police brutality. We go down on our knees to plead for democracy!"*

Barr Seitz heaved a long sigh. He had not left the square in the past twenty-four hours, acting as a runner for the ABC camera crew roaming the area. His job was to set up interviews and carry film back to the nearby Beijing Hotel, where the network had established a base, though it had not sent its star anchorman, Peter Jennings. The sight of the tall, smiling Barr had become a familiar and welcome one to the students. Speaking their language, he had shared with them their dreams, which Chai Ling continued to articulate so eloquently.

"Democracy is life's greatest safeguard. Freedom is our heaven-given right since the beginning of man! Yet now we have to fight for them with our young lives. Can the Chinese people be proud of this?"

Newsweek correspondent Melinda Liu admired the way Chai Ling worked the crowd. The student knew more about public speaking than most seasoned professionals. Melinda decided she would use the student as a sidebar to the main story she would be filing.

Chai Ling continued: *"We have no choice but to go on hunger strike. It is our only choice. We use language which enables us to face death, to fight for the life which is worth living."*

Brendan Ward was once more reminded of some of the great speakers who had made their mark on his own country's history. The Irish diplomat had been about to return to his embassy to send another telegram to the Department of Foreign Affairs in Dublin, describing the day's events, when Chai Ling's words had stopped him. Ward stood mesmerized like those around him.

Her voice beginning to grow hoarse, Chai Ling reminded the crowd of basic truths.

"We are still children! All of us! China is our mother, for all of us! Mother, take a good look at your sons and daughters! Hunger is destroying their youth. Death is stalking ever closer to them. Can you remain unmoved?"

For the first time since she had spoken a sound came from the crowd: part moan, part groan. Then thousands of voices answered Chai Ling's question.

"No, we cannot remain unmoved."

With a quick shake of her head, Chai Ling silenced them. Then she pointed to the hunger strikers.

"I speak for them when I say we do not want to die. None of us. But when we are enduring hunger, fathers and mothers, don't be sad. When we are saying farewell to life, uncles and aunts, please don't break your hearts. We have only one wish. That is to allow all of you to lead better lives. We have only one request. Please do not forget that what we are seeking is in no way death. For we know democracy is not the affair of a few, and we realize it cannot be achieved by one generation."

Around Jenny and her father, people were sobbing. She thought, we are doctors, used to pain and suffering. Yet who cannot be moved by such eloquence? Her mind turned toward little Peter, resting at the back of the first-aid tent. This taut-faced young woman on the pediment was trying to ensure her son's future, the future of untold millions of sons and daughters of Mother China. Finally tears began to run down Jenny's own cheeks. Her father looked at her, then looked away, his own eyes misty.

Over the loudspeakers, Chai Ling was quoting a poem to the hunger strikers. "'When a man is about to die, his words would be kind; if a horse is about to expire, his cries would be sorrowful.'"

Those hunger strikers who still had the strength to do so raised their hands in salute before sinking back on the ground, too exhausted to speak. Doctors moistened their lips with water and tried to make them as comfortable as possible. It was the third day of their hunger strike.

Over the loudspeakers, the voice had risen.

"Farewell, comrades, take care! May those who die and those who live share the same loyalty. Farewell, beloved, take care! I cannot bear to take leave of you, yet there is no choice but to take leave. Farewell, our parents! Please forgive us. Your children cannot manage to be loyal and filial at the same time. Farewell, our people. Please permit us to demonstrate to you our loyalty in this desperate fashion!"

Chai Ling stepped back from the microphone. The silence remained total.

MONDAY, MAY 15, 1989
BEIJING AIRPORT

Soviet Ambassador Troyanovsky liked to quote Balzac on diplomacy: "A science which permits its practitioners to say nothing and shelter behind mysterious nods of the head." He watched the Aeroflot Ilyushin jet coming in to land and smiled ruefully. Balzac's words had taken on a new meaning in the enervating noonday sun.

The sun made the chunky diplomat mop his face with a large silk handkerchief which complemented his Hong Kong tailored blue silk suit and one of the several dozen pairs of custom-made shoes he regularly bought from the colony.

All around him on the airport tarmac, the Chinese delegation waited to welcome Mikhail Gorbachev. They continued to give little Balzac-like nods to each other and murmur in those quick, hissed whispers that the ambassador found hard to understand, though he spoke Mandarin fluently. But it wasn't hard for the diplomat to guess what was on the delegate's minds.

Because of the demonstration, the Party had been forced to abandon its carefully laid plans to greet Gorbachev at Tiananmen Square. Shortly after dinner, Troyanovsky had been telephoned by Qiao Shi. The security chief was calling on his mobile phone from the roof of the Great Hall of the People. He said it had been decided it would be *"more appropriate"* for the welcoming ceremony to take place at the airport. Qiao Shi had added that as there would be so much to discuss during the first Sino-Soviet summit in twenty years, the sooner the diplomatic greetings were over, the better. Therefore the arrival ceremony would be cut to the absolute minimum. Troyanovsky had not been fooled. He could recognize a crisis.

The ambassador had promptly ordered every possible diplomat not involved in the welcoming ceremony to Tiananmen Square to report what was happening. Troyanovsky had then used the embassy communications room to call the airport at Irtytisk, the Siberian city that was Gorbachev's departure point for China. The Ilyushin was already airborne. The ambassador was patched through to the flight deck via a satellite link. Knowing that his conversation was most certainly being monitored by United States intelligence, and probably by the Chinese, the ambassador was circumspect about the latest change of plan.

Nevertheless, Gorbachev did not bother to hide his astonishment. Andrew Higgins, the Beijing correspondent on the British national daily *The Independent*, was one of several reporters who would learn of the exchange between the plane and the ground. *"The Ilyushin's radio crackled with whispers about the extraordinary scenes which lay ahead,"* Higgins would write. *"The reports... sound barely credible. 'How big is the square?' asked the amazed Gorbachev."*

A few minutes ago, as the Ilyushin swept over the airport perimeter fence guarded by, among other PLA forces, Bing Yang's platoon, Troyanovsky's deputy, Minister-Counselor Ivan Fedotov, who was coordinating the reports from the embassy staff on Tiananmen Square, had come through on the ambassador's car phone.

Smiling apologetically at the Chinese, Troyanovsky hurried to the car parked in the official cavalcade waiting to sweep Gorbachev and his hosts away.

"There are nearly a million people here," Fedotov reported. *"They are all singing and dancing. The students have put up Comrade Gorbachev's portrait opposite Mao's on Tiananmen Square. It's an even bigger photo, and they keep calling for perestroika."*

The ambassador's groan of near-despair was heard by the pool of journalists covering the airport ceremonies.

A week ago Troyanovsky had foreseen this could happen: The students would use Gorbachev to embarrass their own government. Three times in the past few days he had gone to Zhongnanhai and spoken to Li Peng's office. The ambassador, with a deserved reputation for attention to diplomatic minutia, had asked whether the state visit should be delayed. He had been told that to do so could have unpredictable consequences for Sino-Soviet relations.

As well as being a student of Balzac, the ambassador was something of a specialist in understanding Chinese face-saving. Deng Xiaoping wanted the visit, even though in Troyanovsky's graphic later description: *"China's leaders were like Nero, fiddling while everything was going up in metaphorical flames around them."*

The ambassador hurried back to take his place with the ranks of Chinese watching the Ilyushin rolling to a stop.

State President Yang Shangkun braced his wiry frame and walked to the foot of the steps. The aircraft door opened and Gorbachev, followed by his wife, Raisa, appeared.

For a moment the Soviet leader stood, composing his face into a smile. Then he and his wife came down the steps onto the bare tarmac. In the near-panic decision to switch the welcome from Tiananmen Square, someone had overlooked laying a red carpet. However, the PLA honor guards were in place and snapped to attention as Gorbachev and the president passed in review, accompanied by the sound of a twenty-one gun salute.

Gorbachev turned and looked about him expectantly. Where was the microphone for the welcoming speeches?

"Later, later," the state president smiled quickly, turning to lead Gorbachev to one of the waiting cars.

Gorbachev's anger was plain. He pursed his lips and hunched his shoulders. Raisa looked faintly bewildered as a Chinese flunky shoved a bunch of flowers into her arms.

One of the Soviet officers rushed to the press pen and handed out copies of the speech Gorbachev had not been allowed to make. It began with suitable allegoric fervor: *"We have come to China in springtime, the good season of burgeoning nature and the awakening of new life. All over the world, people associate this season with renewal and hope."*

As the motorcade swept away, the journalists scrambled for telephones. Gorbachev's words were bound to be interpreted by the students as support, and by his hosts as a calculated slap in the face.

SAME DAY, SAME TIME
TIANANMEN SQUARE

Postgraduate student Sue Tung continued to describe to Rod in Sacramento what was happening, using a mobile phone an American television reporter had loaned her in return for allowing him to film the call. Trying to ignore the camera team, Sue spoke to Rod.

"Even in the two days I have felt a change. People are more open and determined to push this through. The songs have become more militant and more mocking of authority."

"Just like our protests over the Vietnam War," Rod said.

"But different," Sue insisted. *"The people here are fighting for democracy. I'm standing now beneath the flagpole where the hammer and sickle should be flying. Instead the students have run up a huge banner carrying the words* HUNGER STRIKE. *All around are banners. One says 'Mother, we like food, but we like democracy even*

more.' Another says 'Our children are going hungry, Deng Xiaoping. What about your children?'

"Courting couples stroll arm in arm. Fathers carry their children on their shoulders. Many of the kids have headbands with the same two words, FREEDOM and DEMOCRACY. I don't think that you can call this any more just a student movement. It's a people's movement. I've spoken to people who have cycled fifty miles just to be here. One man said he had come from a hundred miles away by train. There are teachers, factory workers, writers, intellectuals. I just don't remember anything like it."

Sue and the camera team eased their way through the cordon of students around the hunger strikers.

"The scene is quite incredible. Just hundreds and hundreds of bodies spread out everywhere. Someone has just told me they've taken away fifty so far to the first-aid posts that are now all around the square. It seems that as soon as they feel strong enough, the strikers will return. In the meantime they are refusing everything except glucose and water — and cigarettes!"

Rod's suddenly excited voice interrupted Sue.

"Honey, are you wearing a yellow dress and a sunhat?"

"Yes. How'd you know?"

"You're on CNN! They've got live pictures coming from the square. I can see you clearly!"

Sue looked around. A few yards away a CNN crew was filming. She waved at its camera.

"I wish you were here," Sue said.

"I'll come, if you like. We could get married right there!"

Sue smiled. "I don't think that would be possible. Besides, I've set myself on having a proper American wedding."

They said they loved each other and hung up.

Dan Rather and the CBS team had gotten into their stride, powered partly by the sheer excitement of being at the center of a major news story, partly by the satisfaction of knowing that they were beating their rivals, ABC and NBC. While those networks had correspondents in the square, none had the stature of Rather.

In the florid prose that so well suited the moment, he continued to paint a portrait of "roller-coaster events."

Because of the thirteen-hour time difference with New York, Rather and the crew were working around the clock from a mobile unit in the square itself. When not on air they trudged back to the Shangri-La, too exhausted even to listen to the tuxedo-clad Chinese musicians playing Brahms.

This semblance of normality encouraged some of the foreign businesspeople who had arrived in Beijing to check on their investments.

SAME DAY, SAME TIME
SAN FRANCISCO

Shao-Yen Wang, the daughter of a senior official in Beijing, was watching Rather's newscast from Tiananmen Square while talking on the phone.

"We must keep up the pressure," she was saying. *"We do that, and maybe one of the diplomats in the consulate will crack. If even one defects, it will be a huge loss of face to the old men in Zhongnanhai."*

The previous day Shao-Yen had been among several thousand Chinese, students and workers from the Chinatown district, who had demonstrated outside their country's consulate in the city. From time to time, faces had appeared at the windows of the building. Some had given V-signs.

The gesture had convinced Shao-Yen that a diplomat might be considering defecting.

"I saw those faces," she said again. *"Everyone in that building is trained to show nothing. But some of them looked as if they wished they were out there with us. If we keep protesting and telling them it's all part of democracy, maybe one will come and join us."*

Shao-Yen was speaking to a woman who was an important member of the local Chinese community. She told Shao-Yen she did not wish to be personally identified with the protest until it was *"absolutely certain the students back home will not fail."*

Trying to enlist support, Shao-Yen had encountered the same hesitancy among a number of wealthy or influential local Chinese. Several had flatly refused to help, explaining they wanted nothing to jeopardize their trading links with their motherland. One or two had warned Shao-Yen of the risk she was taking.

One man had reminded her of the Chinese Secret Intelligence Service agents in the city, who by now had almost certainly reported back to Beijing on those first demonstrations outside the consulate.

Shao-Yen had replied she would do nothing to discredit China but would continue to try and help persuade its leaders to recognize that introducing democracy was the *"only way to make China as great as America."*

In her mind the young actress and aspiring screenwriter had a scenario in which she would one day bring the story to the screen. Perhaps she would even play Chai Ling. The excerpts of her speech broadcast on CNN had moved Shao-Yen to begin to think about a new screenplay. Somehow those Chinese secret agents she had been told were in San Francisco must also be worked into the story.

The FBI had also become involved. Its agents had cast an electronic surveillance net over the consulate. Already they had established that in the wake of the demonstration, coupled with the flow of diplomatic traffic from Beijing, the consulate staff had become polarized. Senior diplomats invariably supported the hardliners in Beijing, while junior diplomats had begun to express support among themselves for the students.

Among them was the consulate's twenty-five-year-old cultural attaché, Zhang Milin. Handsome, carefully groomed, confident, until a few days ago he had been a total believer in his country's political system. But in the past days, the FBI eavesdroppers had picked up hints Zhang had been angered by his government's attitude toward the students. He had been overheard asking his seniors how he should explain what was happening in China to his American contacts. He had been told to say *"reactionaries"* and *"hooligans"* were trying to create trouble with the help of *"imperialist spies."*

About the time Shao-Yen was insisting on the phone to the woman about the need to keep up the pressure outside the consulate, Zhang had been heard on one of the many electronic bugs focused on the building, saying that the latest news from China, that Mikhail Gorbachev was supporting the students, was a further sign that the rest of the Communist world was turning against the old men of Zhongnanhai.

This made the attitude in Washington all the more curious, the cultural attaché had told a colleague. The Chinese embassy there had sent the consulate a lengthy message quoting unnamed White House and State Department officials as still hoping the students would stop confronting their government.

Zhang had *"the strange feeling"* that the U.S. administration had almost as much distaste for what the students were doing as his own government. In one of those moments of black humor that lightened the young diplomat's otherwise serious demeanor, Zhang had joked about whether the United States would find itself on the same side as China in trying to persuade the Soviet Union that it too should be openly discouraging the demonstrations.

SAME DAY, LATE AFTERNOON
BEIJING

Using their separate but equally well placed contacts, Melinda Liu and Jeanne Moore were piecing together what had happened after Mikhail and Raisa Gorbachev had been driven from the airport at high speed to the State Guest House, a palace on the outskirts of the city.

While Raisa had freshened up and studied a schedule that by now bore no resemblance to what was being *"feverishly replanned,"* Mikhail Gorbachev was holding a meeting with Ambassador Troyanovsky and other Soviet officials.

Gorbachev, according to Melinda's sources, was *"close to hopping mad"* at what he was being told. Because of the demonstrators in Tiananmen Square, now estimated to be in excess of 1.5 million, the Soviet leader was going to be driven through the back streets to keep his official appointments.

Gorbachev, in his role as the new liberating force of European Communism, had planned to conquer Beijing with the kind of public relations campaign that had worked so well in other capital cities. He knew how important it was to be seen *"pressing flesh"* and *"gladhanding with the citizens"* if he was to succeed behind the scenes in what he had come to do: persuade the leadership that further reforms were essential to ease the pressure on them and allow them to remain in control.

Now he had been informed there would be no walkabouts, no carefully stage-managed stops to shake hands, no photo-opportunities for Raisa and himself to do what they always did superbly, delivering the few words of their host's language to the local citizens.

Gorbachev's chief spokesman, Gennady Gerasimov, later remembered the Soviet leader's anger was *"quite monumental."* Late in the afternoon of this Monday, though, the personable Gerasimov was doing his best to prevent the press corps camped outside the State Guest House from discovering what was really happening.

In mid-afternoon, when the Gorbachevs were due to be formally greeted by State President Yang in the Great Hall of the People, Gerasimov issued a brief statement that the Gorbachevs were resting.

"In reality Gorbachev, encouraged by Raisa, was demanding to be treated like a world leader, not someone from a banana republic," one of Jeanne's contacts had told her.

Close to 6:00 P.M., the matter still unresolved, the Soviet leader and first lady entered their limousine to go to meet State President Yang. They were already two hours late. But instead of coming down the imposing main driveway of the Guest House compound, the motorcade went round the back of the palace, leaving the grounds through the tradesmen's gate. Entering the city, the cavalcade drove into the maze of hutongs, bouncing and bumping over the cobbles.

Professor Guangzu and Jenny had left Tiananmen Square to eat at the Oriental Restaurant, a modest establishment in one of those back streets, when they were startled to see official cars passing their window table. The Gorbachevs' limousine came to a brief stop. Jenny was convinced Raisa looked *"longingly at our food, then with a little wave and smile they were gone."*

The motorcade drove past warehouses, factories, and gray courtyard homes before it finally reached a gate at the back of the west side of the Great Hall of the People. The entrance was usually used by the cleaning staff.

It took a little honking before the gate was opened by two soldiers. The cars crept past piles of garbage bags before stopping on a disused basketball court.

The Gorbachevs climbed out and stared stoically back at the gate. A group of students had appeared and were unfurling a banner: *"In Moscow they have Gorbachev and freedom! In China we have Deng and corruption!"*

The soldiers closed the gate, and silent, crimson-faced flunkies escorted the Gorbachevs into the Great Hall.

From Tiananmen Square the constant, thunderous chant reached them.

"Give us democracy, Comrade Gorbachev!"

State President Yang smiled stiffly and remarked how glad he was to welcome his guests at such an important moment in China's history.

Gorbachev glanced around the salon where the funeral rites had been conducted for Hu Yaobang just a month ago; perhaps remembering what Hu had tried to achieve, and what he had come to represent to the students. Gorbachev departed from the prepared phrases of his script. He told his hosts that down the generations *"we have become smarter. My hope is that the next generation will be even more smarter."*

The smile left the state president's lips. For the second time in a few hours Gorbachev had delivered a judgment on what was happening outside the windows of the salon.

Worse followed. Still extemporizing, Gorbachev pronounced no society could really exist without *"a sensible balance between the generations."*

He paused to give the eighty-seven-year-old state president a brief, thin smile. Then, deliberately looking toward the windows and raising his voice to overcome the turmoil on Tiananmen Square, Gorbachev delivered his most stinging rebuke so far.

"What is needed is for us all to recognize the energy of young people and their right to speak out against conservatism."

He paused once more, this time to look at his increasingly stunned hosts.

"But also they must recognize the wisdom of the older generation." The balm did nothing to heal the anger of the Chinese.

The message he had come to deliver was plain: There had to be changes.

For a few moments there was an embarrassed silence in the salon. Then a trickle of applause came and went. Gorbachev rocked slightly back and forth on his heels. He looked like a boxer who had delivered his first real body blows. Now he was waiting for the expected counterpunch.

It came at the end of Yang's response. Having delivered a string of banalities, the state president announced: *"My colleagues and I feel the speed is too great. We must reduce it somewhat."*

In a mood that Jeanne Moore likened to the one that *"marks the short step from the death cell to the execution chamber,"* hosts and guests trooped to the welcoming banquet in the magnificent gallery of the Great Hall. One of its many features was the panoramic windows overlooking Tiananmen Square. The drapes had been drawn to help block out the chanting and that endlessly repeated cry for Gorbachev to somehow give the people of China democracy.

The meal passed in desultory small talk. Raisa barely touched her soup, noodles, and chicken. Like her husband she drank only water. Only when it came to the formal toasts did they sip wine.

Standing, glass in hand, Gorbachev said: *"Today we have been able to see at close quarters something of your great city we would not have expected to see. We drove through your streets and saw your people. What most impressed us was their openness and friendliness."*

At that moment another sustained roar came from the square.

"Give us democracy! We need perestroika! Give it to us, Comrade Gorbachev, initiator of glasnost!"

Some of the Chinese looked at the Soviet leader as if somehow he had personally arranged this further humiliation.

Struggling to his feet, visibly shaking, the state president was briefly at a loss how to respond. Then his scratchy voice made a remarkable admission.

"It is not easy for us to have a situation in which to hold these historic meetings."

It was the first official glimpse of what was happening behind the scenes.

The Gorbachevs and their entourage were virtually smuggled out of the building by their hosts, who were determined the students should have no glimpse of the Soviet leader. Three hours later Qiao Shi delivered over the square's loudspeakers what was no longer a threat but an abject plea.

"Please go back to school," the security chief began. *"If you do, be assured that the Party and government will study most carefully all reasonable suggestions and demands and will take feasible measures and steps to resolve the questions."*

Wuerkaixi responded instantly from the pediment. No one must leave. In the meantime, he added, he was joining the hunger strikers.

Cassy watched him swagger across the square to take his place beside the other starving students. Wuerkaixi's behavior troubled her. She had overheard him telling Yang to arrange for a bowl of noodles to be waiting in the back of the car he was using to snatch a few hours sleep. He had explained it was necessary for him to eat because *"as leader, I need to conserve my strength, and I also have a heart condition."*

When Cassy told Daobao what she had heard, he told her not to speak to anyone else about the matter, because they would not understand. But Cassy had begun to wonder whether Wuerkaixi really had the courage of his convictions or whether he was on an ego trip.

DEMILITARIZING THE SOVIET-CHINESE BORDER AND TURNING IT INTO A
BORDER OF PEACE AND GOOD-NEIGHBOURLINESS IS A NOBLE GOAL WHICH WE
COULD ATTAIN THROUGH JOINT EFFORTS.
VAST PROSPECTS FOR MUTUALLY BENEFICIAL COOPERATION OPEN UP IN
THE ECONOMY; THE MAIN SPHERE OF HUMAN ACTIVITY. TRADE EXCHANGES
BETWEEN OUR TWO COUNTRIES HAVE GROWN IN THE PAST YEARS, YET BOTH
THEIR VOLUME AND THEIR DYNAMICS DO NOT AT ALL CORRESPOND TO THE
EXISTING POTENTIAL.
SEEN AGAINST THE BACKDROP OF INTEGRATIONAL PROCESSES, GREATER
INTERNATIONAL DIVISION OF LABOUR, AND RAPIDLY EXPANDING
COOPERATIVE ARRANGEMENTS, SOVIET-CHINESE TRADE, WITH A VOLUME OF
LESS THAN TWO BILLION ROUBLES, PRESENTS A POOR PICTURE.
MORE

TASS-05-17 1302EDT<

Gorbachev speech to the Chinese public.

🖿006

        ¥W 34397   E270001 05-17 0342
        34397, , E270001, 34397

    .GORBACHEV SPEECH TO CHINESE PUBLIC =6.
    17/5 TASS G-1

    AND YET, WE HAVE TWO COUNTRIES WITH TREMENDOUS RESOURCES.
MOREOVER WE ARE NEIGHBOURS SHARING THE LONGEST COMMON BORDER IN
THE WORLD AND THEREFORE HAVING EXCEPTIONALLY FAVOURABLE
CONDITIONS FOR COOPERATION.
    THE POTENTIAL FOR ECONOMIC COOPERATION HERE IS PERHAPS BY
SEVERAL ORDERS OF MAGNITUDE GREATER THAT WHAT WE HAVE NOW. OF
COURSE, HOWEVER MUCH BOTH SIDES MIGHT WANT TO DO SO, THIS
POTENTIAL CANNOT BE REALIZED AT ONE GO. WHAT NEEDS TO BE DONE IS
TO IDENTIFY PROMISING AREAS, SETTLE COMPLEX PROBLEMS OF PRICING
AND HELP ENTERPRISES FIND SUITABLE PARTNERS. IT WILL ALSO TAKE
SOME TIME TO TRAIN PERSONNEL AND TO REGAIN THE EXPERTISE THAT TO
A LARGE EXTENT HAS BEEN LOST OVER THE YEARS WHEN OUR ECONOMIC
RELATIONS WERE VIRTUALLY SUSPENDED.
    HOWEVER, WITHOUT SETTING OURSELVES UNREALISTIC GOALS WE COULD,
I THINK, ENSURE AN EARLY AND SUBSTANTIAL INCREASE IN SINO-SOVIET
ECONOMIC TIES FOR THE BENEFIT OF BOTH COUNTRIES. AND THAT COULD
BE DONE BOTH IN THE TRADITIONAL AREAS, SUCH AS THE EXCHANGE OF
RAW MATERIALS AND MANUFACTURED GOODS AND ASSISTANCE IN BUILDING
POWER GENERATING FACILITIES, AND IN THE DEVELOPMENT AND USE OF
STATE-OF-THE-ART ADVANCED TECHNOLOGIES.
    SPEAKING OF THE FORMS OF COOPERATION, IN ADDITION TO THE
EXPANSION OF TRADE WE COULD PROMOTE THE ESTABLISHMENT OF DIRECT
TIES BETWEEN ENTERPRISES, DESIGN OFFICES AND RESEARCH INSTITUTES,
AND THE SETTING UP OF JOINT FIRMS AND INDUSTRIAL ENTERPRISES,
INCLUDING THOSE WITH THE PARTICIPATION OF THIRD COUNTRIES.

    MORE

    TASS-05-17 1313EDT<

WE ARE AWARE OF YOUR MAJOR ACCOMPLISHMENTS ON THIS ROAD AS WELL AS OF THE DIFFICULTIES YOU FACE. AS YOUR FRIENDS, WE SINCERELY WISH YOU, COMRADES, STEADY PROGRESS TOWARD YOUR PRIMARY OBJECTIVE -- TURNING THE PEOPLE'S REPUBLIC OF CHINA INTO A DEVELOPED MODERN SOCIALIST STATE.

GENERALLY SPEAKING, THE STATUS AND POTENTIAL OF A COUNTRY SHOULD NOT BE JUDGED ONLY BY ITS PER CAPITA PRODUCTION AND CONSUMPTION OR ITS PERFORMANCE IN COMPARISON WITH WORLD LEADERS. WHAT IS NO LESS IMPORTANT IS THE DIRECTION IT TAKES IN ITS DEVELOPMENTS OR, FIGURATIVELY SPEAKING, THE DIRECTION IN WHICH THE STREET IS BEING PAVED FOR FURTHER MOVEMENT.

AS FOR THE DIFFICULTIES, THEY ARE ONLY NATURAL IN A COMPLEX UNDERTAKING SUCH AS THE CREATION OF A NEW SOCIAL SYSTEM. WE KNOW THAT FULL WELL FROM OUR OWN EXPERIENCE.

THE ECONOMIC, SCIENTIFIC AND TECHNOLOGICAL POTENTIAL OF OUR COUNTRY AS WELL AS ITS SOCIAL ACHIEVEMENTS ARE COMMON KNOWLEDGE. HOWEVER, THE RATE AND QUALITY OF OUR DEVELOPMENT BEGAN TO DECLINE IN THE 1970S. AND OUR ANALYSIS SHOWED THAT THE ROOT CAUSE LAY NOT IN SOME INDIVIDUAL SHORTCOMINGS OR MISTAKES, ALTHOUGH THEY TOO PLAYED A NEGATIVE ROLE.

MORE

10/06 '01 SUN 15:44 FAX

TASS-05-17 1343EDT<

M0396
5 W 34456   E270001 05-17 0302
34456, . E270001, 34456

.GORBACHEV SPEECH TO CHINESE PUBLIC =10.
17/5 TASS G-1/

THE MAIN CAUSE WAS THE FLAWS INHERENT IN THE BUREAUCRATIC
COMMAND SYSTEM WHICH TOOK SHAPE IN OUR COUNTRY IN THE LATE 1920S-
EARLY 1930S. IT WAS ONLY BY DISMANTLING THAT SYSTEM AND
COMPLETELY RESTORING LENIN'S IDEALS AND SOCIALIST PRINCIPLES TO
THEIR TRUE STATUS THAT THE COUNTRY COULD BE LED OUT OF STAGNATION
AND THE IMMINENT CRISIS AVERTED. THIS WAS HOW THE IDEA OF
REVOLUTIONARY PERESTROIKA WAS CONCEIVED,
     SPEAKING OF THIS I AM NOW DRAWING ON THE KNOWLEDGE AND
EXPERIENCE GAINED IN THE FOUR YEARS FOLLOWING THE APRIL PLENARY
MEETING OF THE CPSU CENTRAL COMMITTEE IN 1985. HOWEVER, THESE
REALITIES WERE NOT IMMEDIATELY RECOGNIZED. THE PARTY AND THE
PEOPLE HAVE BEEN MOVING TO THEIR +MOMENT OF TRUTH+ STEP BY STEP,
GRADUALLY GOING UP THE STAIRS, AS IT WERE.
     WE STARTED OUT BY SETTING OURSELVES THE GOAL OF STRENGTHENING
ELEMENTARY DISCIPLINE -- IN LABOUR, PRODUCTION AND FINANCE. YET
WE DISCOVERED VERY SOON THAT SUCH MEASURES ALONE COULD NOT
ACCOMPLISH MUCH. GENUINE PROGRESS CAN ONLY BE ACHIEVED IF THE
ALIENATION OF WORKERS FROM PROPERTY IS OVERCOME; IF WORKERS
BECOME REAL MASTERS ENJOYING FULL RIGHTS AT THEIR FACTORY OR
PLANT, AT THEIR COLLECTIVE OR STATE-OWNED FARM, THEIR INSTITUTE
OR RESEARCH LABORATORY.
     LIFE ITSELF HAS LED US TO THE CONCLUSION THAT WE NEED A
RADICAL REFORM OF THE ENTIRE ECONOMIC SYSTEM PLACING OUR
ENTERPRISES ON THE BASIS OF FULL COST-ACCOUNTING, SELF-FINANCING
AND SELF-MANAGEMENT, CREATING CONDITIONS FOR THE DEVELOPMENT OF
COOPERATIVES AND WIDELY USING MARKET INCENTIVES.
     MORE

10/06 '01 SUN 15:49 FAX

N0401

5 W 34467   E270001 05-17 0252
34467, , E270001, 34467

.GORBACHEV SPEECH TO CHINESE PUBLIC =12.
17/5 TASS G-1

AS YOU MAY KNOW, COMRADES, IN A WEEK'S TIME THE CONGRESS OF
PEOPLE'S DEPUTIES OF THE USSR WILL CONVENE IN MOSCOW TO FORM A
NEW SUPREME SOVIET AND GOVERNMENT AND TO DETERMINE BASIC
GUIDELINES FOR THE SOVIET STATE'S DOMESTIC AND FOREIGN POLICIES
IN THE COMING YEARS AND, IN EFFECT, BREATHE NEW LIFE INTO THE
OPERATION ON OUR ENTIRE STATE MECHANISM.
      EQUALLY IMPORTANT TASKS WILL HAVE TO BE ADDRESSED DURING THE
NEXT STAGE OF OUR POLITICAL REFORM TO HARMONIZE RELATIONS BETWEEN
NATIONALITIES. THE FORMULA FOR THE DEVELOPMENT OF THE SOVIET
FEDERATION -- STRONG CENTRE, STRONG REPUBLICS -- HAS MET WITH
GENERAL SUPPORT THROUGHOUT THE COUNTRY.
      IN COMPREHENSIVELY DEMOCRATIZING OUR POLITICAL SYSTEM, WE ACT
ON THE ASSUMPTION THAT THIS ALSO IMPLIES GREATER RESPONSIBILITY
OF ALL MEMBERS OF SOCIETY FOR ITS HEALTHY DEVELOPMENT AND SOCIAL
AND POLITICAL STABILITY. A NORMAL PROCESS OF CHANGE IS
INCONCEIVABLE WITHOUT THAT. THIS IS WHY WE ATTACH GREAT
IMPORTANCE TO THE STRENGTHENING OF LAW AND LEGAL ORDER AND TO THE
CREATION OF ALL OTHER CONDITIONS FOR BUILDING A SOCIALIST STATE
BASED ON THE RULE OF LAW.
      IT WOULD GO AGAINST THE TRUTH IF I SAID THAT ALL THOSE CHANGES
PROCEED SMOOTHLY AND WITHOUT COMPLICATIONS.
      MORE

TASS-05-17 1401EDT

10/06 '01 SUN 15:59 FAX

M0412

```
YY 34491   E270001  05-17  0306
34491,  ,  E270001,  34491
```

.GORBACHEV SPEECH TO CHINESE PUBLIC =17.
17/5 TASS G-1

WHAT NATURALLY FOLLOWS FROM THOSE SELF-EVIDENT PROPOSITIONS IS
ONE GENERAL CONCLUSION -- NAMELY, THAT IN THE MODERN
INTER-DEPENDENT WORLD ISOLATED DEVELOPMENT IN A SELF RESTRICTED
NATIONAL ENVIRONMENT IS NO LONGER POSSIBLE. THE SURVIVAL OF THE
HUMAN RACE AND THE PROGRESS OF THE CIVILIZATION IT HAS CREATED
CAN ONLY BE ACHIEVED THROUGH JOINT CONSTRUCTIVE EFFORTS OF ALL
COUNTRIES AND PEOPLES.

ONE MAY WONDER HOW THIS PROPOSITION CAN BE COMBINED WITH
ANOTHER CURRENTLY POWERFUL SOCIAL TREND, NAMELY: THE ASSERTION BY
INDIVIDUAL NATIONS OF NATIONAL SELF-CONSCIOUSNESS, OF THEIR
UNCONDITIONAL RIGHT TO CHOOSE FREELY THEIR OWN ROAD.

THE WORLD IS GETTING INTEGRATED, BECOMING, FIGURATIVELY
SPEAKING, +MORE TIGHTLY KNIT+; AND AT THE SAME TIME IT IS GETTING
MORE DIVERSE, EXPANDING SO TO SPEAK. HEREIN LIES ONE OF THE REAL
CONTRADICTIONS OF OUR TIME, WHICH CANNOT BE IGNORED. WE WOULD BE
RUNNING A GRAVE RISK IF WE TRIED TO REMOVE THAT CONTRADICTION
THROUGH THE USE OF FORCE, BY IMPOSING UPON THE PEOPLES SOME
SOCIAL SYSTEM, OR BY FORCING ON THEM THE RULES OF CONDUCT DEVISED
BY SOME HIGH COUNCIL OF GREAT POWERS.

OUR TIME'S GORDIAN KNOTS CANNOT BE CUT. THEY OUGHT TO BE
PRUDENTLY UNTIED.

IN THE CONTEMPORARY MULTIDIMENSIONAL WORLD, IT IS ONLY THROUGH
A BALANCE OF INTERESTS AND EQUITABLE PARTNERSHIP THAT REAL
CONTRADICTIONS CAN BE RESOLVED. NEVER BEFORE HAVE POLITICIANS AND
DIPLOMATS BEEN CONFRONTED WITH SUCH DAUNTING TASKS. AT STAKE ARE
THE INTERESTS OF MORE THAN 150 STATES THAT FIND THEMSELVES AT
DIFFERENT RUNGS OF DEVELOPMENT IN THE +LADDER+ OF WORLD HISTORY.

MORE

TASS-05-17 1434EDT<

10/06 '01 SUN 16:08 FAX

.GORBACHEV SPEECH TO CHINESE PUBLIC =21.
17/5 TASS G-1

THREE MONTHS HAVE ALREADY PASSED SINCE THE SOVIET UNION
WITHDREW ITS TROOPS FROM AFGHANISTAN. YET THE SITUATION IN THAT
COUNTRY IS BECOMING EVER MORE THREATENING.THE ATTEMPTS OF THE
PAKISTANI MILITARY TO LAUNCH WHAT IS IN EFFECT AN OPEN AGGRESSION
AGAINST A NEIGHBOURING COUNTRY CAN ONLY BE DESCRIBED AS
IRRATIONAL.

WE BELIEVE THAT THE TIME HAS COME FOR THE WORLD COMMUNITY TO
TAKE A MORE VIGOROUS STAND WITH RESPECT TO THIS CONFLICT WHICH
THREATENS TO SPREAD FIRE TO THE NEIGHBOURING REGIONS. WHATEVER
ONE SAYS OF THE PRESENT REGIME IN AFGHANISTAN, IT IS CLEARLY UP
TO THE AFGHAN PARTIES TO THE CONFLICT TO WORK THINGS OUT BETWEEN
THEMSELVES. AFGHANISTAN'S FUTURE MUST BE DECIDED SOLELY BY THE
AFGHAN PEOPLE.

FOR A DECADE NOW THE SITUATION AROUND KAMPUCHEA HAS BEEN ONE
OF THE SORE SPOTS OF THE ASIAN CONTINENT SEMICOLON IT IS A
WELCOME DEVELOPMENT THAT +LIGHT AT THE END OF THE TUNNEL+ IS NOW
VISIBLE THERE.

IT WOULD, OF COURSE, BE INAPPROPRIATE TO RUN AHEAD OF THE
EVENTS. KAMPUCHEAN SETTLEMENT WILL REQUIRE STILL MORE STRENUOUS
POLITICAL AND DIPLOMATIC EFFORTS. BUT FOLLOWING THE COMPLETE
WITHDRAWAL NEXT SEPTEMBER OF THE VIETNAMESE TROOPS, A
QUALITATIVELY NEW SITUATION WILL EMERGE AND PRACTICAL
PREREQUISITES WILL BE IN PLACE FOR THIS OLD CONFLICT FINALLY TO
BE SETTLED.

WE DISCUSSED THESE ISSUES WITH KAMPUCHEAN AND VIETNAMESE
COMRADES AND, YESTERDAY, WITH THE LEADERS OF YOUR COUNTRY. OUR
IMPRESSION IS THAT KAMPUCHEAN SETTLEMENT IS GRADUALLY TAKING ON A
REALISTIC SHAPE.

AS TO THE MAIN PRINCIPLE ON WHICH IT CAN AND MUST BE BASED, IT
IS THE SAME PRINCIPLE OF NATIONAL SELF-DETERMINATION, WHICH IS
THE ONLY CORRECT ONE. ONLY THE KAMPUCHEANS AND NO ONE ELSE CAN
FIND THE FORMULA OF AGREEMENT AND OF THE FUTURE POLITICAL
STRUCTURE OF THEIR COUNTRY.

MORE

19

The Beckoning Abyss

TUESDAY, MAY 16, 1989
DENG XIAOPING'S COMPOUND

The demonstrations were now in their thirty-second day. Even here, five miles to the north of Tiananmen Square, and despite the immediate area around the compound being an exclusion zone patrolled by Deng Xiaoping's elite guards, what was happening throughout Beijing continued to dominate the discussion going on into the night in Deng's office.

The large, airy room was richly furnished with priceless artifacts from the Forbidden City. On one wall hung a piece of calligraphy commemorating China's twenty-seven-hundred-year-old imperial system, still the longest enduring of all political systems. Beside it hung a quotation from Mao stating that Communism would survive even longer.

With Deng Xiaoping were the handful of men he now most trusted to bring an end to a truly disastrous situation.

Li Peng was there, cold and aloof as always, his fish-eye stare showing nothing of the fury he must have felt at being a prime target of the students' anger.

With him sat Security Chief Qiao Shi, baggy-suited, another pair of chain store socks on his cheaply shod feet. He drew on an eight-inch Cuban cigar, the aroma mingling with the acrid smell of the Panda cigarettes Deng chain-smoked.

Li Xiaming, Party Secretary of Beijing and political commissar of the city's garrison, a key player in any military action against the students, sat, as always, squat and muscled, thick neck chafing against his shirt collar, face suffused with blood. It made his renowned lack of grace and humor more marked, his temper more evident.

State President Yang Shangkun sat beside Deng. If the eighty-two-year-old felt any irritation at being kept from his bed, he did not show it. Like Deng, he wore a dark gray high-buttoning jacket.

Present too was Vice-Premier Yao Yilin. He would soon be seventy-three. But the passing years had not diminished his liking for confrontation. His rough tongue concealed a formidable intellect.

They first dealt with the schedule for the remainder of Gorbachev's visit.

There would be no tour of the Forbidden City, no ceremonial drive along Changan Avenue, no opportunity for Gorbachev to pay homage at Mao's mausoleum. He and Raisa were to be kept virtually incommunicado in the State Guest House in between formal contacts with the leadership. The Soviet leader's meeting with Zhao Ziyang in Zhongnanhai later in the day could proceed, because the route to the compound would avoid the midtown area.

The only time the Gorbachevs would once more come physically close to the students would be during the formal climax to their visit the following day. They were then scheduled to meet Deng himself in the Great Hall of the People in Tiananmen Square.

State President Yang had been driven straight from there after the banquet to report Gorbachev's remarks. According to one European intelligence source, Deng had listened enigmatically, then dismissed Gorbachev's intervention as coming from someone poorly briefed.

By now every foreign intelligence service with officers in Beijing had focused its attention upon Deng Xiaoping's compound. So had many of the foreign journalists.

Nicholas Kristof of the *New York Times* learned that the cabal's anger was not so much directed against Gorbachev as some meddling outsider, but against Zhao. They reportedly warned Deng that the Party Secretary was using the demonstrators *"as pawns"* to further his own ambition.

Melinda Liu's contacts conjured up a scene of the old men grouped around Deng, wan-faced from lack of sleep, demanding he should sack Zhao. Deng had sat impassively, smoking another of his high-tar Panda cigarettes, saying nothing.

Yao Yilin wondered whether Zhao should be asked to produce details of the speech he would deliver to Gorbachev and whether he should be permitted to go ahead with his plan to have it televised. The vice-premier growled, *"We have heard enough of his words lately."*

Deng said he saw no need for Zhao to clear his speech or for his remarks not to be televised. Everyone understood the unspoken portent of the decision. Zhao was being given sufficient rope to hang himself.

SAME DAY, LATER
TIANANMEN SQUARE

From a phone box on the square, Sue Tung had several times tried to telephone Captain Instructor Jyan at the PLA academy without success. Each time the operator said he was not available. Some instinct stopped Sue from visiting his home. Jyan's mother, she suspected, would ask difficult questions as to why she was here. And what would she say if Sue told her she had handed over an unheard-of sum for a Chinese, the $10,000 she had collected in Sacramento, to the student leaders? With her strong Party loyalty, Jyan's mother would regard such support as an act of rank subversion.

Sue still couldn't get over how casually the money had been accepted. When she had asked for a receipt, Daobao had scribbled one on a scrap of paper. She had asked how the money would be used and Yang Li had given her a half-smile, adding it would be spent on *"whatever we need."*

She had found the student leaders friendly but a little distant. She had a feeling that while they welcomed the constant foreign media attention, they were not that interested in having overseas Chinese share in what they were doing. Several Chinese from Hong Kong who had volunteered to join the hunger strikers had been brusquely told there was no place for them.

Sue could see two of the student leaders on the steps of the Great Hall of the People. They were arguing with several young men who did not look like students.

She hurried to see what was happening. She had been struck by the orderliness of the demonstrations. She had not heard or seen a single expression of violence. That made the arguments on the steps that much more surprising and alarming. She was close enough to hear the increasingly angry exchanges between the young men and Yang Li and Daobao.

"*Stand back!*" the men were shouting at the two students. "*We're going to destroy this place!*"

"*No!*" Daobao yelled. "*This is a peaceful demonstration!*"

"*Who are you?*" Yang Li demanded.

"*Your supporters,*" yelled one of the men.

"*You're not students,*" Daobao said. "*We don't need your support.*"

"*Stand back!*" yelled the men, beginning to shove the two students aside.

Daobao shouted for help. Sue turned and repeated the cry. Passing students ran to form a line to stop the men.

When she had last walked past the building, Sue had seen several dozen policemen on duty. Now they had all disappeared. She sensed something sinister was going on.

On the steps Daobao was still shouting for help.

"*We have agents provocateurs here! They are trying to destroy all we have achieved! Come and stop them!*"

Suddenly hundreds of students were running to help. Leading them was Chai Ling. Beside her was a student carrying an electric bullhorn.

But now more rough-voiced men were pushing their way toward the steps. They too were shouting they were there to support the students and wanted to storm the building.

Confused and frightened by what was happening, onlookers began to mill around nervously.

Sue realized that if fighting broke out people could be trampled to death. Already the first scuffles had started between the students and the men driving them back up the steps. Some of the men had produced hammers and other weapons from under their jackets. Sue knew then this was a well-planned provocation to provide an excuse for the security forces to take over the square. Furious at what was happening, she began to shove her way to join Daobao and Yang Li on the steps.

Over the bullhorn came Chai Ling's voice.

"*Citizens! These people have nothing to do with us! They have been sent by the government to cause trouble! Help us stop them! But do not harm them. Only take them from here!*"

Hundreds of people began to escort the men from the square. In moments the last of the twenty or so troublemakers had been removed.

Chai Ling walked slowly back to rejoin the hunger strikers. As she passed, Sue heard her say to Daobao: *"They will try again, but it means we are winning."*

Dr. Jenny Guangzu watched Chai Ling take her place on the quilted coats and blankets that had been given by the public to form a gigantic bedroll. She felt *"a growing love for all the hunger strikers. They were the very symbol of what was going on."*

In the time she had spent on the square she had seen much that made her uneasy, especially the bickering between the student leaders Wuerkaixi and Wang Dan. The pair seemed able to agree on precious little. Wuerkaixi was clearly intent on becoming still more militant; Wang Dan was for a more cautious approach.

The young surgeon was struck by not only their markedly different physical appearances, but also their mental states. In his now-celebrated denims, Wuerkaixi was a hyperactive showman; Wang Dan's face was increasingly drawn, his clothes were stiff with dried perspiration. His eyes still burned bright, but to Jenny he looked like a man burning up his physical reserves.

A short while ago she had heard them arguing again at the foot of the Monument to the People's Heroes. Wuerkaixi had pointed to the crowds.

"Look! Now we must push even harder, because everyone's behind us," he told Wang Dan.

It seemed true. The thousands of banners already on display had been joined by those brought by workers from many of the state-run corporations: iron and steel foundries, auto manufacturers, breweries. Among them marched hotel bellboys and Mao-suited cadres from a ministry. Even the national volleyball team was there, marching between shaven-headed Buddhist monks and students from one of the country's few Christian seminaries. They had finally set up camp under the banner CHINESE CHRISTIANS FOR DEMOCRACY.

But still Wang Dan had urged caution. He said he would only be convinced that the country was indeed fully behind them if the People's Liberation Army sent even a token force of troops to march in the square.

Wuerkaixi had shrugged and walked away to rejoin the hunger strikers.

After only a few hours of lying among them, Wuerkaixi returned to his position on the monument to hold yet another of his *"strategy meetings."*

A short time later Jenny had seen him go to one of the cars parked behind the monument. Her father had later told her he had seen Wuerkaixi wolf down a bowl of noodles. The student had then returned to the monument to urge the hunger strikers again to continue their fast.

As they walked among the hunger strikers, her father now told her they were reaching the critical stage.

"After four days we can expect to see the first serious signs of physical and mental collapse. It is important to keep noise around them to a minimum," Professor Guangzu explained.

Each time they stopped to check a striker's vital signs, he asked how long the student intended to continue. Each time he was given the same response:

"Until our demands are met." Some of the students had swollen faces covered in perspiration, signs of the stress they were experiencing.

By now doctors from almost every hospital in the city were tending them. Professor Guangzu took several of his colleagues aside.

"Those we send to hospital must not be allowed to return," he said. *"And no more must be allowed to start fasting. They have made their point."*

Together with Jenny, Professor Guangzu walked over to the Monument to the People's Heroes and told Wuerkaixi of the medical decision.

"He was quite upset," Jenny was to remember. *"He kept saying how important it was to continue the strike."*

Her father then quietly told Wuerkaixi that if he felt so committed to striking to the death, he should set an example. For a moment they stared at each other. Then Wuerkaixi turned away. A short while later he broadcast an announcement that no more people would be allowed to go on hunger strike, and those sent to the hospital would not be allowed to resume their protest.

Jeanne Moore, Melinda Liu, Dan Rather, and the hundreds of other foreign reporters in the square converged on the strikers.

"Some of the students seem to have lost their reason," Jeanne noted. *"They are no longer lucid. When they try to stand up, they collapse. They lie on the ground side by side, like mummies. When the doctors try to persuade them to quit, they simply shake their heads and say they must continue."*

Melinda noted that everything — the scorching sun, the noise, the polluted air — seemed to have an effect on the strikers. The weaker they became, the greater the anger of those watching them.

"People were saying, the government must stop this now by giving in to the demands. The more onlookers said this, the more determined were the strikers to continue. They were feeding off the anger their condition was generating. If one of the strikers was to die, God knows what would happen. The crowd could become sufficiently enraged to literally trample down the walls of Zhongnanhai. The hunger strike was the most potent weapon the students had. And some of them wanted to die."

Irritated at being confined to the CBS remote unit in a corner of the square, Dan Rather had insisted he should be allowed to do some reporting, though the network had several correspondents on hand to do just that. In the time he had been in the square, Rather had quickly established contacts with the students and, like any other journalist, wanted to exploit these professionally to the full. Now, standing in front of the prostrate hunger strikers, Rather delivered another live broadcast to the United States, describing the courage of young people prepared to die for their country.

A growing number were refusing water and had sealed their mouths with adhesive tape over which they wore smog-masks. Others had stuffed cloth in their mouths. Some had even tied their own hands to avoid any temptation to reach for a drink.

Melinda felt *"a lump in my throat at the sight of such determination and courage."*

Turning away, she glimpsed a solitary figure striding to the platform high on Tiananmen Gate. Though she could not see his face clearly, there was no mistaking that well-cut blue suit. She had seen Zhao Ziyang wear it before. The Party Secretary continued to watch the scene through his binoculars. He struck Melinda as *"an actor waiting in the wings ready to make his entrance."*

Then, as she watched, he lowered his binoculars, turned, and left the platform.

SAME DAY, LATER
THE WHITE HOUSE

Dan Rather's report on the hunger strikers led the CBS evening news on the monitor in the Oval Office. President Bush paused in a meeting about Panama to watch the scene from Tiananmen Square. Then, without comment, he continued discussing how best to remove General Noriega from office.

SAME DAY, LATER
FOREIGN LEGATION QUARTER

In British Ambassador Sir Alan Donald's view, the situation was *"chaos. The government is increasingly having to rearrange its plans for the Gorbachev visit to avoid interruption by the students. The loss of face is considerable. Almost certainly there will have to be a reckoning after the Russians have left. But how far that will go is anyone's guess right now."*

Ambassador Donald was not a diplomat easily surprised by a turn of events. But the televised broadcast he had watched in his office had left him *"just about speechless."* Zhao Ziyang had used his meeting with Gorbachev as an opportunity, in the words of Nicholas Kristof of the *New York Times,* *"to lunge for power."* While Donald would never have stated it so colorfully, he admitted to his staff gathered in his office that Zhao's speech was *"something of a shaker."*

Brian Davidson would remember the ambassador saying that Zhao was clearly blaming Deng for the student unrest. Donald's interpretation was based on his deep understanding of the subtleties of what he sometimes called *"leadership-speak."* In that language, Deng was often *"the helmsman,"* the man at the tail end of China's *"ship of state."*

Zhao's speech had contained a number of flattering references to Deng as *"the helmsman"* and the reminder that *"on important questions we still need him as the helmsman."* Davidson would recall his ambassador explanation: In leadership-speak, Zhao was saying that while he would be quite prepared to meet the students' demands, Deng, as *"the helmsman,"* was against further reform, let alone democracy. The Party Secretary had made a calculated attack on Deng's position and had added insult by choosing to do so in the presence of Gorbachev.

In Donald's view the *"storm cones were being hoisted over Zhongnanhai."*

Zhao's speech had produced similar responses from other diplomats. France's ambassador, Charles Malo, felt it was only a matter of time before Zhao was sacked, as did Canada's ambassador, Earl Drake. Lindsay Watt, New Zealand's ambassador, saw the speech as *"a real cliff-hanger. Everyone was hungering to see what the response would be."*

Diplomatic legmen like Brian Davidson and Brendan Ward were soon reporting the reaction of the students to Zhao's speech. New posters were hurriedly produced attacking *"the helmsman who has lost the way."*

SAME DAY, LATER
DENG XIAOPING'S COMPOUND

At nine o'clock in the evening, a convoy of limousines entered the compound bringing Deng's cabal to meet with him again. *Newsweek's* Melinda Liu's sources would describe how Deng sat *"hunched and hooded-eyed in his armchair, chain-smoking, ignoring everyone."* The others sat tense and watchful.

At nine-thirty, Zhao's car arrived. The Party Secretary wore another of his distinctive suits, a midnight blue two-piece.

As they had on everyone else, weeks of what Deng was repeatedly calling *"chaos under Heaven"* had left their marks on Zhao. His usual self-assurance had gone. In its place was a strained, haunted look. His eyes were red-rimmed behind his tinted glasses. He looked less like a man perfectly cast as a wise adviser, more like someone who knew he had fallen forever from Deng's favor. Now, at best all he could look forward to was spending his remaining years indulging his hobby of watching old war movies on his video player and reading Bismarck at bedtime.

He was shown into Deng's presence. As soon as the formal greetings were over, Deng launched a vituperative attack on Zhao for making such a speech before Gorbachev.

Deng's rage made the Party Secretary blanch. It was the moment of supreme confrontation. Twice Zhao attempted to halt the tirade; he was ordered to remain silent. The dressing down continued for over an hour. Then Li Peng took over. He coldly reviewed the effect so far of *"hooliganism"* on a scale the nation had not seen since the Cultural Revolution.

Next Qiao Shi presented a detailed explanation of the threat to national security the students were increasingly presenting. He added there were *"clear indications of outside influences at work."* The old bogeymen, *"Imperialist spies,"* were on the rampage.

When the intelligence chief had finished, Deng barked a question to Zhao. What did he have to say?

The Party Secretary argued his well-known position: Without further reforms there could be no real conciliation with the students. While Deng's economic policies had invigorated China as never before, these same policies had also produced an unprecedented inflation of 30 percent. The only way to reduce it was by still more reforms.

Zhao was in full flow, arguing that the students were not hell-bent on destroying China or the Party but only giving voice to all those caught in the vise-like squeeze between prosperity and inflation, when Deng interrupted.

He rasped he would not listen any longer to such talk. There would be a vote, here and now, on one issue. The time had come to end the demonstrations. In the affirmative show of hands, Zhao's was the only abstention.

For almost fifty years Deng and Zhao had been close friends and political allies. They had come through purgings and banishment. They had helped guide China through wars. They had together once set the country on a brave new course. People spoke of them in one breath, adding that Deng, deep in his heart, wanted Zhao to succeed him. Now the unthinkable had happened. The rift between them was irreversible from that moment Zhao had refused to raise his hand in silent obedience to his master's wishes.

The Party Secretary stood up and faced Deng.

"I am sorry to see that my way of thinking is not in accord with your way of thinking," he told Deng.

For a moment longer the two men stared at each other. Then, according to one of the officials present, Deng turned away and looked at Li Peng. The prime minister could not quite hide the satisfaction crossing his face.

Zhao Ziyang walked from the room. Deng Xiaoping had begun to tell the others he had decided to introduce martial law and call in the army to reestablish order.

FRIDAY, MAY 19, 1989
CHINA DAILY COMPOUND

By the thirty-fifth day of the demonstration, Jeanne Moore's chronicle of events filled several notebooks. She carried them everywhere with her, a reminder of their importance. They contained a balanced view of not only what others were reporting, often with increasing hyperbole, but also insights that came from her unique position as one of the few non-Chinese journalists working in the state-run media.

Time and again this past week high-level Party contacts she was sure would not have spoken to Chinese journalists had briefed her on what was happening behind the scenes. She believed it was *"because they felt more comfortable and able to trust a foreigner."*

Much of what they had told her, she knew, was too sensitive to be published in *China Daily* or any other Party organ, despite the fact that both her own newspaper and the *People's Daily* had finally begun to report the student protests.

Jeanne herself had helped write several sympathetic editorials about the demands that had caused widespread comment and brought praise from the students. She had smilingly accepted their accolades as she continued to observe how the hunger strikers were fainting or suffering hallucinatory fits after a week of not eating. Over six hundred had been taken away in the past twenty-four hours. In the most recent story she had described how those who remained on the square now *"lie completely still, each with a rose on his neck. They look like the living dead, a pose which subdues the most cynical of foreign journalists. There is a dignity here that cannot be equated with anything elsewhere in living memory. That dignity is summed up by a huge tableau erected over the scene. It shows two naked, writhing figures. Between them are the words 'Save the people.'"*

That kind of reporting had finally found its way into *China Daily* and the American newspaper she also wrote for. So had her careful listing of still more support from all sections of Chinese society, engineers, technicians, and schoolchildren by the thousands. The numbers in the square now never dropped below a million, sometimes it seemed close to two. Though it hardly seemed possible, the thousands of posters had become more provocative, mocking everything the Party and leadership stood for.

The previous day she had seen the unthinkable. A platoon of off-duty, crew-cut PLA soldiers had marched along Changan Avenue into Tiananmen Square behind a banner bearing the legend THE ARMY LOVES THE PEOPLE.

They had been welcomed by thunderous cheers. Even Wang Dan had felt compelled to seize a microphone and ask joyfully, *"With the army on our side, how can we fail?"*

Wuerkaixi, his pretense at being a hunger striker over, had told Jeanne that *"victory is close. Look, there isn't a policeman in sight! We are controlling the crowds, the traffic, everything. We are the government because the other government is invisible!"*

In one sense that was true. In the five weeks since they had first marched to the square, the students had remained a disciplined force.

The key was a deeply ingrained obedience to all orders of their leaders.

"They eat to order, they rest to order, they cheer and wave banners to order," Cassy noted. *"It is the only way that a million people can be marshaled and controlled, by obeying orders."*

Fresh food arrived twice a day and was paid for out of the huge hoard of Chinese and foreign currency kept under constant guard on the Monument to the People's Heroes. Refuse was stacked in great piles for city workers to remove. There were over thirty first-aid posts to deal with minor injuries.

The only problem was the lack of toilet facilities. No matter how many trenches were dug, they quickly filled. The perimeter around the square had become a stinking cesspool, as Dan Rather discovered. He had just completed another report when one of the CBS technicians asked to go to the toilet. *"I took him to that latrine,"* Rather would recall. *"You have to imagine the scene. It was a huge tent, and inside the Chinese had dug slit trenches as far as the eye could see. Well, when he got inside, the combination of the tremendous smell and the shock of the scene, people squatting along trenches, and he just derricked, absolutely derricked."*

Yet despite the terrible stench that drifted like a pall over the square, the mood was upbeat. People came and went, bringing news from other parts of the city and carrying news from the square. This bush telegraph proved surprisingly effective in drawing still more people to Tiananmen.

Jeanne Moore confided to her notebook that the mood was so contagious she would almost have believed victory was indeed possible. Some of her colleagues were reporting rumors that Deng Xiaoping had resigned, that Li Peng had been deposed, that Zhao Ziyang was about to form a new government.

It was that last rumor, swept across Tiananmen Square with Thursday's drizzle, that made Jeanne realize *"how far reality was being sacrificed on the altar of blind hope."* For she knew what had happened to the Party Secretary after he walked out of Deng Xiaoping's office.

As the bemused Gorbachevs were packing their bags in the State Guest House after what the Soviet leader had told one of his hosts (who had passed on the words to Jeanne) was *"the most extraordinary three days of my life,"* Zhao had been driven slowly around Tiananmen Square in his limousine, peering through the car's dark-tinted windows. Another of Jeanne's contacts had told her *"Zhao had wanted to see how big the crowd was, how many he could count on."*

Yet the Party Secretary's career was effectively over. The morning after he walked out of Deng's office, Zhao announced he was going on *"sick leave"* and would no longer participate in *"any Party business."* It had been a move to win over public support, which had not been forthcoming.

Now this Friday morning he was about to make a last desperate bid to elicit support from the people.

Shortly after 5:00 A.M., accompanied by a few trusted aides, Zhao was driven out of Zhongnanhai and brought to the square.

Jeanne Moore was astonished by Zhao's appearance when he stepped out of the car. Whenever she had seen him before, he had epitomized sartorial elegance. Now he was dressed in a baggy suit, crushed shirt, and badly knotted tie. His face was gaunt, his eyes puffed and red-rimmed. He walked *"like a man who is beaten."* His voice echoed the sense of defeat in his appearance.

Daobao handed him a red bullhorn and explained how to work it. After a couple of tries, Zhao managed to get the hang of using the device.

"I have come here to say a few words to you students," he began. Jeanne noted Zhao was close to tears, weak-voiced.

"We have come too late. I am sorry. No matter how you have criticized us, I think you have the right to do so. I am now here to ask for your forgiveness."

Zhao paused and stared at one of the buses the students had commandeered for a makeshift field hospital for some of the hunger strikers. With a visible effort he resumed.

"I just want to say that your bodies are now very weak. Your hunger strike is now in the seventh day. You cannot go on like this. We were once young too, and we all had such a burst of energy. We also staged demonstrations and I remember the situation then. We also did not think of the consequences."

Tears welling in his eyes, the broken Party Secretary climbed into the bus and moved among the semiconscious hunger strikers, peering at them wonderingly.

Then in complete silence he left the square. Jeanne thought *"any hope the students had that this was the man about to form a new government must have gone."*

She watched Zhao's car head back to Zhongnanhai. It would be the last time he would be seen in public.

Walking through the square, Jeanne sensed a sudden feeling of unease. If Zhao was no longer there to support them, the students had no one.

Wang Dan was among those who suggested they should consider ordering a mass evacuation of the square. They had done more than anyone could have thought possible. To leave now would not be seen as a defeat. Wuerkaixi rounded on his fellow leaders. That would destroy everything they had planned. He, for one, would stay to the very end. Wuerkaixi again carried the day.

But only hours later, the quixotic Wuerkaixi once more changed his mind, after a Party broadcast early in the afternoon spoke of the leadership *"having to consider adopting strong measures such as military control."*

Wuerkaixi promptly called another *"strategy meeting"* in the *"command bus"* he now used as a headquarters. Parked behind the Monument to the People's Heroes, it enabled student leaders to eat their meals out of sight of the hunger strikers.

Thirty-six days of running the protest movement had led to polarization within the student leadership.

Wuerkaixi remained certainly the most colorful figure, even if that all-knowing smile had become a little fixed from a thousand television interviews. But his physical stamina was awesome. He radiated energy. His natural ally remained Chai Ling. In her hip-hugging jeans and canvas shoes, she flitted around the square, repeatedly telling people, *"Here we stay and are ready to die so that democracy will live."* No one could doubt she meant it. Daobao, Yang Li, and Liu Gang remained key members of Wuerkaixi's entourage. All three bore signs of strain. Liu Gang had taken to biting his lip nervously; Yang Li had become almost morose. Daobao hid his own exhaustion by working relentlessly to keep up student morale.

Wang Dan continued to be the face of student moderation. He had gathered to him a small coterie of like-minded student leaders. While they did not openly challenge Wuerkaixi, knowing that would fatally wound the movement, they quietly urged that perhaps, after all, the time had come to leave Tiananmen.

Now Wuerkaixi agreed that the students should withdraw, because he had *"just learned there is bloody suppression coming."* He did not say who had told him. It would remain one of his many secrets.

Debate broke out among the group. Some wanted the hunger strike to end but for everyone to remain in the square. Others wanted the strike to continue and for a nationwide appeal to be made to support it. Daobao envisaged *"several million more people"* coming to Beijing to do so. That idea was knocked down by Wang Dan. He thought the most sensible thing would be to keep a *"reasonable number"* of protesters in the square, all from Beijing, and send everyone else back to work. Yang Li was among those who disagreed, saying, *"We have come too far to turn back."*

Then, as if in response to Daobao's suggestion, thousands of workers began to arrive from all over the city. They came by bus and truck, drawn like everyone else simply by a wish to show solidarity with the students. They announced they had formed the country's first Party-free trade union, the Autonomous Union. Its first act would be to organize a nationwide strike of all workers unless the students' demands were met unconditionally by midnight this coming Saturday.

Once again Wuerkaixi changed his mind. Such a strike, he enthused, was bound to tip the balance. Everyone should stay on Tiananmen.

That evening Mikhail and Raisa Gorbachev left Beijing the way they had come, by the back door, driven to the airport at high speed through the back streets. Their state visit had been a fiasco, reduced to a few column inches in the official print media and given only perfunctory treatment on TV and radio. It had achieved almost nothing.

SAME DAY, LATER
TIANANMEN SQUARE

The more than one million people crowded into Tiananmen Square paused as the loudspeakers once again came alive shortly after midnight. Moments later the high-pitched voice of Prime Minister Li Peng echoed in the dank night air.

"This state of anarchy can no longer be tolerated. Law and discipline are being undermined. A handful of people are using the hunger strikers as hostages to coerce and force the Party and the government to yield to their political demands. They have not an iota of humanity."

Students crowded around the CBS monitors receiving pictures of the prime minister addressing the Politburo Standing Committee and rows of military officers. At the back of their ranks among other junior officers sat Captain Instructor Jyan.

The broadcast came from the PLA's General Logistics Department, a walled compound in the western suburbs. Jyan believed the venue had been deliberately selected by the prime minister. Li Peng wanted to show that the army totally supported the action he was now about to outline.

"The intention was plain. Scare the hell out of everyone who was listening or watching," Melinda Liu recalled.

Certainly the television images appeared as intimidating as Li Peng's words. He was dressed in a funeral black Mao suit. Each time he squeaked out a sentence he would pause and raise his fist in the air, forefinger slightly extended as if he were about to pull a trigger. It was crude but compelling theater.

Its effect on the crowd was immediate. All day their tension had built, fueled by rumor: The PLA would parachute into the square. Thousands of troops had already arrived in the Great Hall of the People, brought there by the underground railway from Zhongnanhai. Thousands more were waiting in the nuclear bunkers beneath the city.

Some of the speculation was true. Units were positioned in the bunkers and had been brought underground to the Great Hall of the People. While no one had actually seen the troops, the protesters had convinced each other they must be there. Now the prime minister was suddenly giving substance to the rumors. People looked scared. Some began to leave the square even as Li Peng was speaking.

"The life and future of the People's Republic of China, built by many revolutionary martyrs with their blood, faces a serious threat."

Cassy, standing by the CBS unit, felt *"it was like listening to someone saying the end of the world was coming. It was little comfort to see how calmly the TV crew received the news. They could just pack up and move on to the next story. But for Daobao and the others, it was different. I understood what they meant when they said this is their struggle, theirs and no one else's."*

Cassy had made several appeals for Daobao to leave and go to his family in the country. She had even offered to go with him. Daobao had brushed aside the idea, quietly telling her his place was here. She had both loved him and admired his courage more than ever. Listening to Li Peng, she understood her Daobao was a true revolutionary martyr.

The prime minister was saying something that brought another great murmur of apprehension from the crowd.

" … *the Communist Party of China, as the ruling party, and the government responsible to the people, are now forced to take resolute and decisive measures to put an end to turmoil.*"

Barr Seitz felt the ABC camera teams *"stiffen in anticipation"* when the words were translated.

"Some real action at last," said one.

For the past few days there had been little to film. One of the ABC producers had told Barr that *"when you've shot one hunger striker about to pop off, that's pretty well it."*

The attitude was a reflection of one held by executives at the headquarters of both ABC and NBC in New York. ABC Senior Vice-President Rick Wald had vetoed the idea of sending Peter Jennings to anchor the evening news out of Beijing, because Dan Rather was dominating the coverage. A similar attitude prevailed at NBC. Both networks would make do with correspondents.

On a monitor Barr watched the panning shot and called out the identities of those on the platform with Li Peng: Vice-Premiers Yao Yilin and Qiao Shi; Hu Qili, in charge of propaganda; Vice-President Wang Zhen. Beside him sat the state president himself, Yang Shangkun.

The ABC correspondent Barr was working with wrote down the names.

"Hard to believe old men like these have any real power," said the reporter.

"They don't," replied Barr. *"They're just mouthpieces for Deng. That's why he doesn't have to show up. He's already written the script. They just have to follow it."*

"Sounds like a good producer," the reporter said, grinning.

The previous afternoon, in a belated attempt to defuse the situation, Li Peng had finally received Wuerkaixi and Wang Dan in one of the salons of The Great Hall. The prime minister had been coldly condescending, but the students were in no mood to be patronized. Wuerkaixi had wagged his finger at Li Peng and repeatedly interrupted. Li Peng had fought down his anger, even giving a sickly smile when Wang Dan compared the Party with the regime in South Africa. The *"dialogue"* the students had sought had ended in ill-tempered belligerence on their part and total humiliation for Li Peng. Now the prime minister visibly enjoyed his role as the man chosen to herald Deng's decision.

Li Peng's place on screen was taken by the state president. Yang Shangkun's voice, trembling with anger, boomed around the square.

"To restore normal order and to stabilize the situation, there is no choice but to move a contingent of the People's Liberation Army to the vicinity of the city."

A great roar of protest swept the square.

Sue Tung was standing near the Great Hall. Until then she had been *"a little frightened. But now I knew what was going to happen. I felt very calm. I was certain the troops would harm no one."* Over the loudspeakers the state president continued.

"If this state of affairs is allowed to continue, then our capital will not be a capital."

Jenny Guangzu and her father had momentarily slipped away from tending the hunger strikers to watch a CNN monitor. On the screen the uniformed generals were clapping loudly and nodding to each other. Jenny's son slept peacefully in her arms.

"Jenny," began Professor Guangzu. *"What about Peter? Perhaps you should leave?"*

Jenny shook her head. *"My place is here. They won't harm children. As long as we do nothing foolish the soldiers won't harm anyone."*

A couple of hours earlier she had seen how tense matters had become. She had been passing the Monument to the People's Heroes, bringing fresh water to the hunger strikers, when she had been astonished to see Chai Ling and her husband fighting over a microphone. They both wanted to address the crowd; both were *"almost crazed with exhaustion."* Other student leaders had separated the pair, and Chai Ling had been led away, weeping bitterly. Jenny had told her father; he had shaken his head.

"The hunger strike is turning children into monsters," Professor Guangzu said. *"The sooner they stop the better."*

Watching the monitor, Jenny hoped that the soldiers would somehow be able to persuade the strikers to give up their protest. On the screen the state president continued to speak.

"What's happening is because we have no other choice. But I would like to say that the arrival of the troops is definitely not aimed at dealing with the students."

Sue Tung turned to the person beside her. *"What does he mean?"*

In one form or another the question was being asked by countless others in Tiananmen.

Irish diplomat Brendan Ward, who had been in the square for most of the day, realized that the introduction of martial law had moved *"matters into an unknown but frightening phase."*

A few hours earlier one student had described feelings with which the young envoy could readily identify. The student had spoken movingly about his deep love for his country, which he repeatedly called *"my mother."* The youth had developed the analogy, saying a mother was entitled to be strict with her children. *"But our mother now just keeps misunderstanding us and then beats us when we try and explain."*

Leaving the square to draft another telegram to his superiors, Ward had an overwhelming feeling that when he next returned it could be to a very different scene.

All around him, people began to sing the *"Internationale"* once more.

Jeanne Moore noticed *"people are jeering at what they have just heard."* Then from a million and more voices came the chant. It passed from group to group, from mouth to mouth. The same words, endlessly repeated: *"Down with Li Peng! Down with military rule! Long live the people! Long live democracy!"*

Then over the students' loudspeaker system came the voice of Wuerkaixi.

"Students of Mother China. People of our beloved homeland. I ask you now to join us all in a hunger strike! I ask all students to form a human chain around the square so that the army shall not enter!"

On the pediment of the Monument to the People's Heroes, Daobao and Yang Li were raising a new banner Meili had just written. It read: *"We came on our feet! We will leave on our backs!"*

Over the loudspeaker Wuerkaixi was urging everyone to be ready to die for Mother China, *"for truly she must be weeping for us."*

Writing down his words, *Newsweek's* Melinda Liu felt close to weeping herself.

20

Martial Law

NATIONAL PHOTOGRAPHIC INTERPRETATION CENTER

Throughout the night China watchers fed instructions to their computers. In return they received satellite photographs of the military movements underway throughout China.

Since they had photographed the first student march into Tiananmen Square to mark the death of Hu Yaobang, the satellites had until now reported no military activity of any consequence, apart from the return of a 27th Army troop train from Tibet. The close-up photos of some of the shoulder tabs on the disembarking soldiers confirmed they were the same units that had shipped out of Beijing the previous November. But instead of returning to their garrison in the western suburbs of Beijing, the troops had been positioned some twenty miles beyond the city limits.

After several hours, the photo technicians had produced a set of photographs indicating other troop movements across a wide area of China, together with deployment of naval forces in the Yellow Sea.

The information was transmitted to the CIA's Office of Imagery Analysis. From there it was distributed to the Pentagon, the State Department, and the White House.

President Bush was in Boston, where he and President François Mitterand of France were to receive honorary degrees at Boston University commencement ceremonies the following day.

A set of satellite photographs and Webster's latest report on developments in China were hand-carried to Bush at his summer residence in Kennebunkport. With the President was Brent Scowcroft. After studying the photos, Bush and his national security adviser discussed the situation in China. Both realized China was bound to come up at the news conference following the conferring of the President's honorary degree.

Hunched in a chair opposite Bush, Scowcroft began to advise the President on what he should say.

SAME DAY, LATER
PLA GENERAL LOGISTICS DEPARTMENT COMPOUND
BEIJING

In the situation room adjoining the one from which the prime minister and state president had broadcast a couple of hours before, Captain Instructor Jyan watched and listened with growing astonishment to the reports that had started to arrive. Three hours into the military operation he had helped to plan, the largest internal offensive the People's Liberation Army had ever conducted was grinding to a halt. It was an ominous start to the thirty-sixth day of the demonstrations.

No longer were they confined to Beijing. In the south of the country, in Guandong Province, students at three universities were on hunger strike. In Canton, life had come to a virtual standstill. In the center of the country, in Hubai, students had occupied a bridge over the Yangtze River. At Hunan, birthplace of Hu Yaobang, twenty thousand students had taken over the railway station. In Shaanxi, another ten thousand students in the provincial capital of Xi'an, six hundred miles to the west of Beijing, had burned army vehicles and facilities. In Shanghai, Nanjing, and a score of other cities and towns, the unrest was growing.

At one minute to midnight units from eleven PLA armies had started to move to the centers of disturbance. A group attack division of the air force had been positioned at Shaanxi. The Navy had sent four of its Luda Class destroyers on patrol in the Yellow Sea to intercept anyone from Hong Kong or Taiwan coming to help the students. The sea blockade was also intended to stop any students fleeing by boat.

The wall map in the situation room showed the perimeter that had been established around Beijing. Twenty miles beyond the city limits were stationed units of the 27th Army, which had been withdrawn from Tibet. Ten miles behind this, force units of the 38th Army took up positions. Their function was to stop any more people coming into the capital from the provinces; already an estimated half million had reached Beijing. Roadblocks had been set up and all trains were being checked. All told, seventy thousand soldiers were involved, and over half a million more troops were on standby throughout the country.

The wall map showed that troops had gone to full alert along China's borders with Vietnam and Laos in the south, Burma in the east, and all the way to Mongolia in the north. Any help from those directions would be blocked. Even the long border with the Soviet Union had been sealed. China, as it had so often done in the past, was closing in on itself ready to devour those who were trying to destroy the country from within. The technique went all the way back to the first emperor of the Qin dynasty. Then, the emperor's foes had been slaughtered by flint-head weapons. Now their successors would be killed by the cutting edge of modern technology. The thrust of that assault would be on Beijing. It was an old Chinese maxim that once the capital was secure, the provinces would fall into line.

Jyan had watched as the first column of one hundred trucks had sped along the main western highway leading to Beijing. A similar number swung north, heading for the campuses near the Summer Palace. A squadron of tanks was deployed to enter the city through the eastern suburbs. With them was a force of two thousand soldiers.

The columns had advanced quickly and unopposed until they were a mile from the city limits. There they had waited for further orders, as instructed.

During the pause, intelligence chief Qiao Shi had received the latest news from Tiananmen Square. His agents reported the students were setting up roadblocks with commandeered vehicles on Changan Avenue and broadcasting constant appeals for the citizens to come and help them.

Jyan could now see the effect of those appeals. For the past two hours scores of thousands of people had taken to the streets to block the military advance into the capital. Every truck, tank, and halftrack had come to a halt, stopped by swarms of people clambering over the vehicles or forming human chains.

Over their field telephones unit commanders had reported they could neither advance nor retreat without causing serious loss of life. But the troops had no orders to open fire.

In the situation room, senior PLA commanders had gone into a closed session with, among others, State President Yang and Prime Minister Li Peng. While they deliberated their next step, from outside the compound came the sound of still more people rushing to join the throng. Their continuous chant carried clearly into the situation room. *"The People's Army should love the people!"*

Squatting on top of his T-69 tank, Commander Lee Gang, whose brother, Liu, was one of the student leaders, ordered a crewman to traverse the main gun. Instinctively the crowd drew back against the walls of the buildings on either side of the street.

Then from a doorway a figure in a headband pointed a bullhorn at the truck. It was Daobao.

An hour earlier, when the first report had reached Tiananmen Square that the soldiers were on the move, Wuerkaixi had sent *"flying squads"* of students into the suburbs to alert people. Among those who had gone was Daobao. He had borrowed a motorcycle and, with Cassy riding pillion, driven down Changan Avenue to the suburb of Muxudi. Both wore headbands bearing the word DEMOCRACY. They had stopped at street corners, and Daobao had used the bullhorn to warn those nearby. In minutes people were running into the streets and had started to form barricades; buses were driven broadside across the highway, and then their engines were immobilized. The younger men had followed Daobao's motorcade to this crossroads, where they were confronting Liu's tank and a column of trucks.

"Why do you threaten us? The army is the army of the people. How can you attack your own family?" Daobao yelled.

The tank's gun lined up on the students.

"You will not shoot!" Daobao taunted. *"But even if you do, for every person you kill, ten more will rise up!"*

"No!" came another amplified voice. *"Not ten, twenty!"*

Once more the crowd, many in their pajamas, began to edge toward the tank. Further along the street, buses, trucks, and pedicabs were being used to form another barrier. Behind that obstacle, Liu Lee could see yet another being created.

He turned to look behind him. The trucks had all but disappeared under the sheer number of people on their hoods, on roofs, clinging to the sides, yelling for the soldiers to put down their AK-47 rifles and join *"the people's revolution."*

Seated in the back of the lead truck, Bing Yang felt the same bewilderment as the other soldiers. They had been told by their company commander, Tan Yaobang, that they could expect a warm welcome from the citizens, who had grown tired of the protest.

Yet they had to force their way yard by yard through the crowds even to reach the outer edges of the city. Now they were completely bogged down.

At the rear of every truck stood a student lecturing the soldiers inside on the democracy movement.

"Why are you here?" a student yelled into Bing's truck.

"You sound just like my brother," the exasperated soldier said.

"Who is your brother?"

Bing told him. The student spread the word. More students appeared, trying to coax Bing to give up his weapon and join them. He clutched his rifle more tightly. The students began to taunt him. Then from the back of the convoy came Tan Yaobang's order to withdraw. The trucks began to reverse through the cheering crowd.

Cassy joined those around her in singing the *"Internationale."* Someone grabbed Daobao's bullhorn and addressed the routed column.

"Tell your comrades the truth! That the people of Beijing, no, the people of China, are all behind the students. We all want to reform the country. We want to see an end to the handful of criminals who dare to call themselves our government. Long live democracy!"

In other suburbs, the rest of the soldiers were also pulling back on orders from their commanders. They had bluntly told Li Peng that they would only fire on the youngsters if the order came from Deng Xiaoping himself. In the compound, Captain Instructor Jyan could hear the crowd's chanting had coalesced into one repeated cry: *"Victory to the people!"*

SAME DAY, LATER
TIANANMEN SQUARE

As diplomats Brendan Ward and Brian Davidson walked into the square, the loudspeakers began to boom.

It was 10:30 A.M. on the thirty-sixth day of protest, an hour after the state radio announcement: In eight districts of the city, including Tiananmen, all processions and strikes were forbidden; the army would deal with infringements *"forcefully."*

As the diplomats began another long day of gathering information, the first decree of martial law was announced over the public address system. All journalists were forbidden from that moment to film or report what was happening.

Foreigners were ordered not to *"remain involved"* in any activities by Chinese citizens that broke martial law, such as writing or delivering unacceptable speeches, or distributing leaflets or unauthorized banners or placards. The broadcast ended with the demand that everyone leave the square.

"They've really got the wind up in Zhongnanhai," Davidson told Ward. *"But they're still bluffing, otherwise they'd just cut the power for all the TV feeds. They don't want to do that because it'll be another admission they've lost control. So really this is just an appeal for everyone to be good chaps and pack up and go home, because the action's over, while everyone knows it's just about to start."*

As usual their instructions were to do nothing to embarrass their governments, but to get as close to what was happening as possible. Ward would remember saying to Davidson that if the military did manage to reach the square, they were both protected by diplomatic immunity. Davidson shrugged and asked how many soldiers would recognize a diplomatic passport.

Making their way toward the hunger strikers — always their first point of call of the day, to see how many had given up overnight — they saw that no one had paid any attention to the edict. Foreign journalists remained in force. So did their fellow envoys. Ward and Davidson exchanged greetings with both groups.

"The whole square had become rather like a raffish club," Ward would recall. *"The place stank like a fish market. There was no real sanitation, and refuse was piled everywhere. But everybody kept saying it was 'only for one more day, then it will be over.' The area around the Monument to the People's Heroes looked like a M*A*S*H. clearing station, bodies everywhere, doctors and nurses coming and going. So many were collapsing after seven days of starvation that a special lane had been opened for the ambulances."*

Overnight another seventy students had been taken to the hospital. But over a thousand still remained on hunger strike after eight days. Gray-faced and soaked in perspiration, often too weak to speak, they lay prostrate in the stifling heat. Summer had come early, and the temperature was already up in the eighties.

Music continued to blare. Even at this hour, after another sleepless night, people were moving in time to the sound of the Beatles and the Rolling Stones.

Yet Ward sensed a tension behind the camaraderie that had not been there the night before. Students were writing wills, photographing one another, and autographing each other's shirts. Some of them had begun to dip scarves and handkerchiefs in buckets of water before draping the cloth over their nose and mouth in case they were tear-gassed. They looked like cowboys.

The two diplomats separated after their check on the hunger strikers, Davidson heading toward the Great Hall of the People, Ward to the Monument to the People's Heroes. They would meet later in the day and pool information. This "pairing" arrangement was being operated by many other diplomats in the square.

Their presence had led to Deng Xiaoping once more hesitating over using all-out force to regain control. Governments normally friendly to the regime had now begun to express grave concern to China's ambassadors over the reports coming from their own envoys in Tiananmen.

The Australian government had balanced its substantial trade links with China against a sense of growing moral outrage after reading the telegram from Ambassador David Sadlier, who had maintained a constant presence in the square. So had the Dutch, whose dozen accredited diplomats had all taken turns visiting the square and reporting back to Ambassador Arne Dellira. His telegrams not only reflected the growing health hazard of a million people insisting on remaining in *"a disease trap,"* but also gave an insight into the *"anger and confusion still happening within the leadership. A sign of this was our information that the intention had originally been to declare Martial Law on Sunday (May 21st). Li Peng had persuaded Deng Xiaoping to bring the date forward by a full day in the hope of regaining the initiative."*

Through their assiduous tapping of their government sources, whom they often arranged to meet in the square, other diplomats had also pieced together glimpses of the power struggle going on in Zhongnanhai.

Debnath Shaw, Second Secretary at the Indian embassy, had learned that *"Zhao may be sick, but his supporters are still in good health. It was they who had first persuaded Li Peng that the troops sent into the city must not be given orders to shoot, and then when they were stymied by the crowds, Zhao's men had managed to get the order to withdraw the soldiers."*

Iran's minister-counselor, Huzzan Farazendeh, who had played an important role in getting China to supply his country with Silkworm missiles to defend itself against Iraq, had learned from his contacts that Deng Xiaoping had refused Li Peng's request to tear-gas the entire square from the air.

The Italian embassy's military and defense attaché, Colonel Giulio Fraticelli, a hard-driving figure who walked like the fine horseman he was, had heard the same story and dismissed it as *"impossible to be really effective. Any gas attack from the air could be carried by the wind into Zhongnanhai."*

The most revealing insight of all into the mood in the leadership compound had come from a visit Poland's Marian Woznink had made to Li Peng late the previous evening. Ostensibly it had been a routine call to discuss expanding trade links between their two countries.

Suddenly, Woznink had reported to Warsaw, *"the Prime Minister stood up and began to walk around his office. He grabbed me by the arm and took me over to a window. Outside there were more than the usual security men. Even from here we could hear the voices from Tiananmen. The prime minister then asked me how we had come to the compound. I told him that we had come by a back route. Our Chinese driver had driven us here the same way the Gorbachevs had been brought. The prime minister seized upon this. 'Look what happened to Comrade Gorbachev! His visit was ruined by turmoil. Important people like him and diplomats like us should not have to drive through the back streets because of this turmoil.' The prime minister used the word several times. Then he said his government would have to 'take all necessary steps to halt this turmoil.'"*

Poland's ambassador was not the only diplomat who had been exposed to such a diatribe. A few hours before, Richard Woolcott, an Australian government official who had flown to Beijing on a trade mission, had experienced a similarly surprising encounter with Li Peng.

The splendidly named Alfonso Gualia de Paadin y de Ahumada, defense attaché at the Spanish embassy, had sent a number of telegrams to Madrid stating that the students were not engaged in a violent takeover. The Spanish Foreign Ministry had conveyed its hope that the students would be allowed to continue to protest peacefully. Sweden's ambassador, Bjorn Skala, had sent several of his attachés to the square. Their reports had convinced Skala that the demonstration was *"a genuine expression of widespread discontent."* His government had conveyed that judgment to the Chinese ambassador in Stockholm.

Countries such as Hungary, Pakistan, and Somalia that had all experienced inner turmoil, had expressed the hope that any action against the students would be, in the words of Akran Zak, the Pakistani ambassador, *"kept to the very minimum."*

The only support for completely crushing the students was expressed by Angelo Miculescu, the Romanian Ambassador. In a visit to Zhongnanhai a few days earlier he had reportedly told Li Peng that the Romanian government would do everything possible to help China *"through this unhappy time,"* and that *"whatever action is necessary must be taken."*

Throughout the night, carefully couched diplomatic concern had continued to arrive in Zhongnanhai from other governments.

The exception was the United States. Washington had yet to express any real support for the students or any deep concern about martial law.

Barr Seitz, on a visit to the U.S. embassy compound to pick up press releases for ABC, had found *"everyone was very low-key when it came to expressing attitudes."*

One diplomat, who asked not to be named, later said that *"no one wanted to say or do anything at this stage which could affect long-term situations. At the best of times the Chinese are very touchy about outside pressure. For the United States to go barging in would have been counterproductive. We just sat tight waiting to see how things would develop. Anyway, we weren't going to come out and urge the students on. A lot of us remembered what our own students had done over Vietnam. To us those students on Tiananmen were from the same cut, radicals trying to overthrow an established government that may well be repressive, but was still the government."*

But from the United States had come an unexpected voice supporting the students: Wan Li, the chairman of China's National People's Congress, the country's rubber-stamp parliament.

The gremlin-like Wan was one of those figures all authoritarian regimes need, a smiling face to do the bidding of his masters in the outside world. In his years of service to Deng, the wily, irascible Wan had popped up in Europe, the U.N., Tokyo, and now, all of the United States. Like an old-fashioned door-to-door salesman, he swore by what he was selling. *"Invest in China,"* he would tell businessmen, *"and your profits will multiply."*

On Wan's American trip the message had been endlessly repeated at broiled chicken or beef dinners across the country. His style was feisty, rather like Henry Kissinger's. Indeed, Wan's trip had the full support of the former Secretary of State and all his illustrious consultancy associates, including three former presidents.

Sensing the growing mood of public concern in the country about the fate of the students as a result of reporting like Dan Rather's, Wan had publicly called the students *"patriots"* and was sure the Chinese leadership would *"exercise proper restraint"* and accept that China's problems *"will only be settled through democracy."*

Wan's words could have done little to reassure Kissinger Associates. The consultancy had helped establish more than six hundred U.S.-Chinese joint ventures. Already some of these companies were showing signs of concern over the situation in China. The San Francisco-based Bechtel Engineering and Construction Company had withdrawn all four of its expatriate executives from Beijing. U.S. executives at IBM and Chrysler's Jeep joint venture were also planning to leave.

The Kissinger consultancy was working literally around the clock, lobbying Congress and moving swiftly to stop further departures from China by calling top executives at every joint-venture company.

However, Kissinger Associates could not manage to head off the first signs of public anger in America at what was happening in Beijing. Ohio Governor Richard Celeste, after watching a Dan Rather telecast, had canceled China's participation in the state fair. A number of cities, including Los Angeles, were reviewing their "Sister City" links to China; in L.A.'s case, with Canton. Wan Li's words went some way toward reassuring city councilors in Los Angeles.

On Tiananmen Square, the news of Wan Li's intervention further buoyed student hopes after the success in driving the soldiers out of Beijing's suburbs.

Wuerkaixi predicted that the support of such a powerful figure would lead to a dramatic change. Wan Li was close to Deng; they played bridge together. The chairman of the National People's Congress had also been an open supporter of Zhao Ziyang's reform policies. With one of those boundless leaps of optimism for which he was becoming renowned, Wuerkaixi extrapolated that it would only be a matter of time before the Party Secretary would be back at the helm and it would be Premier Li Peng who would have to go on sick leave.

While Wuerkaixi was exuding such confidence, Sue Tung had come to a decision. The young postgraduate Chinese student from Sacramento who had put her country before her boyfriend had felt increasingly frustrated in her weeks in China. She had still been unable to speak to Jyan, her instructor friend at the PLA academy; its switchboard refused to put through her calls. The student leaders on the square were polite but distant. They had accepted the large donation she had brought from Chinese students in California and then left her to her own devices.

Sue pushed her way past the students standing permanent guard over the Monument to the People's Heroes. Among other duties, the guards decided which foreigners could be allowed into Wuerkaixi's presence. Sue thought it depended on whether the student leader wanted to *"impress that day Europe or the United States."* Sensing it was America's day, she persuaded the guards to let her pass.

On the pediment she found the mood pensive. Wuerkaixi's burst of optimism had just as quickly given way to pessimism. Mood changes had begun to characterize the behavior of several of the student leaders. Unused to such awesome responsibility, they found their moods hard to control. One moment they could feel jubilant, the next gripped with despair. Only Chai Ling maintained her steely determination, masking it behind a cheerful smile on her pixie face, whose eyes missed nothing.

They quickly appraised Sue, then turned back to Wuerkaixi, who was saying he was now sure the troops would return in even greater numbers.

Sue suddenly found herself speaking.

"You need expert advice," she said. "Broadcast a request for anyone with military experience to come forward to tell you what to do."

Chai Ling was the first to react. She grabbed a microphone.

"People of China. A severe counterrevolutionary coup has now been declared against us. It is initiated by Li Peng and Yang Shangkun. They have already sent their troops once to suppress us. They will do so again. We have no weapons. We only fight for freedom and democracy with words. Yet we know that China's fate is in our hands. That is why we must defend this square, defend the democratic movement, and defend this great country to the last drop of our blood. But we need expert help. We ask if anyone has knowledge of military tactics to come forward and advise us!"

No one had asked Sue to leave the pediment. She felt that the student leaders had accepted her. Wuerkaixi kept saying that the student leaders would be the first targets for the soldiers. He thought they would use tear gas and electric cattle prods to force their way to the pediment. Or they could drop paratroops who would simply shoot them on the spot.

Sue watched Wang Dan walk over to Wuerkaixi, firmly take him by the shoulders, and speak quietly to him. Wuerkaixi became calmer.

Chai Ling was about to make a fresh appeal for help when two stocky figures motioned for the student guards to let them through. Sue stepped down from the pediment and introduced herself. The men said they were instructors at the military academy. Impulsively Sue asked if they knew Jyan. They looked at her curiously. One of the instructors said that Jyan was a member of the strategy team planning to remove the students. Sue quickly explained Jyan was an old family friend, then led them to where Wuerkaixi and Wang Dan waited.

That was also the moment Sue decided to give up trying to contact Jyan. "We were on opposite sides. We would probably both be embarrassed to meet under such circumstances."

One of the instructors produced a copy of the strategy plan Jyan had helped to prepare. The man had stolen it from the military academy. He spread the paper on the ground. The students crouched around him. His companion explained they had come to help because like many other officers in the PLA they felt that the military threat against the students was wrong. Using the map as a reference point, they explained to the leaders what they should expect to happen and what they could do to counter the military moves.

The older man said, "Already this morning the order has been given forbidding all civilian planes flying over the city. This will allow military helicopters to operate with complete freedom. Two hundred helicopters are now within five minutes' flying time of here."

Wuerkaixi glanced apprehensively at his companions.

Chai Ling gave him a quick, reassuring smile. Wang Dan blinked behind his glasses. These past weeks had aged him. It was hard to believe he was still only twenty. He looked like a man who had come to terms with life, including coping with the mood swings of Wuerkaixi.

The younger instructor jabbed at the map. "*All public transport is now closed. The underground and trains will be used to move the troops into the city. Already four thousand soldiers are in the railway station a few miles from here.*"

"*What can we do,*" mumbled Wuerkaixi, "*except give up?*"

"*Wait,*" the older instructor said, his voice sharp. "*Before you decide, you must have all the facts.*"

The younger instructor placed a finger on the map, indicating the Forbidden City, the History Museum, and the Great Hall of the People.

"*Over ten thousand troops have arrived in those places.*"

Several of the students glanced toward the buildings and the roofs of the Forbidden City. Everything looked normal.

"*The troops are in the tunnels,*" said the older man. "*In 1976 I was there with them when your predecessors demonstrated. When we came out of the tunnels then, it took us just six minutes to deal with the situation. Hundreds, you remember, were killed or wounded.*" He paused to look out across the square. "*When they come, it will probably only take a little longer to clear this crowd.*"

This time Wang Dan addressed both instructors. "*Okay, so what do we do?*"

The two instructors looked at each other and sighed. The older man began to explain.

"*You probably have little time. The first thing you must do is to prepare against attack from the air. You must get every kite you can and fly them over the square and the surrounds. The kite strings will wrap around the rotors and stop the helicopters from being able to drop paratroopers. You must prepare for tear-gas attack by making everybody wear face masks or handkerchiefs. You must watch out for Public Security agents. They are everywhere, listening and trying to provoke trouble. You need at least three hundred scouts out in the square, reporting back every hour on what is happening. At the first sign of the troops, you must mobilize the crowd so that the troops will dare not fire. They will know they cannot kill everyone and that the survivors will kill them.*"

"*What about tanks?*" asked Daobao.

"*The same tactic,*" said the instructor. "*If you are firm and resolute, no tank commander will dare run over your people.*"

Yang Li stood up, his voice troubled.

"*I have no doubt that what you say is good military tactics. But we are not soldiers. We have come here in the name of nonviolence. If we do what you suggest, more people could die. I suggest that if the troops do come, we should try and reason with them. We should say 'the people love the people's army' and 'the people's army loves the people.' We must not fight the soldiers.*"

Around her Sue could hear murmurs of agreement and dissension. Once more the leaders were divided. While the two instructors watched, the students debated whether they should act on what they had been told.

Agreement was reached on flying kites. That seemed *"appropriately nonviolent,"* said Yang Li. But he remained adamant there must be no violence done by the students. After another hour a compromise was reached. Students would be positioned all around the square to warn of soldiers approaching. At that point Wuerkaixi and Wang Dan would go forward and meet the military commanders and negotiate safe passage for the hunger strikers. In the meantime a general warning would be broadcast for everyone to have a mask ready to deal with any tear-gas attack.

Chai Ling had started to broadcast the terms of what had been decided when the clatter of helicopters filled the air. Swooping in over Zhongnanhai, they whirled across the square, jigging from side to side, dropping until they were only feet above the lampposts. As they veered to either side of the Monument to the People's Heroes, pamphlets rained down on the crowd. The leaflets called for them to leave the square.

A great roar of relief accompanied the helicopters as they headed west across the city. The mercurial Wuerkaixi probably spoke for many when he grinned and said, *"It's going to be okay. We're going to zap them!"*

The effect of long hours spent with American TV crews had begun to show in his speech.

SAME DAY, LATER
THE FOREIGN OFFICE
LONDON

The moment analyst Sue Morton saw the latest telegram from British Ambassador Donald, she felt *"a little surge of excitement."*

Donald had picked up an extraordinary whisper coming out of Zhongnanhai. Within the compound, Zhao was trying to mobilize support to revoke martial law and move to have Prime Minister Li Peng impeached. The supposedly ill Party Secretary had managed to gain support for his action from a third of the members of the National People's Congress, whose chairman, Wan Li, was in the United States.

Zhao appeared to have moved so quickly and discreetly that Li Peng had been completely outmaneuvered. Wan Li's words of support for the students — *"They are patriots"* — and his injunctions to the leadership not to act rashly lest it jeopardize lucrative trade deals, had almost certainly been seen by Zhao as a signal to strike.

Donald's telegram reported the prime minister had rushed to Deng's compound and from there tried to telephone Wan Li to order him to remain in the United States. Unable to contact Wan Li, the prime minister had sent him an urgent fax confirming his instructions. But Zhao had also cabled his own message instructing Wan Li to return *"at once"* to lend his authority to support the students' demands.

Wan Li was in a dilemma. In the next few days he had important speaking engagements, in Baltimore, Orlando, and New York. He planned to use each occasion to drum up more investments in China. He decided to continue with his tour, which would end with a meeting with George Bush in the Oval Office this coming Tuesday, the day after the President flew back to Washington from Boston. To cancel such a meeting would be unthinkable.

Wan Li decided to continue his American tour, much to the relief of Kissinger Associates. The continued presence of Wan Li in the United States was exactly what the consultancy and Prime Minister Li Peng wanted, a symbol that it was very much business as usual as far as the United States and China went.

That sanguine view was not shared by Susan Morton. Ambassador Donald's telegram provided a further glimpse of the serious power struggle still going on behind the walls of Zhongnanhai.

No doubt encouraged by the way the troops had been turned back in the suburbs, Zhao had somehow found the courage to make one last challenge against Li Peng and, ultimately, Deng Xiaoping.

"The struggle for power is a real no-holds-barred affair," the young researcher had scribbled on her note pad. *"There was no real precedent for what was happening."*

The struggle had spilled over even to the pages of the *People's Daily*, the official Party organ. The left-hand side of the front page supported Li Peng and carried stories praising the leadership, while the right-hand columns were devoted to describing the aims of the students. The latest issue of a Shanghai newspaper had even gone so far as to print a huge photograph of Winston Churchill giving his famous V sign; the gesture had been adopted by the students.

Ambassador Donald's cable painted a picture of the sky over Beijing constantly filled with helicopters keeping watch on the crowd as people turned whole areas of the city into fortified bastions. Roadblocks were constructed from commandeered public service vehicles and building site materials.

The mood of the crowd veered between *"foreboding and good spirits,"* the ambassador concluded. He had quoted some of the opinions his tireless press attaché, Brian Davidson, had collected. One of the leaders of the newly formed Autonomous Workers Union had quoted Mao, who had said *"the government has become a tiny handful."*

Susan concluded that government, as such, no longer functioned in Beijing. The country was now being controlled from somewhere called Martial Law Enforcement Headquarters. Her intelligence sources had identified this to be the PLA compound in the west of the city, from which Prime Minister Li Peng and State President Yang had broadcast. But apart from them, no one else had been identified as running the HQ.

The situation, she wrote, is extremely dangerous. China could be on the verge of a catastrophe greater even than the Cultural Revolution.

SAME DAY, LATER
SAN FRANCISCO

With considerable satisfaction Shao-Yen Wang, who was the daughter of a senior officer in Beijing, and whose own hope was to become a Hollywood star one day, saw that the crowd outside the People's Republic consulate had grown even greater this Saturday evening. Staff at every one of Chinatown's scores of restaurants had urged their customers to join in the demonstrations. Many had. They were chanting a succession of slogans urging President Bush to tell Deng Xiaoping to keep the PLA from harming the students.

A number of the demonstrators carried radios to listen to the live broadcasts from Tiananmen Square, where student loudspeakers were repeatedly warning that the troops were once more about to attack.

Then came the bell-like voice of Chai Ling saying the threat had passed; moments later, the protesters outside the consulate heard the loudspeakers in Beijing play Beethoven's *"Ode to Joy."* They began to hum to the music.

Inside the consulate Zhang Milin, the cultural attaché, watched from his bedroom window. The humming strengthened his resolve to defect. He had thought of nothing else for the past two days and nights: how he would do it, when he would leave.

His greatest fear was that one of the consulate's security staff would sense what he was plotting. If that happened, Zhang knew, he would be drugged and, on the pretext he had been suddenly taken seriously ill and was returning home for treatment, escorted on to a flight to Beijing. There he would be sentenced to a term in the Gulag.

The prison camps were in the desert heartland of the country. There, between stints of backbreaking work in the salt mines, would be lectures to *"politically re-educate"* him. Years could pass before his mentors decided he was once more ready to be returned to Chinese society. By then, Zhang feared, he could be both a physical and mental wreck.

The hardest part of defecting would be knowing that almost certainly he would never again see his family. To avoid any harm coming to them he could not tell them what he planned; he could tell no one. His great fear was that in his anxiety he might say something in his sleep. These past two nights he had awakened more than once, convinced he had let something slip that would have been heard by one of the patrolling security men.

So far no one had given him a second look. But he also knew it would only be a matter of time before the already strict security within the consulate would be further tightened, making it virtually impossible for any staff to leave the building. Staring out the window at the chanting crowd in the street, Zhang realized he must make his move soon, before that happened.

14/05 '01 MON 16:32 FAX

SF Consulate Press Release (no date)   SF Consulate

```
          WHY IMPOSE MARTIAL LAW IN BEIJING QUERY PARA
SHI WEI PARA  BY THE THIRD WEEK OF MAY 1989.SERIOUS
TURMOIL HAD  TAKEN PLACE IN BEIJING AMD SOCIAL STABILITY,PEOPLE"S
NORMAL  LIFE AND SOCIAL ORDER HAD BEEN DISRUPTED.IN
VIEW OF THIS AMD  IN ACCORDANCE WITH THE STIPULATIONS

OF THE CONSTITUTION OF THE  PEOPLE"S REPUBLIC OF
CHINA, THE STATE COUNCIL ON MAY 20  ISSUED AN ORDER,
SIGNED BY PREMIER LI PENG,IMPOSING MAR TIAL LAW
IN SOME SECTIONS OF BEIJING.THE PURPOSE WAS TO
CHECK THE UNREST; RESTORE SOCIAL STABILITY IN THE

CITY, SAFE GUARD THE LIFE AND PROPERTY OF THE CITIZENS,PROTECT
PUBLIC  PROPERTY,AND ENSURE THE NORMAL FUNCTIONING
OF CENTRAL   GOVERNMENT DEPARTMENTS AND THE BEIJING
MUNICIPAL GOVERN MENT.IT CALLED TROOPS TO THE CAPITAL
TO ASSIST THE ARMED  POLICE, PUBLIC SECURITY PERSONNEL

AND THE BROAD MASSES,  INCLUDING THE STUDENTS, TO
MAINTAIN BEIJING"S PUBLIC SECURITY  AND RESTORE
NORMAL PRODUCTION, WORK,TEACHING AND SCIENTIFIC
 RESEARCH AND OTHER ASPECTS OF LIFE IN THE CAPITAL.
PARA HOWEVER,SOME PEOPLE HAVE ASKED CLN SINCE

THE STUDENTS ARE  PATRIOTIC, WHY SAY THERE HAS BEEN
TURMOIL QUERY SINCE THE STUDENTS  ARE PATRIOTIC,WHY
SEND IN THE PEOPLE"S LIBERATION ARMY QUERY  THEREFORE,
THE FOLLOWING EXPLANATIONS MAY BE IN ORDER. PARA
  1.WHY DI WE SAY THERE HAS BEEN SERIOUS TURMOIL

IN BEIJING QUERY  PARA FIRST,IT SHOULD BE SAID THAT
THE CHINESE COMMUNIST  PARTY AND THE PEOPLE"S GOVERNMENT
HAVE,FROM THE VERY  BEGINNING,FULLY CONFIRMED THE
PATRIOTIC ENTHUSIASM OF THE  BROAD MASSES OF YOUNG
STUDENTS.THEY HAVE NEVER SAID IT WAS  THE MAJORITY

OF STUDENTS WHO WERE STIRRING UP TURMOIL. THE  PEOPLE"S
DAILY EDITORIAL OF APRIL 26 AND THE MAY 19 SPEECH
 BY LI PENG ON BEHALF OF THE PARTY CENTRAl COMMITTEE
AND  THE STATE COUNCIL,AND THE STATEMENTS BY OTHER
LEADERS HAVE  AIL REPEATEDLY AND CLEARLY POINTED

OUT THAT THE DEMANDS OF  THE BROAD MASSES OF YOUNG
STUDENTS TO PROMOTE DEMOCRACY,  ERADICATE CORRUPTION,PUNISH
OFFICIAL PROFITEERING AND OVER COME BUREAUCRACY
ARE IN CONFORMITY WITH THE WISHES OF THE  PARTY
AND GOVERNMENT,AND THAT THEY HAVE PLAYED A POSITIVE

ROLE IN PROMOTING THE SOLUTION OF THESE PROBLEMS.THE
PARTY  AND GOVERNMENT HAVE ALL ALONG STRICTLY DIFFERENTIATED
BE TWEEN THE YOUNG STUDENTS" PATRIOTIC ENTHUSIASM
AND THE  CONSPIRATORIAL ACTIVITIES OF A VERY SMALL
NUMBER OF PEOPLE  WHO ARE CREATING TURMOIL. PARA

HOW, THEN, DID THESE FEW PEOPLE STIR UP TURMOIL
BY  MAKING USE OF THE WELL-MEANING ASPIRATIONS OF
___ _____ _____ __ _____. BY MAKING USE OF
```

LIES, LIES AND CHINESE WHISPERS
*The Beijing Regime, encouraged by the failure of the West to respond,
set out, as these documents show, on a campaign of global disinformation
intended to prepare the way for the massacre.*

GOVERNMENT AND THE DIFFICULTIES ENCOUNTERED IN
THE COURSE OF CHINA"S ADVANCE QUERY WE HAVE ONLY
TO EXAMINE THE RECENT SERIES OF EXTREMELY ABNORMAL
EVENTS WHICH HAVE OCCURRED TO COME TO THE CORRECT
CONCLUSION. PARA A.THE TURMOIL FOMENTED BY A TINY

MINORITY WAS PREME DITATED. PARA AS EARLY AS THE
END OF LAST YEAR AND THE BEGINNING OF THIS YEAR,
A SMALL NUMBER OF PEOPLE INSIDE AND OUTSIDE UNIVERSI
TIES CONSPIRED TO STIR UP CAMPUS UPHEAVAL AND PROVOKE
INCIDENTS ON THE OCCASIONS OF THE 70TH ANNIVERSARY

OF THE MAY 4TH MOVEMENT,THE 40TH ANNIVERSARY OF
THE FOUNDING OF THE PEOPLE"S REPUBLIC OF CHINA,
AND THE 200TH ANNIVER SARY OF THE FRENCH REVOLUTION.
PARA IN EARLY MARCH THIS YEAR,SOME ANONYMOUS BIG
AND SMALL-CHARACTER POSTERS WERE FOUND IN BEIJING

AND QINGHUA UNIVERSITIES, DIRECTLY ATTACKING THE
LEADERSHIP OF THE CHINESE COMMUNIST PARTY AND THE
SOCIALIST SYSTEM.ONE SMALL CHARACTER POSTER ENTITLED
""LAMENT FOR THE CHINESE PEOPLE"" TERMED THE PRESENT
GOVERNMENT ""AUTOCRATIC AND DESPOTIC,"" AND CALLED

UPON EVERYONE TO ""FIGHT FOR FREEDOM,"" A BIG- CHARACTER
POSTER ENTITLED ""THE CALL OF THE TIMES"" ASKED
""WHETHER THERE IS ANY REASON FOR THE EXISTENCE
OF SOCIALISM"" AND ""WHAT KIND OF PHILOSOPHICAL
SYSTEM CAN BE USED TO REPLACE MARXISM-LENINISM

QUERY "" AT THE CAMPUS OF BEIJING UNIVERSITY, A
POSTER ENTITLED ""A LETTER TO THE BROAD MASSES
OF YOUTH AND STUDENTS"" CALLED UPON THEM TO FIGHT
FOR ""DEMOCRACY,FREEDOM AND HUMAN RIGHTS"" UNDER
THE LEADER- SHIP OF FANG LIZHI, A SCHOLAR WHO ADVOCATES

BOURGEOIS LIBERALIZATION. IN SOCIETY AT LARGE,
CERTAIN PEOPLE BECAME VERY ACTIVE AND HELD INCESSANT
MEETINGS. FANG LIZHI PRAISED THESE MEETINGS FOR
""ADOPTING AN ATTITUDE OF TOTAL BOYCOTT AND THOROUGH
CRITICISM OF THE AUTHORITIES"" AMD ""HAVING A STRONG

SMELL OF GUNPOWDER."" HE PREDICTED THAT ""WITH
THREE MEETINGS OF THIS KIND IN SUCCESSION, PEOPLE
WILL TAKE TO THE STREETS."" WHEN HU YAOBANG DIED
ON APRIL 15,CERTAIN PEOPLE THOUGHT THE TIME WAS
RIPE AND WERE DETERMINED TO STIR UP GREAT DISTURBANCES.

PARA B.THE POLITICAL AIM OF THE TINY MINORITY
WAS TO NEGATE THE LEADERSHIP OF THE COMMUNIST PARTY
AND THE SOCIALIST SYSTEM. PARA A SO-CALLED MESSAGE
TO THE YOUTH AND STUDENTS OF THE NATION,SIGNED
""NANKAI UNIVERSITY,"" INCLUDED THE CALL TO ""ESTABLISH

A COMMITTEE FOR THE REVISION OF THE CONSTITUTION
AND ABOLISH PRINCIPLES" AND "ADHERENCES" IN THE
CONSTITUTION BRACKET MEANING ADHERENCE TO THE FOUR
CARDINAL PRINCIPLES-ED.UNBRACKET, WHICH ARE DEEPLY
HATED BY THE PEOPLE."" REN WANDING, FORMER HEAD

14/05 '01 MON 16:35 FAX

OF THE ILLEGAL ORGANIZATION LEAGUE FOR HUMAN RIGHTS,
SAID IN A SPEECH DELIVERED IN FRONT OF TIANANMEN
GATETOWER CLN ""WITHOUT THE REMOVAL OF THE FOUR
CARDINAL PRINCIPLES FROM THE CONSTITUTION.....THEY
WILL TAKE PRECEDENCE OVER THE PEOPLE"S INTERESTS.""

BRACKET THE FOUR CARDINAL PRINCIPLES ARE CLN KEEPING
TO THE SOCIALIST ROAD, AND UPHOLDING THE PEO PLE"S
DEMOCRATIC DICTATORSHIP, THE LEADERSHIP OF THE COMMUNIST
PARTY AND MARXISM-LENINISM AND MAO ZEDONG THOUGHT. UNBRACKET
HE CONTINUED, SAYING, ""THE FALSE RELAXATION, HARMONY,

UNITY AND STABILITY OF OUR SOCIETY ARE OBTAMED
AT THE PRICE OF AN OVERALL POLICY OF HIGH-HANDEDNESS
OVER THE ENTIRE PEOPLE AND AT THE COST OF THE BLOOD, LIFE,
LOSS OF FREEDOM AND HEALTH OF MILLIONS OF THE BEST
TALENTS,"" PARA A BIG-CHARACTER POSTER AT BEIJING

UNIVERSITY SAID, ""MARXISM EQUALS UTOPIA. MAO ZEDONG
WAS AN OUT-AND-OUT RASCAL. WITHOUT THE NEGATION
OF MAO ZEDONG THOUGHT, THE REFORM CAN HAVE NO PRACTICAL
MEANING."" A POSTER AT THE BEIJING UNIVERSITY OF
AERONAUTICS AND ASTRONAUTICS , SIGNED ""A DOC TORAL

CANDIDATE"" AND ENTITLED ""CHINA"S HOPE CLN PRIVATE
OWN ERSHIP,"" ATTACKED CHINA"S PUBLIC OWNERSHIP
AS ""EXCEEDING THE LAWS OF HISTORICAL DEVELOPMENT,""
AS BEING ""FETTERS ON THE DEVELOPMENT OF THE PRODUCTIVE
FORCES...THE SOIL NURTURING BUREAUCRACY...THE HOTBED

FOR CORRUPTION AND DEGENERATION ...THE CRADLE OF
CENTRALIZED STATE POWER AND AUTOCRACY."" THE POSTER
ADVOCATED ""SOUNDING THE DEATH KNELL OF PUBLIC
OWN ERSHIP AS SOON AS POSSIBLE TO WELCOME THE FUTURE
OF THE REPUBLIC."" PARA IN THEIR ARTICLES AND

POSTERS, THIS TINY MINORITY, COMPLETE LY DISREGARDING
THE GREAT ACHIEVEMENTS THAT TEN YEARS OF REFORM
HAVE BROUGHT, SLANDERED SOCIALIST CHINA AS BEING
""BLACK AS PITCH,"" REACHING A SEVERE CRISIS,""
""RAMPANT WITH PROFITEERING OFFICIALS, FULL OF

CORRUPTION AND DEGENERATION, AND COLLAPSING MORALLY.""
THEY CLAIMED THAT"" CHINA IS MORIBUND, THE PEOPLE
ARE DEGENERATING, EVERYTHING IS DYING."" AND ADVOCATED
THE OVERTHROW OF THE SOCIALIST SYSTEM. PARA AT
THE BEIJING UNIVERSITY OF AERONAUTICS AND ASTRONAU

TICS, SOMEONE POSTED UP A ""MESSAGE TO THE ENTIRE
CHINESE PEOPLE."" DEMANDING THAT THEY ""ABOLISH
THE COMMUNIST PAR TY AND PRACTISE A MULTI-PARTY
SYSTEM"" AND "" ABOLISH THE COMMUNIST PARTY BRANCHES
AND CADRES IN CHARGE OF POLITI CAL WORK IN ORGANIZATIONS, SCHOOLS

AND UNITS."" SOME BIG CHARACTER POSTERS OPENLY CALLED
FOR THE ""ABOLITION OF PARTIES AND ABROGATION
OF THE FOUR CARDINAL PRINCIPLES."" SOME ATTACKED
THE CHINESE COMMUNIST PARTY AS A ""TREACHEROUS PARTY""
WHICH ""ONLY CARES FOR ITS OWN STATUS, WITHOUT

CONCERN FOR THE FUTURE OF THE COUNTRY AND THE NATION,"" AND DECLARED THAT THE PARTY IS ""DISINTEGRATING."" PARA A FEW POSTERS EVEN DECLARCD THAT ""RIGHT FROM THE BEGIN NING, EVERYTHING THE COMMUNIST PARTY HAS DONE IS CORRUPT, AUTOCRATIC AND TRAITOROUS...THE

COMMUNIST PARTY HAS DONE NOTHING GOOD.""SOME BIG-CHARACTER POSTERS ATTACKED THE PAR TY AS ""HAVING LOST ITS ROLE AS THE VANGUARD ORGANIZATION OF THE ADVANCED PROLETARIAT. IT IS JUST ANOTHER AROUP OF AUTO CRATS IN POWER IN CHINA"S THOUSAND-YEAR-OLD FEUDAL DESPOT

ISM."" SOME PEOPLE BRAZENLY CLAMOURED FOR THE OVERTHROW OF THE ""AUTOCRATIC RULE"" OF THE CHINESE COMMUNIST PARTY. OTH ERS PROPSED ""INVITING THE KUOMINTANG BACK TO THE MAIN LAND TO SET UP A TWO-PARTY POLITICAL SYSTEM."" PARA DENG XIAOPING HAS ALWAYS UPHELD

THE FOUR CARDINAL PRINCIPLES, AND INSISTED ON OPPOSING BOURGEOIS LIBERALIZATION. HE IS THE CHIEF ARCHITECT OF CHINA"S REFORM AND OPENING UP TO THE OUTSIDE WORLD AND THE MODERNIZATION DRIVE . HE ENJOYS HIGH PRESTIGE INSIDE AND OUTSIDE THE PARTY, AT HOME

AND ABROAD.THE TINY MINORITY HAVE THEREFORE CONSISTENTLY MADE DENG XIAOPING THE TARGET OF THEIR ATTACK, USING EXTREMELY VENOMOUS AND EVEN SCURRILOUS LANGUAGE TO SLANDER AND ABUSE HIM. PARA THE FOUR CARDINAL PRINCIPLES ARE THE FOUNDATION OF OUR COUNTRY.IF

THE FOUR CARDINAL PRINCIPLES AND THE LEADERSHIP OF THE COMMUNIST PARTY ARE ABOLISHED, WHAT ALTERNATIVE IS THERE BUT CAPITALISM QUERY PARA C. THE TURMOIL STIRRED UP BY THE TINY MINORITY WAS CAREFULLY PLANNED SEMICLN VARIOUS POLITICAL FORCES AT HOME AND ABROAD

WERE INVOLVED. PARA FOR MORE THAN A MONTH,AT EACH STAGE OF THE TURMOIL, EVERY ACTION, SLOGAN AND DEMAND WAS CAREFULLY PLANNED AND ARRANGED. AT THE BEGINNING, ACCORDING TO THE PLANS OF THE SMALL MINORITY, THERE WAS AN ALL-OUT ATTACK ON THE FOUR

CARDINAL PRINCIPLES. PARTY AND GOVERNMENT LEADERS WERE ASSAILED ONE BY ONE.BEFORE AND AFTER APRIL 18 AND 19,WHEN THERE WERE ATTEMPTS TO STORM ZHONGNANHAI WHERE THE PARTY AND GOVERNMENT HEADQUARTERS ARE LOCATED, THE ATTACK WAS CONCENTRATED ON DENG XIAOPING

AND LI PENG. AFTER APRIL 26, WHEN PEOPLE"S DAILY ISSUED THE EDITORIAL EXPOSING THE NATURE OF THE TURMOIL INCITED BY THE SMALL MINORITY, THESE PEOPLE MADE AN ABRUPT AND DRASTIC CHANGE IN THEIR TACTICS. SLOGANS SUCH AS "" SUPPORT THE CHINESE COMMUNIST

PARTY,"" ""SUPPORT SOCIALISM"" AND ""SUPPORT THE CONSTITUTION"" APPEARED. PARA SEVERAL DAYS LATER,WHEN THEY SAW THAT THE PARTY AND GOVERNMENT WERE EXERCISING GREAT RESTRAINT, THEY WITHDREW THESE SLOGANS.WHEN THE SITUATION DETERIORATED ,

14/05 '01 MON 16:38 FAX

""DOWN WITH DENG XIAOPING"" APPEARED AGAIN ----
OVER THE CITY OF BEIJING,CAUSING A TEMPORARY UPROAR.AFTER
MAY 19,WHEN PREMIER LI PENG MADE AN IMPORTANT
SPEECH CALLING FOR RESOLUTE MEASURES TO CURB THE
TURMOIL, THESE PEOPLE FIRST PUT FORTH THE SLOGAN

""DOWN WITH DENG XIAOPING AND LI PENG."" LATER
THE TACTICS WERE READJUSTED AGAIN, AND CARE WAS
TAKEN,IN THEIR WORDS, NOT ""TO SHOUT EXTREMIST
SLOGANS, ESPECIALLY DIRECTED AT DENG XIAOPING""-IN
ORDER TO ""WIN OVER DENG XIAOPING FOR THE BENEFIT

OF THE NEXT STEP OF THE STRUGGLE."" THEY THEREFORE
CONCENTRATED THEIR ATTACK ON LI PENG AND THE ""BOGUS
GOVERNMENT."" PARA SOME PEOPLE HAVE SAID THAT IF
THE LEADERS OF THE CENTRAL AUTHORITIES HAD HELD
DIALOGUES EARLIER WITH THE STUDENTS, THINGS WOULD

NOT HAVE BECOME SO SERIOUS. THIS IS NOT TRUE. AS
PLANNED BY THE TINY MINORITY, THE ORGANIZERS OF
THE STUDENT AGITATIONS ON THE ONE HAND EXPRESSED
THEIR WILLING NESS TO HOLD DIALOGUES WITH THE GOVERNMENT
SEMICLN ON THE OTHER HAND, THEY LAID DOWN A NUMBER

OF PRECONDITIONS AND SPREAD THE WORD THAT THE GOVERNMENT
WAS NOT SINCERE. IN FACT, IT WAS THEY WHO OBSTRUCTED
THE DIALOGUES AND DID THEIR BEST TO ERECT BARRIERS.AT
FIRST, THEY SAID THAT THEY WOULD SEND 20 REPRE SENTATIVES
TO THE TALKS WITH THE GOVERNMENT. WHEN THE GOV ERNMENT

AGREED,THEY ASKED TO INCREASE THE NUMBER TO 200.
 AT THE SAME TIME, THEY STARTED A RUMOUR THAT THE
GOVERN MENT HAD LIMITED THEM TO ONLY 20 REPRESENTATIVES.
AS A RESULT, THE DIALOGUE WAS NOT HELD AS SCHEDULED.
ON THE MORNING OF MAY 13,THE OFFICES OF THE PARTY

CENTRAL COM MITTEE AND THE STATE COUNCIL INVITED
THEM TO A DIALOGUE ON MAY 15. WHILE EXPRESSING
THEIR AGREEMENT TO HOLD A DIA LOGUE,THEY PROMPTLY
ISSUED A DECLARATION, PREPARED BEFORE HAND,ANNOUNCING
THE START OF A HUNGER STRIKE, AND STARTED THE RUMOUR

THAT THE GOVERNMENT HAD REFUSED TO HOLD ANY DIALOGUES,
THUS PUSHING SOME STUDENTS TO THE EXTREMES OF STATING
A HUNGER STRIKE. PARA DURING THE STUDENT AGITATIONS,
A FEW PEOPLE WHO WERE ABLE TO OBTAIN TOP-LEVEL
SECRETS OF THE CENTRAL AUTHORITIES EVEN SENT PEOPLE

TO SOME OF BEIJING"S COLLEGES AND UNIVERSITIES
AND TO TIANANMEN SQUARE TO DIVULGE CONFIDENTIAL
INFORMATION AND STIR UP DISTURBANCES. SOMETIMES,
ONLY A FEW HOURS AFTER A MEETING OF THE STANDING
COMMITTEE OF THE PARTY POLITBURO HAD BEEN HELD,

AND BEFORE THE SUBJECTS DISCUSSED HAD BEEN TRANSMITTED
OFFICIALLY, CERTAIN UNIVERSITY CAMOPUSES WERE AL
READY IN POSSESSION OF THE INFORMATION AND HAD
MADE IT PUBLICLY KNOWN.THE DIFFERENT VIEWS OF LEADERS
OF THE PARTY CENTRAL COMMITTEE WITH REGARD TO THE

STUDENT AGITATIONS WERE WIDELY PUBLICIZED BY A
MINORITY WITH ULTERION MOTIVES, AND THIS CAUSED
SERIOUS IDEOLOGICAL CONRUSION. PARA VARIOUS POLITICAL
FORCES AT HOME AND ABROAD INTERVENED IN THE STUDENT
AGITATIONS. THEY GAVE COUNSEL TO THE STUDENTS AND

ACTED IN CONCERT WITH EACH OTHER. HU PING, CHEN
JUN AND OTHER MEMBERS OF THE REACTIONARY ORGANIZATION
CHINA DEMOCRATIC ALLIANCE JOINTLY ISSUED AN ""OPEN
LETTER TO CHINESE UNIVERSITY STUDENTS"" FROM NEW
YORK.THIS WAS POSTED UP IN MANY BEIJING UNIVERSITIES.

IT CALLED UPON THE ORGANIZERS OF THE STUDENT AGITATIONS
TO PAY ATTENTION TO ""CONSOLIDATING THE ORGANIZATIONAL
LINKS ESTABLISHED DURING THIS MOVEMENT AND TO STRIVE
FOR A STRONG MASS EFFORT IN ORDER TO BE EFFECTIVE.""
IT SAID THAT AT THAT TIME ""THE COMPLETE NEGATION

OF THE ANTI-LIBERALIZATION MOVEMENT OF 1987 SHOULD
BE USED AS A BREAK-THROUGH POINT"" AND ""IT IS
NECESSARY TO STRENGTHEN YOUR CONTACTS WITH VARIOUS
PRESS MEDIA AND OTHER CIRCLES...TO TRY TO WIN THEIR
SUPPORT AND PARTICIPATION."" TWO LEADERS OF THE

ORGANIZATION, WANG BINGZHANG AND TANG GUANGZHONG,
HURRIEDLY FLEW TO TOKYO FROM NEW YORK IN AN ATTEMPT
TO REACH BEIJING TO TAKE A HAND IN THE TURMOIL.
PARA A GROUP OF ORIGINAL MEMBERS OF THE ""CHINA
SPRING"" ORGANIZATION LIVING IN THE UNITED STATES

SET UP A ""CHINA DEMOCRATIC PARTY"" AND SENT A
""LETTER TO ALL COMPATRIOTS"" ON APRIL 16 WHICH
REACHED SOME BEIJING UNIVERSITY CAMPUS ES. IT INCITED
THE STUDENTS TO ""DEMAND THAT CONSERVATIVES AND
BUREAUCRATS STEP DOWN"" AND ""PUSH THE CHINESE

COMMUNIST PARTY TO END ITS AUTOCRATIC RULE."" PARA
ALL THESE FACTS SHOW THAT A SMALL NUMBER OF PEOPLE
AT HOME AND ABROAD COLLUDED WITH EACH OTHER, ACTED
IN COLLA BORATION AND PLANNED THE TURMOIL CAREFULLY.
PARA D. THE TINY MINORITY USED RUMOURS AND INSTIGATIONS
TO STEADILY WORSEN THE SITUATION. PARA SINCE THE

BEGINNING OF THE STUDENT AGITATIONS, BEIJING HAS
BEEN FULL OF RUMOURS OF VARIOUS SORTS. IT IS FOOD
FOR THOUGHT THAT WHENEVER THE GOVERNMENT TOOK MEASURES
TO EASE THE SITUATION AND ONCE THE STUDENTS BECAME
CALM, THERE WERE ALWAYS NEW RUMOURS AND INSTIGATIONS

WHICH LED TO GREATER UNREST. PARA AFTER THE DEATH
OF HU YAOBANG ON APRIL 15,SOME PEOPLE SPREAD THE
RUMOUR THAT ""LI PENG ABUSED HU YAOBANG AT A POLITBURO
MEETING,WHICH MADE HU TERRIBLY ANGRY AND THUS CAUSED
HIS DEATH."" PARA ON APRIL 20, A FEW PEOPLE TRIED

TO BREAK THROUGH ZHONG NANHAI"S XINHUA GATE. SOME
PEOPLE WHO HAD GATHERED IN FRONT OF THE ENTRANCE
WERE FINALLY PUT INTO BUSES BY THE POLICE ON DUTY
AND SENT BACK TO THEIR UNIVERSITIES BEFORE DAWN.
DURING THIS PROCESS, BOTH SIDES PUSHED AND TUSSLED

14/03 01 MO. 10.41 1.M

WITH ONE ANOTHER. THEN CAME THE RUMOURS, ""THE
POLICE BEAT PEOPLE AT XINHUA GATE-NOT JUST STUDENTS,
BUT WORKERS, WOMEN AND CHILDREN"" AND ""MORE THAN
A THOUSAND WORKERS IN SCIENCE AND TECHNOLOGY FELL
IN THE BLOODSHED."" AT THE SAME TIME, ANOTHER RUMOUR

RAN THAT A STUDENT FROM BEIJING NOR MAL UNIVERSITY
WAS RUN OVER BY A POLICE CAR BRACKET IN FACT, A
 STUDENT ON A BICYCLE WAS UNFORTUNATELY KILLED
IN AN ORDINARY TROLLEY BUS TRAFFIC ACCIDENT UNBRACKET
. MANY STUDENTS WHO KNEW NO THING ABOUT THE TRUTH

WERE SYMPATHETIC AND ANGRY. PARA ON APRIL 22, AFTER
THE MEMORIAL MEETING. FOR HU YAO BANG, SOME PEOPLE
SPREAD TO STUDENTS AT TIANANMEN SQUARE THE RUMOUR
THAT ""PREMIER LI PENG HAD PROMISED TO MEET THE
 STUDENTS ON THE SQUARE AT 12 CLN 45."" ACTUALLY,

HE HAD MADE NO SUCH PROMISE, AND WHEN IT DID NOT
HAPPEN, IT WAS RUMOURED THAT ""LI PENG HAS CHEATED
THE STUDENTS,"" WITH THE RESULT THAT 60,000 STUDENTS
STAGED A CLASS BOYCOTT. SO THE STUDENT AGITA TIONS
ESCALATED. ON APRIL 23, AS UNIVERSITY STUDENTS

IN THE CAPITAL BOYCOTTED CLASSES, A SMALL MINORITY
DISTRIBUTED LEAF LETS OF THE SO-CALLED BEIJING WORKERS"
FEDERATION EVERYWHERE IN ORDER TO INCITE WORKERS
TO GO ON STRIKE. PARA ON MAY 13, A NUMBER OF STUDENTS
FROM BEIJING"S UNIV ERSITIES STARTED A HUNGER STRIKE

AT TIANANMEN SQUARE. THE SMALL MINORITY SPREAD
EVERYWHERE THE RUMOUR THAT ""THE WORKERS OF BEIJING
ARE GOING ON GENERAL STRIKE"" IN ORDER TO MAKE
THE SITUATION DETERIORATE FURTHER. PARA ON MAY
20, AFTER THE IMPOSITION OF MARTIAL LAW IN SEC TIONS

OF BEIJING BY THE STATE COUNCIL, THE FOLLOWING
RUMOUR WAS SPREAD CLN ""LI PENG PRESIDED OVER A
MEETING WHICH HAS MADE FOUR DECISIONS CLN 1. THE
NATURE OF THE STUDENT MOVEMENT HAS BEEN DETERMINED
AS A REBELLION SEMICLN 2. ALL THE 200,000 STUDENTS

AT TIANANMEN SQUARE ARE TO BE SUPPRESSED SEMICLN
3. ALL THE LARGE PRISONS IN THE CAPITAL WILL BE
EMPTIED TO HOLD STUDENTS SEMICLN 4. ALL THE STREET
CLEANERS WILL BE MOBILIZED TO CLEAN UP TIANANMEN
THE MORNING AFTER THE SUPPRESSION."" LATER, MORE

RUMOURS CIRCULATED, SAYING THAT ""TROOPS WILL BE
AIR DROPPED"" AND ""THEY WILL USE TEARGAS."" ALL
THIS WAS AIMED AT INTENSIFYING THE CONFLICT BETWEEN
STUDENTS AND CITY RESIDENTS AND THE PEOPLE"S LIBERATION
ARMY. PARA THE TINY MINORITY HAS CREATED TURMOIL

BY FABRICATING RUMOURS TO DECEIVE THE MASSES. WHEN
SOME OF THEIR RUMOURS WERE SPIKED, THEY STARTED
NEW RUMOURS BY CHANGING THE APPEARANCE OF THE OLD
ONES. PARA E. A FEW PEOPLE HAVE WILLFULLY TRAMPLED
UPON DEMOCRACY AND THE LEGAL SYSTEM, AND THEIR

DEEDS HAVE LED TO SERIOUS CHAOS IN THE SOCIAL ORDER.
PARA FOR MORE THAN A MONTH, SOME PEOPLE, INCITED
BY A TINY MINORITY, ORGANIZED PARADES, DEMONSTRATIONS,
SIT-INS AND HUNGER STRIKES,ALL WITHOUT APPROVAL
AND REGARDIESS OF THE 10-POINT REGULATION ABOUT

PARADES AND DEMONSTRATIONS PASSED BY THE STANDING
COMMITTEE OF THE BEIJING PEOPLE"S CONGRESS. THEY
OCCUPIED TIANANMEN SQUARE FOR A LONG PERIOD, AND
AS A RESULT SOME IMPORTANT STATE AFFAIRS, SUCH
AS THE SINO-SOVIET SUMMIT MEETINGS, COULD NOT BE

CARRIED OUT AS PLANNED AND SOME ACTIVITIES HAD
TO BE CANCELLED. THIS SITUATION HARMED THE PRESTIGE
AND IMAGE OF CHINA. PARA AFTER THE BEGINNING OF
MAY THIS YEAR, THE DEMONSTRATIONS STEADILY INCREASED
IN SCALE, GROWING FROM TENS OF THOUSANDS TO HUNDREDS

OF THOUSANDS, EVEN TO OVER A MILLION. THIS SERIOUSLY
DISRUPTED BEIJING"S REGULAR PRODUCTION, WORK AND
SOCIAL ORDER. SOME PEOPLE SURROUNDED OFFICES OF
THE PARTY CENTRAL COMMITTEE, OFFICES OF THE STATE
COUNCIL AS WELL AS THE HOMES OF SOME STATE LEADERS.

SOME ROGUES HARASSED THE BEIJING PARTY COMMITTEE
AND THE BEIJING MUNICIPAL GOV ERNMENT, CURSING AND
USING SCURRILOUS WORDS. PUBLIC TRANS PORT IN BEIJING"S
URBAN AREA WAS SERIOUSLY DISRUPTED AND EVEN PARALYZED
FOR A TIME. INDUSTRIAL RAW MATEIALS COULD NOT BE

BROUGHT IN AND FINISHED PRODUCTS CARRIED OUT.
EVEN THE TRANSPORT OF GAS AND FOODSTUFFS WERE HAMPERED.
SHOPS AND ENTERPRISES COULD NOT MAKE BANK DEPOSITS
IN TIME. PARA SOME PEOPLE TOOK ON THE ROLES OF
POLICEMEN AND PUBLIC SECURITY PERSONNEL WITHOUT

AUTHORIZATION, STOPPING VEHICLES AND CHECKING THE
ID CARDS OF REOPLE AS THEY LIKED. SOME LAWLESS
PEOPLE WILLFULLY ABUSED AND EVEN STRUCK POLICEMEN
AND PUBLIC SECURITY PERSONNEL. AS ANARCHIC CONDITIONS
BE CAME INCREASINGLY SERIORS, LOCAL SECURITY PERSONNEL

AND ARMED POLICE FELT THEY COULD NOT CARRY OUT
THEIR HEAVY TASK OF KEEPING THE CAPITAL IN ORDER,
AND BEATION, SMASHING AND LOOTING REPEATEDLY OCCURRED.
SOME LAWLESS PEOPLE TOOK THE OPPORTUNITY TO ROB
BANKS. ONCE,DOZENS OF BANDITS ROBBED THE HUIYUAN

DEPARTMENT. STORE ON DONGSI STREET.SOME 3,800 BOTTLES
OF MILK CARRIED IN A TRUCK OF THE GUANG ANMEN DAIRY
PRODUCTS PLANT WERE STOLEN. NEAR YONG DINGMEN RAIL
WAY STATION, SOME NO.54 BUSES WERE SMASHED. SIX
RUFFIANS ROBBED SOME HUBEI PROVINCE FARMERS ON

THE HIGHWAY BE TWEEN FANGSHAN COUNTY OF BEIJING
MUMICIPALITY AND LI ANGXIANG, SAYING ""WE HEAR BEIJING
IS IN TURMOIL,AND WE ARE GOING TO GET SOME POCKET
MONEY."" DURING THE PERIOD OF DEMONSTRATIONS, SOME
RUFFIANS WENT TO THE DOWNTOWN AREAS OF WANGFUJING

AND QIANMEN, PREPARING TO ROB SHOPS AND STORES,
BUT THANKS TO THE EFFORTS OF STAFF MEMBERS AND
POL ICEMEN, THEY DID NOT SUCCEED. PARA   WHAT IS
MORE SERIOUS, THE TURMOIL SPREAD FROM BEIJING TO
 OTHER PARTS OF THE COUNTRY, AND DISTURBANCES HAPPENED

ALSO IN MANY OTHER CITIES. IN SOME AREAS, ATTACKS
ON LOCAL GOVERN MENT AND PARTY COMMITTEE OFFICES
OCCURRDE ONE AFTER ANOTH ER. BEATING, SMASHING,LOOTING,BURNING
AND OTHER DISRUPTIVE ACTIVITIES WERE CARRIED OUT.
CHINA"S TRANSPORT NETWORK WAS BROKEN FOR A PERIOD.

STUDENTS IN SOME AREAS FORCED THEIR WAY ONTO TRAINS
TO BEIJING WITHOUT TICKETS SEMICLN SOME EVEN LAY
ON THE   TRACKS TO STOP TRAINS. DURING THIS TIME,OVER
200,000 STUDENTS FROM OTHER PARTS OF CHINA ENTERED
BEIJING. THEY BOARDED TRAINS WITHOUT TICKETS AND

DID NOT PAY FOR THEIR MEALS, JUST AS YOUNG PEOPLE
HAD DONE DURING THE ""CULTURAL REVOLUTION."" PARA
F A FEW PEOPLE ATTEMPTED TO SEIZE POWER BY TAKING
 ADVANTAGE OF THE TURMOIL. PARA   PROVOKED BY A
TINY MINORITY, SOME UNIVERSITY STUDENTS PROCLAIMED

THE ABOLITION OF THE REGULAR STUDENT UNION AND
POSTGRADUATE STUDENT UNION, LEADERS OF WHICH HAD
BEEN ELECTED BY THE STUDENTS,AND THE ESTABLISHMENT
OF A SO-CALLED AUTONOMOUS STUDENT ORGANIZATION
SOME STUDENTS EVEN TOOK OVER CAMPUS BROADCASTING

STATIONS. LATER, THESE GROUPS UNIT ED TO BECOME
THE CENTRE DIRECTING THE STUDENT AGITATION. PARA
  BEFORE MARTIAL LAW WAS DECLARED,THE SITUATION
WAS BE COMING MORE AND MORE SERIORS.SOME WORK UNITS
HAD PRE PATED TO ASK THEIR LEADERS TO ""TRANSFER

THEIR POWER.""IN SOME MINISTRIES OF THE STATE COUNCIL,
CERTAIN GROUPS OF GOVERN MENT EMPLOYEES ASKED THE
MINISTERS TO STEP DOWN. SOME PEOPLE DISTRIBUTED
LEAFLETS PROCLAIMING THE ESTABLISHMENT OF A ""PREPARATORY
COMMITTEE FOR AN ALL-CIRCLES REPRESENTATIVE CONGRESS

OF BEIJING "" TO REPLACE THE CURRENT BEIJING PEOPLE"S
 CONGRESS, AND CALLING FOR THE SETTING UP OF A
""BEIJING REGION AL GOVERNMENT"" TO TAKE THE PLACE
OF THE PRESENT LEGAL MUN ICIPAL GOVERNMENT . SOME
PEOPLE ATTACKED THE LEGALLY SELECTED STATE COUNCIL

AS A "" BOGUS GOVERNNMENT,"" SPREAD RUMOURS THAT
 CHINA"S FOREIGN AFFAIRS MINISTRY AND SOME 10 OTHER
MINIS TRIES HAD DECLARED THEIR INDEPENDENCE FROM
THE PRESENT STATE COUNCIL AND THAT MORE THAN 30
COUNTRIES HAD BROKEN DIPLOM ATIC RELATIONS WITH

CHINA. SOME PERSONS CLAIMED THAT ""DENG XIAOPING
HAS STEPPED DOWN"" AND THAT A ""NEW GOVERNMENT""
WOULD BE FOUNDED IN THREE DAYS" TIME. PARA A FEW
PEOPLE ORGANIZED SOME ROGUES AND LOCAL RUFFIANS
INTO A ""FLYING TIGER TEAM,""WHICH INCLUDED OVER

14/00 01 MON 10:49 FAX

A HUNDRED MOTORCYCLISTS, AND A ""DARE-TO-DIE CORPS""
OF OVER A THOUSAND BICYCLISTS. PEOPLE WERE ASKED
TO RISE, AS THE MASSES HAD IN THE GREAT FRENCH
REVOLUTION, TO ""ATTACK THE BASTILLEBHSS THE HAND
FUL OF PEOPLE THREATENED TO PUT PARTY AND STATE

LEADERS ""UNDER HOUSE ARREST."" PARA DO NOT THESE
FACTS CONSTITUTE TURMOIL QUERY TO RESTORE THE SOCIAL
STABILITY OF BEIJING AND PROTECT PEOPLE"S LIFE
AND PRI VATE AND PUBLIC PROPERTY, AND TO ENABLE
THE CENTRAL DEPART MENTS AND THE BEIJING MUNICIPAL

GOVERNMENT TO CARRY OUT THEIR NORMAL DUTIES, IT
WAS NECESSARY FOR THE STATE COUNCIL, AS PROVIDED
FOR IN THE CHINESE CONSTITUTION, TO DECLARE MARTIAL
LAW IN SOME SECTIONS OF THE CITY. IF THE STATE
DID NOT TAKE DECISIVE MEASURES BUT LET THE SERIOUS

SITUATION DETERIOR ATE, EVEN GREATER DISTURBANCES
WOULD OCCUR IN THE CAPITAL,THE WHOLE COUNTRY WOULD
FALL INTO SERIOUS TURMOIL AND THE RE FORMS AND MODERNIZATION
DRIVE WOULD FALL APATR. THIS, OF COURSE, IS NOT
WHAT THE L.L BILLION CHINESE PEOPLE REALLY WANT

 TO SEE. PARA   2. WHY MATRIAL LAW LS NECESSARY
PARA SOME PEOPLE HAVE ASKED, WHY WAS MARTIAL LAW
IMPOSED ON MAY 20, SINCE THE FASTING STUDENTS AT
TIANANMEN HAD ENDED THEIR HUNGER STRIKE ON THE
EVENING OF MAY 19 QUERY HERE, TWO POINTS HAVE TO

BE CLARIFIED CLN PARA A.THE IMPOSITION OF MARTIAL
LAW ON SOME SECTIONS OF THE CAPITAL WAS NOT JUST
TO SOLVE THE PROBLEM OF SOME HUNGER STRIKING STUDENTS,
BUT TO END THE TURMOIL, ELIMMATE THE SERIOUS, ANARCHIC
SITUATION, RESTORE NORMAL ORDER IN BEIJING AND

PREVENT MORE SERIOUS TURBULENCE. PARA   B.THE NEWS
THAT THE STATE COUNCIL HAD DECIDED TO IMPOSE MARTIAL
LAW WAS LEAKED VERY QUICKLY. SO A SMALL NUMBER
OF PEOPLE IMMEDIATELY MOBILIZED THE STUDENTS TO
CHANGE THE HUNGER STRIKE TO A SIT-IN. THIS SHOWED

THE TACTICS OF THE TINY MINORITY. PARA SOME PEOPLE
HAVE ALSO ASKED ,WHY IS .IT STILL NECESSARY TO ENFOREE
MARTIAL LAW IN BEIJING,SINCE ORDER HAS BASICALLY
BEEN   RESTORED QUERY PARA   FIRST, FOR MORE THAN
A MONTH, UNDER EXTREMELY DIFFICULT CIRCUMSTANCES,

THE BROAD MASSES OF WORKERS, FARMERS, COM MERCIAL
PEOPLE, TEACHERS, MEDICAL WORKERS,CADRES OF STREET
 COMMITTEES ,PARTY AND GOVERNMENT OFFICE STAFF
AND ARMED POLICE AND PUBLIC SECURITY PERSONNEL
HAD REMAINED AT THEIR POSTS, PERFORMED THEIR DUTY

AND MADE GREAT CONTRIBUTIONS TO ENSURE NORMAL PRODUCTION
AND OPERATIONS IN THE CAPITAL. NOTABLY, AFTER THE
DECLARATION OF MARTIAL LAW AND WHEN ENFORCEMENT
TROOPS REACHED BEIJING, PEOPLE FROM ALL WALKS OF
          MADE EFFORTS TO SET THINGS RIGHT.

14/05 '01 MON 17:40 FAX *IN THE END THEY PUT ON A TWO-BIT FARCE OF A "HUNGER'*

STRIKE"" BY FOUR PERSONS FOR 48-72 HOURS.

THEY DISTRIBUTED LEAFLETS INCITING ACOUNTER-REVOLUTIONARY ARMED REBELLION,CLAMOURING THAT THEY WOULD ORGANIZE ""AN ARMED FORCE"" AND ""UNITE WITH VARIOUS FORCES INCLUDING THE KUOMINTANG IN TAIWAN,""AND THAT THEY WOULD ""TAKE A CLEAR-CUT STAND AGAINST THE COMMUNIST PARTY AND ITS GOVERN-MENT"" AND ""WOULD NOT HESITATE TO DIE.""

ALL THIS SHOWS THAT THE TURMOIL CREATED BY A HANDFUL OF REBELS IN A PLANNED AND PREMEDITATED WAY WAS BY NO MEANS TENDING TO SUBSIDE AS IMAGINED BY SOME KIND-HEARTED PEOPLE. RATHER,RNDER A CHANGED APPEARANCE,THESE ELEMENTS' WERE CONTINUING THEIR DESPERATE STRUGGLE.

THEY KNEW FULL WELL THAT ONCE THE MARTIAL LAW INFORCE-MENT TROOPS WERE IN POSITION,THEIR PLOT WOULD FALL THROUGH. SO THEY WAITED FOR AN OPPORTUNITY TO PROVOKE DISTURBANCES AND INTENSIFY THE TURMOIL.

ON JUNE 1,WHEN PUBLIC SECURITY ORGANIZATIONS DETAINED SEVERAL LEADERS OF THE ""AUTONOMOUS UNION OF WORKERS,""AN ILLEGAL ORGANIZATION,FOR INVESTIGATION,THE HANDFUL TOOK AD-VANTAGE OF THIS OPPORTUNITY TO INSTIGATE SOME PEOPLE TO ENCIRCLE AND ATTACK THE BEIJING MUNICIPAL PUBLIC SECURITY BUREAU,THE BEIJING MUNICIPAL PARTY COMMITTEE,THE BEIJING MUNICIPAL GOVERNMENT OFFICE AND THE MINISTRY OF PUBLIC SECURITY.

ON THE EVENING OF JUNE 2,WHEN A JEEP,WHICH THE CHINA CENTRAL TELEVISION HAD BORROWED FROM AN ARMED POLICE UNIT FOR TEN MONTHS TO PRODUCE A FULL-LENGTH DOCUMENTARY TO MARK THE 40TH ANNIVERSARY OF THE FOUNDING OF THE' PEOPLE"S REPUBLIC,WAS ON ITS WAY BACK TO ITS ORIGINAL WORK UNIT,AN ACCIDENT OCCURRED IN WHICH THE JEEP OVERTURNED DUE TO EXCESSIVE SPEED AND A SLIPPERY SURFACE,KILLING THREE PEOPLE AND INJURING ONE.NONE OF THEM WERE STUDENTS.THIS WAS OF COURSE A TRAFFIC ACCIDENT, AND THE DEPARTMENT CONCERNED WAS ALREADY HANDLING THE CASE.HOWEVER,A HANDFUL OF ELEMENTS DELIBERATELY LINKED THIS ACCIDENT WITH THE MARTIAL LAW EN-FORCEMENT TROOPS" PLANNED ACTION OF ENTERING THE CITY.THEY SPREAD A LOT OF RUMOURS,CLAIMING THAT IT WAS THE TROOPS" ""PAVE-THE-WAY""VEHICLE WHICH RAN OVER STUDENTS ON PURPOSE, INCITING PEOPLE NOT CLEAR ABOUT THE FACTS.THEY TRIED TO SEIZE THE THREE BODIES AND CARRY THE COFFINS IN A PROCESSION THROUGH THE STREETS.THE ATMOSPHERE WAS VERY TENSE FOR A WHILE AND THE FLAME OF THE REBELLION WAS THUS IGNITED BY THEM.

2.WHAT HAPPENED ON JUNE 3?

IN THE SMALL HOURS OF JUNE 3, WHEN THE MARTIAL LAW ENFORCEMENT TROOPS WERE ON THEIR WAY TO THE SECURITY AREA ACCORDING TO A SET PLAN,SOME PEOPLE SHOUTED AT THE TOP OF THEIR VOICES AND INCITED OTHERS TO INTERCEPT MOTOR VEHICLES AND CARS,PUT UP ROADBLOCKS,STOP MILITARY VEHICLES,BEAT SOLDIERS AND SEIZE MILITARY SUPPLIES AT THE JIANGUOMEN,NAN-HEYAN,XIDAN AND MUXIDI CROSSINGS ALONG THE CHANG"AN AVENUE.

ATONE O"CLOCK IN THE MORNING,12 MILITARY VEHICLES WERE INTERCEPTED NEAR LUGEZHUANG,SOLDIERS PASSING THE YANJING ____ ____ ___ ___ _____ VEHICLES IN FRONT

AT EITHER END OF YONGDINGMEN BRIDGE AND THE TYRES OF THE
MILITARY VEHICLES IN MUXIDI WERE SLASHED.MORE THAN 400
SOLDIERS MOVING TOWARDS THE CITY WERE STONED BY RIOTERS IN
CHAOYANGMEN.MILITARY VEHICLES WERE STOPPED AND SOLDIERS
WERE PINNED DOWN IN LIUBUKOU AND HENGERTIAO.

ABOUT SEVEN O"CLOCK IN THE MORNING,SOME RIOTERS RUSHED
TO THE MILITARY VEHICLES BESIEGED AT LIUBUKOU AND SNATCHED
LOADED MACHINE-GUNS.FROM JIANGUOMEN TO DONGDAN AND
TIANQIAO,THE MARTIAL LAW ENFORCEMENT TROOPS WERE SPORADI-
CALLY BLOCKED,ATTACKED AND BEATEN.ON THE JIANGUOMEN
OVERPASS,SOME SOLDIERS WERE STRIPPED TO THE SKIN AND OTHERS
WERE REDUCED TO TEARS BECAUSE THEY WERE CO BADIY BEATEN.

IN THE MORNING,THE MARTIAL LAW ENFORCEMEMT TROOPS WERE
ATTACKED NEAR HUFANGQIAO AND SOLDIERS WERE SO BADLY BEATEN
THAT SOME OF THEM WERE BLINDED.SOME WOUNDED SOLDIERS
WERE INTERCEPTED ON THEIR WAY TO THE HOSPITAL.THE AMBU-
LANCE TYRES WERE DEFLATED AND THE WOUNDED SOLDIERS TAKEN
AWAY.FROM HUFANGQIAO TO TAORANTING,21 MILITARY VEHICLES
WERE BESIEGED.WHEN SOLDIERS WERE SHIFTING THE AMMUNITION,
POLICEMEN GOING TO GUARD THE ACTION WERE INJURED.

AT NOON.LIBERATION ARMY FIGHTERS WERE BLOCKED AT THE
SOUTHERN ENTRANCE OF FUYOUJIE,AT THE NORTHERN ENTRANCE OF
ZHENGYI ROAD AND AT XUANWUMEN,HUFANGQIAO,MUXIDI
AND DONGSI.SOMEWERE WOUNDED,AND THE HELMETS,MILITARY
CAPS,"RAINCOATS,KETTLES AND SATCHELS OF OTHERS WERE SNATCHED
AWAY AT SOME CROSSINGS,HARD TACK AND CANNED FOOD WERE
SPILLED ON THE GROUND.SOME RIOTERS INTERCEPTED A MILITARY
VEHICLE LADEN WITH FIREARMS AND AMMUNITION IN LIUBUKOU,
AND THE ARMED POLICE AND PUBLIC SECURITY MEN FAILED TO
RESCUE IT AFTER REPEATED EFFORTS.IF THE FIREARMS AND AMMU-
NITION WERE TAKEN AWAY OR IF AN EXPLOSION OCCUR,THE CONSE-
QUENCES WOULD DE DISASTROUS.IN ORDER TO PROTECT PEOPLE"S
SAFETY AND PROPERTY IN THE CAPITAL,THE ARMED POLICE,OUT OF
ABSOLUTE NECESSITY,FIRED TEAR-GAS SHELLS AND RECOVERED THE
AMMUNITION VEHICLE.AT THE TIME,SOME STUDENTS WERE
WOUNDED AND SENT TO HOSPITAL FOR TREATMENT.

MEANWHILE,SOME RIOTERS BEGAN TO ENCIRCLE AND ASSAULT
GOVERNMENT OFFICES AND IMPORTANT DEPARTMENTS.THEY AS-
SAULTED THE GREAT HALL OF THE PEOPLE,THE PROPAGANDA DE-
PARTMENT OF THE CPC CENTRAL COMMITTEE,THE MINISTRY OF
RADIO,FILM AND TELEVISION AND THE WEST AND SOUTH GATES OF
LM NGNANHAI(WHERE THE STATE COUNCIL AND THE HEADQUARTERS

OF THE PARTY CENTRAL COMMITTEE ARE LOCATED).SEVERAL DOZEN
ARMED POLICE AND PUBLIC SECURITY OFFICERS AND MEN PROTECT-
ING THESE ORGANIZATIONS WERE WOUNDED.

THE RIOTERS BECAME MORE RECKLESS AS THE SITUATION DETER-
IORATED.ABOUT FIVE O"CLOCK IN THE AFTERNOON,SOME PEOPLE OF
THE ILLEGAL""AUTONOMOUS UNION OF UNIVERSITY STUDENTS""AND
""AUTONOMOUS UNION OF WORKERS""ISSUED KITCHEN KNIVES,
DAGGERS,IRON BARS,IRON CHAINS AND SHARPENED BAMBOO POLES
TO THE MASSES WHO WERE UNAWARE OF THE TRUE SITUATION ON THE
TIANANMEN SQUARE,AND WOWED TO ""BEAT THE SOLDIERS AND
POLICEMEN TO DEATH.""THROUGH THE LOUDSPEAKERS THE ""AUTON-
OMOUS UNION OF WORKERS""CLAMOURED FOR ""TOPPLING THE
GOVERNMENT WITH WEAPONS.""A MOB OF SOME 1,000 PEOPLE
INCITED BY A GANG OF RIOTERS PUSHED OVER THE ENCLOSING WALL
··· ···· ···· ····· SEIZED LARGE QUANTITIES OF

AT THIS CRUCIAL MOMENT,THE PARTY CENTRAL COMMITTEE,
THE STATE COUNCIL AND THE MILITARY COMMISSION OF THE CPC
CENTRAL COMMITTEE DECIDED TO ORDER THE MARTIAL LAW ENFORCE-
MENT TROOPS STATIONED IN THE SURROUNDING AREAS OF THE CAPITAL
TO FORCE THEIR WAY INTO THE CAPITAL AND SUPPRESS THE REBELLION.
3.PLA SOLDIERS WERE FORCED TO SHOOT.
    IT IS EVIDENT TO ALL THAT FROM THE ANNOUNCEMENT OF THE
MARTIAL LAW,PLA SOLDIERS IN DOWNTOWN BEIJING HAD ALWAYS
EXERCISED A HIGH DEGREE OF RESTRAINT TO AVOID ANY POSSIBLE
CONFLICT.ON JUNE 3, WHEN THE RIOT BROKE OUT,IN ORDER TO
AVOID INJURING ORDINARY PEOPLE,THE BEIJING MUNICIPAL PEO-
PLE"S GOVERNMENT AND THE HEADQUARTERS OF THE MARTIAL LAW
ENFORCEMENT TROOPS JOINTLY ANNOUNCED AN EMERGENCY NOTICE
AT 6:30 P.M.,URGING""ALL BEIJING RESIDENTS MUST KEEP ALERT,
AND FROM NOW ON MUST NOT GO TO THE STREETS AND TIANANMEN
SQUARE:BEIJING"S WORKERS AND STAFF MEMBERS MUST STAND FAST
AT THEIR POSTS AND RESIDENTS STAY AT HOME SO THAT THEIR
PERSONAL SAFETY CAN BE GUARANTEED.""THIS NOTICE WAS AIRED
REPEATEDLY THROUGH RADIO, TV AND OTHER BROADCASTING DEV-
ICES.
    AROUND 10 P.M.ON JUNE 3,ALLTHE MARTIAI LAW ENFORCE-
MENT TROOPS RECEIVED THEIR ORDERS AND BEGAN MOVING INTO
DOWNTOWN BEIJING FROM ALL DIRECTIONS.HOWEVER,THEY WERE
SEVERELY OBSTRUCTED AND HELD UP AT ALL THE MAJOR INTERSEC-
TIONS.EVEN SO,THEY STILL EXERCISED AN EXTREMELY HIGH DEGREE
OF RESTRAINT.NEVERTHELESS,THE RIOTERS,TAKING ADVANTAGE OF
THE SOLDIERS" SELF-RESTRAINT,LAUNCHED A HAIR-RAISING MELEE OF
BEATING,SMASHING,LOOTING,BURNING AND KILLING.
FROM QP TO 11 P.M.,ALTOGE THER 12 MILITARY VEHICLES WERE
BURNED AT THE SECTION FROM CUIWEILU,GONGZHUFEN AND MUX-
IDI TO XIDAN.SOME RIOTERS BROUGHT IN A TRUCKLOAD OF BRICKS
AND DEBRIS AND HURLED THEM AT SOLDIERS,WHILE OTHERS BLOCKED
THE ROAD BY PUSHING A TROLLEY BUS TO THE INTERSECTION AND THEN
SETTING IT ON FIRE.EVEN A FIRE-ENGINE WHICH WAS ON ITS WAY TO
FIGHTING A FIRE COULD NOT ESCAPE AND WAS SMASHED AND
BURNED ON THE SPOT.
    AROUND 11 P.M.,THREE MORE MILITARY VEHICLES WERE DES-
TRYED AND ONE MORE JEEP WAS OVERTURNED IN THE HUFANGQIAO
AREA.MILITARY VEHICLES WERE INTERCEPTED AROUND THE ANDING-
MEN OVERPASS:SOLDIERS ABOUT THE SIZE OF A REGIMENT WERE
BLOCKED ON CHONGWENMEN STREET:30 MORE MILITARYVEHICLES
WERE ENCIRCLED AROUND THE JIANGUOMEN OVERPASS:AND MORE
THAN 300 MILITARY VEHICLES WERE BESIEGED TO THE WEST OF THE
BEIJING COAL INDUSTRIAL SCHOOL.IN ORDER TO KEEP MOVING
FORWARD,OFFICERS AND MEN GOT DOWN FROM THEIR VEHICLES TO
PERSUADE PEOPLE TO MAKE WAY FOR THEM.HOWEVER,THEY WERE
EITHER BEATEN OR KIDNAPPED AND SOME OF THEM ARE MISSING.
MILITARY VEHICLES BESIEGED AROUND THE NANYUAN AREA IN
SOUTHERN BEIJING HAD TO MAKE A DETOUR TO AVOID CONFLICT WITH
THE MASSES.HOWEVER,THCY WERE ENCIRCLED AGAIN WHEN THEY
ARRIVED AT THE SOUTHERN GATE OF TIANTAN PARK(THE TEMPLE OF
HEAVEN PARK),AND MANY OF THE VEHICLES WERE EITHER DES-
TROYED OR BURNED.WHEN A GROUP OF RIOTERS CLIMBED ON TOP
OF A MILITARY VEHICLE BESIEGED AT THE AREA OF ZHUSHIKOU,A
MAN LOOKING LIKE A CADRE CAME UP AND TRIED TO PERSUADE
THEM TO COME DOWN.HE WAS BEATEN UP AND NO ONE KNOWS
WHETHER HE DIED OR NOT.
    IN THE SMALL HOURS OF JUNE 4, THE SITUATION BECAME EVEN
WORSE.SEVERAL HUNDRED MORE MILITARY VEHICLES WERE SET

ALIGHT WITH GASOLINE,HOME-MADE INCENDIARY BOTTLES AND
FLAME THROWERS AT EAST TIANTAN ROAD, THE NORTH GATE OF
TIANTAN PARK,THE WEST ENTRANCE OF QIANMEN SUBWAY STA-
TION,EAST QIANMEN ROAD,FUYOU STREET,LIUBUKOU,XIDAN,
FUXINGMEN,SOUTH LISHI ROAD,MUXIDI,LIUBUKOU,CHE-
GONGZHUANG,DONGHUAMEN,DONGZHIMEN,CHAOYANG DIS-
TRICT"S DABEIYAO, HUJIALOU,BEIDOUGEZHUANG,THE JIUGONG
TOWNSHIP OF DAXING COUNTY AND AT MANY OTHER INTERSEC-
TIONS.MANY SOLDIERS WERE EITHER BURNED OR BEATEN TO DEATH.
AT SOME OF THESE INTERSECTIONS,SEVERAL AND EVEN DOZENS OF
VEHICLES WERE BURNED,TURNING THE SCENE INTO A SEA OF FIRE.
FOR EXAMPLE,MORE THAN 70 ARMOURED VEHICLES WERE HELD
UP AROUND SHUANGJING INTERSECTION,AND 20 OF THEM WERE
STRIPPED OF THEIR MACHINE-GUNS.MORE THAN 30 MILITARY VEHI-
CLES WERE SET ALIGHT ON THE ROAD FROM JINGYUAN INTERSECTION
TO LAOSHAN CREMATORY.SOME RIOTERS,IRON BARS AND GAS
DRUMS IN HAND,GUARDED EVERY INTERSECTION AND BURNED ALL
VEHICLES IDENTIFIED AS MILITARY IN DEFIANCE OF WARNING SHOTS.
SEVERAL RIOTERS CAPTURED AN ARMOURED VEHICLE AROUND THE
AREA OF THE FUXINGMEN OVERPASS AND FIRED WHEREVER THEY
DROVE.THE ILLEGAL""ARTONOMOUS UNION OF WORKERS""DE-
CLARED IN A BROADCAST THAT THEY HAD CAPTURED A MILITARY RADIO
AND A CIPHER CODE BOOK.SOME MILITARY SUPPLY AND PROVISION
TRUCKS WERE ALSO BURNED OR RANSACKED.

TAKING ADVANTAGE OF THE CONTUSION,SOME RIOTERS ALSO
SMASHED AND DESTROYED CIVILIAN FOCILITIES FOR EXAMPLE,THEY
BROKE ALL THE DISPLAY WINDOWS OF THE YANSHAN AND OTHER
STORES AND SET FIRE TO THE PINE FENCES TO THE WEST OF THE MAO
ZEDONG MEMORIAL HALL AND DESTROYED AND BURNED PUBLIC
BUSES,FIRE-ENGINES,AMBULANCES AND TAXIS.WHAT WAS MOST
RUTHLESS WAS THAT SOME RIOTERS PUSHED A PUBLIC BUS UNDER
TIANANMEN (THE GATE OF HEAVENLY PEACE)AND ATTEMPTED TO
SET THE GATETOWER ON FIRE.

WHILE ATTACKING MILITARY VEHICLES AND INDULGING IV BEAT-
ING,SMASHING,LOOTING AND BURNING,THESE RIOTERS ALSO KILLED
PLA SOLDIERS RUTHIESSLY.

EARLY ON THE MORNING OF JUNE 4,A HORDE OF RIOTERS
ATTACKED THE SOLDIERS WITH WINE BOTTLES,BRICKS AND EVEN
BICYCLES AT THE INTERSECTION OF DONGDAN,WOUNDING MANY OF
THEM.AT FUXINGMEN,ONE MILITARY VEHICLE WAS INTERCEPTED
AND ATTACKED.ED.THE 12 SOLDIERS ABOARD,INCLUDING AQUARTER-
MASTER AND COOKS,WERE FORCIBLY PULLED OUT,BODY-SEARCHED
AND CRUELLY BEATEN.MANY WERE SERIOUSLY WOUNDED.AT LIU-
BUKOU,FOUR SOLDIERS WERE BESIEGED AND ATTACKED,AND SOME
OF THEM WERE KILLED.AT GUANGQUMEN THREE SOLDIERS WERE
BEATEN UP.ONE WAS RESCUED BY SOME PEOPLE BUT THE WHEREA-
BOUTS OF THE OTHER TWO IS STILL UNKNOWN.AT XIXINGSHENG
LANE IN XICHENG DISTRICT,SOME 20 ARMED POLICE WERE AT-
TACKED BY RIOTERS.SOME OF THEM WERE SERIOUSLY WOUNDED AND
THE WHEREABOUTS OF SOME OTHERS ARE STILL UNKNOWN.AT HUG-
UOSI,ONE MILITARY VEHICLE WAS INTERCEPTED BY THE RIOTERS AND
THE SOLDIERS WERE CRUELLY BEATEN UP AND TAKEN AS HOSTAGES.
THE RIOTERS GRABBED MANY OF THEIR MACHINE-GUNS.WHEN ONE
TRUCK LOADED WITH BRICKS BOUND FOR THE TIANANMEN SQRARE
FROM DOAGJIAO MINXIANG PASSED BY,PEOPLE ABOARD THE TRUCK
SHOUTED.""IF YOU ARE CHINESE,COME AND HIT THE SOLDIERS WITH

BRICKS.""
AFTER DAWN,THE HAIR-RAISING ATROCITIES OF BEATING ----
KILLING PLA ARMYMEN SHOCKED THE WHOLE CITY.ONE ARMED
POILICE AMBULANCE CARRYING EIGHT WOUNDED SOLDIERS WAS INTER-

,CEPTED AND ATTACKED BY RIOTERS.THEYKILLED ONE OF THE
WOUNDED SOLDIERS AND THREATENED TO KILL THD OTHERS.
    IN FRONT OF A BICYCLE STORE AT QIANMEN,THREE SOLDIERS WERE
BEATEN UP AND SERIOUSLY WOUNDED,AND THE RIOTERS SHOUTED TO
THE ON-LOOKERS,""/WE"LL KILL WHOEVER DARES TO RESCUE THEM.""
ON CHANG"AN AVENUE ONE MOVING MILITARY VEHICLE BROKE
DOWN SUDDENLY,AND WAS ATTACKED RIGHT AWAY BY ABOUT 200
RIOTERS.THE DRIVER WAS KILLED INSIDE THE CAB.
    THIRTY METRES TO THE EAST OF THE CROSSROAD AT XIDAN.THE
RIOTERS KILLED ONE SOLDIER AND,POURING GASOLINE OVER THE
BODY,SET IT ON FIRE.AT FUCHENGMEN,THE RIOTERS HUNG THE
BODY OF A SOLDIER UP ON THE BALUSTRADE OF THE OVERPASS.AT
CHONGWENMEN,THEY THREW ONE SOLDOER DOWN FROM THE FLY-
OVER AND,POURIND GASOLINE OVER THE SOLDIER,BURNED HIM
ALIVE.AT A PLACE NEAR THE SHOUDU CINEMA ON WEST CHANG"AN
AVENUE ONE PLA OFFICER WAS BEATEN TO DEATH BY THE RIOTERS,
WHO THEN GOUGED OUT HIS EYES AND CUT OPEN HIS BELLY,THE
BODY WAS HUNG OVER A BLAZING MILITARY VEHICLE.THE RIOTERS
ALSO KILLED ONE SOLDIER,GORGING OUT HIS EYES,CUTTING OFF HIS
GENITALS AND THROWING HIS BODY INTO THE MOAT.
    ACCORDING TO INCOMPLETE STATISTICS,THE RIOTERS DESTROYED
AND BURNED MORE THAN 450 MILITARY VEHICLES,POILICE CARS AND
PUBLIC BUSES,INCLUDING SOME 180 MILITARY TRUCKS,SOME 40
ARMOURED VEHICLES,SOME 90 POLICE CARS,SOME 80 PUBLIC
BUSES AND 40-SOME OTHER MOTOR VEHICLES.THEY TOOK AWAY
WEAPONS AND AMMUNITION,KILLING ABOUT 100 MARTIAL LAW
ENFORCEMENT SOLDIERS,ARMED POLICE AND PUBLIC SECURITY PER-
SONNEL AND WOUNDING SEVERAL THOUSANDS.
    SUCH A TRAGIC SCENE CONVINCINGLY TELLS OF THE GREAT RES-
TRAINT EXERCISED BY THE MARTIAL LAW ENFORCEMENT TROOPS.
OTHERWISE,HOW COULD SO MANY SOLDIERS HAVE BEEN KILLED AND
WOUNDED?AND HOW COULD THE TROOPS HAVE SUFFERED SUCH
GREAT LOSSES?DRIVEN BEYOND FORBEARANCE,THE MARTIAL LAW
GREAT LOSSES?
ENFORCEMENT TROOPS.WHO COULD HARDLY MOVE ONE STEP FOR-
WARD,COUNTER-ATTACKED,KILLING SOME OF THE RIOTERS BECAUSE
THERE WERE NUMEROUS ON-LOOKERS AND STUDENTS,SOME WERE
KNOCKED DOWN BY VEHICLES.,SOME WERE COUGHT UP IN CROWDS
AND OTHERS WERE HIT BY STRAY BULLETS.DURING THE RIOT,MORE
THAN 1,000 OF THE PEOPLE WERE WOUNDED AND MORE THAN 100
DIED.NOBODY LIKES TO SEE SUCH A THING HAPPEN.AS TO THE
PEOPLE AND STUDENTS ACCIDENTALLY INJURED,THE GOVERNMENT
AND THE MARTIAL LAW ENFORCEMENT TROOPS HAVE THE SAME
FEELINGS FOR THEM AS HAVE THEIR FAMILY MEMBERS.THE AFTER-
MATH OF THESE ACCIDENTAL INJURIES WILL BE CAREFULLY DEALT WITH
                                        (JUNE 5,1989)

21

Marriage in Mayhem

SUNDAY, MAY 21, 1989
TIANANMEN SQUARE

This was the thirty-eighth day of the demonstrations. Once more climbing the steps to the Monument to the People's Heroes, Cassy sensed a growing defeatism among the student leaders. It was not only because of lack of sleep, absence of proper food, or no chance to wash almost six weeks of grime from their bodies and clothes; hundreds of thousands of others in the square were enduring the same conditions. Rather she felt a *"great malaise"* had settled over the leadership.

It had been there when Cassy woke after a short sleep, squashed between Daobao and Yang Li at the base of the pediment. The first of the Party loud-speaker broadcasts had awakened them all, warning that the square would soon be cleared by force. In a new twist, the broadcast from inside the Great Hall of the People had ordered all doctors and nurses to return immediately to their hospitals to prepare for the expected casualties.

"It's psychological warfare," Cassy had told her companions. *"It means they're not going to actually do anything yet."*

Daobao had said no one could know what the authorities were planning. In a pensive mood he and Yang Li had gone to the command bus to join Wuerkaixi at the first strategy meeting of the day.

Hours earlier Cassy and Daobao had stood and watched Dan Rather addressing millions of Americans glued to the *"CBS Evening News."* The anchorman had shown few signs that he had been in the square for twenty-four straight hours without sleep. He seemed to be operating on pure adrenalin. With Tiananmen Gate as his backdrop, Rather addressed the camera: *"They are still here. The army is not. Incredible! China's Communist government hardliners are finally in control of the government and the Party, and they have called out the army in yet another desperate bid to break the back of the mass movement for freedom and democracy and reform. After weeks of government paralysis, while students took over the streets of Beijing and moved their protest into a national movement, soldiers are now massing to move against the protesters camped right here in the center of Beijing. The problem is, the army has been massing for hours and is still not here."*

As Daobao and Yang Li walked to the bus, Cassy could see Rather and his film crew beside their beat-up Toyota, which was filled with equipment to transmit audio and video tapes via microwave to their "base camp" on the fifth floor of the Shangri-La Hotel. From there the sound and pictures were sent by satellite to New York.

Suddenly Cassy saw the CBS technician gesticulating. She walked over to see the trouble, and discovered the microwave link out of the square was not working. Someone had cut the hookup to the hotel. A short while later it was restored. But Rather presciently asked his colleagues, *"For how long?"*

With a camera crew in tow, the anchorman set off to *"film what we could before they closed us down."*

Overhead more camouflaged military helicopters swooped in over the Beijing Hotel and began to circle the square.

Rather, who knew what panic was from his days of reporting from the streets of Saigon, feared that the helicopters, swooping even lower, might stampede the crowd. To Cassy, raised in the Midwest, the choppers *"resembled cowboys trying to get a herd of cattle to move."*

After a short while the helicopters rose into the air and disappeared westward across the city. Their pilots had thought better of risking their rotors becoming entangled with kite lines.

Wuerkaixi stood in the door of the command bus and watched them depart. Then he returned to the strategy meeting.

Outside the bus, Chai Ling was telling an ABC film crew that while some of the leaders now wanted to abandon the sit-in on Tiananmen, others were considering setting themselves on fire.

"I am ready to sacrifice myself," said Chai Ling in her bird-like voice. *"I will do anything to stop this surrender mentality. Personally, I want the government to launch a bloodbath so that the world can see their true value. At the same time I feel the revolutionary cinders must be preserved to start a new fire."*

She stared uncompromisingly into the camera, her face drained from her six weeks in the square. One of the film crew had offered her a lipstick before the interview started. She had quickly shaken her head, saying it was not what she looked like but what she had to say that was important.

To Barr Seitz her fervor had *"a real touch of Joan of Arc. Every time she spoke to cameras millions of viewers all over the world were stirred by her dignity and courage. She had a dedication to her cause that was both ennobling and a little frightening. She was more than a patriot or revolutionary. There was something almost mesmeric about her. If she, and not Wuerkaixi, had been leading the students, things may have been different by now. As it was, despite her call to fight on to the death, there was a mood of defeatism. Wuerkaixi and the others had no experience of running something as big as this. They'd learned on the job. But the job was simply bigger than they had envisaged. They wanted to change China, to change the lives of one in four people on this earth. They just didn't have the know-how. No one probably had. And as the weeks had passed on Tiananmen, they had come to realize the awful truth. They had started something that was out of their control, but also out of control of the Party, the government, and the old men in Zhongnanhai. It was out of everyone's control, except the military."*

After the strategy meeting, which simply agreed to continue *"as before,"* Wuerkaixi began repeatedly to broadcast messages to students in the square to beware of agent provocateurs. He claimed that during the night *"a division of plainclothes soldiers and security police"* had infiltrated Tiananmen.

"Beware of strangers," Wuerkaixi was still calling out this Sunday afternoon, in what Cassy now called his *"voice of paranoia."*

There was much about Wuerkaixi she neither understood nor liked. The business of his eating secretly while on hunger strike still angered her. But when she had again tried to discuss the issue with Daobao, he had refused.

He too had changed. He was harder, more demanding; nothing appeared to matter except what was happening in the square. In this second full day of martial law, he had become, like Wuerkaixi, convinced the area was now filled with Qiao Shi's agents. This fear had been reinforced by a glimpse of the security chief on the roof of the Great Hall of the People.

Only Wang Dan had retained his calmness. Time and again he had left the pediment to talk to squabbling students in the square. The most common cause of bickering was the lack of space. Protesters who had been in the square for weeks felt proprietary over their particular piece of ground.

Early in the afternoon Cassy had gone with Wang Dan and Yang Li to deal with yet another quarrel, which had started near the Great Hall. A group of Beijing residents who had been on their own hunger strike had wanted to join the students in their enclave and benefit from the close medical supervision. Wuerkaixi had sent word they could not be admitted. He had told Wang Dan they could be *"saboteurs."* Wang Dan had persuaded Professor Guangzu to assign some doctors to tend the residents.

Returning to the monument, Cassy found the mood there had deepened further into gloom. Wuerkaixi was once more talking of *"facing complete defeat"*; he kept saying there was no way the students would be able to stop any military intervention. *"When that comes, we will face a time of great terror. There will be arrests and killings. And we will be the first to die. So we must be prepared to flee first. That is the only way we can carry on the fight."*

Gradually Wang Dan lifted their spirits. He said that if they were forced to leave the square, they must go underground, as their predecessors had done in the purge that led to the downfall of Hu Yaobang. The network of safe houses and cells they had established then still existed. All they would need now were new code names and passwords.

They struck Cassy *"as kids creating a children's secret society. Lots of code words were suggested. Some of them wanted to have animal names, others, more historical. They all became very involved and excited. Maybe this is what they needed to get them going again."*

"It will cost a lot of money," Wuerkaixi said.

"You have the money," Sue Tung reminded him. *"There's the money I gave you. And all the other donations you have received since."*

Sue had seen scores of overseas Chinese, mostly from Hong Kong and the United States, arrive at the pediment bringing donations. Sue estimated over

$250,000 in U.S. one-dollar bills alone had been handed over. Sue thought there could be $1 million in hard foreign currencies stashed on the pediment.

Wuerkaixi began to plan. Cassy was struck by the sheer scope of what he was proposing.

"When Wang Dan spoke of something quite basic, a chain of safe houses for people to hide in, Wuerkaixi was talking of a permanent headquarters in the south of China, somewhere around Guangzhou. He was talking of what sounded like a student government-in-exile. The more he spoke, the more alive he became. It was as if he needed the 'big picture' to get him going again. Soon he was moving around the pediment, full of energy, and once more saying they should really stay and confront the army."

An interruption occurred in the midst of this discussion. Another of the student leaders, Li Liu, announced he wanted to get married. A slim, darkly handsome youth, he had traveled from the provincial campus of Nanjing University because *"my head was full of dreams"* to play his part in what was happening on Tiananmen.

Until then he had struck Sue Tung as a hardheaded young man, a great fixer, devoid of any romantic notions. Now he stood next to a round-faced young woman with a bobbed haircut and shy smile: Zhao Ming, another student from Nanjing. They had been dating before he had come to Beijing. Hearing what was happening there, Ming had traveled to the city to find him.

When they had met at the foot of the monument they had promptly squabbled. Li Liu said she shouldn't have come; Ming said she would not leave without him. He had then swept her in his arms and kissed her to the cheers of onlookers. Then he had brought her onto the pediment and announced he wanted to marry her as soon as possible.

"In my life I've experienced everything but sex and marriage," he declared. *"I may die at any time. I owe myself this pleasure."*

After the whoops had subsided, Chai Ling asked, *"Why not get married now? We'll get you a tent for a bridal chamber. At least you'll have a few hours together."*

The other students crowded around the couple, urging them to marry at once.

"The atmosphere was what it must have been like in wartime, a feeling of needing to live for the moment," Cassy recalled. *"The old taboos on public affection had been loosened. All over the square people were behaving openly like lovers."*

Li Liu turned to Ming. *"Shall we?"*

"Why not?" she said.

Sue said, *"You'll need candy and wine to make it a proper wedding."* She suddenly felt an ache for Rod. Perhaps, after all, she should have told him to come. They could also have been married in the square. Then she reminded herself she wanted to be married in America. The June date she and Rod had set was now less than two weeks away.

For the first time she wondered if she would be able to keep it. If the crackdown came, would she be trapped, driven into hiding, unable to leave? Suddenly Sue felt *"just a little scared. I knew I could go to the airport today and fly back to Rod. But I also knew I couldn't do that. I had come so far with my people; I had to see this through."*

Meili, whose calligraphy had produced many of the more evocative posters adorning the pediment, showed she had a practical side to her. She told Li Liu and Ming that they could eat bread instead of candy and use salt water in place of wine.

"*Without them we would not have survived here so long,*" Meili said.

"*We'll still need a marriage certificate,*" Ming said.

"*No problem,*" Wuerkaixi said. "*It's already being prepared.*"

A student came forward with a piece of paper. On it he had written: "*Li Liu, male, 23, and Zhao Ming, female, 25, are willing to be husband and wife to the end of their lives. We hereby grant the necessary approval.*"

Wuerkaixi stamped the paper with the logo bearing the words *Student HQ.* He handed it to the couple.

"*You are now free to marry, absolutely official,*" he said.

Everyone cheered. Then Chai Ling said the wedding ceremony should take place on the pediment right away. She and her husband volunteered to be bridesmaid and best man. Another student acted as the justice of the peace. Wuerkaixi motioned for the student guard to form a protective cordon around the pediment.

The news that a marriage was taking place swept the crowd. Thousands burst into renditions of the "Wedding March."

Professor Guangzu and Jenny were the first to bring bottles of salt water; in minutes scores of other bottles had been passed up to the pediment.

To Cassy everyone appeared to be toasting everybody. Then the gifts came, items of clothes, pens, sweets, even leaflets signed by the donors. It seemed as if everyone in the square wanted to provide a gift, no matter how small. Children offered buttons. One old man passed forward a bird in a cage. It was politely refused; the newlyweds had no place to keep a pet. Hundreds of gifts were quickly given. The pediment soon looked like a flea market.

Sue understood why there had been such an overwhelming response. "*The wedding was a symbol of what everyone wanted, a new start.*"

After a resounding chorus of what had become the square's anthem, the "*Internationale,*" Li Liu stepped forward, microphone in one hand, the other waving for silence. For once Wuerkaixi seemed content to take a back seat.

The groom thanked everyone for coming. Then he told them a story that brought tears to many eyes.

"*Many of you will remember another young couple who were arrested a long time ago, because their beliefs offended the emperor. He ordered they must die. At the execution ground they announced to the whole world that they were married. They said they wanted to show that though they could be physically killed, what they believed in would never be taken from their souls.*"

He paused and struggled with his emotions. Then, holding his bride close to him, Li Liu continued.

"*We are all now fighting with the courage that defies death for a life that's worth living. My slogan is 'We have to fight, but we must marry too!'*"

All over the square voices took up the refrain: "*We have to fight, but we must marry too.*"

SAME DAY, SAME TIME
BOSTON

On a pleasantly warm New England Sunday afternoon, with the temperature a couple of degrees lower than on Tiananmen Square, President George Bush had finally decided to speak out publicly about what was happening there.

Throughout the weekend Bush had been fully briefed. He had studied the satellite photographs showing the PLA ring of steel beginning to form around Beijing and other major Chinese cities where there was unrest. CIA Director Webster had constantly updated the President on the students' determination to remain in Tiananmen Square in the belief they would achieve their demands for democratic reform. Supporting the intelligence reports were Dan Rather's on CBS and the continuous coverage of CNN. The front pages of the newspapers the President read every day further confirmed the situation. The students were ready, if need be, to die for their belief. Underpinning all the reports was their very clear hope that the most powerful leader in the West would lend them his clearly stated and unequivocal support.

Bush and National Security Adviser Brent Scowcroft had also heard the views of France's president, François Mitterand. Like Bush he was in Boston to receive an honorary degree from Harvard University. Mitterand had described the ramifications of the student protest in Europe.

The French government had come under increasing public pressure to make *"some decisive move to show China our displeasure,"* perhaps by freezing credit, while executives of French companies such as Peugeot, Citroen, Thomson, Alintel, and Framatone were urging nothing should be said or done to upset the status quo.

In West Germany, the Christian Democratic Union Party demanded that the Kohn government threaten to freeze all trade with China unless there was a *"proper accommodation"* with the students. German Foreign Minister Hans-Dietrich Genscher was firmly opposed to any such threat. Executives of Volkswagen, Mercedes-Benz, and Siemens had echoed his view.

"What about Mrs. Thatcher?" Bush asked.

Mitterand had given a Gallic shrug. Britain's prime minister had let Europe's leaders know that she was *"utterly opposed"* to any economic or political move that would isolate China from the West.

Reassured by the support of such a formidable ally, Bush and Scowcroft reaffirmed United States policy. It closely mirrored the views of Kissinger Associates where, until he went to sit at the left hand of Bush, Scowcroft had been a key policymaker.

At a news conference at Harvard University, Bush began by saying that the students should try to *"adhere to the style of protest"* of the late Rev. Dr. Martin Luther King, seemingly forgetting the often violent response of Southern police forces to such peaceful protest.

Warming to his theme, Bush continued. *"I'm one who feels"* — chop, chop with the hand — *"the quest for democracy is very powerful."* More hand chops and a pause to look around the faculty hall to see if anyone would challenge this truism. *"But I'm not going to dictate or try to say from the United States how this matter should be resolved by those students ... I don't want to be gratuitous in giving advice, but I would encourage restraint ... "*

Another pause to glance around the hall. A question from a reporter: Why was the administration being so cautious?

Bush's hands went into overdrive.

"I think this is perhaps a time for caution, for, because, because, we aspire to see the, the Chinese people have democracy, but we do not expect in any way...to stir up a military confrontation ... and so we counsel restraint, as we would counsel powerful means of effecting change. That is sound advice. To go beyond that and encourage steps ... bloodshed would be inappropriate."

Another question: Did the President have anything to say directly to the students?

Bush looked pained. It took him a few moments to formulate a reply. *"It would not be appropriate for the President of the United States to say to the demonstrators and the students in Beijing exactly what their course of action should be."*

Then Bush strode from the podium, watched by Scowcroft. The children of China would find no support from America.

Two days later, when Bush received Wan Li, the chairman of the People's National Congress, in the Oval Office, the President remained equally restrained in his criticism of China. He restricted his comments to asking Wan Li to use his good offices to stop the jamming of Voice of America broadcasts to the People's Republic. Then Bush had walked his guest through the White House rose garden to have coffee with Barbara Bush. Leaving Washington, Wan Li told reporters that relationships between the two countries were *"as always very satisfactory."*

SATURDAY, MAY 27, 1989
PLA BASE
BAO RI DIAN, WEST OF BEIJING

At 4:30 A.M., the loudspeaker in every barracks block came alive. All over the camp thousands of soldiers struggled into fatigues and ran to the parade square for the first of the day's indoctrinations. Among them was Bing Yang.

Every day since the humiliating withdrawal from Beijing's suburbs, he had paraded here to be told what was happening in the city.

A succession of political commissars had repeatedly described how *"reactionaries"* and *"counterrevolutionaries"* had seized control of the center of the capital and declared a *"rebellion"* against the Party and the government.

This morning the assembled ranks listened to a new tape recording of Prime Minister Li Peng and State President Yang Shangkun once more praising the PLA for its loyalty. Then the voices of two of the army's most revered commanders, Marshal Nie Dongzlia and Marshal Xu Xianquan, delivered a homily saying that the army must do its duty without flinching.

Afterward the taped voice of Hu Qili, the Politburo propaganda chief, addressed the soldiers. He told them that Zhao Ziyang had been replaced as Party Secretary by Jiang Zemin, the Party boss in Shanghai.

Jiang was a hardliner who had dealt with Shanghai students firmly since they had marched through the city on the day of Hu's funeral. Initially he had allowed protests up to a point while constantly denigrating the students as only a *"tiny handful"* bent on trying to *"poison the minds of the people."*

When some four thousand Shanghai students and their teachers had begun a hunger strike in the city on May 16, Jiang had kept his nerve, as he had when hundreds of thousands of citizens marched through Shanghai two days later. The protest had been vocal but orderly, requiring little police intervention. Now Jiang's crowd-control skills would be called into play in Beijing.

A great roar of approval swept the ranks. The astute propaganda chief continued to psych up the troops.

"On all fronts your leaders are showing their patience and loyalty. Among them is Wan Li, who upon returning from overseas immediately pledged his full support for martial law." It was less than the full story. The chairman of the National People's Congress had returned from Washington the previous Thursday. Landing at Shanghai airport, he had been met by Jiang Zemin.

Jiang had promptly upbraided Wan Li for his remarks about the students being *"patriots."* The congress chairman had countered by saying he had merely been trying to defuse public concern in the United States. He began to explain the success his trip had been in raising U.S. investment in China, and the outcome of his visit to the White House, where he had left the President firmly convinced there was no cause for American concern over the students. Jiang abruptly said he wanted Wan Li's written support for martial law. Incensed now at his treatment, the congress chairman said he first wanted to fly to Beijing and confer with Zhao. Jiang Zemin promptly informed the tired-looking Wan Li that he needed *"a rest."* The congress leader was then escorted from the airport to a nearby state guest house and told he would remain there until his *"health"* improved.

Twenty-four hours later, Wan Li had *"recovered"* sufficiently to sign a document giving his full support for martial law. That same Friday, the commanders of six of the seven national military regions and heads of twenty-seven of the twenty-nine provinces had also forwarded to Beijing their total support for martial law. Hours later the remaining two provinces and military regions also announced their support.

SAME DAY
WASHINGTON, D.C.

The evidence that a massive military crackdown was unfolding in China continued to emerge from the capital's intelligence communities in the form of satellite photos, intercepts of Chinese signals traffic, and ground intelligence from CIA agents in Beijing. The stream of material was sifted, analyzed, and forwarded by Webster to the White House.

George Bush was now one of the best informed Presidents in history facing a momentous event slowly moving to a climax. He still might have been able to avert it by clearly warning the Chinese leadership not to have the PLA attack the students. Alternatively, the President could have authorized the large number of U.S. intelligence officers and diplomats on Tiananmen Square to warn the students of the exact nature of the terrible threat they faced, in the hope they would leave the square.

Whether President Bush even considered such possibilities was to remain his secret. All that can be said with certainty is that he had made no further public comment on the students since Boston.

SAME DAY, LATER
TIANANMEN SQUARE

This was the forty-fifth day of the demonstrations. Squatting on the ground near the Museum of Revolutionary History, Jeanne Moore realized she had become inured to the sights and smells of the square. She momentarily wondered if she was losing her reporter's skills, which had sustained her in these past weeks. Then she realized it was pure fatigue that enabled her to ignore the stench from the latrines. More slit trenches had been dug during the night.

Her notebook reflected something of the seesaw of events in these past few days.

She had learned that Party Secretary Zhao's attempt to have Prime Minister Li Peng impeached marked the end of Zhao's own career. He was now under house arrest in Zhongnanhai. There was talk that he could face trial for treason. If found guilty he would be executed by having a single bullet fired into the back of his head, which had long been the regime's favored method of dealing with traitors.

A sign that calm had returned had been the sight of Li Peng's kite swooping and soaring over the compound. It had risen higher than the few kites still flying over Tiananmen Square to stop the helicopters returning. A week ago hundreds of kites had formed a protective shield over the square. But no helicopters had been seen for almost three days, and most of the kites had now been reeled in.

After issuing a number of edicts, none of which had been obeyed, the Martial Law Enforcement Headquarters had fallen silent. Its last public statement had been two days ago when it had broadcast to the square a familiar reminder: The army would do everything needed to return the city to social order and stability. Jeers had greeted the threat.

Shortly afterward, a train filled with some two thousand soldiers appeared in the city's main station. Wuerkaixi and Wang Dan had led several hundred students on bicycles to block the station entrance. The troops had remained in their carriages. Finally the train had pulled out. Later, an armored column of seventy-two half-trucks and three hundred trucks had been stoned as it entered the southwestern suburbs. Another column had been stopped as it tried to occupy the area around the Summer Palace. Since then the army had made no attempt to move further into Beijing.

"*Those troops which remain in the suburbs mix freely with the citizens,*" Jeanne had written in a notebook. "*There is a strange carnival-like mood about it all. Everyone knows why the soldiers are there, yet everyone is trying to pretend that there is no cause for alarm. A strange, unreal calm has come to Beijing.*"

Dan Rather's greater experience of such events warned the CBS anchorman this could be the calm before the storm. He told his crew that the soldiers *"could turn at any moment. They could strafe, they could tear-gas. There are a lot of possibilities here."*

But for the moment, he filmed the soldiers mixing with the citizens, sharing their rice bowls, allowing children to clamber over their trucks and tanks. This really was the people's army.

This mingling of soldiers and citizens had led to an easing of tension. Earlier fears that tens of thousands of armed soldiers were waiting in the tunnels beneath the city had proved impossible to verify. All attempts to investigate the tunnels had failed; the doors to the underground labyrinth had been secured. On the street itself the police had relinquished all control. Traffic on Changan, the city's equivalent to Fifth Avenue, and other avenues were controlled by students.

Under Wuerkaixi, Tiananmen Square had become a model of the kind of bureaucracy he had vowed to end. The square had been divided up into various sectors, each of which required its own pass to enter. Only those with *"a full security clearance"* could now go to the Monument to the People's Heroes.

The strain had gone from Wuerkaixi's face. He was his old ebullient self, strutting around the pediment in his denims stiff with dirt and sweat. He was master of all he could survey.

Chai Ling smiled at his behavior. The longer she remained on the square, the greater grew her resolve not to leave. It showed in a newfound intimidating edge to her voice. She spoke sharply to other student leaders who asked how much longer they should stay.

Wang Dan too had undergone a change, finally shaking off his caution. He moved from one group to another offering support and promising *"the end is close, victory will be ours."*

Daobao had lost a personal battle. After three weeks of not smoking he had succumbed, taking a cigarette from Yang Li. Soon Daobao was back to almost chain-smoking.

By this Saturday afternoon, forty-five days into the demonstrations, many of the students and citizens had begun to drift away from Tiananmen Square. Barricades had come down on Changan, and buses had started to run freely for the first time in a week. Shops and factories along the avenue had reopened.

At the Beijing Hotel it was very much business as usual, tending to the demands of the hundreds of foreign media people who had made it their headquarters. In a day the hotel earned more hard currency from overseas telephone and fax charges than it normally did in a month. Its restaurants and bars stayed open around the clock to feed reporters and camera crews with almost nothing to do except pick through the overpriced souvenirs on sale in the lobby.

Qiao Shi's security men and officers of Western intelligence agencies mingled with them. A CIA agent had taken up a more or less permanent corner in the coffee shop near the telex room. There was a persistent rumor that he had bribed one of the telex clerks to let him read all the reporters' messages.

"The hotel had become a real haven for spies," Melinda Liu would remember. *"The Chinese had the place bugged. Everybody was watching everybody and feeding rumors to each other. You got more disinformation walking the lobby than you would get in the whole square. It got worse as nothing was happening. The big-time stars of prime TV couldn't accept that. You'd hear Dan Rather saying to one of his producers, 'What do you mean, there's nothing to report. There has to be something!'"*

The antics of the media continued to fascinate Barr Seitz. *"The networks were spending hundreds of thousands of dollars a day, and it was all going suddenly flat. Reporters were now interviewing each other, or anybody else who had an opinion. If you wanted to start a stampede, all you had to say was 'I hear there's some movement up on the square.' The hotel lobby would empty as if the place were on fire."*

"And Tiananmen itself," wrote Jenny Guangzu, as she squatted on the ground, *"is a sad and sorry sight. A great dust storm has left many of the banners in tatters. Empty food packages, plastic wrappings, and leaflets lie everywhere. So do bits of clothing."*

On the square itself a hard core of protesters remained. In number they fluctuated between an estimated half million at noon to half that number at dusk. People went home for meals and returned, often with food for the students. The hunger strikers continued to draw a crowd. Some of the Chinese gamblers in the crowd had started to bet on how long it would be before the first striker died. The strikers were now into their third week without food.

Despite the military cordon around the city, thousands of provincial students had still managed to reach the square.

Jeanne Moore thought *"they lack discipline and purpose. They have often come out of curiosity, a feeling of wanting to be part of the action. But nothing much is happening. So in the frustration and sordid living conditions, it's inevitable that rows have broken out. Students are actually fighting about who should say what and when over the public address system. The newcomers are accusing Wuerkaixi and the Beijing student leaders of taking the best food and sleeping equipment."*

There had also been angry questions about the large sums of money that had been donated. Wuerkaixi had furiously denied he or his companions had pocketed any for themselves, but he refused to give a detailed accounting of how much they had received and what it had exactly been used for. All Wuerkaixi would concede was that the money was being kept in *"a safe place"* ready for the time it would be needed to *"continue our struggle far from here."* Most reporters had assumed this meant the money was to be used to finance the escape of the leaders.

"It's very sad," thought Jeanne Moore, *"that everything has come down to such basics."*

The young reporter rose and once more began to walk through the debris-strewn square. How long could this go on?

The answer came minutes later. Over the loudspeakers came the voice of Wuerkaixi. He announced there would be a *"final"* rally this coming Tuesday, May 30, after which the students would return to their campuses to prepare *"a new form of protest."* By then their protests would have lasted fifty days.

No one knew what had prompted Wuerkaixi to make the announcement. He had consulted no one.

However, howls of anger greeted the news. Suddenly Chai Ling's voice rose over the turmoil.

"I will not leave! I shall stay here to fight to the end! Long live democracy!"

Anger turned to cheers.

"We want Chai Ling to lead us," rose the chant. *"We stay to fight with her."*

At that moment the mantle of power fell from Wuerkaixi and Wang Dan onto the narrow shoulders of Chai Ling. Only some two hundred thousand were there to witness it.

She promptly called for a *"march of reaffirmation"* around the square, and for all the demonstrators to prepare to stay and ready themselves for the next great day in the Party calendar: the meeting of the National People's Congress on June 20.

"We will stay forever," she promised, *"if that is as long as it takes to bring democracy!"*

The cheer was the loudest Jeanne Moore had heard.

TUESDAY, MAY 30, 1989
SAN FRANCISCO

Inside the beleaguered consulate Zhang Milin watched the television screen that had become his one link "with reality." For days now all normal work in the consulate had been halted by the continuous demonstrations outside. The protest from the street echoed the tumult on the screen relaying live pictures from Tiananmen Square.

As Zhang watched, an extraordinary procession was making its way into view. It was dominated by a thirty-foot tall, white plaster statue of a Caucasian-faced woman holding aloft a flaming torch in both her hands. The CNN commentator was saying she was called the *"Goddess of Democracy."*

Supported by scores of students, Lilliputian figures around this towering figurine, the statue rose serene and proud over the square, confronting the portrait of Mao on Tiananmen Gate as Hu Yaobang's photograph had done all those weeks before.

The commentator described how the statue had arrived on flatbed pedicycles from the Central Institute of Fine Arts and how it was being likened to the Statue of Liberty.

The moment he heard the comparison, Zhang knew that the students were *"trying to involve the United States in their protest. They hoped the statue would make Bush say something to support them."* But the cultural attaché realized there was no way that President Bush would do that. The Chinese embassy in Washington continued to report that the administration was refusing to become embroiled *"in China's internal affairs."*

However, the arrival of the statue had put the demonstrators firmly back at the top of the newscasts. The figurine would become a "rallying symbol" for the demonstrators outside the consulate. In the past few days their numbers had dwindled. Now they would dramatically increase.

But Zhang also recognized that the arrival in Tiananmen of this *"potent symbol of the capitalist world"* would be seen as the ultimate provocation by the

Chinese leadership. Already some of his fellow diplomats, watching the TV screen, were saying the time for action had finally come.

Zhang also knew the moment had come for him to defect. As a still trusted diplomat, he was allowed to leave the consulate. Each time he did, he smuggled out extra items of clothes under his suit and left them with a young American he had come to know and trust. He knew he must only take the bare minimum in case one of the consulate security guards ran a spot-check on his room and found his wardrobe visibly depleted. He would not be able to smuggle out his books or records; all he could risk taking would be letters from his family. When he felt he had removed all he could, he would make one last trip, to freedom. He had not thought beyond that point. He suspected the FBI would wish to question him. But he had vowed to himself to tell them nothing that would compromise the national security of China.

His scruples were commendable but unnecessary. The FBI's bugs had ensured it knew a great deal of what was going on inside the consulate, including those angry words from the consul to his staff for their government to deal with this latest *"outrage"* by the students in Beijing.

THURSDAY, JUNE 1, 1989
TIANANMEN SQUARE

Again British press attaché Brian Davidson and Irish envoy Brendan Ward agreed on a number: Probably fewer than ten thousand remained encamped in the square.

In the past few days, despite Chai Ling's *"march of affirmation"* and her promise to remain in the square, there had been a steady exodus. Many of the public complained they could no longer tolerate the stench from the latrines. Others said they could no longer stay away from their work. Many of the students felt too exhausted to camp out. Others wanted to go home for the summer vacation. Hour by hour the million-plus who had occupied the square only a week ago had drifted away. Now, on this hot, sultry morning, only a relatively small number remained.

Moving among them were scores of Public Security photographers. They would stop before each group of students and carefully photograph them before moving on.

Ward thought it *"quite extraordinary the way the students made no protest. Several just smiled defiantly into the cameras. Some even posed proudly beneath the goddess's statue."*

As an attraction, the figurine had not been a success. The crowds who had come to stare had quickly dwindled. Davidson felt it was *"because the figurine was alien to most Chinese. The similarity with the Statue of Liberty meant nothing to people who knew nothing of the world outside their hutongs."*

Nevertheless, the authorities had been quick to attack the statue as *"proof that the counterrevolutionary rebellion is inspired by outside enemies of the people."* A number of *"outraged intellectuals"* had written to the state media pointing out that the *"foreign monument actually was standing on the very spot where the portrait of Sun Yatsen, the founder of China's Republican movement, was displayed on high days in the Party calendar. Such 'heresy' must be punished."*

This had been also one of the themes of several demonstrations organized by the Party in the past few days. Several thousand demonstrators had been bused to a football stadium in the Suburbs to chant slogans such as *"crush the People's enemies"* and wave banners proclaiming OPPOSE TURMOIL.

The state media had called the occasion *"a spontaneous display of anger against bad elements."*

That image had been spoiled for Ward because most of the demonstrators had spent their time giggling into the TV cameras while Party cadres tried to stoke their fury. The demonstration had ended with the burning of an effigy of astrophysicist Fang Lizhi, who was China's most renowned dissident, and an unnamed "conspirator."

"It has to be Zhao Ziyang," Ward had told Davidson.

"Who else?" the press attaché had agreed as they walked on through the square.

Several of the other foreign diplomats in the square had heard the story that Zhao was now under house arrest in Zhongnanhai.

Geert Andersen, a counselor at the Danish Embassy, had been told that Zhao had suffered the ultimate indignity of having his limousine taken away. Horst Lohmann, the military attaché of the German Democratic Republic, had heard that Zhao might soon face trial for treason.

"So many reports were always a sure sign no one really knew," Ward would say.

Chai Ling remained encamped on the pediment of the Monument to the People's Heroes. With her were a tired-looking group of students. But there was no sign of Wuerkaixi and Wang Dan.

Melinda Liu had spotted both asleep in the back of a bus. It would make a line in the story she was preparing for *Newsweek*. She had decided it would probably be a wrap-up. The simple truth was that the students had begun to lose the interest of her editors. It happened with any long-running story. And this one had run longer than most, since April 15, forty-nine days now.

Melinda decided she would return to Hong Kong the coming weekend.

Glancing around the square she thought, *"They've achieved very little. But that's the way it often is in China."*

FRIDAY, JUNE 2, 1989
DENG XIAOPING'S COMPOUND

Shortly after midnight, the small group of Politburo members once more arrived to confer with Deng Xiaoping. With them was General Hongwen Yang, commander of the 27th Army. He had driven there with his relative, the state president.

Grouped in the obligatory semicircle of armchairs facing Deng, the cabal spoke in turn. Western intelligence sources would later agree there was little debate. In the words of one European operative monitoring the situation through his Chinese contacts *"they were just rubber-stamping what Deng had decided."*

Those same intelligence sources would concur that what had finally driven Deng to action was a combination of developments.

Intelligence chief Qiao Shi presented a report showing that unrest in other parts of the country had spread. In the southern city of Guaidong, a thousand miles from Beijing, a crowd of thirty thousand continued to keep a permanent vigil in support of local students. In Hunan province, Hu Yaobang's birthplace, six hundred miles south of the capital, there was a continuous sit-in outside the local government headquarters. In another provincial capital, Xian, up to three hundred thousand protesters were continuously marching. In all, some twenty cities across China were now in a state of "turmoil."

Qiao Shi insisted that the widespread disruption was being masterminded by the Beijing students. His agents had intercepted their phone calls and obtained copies of their faxed messages. They all clearly showed that a small group of students were determined to create what the security chief now also called *"chaos under Heaven"* throughout the country, led by Wuerkaixi, Chai Ling, and Wang Dan.

When Deng finally spoke he said he was now convinced that he had little to fear from the United States, Britain, or West Germany in terms of military reprisals for acting decisively against the students.

Chinese ambassadors in all those countries had told him that the official protests likely to follow would be short-lived, coupled to short-term diplomatic and trade disruption. But no more.

There would be absolutely no question of any covert military support. Not even the CIA was going to think of arming the students.

The way was clear to deal with the students once and for all.

General Yang was the last to speak. He assured the others that his forces were ready to end the rebellion.

No one asked for operational details. Yang did not offer any.

At 2:00 A.M., the meeting broke up. While other members of the cabal returned to the Zhongnanhai compound, Prime Minister Li Peng and State President Yang Shangkun drove with General Yang to the General Logistics Department compound in the western suburbs. From here they would watch the final operational plans being activated. This time there would be no turning back.

SAME DAY, LATER
TIANANMEN SQUARE

Sue Tung strolled through the square in the early afternoon sunshine planning her return to Sacramento. There was a flight in the morning. Sixteen hours later she could be back with Rod, telling him how everything had fizzled out. She was still glad she had come. But the trip had ended in disappointment and, she had to admit, in downright farce.

Near the goddess's statue, a new hunger strike had started, but it was a far cry from that of the two thousand students who had vowed to starve to death until they had been ordered by Wang Dan to stop after twenty-three days. Many had been hospitalized, but they were now recovering.

This strike consisted of just four people, led by Hou Dejian, a pop singer and self-publicist, who had come from Taiwan. He had announced he could *"only starve"* for two days because he had to be in Hong Kong this coming

Monday to cut a new record, and he could not afford to damage his voice by going hungry too long. His companions had also set a strict time limit on their fasting, no longer than three days.

Nevertheless, Chai Ling had welcomed what she called their *"courageous act."* She had struck Sue as prepared to endorse anyone who *"could get things going again."*

But already, after a couple of hours' squatting on the ground, the quarter of hunger strikers had become an object of wry comment. Some of the students were teasing Hu and his companions, offering them sweets and drinks.

Jenny Guangzu and her father had walked over to cast a professional eye on the four and then returned to the first-aid tent.

"They've got enough fat on their bodies to last a week," Professor Guangzu grunted. He left the square to return to the hospital to look at some of the student hunger strikers who were recovering there.

Jenny had curled up in the back of the tent to snatch a few hours' sleep. One of the medical students had volunteered to look after Peter. The girl had taken the child to the Beijing Hotel. A TV reporter had told her she could use his bathroom to freshen up. A number of students had established the same relationship with the media.

For the first time in weeks Cassy Jones felt she had nothing to do. Daobao had gone back to his dormitory on the campus to change his clothes. She sat near the goddess's statue to write postcards home. She had actually brought the cards on the day Hu Yaobang died. They were views of Tiananmen Square.

To a friend in Chicago Cassy wrote: *"After all the weeks of tension, it's all over. No doubt you've seen the Goddess of Freedom (the first version actually went up in Shanghai a week before the one here) on TV. People just drop by from work to see if it's still here. But it's no big deal."*

Behind her Hou Dejian had started to sing another number from his repertoire.

"This place is a bit like Woodstock," Cassy added.

Suddenly she longed to go home.

SAME DAY, LATER
PLA BARRACKS
BAO BI DIAN

Shortly before dusk, Bing Yang and several thousand other troops were paraded to be lectured by their political commissar. They were once more told the center of Beijing was now in the hands of *"armed and highly dangerous counterrevolutionaries"*; that *"foreign mercenaries"* were helping them; that the citizens were in *"mortal terror of their lives."*

After the harangue, Bing and his companions were told they must be ready to move out at a moment's notice.

One of the U.S. satellites positioned over the area gathered up the order and transmitted it to Washington. The technicians at the National Photographic Interpretation Center sent the order on up the intelligence community chain of command. It would form part of the next President's Daily Brief, ensuring

George Bush would be among the first to know that full-scale military action was now under way against the students. There would still be time for him to warn the Chinese leadership against such a response, if he chose to do so.

22

Massacre

SATURDAY, JUNE 3, 1989
MUXUDI DISTRICT
BEIJING

At a little after 2:00 a.m. on this fifty-fourth day of the protest, Daobao brusquely ordered a PLA officer out of the telephone booth outside the Military Museum on Fuxing Avenue in the western suburbs. The officer had tried to call his headquarters to get fresh orders for his squad of unarmed recruits. They were surrounded by a crowd, most in their nightclothes, who taunted the soldiers.

A couple of hours earlier some five thousand troops had passed into the city on foot east and west, planning to meet on Tiananmen Square. Dressed in green baggy fatigues and rubber-soled boots, they had run like marathoners through the silent streets of sleeping suburbia.

When they had reached a crossroads in the Muxudi District, four miles to the west of Tiananmen Square, where they were supposed to rendezvous with a police jeep that would lead them into the city, the vehicle had been involved in an accident, killing three people. The incident had brought residents into the street. Seeing the soldiers, they swung into action.

Barricades had once more been swiftly erected from buses, trucks, vans, handcarts, and bicycles. No one expected the barrier would hold back the troops for long, but they might buy enough time for more substantial defenses to be erected further back in the city.

A pedicab driver had cycled up Changan Avenue yelling, *"They're coming, they're coming!"* Along the avenue, which was three times the width of New York's Fifth Avenue, people appeared at windows, realized what was happening and took up his cry.

Alerted by the shouting, students in the square had begun to run down the avenue as Wuerkaixi and Wang Dan joined Chai Ling on the pediment of the Monument to the People's Heroes. All previous bickering was forgotten. This was a time for concerted action.

They dispatched students to report back on what was happening. Daobao was sent to the Muxudi District. Cassy had again ridden with him on a motorcycle as it sped down Changan Avenue, passing students ripping up traffic dividers and using them to reinforce barricades. Others were using tools to pry up paving stones, which were broken into handy pieces to throw at the troops.

Reaching Muxudi, Daobao and Cassy found that most of the soldiers had run into side streets to bypass the barricades rather than try to dismantle them. They were reduced to small groups that were easy to surround, like those trapped on the steps of the Military Museum.

Having evicted the officer from the phone booth, Daobao called one of the kiosks on Tiananmen Square. Another student answered, and Daobao reported what he had seen. A third student ran to the pediment with the news. Reports in this manner were coming in from all quarters, enabling those on the pediment to have a clear picture of events.

By now the first TV crews were coming from the Beijing Hotel, led by Barr Seitz. Running into Changan Avenue, he was astonished to find that *"out of nowhere"* a crowd of several thousand had pinned a column of soldiers against the walls of the China Ocean Shipping Corporation.

Barr shouldered his way to the front of the crowd, which was jeering at the troops. He saw that several of the soldiers were weeping. Most looked cowed or bewildered. Barr began to question them.

"They were teenagers, mostly country kids. They'd run some fifteen miles into the city without a gun between them, or seemingly any clear orders. Their officers kept saying they would be told what to do once they reached Tiananmen Square," Barr recalled.

The ABC crew filmed several of the soldiers simply walking away into the crowd, repeatedly saying they didn't want to harm anyone.

"For a military operation, this is a real fiasco," Barr told his producer. *"Let's go see if we can find some real action."*

Half a mile further back along Changan, Jeanne Moore had been awakened by the commotion. By the time she reached the street, a crowd had surrounded another squad of soldiers.

The boldest of the onlookers prodded at the backpacks the soldiers carried and removed biscuits, rice cakes, and water bottles. They tasted the food and wrinkled their noses in disgust.

"If this is what they feed you, no wonder you look so scared," a man said, spitting out a biscuit. There was good-natured laughter. The tension was broken.

The crowd now began to coax the soldiers. *"Go back to your bases. Or join us in supporting the students. You're just being used."*

More soldiers drifted off with members of the crowd or began to walk back along Changan. Finally only officers remained. They glanced at the crowd, and then they too began the long walk back to base.

A half mile to the west of Tiananmen Square, *Newsweek's* Melinda Liu once more found herself in the right place at the right moment.

She had been awakened in her room on the seventeenth floor of the Beijing Hotel by an informant with news that troops were *"surging in from the west."*

She ignored her colleagues heading for the square and ran on down Changan, keeping to the center of the great boulevard that bisected the city. At the intersection leading to Zhongnanhai she found a couple of thousand people pressed around four buses filled with armed troops. The sight of gun muzzles sticking out of sacks had inflamed the crowd. They were rocking the buses in an effort to tip them over. The soldiers were trying to scramble through the windows.

Melinda spotted ammunition boxes hidden beneath blankets inside the buses.

The crowd's anger deepened. They began to scream at the soldiers. *"Why do you want to kill us?"*

Some of the troops began to tremble and weep. In her notebook Melinda jotted: *"Scene very adrenalin provoking and disturbing."*

As one of the soldiers tried to climb out of a window, he changed his mind. *"Too late. The crowd grabbed his arms; a tug-of-war began. The trooper has his hat in his mouth, as if he's scared to lose it. The crowd took off his shoes. They know the greatest humiliation they can do to a Chinese soldier is to leave him barefoot,"* Melinda noted.

"In minutes they had removed the footwear of a score of soldiers. The shoes and boots piled in the form of a mock shrine, consisting of boxes of ammunition, rifles, copies of Mao Tse-tung's textbook on military themes and the Communist Party manual, both of which are obligatory for all soldiers to carry."

The mood of the crowd lightened. They began to laugh and chant:

"The army and the people are as close as fish and water."

The soldiers grinned sheepishly.

Melinda continued on down Changan Avenue, noting the students standing over their piles of broken paving stones and the traffic dividers strewn across the streets. Did they really think any of this could stop a determined army? The sight of those guns and ammunition boxes continued to trouble her.

She remembered what China's most revered military philosopher, Sun Tzu, had written: *"When capable, feign incapacity; when active, inactivity. When near, make it appear you are far away; when far away, that you are near. Offer the enemy a bait to lure him; feign disorder and strike him."*

THE WHITE HOUSE

It was Friday night in Washington, D.C., and Barbara Bush, like millions of Americans, had settled down to watch the latest episode of "Dallas" when a bright red "CBS News Special Report" sign filled the screen. J.R. Ewing was cut off in the middle of trying to justify another piece of skullduggery, to be replaced by Dan Rather, live from Beijing, confronting two Chinese officials over his right to broadcast.

Rather was using all his skills and authority to persuade the officials. CBS still had a firm agreement with the Chinese Foreign Ministry allowing them to broadcast live. The Ministry now wanted him to end all such transmissions, clearly because of the powerful effect they were having on U.S. public opinion.

While Rather negotiated with the two officers, he continued to describe to his audience what was happening all around him.

"At almost every intersection, there are crowds," Rather said into his handheld microphone. *"Though martial law has been declared, the army has engaged in tremendous restraint...."*

In the Oval Office, the President had continued to receive hard intelligence of what the army was doing out of range of Rather's cameras, but all too clearly caught in the lenses of U.S. satellites and other intelligence gathering methods. Prints from the National Photographic Interpretation Center had been hand carried all day to the White House, together with summaries of PLA radio traffic. The CIA's Beijing station had continued to send updates, while U.S. diplomats in Beijing had transmitted situation reports to the State Department.

They ensured that Bush had the clearest possible view of what was already happening in Beijing, and what was almost certainly going to happen. A massive pincer-like movement, involving over a hundred thousand troops, was encircling the city and preparing to move forward. Supporting it were battle tanks and weaponry of a kind more suitable to full-scale war: rocket launchers, heavy-caliber machine guns.

American surveillance reports also showed that the People's Liberation Army was poised to support armed police in other cities. From Canton in the far south, to Shanghai five hundred miles up the coast, all the way inland to the industrial cities of Wuhan and Chengdu, the PLA had deployed close to another fifty thousand troops.

Although he joined his wife to watch the CBS report, the President did not need Dan Rather to tell him that almost eight weeks of high drama was moving to a terrible climax.

Outside the White House events were being monitored by non-government analysts. One was Joseph Brewda of the Washington-based Economic Intelligence Bureau. To Brewda it seemed *"incomprehensible that even now George Bush, who knew the Chinese mind-set every bit as well as did Rather, and who, in turn, was respected and probably feared a little by the old men in Zhongnanhai, made no move to warn them that America would react strongly to any military move against the students. The President could have threatened to cut all diplomatic ties, to freeze all credits, to withdraw all economic and technical assistance. He could have consigned China to the boonies. Or, at the very minimum, he could have given other Western leaders a lead by telling the students we were with them 100 percent in calling for democracy."*

SAME DAY, LATER
THE FOREIGN OFFICE
LONDON

Analyst Susan Morton had found that the best way to cope with the almost overwhelming flow of material arriving on her desk was to strictly segregate it. Her growing piles of accounts included those from Brian Davidson.

The press attaché had reported that well-armed units inside the Great Hall of the People and in the tunnels under the city could now number twenty thousand soldiers.

Other reports claimed that Deng Xiaoping had suffered a sudden collapse with his invasive cancer, that Li Peng had been fired. A short while ago these reports had been formally denied by a Chinese Foreign Ministry spokeswoman in Beijing.

Another item that had caught Susan's eye was an intelligence report about China's minister of defense, Qin Jiwei, and the deputy chief of the PLA general staff, Xu Xin, visiting military units to the west of Beijing. The two men had urged troops *"to make martial law a success, so as to add glory to the armed forces and make new contributions to stabilizing the situation."*

SAME DAY, SAME TIME
NORTHEAST SUBURBS OF BEIJING

Sue Tung had been sent to Andingmen Avenue, four miles to the north of the square, to watch for any approaching troops.

Like everyone else who had spent time in Tiananmen Square, the young postgraduate student was operating on adrenalin. She had snatched food and sleep when she could and washed her underwear under a cold-water tap in one of the alleys behind Tiananmen Square. She had lost weight and at times, she had admitted to herself, faith in some of the student leadership.

Only Wang Dan and Chai Ling seemed to Sue to have retained their ability to focus. Both of them showed an iron resolve to see this through. Wuerkaixi still vacillated, one moment rousing those around him, the next bowed down with despair. Yet Sue was sympathetic and understood his feelings.

"No twenty-year-old should have such a great responsibility," Sue had told her boyfriend, Rod, in one of her telephone calls to him back in Sacramento.

Despite the threat by the martial law authorities to cut all overseas TV and radio transmissions, the Beijing telephone system was functioning normally, enabling foreign journalists to call their offices and file reports. Anxious to reassure Rod, Sue had telephoned him collect every day from a pay phone on Changan Avenue. In her last call a few hours ago, she had told him that she planned to stay on in Beijing *"a day or two longer, as things have become interesting again."*

Rod told her he had just seen the Chinese pull the plug on Rather's last transmission and said, *"Things look really bad."*

Swept along by the bullish mood on Tiananmen Square, Sue had once more tried to reassure him.

"The troops are a ploy. Like the helicopters and the Party broadcasts," she told Rod. *"The army can see the entire population does not want them to harm the students. It could well be that the soldiers will now side with us. Then we would have a bloodless coup, just like in the Philippines. People power worked there. It will do so here."*

In that optimistic mood she had hung up and cycled to her assigned post on the broad expanse of Andingmen Avenue.

She arrived shortly after dawn to find several trucks filled with soldiers parked inside Ditan Park, unable to leave because of the crowd.

The soldiers reminded Sue *"of caged animals, pacing back and forth among the trucks, and rather frightened."* Several asked for cigarettes and for water to refill their canteens. The crowd, numbering several thousand, Sue thought, said they would only provide supplies if the soldiers handed over their weapons.

They began to do so early in the afternoon. Soon AK-47 assault rifles were stacked on the road alongside piles of helmets and backpacks.

A little later several Chinese photographers arrived, equipped with video cameras. They said they worked for the Hong Kong media and had come to record *"the people's victory."* They were cheerful and polite and soon persuaded youths in the crowd to pose with the seized weapons. The youths donned helmets and began to mock-threaten the soldiers. The troops looked even more scared.

It struck Sue as *"all a bit childish, but harmless fun."* After a while the photographers left. Sue didn't think the incident was worth reporting to the student leaders on Tiananmen Square. Some four miles south of where Sue kept watch, Jenny Guangzu and her father emerged from the hospital where he worked and walked toward the square. Both wore white coats to distinguish them. In the early hours of the morning, Jenny had brought her year-old son, Peter, from the square to her father's tiny apartment at the rear of the hospital. One of Professor Guangzu's nurses had volunteered to look after the child, freeing Jenny to return to the square.

Father and daughter continued an argument that had begun in the apartment. He felt it was time for Jenny to return to Los Angeles and resume her studies.

"Things are moving to a new level of uncertainty," her father said.

"All the more reason for me to remain," Jenny said. She smiled at her father. *"Besides, you know how much you like having Peter here."*

It was true. The professor had spent every available free moment playing with his grandson. He had even brought Peter to his office and pointed out his precious collection of bottled tongues.

On Changan Avenue they were suddenly confronted by men wearing construction helmets and carrying clubs fashioned from chunks of wood. Several were stripped to the waist and appeared to have been drinking. With them were two men operating video cameras.

The men were cursing volubly and saying they would beat up any soldiers they encountered. Professor Guangzu moved to remonstrate. They pushed him aside. Jenny confronted them.

"The students don't need people like you," she said. *"You're just troublemakers."*

Passersby stopped and joined in, accusing the men of being agent provocateurs. In moments the crowd had grown to hundreds. The men were disarmed and sent on their way with a warning not to harm any of the soldiers. Jenny noticed that the cameramen had disappeared.

Further along Changan Avenue she heard the sounds of explosions and saw clouds of smoke drifting in the air.

"Tear-gas grenades," her father said. With others they ran into an alley.

SAME DAY, SAME TIME
WASHINGTON, D.C.

Lights continued to burn throughout the night on the top floor of the State Department, where the China Desk analysts worked furiously to prepare yet another briefing paper for Secretary of State Baker. It would form part of his breakfast reading along with other reports from the National Reconnaissance

Agency, responsible for collecting satellite intelligence for the Department of Defense, and the National Security Agency. He would also receive a copy of the President's Daily Brief, containing CIA Director Webster's overnight assessment of the situation.

Like Bush, Baker would be in no doubt that China's leaders were finally ready to silence the students' call for democracy.

SAME DAY, SAME TIME
BEIJING

On Changan Avenue the "action" Barr Seitz, the son of one of Secretary Baker's more senior aides, had waited so long to experience was suddenly erupting all around him. He had been returning with a cameraman from filming in the Muxudi District and had actually been passing Zhongnanhai when several hundred police in full riot gear with tear-gas grenade launchers emerged from the compound's western gate.

"They just opened up as they ran, firing point-blank into the crowd," Barr would remember. His cameraman kept his professional discipline, filming the unprovoked attack that sent people scattering. As the students regrouped, the pair found themselves in a deadly crossfire. Retreating before the grenades and the swinging truncheons of the police, they had to duck the pieces of paving stones the demonstrators were hurling. Then, as suddenly as it had begun, the incident was over. On command, the police turned and ran back into Zhongnanhai.

Eyes streaming from the tear gas, people crowded back into Changan Avenue. They displayed their tears with pride and told each other that if this was the best the army could do, then there was nothing to fear.

SAME DAY, LATER
TIANANMEN SQUARE

Brendan Ward and Brian Davidson were back in the square, two of several score foreign envoys keeping watch. Some had mobile telephones to report instantly any developments to their embassies. News of the tear-gas attack was already being relayed to foreign ministries around the world.

Ward and Davidson had become inured to the stench, the refuse, the feeling, in Ward's words, *"that Tiananmen had become 'one big toilet.'"* They still had a job to do, to be the eyes and ears of their respective governments. In the seven weeks they had been coming to the square, they had made friends with many of the students. Yet under strict orders from their own superiors, neither Ward nor Davidson was allowed to alert those students to the pincer-movement the PLA was tightening around the city on this fifty-fifth day of the demonstrations.

The two diplomats began to carry out another of their routine checks, walking through the wide underpass that led from one side of Changan into the square. The walls of the underpass had become a vast bulletin board, a jungle of posters and notices. Some announced where people could be found. Others were political declarations. Reading them gave Davidson a clue to the mood of many of the demonstrators.

"*A lot more think it's time to pack up*," the press attaché told Ward as they picked their way through groups of students who were sprawled exhausted in the underpass.

Even though the light was poor, Ward could see "*a lot of them looked pretty sick. They had that flushed appearance that comes from no real sleep or proper food. The air was awful, as if they were lying in their own excrement.*"

From the square came sudden shouts and the sound of people running.

Davidson and Ward bounded up the steps of the underpass and emerged back on Tiananmen in time to see a thousand or more soldiers wearing steel helmets and carrying rifles at the ready, rushing out of the Great Hall of the People onto Changan Avenue.

The crowd, about two hundred thousand people, did not flee. The events of the past few hours had once more drawn them back to Tiananmen. To Ward, the great mass seemed to symbolically consume the soldiers. "*One moment the troops were a disciplined force, the next they had been broken up into small groups, each with its 'minders.' The soldiers were led to the center of Changan Avenue and invited to sit on the tarmac.*"

Once the troops squatted on the ground, students moved among them, checking their weapons. None was loaded.

The incident had also been seen by Jeanne Moore, the young American reporter on *China Daily*, the English-language Party newspaper.

"*The mood changed at once*," she noted. "*Everybody is very relaxed and cheerful. They keep trying to get the soldiers to sing the 'Internationale.' When that fails, the students encourage them to sing army songs. But that doesn't work either. The soldiers just sit there in the baking sun. People are buying them ice cream and offering them water. It's the weirdest thing.*"

Seeking a possible explanation for the reaction of the troops, a number of foreign military attachés in the square echoed the conclusion of Horst Lohmann. The military attaché of the German Democratic Republic had seen the *Volkspolezei* of his own country use similar tactics.

"*It's called testing the ground*," he would say cryptically. "*Make the people relax before attacking them.*"

Watching the soldiers, *Newsweek's* Melinda Liu was once more reminded of those words of Sun Tzu. Was this indeed a bait to lure the students into a false sense of security?

As the sun lost its heat, the soldiers suddenly rose to their feet and ran back into the Great Hall.

An hour later the hundreds of reporters and TV crews in the square were joined by a tall, white-haired patriarchal figure, Harrison E. Salisbury, the veteran American journalist and author. He had visited China perhaps more times than any other correspondent. He was back to make a documentary for Japanese television. Quickly recognized by many of the students, Salisbury was soon signing autographs.

Watching him stride, still erect and proud at an age when most men would "*be hanging up their boots*," Jeanne Moore thought Salisbury was like a character in Evelyn Waugh's novel *Scoop*.

Salisbury had left the square to return to his suite in the Beijing Hotel when the disembodied voice of Qiao Shi, the country's security chief, once more came over the loudspeakers.

He broadcast an *"urgent warning that lawless acts still continue, and have infuriated the officers and men of your army and will no longer be tolerated."* He listed a series of infractions: soldiers being threatened and impeded in their lawful duties; their equipment being stolen.

In a café on Andingmen Avenue, Sue Tung watched a TV news bulletin. She was stunned to see herself standing near some of the youths who had been persuaded to act as if they were threatening the soldiers. Now the youths were being described as *"dangerous counterrevolutionaries who have seized weapons to worsen the rebellion in our city."* The onlookers were called *"reactionaries"* who were supporting them.

Sue's first instinct was to burst out laughing. Then she realized everyone around her was leaving the café.

"If the Public Security find you, you will be arrested," an old woman told Sue. *"You must hide."*

But Sue could think of nowhere to go. She had given up her hotel room days ago to sleep in Tiananmen Square.

There, Jenny saw on the same newscast the group of men she and her father had watched being disarmed. The men were described as plainclothes policemen being stopped from keeping order by the mob. She realized then that *"we were being set up."*

Further items in the bulletin went on to show photographs of similar stage-managed scenes in several parts of the city.

Watching the newscast, Louise Branson had a *"sinking feeling this is it."* The tall, faired-haired, thirty-four-year-old correspondent for Britain's *Sunday Times* had earned high praise for her reporting. She turned to her husband, Dusko Doder of *U.S. News and World Report* and said, *"All hell is about to break loose."*

"As long as the circuits remain open, we'll go on reporting it," he said cheerfully.

The sound of their small son, Thomas, gurgling happily in his playpen came from another part of their apartment-office, located four miles to the east of Tiananmen Square.

Melinda Liu had left the TV set permanently on in her room in the Beijing Hotel. She divided her time between standing on the balcony overlooking the roofs of the Forbidden City and Tiananmen Square and watching the TV screen. In between she kept up the pressure on the switchboard staff to connect her to her editors in New York. She wanted to warn them that *"we all could be in for a long night."* But many of the hotel telephone operators, like most of the other staff, had abandoned their posts to go to the square. From her balcony Melinda estimated there could now be *"close to a million or more around Tiananmen."*

As she once more pleaded with the switchboard operator, the TV screen went blank. A caption card appeared bearing the words MARTIAL LAW ENFORCEMENT HEADQUARTERS. An anonymous voice began to speak.

"Citizens of Beijing. We are all facing a most serious situation. Thugs are creating turmoil. At the request of the broad masses of city residents the army will take strong

and effective measures to deal with those thugs. They will be shown no softness. But to avoid the innocent being involved in our measures, we ask that all residents should leave the streets and stay away from Tiananmen Square. You must all remain in your own houses until further notice."

Once more the screen went blank.

SAME DAY, LATER
PLA CAMP
BAO BI DIAN

Late in the evening Bing Yang and the other soldiers were ordered out of their barracks and marched to the parade ground. The space was dotted with tables. At each one was an army doctor or medical assistant. A loudspeaker announcement explained their presence.

"The situation in Beijing has become medically dangerous. The counterrevolutionaries are spreading disease. To avoid any damage to your health, all of you will now receive an injection to protect you."

When Bing received his shot, he felt a warm sensation through his body. Climbing into a truck, he felt even more determined to deal with the enemies of the people. A magazine of live ammunition was locked in place in his gun; several spares filled the pockets of his fatigues. On the floor of the truck were more boxes of ammunition.

Tan Yaobang, their company commander, gave a final reminder: *"Shoot to kill when the order comes."*

Bing Yang and the others would be helped to do so by the injections they received. No one would be certain what drugs were used.

At 10:30 P.M., the trucks drove out of the base. Already their "victory" had been proclaimed by the country's state-controlled news agency. An hour before the wire service had distributed a proclamation: *"The glorious army of the people has the trust of the people. By their great deeds the army has ardently shown its love for the capital and its people, and all law-abiding students. The officers and soldiers of the PLA have once more shown they are the people's own army."*

A night of tragedy was under way.

SAME DAY, LATER
MUXUDI DISTRICT

Three miles to the west of Tiananmen Square at a little after 11:30 P.M., almost twenty-two hours since he had ordered the PLA officer out of the telephone booth on Fuxing Avenue, Daobao was making another phone call to the square.

"Zhendan!" he screamed. *"Zhendan — Live fire! Live fire!"*

Company commander Tan Yaobang had relayed the order to open fire, which he had received moments before through the headset of his field wireless set. The commander was in the back of a small truck. The order had come from General Yang's headquarters in the PLA situation room in the city's western suburbs. The attack was being directed from there.

The company commander would later justify the order by insisting that *"the counterrevolutionaries were armed and dangerous. They had been trying to raise rebellion for weeks. They had been given every opportunity to surrender. In the end we had no alternative but to take firm and decisive action."*

Behind Yaobang another burst of automatic fire raked the barricade of buses, trucks, and pedicabs strewn across the street. Already bodies lay on the ground.

"Zhendan!" Daobao screamed once more. Then he dropped the phone and ran to where he had left Cassy, in the gateway of the compound of Building Number 22 and Building Number 24. The high-rises in the center of Muxudi District housed senior Party officers and their families.

When he reached the gateway, Daobao found no sign of Cassy. He assumed she must have fled back into the city when the shooting started.

When the firing began, Cassy had decided the gateway was no longer safe. Despite the rank of those who lived in the high-rises, the soldiers had raked both buildings with gunfire. Cassy, like others, could only assume *"the troops were either drugged or gung-ho to the point where they'd shoot at anything."*

In a momentary lull in the firing, she dashed from the compound gateway to seek shelter behind a barricade in the road. As she reached it, the shooting resumed. Cassy saw the arriving troops were throwing stun grenades to terrify the crowd crouching around her. The grenades exploded in the air with deafening effect. Then another burst of small-arms fire raked the barricade's jammed-together trucks, buses, and handcarts. The cries of the injured rose above the shooting. All around her people suddenly fell from the murderous fire. Cassy retreated to shelter in a doorway a little further up the street. Standing on a pile of refuse, she could see over the barricade. She would recall, *"The troops took their time, often kneeling to fire. They would advance for a few yards, then once more kneel, load, and fire. It was pure murder."*

Cassy saw Daobao. He was running diagonally across the street, crouching and weaving like a running back, sprinting toward the barricade. She saw him spin around and fall. At the same moment a huge burst of flame leaped from the barrier as the fuel tanks in the vehicle exploded under the gunfire. A fireball rose into the air. People were screaming in agony, running in blind panic, their clothes on fire. Cassy found it impossible to make herself heard, let alone understood. There was no way she could make her way back to the barrier to reach Daobao. Swept along by the near-demented crowd, she saw other bodies on the ground around him. Several appeared to be burning.

The troops continued to pour gunfire into the backs of the fleeing crowd. Scores more fell.

Among the marksmen was Bing Yang. He had remembered his company commander's order to shoot to kill.

Behind the troops came the first of the tanks, a T-69, commanded by Liu Lee, the brother of one of the student leaders. He smashed through the barrier, scattering flaming wreckage. Behind came halftracks and trucks. Company commander Tan Yaobang reported to headquarters that the advance into Beijing continued unopposed.

As a tank passed the mouth of a *hutong,* gasoline-filled bottles showered over it, enveloping it in flames. Then people swarmed back into the street to launch more gasoline bombs against the other vehicles. Battened down, the tank drove on up the avenue, its machine gun firing long bursts into the retreating crowd. Its tracks passed over more bodies.

The bravery of the people of Muxudi District, Andrew Higgins of Britain's *Independent* later noted, was *"extraordinary and foolhardy, as people regrouped against the soldiers, only to face fresh fusillades."*

SAME DAY, SAME TIME
GENERAL LOGISTICS DEPARTMENT
PLA COMPOUND

Prime Minister Li Peng and Yang Shangkun, along with General Hongwen Yang and other officers continued to monitor the attack from the situation room.

To the west of the city, ten thousand troops were now advancing on a half-mile-wide front. In the east a convoy of thirty vehicles led another ten thousand in a similar movement. In the south, a brigade of infantry and paratroopers had swept out of Nanyuan military airbase behind a screen of tanks and raced through the suburbs. In the north of the city, five thousand more troops were sweeping down Andingmen Avenue, systematically destroying the barriers there. Behind them waited an additional seventy-five thousand soldiers. Sue Tung, who had dashed into an apartment building on Andingmen Avenue, saw the soldiers running down the street and felt *"suddenly terrified. There was a look about them, as if they were on drugs. A glazed-eyed look."*

Troops were being ferried by underground train from Zhongnanhai to the Great Hall of the People. All entrances to the nuclear shelter tunnels in the city had been opened so troops waiting there could make their way up into the city.

Word of what was happening spread like a brush fire. Students who had left the square to go back to their campuses either to sleep or prepare to go on vacation, returned to Tiananmen Square by the fastest way they could. Some commandeered buses and trucks, others pedaled furiously through the alleys. Many just ran. With them came the citizens of Beijing. Construction workers downed tools, housewives left their kitchens. In a pell-mell dash to the square, office workers ran alongside factory hands. Thousands became tens of thousands, who became hundreds of thousands. In an hour a million and more were once more converging on Tiananmen Square. Among them they did not possess a weapon worth its name. All they could do was to scream for the soldiers not to harm the students.

In soft-soled shoes, the soldiers moved almost silently, just the thump of rubber on the asphalt of six-lane Changan Avenue, advancing along the road that slices Beijing in half from east to west. They wore white shirts and green pants and carried small backpacks and metal helmets as well as their assault rifles. They marched swiftly, urged on by platoon leaders counting cadence in the night air. The citizens of Beijing continued to assemble on the streets. Students on bicycles swept them along, windmilling their arms as they rode. Truckloads of workers in yellow hard hats, looking tough, alert, and confident, sped down the city's Second Ring Road, the six-lane highway that encircles the inner city and skirts the diplomatic compound. Behind them drove Edward A.

Gargan, a former Beijing bureau chief for the *New York Times* who was back in China to write a book about economic and political changes in the country.

He would write that *"the commotion in the streets was intense.... The stutter of automatic weapons cracked in the air. Someone hollered at me, 'they're firing at children!' A man, almost hysterical, said that he had seen thirty people shot, old people, young people."*

Close by, Associated Press photographer Mark Avery had been dragged by a crowd to take a photo of a dead man. *"Show the world what is happening!"* screamed the crowd. Avery's photo ended up on the cover of *Time*.

From the PLA situation room, Prime Minister Li Peng continued to relay reports to Deng Xiaoping, whose compound was now guarded by over a thousand soldiers. They were already shooting at anyone they spotted, including women and children who were hurrying home from Tiananmen Square in obedience to the broadcast ordering them to do so.

SAME DAY, SAME TIME
HOSPITAL FOR TRADITIONAL MEDICINE

The wail of ambulance sirens announced the arrival of the first casualties. Though it was years since he had worked in the emergency room, Professor Guangzu realized his presence would help. Many of the younger medical staff were visibly nervous. He walked among them, speaking softly and calmly.

"Think of this as any other disaster," he repeated.

"But I have no experience of dealing with bullet wounds," said one doctor.

"Then watch me," Jenny said. She knew the knowledge she had gained in Los Angeles treating victims of violent crime would be invaluable.

Then there was no time for reassuring conversation. The ambulance crews were wheeling in the first victims. In minutes every emergency room bed was filled. The wounded were placed on the floor, then out in the corridors. Almost all had bullet wounds in the back. Several died before they could receive medical attention. Their bodies were quickly taken away by relatives.

By midnight Professor Guangzu estimated that over sixty victims of gunshots had been admitted. And still the ambulances were arriving. He would remember *"feeling nothing, not anger, not shock, just nothing. How could any emotion cope with what was happening?"*

He turned to deal with another patient, using the techniques of traditional medicine to cope with gaping wounds. Behind him Jenny used the surgical methods she had learned in Los Angeles.

Elsewhere, news correspondents such as Keith Morrison of NBC were calling the city hospitals to establish casualty figures. Morrison was to remember *"talking to a student nurse in one of the hospitals. She said soldiers were pulling life-support systems from the wounded. She ran from the emergency room after she saw soldiers fighting with the staff and soldiers shooting the doctors."*

As the night wore on, the reports of dead and injured grew. The Capital Hospital, a few blocks from Tiananmen Square, had received 121 injured and 46 dead by midnight. The Children's Hospital, a three-mile ambulance drive from Changan Avenue, had received 150 victims; 43 were pronounced dead on arrival, and many of the remaining 107 were in critical condition. The Xuanau Hospital, a mile south of Tiananmen Square, had accepted 38 seriously wounded and 16 bodies. The Railway Hospital, three miles to the east, had admitted 172 casualties, of whom 61 would die. At Hospital No. 2 on Youfung Avenue, to the west of Tiananmen Square, 107 victims arrived in the two hours following the shooting in the Muxudi District. Most of the victims from there had been taken to the nearby Fuxinn Hospital, 284 injured and 119 dead.

In all, Beijing's thirty-seven hospitals admitted about 4,000 dead or injured before midnight this Saturday, June 3.

SUNDAY, JUNE 4, 1989
ANDINGMEN AVENUE

Four miles north of Tiananmen Square, Sue Tung told herself that if she were to die, she wanted *"a record left of the moment."* From her purse she produced a small tape recorder her boyfriend, Rod, had given her before she left California. Sue placed it on the window of the room in the apartment in which she had found shelter for the past hour. The family who had brought her here stared in wonder. She could hear the mother whispering to her husband that Chinese who went abroad acquired some very peculiar ways.

From below in the street came the sound of tank tracks. They had been grinding down the broad avenue for the past hour, crashing over one makeshift barrier after another. Now, a little after midnight, a tank had stopped before a more substantial obstacle. Buses and trucks had been piled one on top of the other by a couple of bulldozers. To the tangle had been added tons of rubble and huge planks of wood. The great barrier blocked the way into the city.

The order of the tank commander was followed by the roar of the vehicle reversing. A little way up the avenue, there was a brief silence, broken by the shattering roar of the tank's main gun blasting a path through the barricade.

The vibration toppled Sue's recorder off the window-sill into the street. From below came excited voices. Some of the soldiers following behind the tank had found the recorder and were shouting up at the windows, demanding to know who owned it.

Sue shrank back into the room. A burst of gunfire flashed across the adjacent building windows. Then came the sound of the tanks grinding forward through the breached barrier. Behind them ran the soldiers. To Sue it sounded as if thousands were running past her window, firing at random and laughing as they did so.

"They sounded more than ever like crazies, as if they were drugged to the eyeballs," Sue would recall. *"They laughed even louder when they heard people who had been hit, screaming. Their laughter was more frightening than the shooting."*

SAME TIME, A LITTLE LATER
CHANGAN AVENUE

Reporter Edward Gargan could see an armored personnel carrier ablaze near the Forbidden City. People were heaving cardboard boxes and blankets onto the searing metal surface. Gargan photographed the fractured silhouette of the vehicle's .50-caliber machine gun pointing crazily into the starless sky. Nearby, buses were on fire, their window frames white with flames billowing from the vehicles' innards. Another bus rocketed through the throng on Changan Avenue, its driver wrestling with the huge steering wheel as he careened to the entrance of the Forbidden City and parked the vehicle to block any troops from emerging. Over the heads of the crowd flashed the blue lights of some of the city's 780 ambulances, all now ferrying the dead or wounded to hospitals.

Then people stopped, staring open-mouthed at the apparition calmly walking down the center of Changan Avenue. A woman with long black hair, wearing a spotless white satin dress, moved through the crowd, swinging a white patent-leather purse. Gargan *"watched her for a moment, stopped by the sight of her effortless progress, her studied obliviousness to the building storm."* Then, all too quickly, she was gone, turning into one of the alleys.

From the west came the thunder of engines and the churn of tank tracks. As if mesmerized, the crowd turned and saw, far down broad Changan Avenue, closely set pairs of headlights. The tanks were advancing six abreast, the barrels of their guns almost parallel to the ground. In the gap between the vehicles were troops firing up the avenue. From the east more tanks were appearing, with more troops shooting.

Edward Gargan saw *"not more than a hundred people forming a thin line, not linking arms, but standing quietly. I ran up behind them. I wanted to see their faces, to look in their eyes, to see the people who stood unarmed in front of the Chinese army. The people, baby-faced students and weathered workers, gazed toward the army without fear. Suddenly there was a sharp popping sound, then a rattle, like firecrackers going off in a neighbor's backyard. Some people in front of me fell to the ground, awkwardly, as if broken apart."*

Watching the Dantean scene, Jonathan Mirsky, a distinguished China specialist, whose reporting these past weeks had been a benchmark for one of Britain's national Sunday newspapers, *The Observer,* remembered the words of a tank commander. The officer had told him a few days before that *"the students were like his younger brothers and sisters, but said they were also his* duixima, *his target. Why? Because Deng Xiaoping, who was giving the orders 'is like my father.'"*

The unreality of the scene was summed up for Mirsky by the voice howling out of the loudspeakers around Tiananmen Square. Now the implacable announcer was repeating two reminders: *"These are disorderly times. Look out for pickpockets";* and *"The People's Liberation Army loves the people. The people love the PLA. Only bad people do not love the army."*

Already the first bodies were being stacked by troops on Changan Avenue, doused with gasoline, and set alight. In the early hours of Sunday morning several such pyres were ablaze. By a quirk of the wind, the stench of burning flesh carried over the walls of Zhongnanhai.

SAME TIME
TIANANMEN SQUARE

The young American teacher, Barr Seitz, found himself in a new role: on-the-spot reporter, broadcasting live to the ABC radio network in the United

States. A short while earlier the network's executive producer had told Barr to use his mobile phone as a microphone. *"Just tell us what you see, as you see it,"* the producer had instructed from his improvised control room in a bedroom in Beijing Hotel. Barr's colleagues had already withdrawn from the square.

Loping through the already panicked crowds, Barr was faithfully following his orders.

"I am standing near the Great Hall of the People. As I watch, all its doors suddenly open and hundreds of troops pour out. They are all helmeted and armed. They're forming lines and coming down the steps, guns at the ready. Oh my God, people are throwing rocks and sticks at them. This is the start of a riot in the square. People are so worked up, so frightened, that they're just totally panicking. From the pediment Wuerkaixi, I think it's him, is calling out 'Don't get those soldiers angry. They've got guns!' Nobody is listening. The soldiers are still coming on down the steps. It's real scary to watch them. Just advancing on in their hundreds, row after row, guns extended. People are backing away. Now there's a new situation developing. An armored personnel carrier has just come up Changan and swung into the square. People are attacking it with sticks, as if they would beat it into the ground. In the distance I can hear a new sound. It sounds like more tanks coming up Changan from the west. Somebody is saying it is tanks. I'm running on to Changan to see what's happening."

Behind him the armored personnel carrier had been set alight by gasoline bombs. As its two-man crew tried to scramble to safety, one was bludgeoned to death, the other rescued by, among others, Liu Gang, the brother of a T-69 tank commander. The young student kept saying to the terrified crewman that it was not students who had killed his companion, but government-sponsored "troublemakers."

As Barr reached Changan Avenue he heard a volley of shots coming from in front of the Great Hall; unable to see if the troops were firing into the air or at people, Barr reported only the sound of gunfire.

Towering over those around him, he could see some distance down the broad avenue. What he saw tested his nerve.

"Tanks. I can't see how many, but many. Each time they reach a barricade they crush it. They are rolling over everything. Buses that have been upturned, trucks, pedicabs, everything. Behind them are soldiers. They are marching in orderly lines, firing from the hip into the buildings, into the mouths of the alleys. They just load and fire, load and fire. It's like a turkey shoot for them. All around, as you can hear, people are screaming at them, 'Why are you attacking the Chinese people? Why are you killing us?' The army seems to be behaving as if it is facing another army, and not a bunch of civilians using sticks and stones."

Barr felt something whistle past his face. Behind him a woman fell, shot through the head by a bullet.

Close by, reporter Edward Gargan dived onto the pavement and began to crawl to safety.

"Two young men ran by me furiously pushing a bicycle cart. On the cart a man lay bathed in blood. More people ran by, carrying a woman whose shoulder was soaked red.

There were some screams, but now I cannot remember how many. Instead, there was a silent anger and a frenzy to move the wounded to the ambulances. A chant of 'ji shao shu, ji shau shu' — 'very, very few' — erupted from the mob, which regrouped in straggly lines of forty to fifty to face the troops. Again a wave of people moved to meet the army, and again the rifles cracked. More people fell.

"I ran farther east, past the edge of the square. Helmeted troops ran around the line of tanks, their engines thundering as they crept forward. Another bus sped through the retreating crowd, young men leaning from the windows waving bamboo poles fixed with crimson flags, the driver, in a snow-white headband, barreling suicidally toward the oncoming tanks.

"'Ba gong, ba gong, ba gong,' the crowd chanted. 'Strike, strike, strike.'

"People swarmed by me, some moving to the square. Many were weeping. Now the sound of gunfire was almost continuous. Threads of yellow light shot from the southern edge of the square, machine-gun tracer bullets, I later learned.

"I stopped a young man to talk for a moment. 'I don't believe it,' he said, his voice shaking. 'How is this possible? How could we prepare?' He stopped abruptly as another young man lying face down on a cart, blood seeping through his clothing, was pushed past us. The first young man put his hands on his face. 'You must support the Chinese people,' he said, turning to me. 'You must go to your country and support the Chinese people.'"

SAME TIME
WASHINGTON, D.C.

In the White House, in the State Department, out at Langley, President Bush and his key advisers continued to hear the live reports of the massacre being broadcast by the radio networks. They were also receiving reports from U.S. diplomats and CIA agents. Yet no one, not President Bush, Secretary of State Baker, or any of their aides, at once publicly deplored the carnage, or even called the Chinese embassy to formally protest what they could clearly hear was happening.

A LITTLE LATER
TIANANMEN SQUARE

On Tiananmen Square, Edward Gargan had become numbed by the wail of the crowd: "*Si duo le, si duo le! Many are dead, many are dead.*" All around him the cautious and highly experienced reporter heard people say bodies were being burned with flamethrowers.

Louise Branson gathered impressions for her next report to the *Sunday Times* in London.

"*They're building another barricade beneath our window. People have dragged one of the trucks filled with suddenly frightened soldiers to form a barricade.*"

The crowd had marshaled them to one side of the barricade and were trying to persuade them to desert.

Suddenly an armored personnel carrier raced down the street. To Louise it seemed the driver was intent on killing as many as he could. It plowed into the crowd, scattering soldiers and civilians alike, and overturned the truck. Bodies flew everywhere. The carrier continued on its way.

"A man lay dead, completely flattened, with a pool of blood oozing from where his head had been. Two soldiers and three civilians lay clearly dead, many others were wounded."

She knew that she had witnessed *"just one small incident in a bloodbath."*

Melinda Liu of *Newsweek* crouched low on Tiananmen Square. From further down Changan Avenue, near the intersection with Zhongnanhai, came continuous gunfire. *"Heavy stuff, machine guns, mixed with the 'putt-putt' of automatic rifles. The reviewing stands in front of the Forbidden City are covered in smoke; Mao's portrait looks like it could go up any moment. There are vehicles on fire. The dead and wounded are everywhere. Not enough ambulances, so pedicabs are being pressed into service. The soldiers on Changan Avenue continue to shoot. Others are in trucks, which they use as firing platforms, driving past the square and pouring down a deadly fire,"* noted Liu.

She ran back down Changan Avenue to the Beijing Hotel, to file her latest eyewitness account. She passed several bodies, and more than once her feet skidded in pools of blood. If anything the shooting had become more intense and was coming closer to the square.

Jeanne Moore had been at the Monument to the People's Heroes when news came of the shooting in Muxudi District. Since then she had remained close to the pediment, observing the student command structure reacting to the unfolding tragedy.

"The mood is surreal. People are dying, and here they are talking at 2:00 A.M. of holding a news conference to once more attack Li Peng. There is no sense of reality," Jeanne noted.

Now, thirty minutes later, Chai Ling had led the other visibly exhausted students to the statue of the Goddess of Democracy.

Despite the fatigue lines around Chai Ling's mouth, her eyes glowed. She was now the undisputed leader of the student movement. Even Wuerkaixi had conceded she was in command.

Wuerkaixi's bombast and ebullience had gone: In their place was a frightened young man, repeatedly saying that the soldiers would kill him.

Wang Dan remained his usual controlled self, but behind his glasses his eyes looked heavy and defeated.

The remaining half dozen student leaders were now mere ciphers for Chai Ling.

Fifty yards away from the Democracy statue, the troops were still firing into the crowd.

"People are running like wild animals," Jeanne scribbled. *"Yet Chai Ling and the others seem to be touched by some magic protection. No bullets come near them. They just march on, serene and indifferent to what is happening. They seem to be living on another plane, perhaps in another world."*

Reaching the statute, already pockmarked by gunfire, Chai Ling addressed her companions. She was dedicating this spot as the site of *"the University of Democracy."* In years to come, she trilled, people would stand here and know the meaning of freedom. Her voice rising, she pronounced an oath.

"I swear to use my young life to protect Tiananmen Square. Our heads may be cut off, our blood may flow, but the People's Square must not be lost."

One by one, the other student leaders repeated the words.

As they turned away, Cassy staggered into the square. She had run all the way from Muxudi, a distance of three miles. She started to tell them what had happened to Daobao, then she fainted. Meili and Yang Li waved down a pedicab and told the driver to take Cassy to the nearest hospital. As she was loaded onto the back of a cart, a few spent bullet casings fell from her hand.

On Changan Avenue, Barr Seitz had also picked up several casings. He wanted a souvenir of this night as a makeshift radio news reporter.

"Bullets are smashing glass and brickwork all along the avenue," he told ABC's radio audience. *"There are fires everywhere. The biggest one is in front of the Forbidden City, where the blaze is casting a great fiery glow on the face of Mao's portrait. It would be interesting to know what he would think of all this. We're getting tragic reports all the time. A mother has just gone running by screaming that her husband and son have both been killed. There is a story that the soldiers have gunned down a row of schoolgirls outside Quanjude, the city's most famous roast-duck restaurant. There are so many stories. All I can tell you is that the people are fighting back with stones and bottles. Whenever they get their hands on a soldier, they beat him mercilessly. But this is really a no-contest. The soldiers are well equipped. Even as I speak, another convoy of armored troop carriers is coming up the avenue."*

On the corner of Jianquomen Avenue, two miles to the east of the foreign legation quarter, Brian Davidson watched an advancing army column come to an inglorious stop. Nails and broken glass liberally sprinkled on the road had punctured the tires of their trucks. The troops disembarked and began to jog toward Tiananmen Square. Davidson estimated they numbered two thousand.

Away to his right, from just behind the main railway station, came the sound of more tanks turning on to Changan and heading toward the square.

To Davidson, *"It was a grim showpiece of military power, not just designed to quell the students, but the whole country. A quarter of the world's population was being told what to expect if they ever dared again to ask for democracy, or anything else the leaders did not approve."*

A couple of miles away on Wenjin Road, to the east of Tiananmen Square, the CIA officer known as Tom sat in a car with diplomatic number plates and watched another column of trucks pass. From time to time the vehicles slowed long enough to allow soldiers to jump into the road and remove all the student banners and posters from the walls. These were piled up in the street and set on fire.

From her vantage point in the Beijing Hotel, Louise Branson watched *"four people fall dead under a fresh burst of gunfire. Everywhere there were burning buses, wrecked military vehicles, twisted metal barriers, and blood. A student truck drove past, three bloodied corpses displayed on the back. It stopped every few yards. A young man with a bullhorn called for people to see for themselves the horror perpetrated by the People's Army."*

Other reporters, including NBC's Keith Morrison, continued to try to measure the massacre in terms of the numbers admitted to hospitals. As hospitals in the center of the city filled to overflowing, victims were being taken farther and farther afield. By the early hours of Sunday morning, the well-equipped Andima Hospital, fourteen miles north of Tiananmen Square, had received 196 gunshot victims; 41 had died despite the efforts of the surgeons. Three miles to the east of the square, the dozen doctors and seventy nurses on duty at Hospital Number 4 found themselves unable to cope with 177 casualties, all serious emergencies. Normally they could have transferred their overflow to one of the other four nearby hospitals. But they were also swamped, having among them 700 victims.

Professor Guangzu and his daughter, Jenny, were working *"like demons. We all were,"* she would recall.

Matters were made worse by the number of wounded who had been taken home by families fearing troops would invade the hospitals to kill the survivors. Now, realizing that the wounded were dying from their injuries, relatives had come to the hospitals to plead for doctors to make house calls. They were told their only hope was to bring their loved ones back.

They had begun to arrive in handcarts and stretchers, or carried on mattresses. They lay on the floor, joining all the others needing urgent attention. Throughout the city's hospitals, the number of dead and injured continued to climb. No one had precise figures. There was no longer time to keep them.

Down on the northwest corner of Tiananmen Square, close to the Great Hall of the People, Jeanne Moore watched yet another column of troops. They looked pale, as if they had spent some time underground. They carried assault rifles.

At 3:00 A.M., the metallic voice of Qiao Shi bellowed forth. *"A serious counterrevolutionary rebellion was broken out. The People's Liberation Army has been restrained for some days. However, the counterrevolutionary rebellion must now be resolutely counterattacked."*

Immediately Chai Ling responded. *"There is no revolution! Many students, workers, and ordinary citizens have asked the student command for permission to use weapons. We share their rage at the attack on the innocent. But we remain true to the spirit of Hu Yaobang. We uphold the principle of peaceful demonstration."*

Even as Chai Ling spoke, Jeanne could see people seizing whatever came to hand, ready to defend themselves against the next attack.

It came with a suddenness and ferocity that left no room for resistance. The troops at the northwest corner were joined by others coming from Zhongnanhai compound. At the same time several hundred paramilitary police, armed with long wooden stakes, swept out of the Forbidden City. Someone threw a gasoline bomb toward them. It exploded in midair, shot to pieces by a burst of gunfire.

The troops moved at a walking pace firing nonstop into the crowd on the edge of the square. Behind came tanks. Advancing up Changan Avenue from the east was another force of troops, firing into buildings and side streets. Passing the Beijing Hotel, they raked its balconies, driving Melinda Liu to duck for cover.

On the square, Barr Seitz realized he was *"probably the last foreign journalist still broadcasting. My producer was yelling on the mobile for me to get the hell out of there. With my height I was a good target."*

But Barr continued running toward the Monument to the People's Heroes. He wanted to convey the words of Chai Ling to his audience. With his fluent Mandarin he had no difficulty translating them into English.

Her voice somehow rising above the continuous firing, Chai Ling continued to try and reason with the army.

"You are our brothers! You promised you would not use violence against the people! Please do not break that promise!"

A volley of shots answered her. On Changan Avenue, still more buses burned against the walls of the Forbidden City. A great pall of smoke drifted toward Zhongnanhai. Through it came the constant muzzle flash of guns firing.

Barr's producer was still screaming for him to pull out. But Chai Ling had chosen this moment to attempt to rally the students with a story.

She was *"like a teacher addressing an unruly class,"* Barr would recall. *"She asked the students to ignore everything and gather round. Incredibly, such was her charisma that they did."*

When there were several thousand around the pediment, she began, one hand on the hips of her faded jeans, the other holding a microphone close to her lips. She spoke calmly.

"There was once a colony of a billion ants living on top of a hill. One day their hill caught fire. The ants formed a giant ball and rolled down the hill. Those on the outside were burned and crushed to death, but the majority inside survived. Fellow students, we in the square, we are the outer layer of people. We know deep in our hearts that only with sacrifice can we save the Republic."

Close to tears, Barr joined with them in singing the *"Internationale."* Then he ran from the square. Over the loudspeakers, Chai Ling was saying that those who wished to stay could do so, but those who wanted to leave could now go.

Renewed gunfire drowned out everything else. It was the signal for Wuerkaixi to board an ambulance, already filled with four people with bullet wounds. Later he would say: *"I left because I knew if I did not, students who had remained just because of me would now die."*

Like much else about Wuerkaixi, where he went would remain his secret. When he next emerged in public it was in Paris. He would steadfastly refuse to confirm or deny the persistent story that French intelligence smuggled him out of China.

As he ran, Barr wondered if he would be able to escape. The entire square was now surrounded by troops who were systematically firing into the crowd.

But now an unlikely negotiator had emerged to try and stay their hand. Hou Dejian, the pop singer, had abandoned any pretense of a hunger strike. With the verve and showmanship of someone used to making an entrance, Hou emerged on the pediment. Grabbing one of several microphones he shouted: *"Testing, one, two, three,"* and then launched an appeal for the crowd to give up all their weapons.

"Show them you will obey," Hou cried.

And they did. All over the square, people dropped what weapons they had. Convinced he could stop more carnage, Hou commandeered an ambulance and ordered it to drive to the north side of the square. There he told a political commissar he had come to negotiate an orderly withdrawal. The students would leave the square if there were no more firing. The commissar ordered a ceasefire and then disappeared into the Great Hall of the People to consult with his supervisors.

Suddenly the square was plunged into darkness as the streetlights went out. Flares from burning vehicles lit the scene. Thirty minutes later the commissar returned and announced that if the students left at once they would not be attacked. Hou hurried over to the pediment and once more pleaded with the students.

"You have made your point. You have shown you are not afraid to die. So now leave."

A wave of uncertainty swept the students. There were calls for a vote. Others said it would be a "betrayal" to leave. They called for Chai Ling. But she refused to come to the microphone. No one knows why.

The lights came back on. Again, no one knows why, the students saw that the soldiers had moved further into the square. With them was a PLA commando unit, faces blackened, wearing camouflage and combat boots. They had bayonets fixed to their rifles. They raced to the Monument to the People's Heroes and began to smash the microphones and other equipment.

The students had lost their voice and their platform. Their fifty-five days on the pediment were over. That was the moment their hope for democracy died.

On the largest square in the world lay the bone-white shards of the Goddess of Democracy, which had been faithfully modeled on the Statue of Liberty.

```
      C116                    01           1739    03-06-89

               =1800 CHINA ASSAULT=

     Armed troops have been converging on Peking's Tiananmen Square,

the stronghold of the pro-democracy demonstrators for the last few

weeks.  Troops using armed personnel carriers crashed through

barricades on the outskirts of the square.  Eyewitnesses described

how the night sky was lit by tracer bullets being fired into the air.

Announcements were broadcast ordering everybody to get clear of the

square.  However, students and other demonstrators in the square

showed no signs of giving way and tried to commandeer buses and build

new barricades around the square.  Thousands more people were seen

flooding into the square on bicycles.  Ambulances were also moving in

the neighbourhood of the square, but it was not clear what casualties

there had been.  Earlier, eyewitnesses said troops trying to reach

the square from the west fired into a crowd and at least four people

were said to have been killed.

Attack on square snap 1720 (C112)
with more CNN on ambulances, cyclists.
14/05 '01 MON 14:29 FAX
```

Dispatches From Tiananmen Square
These show the raw, unedited coverage of foreign correspondents reporting from
Tiananmen Square in the run-up to the massacre.

```
   C124                        01            1834   03-06-89

                 =1830 CHINA ASSAULT TWO =

    A few miles (km) to the west of the square, troops opened fire

on demonstrators and reports say at least four people were killed.

Many more are said to have been wounded.  People armed themselves

with crowbars and bricks to try to beat back the soldiers advancing

towards the city centre.  A correspondent who was near the scene said

people were horrified that troops of the People's Liberation Army

were shooting Chinese citizens and pleaded with him to get the news

to the outside world.  In another area of the city, an armoured troop

carrier crashed into a barricade of army trucks which had been placed

across the road by demonstrators with the soldiers still inside.

Witnesses said several people were killed and others wounded.




Shooting in west snap 1621
with MILES r'main on reaction;
LUARD XN51 apc crash                        GWL     END  11   jac
```

```
 C127                    01          1904    03-06-89
```

=1900 CHINA ASSAULT - ONE=

The Chinese army has finally intervened to end the occupation of

Peking's Tiananmen Square, the stronghold of the pro-democracy

demonstrators for the last few weeks. It was around two in the

morning that troops using armoured personnel carriers crashed through

barricades on the outskirts of the square. Eyewitnesses said

thousands of troops later poured into the square from the entrance to

the Forbidden City, firing as they advanced. They were said to be

sweeping the north side of the square systematically to clear it of

protesters. Tens of thousands of demonstrators were crouching in the

centre of the square; some tried to turn the soldiers back by

throwing petrol bombs, while others were said to be fleeing and

trying to regroup. In one incident witnessed by a BBC correspondent,

an armoured vehicle became stuck on a concrete barricade and was set

on fire -- as soldiers tried to escape from it they were attacked and

beaten by the crowd. Some reports say deaths run into the twenties,

with dozens more wounded. As the assault began, eyewitnesses

described how the night sky was lit by tracer bullets being fired

into the air. Announcements were broadcast ordering everybody to get

clear of the square.

```
RW 1830 (C121) with LUARD CNN on troops entering sq (snap 1853)
RTR ADIE on 28 dead; SIMPSON on apc attack from 1830;
```

C131   01   1924   03-06-89

=1930 CHINA PROTEST HISTORY=

The assault on Tiananmen square ended nearly two weeks of
uncertainty after the declaration of martial law. This followed
nearly a month of China's most serious anti-government protests in
forty years of communist rule. They began with the death of the
former Communist party leader, Mr Hu Yaobang, when students held
memorial at which they called for more democracy, an end to
corruption in the Communist Party and the resignations of China's
senior leader, Mr Deng Xiaoping and the Prime Minister, Li Peng. The
protests came to a head when the Soviet leader, Mr Gorbachev was in
Peking. More than ten-thousand students staged a sit-in. Tiananmen
square -- three-thousand of them began a hunger strike. The protests
grew as students were joined by workers, government officials and
even the police. The country's leadership was plunged into turmoil
and there were reports of a power struggle which saw the eclipse of
the man the students had adopted as their hero -- the party leader,
Zhao Ziyang.

NEWSINF,RTR,UPI,THOMAS   BOL   15

C141   01   2043   03-06-89

=2100 CHINA ASSAULT TWC=

There was more shooting in streets leading to the square. An
eyewitness said soldiers fired from passing trucks at people standing
in the streets, shooting indiscriminately. Hundreds were admitted to
nearby hospitals. People shouted angrily at the troops to go back.
Others ran in panic as volleys of shots rang out, some falling to the
ground as they were hit. Many army trucks were set on fire, but
hundreds more continued to pour into the city centre. The first
outbreak of shooting had been a few miles (KM) west of the square.
As the troops opened fire on unarmed protesters, people at the scene
pleaded with foreign reporters to tell the world that troops of the
People's Liberation Army were shooting Chinese citizens.

RW 2030 C137 with more ADIE XN66 new then
west shooting snap 1621   GWL   11

```
        C154                    01          2225    03-06-89

                 =2230 CHINA ASSAULT -- TWO=
```

Some of the worst violence was in other parts of the city, from
which the sound of heavy explosions could still be heard towards
dawn. Hospitals were unable to cope with the number of wounded --
one small hospital alone had three-hundred casualties. In streets
leading to Tiananmen Square, soldiers were seen firing at people from
passing trucks, shooting indiscriminately. People shouted angrily at
the troops to go back. Others ran in panic as volleys of shots rang
out, some falling to the ground as they were hit. Hours later, the
streets were still filled with people expressing their defiance and
their outrage at what had taken place. Many said they could not
believe that they had been fired on, and they pleaded with foreign
reporters to tell the world that troops of the People's Liberation
Army were shooting Chinese citizens. The soldiers are said to be
from the Twenty-seventh Army, loyal to the hardline president, Yang
Shangkun.

```
RW 2200 (C148) when later defiance new
with LuARD r'main on outlying explosions,300,Yang's men
ADIE on near square 2100          GWL              14
```

```
  C002                    01           0038  04-06-89
```

=0100 CHINA ASSAULT · ONE=

The Chinese army has seized control of Tiananmen Square in central Peking after mounting a bloody assault to drive out the pro-democracy demonstrators. A BBC correspondent says it was a devastating and ruthless use of force against the unarmed protesters trying to stop them. At five thirty in the morning, he watched as a column of more than fifty tanks and troop carriers tossed aside the remnants of the barricades and drove into the square from the east. Three hours earlier, troops had entered from other directions and gradually sealed it off. Nobody knows the extent of the casualties. Our correspondent says he saw five corpses on stretchers, but eye-witnesses suggest that far more than that may have died in the square -- not only from gunshots, but also from being crushed by tanks, which ploughed relentlessly through obstacles in their way.

```
RW 2300 (C157) with LONG XN1 on army control
(Snapped 2357) and colour
Troops entering 1853
Assault 1720, hospitals filling 2030.        DRM    MORE  13   jk
```

```
     C005         ξ           01         0054   04-06-89

              =0100 CHINA ASSAULT - TWO=
```

Another of our correspondents says much of the worst violence
was in outlying districts where hospitals said they could not cope
with the number of wounded. One small hospital alone reported three
hundred casualties. Diplomats said that two members of an American
television crew had been beaten up by soldiers and taken away at
gunpoint. Students have asked the people of Peking to strike in
protest at the military action, and our correspondent says it is
likely to be some time before the political effects become clear.
During the assault, many people in the streets said they could not
believe that they had been fired on and pleaded with foreign
reporters to tell the world that troops of the Peoples Liberation
Army were shooting Chinese citizens. The soldiers are said to be
from the Twenty-seventh Army, loyal to the hardline President, Yang
Shangkun.

```
RW 2230 (C154) with
LUARD XN2 on TV crew, strike
Outlying, Yang s men 2230.          DRM        END     13      jk
```

```
THOMAS    C045                     01          0840   04-06-89
                =0900 CHINA ASSAULT - ONE=
```

The people of Peking are said to be in a state of shock after

the army stormed into Tiananmen Square using automatic weapons and

tanks to suppress the student occupation. It was the worst bloodshed

in the city since the Communists came to power forty years ago -- but

the full extent of the casualties is still not known. Hospitals have

been flooded with casualties; at one alone forty deaths were

reported, with another three-hundred people wounded. Latest reports

say sporadic shooting has been continuing near Tiananmen Square which

has now been sealed off. The army action began at two o'clock in the

morning when thousands of troops swarmed into the square from various

directions, opening fire on the demonstrators. They were supported

by tanks and armoured vehicles which ploughed through the makeshift

barrices which had been put up by the students.

Sources: to come   MHF   13   MORE   YAS

23

A Time of Pain

SUNDAY–TUESDAY, JUNE 4–6, 1989
BEIJING

In the hard light of a new day, the carnage on Changan Avenue became clear. Along a ten-mile length of the great avenue lay the bodies of scores of men, women, and even children. Many were heaped into funeral pyres by soldiers. No doubt the soldiers were not anxious to dispose of corpses in this way under the gaze of foreign reporters watching from the balconies of the Beijing Hotel. So they were loading the dead around Tiananmen Square aboard helicopters and carrying them to the hills to the west of the city.

From there the stench of burning flesh had begun to drift back across the city, adding to the charnel-house smell of the smaller pyres on Changan Avenue. Brian Davidson, the British Embassy press attaché, thought the air around the Nazi concentration camps must have been as sickening.

Like almost everybody else, Davidson was numbed by the ferocity of the Chinese response. Uppermost in his mind was the fate of the students, especially their leaders. Davidson feared that the sporadic gunfire still coming from the north of the city, where most of the university campuses were, boded ill for them.

The student leaders had left Tiananmen Square separately, as they had planned they would, to avoid being captured as a group.

Reaching the labyrinth of alleys on the far side of Changan Avenue, Chai Ling went to the first of a chain of safe houses set up by the student leaders for just such a contingency. There she changed her clothes and put on a wig and a pair of steel-framed glasses. She was ready for the next stage of her long journey. She was taken by pedicab through the southern suburbs of the city, her driver successfully taking them past several military roadblocks, claiming they were on their way to visit a dying relative in the village of Guan just outside the city limits.

By noon Chai Ling was hidden in Guan in another safe house. When she had eaten, she insisted on preparing a tape for the country's students. That night it was hand-carried by road and rail all the way south to Canton. From there it was smuggled the short distance into Hong Kong. Two days later, Chai Ling once more addressed not only her fellow students, but the entire world over a Hong Kong radio station.

"*I am Chai Ling,*" she began. "*I am still alive. Ours was a peaceful protest. The ultimate price of a peaceful protest was to sacrifice oneself. Arm in arm, shoulder to shoulder, we sang the 'Internationale' and slowly walked toward the Monument to the People's Heroes. We sat quietly at the monument awaiting with dignity the arrival of our executioners. We realized that what was happening was a conflict between love and hate and not a battle of brute forces. My compatriots, even at the darkest moment, dawn will still break.*"

Wang Dan did not hear her broadcast. After leaving Tiananmen Square, he returned to Beijing University to collect some of his favorite books to take with him into hiding. Waiting her him was the senior political officer on campus, Pang Yi, with a number of his staff. They arrested Wang Dan. He was taken to Public Security headquarters a few blocks from Tiananmen Square. Later that day his interrogation began. It would last many weeks.

During Sunday other student leaders were brought in. One of the first was Liu Gang. His Western-style sports clothes were in tatters. His face bore marks of the severe beating he had received when he was arrested at Beijing's main railway station. Just before he boarded a train for Shanghai, a security agent had recognized him from the days in 1986–87, when Liu Gang had also been a student activist.

Yang Li, whose brother, Bing, had taken part in the massacre, and Li's girlfriend, Meili, were also arrested at the train station. They had been trying to catch a train to Li's village on the banks of the Yangtze River. Instead they found themselves incarcerated in basement cells in the public security headquarters.

Forty-seven students were brought there in those first few hours after leaving Tiananmen Square. Almost all showed signs of having been beaten.

Bing Yang had been among the troops occupying Tiananmen Square. They had been recalled to barracks at 7:00 A.M. to have a meal of rice and pickles. They had then gone to sleep, with the praise of company commander Tan Yaobang for a job well done echoing in their ears. Not for a moment, Bing would later say, had he or the other soldiers had doubt about what they had done.

On Andingmen Avenue, twelve miles north of where the students were held prisoner at police headquarters, Sue Tung was planning her escape. At dawn the sound of gunfire had eased outside the apartment block where she was hiding. The family who had sheltered her was now as anxious as Sue was for her to be on her way out of the city, beginning her long journey back to Sacramento.

Sue had thought of telephoning Rod to reassure him she was alive, but the nearest public phone was several blocks away. Then she remembered that because of his position at the military academy, Captain Instructor Jyan had a telephone in the apartment he shared with his mother. The building where they lived was only a short walk from Andingmen Avenue.

Profusely thanking the family, Sue stepped out onto the avenue. There were bodies on the street, some being hefted onto bicycle carts, others just lying on the pavement. Soldiers stared indifferently at the corpses. Once more Sue was struck by the idea that the soldiers had been drugged. *"There was a strange look in their eyes, sort of glazed. I'd seen that look when I'd visited friends in hospital,"* she said later.

The soldiers ignored her. Trying to walk as calmly as possible, Sue cut through the alleys to reach her destination.

Jyan's mother was astonished to see Sue when she opened the door. Sue decided that despite the old woman being a member of her local street committee, she had no alternative but to trust her. Once inside the apartment, Sue told her why she had returned to China, and what she had witnessed on Tiananmen Square and during the night, ending by describing the bodies she had seen on Andingmen Avenue.

Jyan's mother listened intently and without interruption. Finally she looked at Sue.

"My son had no part of this," the old woman said firmly. *"He would never allow the army to harm the people."*

Sue felt a sudden tension in the room. She regretted having come; she feared Jyan's mother would call the police. Sue suspected that what she had told the old woman was sufficient to send her to prison for many years.

At that moment Jyan arrived. His appearance shocked both women. To Sue *"he looked like a man who had looked into hell."*

In little more than a whisper, Jyan described what he had seen when he left the situation room in the PLA compound after he drove past Tiananmen Square: tanks and armored personnel carriers rolling over bodies, grinding them to pulp, soldiers mowing down the fleeing crowd, more tanks flattening the bodies.

"So many bodies," Jyan kept repeating. *"It is terrible, terrible."*

"He spoke for an hour as if by doing so he could exorcise what he had seen," Sue would recall. *"By then his mother had no doubt about what had happened. Her attitude changed. She was like someone who has seen a terrible truth about someone she had trusted, the leaders of China. She started to say they had betrayed the people."*

Jyan cut her off, insisting this was not the time for recriminations. What they must do was help Sue leave China so she could spread the word about what had happened.

"The leadership will lie," Jyan predicted. *"They will say there was no massacre."*

While Jyan and his mother helped Sue plan her escape, his political commissar, Zhang Gong, was already briefing Deng Xiaoping and the other members of the Politburo on the official version of events to be broadcast on radio and published in the *People's Daily,* the official mouthpiece of the Chinese government.

The version began as it would continue to be given.

"The whole people of the capital and the country will understand the fact that the troops did not kill or hurt one single person. In fighting against the counter-revolutionary riot, the troops were forced to defend themselves, but they only fired blank rounds.

Four officers, soldiers, and police were murdered brutally by those inhuman protesters. Their brutality cannot be imagined by ordinary people!"

Deng Xiaoping ordered the Big Lie to be promulgated even as the slaughter continued.

Throughout Sunday, June 4, the gray-brown haze over the city thickened and grew more obnoxious as the smoke from the funeral pyres added to the natural air pollution.

Reporters continued to revise upward the number of dead and injured. By noon all the city's thirty-seven hospitals were completely filled with casualties, the vast majority with gunshot wounds, usually in the back. There were 107 such victims in the city's main children's hospital, all under the age of fifteen.

The Friendship Hospital reported 134 admissions; Tongren Hospital, 198; Xyum Hospital, 209; Hospital Number 1, 181. Even the city's two hospitals specializing in treating infectious diseases had between them admitted close to 400 wounded.

By noon the totals were 6,500 wounded and 4,000 dead.

No one could be certain of the numbers. The only certainty was that they continued to climb.

Having cleared the square, the army set off in pursuit of the students, who were fleeing northward toward the university campuses. They carried with them the bodies of their fallen. The corpses were displayed on tables in their classrooms and adorned with white paper flowers, a reminder of the bouquets the students had borne to Tiananmen on that day they marched to mourn Hu Yaobang.

By nine o'clock on that Sunday morning, Tiananmen Square had become an armed camp. Twenty thousand troops and over a thousand armored vehicles guarded its ninety-eight bloodstained acres. Every few yards was the same sign: MARTIAL LAW AREA. ENTRANCE STRICTLY FORBIDDEN.

Hundreds of troops were stationed outside the Beijing Hotel. In the hotel compound small groups of people stood and watched. They were orderly in their behavior.

Edward Gargan was one of the correspondents running through the upper floors of the hotel, trying to find a better vantage point for observing the square. *"We tried locked door after locked door. One door opened into an office full of Chinese security officers with walkie-talkies. We rushed to the balcony, but the security people forced us back. Racing back down the hall, we found a stairwell to a fire escape that led to the roof. Shoving aside planks that had been piled on the exit to block access, we ran to the edge of the roof. Chinese security people on another corner of the roof began moving toward us. We stared for a minute, perhaps two, toward the square, the scene of the previous night carnage."*

At one minute past ten, without warning, the soldiers positioned outside the hotel opened fire on the crowd that had gathered in front of the building. Scores of people fell dead. An ambulance called to the scene was machine-gunned. It burst into flames, its crew killed by the gunfire.

All over the city similar unprovoked attacks were taking place.

At the Hospital for Traditional Medicine, Professor Guangzu was about to snatch a few hours sleep when troops arrived in the emergency room. They demanded to know if any "counterrevolutionaries" were receiving treatment.

When the professor remonstrated, one of the soldiers shoved a rifle butt in his chest and threatened to execute him on the spot. Jenny rushed forward and pulled her father away. To her experienced eye *the soldiers seemed to be doped. They were extremely high.*

With two of the soldiers standing guard over the medical staff, the others entered a postoperative room. What happened there is forever etched in Jenny's memory.

"The soldiers just pulled out all the IVs from our patients." Several would not survive the abuse.

Once more Professor Guangzu urged his daughter to leave China with her small son, Peter. Jenny firmly refused, cutting short further argument by saying *"we have work to do."*

She had decided that she would remain in China, that in its *"hour of darkness"* she had an important role to play. She knew she would miss America, but life often demanded sacrifices, she reminded herself.

In their apartment Captain Instructor Jyan and his mother had completed preparations for Sue Tung's escape. His mother had given Sue the only suitcase she possessed, a large battered relic of the old woman's only trip outside the city, to see relatives in Shanghai. She had filled the case with old clothes and bedding. These would provide cover for Sue's story if she were stopped by troops at the railway station: that she was traveling to Shanghai to get married.

Jyan would accompany her to the station. Before leaving the apartment, Sue tried to call Rod. The line was dead. Jyan said the authorities had probably cut all communications with the outside world.

Jyan's mother insisted Sue should eat, and take food with her for the journey. While this was being prepared, Sue turned on the English-language waveband of the small radio in time to hear a brave attack on what had happened. Defying the Great Lie being broadcast in Mandarin on other channels, an announcer told something of the truth in a voice vibrant with emotion.

"A most tragic event has happened in our capital. Thousands of people, most of them innocent civilians, have been killed by fully armed soldiers who forced their way into our city. The soldiers arrived in armored vehicles and used machine guns against thousands of local people and students who tried to stop them. When the army succeeded in overcoming the opposition, they continued to fire indiscriminately at crowds on the street. Some armored vehicles even crushed foot soldiers who hesitated in front of the resisting civilians. We appeal to all our listeners to join our protest for the gross violation of human rights and the most barbarous suppression of the people."

The radio then played Beethoven's Fifth Symphony, the opening notes of which echo three dots and a dash, a symbol for the "V" for victory.

Suddenly the broadcast went off the air. Troops had invaded the studio and arrested the announcer. His fate, like so many others, would remain unknown.

A little while later, sitting on the back of a pedicab and clutching the suitcase, Sue was taken through the streets by Jyan. Because of his uniform, they were waved through the roadblocks. They passed piles of burning bodies. When they reached Changan Avenue, they saw the slaughter was even more widespread. By the time they arrived at the railway station they had counted over one hundred corpses. They had to stop frequently to allow helicopters to land and disgorge more troops before airlifting out some of the corpses.

The station was surrounded by a cordon of troops. Once more Jyan's rank enabled them to pass untroubled. Sue recognized several students from the square being arrested by police and bundled into waiting trucks.

Her ticket purchased, Jyan escorted her to the train. In one of the carriages Sue spotted Cassy Jones.

Cassy had made her way from the hospital to her room in the Friendship Hotel. She had packed her belongings and headed for the station. With her fluent Mandarin Cassy had convinced the soldiers she was an American diplomat traveling to Shanghai on urgent business.

"They were country boys, who had not seen many foreigners," Cassy would remember.

Sue decided that to travel with a foreigner now would be to attract attention. She wedged herself into a carriage of elderly Chinese.

Jyan formally wished her a safe journey and was gone. She sensed that she would never see him again, and she was right.

On Monday, June 5, fifty-six days after the first demonstrations, the army continued to shoot the people. That morning Melinda Liu of *Newsweek* saw several dozen cyclists outside the Beijing Hotel *"simply shot out of hand for biking too close to the troops."* Their bodies lay for several hours in the street before they were taken away in army trucks.

That afternoon from a balcony of the hotel, Barr Seitz witnessed an encounter that brought tears once more to his eyes. A young man strode out on Changan Avenue and confronted a squadron of tanks driving out of Tiananmen.

"He just stood there, arms outstretched, daring the lead truck to run him over while we all watched. The first truck rocked on its tracks, with a great grinding noise. When the tank moved to the right to get around the man, he just went with it. When the tank moved to the left, the guy moved with it. Back and forth. We just held our breath. Then the man climbed on the tank and shouted at those inside. 'Go back! Turn around. Stop killing our people!' Then his friends rushed and pulled him from the tank. The man just walked away as calmly as if he did this for a living."

The footage of the incident Barr's colleagues had shot would become one of the lasting images of the rape of Beijing.

That Monday in Spook City, the building in the U.S. embassy compound that housed the CIA station chief and his staff, operatives were preparing the first analysis of what had happened.

The document was a masterpiece of CIA-speak, presenting its intelligence agents as having forecast events accurately. A part of the draft document read:

"It is widely reported that some of the soldiers were heavily drugged so that they would not be scared by their own action. The use of drugs, however, can only explain the behavior of individual soldiers. It cannot explain some actions of the military as a whole. Soldiers were reported to gun down everybody in sight; they even chased people all the way to back lanes just to kill them. Not only did they try to prevent medical workers from rescuing the wounded, but they even rushed to the hospitals to pull off life-supporting systems from the wounded. This was not trigger-happy, individual behavior, but the carefully planned and organized efforts to kill all the eyewitnesses if possible.

"The government effort to prevent any eyewitness from escaping was also achieved in Tiananmen Square. The square was completely sealed by the military vehicles and troops before the killing started. Though both the Chinese government and some eyewitness accounts mention the negotiated withdrawal of the students from the square, there were some students left in the square. While outsiders did not know what exactly happened inside the square, the potential eyewitnesses were perhaps all killed. The Chinese government has insisted that no one was killed in Tiananmen Square. This is largely because no one actually saw the killing.

"The post-massacre roundup of student leaders and execution of those participants is a continuation of the 'no eyewitness' policy.

"Given the above analysis, which indicates a violence-maximization policy by the government, the remaining question is, who was actually in charge of all this?

"There was no doubt that Deng was the commander-in-chief; he made the decision to crack down on the student demonstrations on April 25. But in China, it is those who are able to carry out the decision that actually obtain the greatest power and benefit most. On the other hand, it was just impossible for an eighty-four-year-old man to oversee every operational detail.

"What the hardliners needed was not simply the recapture of the square. They needed a redistribution of political power at the top without any moderate elements, not only for the present situation, but also the post-Deng era.

"The hardliners have succeeded, but only for the time being. By removing the moderates from the top, the link between top leaders and the reforming forces at various levels of the society has finally been severed. By so doing, they have polarized the entire political spectrum in China. They have done so with the support from the old guard. It is doubtful if they can continue such a policy without the old guard, given a disastrous economy, a discredited image of the Party, and discontented population.

"In the next few months up to the fortieth anniversary of China's national day on October 1, Chinese leaders have to convince the population that China's economy will be better off with the political crackdown. The prospect, however, is so bad that it will be very difficult, if not impossible, to re-centralize the economy, to control the inflation and investment. Failing that, what the Chinese government will face won't be another intellectual revolt, but serious and large-scale social unrest."

The CIA version of events was one of several reports on the massacre that were faxed from the U.S. embassy compound to Washington. They would be endlessly scrutinized by those composing what President Bush was saying would be "a measured response."

It took a full day before the presidential reaction emerged.

On Tuesday, June 6, in an evening news conference, Bush announced he would suspend U.S. military sales to China and end contacts between U.S. and Chinese military officials. He offered to extend the visas of Chinese students studying in the United States. He also recalled a number of U.S. diplomats from Beijing.

Bush then revealed he had tried to telephone a Chinese leader whom he refused to name, to underscore the point that America still viewed its relationship with China *"as important, and yet I view the life of every single student as important."*

The President admitted the Chinese leader had refused to take his call. *"Nonetheless,"* he added, *"there's a relationship over there that is fundamentally important to the United States that I want to see preserved. And so I'm trying to make a proper, prudent balance ... and I think we found a proper avenue."*

The President then went on to lambaste the regime in Iran for underwriting terrorism. One reporter murmured to a colleague that the United States trade links with Iran were currently zero.

In Washington analyst Joseph Brewer later said, *"Bush's implicit message to U.S. corporations with a total of many billions of dollars invested in China was clear. Despite the massacre, they should regard the situation very much as business as usual. The apologists of Kissinger Associates could not have expressed their position more clearly than had the President."*

In Beijing and elsewhere in China, few U.S. firms felt it necessary to withdraw their executives as a protest over the killings. And after all, nobody else was doing that. The Japanese, British, and Europeans were staying put. The prevailing mood in the foreign business community was perfectly summed up by George Kenneth Liu, chief executive in China of General Foods Corporation. *"We are vigilant but we are not pulling out."* George F. Truber, in charge of American Telephone and Telegraph Company operations in China said: *"We are not in a panic. We still regard China as a market for the future."*

That Tuesday in Beijing, in her apartment in the *China Daily* compound, Jeanne Moore wrote her wrap-up story for her American newspaper.

"With so much killing, a death fatigue sets in and the stories people trade of what they've seen and what they've heard can only be endured if they contain distinctively unusual features: The young man whose beautiful face was left in the doorway, or the five provincial tourists who, according to a Chinese journalist, had just arrived in Beijing's main railway station. Knowing nothing of the situation and eager to see the city, they wandered too close to the soldiers and were mown down. The unthinkable becomes the norm and then even natural."

Jeanne had decided to remain in China for the foreseeable future, in the hope of *"being able to report a change for the better."*

That same Tuesday, Chai Ling was making her way out of China. Repeatedly changing her disguise, the young student visionary traveled from one safe house to another. Her exact route would remain a closely-guarded secret shared only by a handful. It would be many weeks before she would emerge in Hong Kong. From there she would fly to Paris to join Wuerkaixi.

While Chai Ling wended her way to safety, a young American actress, Debbie Gates, was also making her escape.

She had arrived in China two months before to star in the role of reporter Helen Shaw, an American journalist who had been caught up in the Chinese Civil War in the 1930s, in a feature film to be shot on location some six hundred miles south of Beijing. Her co-star was Hollywood actor John Perry.

Filming had all but finished when news of the massacre in Tiananmen Square reached the location. Gates immediately turned on the Chinese crew and its director and accused them of *"complicity in the murder of women and children."*

The film's producer promptly confined the two Americans to a hotel, well away from the Chinese cast and crew. Gates and Perry were warned they would be imprisoned if they *"spread any more lies."*

The next day they learned their contracts had been canceled and the Chinese would not help them leave the country.

Finally they escaped from their hotel and went to the local airport. They waited six hours for a flight. Strapped to her body was Gate's diary of life on a Chinese location, along with photos she had taken of local demonstrations in support of the students. The couple flew to Canton. From there they took a boat to Hong Kong, where they stayed for three days, sleeping on the airport floor among the throngs of people waiting for a flight out.

A week later Gates and Perry were back in Hollywood. She was ready to sell her story to the highest bidder among its two thousand producers. There were no takers.

That same boat that brought Gates and Perry to Hong Kong also carried Cassy Jones and Sue Tung out of China.

Sue and Cassy flew home together, landing at San Francisco. Rod was waiting at the airport. Over a celebratory drink they watched the local evening news. The headline story was the defection of Zhang Milin. The young Chinese diplomat had finally walked out of the consulate, vowing he wanted to help China to a better future.

His words were yet another epitaph to the fifty-five days that had shocked the world.

24

For the Moment

JUNE 1989 TO THE PRESENT DAY

The world's response to the massacre was vocal but, in practical terms, limited. Public opinion may have made China a pariah, but politically its leadership was barely touched.

A week after the massacre Deng Xiaoping appeared on television, surrounded by his Mao-suited Politburo. The supreme leader looked surprisingly chirpy; there were reports that he had been given a number of blood transfusions. He praised General Yang and other military commanders for crushing the *"rebellion"* and described the People's Liberation Army as China's new *"Great Wall of iron and steel."*

In those days after the massacre, people came to the administration building of the Institute of Politics and Law in Beijing to stand before the battered body of a student. His skull crushed, he lay on a table surrounded by blocks of ice. Students filed slowly past, small swatches of black fabric pinned to their sleeves. No one knew the student's name, only that he had died when the army moved into Beijing.

One day the remains were gone. It was another signal that the past was as dead as that corpse.

Weeks after the massacre it was almost impossible to know what had happened. Flowers bloomed along Changan Avenue and the city's other thoroughfares. Shops were as busy as ever. Women, as the city's mayor announced proudly, *"continue to have babies."*

A closer look at buildings like the Beijing Hotel showed that the bullet holes had been repaired, but imperfectly. On Changan itself, spruced up and constantly bedecked with Party banners, the millions who cycled along found the smooth ride gave way to a bumpy passage as tires rode over the few remaining furrows of tank tracks. The furrows were what Melinda Liu called an *"absolutely small, yet potent, reminder of what had really happened."*

From time to time she and the other journalists who reported those fifty-five momentous days in China have returned not just to monitor the physical cover-up of what had occurred, but also to continue gathering the recollections of those who experienced the nights of horror, those millions who took to the streets demanding change, asking for democracy. Memories are less easy to erase than tank tracks.

In the months after the massacre Amnesty International and other human rights groups estimate that ten thousand had died and perhaps twice that figure had been injured in the massacre in Beijing. The figures for the rest of China were put at twenty thousand killed and around forty thousand injured. In truth no one could really be sure how many bodies had been burned and how many of the wounded had been snatched from their hospital cots and taken away for interrogation.

The six prisons in and around Beijing were allegedly crowded with students. There were persistent reports that up to three thousand were being held for questioning. Many of those were said to have made abject confessions and been sent to that string of prison camps in the inhospitable heart of the country. Again, it was impossible for even the most diligent reporter or intelligence officer to get precise figures or exact details of the files of those being held.

To all intents and purposes, China had become a closed society, suffocating under a blanket of repression.

During a few brief weeks in 1989 areas greater than the British Isles, with populations larger than those of some European countries, had been in uproar. In the Yangtze Delta alone some sixty million people had raised their voices and taken up the nearest weapon in support of the students. Now they had all been brutally silenced under the pall that had fallen across the land.

But uncomfortable questions were being whispered from mouth to mouth in the alleys of Beijing.

Why had the superpowers, the United States, Russia, Great Britain, France, and West Germany, who had known *beforehand* that thousands were going to be butchered in Tiananmen Square, done nothing to warn or help the students?

The suspicion that the West had sold out the students added to the anguish of those who asked the question. Of course, they had no proof either way.

The first anniversary of the massacre found Dr. Jenny Guangzu still in China. The authorities had told her she was not permitted to return to Los Angeles to complete her studies. In the summer of 1989 she was sent to work in a provincial hospital. Her small son, Peter, accompanied her. They are still there at the time of writing. Her father died suddenly three months after Jenny left Beijing.

By then Barr Seitz had departed from China and returned to the United States. In May 1991, shortly before the second anniversary of Tiananmen Square, Barr's father, Raymond, was appointed United States ambassador to the Court of St. James. Part of his brief was to help maintain a common Anglo-Saxon policy toward the Beijing regime — that the recent past was over. Barr meantime had found romance — falling in love with a pretty German girl, Brigitte, who, coincidentally, had the same surname as his. Currently they live in Munich, where Barr is learning the hotel business.

Shortly after Barr left China, Cassy Jones was granted a visa to return as a foreign expert at Beijing University. She remained there for six months, during which she tried and failed to discover what had happened to Daobao. Most likely he was cremated on one of the funeral pyres, which burned for a week in the streets of the city and even longer in the hills to the west of Beijing.

Cassy once more left China. She has no further plans to return.

Sue Tung married Rod a few days after she landed in San Francisco, where Shao-Yen Wang has begun a career as a model. Zhang Milin, one of several Chinese diplomats who defected, has found *"some problems"* in establishing a new life for himself in California.

In China, Captain Instructor Jyan was promoted later in 1989, much to the delight of his mother.

Yang Li, whose brother, Bing, took part in the massacre, was among several student leaders who reached Hong Kong some months after the massacre. He and his girlfriend, Meili were released after two months of detention. They still do not know why they were freed. The young couple remained in Hong Kong until late 1990, when they successfully applied for immigration to Australia.

For a few months they lived together in Sydney until Li took up with another Chinese girl student he had briefly encountered on Tiananmen Square. The couple have no plans to marry. Meili remains single.

Li has written several letters to Bing but has received no reply. Bing Yang remains in the People's Liberation Army.

While those young lives were being rearranged, two former U.S. secretaries of state, Henry Kissinger and General Alexander Haig, and President Bush's brother, Prescott, were engaged in the delicate task of fully re-establishing China as America's most valued trading partner in the next decade.

Haig was currently chairman of Worldwide Associates, Inc., a consultancy with powerful connections in Washington, not the least to Kissinger Associates. He was personally conducting discussions to fund new joint ventures with CITIC, the merchandise banking arm of the Chinese government. The value of the proposed joint ventures was put at $4 million.

Kissinger was also in active discussions with CITIC. In September 1989 the *Wall Street Journal* reported that Kissinger Associates *"could be on the verge of earning hundreds of thousands of dollars from a limited partnership set up to engage in joint dealings with CITIC."*

Prescott Bush, with the full knowledge of his brother, the President, was touring China in September, once more as a consultant to Asset Management, International Financing and Settlement Ltd. He had $60 million to invest in joint-venture agreements. In Shanghai he told U.S. businessmen that *"if we don't get back into this market fully here and now, we'll lose out to the Japanese and Germans."*

Other businessmen were also beating a path to China. From Baghdad had come Saddam Hussein's arms buyers, seeking Silkworm missiles and other weaponry in preparation for the attack on Kuwait that Saddam was already beginning to plan. China obligingly filled their order books with an arsenal of weapons, paid for in the U.S. dollars China so badly needed.

On August 7, 1990, Chinese weapons formed the spearhead of the attack on Kuwait.

In the months that followed, as America prepared to go to war with Iraq, the importance of China in the administration's strategic thinking became increasingly clear.

China was a permanent member of the United Nations Security Council. Its veto would throttle President Bush's plan to go to war with the full support of the U.N.. China also knew exactly where Iraq had positioned the arms it had supplied. That information was crucial to the Pentagon as it planned Operation Desert Storm. China, because of its close ties with Iraq's neighbors, could provide a critically important insight into Arab thinking that would not be available to U.S. diplomats.

China, then, had to be accommodated. In Washington, as the clock ticked inexorably closer to war, it became an article of faith that it was *"time to put Tiananmen behind us."*

From December 1990 onward it became a prime objective for Secretary of State Baker to explore with the Chinese what they wanted in return for their support. Baker was told in a New York meeting with Zhang Tuobin, China's minister of foreign economic relations and trade, that China wanted an end to all trade restrictions imposed after the Tiananmen Square massacre, as well as Washington's help to enter the world trade organization, GATT, and secure for China a full resumption of World Bank lending, suspended since the slaughter.

Baker agreed.

China then provided the United States with data on its military deals with Iraq that NSA satellite surveillance and CIA ground intelligence had not been able to discover.

By early January 1991 the Pentagon had been given the exact location of every Silkworm missile site in Iraq and details of other weapons provided by China. Included in this intelligence data were details of the amount of lithium 6 deuteride — a compound used in the manufacture of the hydrogen bomb — which the Chinese had supplied from its nuclear facility in the deserts of Inner Mongolia.

The United States now possessed all the information it needed to launch a spectacularly successful air war against Saddam's key targets.

A week before the Persian Gulf War started, Beijing informed Washington there was one other matter over which it wanted *"understanding."* Before the Chinese New Year started on February 15, the Beijing regime intended to try the student leaders it still held. The old men of Zhongnanhai made it clear they neither wanted, nor expected, any official U.S. protest over what would be a series of short trials. The public would be barred from attending. The only crime the accused had committed was to have demonstrated peacefully for democracy.

Despite the passionate plea of the distinguished Chinese writer Liu Binyan, then scholar-in-residence at the Woodrow Wilson International Center for

Scholars, for the Bush administration *"to stop stroking Beijing's butchers,"* neither the President nor his aides condemned what was once more unfolding in Beijing. In a passing reference, the State Department confirmed that *"at least 1,000 have been sentenced since the troops moved in on Tiananmen."* Spokeswoman Margaret Tutweiler, no doubt wishing to be helpful, added that the sentences appeared determined by the degree of remorse shown by the accused.

On an icy cold morning in late January 1991, Wang Dan stood before the People's Intermediate Court in midtown Beijing. He wore the sweatshirt and black baggy pants that had been his distinguishing uniform on Tiananmen Square twenty months before. He had lost weight, and his glasses kept slipping down his nose as he blinked owlishly around the courtroom. Paneled in light-colored wood, it was a stark, functional room. Wang Dan stood before his judges, three middle-aged men dressed in Mao jackets.

When he spoke his voice was little more than a whisper. He offered no defense to the charge that he had attempted to overthrow the Chinese government.

He stood, head bowed, looking shrunken and far older than his twenty-two years. The senior judge explained that one of the court's functions was to *"redeem criminals"* who oppose the state by re-educating them, by sending them to remote border areas, or prison, where they would be taught that the way back into Chinese society is through a *"full understanding"* of Marxism, together with a *"proper understanding"* that the sentence about to be passed was only for Wang Dan's own good.

He was sentenced to an undisclosed term in a maximum security prison in central China. As he turned to leave the court, Wang Dan addressed the judges.

"The series of concrete criminal acts listed in the indictment were objective facts. I keenly regret and feel sorry for the consequences arising from the turmoil and rebellion, and I am willing to assume full responsibility for my actions. I will conscientiously draw a lesson from the past. I will never again create chaos under Heaven."

Then he was led away.

Throughout the day, students came and went, each reciting an act of contrition that seemed well rehearsed. Liu Gang received four years in a labor camp. Other sentences varied from three to thirteen years. By late afternoon, seventeen students had been sent to prison.

Two months later, on March 20, 1991, a remarkable poem appeared in the *People's Daily*:

> *East Wind urges plum to flourish its petals, soft as DOWN;*
> *The hawk unfurls its wings, soars far away, WITH the wind.*
> *The moon shines, sheds tears on the LI-ward sea,*
> *And a sojourner in the PENG-hu islands thinks of home.*
> *I'll strive to the END and realize our hopes for the motherland.*
> *The PEOPLE'S gift to me is worth more than millions.*
> *RAGE, impetuous rage, invigorates the good earth,*
> *As we wait for spring to spread all over the land.*

The seemingly innocuous words had been penned by a Chinese student in the United States. The words caused a furor after it was studied by Party scholars in Beijing. For the poem was what is known as *"a diagonal acrostic,"* and its literal meaning was *"Li Peng step down; mollify the people's anger."*

Professor Eugene Eoyang, who teaches comparative literature and East Asian languages and cultures at Indiana University, explained in the *New York Times* the challenge in translating the poem.

"First it must be rendered in a way that demonstrates why the People's Daily *was eager to publish it. The lines must reflect the patriotic devotion of a student sojourner at spring (something like Robert Browning's 'Oh to be in England, Now that April's there'). The second challenge is to hide the protest, yet let it be visible. In the transliteration of Li Peng's name, I resorted to a few devices. His family name, Li, means 'plum'; his given name, Peng, signifies a mythical bird, like a roc, that flies huge distances. But neither 'plum' nor 'roc' conjure up a person's name. To retain Li, I resorted to a phonetic pun in English, and, as there is no phonetic equivalent to 'Peng,' I introduced a reference to 'Peng-hu,' the Pescadores Islands between Taiwan and the mainland, on which a homesick sojourner might be imagined to be brooding. Inevitably, there are some distortions and deletions, but perhaps the spirit of the poem has not been lost altogether."*

A month after the poem appeared, reports reached the United States that the editor responsible for publishing it had been arrested.

The reports came at the same time as Li Peng gave what Nicholas D. Kristof of the *New York Times* described as *"a vigorous defense"* of the Tiananmen Square massacre. China's prime minister concluded his press conference by saying that his government was ready to use similar methods to crush further protests. As he left the conference, called to mark the end of the 1991 session of the National People's Congress, China's rubber-stamp parliament, Li Peng continued to smile and attempt, in Kristof's view, *"to foster a more friendly and down-to-earth image."* The prime minister was still smiling when a reporter asked him about the poem.

"Not worth mentioning," said the prime minister, adding that Deng Xiaoping, now eighty-six, was *"in good health."* But even if the country's senior leader was to die, nothing would change, Li Peng assured the reporters. *"The Party will remain totally in control."*

A few days later the *People's Daily* announced that 72,000 Party members had been expelled, and a further 256,000 *"punished."* They were deemed to be *"unreliable and corrupt."* It was the biggest purge in recent years of the 49 million member Party.

A week after the Gulf War ended, Qian Qichen, China's foreign minister, announced that all those involved in the *"counterrevolutionary rebellion in 1989 have been dealt with."* In one of those chillingly memorable phrases that will ensure Qian's footnote in history, he promised: *"Those who should be freed have been freed, and those who should have been shot have been shot."*

The words were a reminder of the ancient Chinese saying, *"By killing one we educate one hundred."*

Early in April 1991 Britain's Foreign Secretary, Douglas Hurd, became the first world-ranking Western diplomat to visit China since the Tiananmen Square massacre. As he was escorted past the square by Qian, the foreign minister reminded Hurd *"that the standards of one country or group of countries must not be imposed on other countries."* Hurd nodded politely.

Shortly after, ex-President Jimmy Carter visited Beijing. He told Deng Xiaoping that China should now have most-favored-nation trade status with the United States and it was high time to *"put the Tiananmen Square tragedy behind us."*

A few days later President Bush confirmed he wanted to give China those special trading privileges. Most-favored-nation status fixes tariffs on imports at the lowest prevailing rates, and is not usually granted to communist countries. But the President insisted he did not wish to *"isolate Beijing"* and indicated he was trying in part to reward China for not blocking actions at the United Nations during the Persian Gulf crisis.

"I look at the big picture," Bush said. *"I look at the support we got from China back in Desert Storm, the importance of China as a country. And I don't want to see us isolate them ... I got back to the days when I was in China as the equivalent of an ambassador, and though there are major problems in China, things we don't like about their system, things are an awful lot better than they were back in 1975,"* the President said.

Meantime, the Bush administration continued to secretly draw even closer to the Beijing regime. Undaunted by the failure of a highly secret mission in December 1989 to Beijing by National Security Adviser Brent Scowcroft and Deputy Secretary of State Lawrence S. Eagleburger, both old Kissinger Associate hands, Bush dispatched another envoy to China, Robert M. Kinsmitt, the Under-Secretary of State for political affairs. The ostensible purpose of the visit was to hold *"candid discussions on human rights, trade, and weapons sales."*

Like the Scowcroft-Eagleburger venture, the Kinsmitt mission was also to explore with Beijing the Bush administration's growing fears that Japan was becoming an intolerable threat to U.S. economic interests.

In one of his last actions before leaving office in May 1991, CIA director Webster had approved plans to recruit moles in the boardrooms of Japanese corporations, such as Sony, Honda, and Mitsubishi. Webster had done so on the direct orders of Bush, who has come increasingly to fear that the United States could be embroiled within the next twenty years in an increasingly bitter economic war with Japan, one which could even eventually flare into fighting.

Bush's fears had been synthesized by a most secret CIA-sponsored report, describing the Japanese as *"creatures who are amoral, manipulative and live by a controlling culture that is intent on world economic dominance."* The same report also described Japan as *"a racist, non-democratic country whose population believes might is right and who feel superior to other people."*

Two recent books had helped to fuel Bush's fears of the Japanese. The first, *The Coming War with Japan* by George Friedman and Meredith Lebard, respected American economists, argued that economic competition for markets between the world's two largest economies will almost certainly end in war as Japan tries *"to force the U.S. out of the Western Pacific."* The authors claim that the United States will see this move as Japanese aggression and, as in the 1930s, both sides will engage in a cold war which will eventually end in physical fighting. Some White House aides sensed the President already felt the cold war was coming to some sort of climax.

The second book, by Japanese businessman Shintaro Ishihari, titled *Japan Cannot Say No,* claims that Japan was poised to sabotage American military might by withholding the delivery of crucial microchips.

Bush had ordered his aides to study both books and use them as a reference in the administration's dealings with China. Webster had told his own analysts that nowadays the President increasingly saw China as America's ally in the Pacific against Japan, with its *"win-at-any-cost society,"* where *"the poor are down-trodden and there is a systematic discrimination against foreigners."*

The President insisted that China must not only have most-favored-nation status, but in every way possible be drawn ever closer to his administration to help defeat what Bush saw as Tokyo's aspiration to dominate the world. In that overview there could be no room for justice for a handful of students.

On Wednesday, April 24, 1991, a group of university students in Beijing circulated an eleven-page document describing continued student opposition to the regime. They appealed for *"energetic"* help from, in particular, the United States to bring democracy once more to China.

The document described failed *"attempts to brainwash us. During these sessions we pretend we cannot remember anything that happened on Tiananmen Square."*

At the end of the document its authors issued a blunt warning. *"The students of China are no longer scared by blood or by punishment. The blood that was spilled in 1989 has taken students from fanaticism to calmness and awareness. We now recognize how formidable is the process of pursuing human rights and democracy. But we will pursue them and we will succeed, if not today, then certainly soon."*

The old men who still run China must surely know that the farther they are from the events of 1989, the closer they come to the next uprising. Next time they may not be able to crush it.

DECEMBER 2000
WASHINGTON D.C.

On that December morning in 2000, on his way to meet the Bush transition team, CIA Director General George Tenet sat in his preferred position immediately behind the limousine driver. Tenet wore the formal business suit that went with the job: Pressed, he had come up with his own job description as *"essentially speaking truth to power. I will always do so whether it fits with Administration policy or not."*

He planned to re-state those words to the transition team. Dick Cheney, Vice-President-elect, would chair the meeting. The incoming President, George W. Bush, had already made it clear he preferred to spend as much time as possible back on the family ranch in Texas until Inauguration Day. Tenet regarded Cheney, despite his recent health problems, as a safe pair of hands. Colin Powell, the future Secretary of State, would be there. He was as close to the Bush family as anyone could be.

In a CIA psycho profile marked "DCI-Eyes Only," Powell had been described as "*a reluctant interventionist*" and "*the apostle of restraint.*" The paper had contained, among much else, a full account of a stormy confrontation during a crisis meeting in the windowless White House Situation Room. It had been in 1993 and the siege of Sarajevo was at its height. Colin Powell had argued vehemently against U.S. military intervention.

"*What's the political objective? What's the exit strategy?*" Powell had repeatedly demanded.

Finally losing her patience and coming close to allowing her temper to show, Madeleine Albright, then America's ambassador to the United Nations, had shouted across the table at Powell:

"*What's the point of your having this superb military machine you're always talking about if you won't use it?*"

Powell had refused to back down: to do so would have meant relinquishing the core of his philosophy. It was synthesized in a plaque Tenet had once seen on Powell's desk. It was a framed quote from the Greek historian Thucydides. "*Of all manifestations of power, restraint impresses men most.*"

When Powell had effectively masterminded the Persian Gulf War in 1991, that doctrine had been his driving force behind the economic sanctions and finally the overwhelming fire-power which had forced Saddam Hussein to his knees. But that was nine years ago. Was Powell going to be the same man now?

In a private meeting with Tenet, Powell had acknowledged the enormous changes that had occurred since he had worked in the last Bush Administration. How much influence would Bush Sr. have now, especially on foreign policy? His son, according to another CIA briefing paper, was "*at best inexperienced in global matters.*" Would President-elect George Walker Bush rely too much on his father's style of doing things? In Tenet's view on this winter's morning, the jury was still out.

But a balance may have been struck by the appointment of Condoleezza Rice as National Security Adviser to the new President. At 46 she not only retained the stunning good looks that could have made her a beauty queen, but she had brains no Miss America would ever equal. A former provost of Stanford University, Condoleezza was not only a former aide to President George W. Bush's father, but was also the first black woman to hold the post of National Security Adviser. But was she strong enough to face down the old men in Beijing?

From her office on Washington's G Street, she would certainly cast a cool eye over each one of the 8,000 appointments the new Administration would make, starting with the twelve Cabinet secretaries.

Like all good intelligence chiefs, Tenet was prepared to answer questions he had discovered were of special interest to Rice. One was India. Tenet suspected that Rice had at least an inkling of the planned revamp in India's intelligence services that could turn out to be the most radical since the country achieved independence 54 years ago. While these changes had directly come about following the infiltration of Pakistani troops and Islamic mercenaries into the disputed state of Kashmir, the wider, long-term implications would impinge upon the United States' position in the Far East.

The incoming Bush Administration might find itself facing a delicate question: how far should the CIA support India's two intelligence agencies — the IB, responsible for internal security, and RAW, whose task was gathering intelligence outside India. This included "deep penetration" operations.

This question had to be weighed against the present cooperation where India still allowed the CIA to operate on the Indo-China border, something the Agency had been doing since 1962. But in the revamp, RAW might want something more in return from the United States: access to sensitive information that would include an overall upgrading of technical, imaging, signals and electronic counter-intelligence. Yet, in Tenet's view, properly handled, RAW's "deep penetration operations" could be turned against the real threat: China.

Tenet was certain that Rice would appreciate the significance of what he would, at an early stage of the briefing, merely plant.

He would also touch upon how China would almost certainly exploit the election due in June 2001 in Iran. Already China had nodded approvingly in the direction of Iran's anti-reformists and their campaign of intimidation against the country's leading intellectuals and writers; the closure of over thirty newspapers as "*bases of the enemy, the Great Satan, America*"; attacks on Iran's judiciary, accusing them of *moharabeh* — "*warring against the system.*"

Tenet would explain how the CIA had tried to discreetly encourage the reformists, pointing to the fact that 65% of Iran's population is under the age of thirty and would like to see the country reconnecting with the global system. But the risks were that the conservative elements would continue their vicious repression and this could lead to confrontation that might result in bloody conflict in Iran. Again, Tenet would sow the seeds that both China and Iraq would exploit such a situation; the former to increase its support for the anti-reformists, the latter to actually restart the still-simmering conflict between Iran and Iraq. Rice would readily understand the effect this could have on not only the balance of power in the region, but how it might spread beyond.

On this cold December morning in 2000, it was too soon yet for even the astute Tenet to predict what would happen in the aftermath of the Iran elections.

But he would make sure Rice would grasp that much of what he would be revealing would be for her attention. He would choose his words with care, in marked contrast to his predecessor who had often sounded as if his speech had gone through an ideological prism. Tenet's style was to speak softly but with full mastery of the facts. He knew that, for one, Al Gonzales, the new chief White House lawyer, would appreciate such an approach.

Donald Rumsfeld would also be there. It was an open secret that the 63-year old wanted the post of Secretary of Defense, one he had held all those years ago under President Ford. Rumsfeld was a hard-liner whose smile rarely reached behind his spectacles. He was a strong advocate for the "Star Wars" missile project and shared Powell's opposition to America's involvement in the Balkans and what Rumsfeld had called "*all those half-hearted wars for half-baked ideas that Africa likes.*"

Another certainty to be at the meeting was John Ashcroft, tipped to be the 58-year-old next Attorney General. He would run the Justice Department with an iron fist if he got the job. But Tenet knew that already Washington influential Democrat and black groups had begun a campaign to block Ashcroft's appointment, dubbing him a right-wing extremist, and citing his opposition in 1988 to a black judge in Missouri being elevated to the federal bench.

Gale Norton, proposed to be the new Secretary of the Interior, would win few friends out at Langley with her determination to limit government control over environmental regulations and, as she once had put it, "*less Washington interference. Period.*"

There would be a number of people at the meeting Tenet had never met: Don Evans, tipped to be Commerce Secretary. Carl Roe who had masterminded the new president's narrow election victory and Karen Hughes, the Bush campaign communications director. All were tipped for office in the White House. Their presence at the transition briefing would be a sure sign that their futures were assured.

In advance of this meeting Tenet had sent Colin Powell a note of areas he intended to focus upon. He had prefaced them with words that still stood as his leitmotif for his time in office.

"*When I became DCI, I made it clear to President Clinton that I had certain priorities. I wanted to recruit more analysts and case officers. I wanted them to focus on what was going to be important in intelligence gathering in the 21st century. That would include countering money-laundering, countering narcotics and countering terrorism. I wanted the Agency to go back to basic espionage. I wanted our field agents to work in alleys which have no names, I didn't want to hear about our failure. But I also did not want to read in the newspapers about our successes.*"

Tenet's policy had remained in force to this December day in 2000. His colors nailed to the Langley mast, he had led from the front. He had increased ground surveillance in Iran and Iraq and within the Islamic republics of the former Soviet Union. He had strengthened the CIA Asia Desk to focus on money-laundering through Hong Kong and other Pacific Rim nations. Conversely he had reduced the CIA's presence in London, Paris and Berlin. He believed that domestic intelligence services in those cities would continue to liaise closely with their counterparts in Langley. He had reminded his heads of department that a good deal of the work the CIA was doing in those countries was little more than confirming what was openly coming across their desks from MI5 and MI6 and the French and German intelligence services.

One key to his style was the way he had insisted that the President's Daily Brief — his "Eyes Only" intelligence summary and brought by CIA courier to the White House at dawn every day — should be more sharply written and include even excerpts from classified raw intelligence and transcripts of intercepted messages. Sometimes he would add a note in his own neat hand, knowing the touch had pleased President Clinton. Would Bush want the same?

In his note to Powell, Tenet had written: "*It is a mistaken notion that the break-up of the Soviet bloc has rendered intelligence collection less necessary. Meeting today's priorities will require re-directed and more targeted deployment of intelligence officers, especially outside west European democracies where intelligence reporting and State Department reporting are the most likely to overlap.*

"*In my judgment, Europe will welcome the prospect of our spies being diverted elsewhere: relations with Washington have been strained by reports of American intelligence using our communications network, Echelon, to eavesdrop on European businesses.*"

Powell had personally thanked Tenet for the note.

In Tenet's briefcase was a 70-page document entitled "Global Trends up to 2015." An advance copy had been sent to each member of the transition team. Tenet suspected that many of them would think the contents resembled the screenplay for a new James Bond film; a series of scenarios predicted that the CIA would have to deal with large and powerful criminal groups "*who will corrupt leaders of unstable, economically fragile or failing states, insinuate themselves into troubled banks and businesses and cooperate with insurgent political movements to control substantial geographic areas. Their income will come from narcotics trafficking in women and children smuggling toxic materials, hazardous wastes, illicit arms, military technologies and other contraband; financial fraud and racketeering. The first five years of the new century in particular will be filled with perils that will far outweigh peace.*"

The document had been compiled by over fifty CIA analysts plus those attached to the Institute for International Studies in London. Its highly classified contents predicted that "*governments will have less and less control over flows of information, technology, diseases, migrants, arms and financial transactions, both licit or illicit.*"

As Russia economically declined and India and China grew, "*terrorist tactics will become increasingly more sophisticated and designed to achieve mass casualties.*

"*China, as it becomes increasingly the new superpower of the Third Millennium, is likely to provide the biological and chemical weapons and 'suitcase' nuclear devices to wage terrorist war against the United States. Rogue states such as Iraq and Iran will have developed long-range missiles by the year 2005. Ten years later those weapons will be capable of hitting the United States, carrying nuclear, chemical and biological warheads.*"

The document predicted that as the world population grew by another billion, coming close to eight billion, the mega-cities in the developing world would become a potent breeding ground for terrorism. In Europe and Japan an aging population and virtually static birthrate would mean that allowing more immigration would be the only way of meeting the chronic shortage of workers. Many of those workers would be trained in terrorist activities.

Africa would face such a blight of AIDS, famine and continuing economic and political turmoil that populations in many of its countries would have fallen, often by 70%, by the year 2015.

China's economic growth would overtake that of Europe by the year 2010 while Russia's would have contracted to barely a fifth of that of the United States. China would exploit a trade war, likely to start before the end of the first decade of the Third Millennium and encourage an alliance between terrorist groups to attack the West.

"Israel may find itself driven to make use of a limited nuclear war to survive unless the Second Intifada shows signs of stopping. There is no evidence to indicate it will."

Most alarming of all, the report predicted a period of global economic stagnation as a result, *"possibly by the year 2015; of America abdicating its role as the world's policeman. This will come at a time of rising tension in the Far East; on present indications, when China orders Japan to dismantle its nuclear program leaving the United States with no alternative but to engage itself in Asia under conditions that could see a major war breaking out before the year 2015. The protagonists would most likely be China and America."*

Now, as the Lincoln made its smooth way over the final of the nine miles into Washington, George Tenet continued to review what he would tell the transition team. Much of the input had come from Jack Downing, the head of the Directorate of Operations, the clandestine side of the CIA. A former station chief in Moscow and Beijing, Tenet had persuaded Downing out of a well-earned retirement. He had told the old spy *"Jack, I need a hard-nose to run some very hard-nosed operations."* Downing had certainly proven his ability to do that: he had managed to get agents into Teheran and Kabul and one deep inside the Syrian regime.

Going to the transition meeting, Tenet knew his own years as deputy-director of the CIA were an asset: he had been the silent assistant who sat behind his chief at a meeting ready to whisper a fact or opinion when it was needed. His tact had become legendary from the day he assumed office and invited foreign intelligence chiefs to lunch in his private dining room. Before, he had asked them all to join Downing for a cocktail, except Amiram Levine, the deputy-director of Mossad. When they were alone, Tenet had said to Levine, *"Excuse me, general, but your fly zipper is undone. I sense there is enough competition among your colleagues for you not to wish to add to it, purely speaking in size of course."*

Levine had burst out laughing and zipped up. The story had helped to create the legend that Tenet was a gentleman spy. But that image died a few months later. In less than fifty words, Tenet had destroyed the long career of his predecessor, John Deutch. On that day, Tenet had summoned to his office and announced to the stunned chiefs of the U.S. intelligence community that he had suspended *"for an indefinite period"* the security clearance of Deutch, the man who had groomed him for office. A CIA internal enquiry had found Deutch *"guilty of improperly storing national security secrets in a desktop computer at his home."*

The classified information consisted of thirty-one documents relating to Iraq and the 1996 terrorist bombing in Saudi Arabia that had killed 19 American servicemen.

Tenet had known of the offense Deutch had committed soon after becoming director. He had challenged Deutch. Deutch had freely admitted his guilt. Later he had told friends he had expected no more than a reprimand. Instead, George Tenet had ensured Deutch would never again work in any position of high trust in Washington — perhaps in any United States company which normally would value having a former intelligence chief on its payroll.

When it became known what Tenet had done, his action was viewed by many intelligence professionals as a deliberate attempt to shake off Tenet's image as "the gentleman spy." He had been dubbed that by a senior Mossad officer and the image had dogged him in his years as deputy director of the CIA. During that time, Tenet had worked hard to remain out of the public gaze. Where others in Washington boasted of being part of the grinding pace of national destiny, Tenet found strength in concealment. He took pride in his obscurity. If he knew something, he did not let on that he did. And nearly everyone assumed he knew even more.

To insiders he was the quintessential CIA chief, the man inured in its friend-less discipline. He had survived the corrosive rumors, the tales of disgrace and ruined careers. But nothing had touched him personally. Within the Agency he had a reputation as a methodical and careful manager. In everything he did there was a steady conformity with expectations.

The transition team would learn that — and much more. There was, for a start, the intriguing story of how Saddam Hussein had become a billionaire.

The foundation for Saddam Hussein's fortune was laid in a secret deal Iraq made with the late Shah of Iran. The story of how Saddam came to join the world's billionaires has all the hallmarks of his ruthless style.

In 1978 the Shah knew his rule was about to end, and that the gilded Pea-cock Throne from which he had ruled with such brutality was about to go into meltdown. Entire cities in Iran had become closed citadels controlled by the clergy of the Ayatollah Khomeini.

Beyond the expanding borders of Islamic fundamentalism, teams of the Ayatollah's accountants, trained by Wall Street and the Swiss banking systems, were combing the world to try and confiscate the Shah's huge fortune. Over the years he had built up portfolios in every financial market. His investments on Wall Street alone were estimated at over 200 million U.S. dollars.

Anticipating Khomeini's determination to confiscate the money in the name of the Islamic revolution, the Shah had made an astonishing move to try and protect his wealth. For months in 1978 his most trusted aides had held secret meetings in Paris and Geneva with representatives of Iran's sworn enemy — Iraq. The Shah had reasoned that even the most diligent of the Ayatollah's accountants would be unable to gain access to Iraq's banks.

Stripped to its essential the deal the Shah's men were proposing was breath-takingly simple. The Shah would transfer a substantial portion of his personal fortune that had not already been frozen by the Ayatollah's accountants into accounts to be managed by the Shah's surrogates. They would place the funds in Iraqi banks.

The bankers in Baghdad would receive a "handling fee" of 1.5 percent for arranging this unique facility.

Until he came to power in July 1979, Saddam had been relatively impoverished. Raised in almost abject poverty, he had never had sufficient money to finance his grandiose schemes. The war with Iran was biting ever deeper into the Iraqi economy. Loans from the United States, Britain and Europe were all tightly controlled. There was little opportunity for him to get his hands on ready cash.

The deal with the Shah changed all that. In a matter of days after the arrangements had been agreed, some one billion U.S. dollars were withdrawn from U.S. banks and transferred into accounts held by Iraq in Swiss banks.

From there the money was transferred to the numbered accounts Saddam Hussein held in Geneva, Paris, the Cayman Islands and the City of London.

The Shah was unaware of what had happened until he fled to the West in 1979. There he learned where his money had gone.

His appeals to Washington to intervene fell on deaf ears. The United States realised they had made a bad move in not backing the Ayatollah. The only card they could play was to support Saddam. There was no way Washington was going to ask him to pay back the Shah. The Shah was yesterday's man.

With his first billion safely stashed away, Saddam then turned to another unlikely source to advise him on how to enhance his easy-won fortune.

Financier Roland Rowland was invited to Baghdad by an Egyptian lawyer, Soubi Roushdi, a legal adviser to one of the Iraqi banks involved in ripping off the Shah. For Saddam it was a perfect choice. Until his death, Rowland had a deserved reputation as a financial terrorist, a manipulative conspirator. In the City of London he had become a detested figure. But in personality and ruthlessness, he matched Saddam.

Rowland, known as "Tiny" to his friends, had been born in India, the son of a German businessman and an Englishwoman. In his youth he had become a supporter of Hitler, a liking he shared with Saddam. The other attraction they shared was anti-Semitism.

Impressively rich and powerful, Rowland dazzled Saddam with his tales of financial acumen. Soon Saddam moved in exalted circles. From London came figures like Edward du Cann, then a senior member of Britain's Conservative Party, and Duncan Sandys, who had been Winston Churchill's son-in-law.

From them and others, Saddam learned the lessons of making his money work. His portfolios began to grow. Ten years after he had acquired the Shah's money, Saddam Hussein had doubled his fortune. He arranged for the world's leading financial journals to be flown in from New York and London on the day of publication. Later, when the newspapers established Web sites, Saddam would pore over them.

The Gulf War proved to be a mere blip on his race to join the world's leading billionaires.

Mossad monitored a meeting between Saddam and the late King Hussein of Jordan in which the Iraqi leader threatened to bomb Amman — unless the king made "a contribution to the poor people of Iraq." The king refused.

After the Gulf War, Saddam turned the business of building his fortune over to his son, Uday.

One way Saddam and his son have been able to manipulate money is through the Internet. There is no way to check on their activities on the Internet. By the time any investigation can get close, Saddam and his people have moved on. Patrolling the Internet financial world is something that has yet to be effected. You can hide anybody and anything behind a Web site.

One thing for sure is that Saddam will have invested part of his billionaire's fortune in the most advanced computer system to roam the Internet.

Tenet would open his briefing with an overview of how the end of the Cold War had thrown the world's intelligence services into turmoil. The old days of superpower confrontations — the United States and the Soviet Union — had long gone. Into its place had come what George Herbert Bush, the President-elect's father, had called *"the new order."* And with it had come a new search for work for the spies of the world. Not just in Langley but in Moscow, London, Berlin and, of course, Beijing. At stake was a global industry that, by the end of 2001 would cost out at over $60 billion and employ well over a million people.

Then, nation by nation, beginning with Israel, he would deliver an assessment of each service.

Fifty years old, only a little younger than the CIA, Israel's Mossad was no longer seen as a derring-do agency, its deeds burnished bright in the collective memory of Israelis everywhere. Nor, in those memorable few years in which Israel had built a new world for itself, was Mossad any longer a guarantor that it would survive.

Next he would quickly deal with the CIA's relationship with Britain's intelligence services: *"One word will sum that up,"* he had jotted, *"workable."* The truth was a little more shaded. The days of the Thatcher-Reagan alliance had gone. Britain's prime minister, Tony Blair was not so ready to rubber-stamp all that the Washington intelligence community required. This had led to friction and even tensions.

Tenet planned to devote considerable time to the activities of the various Russian intelligence services. He would begin with the monolithic Federal Counter Intelligence Service, the FCS. With a staff, in 1999, of 142,000, it was really the former KGB updated. It worked closely with the SVR, which ran a worldwide multi-layered intelligence-gathering operation. Its various specialist units gathered industrial and commercial intelligence. Its covert operations included assassinations, some of which had been carried out within the United States and Canada. He would devote time to the GRU. Operated directly by the Kremlin, it provided worldwide military intelligence. It was staffed with the best operatives and equipped with extensive satellite surveillance equipment.

France and Japan would each be given their space. But apart from gathering commercial and economic data, neither was in the major league of global intelligence gathering.

Tenet would then develop themes he had touched upon earlier: Iran and China, this time adding a new element: Russia.

He would explain how Russia was continuing to re-establish growing control over its neighboring former Soviet states. It had also begun to deepen its relationships with Iran and China; those alliances provided Moscow with a counterweight to what it saw as NATO's expansion on its own borders.

In Tenet's briefcase was a report from the CIA station chief in Moscow which detailed how Russia was now Iran's main source of sophisticated arms and civilian nuclear technology. The report estimated that by the year 2005 Russia would have supplied Iran with "*up to $7 billion of military hardware, including S-300 air defense missiles, MI-17 combat helicopters and SU-25 fighter aircraft.*"

The station chief had sent a photocopy of a document bearing the signature of Viktor Komardin, head of Rosonoron Export — Russia's arms export corporation, confirming the deal. The agreement also included tanks, diesel submarines and materials for the construction of Iran's first nuclear power plant at Bushehr on the Persian Gulf. The actual work was to be done by Atommash, Russia's largest manufacturer of nuclear power plant equipment. In all, stated the CIA report, Russia was planning to build three more reactors at Bushehr, making Iran second only to Israel in nuclear power in the region. Russia was also updating Iran's oil and gas resources using the latest technology to do so.

A similar pattern was developing in Moscow's relations with China. Beijing had just bought four Russian A-50 early-warning aircraft from Russia. By 2001, China would have some twenty multi-role Russian 20SU/30MKI warplanes capable of matching any combat aircraft in the West.

Tenet would reveal his agents in Beijing and Moscow had confirmed a new Russian-China interstate treaty was under discussion. It had been twenty years since the last treaty had expired. The new one, according to the CIA, would focus on providing strategic weapons. "*This will include lasers and interceptor missiles and linking China's space program with the Russian Global Navigation System with its three satellites. Russia would also provide an unspecified number of 949- and 971-class nuclear submarines, armed with batteries of long-range cruise missiles. Each was capable of devastating a major U.S. city from mid-Atlantic or mid-Pacific.*"

Russian engineers were working alongside China's to build a massive nuclear power plant near the South China Sea port of Lianyangang. It would contain a 60MW fast reactor, one of the most advanced in the world.

The CIA document concluded on a somber note: "*Russia will continue to secure its southern and eastern borders at all possible levels. This will allow it more freedom to deal with any potential threat from the West, especially the United States, and to enjoin China, should such a threat come, in launching a pre-emptive strike. As well as mainland Russia and China, that strike would be reinforced by the increasing Russian entrenchment in Iran.*"

Tenet knew that his revelations would find a ready response from his transition team audience. They would confirm that Bush was right to push ahead to build a shield against missile attacks. It had originally been hoped to have it in place by 2004. But Tenet realized his revelations would put the shield on the fast track. The first part of the system could be in place a full year earlier. Tenet would explain why the new Administration could be certain that its every move would be monitored by China's intelligence services.

China had five separate intelligence services. Each was powerful, well-funded and staffed, and shared a common brief: to wage an all-out intelligence war against the United States. It did through its ILD, the harmless-sounding International Liaison Department whose prime target was to steal secrets from the United States. In close support came MID, the Military Intelligence Department that reported to the general staff of the People's Liberation Army. Its spies were attached to every embassy and consulate in the United States.

Working in close liaison with both these organizations came STD. Based in the Ministry of Defense in Beijing, the Science and Technology Department had two prime functions: to collate all signals traffic from China's satellites and from those picked up by its Navy monitoring overseas facilities, and to target American firms working at the cutting edge of military and civilian technology.

Finally there was NCNA. Nominally a news agency reporting on Chinese affairs, in reality NCNA was a cover for CSIS operatives.

Untold billions of dollars had been spent by the old men who ruled from Beijing to maintain these agencies in the nine years that had passed since those students had been so murderously crushed on Tiananmen Square.

Even more billions had been spent by China's rulers to develop plans which every day brought China closer to its dream of being the new superpower of the Third Millennium, one strong enough to confront the United States, its partners in the Western world, indeed the whole globe.

JANUARY 1, 2001
BEIJING — WASHINGTON D.C.

By the year 2001, technology had become like drug addiction in China. People couldn't get enough of it. It manifested itself in more being spent on leisure than on food. Technology had created the illusion it offered a cure for every ill; that computers in every classroom would improve education; that genetically engineered crops would eradicate hunger and genetically engineered humans would eliminate diseases.

In an attempt to meet the insatiable demands of China's new consumer society, technology churned out more and more gadgets, faster and faster. Only the most incorrigible Luddite or romantic could deny that technology has brought untold benefits to China, as elsewhere. But it is steadily creating a monster roaring out of control and further undermining the understanding of what it was to be a human being in China.

Nowhere was this more evident than in the world of surveillance.

Already in Beijing and other Chinese cities, the techniques were coming to be well established: ultrasonic detectors sensitive to noise or motion; electric eyes which activated cameras and silent alarms in *"high security areas"*; motion detectors; bugging devices; de-bugging devices. Long before the year 2010 no Chinese street would be without its CCTV; employees' phones would be routinely monitored and the monitoring accepted because of cleverly-organized campaigns to make people accept this imposition as a condition of employment.

Voice analyzers would monitor the tension in a job-seeker's voice. A company would ask a job applicant to complete the questionnaire and ask him to read the answers over the phone. The responses would be recorded and fed through the analyzer. The machine would judge the level of stress and decide if the prospective employee was suitable to be employed. The questions would probe every area of a person's private life.

Reports had begun to reach the West from China, sent by diplomats and foreign intelligence agents based in the country. They all basically told the same story. Chinese neurosurgeons working at a research center on the outskirts of Beijing were exploring the feasibility of attaching clip-on microchips to the human brain. Supposedly the chips would serve different and beneficial purposes: one to stimulate a fading memory, another to enhance processing skills, another to improve musical abilities, yet another to improve a person's sporting prowess. Eventually it was predicted that people fitted with the chips would, for instance, not need to watch a film; with the relevant memory chip they would instantly "have seen" the movie.

The reports were received with understandable astonishment. Human brains are complex biological organisms; simulations or attempted copies of the action of the brain are usually done with electronic circuitry. The problem was that no matter how good the simulations, the created brain will behave differently from its human version. To place clip-on microchips to human brains was a major step forward. But the Chinese seemed to be advanced in overcoming the many hurdles.

The "clip-ons" could also be fitted with a microchip that could, one day, read a person's mind and report what it was thinking to a computer.

To those in the CIA who still dimly remembered the infamous MK-ULTRA "mind control" experiments the agency funded in the Fifties, the reports were a reminder of what might have been if Congress had not intervened to stop the research. Just like the Chinese, the CIA had used human guinea pigs — patients at the Allan Memorial Hospital in Montreal — for its purposes. None of the Canadian patients had given permission to be subjected to a battery of inhuman experiments. Almost certainly the patients in China would not have given their consent to having themselves experimented on for what would be the ultimate surveillance system: a microchip attached to a human brain which would read its very thought and report it to others.

In other areas too, China had been dramatically upgrading its surveillance techniques and spying. While the Bush Administration had already indicated it would not object to increased cooperation with the Beijing leadership, China had shown itself as a potential threat to America's military planners. That threat included a number of new surveillance systems. One was China's so-called "fast ship," able to travel at 120 mph, and equipped with a whole new range of surveillance equipment with the original Enhanced Promis software. China had developed new radar capable of detecting America's most advanced Stealth jet fighters. Instead of emitting electromagnetic energy pulses which bounced off an enemy aircraft and betrayed its shape and size, the Chinese system depended on analyzing fluctuations in commercial television and radio signals filling the air. Even the Stealth fighter, whose bat-like shape is designed to fool conventional radar by reducing its own radar "signature" to that of a large bird, could not avoid causing fluctuations to radio and television signals. The fluctuations could also be adapted for surveillance purposes.

Long inured with its mistrust of foreigners, the Chinese were already spending billions of dollars updating their surveillance systems to track those who visit their country.

Privacy International, a London-based human rights group, claims that, from 2001 onwards, visitors to China will end up on anywhere up to 300 interlinked databases. Within this system every foreigner becomes caught in a surveillance web enveloping everything they do and spend: what they order from hotel room service; what e-mails they send via their laptops; when and how they change their money into Chinese currency; who they talk to and dine with; what kind of transport they use. It is all recorded on one of those databases. Like much else it was creating, China was determined to be a leader of a surveillance society through information technology to police the morals, thoughts and behavior of all its citizens.

Already hundreds of thousands of cameras have been placed on buses, trains and elevators. Many Chinese expect to be routinely filmed from the moment they leave home. Hidden cameras are installed in cinemas, alongside roads, in bars, dressing rooms and housing estates. Once viewed as a blunt tool of surveillance, such devices in the space of 15 years have become a benign, integral part of the urban Chinese infrastructure. It is the integration of surveillance with their day-to-day environment that is most telling.

Visual surveillance has also become a fixed component in the Chinese design of modern urban centers, new housing areas, public buildings and even throughout the road system. Soon people spy technology will be engineered into all forms of architecture and design. It is perhaps only a matter of time before the regime installs the cameras into all homes.

Surveillance has become a design component in all Chinese information technology. Systems architects are required to design technology that will capture, analyze and present personal information. Accordingly, the workplace is fast becoming a surveillance zone. Electronic supervisors analyse every minute of the working day, checking on performance rates, toilet breaks and personal activities.

Chinese citizens are routinely entrapped into handing over their data. Dozens of laws force them to disclose personal information that is then used for unrelated purposes. Government surveillance has infiltrated every element of communications networks. Telecommunications companies are required by law to ensure that their equipment is "wiretap friendly."

The state can do more or less as it pleases with data in the name of law enforcement, public interest, public health, national security or national revenue. Chinese are obliged, through an increasing number of laws and technologies, to disclose details.

Disclosure of their identity sits at the heart of all Chinese technology. But the nightmare vision of Big Brother is a reality of every entity — citizen, state and corporation — working in partnership to achieve an alleged "common good." Chinese citizens and businesses routinely are advised that they have a responsibility to support authoritarian measures. At a variety of levels, they are all expected to become partners in surveillance.

The last vestiges of trust and privacy — two treasured concepts — have long ago been removed from Chinese minds.

No building in Beijing or any other Chinese city, town or hamlet across the country could operate efficiently without microchips which constantly feed the great banks of computers by which the government keeps track of its citizens from the moment they were born until death.

Ironically much of this has been possible due to China's theft of U.S.-created technology.

The country had survived the economic meltdown that had been predicted for it in the 1980s and 90s. It had set about establishing itself as the flagship of what would become the Asian Century. By the year 2005, of the thirteen world cities with populations of over ten million, seven would be around the Pacific Rim. By then, China's predicted economic growth of eight per cent per annum would allow its technicians to continue creating a multi-media super corridor to rival Malaysia's Cybercity. China's reserve of foreign currency would, by the year 2010, exceed that of Japan. One of every ten corporations around the Pacific Rim, would have Chinese investors, many the largest single stockholders. Singapore would be a Chinese city. The one-third Chinese population of Malaysia would have tightened its control over trade and investment. In the year 2001 that already accounted for 50 per cent. At the start of the century the small Chinese populations of Thailand and the Philippines controlled 60 per cent of those nations' economies. By the year 2015 that figure would have increased by a further twenty per cent. Much of China's success came from its export of technology, including surveillance systems.

Even nations in Africa and Asia, still impoverished at the start of the New Millennium would, thirty years later, possess its gadgets and built-in robotic brains to understand the likes and dislikes of those they served.

These machines, with their artificial intelligence skills, would be the modern-day equivalent of the trusted human servants of the early 20th century. But, unlike those butlers and parlour maids who only gossiped to each other about their employers, by 2020, the robots who came in so many differing forms, shapes and sizes, would be capable of analysing and assessing and reporting on everything which happened in their environment. They combined their roles of Jeeves and master spies with effortless ease.

In China itself, unnoticed and usually unchallenged, surveillance continued to make new inroads into privacy, establish beachheads in Chinese homes and workplaces, and change forever life as people once knew it.

Such monitoring has become routine. Chinese visitors were among those at a conference hosted by Codex Data in New York in December 1999. Their hosts had promised they would "*learn how to trace e-mail, crack passwords, monitor* computers remotely, track online activity, find and recover hidden and deleted data, create trackable files and locate stolen computers."

They were told that surveillance is increasingly an important intelligence-gathering tool. "It is no more than an extension of opening mail, electronic eavesdropping and planting bugs. The difference is that was once the province of the security services. Now all sorts of companies and corporations are doing it. We are moving into a world of those who are under surveillance and those who do the surveillance."

Technologies, mostly developed or introduced in the past twenty-five years, have made possible to already extend surveillance so that hundreds of millions of Chinese who have never been subject to it before, are now closely monitored. The results of such surveillance can reshape, reform, or at least control, the thinking and behavior of any individual. In China, such surveillance is liberated from any legal or moral obligations or restraints.

Consequently surveillance has become part of a burgeoning industry that spreads itself from welfare institutions to university campuses, reaching through hospitals to all levels of industry and, of course, government. Surveillance is interlocking and in one form or another, touches everybody.

In China, surveillance is an integral part of pacification, intimidation, obfuscation, propaganda and control. In its most pernicious form, surveillance is used for behavior modification, including adverse conditioning. Surveillance is always promoted as being done with the best intentions; that it is a less stigmatizing and more human form of control than other sanctions. Surveillance is presented as offering a means to avoid prison, school suspension, eviction from public housing or an appearance before a court. Surveillance is promoted with the unspoken reminder that if you do no wrong while being watched, you will not be punished. In China, no one ever speaks about the gross intrusions into privacy that any surveillance brings.

Becoming technologically as advanced as any industrialised country on earth, China still had, in 2001, a per capita national income less than that of many countries generally accounted as poor. Child-loving to a fault, the regime still made it a crime for a couple to have more than one child. China's ancient political theorists had rivalled those of the Greeks, yet their modern political theory remained crude and derivative.

But, most important of all, China's technology was at the cutting edge.

Nowhere was this more important than how the Chinese had exploited the original Enhanced Promis software that Robert Maxwell had originally sold to Beijing. Just as all those years ago Rafi Eitan had arranged to have deconstructed the version of the software which had come into his hands after he had posed as "Dr. Orr," so the Chinese had taken apart, then rebuilt the version Maxwell had sold them. Over the years many improved versions had been constructed until, by the year 2000, China was ready to use it for its greatest ever coup against the United States. It would become known as the most significant software theft in history.

The theft was prepared in an annex at the rear of the Ministry of Defense headquarters in Beijing's Dongcheng district. The annex houses the Science and

Technology Department. In 1998, when the plan to electronically rob Los Alamos was first mooted, it was under the control of Wang Tomgye; he had a staff of less than one hundred persons. Many were experts in the difficult art of undetected computer hacking. Some of them had learned their skills while working for various companies in California's Silicon Valley. One by one they had been recalled to Beijing to take up their specialist work inside the annex.

Undoubtedly it would have taken even longer but for the help Mossad technicians provided. They were part of a still-secret relationship, one totally unsuspected by the CIA or its fellow members of the Washington intelligence community, that had developed between Mossad and China's Secret Intelligence Service, CSIS.

This relationship between the two countries had started in the aftermath of the Persian Gulf War. China had provided Israel with valuable information about the various types of Iraqi weapons systems that had survived the Allied attacks on Iraq — and which could still be a threat to Israel. Israel's own relationship with the American-led coalition during the war had been an abrasive one, not least because Iraqi Scud missiles had hit Tel Aviv and Israel had been, in the later words of the then Prime Minister Yitzhak Shamir, *"bloody coerced by that bastard Bush* (President George Herbert Bush) *into not retaliating."* Shamir had welcomed China's initial overtures. As simply as that, the relationship between the two nations had begun. Over the ensuing years that cooperation had developed on all levels: China had provided Israel with experts on water desalination and agricultural techniques; Israel had provided the Chinese with details of various weapons systems provided by the United States. But it was in the secret world of intelligence — the one inhabited by Mossad and CSIS — that the closest ties had been developed. These had culminated in 1999 when Efraim Halevy, then director-general of Mossad, had made a secret visit to CSIS headquarters in Beijing. Shortly afterwards, senior members of CSIS had visited Mossad in Tel Aviv. This relationship between the two services would prove to be crucial in what was to follow.

The entire break-in to Los Alamos was coordinated by Wu Xingtang, whose official title was a director of ILD, China's Internal Liaison Department. He was one of China's best spymasters.

The date for the unprecedented robbery was set for May 5, 2000. The target was the high security vaults in what was itself Los Alamos' most secret facility. It was known only as X Division. Around 3000 people worked inside a network of cramped offices on the third floor of the main laboratory building. Guarded by coded swipe cards whose entry numbers changed every day, the most sensitive of X Division's data was stored in a vault. The strong room had every device known to U.S. security experts. Inside the vault was a fireproof bag that could only be opened by using a special password. Throughout the entire Los Alamos complex only 24 people had access to the locked bag.

Inside the bag were the computer hard drives. Each disc contained detailed technical information including how to dismantle the bomb designs by terrorist or rogue states. The computer drives were each the size of a pack of playing cards.

Every week members of NEST, America's Nuclear Emergency Response Team, based at Nellis Air Force Base outside Las Vegas, checked that the bag had not been tampered with.

Access to the hard drives would enable a country like China, or a terrorist group, to use the information to conceal suitcase-type nuclear bombs and make them more difficult to disarm.

The contents of the hard drives would also give anyone who obtained them a massive advantage in knowing the nuclear secrets that the United States possessed.

Firstly, Chinese and Israeli technicians, who had flown to Beijing to work in the annex, devised a hacking system that could electronically penetrate all the X Division defenses at Los Alamos. They were helped by the updated version of the Enhanced Promis software Maxwell had originally sold to China.

A replica of the Los Alamos vault was specially built in the basement of the Science and Technology Department in Beijing. Inside the vault's steel walls was placed a fireproof bag. Inside the bag were put hard drives containing non-secret information.

The task of the hackers was to remove that information without revealing signs they had done so. They were to do so not from somewhere in Beijing, but at a considerable distance from the Chinese capital.

The hackers were dispatched to Shanghai, several hundred miles away. They set to work. The vault was later opened. There was no evidence the fire-proof bag had been penetrated. The team of hackers returned to the annex. With them they brought true copies of the information electronically lifted from the hard drives stored in the bag.

The Chinese planners had worked on the premise that from time to time the hard drives in Los Alamos would be removed from their fireproof bag and placed in a computer they were certain would be inside the American vault. This would either be done to check for a piece of information or to make sure the discs were in perfect working order. In Shanghai, the hackers had waited several days for the discs in the replica vault to be removed and inserted in a computer inside the Beijing vault.

Their success was proof that distance was not going to be a problem.

The next test took place in the Luzon Strait between Taiwan and the Philippine Islands. This time the hacking team was on board a Chinese nuclear-powered submarine of the blue-water fleet of the People's Liberation Army-Navy. The submarine rose close to the surface. Once more the hackers went about their business. Once more they succeeded in electronically penetrating the vault in the Beijing annex. They returned to report their success to Wu Xingtang.

Everything was ready. A month later, in late April 2000, the team of hackers arrived in Puerto Penasco, at the upper reaches of Mexico's Golfo de California. They were equipped with fishing equipment and boxes of tackle. Their journey to the port had been a long one. From Hong Kong, now part of China, they had flown into Mexico City. From there they had driven to Puerto Penasco. Waiting for them was their rented fishing boat. Hidden on board, placed there by a CSIS agent in Mexico, was their equipment for hacking. They set to sea, ostensibly on a fishing trip.

Using the coordinates they had been provided with, the hackers had homed in on the vault in X Division at Los Alamos. Just as they had waited in Shanghai for the right moment, so they had electronically lifted all the data from the hard drive discs in the fireproof bag when they had been briefly removed for some purpose.

A week later they were back in Beijing.

Late in November 2000, a meeting was held at Los Alamos to discuss not only the electronic theft of the contents of the hard drives, but also the new relationship between Mossad and CSIS that the CIA had finally discovered.

Gathered in a conference room in X Division was George Tenet, Director General of the CIA; Britain's MI6 Chief Dearlove; Director Freeh of the FBI; and Los Alamos security chief, Eugene Habinger.

There was a consensus the theft had changed, almost certainly for the foreseeable future, the close intelligence links between Washington and London with Israel.

Those present could not be absolutely certain how the theft had been carried out. A check on the vault computer gave no clue. The only hint that a break-in had occurred was that the hard drives had *not* been replaced in the precise way the NEST team had last left them. After each visit the team rearranged the discs in a certain order only they knew. When they had next inspected the fireproof bag, they had found the discs were not in that order. An internal security inquiry had begun at Los Alamos. It established that a member of X Division, Dr. Lee, had inadvertently (so he said) replaced the discs in a different order. This had led to his immediate suspension and eventually being charged with espionage. Meanwhile, the inquiry had continued. This had lasted some weeks. Then the FBI had been brought in. Finally the CIA had entered the scene. There were many in the FBI and CIA who felt such a casual approach to security was typical of Los Alamos.

The implications would conclude Tenet's briefing to the Bush transition team. It would not be many months before signs would emerge as to how they had responded to all he would have said.

But for two fine, unassuming Americans, William and Nancy Burke Hamilton whose pioneer work in creating the world of modern day surveillance, and who had been so cruelly betrayed in return, the Third Millennium would merely mark the arrival of a new era in which they would fight on for justice.

On January 5, 2001, the couple blinked at each other, not quite able to believe what they were reading. But there was no doubt. *Insight Magazine*, the powerful arm of the *Washington Times*, had blown wide open the secret of Enhanced

Promis. The magazine had published revelations about the investigations of McDade and Buffam, two senior investigators of the National Security Section of the Royal Canadian Mounted Police, RCMP.

The evidence McDade and Buffam had uncovered supported the contention of Bill and Nancy Burke Hamilton that during the Reagan Presidency, Justice Department officials allowed one of the most valuable pieces of software ever created to be stolen. The Hamiltons continue to allege not just bad faith on the part of the Justice Department officials but criminal conduct on the part of high government officers. The late Attorney General, Elliot Richardson said that the implications of what happened in the saga of Enhanced Promis *"is even more damaging to what government should represent in the United States and indeed any democracy, than Watergate or Irangate — or all the other 'gates' in recent memory."*

To this day the Hamiltons fight on, still firm in their belief that the Constitution will finally give them justice. That belief is the one ennobling element in a story that raises deeply disturbing questions about justice.

Would President Bush order them to be answered? The Hamiltons asked the same questions when President Bill Clinton came to office. They asked the same questions when they pondered if the software they had developed would eventually help make China the superpower it is fast becoming. The one certainty is that when it does achieve that aspiration, the events of that terrible day and night in Tiananmen Square in June 1989 would be forever buried. There is little doubt that doing so is part of the price the Bush Administration will have to agree to if it is to enlarge its business and economic ties with China.

In late January 2001, the Tiananmen Trump returned to haunt both the present Chinese regime and the new Bush Administration. Secret documents smuggled out of Beijing that month revealed the fear of the Chinese leadership in 1989 that they would be overthrown by a mass uprising — if the United States indicated it would support such a revolution.

Deng Xiaoping, in a memo dated 13 May 1989, expressed *"a real fear"* of being placed under house arrest — prior to a possible execution — if the students were allowed to go on protesting with the backing of the United States and the Western world.

Wang Zhen, a Party elder at the time, is quoted as saying in one of the documents, *"these students are really asking for it…give them no mercy."*

The documents, smuggled into the United States, were bound to cause huge embarrassment to President Bush's hopes of bridge building with China's present president, Jiang Zemin. His father, the then president at the time of the slaughter, emerges from the documents as so ambitious for power that he endorsed the massacre of the students.

The former Chinese premier, Li Peng, is confirmed in the documents as another strong advocate for the mass killing of the students.

Two of America's leading sinologists, Andrew Nathan of Columbia University, and Percy Link of Princeton, have authenticated the documents, as has James Lilley, the U.S. ambassador to Beijing at the time of the massacres.

All three experts believe the documents are deliberately intended to rock the present Chinese leadership and its relationship with the United States before the major political changes due to take place in Beijing after 2002. Then Jiang steps down from all formal offices.

But by then the effect of the revelations in the documents could have led to growing embarrassment to President George W. Bush — and his own father, who failed to utter a word in support of the students about to die as they cried out for democracy.

In late January 2001, Amnesty International confirmed that some 700 students who had been executed for their part in the Tiananmen Square demonstrations had their vital organs — kidneys, hearts, lungs and eyes — sold to wealthy Chinese in need of transplant surgery.

It emerged that the Chinese authorities have established a system in which the prison authorities nowadays inform hospitals in advance of any executions. Transplant patients are then alerted by telephone or fax that an organ will be available so that they can reach the transplant centers in time. Almost all of these are in the province of Guandong, though since Hong Kong was returned to the mainland, the island has established two clinics for transplant purposes.

The organs are removed according to a well-established ritual. The usual form of Chinese execution is a gunshot in the base of the skull. But human rights observers say executions are so planned that if, for instance, eyes are needed, prisoners are shot in the heart. The Chinese authorities also ensure that prisoners scheduled to have their organs removed are not tortured and are fed special diets. Immediately after execution, a prisoner's corpse is transferred to the adjoining Operating Room where the organs are removed by surgeons. The body is then disposed of and the organs taken to a transplant center.

In February 2001, the Nangfang Hospital in Canton remained the leading hospital for such transplant surgery using the organs of prisoners. In 2000 it had performed, according to Amnesty International, over one hundred such operations. The majority of patients were wealthy Chinese who had traveled from the United States. The hospital has a special medical wing for foreigners and advertises its unique services in the Chinese-language media.

Pressed to explain this, a hospital spokesman told the author in late January 2001 that *"there is nothing unethical about what we do. These are criminals whose organs we use. There is no need for us to obtain their consent when they are going to be executed. They might as well do something for other people with their organs."*

The butchers of Tiananmen Square live on in another guise.

On Saturday, March 17, 2001, CIA Director George Tenet was woken from a deep sleep at his home in Georgetown, Washington D.C., by a telephone call from the duty officer at Langley. There had been talk that the CIA HQ was about to become informally known as the George Herbert Bush Center for Intelligence, the President's tribute to his father when he had once directed the CIA. Tenet did not care what the building complex was called.

The late Robert F. Kennedy, then attorney general, and President Kennedy's overseer of the agency, had once witheringly called Langley *"the home of the only secret service to advertise its presence on the freeway."*

Tenet's caller, in a throwback to the lingu-franca of the Cold War days, was typically obtuse. He simply said *"the jumper is coughing."*

It was the call that Tenet had been waiting for during the past two months. On that frosty morning in January 2001, Senior Colonel Xu Junping of China's People's Liberation Army, and one of his nation's new breed of military high fliers, a strategist with fluent English and a year at Harvard University on his CV, had defected to the United States.

Xu had simply caught a China Airlines flight to Bangkok. From there he had booked a business class seat on Thai Airlines to New York. Next he had boarded the shuttle to Washington D.C. From the capital's National Airport he, Xu, used one of the few quarters in his pocket to call an unlisted number. It was the one he had been given by a CIA agent in Beijing. Xu told the man at the other end of the phone who he was and why he was in Washington.

Within an hour a government unmarked car had collected Xu and whisked him from the airport to a CIA safe house in a Washington suburb.

So important was Xu's defection that President George W. Bush was immediately informed by the director. Tenet called it *"the best news we have received out of China for a long time."*

Given his importance, Xu was afforded all the courtesies of a top-level defector. He was allowed to order-in the finest cuisine to the safe house. His "handlers" — the team of interrogators assigned to debrief him — were told by Tenet to *"take things at Xu's pace."*

For weeks Xu revealed little other than what the CIA either needed confirming or already suspected.

Xu chose to open his debriefing with news which brought a wry smile to the lips of his listeners. He told them that Israeli scientists trained at the PLA's super-secret intelligence and security command in the Western Hills outside Beijing had been trained to perfect the technique of morphing, among others, the images of Yasser Arafat and Saddam Hussein onto television screens.

Using specially doctored voice tapes of the actual Arafat and Saddam speaking, these have been re-spliced and perfectly lip-synced so that either leader appears to be making totally outlandish statements against their own people — which could lead to them being toppled.

Xu had witnessed these close-circuit test transmissions later carried out deep inside the Kirya, Israeli Defense Force headquarters, in Tel Aviv.

The transmissions could be relayed to both PLO and Iraqi television stations. They would then replace real-time programmes and cause panic, anger and havoc.

The CIA debriefing team knew this development was an extension of what had been done by the United States 193rd Operations Group during the Persian Gulf War in 1991. Then a specially converted 737 flew over Iraq and broadcasted reports directly into Baghdad radio stations urging Iraqi soldiers to desert before the next bombing.

Xu's debriefers had been more interested to learn that other Israeli scientists had returned from China with the capability to arm Shin Bet agents with radioactive aerosol sprays that their Chinese counterparts had shown them how to create. These had been used in the Second Intifada still raging in Israel.

The debriefers were shocked to hear Xu admit that the sprays contained Scandium-64, an element whose side effects include creating impotency in a male and severely damaging the fallopian tubes of a woman.

He said that when PLO dissidents were arrested and taken to an Israeli police station or detention center, they were strip-searched. Their clothes were then given a small squirt from an aerosol that contained the radioactive chemical. The chemical was invisible, odorless and left no detectable residue on the clothes. It also quickly penetrated skin.

A small squirt of the substance enabled Israeli agents and Defence Force "snatch squads" to detect a person previously arrested.

Xu explained this was done by Israeli detector vans equipped with ultra-sophisticated Geiger counters that pinpointed a person previously sprayed. The vans were identical to those already used by Israeli Defence Force patrols.

The Chinese-trained Israeli scientists had set up a lab to make aerosol and detector equipment at Israel's top-secret Institute for Biological Research situated in the Tel Aviv suburb of Nes Ziona. Most of its twelve acres of laboratories were underground and protected by state-of-the-art security systems.

Within its laboratories and workshops are manufactured a wide range of chemical and biological weapons. The Institute's chemists — some of whom once worked for the Soviet KGB or East German Stasi intelligence services — had a current research program which included developing a range of pathogens which would be, according to a secret CIA report, "ethnic-specific." The CIA report claims that the Institute scientists were *"trying to exploit medical advances by identifying distinctive genes carried by some Arabs to create a genetically modified bacterium or virus. Still at the early stages, the intention is to exploit the way viruses and certain bacteria can alter the DNA inside their host's living cells."* This research mimics work conducted by South African scientists during the apartheid era to create a *"pigmentation weapon that would target only black people."*

The research was abandoned when Nelson Mandela came to power but at least two of the scientists who worked in the program in South Africa later moved to Israel.

The idea of the Jewish State conducting such research has triggered alarm bells — not least because of the disturbing parallel with genetic experiments conducted by the Nazis. Dedi Zucker, a member of the Israeli Parliament, the Knesset, is on record as saying: *"We cannot be allowed to create such weapons."*

It was the raw materials for such weapons that an El Al jet was carrying on that October night in 1992. In its 114 tons of cargo, that also included

Sidewinder missiles and electronics, were twelve barrels of DMMP, a component of Sarin gas. The chemicals had been bought from Solkatronic, the New Jersey-based chemical manufacturer. The company has steadfastly insisted it had been told by Israel the chemicals were *"to be used for testing gas masks."*

The Institute was founded in 1952 in a small concrete bunker in an orchard. The fruit trees have long gone, replaced by a high concrete wall topped with sensors. Armed guards patrol the perimeter. Long ago the Institute disappeared from public scrutiny. Its exact address in the suburbs of Nes Ziona has been removed from the Tel Aviv telephone book. Its location is erased from all maps of the area. No aircraft is allowed to over-fly the area.

Only Dimona, Israel's nuclear facility in the Negev Desert, is surrounded by more secrecy. In the classified directory of the Israeli Defense Force, the Institute is only listed as "providing services to the Defense Ministry." Concealed deep underground, the biochemists and genetic scientists work with their bottled agents of death: toxins that can create crippling food poisoning and lead to death; the even more virulent Venezuelan equine encephalomyelitis and anthrax.

In other laboratories, reached through air locks, scientists work with a variety of nerve agents: choking agents, blood agents, blister agents. These include Tabun, virtually odorless and invisible when dispensed in aerosol or vapor form. Soman, the last of the Nazi nerve gases to be discovered, is also invisible in vapor form but has a slightly fruity odor. The range of blister agents include chlorine, phosgene and diphosgene which smells of new-mown grass. The blood agents include those with a cyanide base. The blister agents are based upon those first used in World War One.

Outwardly featureless, with few windows in its dun-colored concrete walls, the Institute's interior has code words and visual identification control access to each area. Guards patrol the corridors. Bombproof sliding doors can only be opened by swipe-cards whose codes are changed every day.

All employees undergo health checks every month. All have been subject to intense screening. Their families have also undergone similar checks.

Within the Institute is a special department that creates lethal toxin weapons for the use of Mossad to carry out its state-approved mandate to kill without trial the enemies of Israel. Over the years at least six workers at the plant have died, but the cause of their deaths is protected by Israel's strict military censorship.

The first crack in that security curtain has come from a former Mossad officer, Victor Ostrovsky. He claims that *"we all knew that a prisoner brought to the Institute would never get out alive. PLO infiltrators were used as guinea pigs. They could make sure the weapons the scientists were developing worked properly and make them even more efficient."*

Israel has so far issued no denial of these allegations.

Xu had confirmed all this and much more to his silent and undoubtedly shocked listeners in the CIA safe house. What he had described was far more disturbing than anything they had previously learned — which itself was precious little — about the laboratories at the Institute. Suddenly Washington must have seemed a long way from the sinister work going on in Israel.

Xu had next described how the labs had developed another weapon with the help of the Chinese, which contravened all international treaties. These had begun to be used by special undercover IDF squads on the West Bank and in Gaza.

The weapons included a variety of fast-acting poisons that left no trace unless a victim was subjected to minute examination by a specially trained pathologist.

No fewer than six varieties of poison had been developed in the past two years.

The first time the weapon was used was in September 1997 when a Mossad *kidon* unit attempted to assassinate Hamas leader Khaled Meshal on an Amman, Jordan street. That operation was bungled by the team.

Since then, chemists at the Institute had created more sophisticated delivery systems. These included powerful pistols that could fire such weapons at up to 50-meter range. On impact, the specially designed actual bullet-head releases a needle-thin dart containing the poison. Israeli marksmen were taught not to fire at a target's head, but into his body. All the poisons were fast-acting and leave no trace.

The pistols that fired them were completely silent. The bullet that acts as the delivery system was designed to have minimum body penetration. The killing was done by the needle-like dart. It left no more than a pinprick. The Israelis calculated that in the mayhem of fighting in the West Bank and Gaza, no one would spot the pinprick.

The full range of weapons supplied to the undercover teams included a number of nerve agents, choking agents, blood agents and blister agents.

All were designed to bring about quick deaths. Also available to the undercover teams were other killer gases that were strictly outlawed under international treaties.

All these revelations had been transcribed and delivered on a daily basis to Tenet. Summaries had then been sent to the White House.

The new President was said to be "deeply disturbed" by all he read. But more was to come from Xu. Comfortable in his safe house and with his debriefers, Xu began to widen the scope of his extraordinary knowledge.

He spent an entire morning telling his debriefers about possibly the most secret island in the South China Sea that Beijing used as a top-secret listening post far out into the ocean. Heavily protected, Hainan Island was one of the most secret of all the PLA bases. In one of those stranger than fiction twists that no novelist dare invent, two weeks later, on April 1, 2001, a U.S. Air Force EP-3 spy plane, trying to test the island's electronic defenses, was forced to land there by Chinese fighters, one of which ditched in the sea, killing its pilot. The twenty-four U.S. air crew and specialist technicians on board brought the first international crisis to the Bush Administration. There was an element of panic in the way it was handled from Washington. The President's bellicosity did little to impress Beijing. But that was still a little ways away on that St. Patrick's Day.

Xu had decided to begin to unburden himself on how China's military strategists viewed the West and its strategies towards the People's Republic. He described the People's Liberation Army's fears and the arguments it was prepared to lose and those for which it was ready to go to war. But above all, Xu had begun to confirm the full details of China's Secret Intelligence Service's dealings with Israel's Mossad.

It was what Tenet later called *"the wider panorama"* that had led to Tenet being once more awoken from a deep sleep.

On that March Saturday, Tenet put down the bedside phone, summoned his driver, shaved and showered and cancelled his St. Patrick's Day breakfast which neighbors were holding. Putting on a sports jacket and pants — his regular weekend outfit — he slipped a sprig of shamrock in his lapel button, a sign he had not forgotten Ireland's national day. Forty minutes later his driver had deposited Tenet outside the safe house where Xu was staying.

Tenet was soon joined by members of Bush's inner team — headed by Condoleezza, his new senior policy adviser and several of her assistants.

Over what was to become a long weekend, the Bush team and Tenet listened as Xu took them on a detailed tour of China's policy towards Iraq, Iran, Russia, Taiwan, Britain, Europe and, of course, the United States.

Xu spoke in a flat, unemotional voice, the one he had until recently used when briefing senior cadres in Beijing. He filled in details of China's flagrant sanctions-busting in Iraq, with Chinese corporations helping Saddam Hussein to update his air defense networks.

The importance of what Xu revealed was hard to overestimate. He had been director of the North America and Oceania Department of Foreign Affairs Office of China's Defense Ministry. Part of his job was to socialize and "come alongside" U.S. embassy military attachés in Beijing. He had also acted as a translator at high-level summits and was the author of secret briefing papers on Pentagon thinking.

What stunned the Bush team was how close he had come to explaining Washington's thinking to his Chinese leaders. Part of this, he said, had come from knowledge gleaned during his year at Harvard, at the Kennedy School of Government. Upon his return to Beijing, he had been appointed to the Central Military Commission. It was there that he supervised the growing contacts between Israel and China, between Mossad and the CSIS.

It was Tenet who had posed the question: Why had Xu decided to defect?

His answer was to the point. He had written a detailed analysis of the bombing by the United States of the Chinese embassy in Belgrade during NATO's air war over Kosovo. His analysis pointed to a "genuine but most unfortunate accident" by the U.S. pilots. This view was not accepted by his seniors at the Central Military Commission.

Xu told his attentive listeners in the safe house on that holiday weekend that that was when he decided to defect.

Like all good intelligence officers, Xu continued by describing a visit he had made in January 2000 to Cape Town in South Africa. He had flown there from Tel Aviv via Johannesburg with Danny Yatom, once head of Mossad but then

Prime Minister Ehud Barak's personal security adviser — a watchdog to keep an eye on his old service's activities and those of other agencies within the Israeli intelligence community.

He and Yatom had traveled on false passports. Yatom's had been a British one, Xu's a Thai document. Both identified them as "businessmen."

In Cape Town, Xu and Yatom had met with two Mossad *katsas*, field agents, in the city to monitor the activities of the growing number of Islamic fundamentalists in the country. Yatom had explained that had brought the total number of Mossad agents in South Africa to seven; they were supported by analysts at the newly reinforced "Desk" at Mossad HQ. Initially, the two *katsas* explained, they had collaborated with South Africa's National Intelligence Agency (NIA) responsible for internal security, the country's poor relation version of the FBI. The intention had been to collaborate, Yatom had explained to Xu, on a shared intelligence basis.

But following what the *katsas* called an "intelligence shambles" over Islamic car bomb attacks in Cape Town against a number of foreign-franchised companies in the city, Yatom had ordered the agents to break off collaborating with NIA. A Mossad report on the matter stated NIA *"is poorly led and that cooperation with its sister service, the South African Secret Service (SASS), is at a minimum. So great was the dissension that the country's already over-burdened police force had created a special unit to do the work that NIA should be doing. The unit was called 'the Scorpion Force.'*

"But Mossad felt it lacked the essential 'prior knowledge' that is a prerequisite for any successful intelligence gathering.

"In recent months there had been a spate of car and pipe bombings in the city. The targets included a McDonalds, New York Bagels and the city's popular Hard Rock Café.

"The attacks had been laid at the door of an extremist Muslim group, People Against Gangsterism and Drugs (PAGAD).

"Despite the effect they have had on foreign tourism, PAGAD gained a deal of sympathy with local people — by driving out Cape Town's drug barons who used the targets as meeting points to dispense their drugs."

With the South African security services at loggerheads with each other — a situation the Mossad *katsas* called the *"usual turf war that should have been resolved a long time ago"* — Mossad's presence in the country had led to renewed speculation.

Mossad's presence in South Africa was a long-standing one. It began in 1972 when Ezer Weizman, then a senior official in the Israeli defense ministry, met then Prime Minister P.W. Botha in Pretoria to further intelligence cooperation. At that time South African security was in the hands of the notorious BOSS, the Bureau of State Security.

It was Mossad who taught BOSS the more sophisticated means of interrogation that had worked for the Israelis in Lebanon: sleep deprivation, hooding, forcing a suspect to stand against a wall for long periods, squeezing genitalia and a variety of mental tortures including mock executions. Those were the halcyon days of Mossad's great African safari.

Then, when the apartheid regime finally ended, Mossad was among the first foreign intelligence services to offer its expertise to Nelson Mandela. It helped his fledgling regime target the white extremists Mossad had previously worked with.

Tenet then told Xu what had happened since he had arrived in Washington. The CSIS had begun an intensive search for Xu, quickly tracking him to Bangkok. CSIS agents in London and Europe were alerted in case Xu had chosen to defect to one of their security services.

When it was discovered by a CSIS agent in New York that Xu had traveled directly to the United States, the Chinese government had reacted in typical fashion.

Firstly, the Foreign Ministry asked the U.S. embassy in Beijing *"for assistance in locating a Chinese military officer who had disappeared in New York."*

The implication was that Xu had been kidnapped either by the CIA or FBI and was being held under duress.

The United States embassy in Washington solemnly handed a diplomatic note to the Chinese Foreign Ministry that Xu was indeed in the United States but was in good health and "had not been kidnapped."

Stymied, the Chinese Foreign Ministry raised the matter with Admiral Dennis Blair, commander of the U.S. Pacific forces in a meeting in Beijing. Blair, truthfully, said he knew nothing of the episode.

On March 22, China sent its foreign policy chief, Qian Qichen, to Washington. In a face-to-face meeting with Condoleezza Rice, he warned her *"of the dangers for peace if the United States continued to supply arms to Taiwan and went ahead with its missile defense shield."*

Condoleezza Rice listened politely. But she knew Qian was bluffing. Xu had told her.

For the moment the Bush Administration could use Xu's inside knowledge to thwart China's intentions to challenge America. But no one could predict how long that advantage would last.

While Xu Junping settled into his secret home in the Witness Protection Program, the crisis over the EP-3 spy plane ended as swiftly as it began. On Friday, April 13, 2001, the Beijing regime ordered that the crew of twenty-four — fliers and the spy technicians they carried — should be released. The plane, gutted of all its secrets, remained on the ground on the island of Hainan. In keeping with the mood of self-satisfaction and patriotism which swept the United States, one of the crew, Josef Edmonds, proposed to his girlfriend, Sondra White, in Texas; the moment was captured by CNN as Edmonds made his proposal on a brief stopover at Guam on his way back to the United States mainland.

More significantly, hawkish Americans demanded that President Bush should harden his stance against China. The conservative *Wall Street Journal* spoke for many when it editorialised that *"Mr. Bush now needs to extract a price for this behavior."*

The editorial, understandable from the American standpoint, indicated a major misunderstanding of the reality of how the crash-landing of the spy plane on Chinese sovereign territory was seen in Beijing.

While America was bedecked with yellow ribbons of rejoicing at the homecoming of the crew, and the spin doctors in Washington coined the phrase for this as *"Operation Valiant Return,"* on the other side of the world, in China, the entire incident was seen as another blip, no more, in Beijing's long-term goals. How much Xu Junping warned his debriefers on the matter; how much attention they paid to his words during what, in the U.S., had become a superheated crisis, we will never know for sure.

But publicly in America there was a dissenting voice, and one not easily dismissed. Despite his self-proclaimed title as *"America's foremost whistle-blower on government fraud and corruption,"* former U.S. Navy Lt.-Commander Al Martin had worked in the office of Naval Intelligence, coincidentally not far from where the Israeli spy, Jonathan Pollard, had once had an office. But Martin is no spy. He is passionately — some would say obsessively — concerned about government cover-ups which have been handed down from one Administration to another.

By May 2001, he had concluded that the "entire spy plane saga" was just such a cover-up; that the Department of Defense, DOD, had tried and failed to hide the truth about what the spy plane was doing and what happened when it was forced to crash.

While some of Martin's assertions have failed to check out — despite the author's exhaustive checks with sources in European and Russian intelligence services, who would have no reason to cover up the truth — there are some uncomfortable matters which the Department of Defense have failed to explain.

Initially the DOD stated that the crew had used "axes" to smash the top-secret equipment on board. But when the U.S. Navy Department released a detailed inventory on all the non-secret equipment on the aircraft, no axes were listed.

So far the DOD has refused to explain their "axes." But in one of the later press releases — a staggering 142 in all that were issued by the DOD — one contained the admission that *"not as much technology was destroyed as previously claimed and that the Chinese are in possession of certain technology."*

Then, on April 27, 2001, the DOD made a more staggering admission: *"No technology was destroyed ... it is reasonable to assume that the Chinese are now in possession of our Entire Story Classic System."* This technology interprets data. No other nation in the world has such a system.

Martin insists this revelation means that, with the full knowledge of the burgeoning relationship between China and Russia, the Bush Administration has secretly decided to arrange a "technology transfer" to China to try and keep Beijing on side. In other words, all the bellicosity from President Bush was a cover-up to what was really going on.

Martin's long and complex argument in support of this gained credibility when, days after Martin had publicly made his claims, the office of Defense

Secretary, Donald Rumsfeld, ordered the suspension of military exchanges and all Chinese armed forces. Hours later the order was cancelled by President Bush. The Pentagon admitted the cancellation was *"an unusual retraction."*

Martin insists *"it is all part of the cover-up over the spy plane that has gone wrong."* He continues:

"What gummed up the works is that not everyone on the aircraft was in the loop. The only people who were in the loop were the five so-called unidentified non-military personnel which incidentally the Department of Defense still refuses to identify. Conveniently, when they show photographs of the people who have been returned, they only show the Navy personnel. They have still never shown these other civilian personnel. No pictures of them landing or being transported. Nothing. It's very convenient."

The use of hammers to bang the high-tech equipment on the plane has been confirmed — but they were ball-peen hammers, not the eighteen-pound hammers the Department of Defense claimed. The only axes ever known to be around the aircraft were the axes the Chinese soldiers used to break down the doors. The plane has an internal fire extinguishing system so there is no need for the typical breaking of glass cabinets on board. The only axes were the axes the Chinese soldiers left behind after they broke down the door.

The Department of Defense Statement No. 16 out of the 142 they've now made, said that the crew had time to destroy the technology while the plane was still in the air. Then they said — no, that's not true, because the plane was so severely damaged they were busy trying to land so they didn't have time.

Then they went to a second line where the crew got hammers after the plane was on the ground in order to try to destroy it. Despite this story, subsequently a press release from the Chinese Army through the Chinese State Media claimed that the Chinese soldiers were inside the aircraft within 60 seconds after it came to a stop on the ground.

On May 15, 2001, further evidence to support Martin's claims came from the Pentagon. It confirmed that classified manuals *"and other documents"* had been left on board the plane that *"detailed tactics and operations."*

"It would have been impossible to eliminate totally the loss of intelligence, short of setting charges to the plane," said the Pentagon spokesman, Admiral Craig Quigley.

"The aircraft was not equipped with a shredder so the crew would have had to push manuals and documents out of a hatch or, perhaps, use a specially designed acid during the emergency landing.

"But you can't set fire to documents inside an airplane that is falling like a rock," added Quigley.

While the DOD takes the line it would not dignify Martin's allegations with a denial, there is a record of it playing fast and loose with the truth.

In September 1985, the DOD issued videotape of a high altitude anti-satellite missile launch from an F15 successfully destroying a low orbit satellite. Later the Department of Defense admitted it was a fake and that the missile in fact didn't hit anything.

In 1989, Department of Defense videotape showed one of the new Patriot missile systems striking a target. Subsequently they admitted that the videotape was also faked.

In 1996, the DOD showed the V-22 Osprey aircraft on *"successful military maneuvers"* stating that the aircraft performed *"to its full specifications."* Later it back-pedaled on that too, saying that this video and the accompanying photographs had also been faked.

All these incidents give further credibility to Martin's claim that the United States, under Bush's leadership, will draw closer to the People's Republic of China — so as to try and keep its old Cold War enemy, Russia, still out in the cold.

Martin is right when he says that when President George Herbert Bush reiterated American support for Taiwan in April 2001, it was actually a reversal from the previous Reagan statements. Bush backed away from the protocol that an attack on Taiwan from the PRC was an aggressive act of war against the United States, the Reagan interpretation.

What President Bush intimated in his statement is that an aggressive act against Taiwan would no longer be considered an act of war against the United States. As time goes by, the U.S. will slowly back away from Taiwan. Then it is likely that the Taiwanese will buy weapons from the Russians. It is the only place where they can buy sophisticated weapons that actually work.

But one certain truth is that Beijing never panicked over the spy-plane incident. Proof of this was that, while President Bush was fulminating on the lawn of the White House to the world, China's own president, Jiang Zemin, had gone off on a state visit to Latin America.

Better than anybody, he knew that in Beijing was a well-oiled machine into which any unexpected event is fed and used accordingly. That machine is not distracted by such concerns as the truth or public opinion — its ability to use censorship and propaganda on its population sees to that.

To better understand that machine it is essential to grasp that if the position were reversed — and twenty-four Chinese were held captive by another country — China would never sacrifice its national interest. Its newspapers would not call for, as the *Wall Street Journal* did, *"a price"* to be paid. The machine would simply log what had happened — and wait. It knows the day would surely come when it would effectively exert its own price.

At the core of the Chinese machine — its intelligence services, its propaganda — its military leaders, its politicians — is one belief: it despises America's fear of casualties. It witnessed this fear in the Korean War, in Vietnam, in every war in which the United States has been involved. In Beijing it is known as "the body bag syndrome." The United States has magnificent weapons systems. But China's soldiers are taught from the day of their induction into the People's Liberation Army, that the Americans who man those machines fear death — and that is why they can be beaten.

This is yet another reason why China admires Israel; their men have the same lack of fear. It is why Beijing will continue to work closely with Tel Aviv.

A team of Israeli technicians had secretly flown to Hainan Island — where the U.S. "spy plane" was still being held.

They had been promised full access to the ultra-sophisticated data the Chinese had removed from the aircraft. It was the first tangible evidence of the new links between Israel and China, established since the Bush Administration.

The EP-3 spy plane, costing some U.S. $ 90 million, had last year been requested by Israel as part of its updating of military equipment. The request had been provisionally agreed by the Clinton administration. President Bush cancelled it.

The Chinese decision to allow Israeli military technicians to study the contents of the downed EP-3 was an invaluable intelligence coup for Israel.

Mossad sources said the EP-3 would be invaluable in hovering up conversation from all its Arab neighbors. The U.S. ambassador in Beijing has said he was certain *"the Chinese have learned the secrets of the EP-3 and would be able to build their own version."*

It is then possible the aircraft could be sold to Israel.

"That will further seriously affect the uneasy relationship currently existing between Israel and the United States," said a Washington State Department analyst.

In Israel, Mossad followed the spy-plane crisis and accurately predicted its relentless course. There were the impossible demands that China made of Washington — all designed to leave Beijing nursing a useful set of grievances when they were not met.

There was the steady escalation of Chinese propaganda as the missing Chinese pilot was first named, then eulogised and his sobbing family produced on television night after night. This was imagery-making at its cynical best. The American networks fell into the trap of using it, as did TV networks around the globe.

The machine in Beijing brilliantly used selective reporting and edited translations of American statements. These were also rebroadcast, leaving Washington's spin doctors in a spin.

There was nothing new in any of this. The same technique had been used in 1999 after U.S. planes bombed the Chinese embassy in Belgrade.

In all the euphoria over the release of the spy plane crew, several goals have been overlooked by many Americans. The spy-plane standoff improved China's chances of taking back the island of Taiwan, by force if necessary. It also positioned Beijing's authority in East Asia, its next step to becoming a global superpower. It served a clear warning to Washington that the day is coming when Beijing will drive the American military might — primarily the Seventh Fleet — out of China's backyard, possibly as far back as Hawaii.

China wants the South China Sea all for itself. It wants all U.S. spy plane flights stopped. So far Washington has not agreed. President Bush has spoken of keeping up the flights. But for how long? For the moment he has one card to play: China still needs America's technology. It cannot get it all through the good offices of its new friend, Israel.

But the problem that the Bush Administration faces is that China can never be a simple exercise in foreign policy analysis. The spy-plane incident showed that Beijing was able to display a masterly command of international tactics. In 1986, the Chinese philosopher, Sun Lomgli, said, *"There are many walls within the Chinese world; the Great Wall itself merely protects the Chinese against the Devils from without."*

The spy-plane incident reveals that the "devils" within the Great Wall are getting ready to come out and confront those outside. The further the world is from that last confrontation, the closer it is to the next. And that may not end so fortunately for the West as the spy-plane incident.

FOR THE MOMENT:
JUNE 2001:

George Tenet remained Director of Central Intelligence. Once Bush had confirmed Tenet was staying on, the DCI made a surprising decision. He agreed Langley could be used as a film set for a CBS TV series about the Agency called, what else, "The Agency." Tenet said he was *"only interested in cooperating with Hollywood if the subject of the script is sympathetic."*

Louis J. Freeh, Director of the FBI, resigned after an eight-year tenure in which he had energetically expanded the Bureau's reach around the world. President Bush said Freeh's decision to go *"did catch me by surprise."* Freeh had led the FBI's failed investigation into the theft by China's CSIS from Los Alamos.

President George W. Bush put his missile shield plans into full production. Mounting criticism came from both the West and from China and Russia.

Bush held open the *"prospect that the United States and Russia would one day cooperate in operating a joint missile defense system."*

Russian President Vladimir Putin stressed in response that Washington should not make any unilateral decisions *"on strategic stability."*

In Beijing, the regime noted that the latest anniversary of the massacre of Tiananmen Square passed almost peacefully. It was a further sign their Tiananmen Trump would dampen the Seeds of Fire which had once burned so brightly in the hearts of all those who believed in true democracy for China.

Rafi Eitan, the man who probably more than any other spy, has done more damage to the United States — his many thefts, including that of "Broken Promis," had led to the establishing of the relationship between Israel and China — continued in 2001 to escape censure — and to plot and plan how he might strike again.

In June of that year, he sent a Beirut lawyer to see Bill Hamilton, still battling to win his case of the theft of his software.

The lawyer was Muhamad Mugraby, head of one of the most successful legal firms in Lebanon.

Mugraby had an intriguing proposition for Hamilton. After introducing himself as an *"old and valued friend"* of Rafi Eitan, Mugraby suggested that Hamilton could meet Eitan in Vienna.

"There if all went well, Rafi and I could form an off-shore company to market the latest version of Enhanced Promis software to all those many intelligence services that Israel had previously sold the doctored version to through Maxwell," Hamilton was to recall Mugraby proposing.

Hamilton, older and wiser now to the ways of men bearing gifts, declined.

"*First I thought this could be a set-up. Then I remembered that Vienna was a place where Rafi had operated with great success. You might say it was one of his favorite killing fields. There was no way I was going to go there to meet Rafi Eitan,*" Hamilton said.

Eitan, true to form, when asked if he knew Mugraby, said he had never heard of him.

That Tuesday morning, September 11, 2001, was one of those September idylls that Xu Junping, unlike countless Americans, could not yet take for granted. At this time of year the weather in Beijing would still be humid and the temperature up in the high eighties. But that was not the only change he was learning to cope with.

Like everyone who entered it, he had been told that settling into the Witness Protection Program was never easy; it was not just getting used to his new identify and all that went with it — a Social Security number, a driving license, the kind of paperwork which confirmed he was now an American citizen; it was the minutiae of a very different lifestyle that he had to absorb: shopping at a supermarket, using a laundry service, a parking lot, how to access a freeway, navigate his way back to where he now lived. There had been endless coaching by men and women trained in the art — teaching him to use American idioms, how to follow TV listings, tune in his radio — do all those things that all Americans take for granted.

In those months in the Program he had been tested on a weekly basis. As he had become more proficient, he had increasingly been encouraged to widen his horizons. But wherever he went, he was shadowed by a small team of U.S. Marshals, again specially trained for the job.

Junping had not yet been placed in a suitable employment; he had been told it would probably be some months before he was found a position, probably within the U.S. intelligence community working with one of the 45 separate agencies within that closed world. For the moment he received a generous allowance out of the secret fund that the CIA had for supporting defectors. Like everything else about Xu Junping's new life, the amount of his stipend remained a secret.

But on that Tuesday morning his routine in his new home had assumed part of his new life. He had showered, dressed and eaten his breakfast, readying himself for the first visit of the day from one of his Marshal minders.

Outside, commuters were hurrying to work, children to school; rail stations and airports in the countless other cities and towns — each probably little different from the one where he lived — were bustling with early morning travelers.

At 8:30 A.M., he would later recall, he turned on his TV set to CNN; a news channel he had come to watch because of its reports from Asia.

Fifteen minutes later, as seamless as a champion diver into water, a passenger plane passed through the glass wall of the north tower of the World Trade Center. Eighteen minutes later, at 9:03 A.M., another passenger plane swallow-dived into the second symbol of America's premier position as the world's leading financial power. By then the Pentagon had been dive-bombed by a third passenger plane. Then, at 10:10 A.M., eighty miles southeast of Pittsburgh, a fourth passenger plane crashed, its crew like all the others overpowered and the flight deck manned by kamikaze terrorists in the pay of Osama bin-Laden.

Only later would Xu Junping ask the questions that everyone else would ask. How had it been possible to carry out such a devastating strike on the twin symbols of American economic might, the World Trade Center, and the heart of its military pride as a superpower, the Pentagon? How was it possible that such a devastating strike on the American tradition of swaggering gung-ho invulnerability — the rarely wavering conviction that American intelligence is smarter than any other in the world — had proven to be so easy to carry out? There would, in the days, then weeks to come, be hundreds of questions that would narrow down to one. How?

But on that Tuesday morning, Xu Junping, it later emerged, had an initial question of his own. What part had China played in this unprecedented assault on the United States?

On the other side of the world in Kabul, Afghanistan, it was already late afternoon when the attack on America had occurred. Earlier that day a transport aircraft from China's People Liberation Army (PLA) had landed at the city's ramshackle airport. It had brought to Kabul the most important delegation the ruling Taliban had ever received. It included senior officers of the PLA and the Bureau of State Security and managers from two of China's leading defense contractors, Huswei Technologies and ZTE.

They had come to sign a contract that would provide the Taliban with state-of-the-art electronic defense equipment. It would include electronic advance-warning systems, missile tracking systems and various weapons systems that would, overnight, bring the Taliban army out of the Stone Age in terms of modern warfare to something resembling a formidable fighting force.

Until that Tuesday the Taliban had some 50,000 soldiers under arms, 150 tanks, 200 heavy artillery, 15 helicopters and 20 fighter bombers. Supporting this was the Al-Qaeda brigade of Osama bin-Laden; this consisted of some 5,000 Algerians, Yemenis and Egyptians. As a force, they were more suitable to terrorist attacks than fighting a conventional war. They were equipped with Kalashnikov rifles they had captured from the Soviets during their failed attempt to overcome Afghanistan. They also had Stinger missiles, supplied by the CIA when the United States had supported the Taliban against the Russian invaders. Iraq had provided the Taliban with a small arsenal of ZSU-23s, a three barrel, 50-calibre machine gun, usually arranged in groups of three or four. With a range of some 4,000 yards, they were an effective defense against helicopter attack, or an advancing enemy trying to pick its way through the mountains and the vast expanse of the Hindu Kush.

That Tuesday evening, over cups of mint tea, the Taliban and the Chinese delegation had signed an historic agreement. In return for providing military equipment, the Taliban would order Muslim Fundamentalists to stop their long-running terror attacks against China's western provinces.

In his seventh-floor office at Langley, George Tenet, the CIA's 45-year old director, had come to one important conclusion. The attacks had been orchestrated by Osama bin-Laden. All else would flow from that conclusion.

From that had flown hundreds of questions, orders and instructions to his staff and through them to the entire U.S. intelligence community. At some point in those first hours of Tuesday, Tenet had recalled what Xu Junping had said during his debriefing sessions. President Bush had asked Tenet to try and have Col. Xu focus on what China was doing to support global terrorism through its secret intelligence service, CSIS.

The question had "deeply disturbed" Mr. Bush, since he had learned that his predecessor, Bill Clinton, had authorized an assassination attempt on bin-Laden after the destruction of the U.S. embassy in Nairobi. The hit-team failed because bin-Laden had been warned by the CSIS and escaped into his warren of hideouts in the mountains of Afghanistan. Col. Xu had informed Tenet and Condoleezza Rice, also present at the debriefing, that bin-Laden had made several visits to China in the past two years.

After learning from Col. Xu of bin-Laden's "shopping list" from China, Ms. Rice had telephoned President Bush. There had been one question uppermost in her mind — should Mr. Bush warn China of the consequences if the deal with the Taliban went ahead?

Mr. Tenet had been instructed to monitor the situation, but he had a problem — there was no one on the CIA's 22,000 staff who spoke Afghan or had any direct knowledge of Afghanistan.

Once more, Mr. Tenet had turned to an old and trusted ally, Israel's Mossad. It was — and is — the only intelligence service with spies on the ground in Afghanistan.

On Saturday, September 8, the Mossad had sent a short transmission "burst" that the previously troubled Chinese western provinces were now quiet — and that a delegation from Beijing was due in Kabul on Tuesday, September 11.

When Osama bin-Laden had visited China, he had usually been accompanied by China's most senior diplomat in the region, its ambassador to Pakistan. By sheer coincidence, Lt-General Mahood Ahmed, the head of Pakistan's powerful many-tentacled intelligence service, PIS, was in Washington. He was in the city to discuss with various intelligence agencies a PIS request for additional funding. He was due to meet Tenet in two days' time.

By lunchtime on that terrible Tuesday, Ahmed's schedule had been cleared for him to join Tenet at Langley. For the rest of the day, Ahmed briefed the CIA director and his senior staff on the links between bin-Laden and China. It matched everything Junping had earlier said during his debriefing. Ahmed told him that China had made a decisive decision: It was prepared to infuriate

America and its allies in supporting bin-Laden and the Taliban because Afghanistan fitted into China's own long-term strategic plans.

Hours later, Tenet received a coded "red alert" message from the Mossad's Tel Aviv headquarters. The CIA chief was presented with what he called a "worse case scenario" that Tenet had always feared — that China would use a ruthless surrogate to attack the United States.

In his first briefing to President Bush, Tenet predicted that China would refuse to support any military action against Afghanistan. Part of the reason stemmed from Beijing's fury over the American bombing of the Chinese embassy in Belgrade in 1999, during the war against Serbia, and the loss of the Chinese fighter plane during the spy plane "incident" the previous April.

Three days later, on Friday, September 14, President Bush received a telephone call from China's President, Jiang Zemin, to express China's formal regret over the attack on America. The call came long after all other world leaders had hurried to express not only their horror, but support in taking decisive action against bin-Laden and Afghanistan.

Jiang Zemin, however, had a message for Bush. Through a translator he made it clear that China would find itself in a *"difficult situation, given our well-known position of opposing any interference in the internal affairs of any country."*

Washington sources later said that Bush *"gritted his teeth and said he would move without China's blessing."*

So it would prove.

But the war on terrorism would be long and costly. It would be waged on an unknowable scale and duration. It would not be made easier by the mythology that would arise about the origins of the war. It would be a war where the role of public opinion would prove to be as important as technological power. It would be a war on not only a relatively small group of fanatics supported by a small number of clearly identifiable states: Iraq, Libya, Algeria among them.

It would be a war that would test Bush's entire relationship with China. To succeed he would have to put aside all he had previously thought and recognize that China has grown contemptuous at the softness of America and its allies. That is why China had calculated in the first place that by supporting the Taliban, a group of religious zealots, it could escape retribution itself.

It is a cliché that truth is the first casualty of war. But the inescapable truth is that the CIA's *Global Trends to the Year 2015* is a powerful reminder that the further the world is from the last outrage, the closer it is to the next. And, on all the evidence available, China is the ultimate perpetrator.

President Bush will have to consider a number of issues that a decade ago did not face his father when he confronted Saddam Hussein in that memorable image of a line drawn in the Iraqi sands. In the Persian Gulf War Saudi Arabia, Kuwait and Japan paid most of the bill, well over $100 billion.

But Bush's declared war on global terrorism did not show any immediate indications of who would finance it, apart from the United States. In part this may be because Bush did not spell out for his European and Middle East allies how he intended to wage not only his war against terrorism, but how he also intended to deal with equally important other conflicts: the continuing Arab-Israeli dispute; the equally serious one in Kashmir that could trigger an open conflict again between Pakistan and India; to lift sanctions against both countries may well be a short-term solution that could rebound, given that Pakistan and India have a nuclear capability and would use it. There is also a price to pay for Turkey's support, a rescue plan that would run to the end of the next decade and be a further drain on America's finance. There is also the huge bill, running at hundreds of million dollars a day, to maintain military deployment in the Persian Gulf and Southwest Asia.

And, once the issue of bin-Laden was laid to rest, there was the need for President Bush to define what he actually intended in his speech to Congress, with that carefully crafted threat: "From this day onward, any nation which continues to harbor and support terrorism will be regarded by the United States as a hostile regime."

If those words were merely intended to try and persuade Saddam Hussein of Iraq, the ayatollahs of Iran or the Assad dynasty in Syria to renounce terrorism, then the Bush Administration will find they have seriously miscalculated; those regimes, and others like them, have been strengthened by decades of war and support of terrorism. The present evidence is that it will remain so.

Osama bin-Laden and all those like him have spawned a whole generation of future terrorists. Over 15,000 of them have been trained in Afghanistan alone. They are now scattered across the globe. In all, intelligence services suggest there may be as many as 500,000 well-trained and totally ruthless terrorists, tutored in the use of nuclear, chemical and biological weapons, scattered around the European Community and North America.

In turn they have trained other terrorists. In turn they will themselves train others. It is an endless cycle of well-financed terrorism the like of which the world has not seen.

A substantial portion of the money to achieve this comes out of China. Only sustained American leadership and matching amounts of foreign aid can in the end combat this. But even then there is no certainty. That is the grim forecast as this book goes to press.

Global Trends 2015:

The Middle East
Global trends from demography and natural resources to globalization and governance appear generally negative for the Middle East. Most regimes are change-resistant. Many are buoyed by continuing energy revenues and will not be inclined to make the necessary reforms, including in basic education, to change this unfavorable picture.

- Linear trend analysis shows little positive change in the region, raising the prospects for increased demographic pressures, social unrest, religious and ideological extremism, and terrorism directed both at the regimes and at their Western supporters.

- Nonlinear developments—such as the sudden rise of a Web-connected opposition, a sharp and sustained economic downturn, or, conversely, the emergence of enlightened leaders committed to good governance—might change outcomes in individual countries. Political changes in Iran in the late 1990s are an example of such nonlinear development.

China
Estimates of developments in China over the next 15 years are fraught with unknowables. Working against China's aspirations to sustain economic growth while preserving its political system is an array of political, social, and economic pressures that will increasingly challenge the regime's legitimacy, and perhaps its survival.

- The sweeping structural changes required by China's entry into the World Trade Organization (WTO) and the broader demands of economic globalization and the information revolution will generate significantly new levels and types of social and economic disruption that will only add to an already wide range of domestic and international problems.

Nevertheless, China need not be overwhelmed by these problems. China has proven politically resilient, economically dynamic, and increasingly assertive in positioning itself for a leadership role in East Asia. Its long-term military program in particular suggests that Beijing wants to have the capability to achieve its territorial objectives, outmatch its neighbors, and constrain US power in the region.

- We do not rule out the introduction of enough political reform by 2015 to allow China to adapt to domestic pressure for change and to continue to grow economically.

Two conditions, in the view of many specialists, would lead to a major security challenge for the United States and its allies in the region: a weak, disintegrating China, or an assertive China willing to use its growing economic wealth and military capabilities to pursue its strategic advantage in the region. These opposite extremes bound a more commonly held view among experts that China will continue to see peace as essential to its economic growth and internal stability.

Russia
Between now and 2015, Moscow will be challenged even more than today to adjust its expectations for world leadership to its dramatically reduced resources. Whether the country can make the transition in adjusting ends to means remains an open and critical question, according to most experts, as does the question of the character and quality of Russian governance and economic policies. The most likely outcome is a Russia that remains internally weak and institutionally linked to the international system primarily through its permanent seat on the UN Security Council. In this view, whether Russia can adjust to this diminished status in a manner that preserves rather than upsets regional stability is also uncertain. The stakes for both Europe

Future Conflict

Through 2015, internal conflicts will pose the most frequent threat to stability around the world. Interstate wars, though less frequent, will grow in lethality due to the availability of more destructive technologies. The international community will have to deal with the military, political, and economic dimensions of the rise of China and India and the continued decline of Russia.

Internal Conflicts

Many internal conflicts, particularly those arising from communal disputes, will continue to be vicious, long-lasting and difficult to terminate—leaving bitter legacies in their wake.

- They frequently will spawn internal displacements, refugee flows, humanitarian emergencies, and other regionally destabilizing dislocations.

- If left to fester, internal conflicts will trigger spillover into inter-state conflicts as neighboring states move to exploit opportunities for gain or to limit the possibilities of damage to their national interests.

- Weak states will spawn recurrent internal conflicts, threatening the stability of a globalizing international system.

Internal conflicts stemming from state repression, religious and ethnic grievances, increasing migration pressures, and/or indigenous protest movements will occur most frequently in Sub-Saharan Africa, the Caucasus and Central Asia, and parts of south and southeast Asia, Central America and the Andean region.

The United Nations and several regional organizations will continue to be called upon to manage some internal conflicts because major states—stressed by domestic concerns, perceived risk of failure, lack of political will, or tight resources—will wish to minimize their direct involvement. When, however, some Western governments, international and regional organizations, and civil-society groups press for outside military intervention in certain internal conflicts, they will be opposed by such states as China, India, Russia and many developing countries that will tend to view interventions as dangerous precedents challenging state sovereignty.

Transnational Terrorism

States with poor governance; ethnic, cultural, or religious tensions; weak economies; and porous borders will be prime breeding grounds for terrorism. In such states, domestic groups will challenge the entrenched government, and transnational networks seeking safehavens.

Bombed US Embassy in Nairobi

At the same time, the trend away from state-supported political terrorism and toward more diverse, free-wheeling, transnational networks—enabled by information technology—will continue. Some of the states that actively sponsor terrorism or terrorist groups today may decrease or even cease their support by 2015 as a result of regime changes, rapprochement with neighbors, or the conclusion that terrorism has become counterproductive. But weak states also could drift toward cooperation with terrorists, creating defacto new state supporters.

- Between now and 2015 terrorist tactics will become increasingly sophisticated and designed to achieve mass casualties. We expect the trend toward greater lethality in terrorist attacks to continue.

Current World Illicit Trafficking

Criminal Organizations and Networks
Over the next 15 years, transnational criminal organizations will become increasingly adept at exploiting the global diffusion of sophisticated information, financial, and transportation networks.

Criminal organizations and networks based in North America, Western Europe, China, Colombia, Israel, Japan, Mexico, Nigeria, and Russia will expand the scale and scope of their activities. They will form loose alliances with one another, with smaller criminal entrepreneurs, and with insurgent movements for specific operations. They will corrupt leaders of unstable, economically fragile or failing states, insinuate themselves into troubled banks and businesses, and cooperate with insurgent political movements to control substantial geographic areas. Their income will come from narcotics trafficking; alien smuggling; trafficking in women and children; smuggling toxic materials, hazardous wastes, illicit arms, military technologies, and other contraband; financial fraud; and racketeering.

- The risk will increase that organized criminal groups will traffic in nuclear, biological, or chemical weapons. The degree of risk depends on whether governments with WMD capabilities can or will control such weapons and materials.

Crime and Corruption Pay

Available data suggest that current annual revenues from illicit criminal activities include: $100-300 billion from narcotics trafficking; $10-12 billion from toxic and other hazardous waste dumping; $9 billion from automobile theft in the United States and Europe; $7 billion from alien smuggling; and as much as $1 billion from theft of intellectual property through pirating of videos, software, and other commodities.

Available estimates suggest that corruption costs about $500 billion—or about 1 percent of global GNP— in slower growth, reduced foreign investment, and lower profits. For example, the average cost of bribery to firms doing business in Russia is between 4 and 8 percent of annual revenue, according to the European Bank for Reconstruction and Development.

Changing Communal Identities and Networks
Traditional communal groups—whether religious or ethnic-linguistic groups—will pose a range of challenges for governance. Using opportunities afforded by globalization and the opening of civil society, communal groups will be better positioned to mobilize coreligionists or ethnic kin to assert their interests or defend against perceived economic or political discrimination. Ethnic diasporas and coreligionists abroad also will be more able and willing to provide fraternal groups with political, financial, and other support.

- By 2015, Christianity and Islam, the two largest religious groupings, will have grown significantly. Both are widely dispersed in several continents, already use information technologies to "spread the faith," and draw on adherents to fund numerous nonprofit groups and political causes. Activist components of these and other religious groupings will emerge to contest such issues as genetic manipulation, women's rights, and the income gap between rich and poor. A wider religious or spiritual movement also may emerge, possibly linked to environmental values.

Criminal Networks and New Technologies

Estimates of the number of distinct ethnic-linguistic groups at the beginning of the twenty-first century run from 2,000 to 5,000, ranging from small bands living in isolated areas to larger groups living in ancestral homelands or in diasporas. Most of the world's 191 states are ethnically heterogeneous, and many contain ethnic populations with co-ethnics in neighboring states. By 2015, ethnic heterogeneity will increase in almost all states, as a result of international migration and divergent birthrates of migrant and native populations.

Interstate Conflicts

Over the next 15 years, the international system will have to adjust to changing power relationships in key regions:

- **China's potential**. Estimates of China beyond five years are fraught with unknowables. Some projections indicate that Chinese power will rise because of the growth of its economic and military capabilities. Other projections indicate that the array of political, social, and economic pressures will increasingly challenge the stability and legitimacy of the regime. Most assessments today argue that China will seek to avoid conflict in the region to promote stable economic growth and to ensure internal stability. A strong China, others assert, would seek to adjust regional power arrangements to its advantage, risking conflict with neighbors and some powers external to the region. A weak China would increase prospects for criminality, narcotics trafficking, illegal migration, WMD proliferation, and widespread social instability.

- **Russia's decline**. By 2015, Russia will be challenged even more than today to adjust its expectations for world leadership to the dramatically reduced resources it will have to play that role. The quality of Russian governance is an open question as is whether the country will be able to make the transition in a manner that preserves rather than upsets regional stability.

- **Japan's uncertainty**. In the view of many experts, Japan will have difficulty maintaining its current position as the world's third largest economy by 2015. Tokyo has so far not shown a willingness to carry through the painful economic reforms necessary to slow the erosion of its leadership role in Asia. In the absence of an external shock, Japan is similarly unlikely to accelerate changes in security policy.

- **India's prospects**. India will strengthen its role as a regional power, but many uncertainties about the effects of global trends on its society cast doubt on how far India will go. India faces growing extremes between wealth and poverty, a mixed picture on natural resources, and problems with internal governance.

Current Ethnic Diversity States

The changing dynamics of state power will combine with other factors to affect the risk of conflict in various regions. Changing military capabilities will be prominent among the factors that determine the risk of war. In South Asia, for example, that risk will remain fairly high over the next 15 years. India and Pakistan are both prone to miscalculation. Both will continue to build up their nuclear and missile forces.

India most likely will expand the size of its nuclear-capable force. **Pakistan's** nuclear and missile forces also will continue to increase. Islamabad has publicly claimed that the number of nuclear weapons and missiles it deploys will be based on "minimum" deterrence and will be independent of the size of India's arsenal. A noticeable increase in the size of India's arsenal, however, would prompt Pakistan to further increase the size of its own arsenal.

Russia will be unable to maintain conventional forces that are both sizable and modern or to project significant military power with conventional means. The Russian military will increasingly rely on its shrinking strategic and theater nuclear arsenals to deter or, if deterrence fails, to counter large-scale conventional assaults on Russian territory.

- Moscow will maintain as many strategic missiles and associated nuclear warheads as it believes it can afford but well short of START I or II limitations. The total Russian force by 2015, including air launched cruise missiles, probably will be below 2,500 warheads.

As Russia struggles with the constraints on its ambitions, it will invest scarce resources in selected and secretive military technology programs, especially WMD, hoping to counter Western conventional and strategic superiority in areas such as ballistic missile defense.

China's People's Liberation Army (PLA) will remain the world's largest military, but the majority of the force will not be fully modernized by 2015. China could close the technological gap with the West in one or more major weapons systems. China's capability for regional military operations is likely to improve significantly by 2015.

- China will be exploiting advanced weapons and production technologies acquired from abroad—Russia, Israel, Europe, Japan, and the United States—that will enable it to integrate naval and air capabilities against Taiwan and potential adversaries in the South China Sea.

- In the event of a peaceful resolution of the Taiwan issue, some of China's military objectives—such as protecting the sea lanes for Persian Gulf oil—could become more congruent with those of the United States. Nevertheless, as an emerging regional power, China would continue to expand its influence without regard to US interests.

- China by 2015 will have deployed tens to several tens of missiles with nuclear warheads targeted against the United States, mostly more survivable land- and sea-based mobile missiles. It also will have hundreds of shorter-range ballistic and cruise missiles for use in regional conflicts. Some of these shorter-range missiles will have nuclear warheads; most will be armed with conventional warheads.

China: How to Think About Its Growing Wealth and Power

China has been riding the crest of a significant wave of economic growth for two decades. Many experts assess that China can maintain a growth rate of 7 percent or more for many years. Such impressive rates provide a foundation for military potential, and some predict that China's rapid economic growth will lead to a significant increase in military capabilities. But the degree to which an even more powerful economy would translate into greater military power is uncertain.

The relationship between economic growth and China's overall power will derive from the priorities of leaders in Beijing—provided the regime remains stable. China's leaders have assessed for some years that comprehensive national power derives both from economic strength and from the military and diplomatic resources that a healthy, large economy makes possible. They apparently agree that, for the foreseeable future, such priorities as agricultural and national infrastructure modernization must take precedence over military development. In the absence of a strong national security challenge, this view is unlikely to change even as new leaders emerge in Beijing. In a stable environment, two leadership transitions will occur in China between now and 2015. The evidence strongly suggests that the new leaders will be even more firmly committed to developing the economy as the foundation of national power and that resources for military capabilities will take a secondary role. Existing priorities and projected defense allocations could enable the PLA to emerge as the most powerful regional military force.

- Beyond resource issues, China faces daunting challenges in producing defense systems. Beijing has yet to demonstrate an assured capacity to translate increasingly sophisticated science and technology advances into first-rate military production. To achieve this, China must effect reforms in its State Owned Enterprises (SOEs), develop a capacity for advanced systems integration skills, and recruit and retain technologically sophisticated officers and

Japan has a small but modern military force, more able than any other in Asia to integrate large quantities of new weaponry. Japan's future military strength will reflect the state of its economy and the health of its security relationship with the United States. Tokyo will increasingly pursue greater autonomy in security matters and develop security enhancements, such as defense improvements and more active diplomacy, to supplement the US alliance.

A unified Korea with a significant US military presence may become a regional military power.

For the next 10 to 15 years, however, knowledgeable observers suggest that the process of unification will consume **South Korea's** energies and resources.

Absent unification, **North Korea's** WMD capabilities will continue to cloud regional stability. P'yongyang probably has one, possibly two, nuclear weapons. It has developed medium-range missiles for years and has tested a three-stage space launch vehicle.

P'yongyang may improve the accuracy, range, and payload capabilities of its Taepo Dong-2 ICBM, deploy variants, or develop more capable systems. North Korea could have a few to several Taepo Dong-2 type missiles deployed by 2005.

In the **Middle East**, the confluence of domestic economic pressures and regional rivalries is likely to further the proliferation of weapons of mass destruction and the means to deliver them. By contrast, spending on conventional arms probably will remain stable or decline in most countries. Some governments may maintain large armed forces to absorb otherwise unemployable youths, but such armies will be less well trained and equipped. Rather than conventional war, the region is likely to experience more terrorism, insurgencies, and humanitarian emergencies arising from internal disparities or disputes over ethnic or religious identity.

- **Iran** sees its short- and medium-range missiles as deterrents, as force-multiplying weapons of war, primarily with conventional warheads, and as options for delivering biological, chemical, and eventually nuclear weapons. Iran could test an IRBM or land-attack cruise missile by 2004 and perhaps even an ICBM or space launch vehicle as early as 2001.

- **Iraq's** ability to obtain WMD will be influenced, in part, by the degree to which the UN Security Council can impede development or procurement over the next 15 years. Under some scenarios, Iraq could test an ICBM capable of delivering nuclear-sized payloads to the United States before 2015; foreign assistance would affect the capabilities of the missile and the time it became available. Iraq could also develop a nuclear weapon during this period.

Reacting to US Military Superiority

Experts agree that the United States, with its decisive edge in both information and weapons technology, will remain the dominant military power during the next 15 years. Further bolstering the strong position of the United States are its unparalleled economic power, its university system, and its investment in research and development—half of the total spent annually by the advanced industrial world. Many potential adversaries, as reflected in doctrinal writings and statements, see US military concepts, together with technology, as giving the United States the ability to expand its lead in conventional warfighting capabilities.

This perception among present and potential adversaries will continue to generate the pursuit of asymmetric capabilities against US forces and interests abroad as well as the territory of the United States. US opponents—state and such nonstate actors as drug lords, terrorists, and foreign insurgents—will not want to engage the US military on its terms. They will choose instead political and military strategies designed to dissuade the United States from using force, or, if the United States does use force, to exhaust American will, circumvent or minimize US strengths, and exploit perceived US weaknesses. Asymmetric challenges can arise across the spectrum of conflict that will confront US forces in a theater of operations or on US soil.

Central Asia: Regional Hot Spot?

The interests of Russia, China, and India—as well as of Iran and Turkey—will intersect in Central Asia; the states of that region will attempt to balance those powers as well as keep the United States and the West engaged to prevent their domination by an outside power. The greatest danger to the region, however, will not be a conflict between states, which is unlikely, but the corrosive impact of communal conflicts and politicial insurgencies, possibly abetted by outside actors and financed at least in part by narcotraffickers.

It is also generally recognized that the United States and other developed countries will continue to possess the political, economic, military, and technological advantages—including through National Missile and Theater Missile Defense systems—to reduce the gains of adversaries from lateral or "side-wise" technological improvements to their capabilities.

Threats to Critical Infrastructure. Some potential adversaries will seek ways to threaten the US homeland. The US national infrastructure—communications, transportation, financial transactions, energy networks—is vulnerable to disruption by physical and electronic attack because of its interdependent nature and by cyber attacks because of their dependence on computer networks. Foreign governments and groups will seek to exploit such vulnerabilities using conventional munitions, information operations, and even WMD. Over time, such attacks increasingly are likely to be delivered by computer networks rather than by conventional munitions, as the affinity for cyber attacks and the skill of US adversaries in employing them evolve. Cyber attacks will provide both state and nonstate adversaries new options for action against the United States beyond mere words but short of physical attack—strategic options that include selection of either nonlethal or lethal damage and the prospect of anonymity.

Information Operations. In addition to threatening the US national infrastructure, adversaries will seek to attack US military capabilities through electronic warfare, psychological operations, denial and deception, and the use of new technologies such as directed energy weapons or electromagnetic pulse weapons. The primary purpose would be to deny US forces information superiority, to prevent US weapons from working, and to undermine US domestic support for US actions. Adversaries also are likely to use cyber attacks to complicate US power projection in an era of decreasing permanent US military presence abroad by seeking to disrupt military networks during deployment operations—when they are most stressed. Many countries have programs to develop such technologies; few have the foresight or capability to fully integrate these various tools into a comprehensive attack. But they could develop such capabilities over the next decade and beyond.

Terrorism. Much of the terrorism noted earlier will be directed at the United States and its overseas interests. Most anti-US terrorism will be based on perceived ethnic, religious or cultural grievances. Terrorist groups will continue to find ways to attack US military and diplomatic facilities abroad. Such attacks are likely to expand increasingly to include US companies and American citizens. Middle East and Southwest Asian-based terrorists are the most likely to threaten the United States.

Weapons of Mass Destruction. WMD programs reflect the motivations and intentions of the governments that produce them and, therefore, can be altered by the change of a regime or by a regime's change of view. Linear projections of WMD are intended to assess what the picture will look like if changes in motivations and intentions do not occur.

Short- and medium-range ballistic missiles, particularly if armed with WMD, already pose a significant threat overseas to US interests, military forces, and allies. By 2015, the United States, barring major political changes in these countries, will face ICBM threats from North Korea, probably from Iran, and possibly from Iraq, in addition to long-standing threats from Russia and China.

- Weapons development programs, in many cases fueled by foreign assistance, have led to new capabilities—as illustrated by Iran's Shahab-3 launches in 1998 and 2000 and North Korea's Taepo Dong-1 space launch attempt in August 1998. In addition, some countries that have been traditional recipients of missile technologies have become exporters.

- Sales of ICBMs or space launch vehicles, which have inherent ICBM capabilities, could further increase the number of countries that will be able to threaten the United States with a missile strike.

The probability that a **missile armed with WMD** would be used against US forces or interests is higher today than during most of the Cold War and will continue to grow. The emerging missile threats will be mounted by countries possessing considerably fewer missiles with far less accuracy, yield, survivability, reliability, and range-payload capability than the strategic forces of the Soviet Union. North Korea's space launch attempt in 1998 demonstrated that P'yongyang is seeking a long-range missile capability that could be used against US forces and interests abroad and against US territory itself. Moreover, many of the countries developing longer-range missiles assess that the mere **threat** of their use would complicate US crisis decisionmaking and potentially would deter Washington from pursuing certain objectives.

Other means to deliver WMD against the United States will emerge, some cheaper and more reliable and accurate than early-generation ICBMs. The likelihood of an attack by these means is greater than that of a WMD attack with an ICBM. The goal of the adversary would be to move the weapon within striking distance by using short- and medium-range missiles deployed on surface ships or covert missions using military special operations forces or state intelligence services. Non-missile delivery means, however, do not provide the same prestige, deterrence, and coercive diplomacy associated with ICBMs.

WMD Proliferation and the Potential for Unconventional Warfare and Escalation

The risks of escalation inherent in direct armed conflict will be magnified by the availability of WMD; consequently, proliferation will tend to spur a reversion to prolonged, lower-level conflict by other means: intimidation, subversion, terrorism, proxies, and guerrilla operations. This trend already is evident between Israel and some of its neighbors and between India and Pakistan. In the event of war, urban fighting will be typical and consequently, civilian casualties will be high relative to those among combatants. Technology will count for less, and large, youthful, and motivated populations for more. Exploitation of communal divisions within an adversary's civil populations will be seen as a key to winning such conflicts—increasing their bitterness and thereby prolonging them.

Chemical and biological threats to the United States will become more widespread; such capabilities are easier to develop, hide, and deploy than nuclear weapons. Some terrorists or insurgents will attempt to use such weapons against US interests—against the United States itself, its forces or facilities overseas, or its allies. Moreover, the United States would be affected by the use of such weapons anywhere in the world because Washington would be called on to help contain the damage and to provide scientific expertise and economic assistance to deal with the effects. Such weapons could be delivered through a variety of means, including missiles, unmanned aerial vehicles, or covertly via land, air, and sea.

Trends in Global Defense Spending and Armaments

Defense-related technologies will advance rapidly over the next 15 years—particularly precision weapons, information systems and communications. The development and integrated application of these technologies will occur mostly in the advanced countries, particularly the United States. Given the high costs and complexity of technical and operational integration, few nations will assign high priority to the indigenous development of such military technology.

- Non-US global defense spending has dropped some 50 percent since the late 1980s. "Military modernization accounts, particularly procurement, have been hit hard.

- The global arms market has decreased by more than 50 percent during the same period.

- Indications are that global defense spending may be recovering from mid-1990s lows; part of East Asia, for example, could experience rises in defense spending over the next decade, but, overall, long-term spending patterns are uncertain.

Over the past decade, a slow but persistent transformation has occurred in the arms procurement strategies of states. Many states are attempting to diversify sources of arms for reasons that vary from fears of arms embargoes, to declining defense budgets, or to a desire to acquire limited numbers of cutting-edge technologies. Their efforts include developing a mix of indigenous production; codeveloping, coproducing, or licensing production; purchasing entire weapon systems; or leasing capabilities. At the same time, many arms-producing states, confronted with declining domestic arms needs but determined to maintain defense industries, are commercializing defense production and aggressively expanding arms exports.

Together, the above factors suggest:

Technology diffusion to those few states with a motivation to arm and the economic resources to do so will accelerate as weapons and militarily relevant technologies are moved rapidly and routinely across national borders in response to increasingly commercial rather than security calculations. For such militarily related technologies as the Global Positioning System, satellite imagery, and communications, **technological superiority will be difficult to maintain for very long**. In an environment of broad technological diffusion, nonmaterial elements of military power—strategy, doctrine, and training—will increase in importance over the next 15 years in deciding combat outcomes.

Export regimes and sanctions will be difficult to manage and less effective in controlling arms and weapons technology transfers. The resultant proliferation of WMD and long-range delivery systems would be destabilizing and increase the risk of miscalculation and conflict that produces high casualties.

Advantages will go to states that have a strong commercial technology sector and develop effective ways to link these capabilities to their national defense industrial base. States able to optimize private and public sector linkages could achieve significant advancements in weapons systems.

The twin developments outlined above—constrained defense spending worldwide combined with increasing military technological potential—preclude accurate forecasts of which technologies, in what quantity and form, will be incorporated in the military systems of future adversaries. In many cases, the question will not be which technologies provide the greatest military potential but which will receive the political backing and resources to reach the procurement and fielding stage. Moreover, civilian technology development already is driving military technology development in many countries.

Worldwide Adherents of Selected Major World Religions, Mid-1998

Communal tensions, sometimes culminating in conflict, probably will increase through 2015. In addition to some ongoing communal frictions that will persist, triggers of new tensions will include:

- **Repression by the state.** States with slow economic growth, and/or where executive power is concentrated in an exclusionary political elite and the rule of law and civil or minority rights are weak, will be inclined to discriminate against communal minorities. Such conditions will foment ethnic tensions in Sub-Saharan Africa, Central and South Asia, and parts of the Middle East, often in rapidly growing urban areas. Certain powerful states—such as Russia, China, Brazil, and India—also are likely to repress politicized communal minorities.

- **Religious, often fused with ethnic, grievances.** Few Muslim states will grant full political and cultural rights to religious minorities. At the same time, they will not remain indifferent to the treatment of Muslim minorities elsewhere: in Russia, Indonesia, India/Kashmir, China, and the Balkans. Other religious denominations also will support beleaguered coreligionists.

- **Resistance to migration.** Some relatively homogenous countries or sub-regions in Asia and Europe will resist ethnically diverse migrants, creating tensions.

- **Indigenous protest movements.** Such movements will increase, facilitated by transnational networks of indigenous rights activists and supported by well-funded international human rights and environmental groups. Tensions will intensify in the area from Mexico through the Amazon region; northeastern India; and the Malaysian-Indonesian archipelago.

Overall Impact on States

The developed democracies will be best positioned for good governance because they will tend to empower legitimate nonstate actors in both the for-profit and nonprofit sectors; will favor institutions and processes that accommodate divergent communal groups; will press for transparency in government and the efficient delivery of public services; and will maintain institutions to regulate legitimate for-profit and nonprofit organizations and control illegitimate criminal groups. Countries in Western Europe, Canada, Australia, New Zealand, and Japan have the requisite agility and institutions to meet the challenges. Countries in Eastern Europe as well as Turkey, South Korea, India, Chile, and Brazil, among other developing countries, are moving in these directions, despite some continuing obstacles.

Some newly democratic states and modernizing authoritarian states will have leaders amenable to technological change and access to substantial human and financial resources. They will encourage business firms, nonprofits, and communal groups supportive of the government and discourage or suppress those that are independent-minded or critical of government policies. They will have some success in coping with the energy, ideas, and resources of nonstate actors. Several Asian countries, such as Singapore, Taiwan, and perhaps China, as well as some states in the Middle East and Latin America are likely to take this approach.

Other states in varying degrees will lack the resources and leadership to achieve effective governance. Most autocratic states in the Middle East and Africa will not have the institutions or cultural orientation to exploit the opportunities provided by nonstate actors—apart from certain forms of humanitarian assistance. In many of these countries, nonstate actors will become more important than governments in providing services, such as health clinics and schools. In the weakest of these countries, communal, criminal, or terrorist groups will seek control of government institutions and/or territory.

Overall, the number of states—which has more than tripled since 1945 and has grown 20 percent since 1990—is likely to increase at a slower rate through 2015. This growth will result from remaining cases of decolonization and to communal tensions leading to state secession, most likely in Sub-Saharan Africa, Central Asia, and Indonesia. In some cases, new states will inspire other secessionist movements, destabilizing countries where minorities were not initially seeking secession.

EXPLANATIONS

Early in my career I had the good fortune to work for two of the great editors of modern journalism, Arthur Christiansen of the *Daily Express,* then Britain's foremost mass-circulation newspaper, and Ed Thompson of the *Reader's Digest.* Both were absolutely firm about always using two sources for an important fact, and both believed that attributed reactions such as "felt," "sensed," "thought," "understood," or "believed," must accurately reflect the particular portion of the interview being written up.

Ken Auletta, another veteran of our business — the re-creation of historical events after the dust has settled — has synthesized the whole complex question of primary and secondary sources, on- and off-the-record conversations, and describing an event through the use of unpublished documents, letters, diaries, and file notes. Auletta has written that *"no reporter can with 100 percent accuracy re-create events that occurred some time before. Memories play tricks on participants, the more so when the outcome has become clearer. A reporter tries to guard against inaccuracies by checking with a variety of sources."*

Luckily for me, the time frame of the story comes when the memory is still clear. That is why a few of those who were directly involved asked for guarantees that their identities would be suitably protected for professional or personal reasons; in some cases the reminder of their experiences still traumatizes them. Those persons chose the identities by which they wished to be known in the text. Cassy Jones and Sue Tung were two who did. Their decision in no way diminishes the honesty of their eyewitness accounts.

In all, some 240 hours of taped testimony were taken.

Immediately after the massacre, interviews were conducted in China, Hong Kong, the United States, and Europe between June and October 1989. Follow-up interviews by telephone and correspondence took place between December 1989 and February 1990. In all some one hundred persons, the vast majority eyewitnesses, were spoken to either directly by me or by researchers acting on my behalf.

All serving intelligence officers insisted they would only speak off-tape and without direct attribution. This is an accepted form of briefing by them, though a word of explanation will perhaps be helpful.

In 1986 I interviewed the late William Casey, then director of the Central Intelligence Agency. We met at the International Club in Washington, D.C., on Friday, March 21, and at the same venue four days later. Casey said he would "mark my card" on how to deal with him and anyone else in the U.S. intelligence community. All information they supplied must be written up as "background," a catch-all phrase that means information provided can be fully used, but not directly attributed.

It worked for the project I was researching at the time; it has continued to do so for this book. Long before Casey's guidance, when I was reporting on intelligence matters for the *Daily Express,* the *Sunday Express,* and the Press Association, Britain's major wire service, I had never subscribed to the canard that intelligence services constantly spend their time and money creating stories to deceive journalists and authors. While all agencies spread disinformation among the more gullible in any profession, they do not do so all the time.

The contribution of the diplomatic community in Beijing is generally acknowledged throughout the text; a few diplomats asked to speak off the record, fearing that direct attribution could embarrass their governments. Special thanks are due to Brian Davidson, Brendan Ward, and Susan Morton. They gave freely of their time and experiences.

A word of similar thanks is due to the martial law authorities in Beijing. They turned out to be surprisingly willing to state their side of the story, that "rebellion" had been in full cry and that the People's Liberation Army had no alternative but to intervene. To support that view, the Chinese authorities provided me with a pass allowing me to visit Tiananmen Square when it was still a proscribed area. There I interviewed Captain Instructor Jyan, company commander Tan Yaobang, and the young PLA soldier, Bing Yang. I was also given a conducted tour of the National Military Academy in the western suburbs of the city, various PLA bases in and around Beijing, and, most gratifying of all, a short visit to Zhongnanhai. At all times the PLA provided translators, and I have no reason to think they were less than accurate in putting my questions and translating the answers.

From April until June 1989, the story was front-page news on every major newspaper around the world. Some of the best reporting was in the *New York Times;* the *South China Morning Post;* and the other Hong Kong-based English-language daily, *The Standard.* However, anxious to obtain a spread of the coverage, I compiled chronologies from the *Los Angeles Times, Washington Post,* and *San Francisco Chronicle.* From Britain I collated the reporting of the *Sunday Times,* the *Independent,* the *Guardian,* the *Daily Telegraph,* the *Times,* and the *Independent on Sunday.*

I was especially drawn to the reporting of Louise Branson of the *Sunday Times,* London, and I express my gratitude for her generosity in making available to me her original stories and background notes for the period. They provided a revealing and invaluable insight.

In assessing the value of what was published, I used the guidelines of that most estimable of investigative authors, William Manchester.

He has written that the only way to successfully approach our kind of work is to accept that no one can ever root out the truth, the whole truth, and nothing but the truth. That is a game lawyers play, and as Bill says, *"there is something touching about their naive assumption, that we get the full story by putting a man under oath. In practice, you get very little of it. Anxious not to perjure himself, the witness volunteers as little as possible. The author, with his tape recorder, or shorthand notebook, gets a great deal more chaff, but in the long run, he harvests more wheat too."*

Once more, so it was for me.

As so often in the past, colleagues proved accommodating. The Press Association, for which I am a special news features correspondent, a post that allows me to cover stories anywhere in the world, extended my beat to include China. I owe David Staveley and Neal Williams, my editors at the PA, a great deal for their support during those months I spent in the field. Through them my reports from China received wide distribution.

In the end, however, it was colleagues in China who made the book work. First and foremost, I must thank Melinda Liu of *Newsweek*. In the late summer of 1989 she found time in her hectic schedule to sit down with me for a series of lengthy taped interviews. She also provided copies of all her original stories and the telex traffic between her and her editors. Jeanne Moore of the *China Daily* was also a prime source. She gave a lengthy interview, then made available the deeply moving diary she had kept during those fifty-five days in Beijing. Several other Chinese journalists in the city spoke long and frankly, in return for guarantees of anonymity. The book owes much to them.

I also gratefully acknowledge the invaluable help of Barr Seitz. His testimony proved to be that cliché come true, a real treasure trove. He had a born reporter's eye for detail. And his astonishing memory was reinforced by his diary.

In Hong Kong, I was repeatedly helped by Nelson K. Fung, manager of the Broadcast Department at Hill & Knowlton, the international consultancy and public relations agency. His colleague, Gordon Chan, senior consultant in Corporate and Government Affairs at the agency, was another valuable source. Deborah Biker, head of the same agency's Creative Services Division, provided unlimited access to news footage and media coverage from China, Japan, Korea, and Indian sources, little of which has surfaced in the West.

Many of the interviews with students who had managed to escape to Hong Kong were conducted in the colony's Kowloon Hotel during September and October 1989. I was greatly assisted by the translations of Suzanne Chan, Tan Li, and, briefly, Gali Kronenberg.

But my greatest support was David Jensen, a former White House correspondent. David still has his tabs on Washington, and time and again he pointed me in the right direction, not only around Capitol Hill, but around the Pacific Rim. He probably has as many good contacts there as any working journalist. Quite simply, without him this book would not have been written.

NOTES

1. THE THIRD MILLENNIUM

This chapter is based on interviews with William Hamilton, President of Inslaw; Ari Ben-Menashe, former adviser of counter-terrorism to the Israeli government; Rafi Eitan, former Director of Operations of Mossad; General Meir Amit, former director-general of Mossad; various serving officers in the CIA who asked not to be named; members of a number of Chinese organizations involved in the battle to bring democracy to their country. Again, for obvious reasons, they requested anonymity.

2. THE TIANANMEN TRUMP

This chapter is based upon an interview conducted by the author with Jeanne Moore and on articles in the *New York Times,* Dec. 1, 1990; *Newsweek,* Jan. 6, 1990; *The Times* (London), Jan. 6, 1990; *Independent on Sunday,* Jan. 6, 13, 21, 1990.

3. SEEDS OF FIRE

For this chapter I have relied upon my interviews with Melinda Liu, Jeanne Moore, Brian Davidson, and members of the U.S. intelligence community.

4. ILLUSIONS

For "Illusions" I interviewed Cassy Jones, Jia Guangzu, Jenny Guangzu, and Li Yang, and relied on interviews by others of Wuerkaixi, Chai Ling, and Meili Chang. Additional sources were the *China Daily* (all issues for Oct.–Dec. 1989), the letters of Jenny Guangzu and Jia Guangzu, the diaries of Jenny Guangzu and Cassy Jones, and photos by Cassy Jones and Jenny Guangzu. Also helpful was the Emergency Action Plan for the City of Beijing, published by the mayor's office, Nov. 11, 1989.

5. SECRETS

Various members of the U.S. intelligence community in Washington, D.C., and Beijing were interviewed for this chapter; as well as Melinda Liu, Jeanne Moore, and Jenny Guangzu. James Laracco was also interviewed. Other sources were the diary of Jenny Guangzu, letters to Jenny Guangzu from her father, and a report by Laracco on the economic situation in China.

6. THE WATCH KEEPERS

This chapter was based on my interviews with Li Yang, Tan Yaobang, Kao Jyan, Zhang Zhen, General Bull, and Susan Morton, and interviews by others of Earl S. Drake, Gerard Chesnees, Nicholas Chapuis, and Charles Malo. Other sources were the *China Daily* (all issues for Oct.–Nov. 1988); the *South China Morning Post*, Dec. 10, 12, 1989; the *Standard*, Dec. 20, 1989; and *The Chinese Secret Service* by Richard Deacon (Grafton Books, 1989).

7. STATES OF MIND
For this chapter I relied upon my interviews with Shao-Yen Wang, Kao Jyan, Cassy Jones, and Sue Tung, and various members of the U.S. intelligence community. Other sources were the diary of Cassy Jones, letter of Sue Tung, and screenplay of Shao Yen Wang; the *Washington Post*, Nov. 22, 1988; and the *South China Morning Post*, Nov. 29, 1988.

8. THE ROOF OF THE WORLD
This chapter is based on my interviews with Li Yang, Tan Yaobang, Bing Yang, and Kao Hyan, and an interview by another of Liu Lee. Other sources were the *People's Daily*, Jan. 2, 1989; the *China Daily*, Jan. 7, 1989; and *The Chinese Secret Service* (Deacon).

9. PERSUASIONS
For "Persuasions" I interviewed Cassy Jones, Brendan Ward, Brian Davidson, and Li Yang, and relied on interviews by others of Liu Gang, Wuerkaixi, Ian McGuinness, and Fang Lizhi. Other sources were the *World Economic Herald* (all issues from Dec. 1, 1989–Feb. 1, 1990) and a letter from Fang Lizhi to Deng Xiaoping, Dec. 31, 1989.

10. CAMELOT, ALMOST
I based this chapter on my interviews with Jia Guangzu, Jenny Guangzu, and Cassy Jones, and on an interview of Li Zhao Hu. Other sources were the *People's Daily*, Jan. 6, 1989, and the *China Daily*, Jan. 6–7, 1989; letters between Jia and Jenny Guangzu; and *The Yellow Emperors' Classic of Internal Medicine* (Chinese Academy of Traditional Medicine).

11. PRESIDENTIAL PRAGMATISM
For this chapter I relied on my interviews with Cassy Jones, Li Yang, Barr Seitz, Melinda Liu, Jeanne Moore, and Bing Yang, and interviews by others of Wuerkaixi, Chai Ling, Qian Qichen, and Fang Lizhi. Other sources were the diaries of Cassy Jones and Jeanne Moore, the *China Daily*, Feb. 1–10, 1989, and the *People's Daily*, Feb. 1–10, 1989.

12. DEATH IN THE POLITBURO
I based this chapter on my interviews with Melinda Liu, Jeanne Moore, Barr Seitz, Jia Guangzu, Li Yang, Vladimir Troyanovsky, Brian Davidson, Brendan Ward, Charles Malo, and members of the U.S. intelligence community in Washington, D.C., and Beijing, and on interviews by others of Li Zhao Hu and McKinsey Russell. Other sources were the *People's Daily*, Mar. 9, 1989; the *China Daily*, Mar. 9–14, 1989; *Time*, Mar. 8, 1989; *Newsweek*, Mar. 8, 1989; Melinda Liu's faxes to *Newsweek;* diaries of Jeanne Moore and Barr Seitz; and *The Chinese Secret Service* (Deacon).

13. OVERTURES

"Overtures" is based on my interviews with Cassy Jones, Barr Seitz, Jeanne Moore, Melinda Liu, Alan Donald, Brian Davidson, Brendan Ward, and Susan Morton, and interviews by others of Wuerkaixi, Chai Ling, Wang Dan, Liu Gang, and Li Liu. Other sources were the diaries of Jeanne Moore and Cassy Jones; faxes from Melinda Liu; the *China Daily*, Mar. 15–31, 1989; the *People's Daily*, Mar. 15–31, 1989; and the *South China Morning Post*, Mar. 15–31, 1989.

14. SURGES

"Surges" is based on my interviews with Cassy Jones, Jenny Guangzu, Barr Seitz, Jeanne Moore, Melinda Liu, Alan Donald, Brian Davidson, Brendan Ward, Sue Tung, Jia Guangzu, Kao Jyan, Shao-Yen Wang, and Li Yang, and interviews by others of Wuerkaixi, Chai Ling, Wang Dan, Fang Lizhi, Boris Klimonko, Vladimir Kudinov, Anatole Bykov, and Raymond Burghardt. Other sources were the *China Daily*, Apr. 19–24, 1989; the *People's Daily*, Apr. 19–21, 1989; the *South China Morning Post*, Apr. 20–21, 1989; the *Standard* (Hong Kong), Apr. 20–24, 1989; the diaries of Cassy Jones, Jeanne Moore, Melinda Liu, and Sue Tung; faxes of Melinda Liu; and a letter from Jenny Guangzu to her father.

15. A TIME OF DECISION

For this chapter I relied on my interviews with Cassy Jones, Jia Guangzu, Yang Li, Melinda Liu, Barr Seitz, Sue Tung, Brian Davidson, and Brendan Ward, and interviews by others of Wang Dan, Wuerkaixi, Chai Ling, Feng Conde, Liu Gang, Xiong Yan, and Yang Tao. Other sources were the diaries of Cassy Jones, Jeanne Moore, and Sue Tung; an "Open Letter to Beijing College," published Apr. 22, 1989; various transcripts of Radio Beijing broadcasts, Apr. 21–30, 1989; the *New York Times*, Apr. 21–30, 1989 (especially the reports of Nicholas D. Kristof); *Newsweek* for Apr. 1989; *Time* for Apr. 1989; the *Reader's Digest*, Apr. 21–30, 1989; and the *China Daily*, Apr. 21–30, 1989.

16. POWER PLAYS

"Power Plays" is based on my interviews with Melinda Liu, Jeanne Moore, Cassy Jones, Barr Seitz, Jenny Guangzu, Jia Guangzu, Sue Tung, Kao Jyan, Li Yang, Brian Davidson, and Brendan Ward, and interviews by others of Wuerkaixi, Chai Ling, Liu Gang, Xiong Yan, Yang Tao, and Wang Dan. Other sources were the diary of Jeanne Moore and faxes of Melinda Liu.

17. COUNTERMOVES

For this chapter I relied on my interviews with Jenny Guangzu. Melinda Liu, Susan Morton, Barr Seitz, Bing Yang, Jeanne Moore, Cassy Jones, and various members of the U.S. intelligence community in Washington, D.C., and Beijing, and on interviews by others of Wuerkaixi, Wang Dan, Jenny Guangzu, and Cassy Jones. Other sources were the diaries of Barr Seitz and Jeanne Moore; faxes of Melinda Liu; the *People's Daily*, May 2–4, 1989; the *China Daily* (all issues for May 1989); and *Newsweek* for May 1989.

18. TURMOIL ON TIANANMEN

I based this chapter on my interviews with Jia Guangzu, Jenny Guangzu, Barr Seitz, Jeanne Moore, Brian Davidson, Brendan Ward, Alan Donald, Sue Tung, Shao-Yen Wang, Zhang Milin, Melinda Liu, and Cassy Jones, and on interviews by others of Wuerkaixi, Wang Dan, Chai Ling, Feng Conde, and Vladimir Troyanovsky. Another source was the *Independent* (all issues for May and June 1989, especially the reports of Andrew Higgins).

19. THE BECKONING ABYSS

This chapter is based on my interviews with Brendan Ward, Brian Davidson, Melinda Liu, Jeanne Moore, Sue Tung, Kao Jyan, Li Yang, Jia Guangzu, Jenny Guangzu, Cassy Jones, and Alan Donald, and on interviews by others of Wuerkaixi, Wang Dan, and Chai Ling. Other sources were the diaries of Jeanne Moore, Cassy Jones, Sue Tung, and Barr Seitz; the *New York Times* (all issues from May 15–June 6, 1989, especially the reports of Nicholas Kristof); and the *China Daily*, all issues from May 1–June 6, 1989.

20. MARTIAL LAW

"Martial Law" is based on my interviews with Kao Jyan, Melinda Liu, Brian Davidson, Brendan Ward, Jeanne Moore, Sue Tung, Bing Yang, Debnath Shaw, Huzzan Farazendeh, Susan Morton, Shao-Yen Wang, and Zhang Milin, and interviews by others of Liu Lee, Wuerkaixi, Wang Dan, Arne Dellira, Giulio Fraticelli, Marian Woznink, Alfonzo Alumada, Bjorn Skula, and Angelo Miculescu. Other sources were the "Proclamation to the People of China" by Chai Ling, mimeographed on Tiananmen Square, May 20, 1989; the diaries of Jeanne Moore and Sue Tung; and the faxes of Melinda Liu.

21. MARRIAGE IN MAYHEM

This chapter is based on my interviews with Cassy Jones, Li Yang, Barr Seitz, Sue Tung, Jia Guangzu, Jenny Guangzu. Bing Yang, Melinda Liu, Zhang Milin, Brian Davidson, and Brendan Ward, and on interviews by others of Chai Ling, Wang Dan, Wuerkaixi, Li Liu, Zhao Ming, Geert Andersen, and Horst Lohmann. Other sources were the diaries of Jeanne Moore, Sue Tung, and Barr Seitz; and the faxes of Melinda Liu.

22. MASSACRE

"Massacre" was based on my interviews with Cassy Jones, Sue Tung, Brian Davidson, Brendan Ward, Melinda Liu, Jeanne Moore, Barr Seitz, Alan Donald, Susan Morton, Jenny Guangzu, Jia Guangzu, Louise Branson, Bing Yang, Tan Yaobang, Kao Jyan, David Blackstock, Lindsay J. Watts, Earl Drake, Patricia Martinez, Denis Biggs, Brix Andersen, and Hou Dejian, and interviews by others of Wuerkaixi, Wang Dan, Chai Ling, Charles Malo, Gerard Chesnees, Rolf Berthold, Horst Lohmann, Hans-Peter Hellbeck, Bjorn Skala, Bilal Simisar, and James W. Brown. Other sources were reports by Louise Branson in May–June, 1989, and the diaries of Jeanne Moore and Barr Seitz.

23. A TIME OF PAIN

For this chapter I relied on my interviews with Jenny Guangzu, Sue Tung, Melinda Liu, and Barr Seitz.

24. FOR THE MOMENT

This chapter is based on my interviews with Sue Tung, Jenny Guangzu, Li Yang, Shao-Yen Wang, and Zhang Milin; Global Trends 2015 (CIA document, unpublished); *The Dragon's Teeth* (Wm. Hutchinson, U.K. 1987)

Index

About the Author

GORDON THOMAS is the author of thirty-eight books. They have achieved total sales of 45 million copies in 36 countries. Seven of his books have been made into major motion pictures, including the five-times Academy Award-winning *Voyage of the Damned*. Currently his series of best-selling David Morton novels are being filmed by IAC International for a 22-hour television series to be screened internationally in 2002. *Gideon's Spies* is also in the process of being filmed by Helkon International Media. Gordon Thomas's next book, *Mindfield*, has already been pre-sold around the world. He is a daily commentator for TV-3 of Ireland and the UK and his up-to-the-minute reportage appears throughout Europe in major independent and syndicated newspapers. He lives in Ireland with his wife, an interior designer, and his two children.